T&T Clark Companion to Methodism

Titles in this series include

T&T Clark Companion to Reformation Theology, edited by David M. Whitford
T&T Clark Companion to Nonconformity, edited by Robert Pope
T&T Clark Companion to Augustine and Modern Theology, edited by
    C.C. Pecknold and Tarmo Toom

T&T Clark Companion to Methodism

Edited by
Charles Yrigoyen, Jr.

BLOOMSBURY
LONDON · NEW DELHI · NEW YORK · SYDNEY

Bloomsbury T&T Clark
An imprint of Bloomsbury Publishing Plc

50 Bedford Square	1385 Broadway
London	New York
WC1B 3DP	NY 10018
UK	USA

www.bloomsbury.com

Bloomsbury is a registered trade mark of Bloomsbury Publishing Plc

First published in hardback 2010, published in paperback 2014

© Charles Yrigoyen Jr., 2010, 2014

Charles Yrigoyen Jr. has asserted his right under the Copyright, Designs and Patents Act, 1988, to be identified as Author of this work.

All rights reserved. No part of this publication may be reproduced or transmitted in any form or by any means, electronic or mechanical, including photocopying, recording, or any information storage or retrieval system, without prior permission in writing from the publishers.

No responsibility for loss caused to any individual or organization acting on or refraining from action as a result of the material in this publication can be accepted by Bloomsbury or the author.

British Library Cataloguing-in-Publication Data
A catalogue record for this book is available from the British Library.

ISBN: HB: 978-0-567-03293-5
PB: 978-0-567-65712-1
ePDF: 978-0-5672-9077-9
ePub: 978-0-5676-6246-0

Library of Congress Cataloging-in-Publication Data
A catalog record for this book is available from the Library of Congress.

Typeset by Newgen Knowledge Works (P) Ltd., Chennai, India
Printed and bound in Great Britain

Contents

	Preface	vii
	Abbreviations	ix
	Part I	
1	John and Charles Wesley: Life, Ministry, and Legacy *Richard P. Heitzenrater*	3
2	Theology of John and Charles Wesley *Randy L. Maddox*	20
3	Hymnody of Charles Wesley *S T Kimbrough, Jr.*	36
4	Authority and the 'Wesleyan Quadrilateral' *Ted A. Campbell*	61
5	Methodism in the UK and Ireland *Martin Wellings*	73
6	Methodism in North America *Russell E. Richey*	89
7	Methodist Missions/Missiology *Norman E. Thomas*	112
8	Methodism in Africa *John Wesley Z. Kurewa*	133
9	Methodism in Asia and the Pacific *Luther J. Oconer*	152
10	Methodism in Northern and Continental Europe *Ulrike Schuler*	166
11	Methodism in Russia and the Baltics: Old and New Beginnings *Rüdiger R. Minor*	188

12	Methodism in Latin America and the Caribbean *Paulo Ayres Mattos*	204
13	Evangelism in the Methodist Tradition *Paul Wesley Chilcote*	221
14	Methodist Worship *Karen B. Westerfield Tucker*	240
15	Methodism and the Sacraments *Laurence Hull Stookey*	257
16	Spirituality in the Methodist Tradition *Thomas R. Albin*	275
17	Social Ethics in the Methodist Tradition *Manfred Marquardt*	292
18	Methodism's Polity: History and Contemporary Questions *Thomas Edward Frank*	309
19	Methodism and the Ecumenical Movement *Geoffrey Wainwright*	329
20	Methodism and Its Images *Peter Forsaith*	350
21	Methodist Printed and Archival Research Collections: A Survey of Materials in UK/USA Repositories *Gareth Lloyd*	369

Part II

Methodism A to Z   389
John G. McEllhenney and Charles Yrigoyen, Jr.

Part III

Bibliography *Susan E. Warrick*	515
Contributors	533
Notes	535
Index	587

Preface

John and Charles Wesley never dreamed of the success that would bless the eighteenth-century Methodist movement in which they were primary leaders. Two hundred fifty years later Methodism had spread to every continent and numbered approximately forty million members in more than 130 nations. Over the centuries it spawned a diverse group of denominations as widely different as the British Methodist and United Methodist churches and the Salvation Army, and gave rise to a host of larger and smaller ecclesiastical bodies including those which evolved in the Holiness and Pentecostal movements.

Cofounder Charles Wesley was unhappy with his brother's decisions which led to Wesleyan Methodism's separation from the Church of England. Nevertheless, Methodism became a distinct church (and, later, many churches), a major force in Protestantism, and influential throughout the world powered by the twin emphases of evangelical outreach and social activism.

The literature describing and analyzing the origins and development of Methodism is voluminous. Since its earlier years, historical studies, autobiographies, and biographies have appeared regularly. Special historical celebrations have produced flurries of publications, for example, the bicentennial of American Methodism in 1984, and the tercentenaries of the births of the Wesley brothers (John in 2003, Charles in 2008). Furthermore, the abundant roll of possible commemorations of historic Methodist mileposts – birth and death years of other significant leaders, establishment of denominations, missions, institutions, etc. – provides almost limitless prospects for appropriate celebrations and fresh research and writing on a variety of topics. Hardly a year passes without some opportunity to recognize the anniversary of some important Methodist person, event, denomination, or organization.

Denominational and secular presses have turned out an assortment of first-class books and periodicals focused on the history, theology, and polity of Methodism. *The Bicentennial Edition of the Works of John Wesley* (Oxford University Press and Abingdon Press), a full-scale critical edition of Wesley's writings, is an outstanding example. The *Historical Dictionary of Methodism* (Scarecrow Press), *A Dictionary of Methodism in Britain and Ireland* (Epworth Press and online editions), and *The Oxford Handbook of Methodist Studies* (Oxford University Press) are also worthy of note.

The present volume is another contribution to publications on Methodism. Although it is not intended as an introductory text, it contains basic information on the origins and development of Methodism. Part I includes chapters on the life, ministry, theology, and legacy of John and Charles Wesley. It also contains chapters on the organization of Methodism in Great Britain/Ireland and North America, and its missionary spread to Africa, Asia and the Pacific, Europe, Russia and the Baltics, and Latin America and the Caribbean. Chapters on evangelism, worship and the sacraments, spiritual formation, social ethics, polity, and the ecumenical movement – major emphases of Methodism – highlight a few of its core features. Part I concludes with chapters on Methodism in art and architecture, and a survey of the types and locations of printed works and archival collections pertaining to Methodism. Each major chapter has a short list of bibliographic recommendations for further reading and raises questions for further research.

Part II, titled Methodism A to Z, contains a series of short encyclopedic chapters on geographic areas, denominations, concepts, important leaders, and other topics. Each chapter has suggestions for further investigation by those who wish to dig deeper.

Part III is a formal bibliography which lists general reference works (bibliographies, encyclopedias/dictionaries), general histories (world Methodism, Great Britain/Ireland, North America, Africa, Asia/Australasia, Latin America/Caribbean, Europe), topical studies (evangelism, holiness, missions, social reform, Sunday schools), theology and doctrine (John and Charles Wesley, doctrine, representative Methodist theologians), worship, sacraments, and hymnody, polity, and representative journals of Methodist history and theology. Bibliographic references are an important component of all three parts of the volume.

Appreciation is expressed to the outstanding cadre of chapter authors. These contributors not only represent an international group of writers, but also younger and seasoned experts on Methodist history, theology, and church life. Readers will note the indebtedness to John G. McEllhenney who has supplied more than half of the articles for the A to Z section, and to Susan Eltscher Warrick who provided the main bibliographic section. We are also grateful to Thomas Kraft, associate publisher of T&T Clark/Continuum Publishing, and his able staff for their assistance.

Charles Yrigoyen, Jr.
Willow Street, Lancaster County, Pennsylvania

Abbreviations

ANB	John A. Garraty and Mark C. Carnes, eds, *American National Biography*, 24 vols., New York: Oxford University Press, 1999.
BDE	Timothy Larsen, David Bebbington, and Mark A. Noll, eds, *Biographical Dictionary of Evangelicals*, Downers Grove, IL: Intervarsity Press, 2003.
DCA	Daniel G. Reid, Robert D. Linder, Bruce L. Shelley, and Harry S. Stoudt, eds, *Dictionary of Christianity in America*, Downers Grove, IL: Intervarsity Press, 1990.
DMBI	John A. Vickers, ed., *A Dictionary of Methodism in Britain and Ireland*, Peterborough, UK: Epworth Press, 2000.
EA	Evangelical Association.
EUB	Evangelical United Brethren Church.
EWM	Nolan B. Harmon, ed., *The Encyclopedia of World Methodism*, 2 vols., Nashville: United Methodist Publishing House, 1974.
HAM	Emory Stevens Bucke, ed., *The History of American Methodism*, 3 vols., Nashville: Abingdon Press, 1964.
HDM	Charles Yrigoyen, Jr., and Susan E. Warrick, eds, *Historical Dictionary of Methodism*, 2nd ed., Lanham, MD: Scarecrow Press, 2005.
HMGB	Rupert Davies, A. Raymond George, and Gordon Rupp, eds, *A History of the Methodist Church in Great Britain*, 4 vols., London: Epworth Press, 1965–1988.
MEA	Russell E. Richey, Kenneth E. Rowe, and Jean Miller Schmidt, eds, *The Methodist Experience in America: A Sourcebook*, Nashville: Abingdon, 2000.
MEC	Methodist Episcopal Church.
MECS	Methodist Episcopal Church, South
MP	Methodist Protestant Church
ODCC	F. L. Cross and E. A. Livingstone, eds, *The Oxford Dictionary of*

Abbreviations

	the Christian Church, 3rd ed., Oxford: Oxford University Press, 1997.
ODNB	H. C. G. Matthew and Brian Harrison, eds, *Oxford Dictionary of National Biography*, 60 vols., Oxford: Oxford University Press, 2004.
PWHS	*Proceedings of the Wesley Historical Society*.
UB	Church of the United Brethren in Christ.
UMC	United Methodist Church.
WJW (Jackson)	Thomas Jackson, ed., *The Works of John Wesley*, London, 1831; reprint, 14 vols., Grand Rapids, MI: Baker Books, 1996.
WJW (B)	The Bicentennial Edition of the Works of John Wesley, Nashville, Abingdon Press, 1976–.

Part I

This page intentionally left blank

1 John and Charles Wesley: Life, Ministry, and Legacy

Richard P. Heitzenrater

John Wesley's obituary in the *Gentleman's Magazine* in March 1791 stated that, 'as the founder of the most numerous sect in the kingdom, as a man, and as a writer, he must be considered as one of the most extraordinary characters this or any age ever produced.' Although the Methodist movement at his death numbered only about 75,000 members in a general population of some ten million, Wesley was certainly one of the most visible British citizens of the eighteenth century, which his life nearly spanned. As leader of the Methodist movement within the Church of England, he developed views on how scriptural theology could impact the daily lives of ordinary people and created patterns of organizing the people of God into effective groups of disciples, both of which became foundational for the Methodist family of denominations. These churches have spread to every part of the globe and together make up one of the largest of the Protestant religious groups.

Charles Wesley, though not as notable as his older brother during his lifetime, was in many ways a co-worker with John. His theology and his staunch support for the national church certainly influenced the nuances of his older brother's opinions. But his most notable contribution, in his own day and subsequently, was the religious poetry he produced so prolifically. Hundreds of his poems, from a corpus that totaled thousands of individual pieces, became the lyrics of hymns that have graced the hymnbooks of Christian churches down to this day. Although he never wrote any music, his hymns are among the favorites of many people for a wide variety of occasions in all seasons of the church year. In his sons and grandson he also produced a lineage of composers and organists that made a significant mark on British sacred music.

Methodism today is more than the lengthened shadow of the Wesley brothers. But one cannot understand the heart of the tradition without catching the vision of Christian holiness that motivated these men of God. Their life and thought reflected their faith, lived out in the context of a world that was stretching beyond old boundaries in many ways. The study of the rise of Methodism comprises a study of the eighteenth-century north Atlantic world, with all its stories of exploration, settlement, conflicts, and revolutions. One exciting aspect of doing such a study is that, if done adequately, it entails looking at nearly all the facets of the culture of the day – political, economic, ethical, artistic, scientific, religious, and social. The Wesleyan movement starts in the spiritual journey of the Wesley brothers in Great Britain, but before the century was out, the movement had begun to reach around the globe.

The focus of Wesleyan theology is the Christian life – how scripture and tradition could become the framework and pattern for everyday living. The perspective that focuses on the practice of Christian living is often tagged today 'practical theology.' John Wesley's theology grew out of his daily attempts to embody a 'way of salvation' that he discerned in the Bible and saw in the lives of Christian believers from the earliest days to his own. His developing theology, therefore, reflects his own spiritual pilgrimage, his serious search for assurance of salvation, a lifelong process that formed the matrix for his continual encounters with God and his neighbors – contemporary and historical, friends and critics. In the long history of Christianity, such a view centering on the virtues and habits of the faith is considered part of the 'holy living' tradition.

The spiritual genealogy of the Wesley brothers falls well within this long-standing heritage which is grounded in scripture and manifest in many leading Christian figures, from the early church through the Reformation and into various parts of the church in the Wesleys' day. In order to understand this heritage fully, one must have a competent grasp of scripture and a basic knowledge of Christian thought. Then it is necessary to work through the breadth and depth of the Wesleys' life and thought, no mean task in itself.

Present State of Research

Wesley studies have only recently entered the world of modern historical and theological scholarship. For generations after John Wesley's death in 1791, his followers told the stories of early Methodism that focused on the 'great man' who had given birth to the movement through his spiritual biography, effective preaching, prolific publishing, indefatigable traveling, and persuasive personality. Wesley was the hero, the religious leader who could do no wrong and represented the epitome of Christian experience. His biography looked larger than life and took on the function of a spiritual paradigm for faithful followers. He was seen as a doer, not a thinker – an organizer who was concerned more about practice than theology. For generations, faithful Methodists perpetuated and enhanced the legends that Wesley himself had helped to create.

Modern thinkers should not feel they are being faithful to Wesley by simply transferring his own method of thinking and acting to the present age. Wesley's own methodology was based on an eighteenth-century framework of perception and his intentions were often apologetic and propagandistic. As a historian, he falls short of modern critical approaches to the past; as a biblical interpreter, he was unable to benefit from the scholarly advances made in the last two centuries; as a theologian, he was inclined to be more dogmatic than constructive; as a person interested in science, he was bound by a worldview that was excited about the invention of the steam engine and never conceived the possibility of visiting the moon.

Wesley's views may represent an important perspective on many issues of his day, but modern observers must take into account those aspects of his life and thought that demonstrate the limits of his time and place. They should also consider Wesley's own sources – the fact that many of his ideas are based on sources that influenced him in various ways.[1] Most of his ideas did not appear *de novo* as totally original with him, but fit into a long history of developments on various issues, whether theological, political, social, artistic, scientific, or economic. Many of the general frameworks used by Wesley are still beneficial, but certain assumptions and approaches are no longer as useful as they once were. In today's quite different contexts, many social attitudes and prejudices are now quite different regarding such things as heresy, other Christian and non-Christian groups, women, class structure, witchcraft, democracy, and capitalism. These differences, beginning during Wesley's lifetime, have caused numerous tensions within the heritage.

In Wesley's own day and for a time thereafter, detractors split off from the mainline Wesleyan tradition (a term often used to designate the largest groups, as if the majority should be equated with orthodoxy and therefore truth) and formed other denominations, often using 'Methodist' as part of their name, but at times differing from Wesley on some issues that represented a different, sometimes new, perspective on the world: the place of democracy, the role of bishops, the power of laity, the particulars of social behavior, the implications of race, and other matters that differentiated them while they remained clustered around a shared body of doctrine. Some groups claimed that their view of Wesley was more correct than the mainline 'orthodox' position, while others differed from Wesley in, what was to them, critical areas of thinking or action.

Even within Methodist or Wesleyan denominations, heated debates arose over just what Wesley intended on certain issues. In many instances, opposing parties chose to emphasize a favorite passage or interpretation that agreed with their own prejudices or preconceived notions. Such proof-texting often simplified complex issues, ignored contrary materials from Wesley's own writings, overlooked changing forces in the historical context over his long lifetime, or differed on the implications of his subsequent perspectives. The constant retelling of stories often led to the loss of earlier hesitations, the growing assumptions of authenticity, the simplifying that comes from continuing defensiveness, and ignoring contrary positions. Some people shaped their hero as much as (or more than) their hero shaped them.

The twentieth century witnessed an important shift in the presentation and portrayal of Wesley in new ways similar to the more objective approaches that had become more apparent in other areas of religious studies, such as the Reformation or the New Testament. First came an increase in monographic studies of Wesley in relation to particular groups or ideas: 'Wesley and . . .' Puritanism, Roman Catholicism, the Moravians, the early church, social concerns, medicine, the family, revivalism, authority. He was examined as a preacher, an organizer, a publisher, and a reformer. Also in the first half of the century, some probing questions about the stereotypical Wesley image by non-Methodists resulted in some major writings that tried to defend and define him.[2]

Then after mid-century came a whole new approach, based on an increasing emphasis on primary sources, accompanied by a more critical historical and literary approach to the documents, that resulted in quite different perspectives in many areas of inquiry that had become dominated by clichés and stereotypes.[3] A new wave of scholars began asking different questions and seeing Wesley afresh through a more comprehensive study of his own writings, seeing them in the light of sources that Wesley himself read and the historical context in which he lived and thought.[4] Frank Baker, an indefatigable research historian, and Albert C. Outler, a forceful theologian and church leader, set a new standard for the field.

By 1983, Outler saw that the previous twenty years had witnessed a new level of Wesley studies, which he defined then as 'phase three.'[5] The first phase had entailed the triumphalistic stories about Wesley the hero; the second phase was marked by the monographic studies of Wesley in relation to selected themes. The new third phase gave rise to the Wesley Works Editorial Project, an ambitious international endeavor that began to produce a new, critical edition of the published Wesleyan literary corpus. Baker's concern was to produce the most accurate text possible, with a special interest in historical and literary issues. Outler's concern was to make the material accessible and understandable to modern readers so that Wesley would become a shaping force in current religious dialogue.

Since the turn of the twenty-first century, yet another development in Wesley studies has appeared on the scholarly scene, one which might be seen as 'phase four' (using Outler's typological framework). Authors who have approached Wesley in phase three are now on occasion applying this more critical and comprehensive view to particular issues and problems in the present in creative and constructive studies.[6] This approach is quite different from the design that characterized the work of earlier phases. The main focus is not so much to unfold Wesley's views on a particular issue as to apply the main Wesleyan principles or ideas on that issue to the new situations that exist more than two centuries later. This appropriation of Wesleyan views attempts to be faithful to his basic principles while confronting problems and positions that are quite different from those of the eighteenth century.

Methodology and Techniques for Wesleyan Studies

Many people ask, what is the best book that one can read in order to understand the Wesleys? The answer is that there is no single book that will provide a comprehensive understanding of either or both of the brothers. At the very least, any person who wants to understand the Wesleyan heritage must first read and know the Bible (which contains the worldview, imagery, and vocabulary context for the Wesleys' own life and thought), and obtain a grasp of the history of Christian thought (which provides the historical matrix for the Wesleys' own understanding of scriptural Christianity and the context for their own controversies with other segments of the tradition). Then the best approach is not to read secondary works about the Wesleys, but rather to read the Wesleys themselves (especially in a critical edition that provides helpful annotations), examine the works of other people that they abridged and published, and look at the material that was written by both critical and friendly observers in their own day. It is important to see the whole picture, remembering that both brothers experienced many controversies and developments during their long lives. John especially became somewhat legendary in his own day, and the facts of his life must be separated from the myths that developed very early (to which John himself often contributed and shaped) and have been perpetuated for generations.

People who are studying the Wesley brothers, as well as those who are writing studies of these early Methodist leaders, should be aware that there are several types of literature that have been produced over the years. These works generally fall into four categories or levels of study: primary source materials, monographic studies, comprehensive works, and popular writings. The best work in each area has an important place in bringing the Wesleys into public view and should be evaluated in terms of the role that it is expected to play. The basic knowledge of the period relies upon careful and critical editing of primary source materials from the time itself. These works, the foundation of the scholarly enterprise, provide the basis for well-done monographic studies on particular areas of investigation, no matter what the discipline. These works are usually produced by experts in the various topical, theological, historical, or biblical fields. From the collective wisdom represented in these specialized studies, mature scholars can glean general interpretations that will then form the framework for comprehensive studies. These summative books, if well done, represent the latest scholarship in the previous two levels of work and necessarily depend upon them for shaping their study. These three levels of work are generally done by scholars and are mostly used by scholars, so that another step is required to get this material to the general public. Popular works that summarize these other materials are therefore crucial in transmitting the scholarly research and writing to a wider audience. Each of these types of publications should be recognized for the kind of information that it represents and used accordingly. Popular works are often scorned by scholars, but well-done material of this kind plays an important role in disseminating the best ideas from the most recent scholarship.

There is often a time lapse from the appearance of new information in primary source editing, its use in monographic works, its incorporation into comprehensive studies, and its eventual appearance at the level of popular writing. Some scholars at the more basic levels of research therefore help reduce that gap by producing books at more than one level, even at times introducing comprehensive and popular studies into their own repertoire of writings. Whether producing these works, or simply reading them for information or pleasure, one should be aware of the different levels at which works function within a particular field such as Wesley and Methodist studies.

Most of the criteria for good modern scholarship apply to Wesley studies as well as to any other attempt to further our understanding of the past. The *Bicentennial Edition of the Works of John Wesley* represents the best of careful research that is produced relative to the primary sources upon which the whole story of early Methodism is based. The series is called a 'critical' edition for several reasons:

1. the text is produced through a careful comparison of all the editions produced in Wesley's lifetime, with the best edition providing the basic text, with important emendations entered into the text (with the source edition carefully noted in the footnotes), and all the variant readings from other editions in the Wesleys' lifetime noted in an appendix, so that the reader can in effect recreate the text of any of the early editions;
2. quotations, whether scriptural or otherwise, are identified for the reader, so that the background of Wesley's classical and contemporary reading becomes transparent and his reliance upon scriptural vocabulary, stories, and indeed worldview, is unfolded for the reader;
3. the introduction to each separate publication (such as sermon, treatise, letter, or journal segment) provides the historical and theological context for that particular piece, with any comments that might tie the material to Wesley's life and thought, as seen in other parts of the literary corpus;

4. the general introduction to each major unit of material provides a careful analysis of the material and its relationship to the important developments in that literary genre in the eighteenth century, whether it be letter writing, preaching, autobiography, or theological controversy and apology, putting Wesley and his writings into context and in some cases producing the equivalent of a small but significant monographic study on the subject;
5. the appendices usually include related Wesleyan manuscript material, a scripture index, a bibliographical index, and a very complete general index that helps tie together the various topics in the literary corpus.

This careful approach to primary materials has been used within the broader field of historical studies for less than two centuries. Such care was not evident during Wesley's time and his own productions were not nearly as reliable as historians expect to find today. Even when producing historical works, Wesley did not write as an objective historian any more than he could be a non-partisan theologian. His own writings more often fit the scheme of propaganda or *apologia*, and should be read that way.

Wesley is not a less reliable writer than other people of his day, but the approach of writers at that point in history was simply quite different from those of our own time. The same rules of plagiarism did not apply, for instance, and many of Wesley's publications consisted of his abridgements of other people's writings – reduced, edited ('collected,' in his terms), and sometimes 'corrected' for his readers. At times, he acknowledged his debt to other authors; at other times, he simply produced such abridged works without attribution, or perhaps even anonymously. That he would include these publications in his collections of published *Works* is a tribute to their importance in his efforts to help fulfill God's design to 'spread scriptural holiness' through the work of the Methodist preachers.

Recognizing the sources and context of Wesley's thought is only part of the approach that one must consider today. One must also recognize that Wesley became a legend in his own day, and that he had no qualms about reinforcing that image. Many of the myths of Methodism at least can be partially attributed to Wesley's pen, or perhaps a more recent misconstruing of what Wesley was trying to say. In either instance, the real John Wesley becomes as elusive as any other major historical figure who is seen as larger than life.

To understand the Wesleys in their own day, the present-day interpreter must realize that we cannot simply say that they thought or said a particular thing demonstrating a particular point of view. One must realize that, like everyone else, the Wesleys grew and changed. They developed and matured. Therefore, quotations from the earlier years may betray a position that is not evident in mid-life or later. One must remember that neither John Wesley nor anyone else in 1745, for instance, knew how the century would turn out or what direction the Wesleyan and Methodist stories would take. The tendency these days is often to say that 'Wesley thought such and such,' as though his whole life exhibited a particular point of view, without indicating that there are important developments and nuances in his thought over the years. To provide the best help in this regard, writers should indicate the period, the context, the particular controversy, or whatever else is appropriate to help interpret a particular point of view that the Wesleys exhibit in a specific way.

The internet represents an important element of current research, combining the best and the worst of materials relative to understanding the 'real' Wesleys. Many people head to the computer to find out information that they used to look for in books written (at least presumably) by experts. The electronic media, however, represent both great possibilities and horrible problems. While many reliable institutions have made source collections available, some of the material available on the internet is simply a reproduction of nineteenth-century editions and reflects all the problems of pre-critical materials. Thousands of sites, especially personal sites and local church home pages, contain misinformation about the Wesleys, which is often hard to distinguish from reliable sources. The best rule to follow seems to be to trust only those sites that are produced by reliable institutions with solid scholarly reputations.

Charles Wesley Studies

Serious study of Charles Wesley began in the last two generations. Prior to that, most of the publications relating to Charles tended to repeat many of the time-worn tales about his reputation as a great hymn writer and how his work carried the Wesleyan message to the singing masses. There is some truth in both perspectives, but modern scholarship has gone far beyond the simplistic praise of earlier work.

An indication of the general lack of knowledge about Charles can be seen in the fact that most people do not realize that he did not write any music, and in fact (according to his son) was not much of a singer.[7] His lifetime production of hymns is variously indicated as being somewhere between six and nine thousand. As more recent scholarship has pointed out, however, those numbers often do not take into account the duplicated publication of many poems, the absence of any publication of some other poems, and a lack of awareness of the complications involved in trying to number his poetic production.

Charles is not remembered by scholars as either a great literary figure of his time or an outstanding theologian. He was, however, a master craftsman of religious and devotional poetry, which we could call 'hymns,' whether or not they were ever put to music. Perhaps most of his 'sacred poems' were simply read devotionally and never sung – only a fraction of his poetry was sung in a service, either during his lifetime or since. But the attractiveness of his material to the public gave rise to a comment by Isaac Watts that Charles' single poem, 'Wrestling Jacob,' 'was worth all the verses he himself had written.'[8] That is not to say that Charles ranked among the great poets or notable theologians of his day, but it does recognize that he had a talent for expressing spiritual experiences through powerful images and striking phrasing.

His marriage to Sarah Gwynne presents an interesting twist in the relationship of the Wesley brothers on several levels – with regard to marriage, family life, use of money, position in society, relationship to the Church of England, and many other areas. Although there remains a great deal of work to do on John Wesley's personal attitude toward and practices concerning personal finances, Charles' marriage raises even more critical questions in this regard. Although there are not as many personal resources available from Charles' hand, the extant materials provide sources for a useful field of study. The published appearance of more personal materials such as letters and journal letters, currently underway, should allow for a new renaissance of studies of Charles Wesley.

Areas That Require Further Attention

Some areas of Wesley studies are currently being considered in the introductions to units in the *Bicentennial Edition*, placing John Wesley in the context of his day. The pattern has already been set by Frank Baker's introduction on letter-writing and postal system, Albert Outler's work on preaching and sermon-writing, and Reginald Ward's study of the developments in autobiographical writing in Wesley's day. The purpose of these introductions is to put the work of the Wesleys in the context of their time and to examine the state of the field to which they were contributing, such as New Testament scholarship, folk medicine, theological reflection, diary-writing, editorial work, and publishing. While this contextual approach is expected as complementary to the critical textual work in preparing the Works project, such critical analyses of the context should also be a normal part of most Wesley studies.

Several areas of investigation are being studied carefully in dissertations and other monographic studies that are presently underway, such as the influence of John Wesley on American holiness traditions, the shaping of the Methodist tradition in wider global settings (such as Jamaica and Korea), and various issues about the *Christian Library*. A dozen or more of these topics comprise the projects of scholars every year who participate in the Summer Wesley Seminar at Duke Divinity School, which has brought together different groups of both senior and junior scholars from around the world for a month every summer for several years.

Many other topics are still in need of scholarly attention and are worthy subjects of continued investigation. A few of the general fields that present issues for consideration are:

1. *Psychological studies.* Although there has been some previous study of this aspect of John Wesley's life,[9] the wealth of private material in many of John's diaries lends itself to an in-depth study of the man from this perspective which no one has done. The prior studies tend to use the perspective of a particular psychological school of thought, but the success or failure of their endeavor depends more upon the Wesleyan material that is examined than on the theories that are applied. To use recent secondary reflections as the basis for a psychological examination, which has usually been the case, is as inadequate as sending your cousin's wife to the doctor for a diagnosis, based on a distant relative's comments regarding what her medical problems might be. From first-hand study of detailed primary sources, scholars should be able to develop useful conclusions about such topics as Wesley's motivation for and personal approach to leadership, about the various pressures that were exhibited in the tensions between the brothers, about the relationship between scriptural principles developed by the Wesley brothers and the personal relationships that they developed, about the relationship between their state of health and their outlook on life (especially in comparing the Wesley brothers), about the differences in their handling of relationships with women, and about the difference between their understanding of the role of lay preachers in the Methodist movement.
2. *Women and gender issues.* While the question of women's roles in the Methodist societies and the Wesleys' attitudes toward women has occupied the attention of several scholars in recent years,[10] much remains to be done in this field. More primary material is constantly becoming known and available to interested scholars, as is the case with women's studies in general, which then provides the basis for a broader and deeper examination of the various issues relating to women in the Wesleyan movement. The Wesley brothers each had peculiarities in their personal relationships with women, although Charles was much more contented as a married family man. No one has satisfactorily explained the reason why John, whose whole life was spent proclaiming the Christian gospel, grounded in love, never seemed to experience a lasting loving relationship with a spouse.
3. *Wealth and economics.* The last half of the twentieth century became

enamored with God's 'preferential option for the poor.' This perspective was then applied to Wesley, who had a flourishing ministry to those who had been disenfranchised by society.[11] But the topics about poverty and the concomitant questions about wealth have generally been dealt with in a very hackneyed fashion in Wesley studies. Everyone knows that Wesley was in favor of earning and saving as much as possible and also then giving as much as possible to others. But this view overlooks the fact that, while the Methodist societies did consist of slightly more poor members than the societal average, those societies had twice as many rich members as one might find generally in the population. Charles himself married into a wealthy family, which had an effect on his ministry and his relationship to his brother. John Wesley's ministry to the poor was made possible by his ministry to the rich, a situation virtually unexamined in previous studies. British historians have begun to emphasize social and economic history in their work, and Wesleyan studies would benefit from more use of these same approaches to look at some new questions relating to the evangelical revival.

4. *Political and social issues.* The eighteenth century experienced a great deal of political and social unrest, and is marked by revolutionary movements in several countries such as France. Wesley's role in this context has been the subject of some speculation ever since the formulation of the Halévy thesis which claims that Wesley prevented such a revolution from occurring in England.[12] But Wesley's views and actions on the public scene raise both larger and smaller issues that await asking the right questions. In order to proceed in the best possible manner, the researcher must get beyond the tendency of past writers to see things in terms of simple dichotomies (did he or did he not) and current writers to blanket the past with political correctness. While John Wesley was opposed to war and felt that it was an illustration of the reality of original sin, he also was not opposed to the raising of a 'Methodist militia' to protect English soil from a French invasion. The tensions inherent in such views, in this and other similar issues, remain to be dealt with in a careful and satisfactory way.

5. *Arts and aesthetics.* Aside from a brief moment in the mid-twentieth century, the role of the arts in Christianity has remained by and large a critically unexamined field in the history of Christian thought and practice until recently. Wesley studies shares this vacuum, except perhaps for the studies that have attempted to look at the role of hymn-singing in the revival. The Wesleys, however, had quite specific and thoughtful views on other artistic fields as well as hymn-singing – architecture, literature, poetry, music, painting, and other expressions of the aesthetic impulse in society. John's *Journal*, for example, has comments upon

many of these fields of human expression. He even mentioned the aesthetic character of some forests and mountains that he viewed while traveling around the British Isles, and made comments upon some of the paintings that he saw when visiting country homes of the wealthy. John and Charles both had very definite views on what kind of music they liked and which composers were worthy of their art. John was conscious of the architecture of churches, in terms of their aesthetic appeal, acoustics, comfort, and cost. These are only a few of the topics that bear further investigation.

6. *Extra-sensory perception and spiritual reality.* When John was attending Charterhouse School in London, the Wesley household became somewhat notorious by claiming that it had experienced several visitations by a ghost, whom they nicknamed 'Old Jeffery.' John wrote several letters to various people who had been present or heard firsthand accounts of these events. His diary includes several records of having visited supposed 'haunted' houses and gives an account of a mysterious closing of the door while he and Charles were chasing a chicken around an upstairs room. He continued to be interested in these phenomena throughout his life, partly in terms of their being a manifestation of the reality of the spirit world in a world increasingly influenced by the skepticism of Deism. During the last century, this whole area became a field of investigation in its own right, and the methods and results would provide an interesting avenue to wander down in relation to the Wesley's persistent belief in the reality of the interventions of supernatural divine reality in the everyday lives of human beings.

7. *Publishing and editing.* Frank Baker spent a great deal of his time and effort prowling around the printing history of the eighteenth century. Among his papers remain unpublished works on some of the trivia that had previously remained largely unexamined, such as the history and use of 'printer's flowers' – those fancy little printed designs that often add flourishes to title pages, make up the introductory borders of the preface or body of the work, and provide the final artistic punctuation of printed works. Such details often provide clues as to who the unnamed printer might be, the date of an undated pamphlet, or other elusive information. In addition to such physical details, a host of topics remain that bear careful study in the multitudinous pages of the *Christian Library* and the *Arminian Magazine*. Not only do the editorial policies and practices entailed in such enterprises bear closer examination,[13] but the vast amount of information contained therein remains a storehouse of topics related to the interests of the editors, the society members, and the evangelical revival in general. Beyond these two collections, Wesley's publishing enterprise represents an interesting

subject for his views, not only on the topics of his own creation and of the abridgements that he created, but also of the editorial practice and intentions that gave rise to such a large endeavor that was so important to both the revival and to his method of communicating with the public.

8. *Wesley family.* The story of the Wesley family has been told many times, but usually by authors who are basically popular lecturers. The family dynamics in the Epworth household bear careful study. On the surface, it looks like what one might call today a dysfunctional family – the parents interfere unduly in the romantic lives of the children; the father forces at least one daughter to marry a man she does not love; the mother grows to despise a son-in-law who she thinks is unworthy of her daughter; two of the daughters are engaged to the same man at the same time (he marries one of them, and the other lives with the couple for a time); thirty-two-year-old John falls in love with an eighteen-year-old girl; and several other anomalies that raise some interesting questions for the modern investigator. Some members of the family, other than John and Charles, made important contributions to the literature of the day and deserve more attention, as do the children of Charles and Sally, two of whom were serious musicians. Careful study of the views of the Wesleys on the nature and role of children has only just begun.[14]

9. *Influence and legacy.* Most Wesleyan and Methodist denominations have openly expressed their dependence upon the Wesley brothers, but the exact nature of that influence or dependence has often varied in different times and places. It is much easier to give a pious nod in the direction of a founder than to explain the continuing influence of his ideas on the developing group over the generations. The various natures of groups around the world that rely in some way or another on the Wesleyan tradition for their very existence is vastly different – look at the Church of God in North America, the United Methodists in Brazil, the Methodists in China, Africa, or Sri Lanka (to say nothing of the Wesleyans who are now a part of united or uniting churches), and one begins to understand that the legacy of the Wesleys is not uniform and the interpretation of the Wesleys is not singular. Seventy-five of these Wesleyan and Methodist communions gather together regularly at meetings of the World Methodist Council, but their discussions are quite general concerning such specific topics as doctrine, liturgy, and polity. Very little work has been done comparing these Methodist and Wesleyan groups, as well as looking at the ways by which they each reached their different destinations.

Some areas have seen new work in recent years, but many questions must be pursued further. John Walsh has peered into the eighteenth-century hinterlands of Great Britain for years, looking at the fringes of Methodism and the ways that the Wesleyan message was filtered through the local imagery of such things as magic and superstition. Bruce Hindmarsh is expanding Reginald Ward's work on the relationship of the Wesleys to the larger 'holy living' tradition that flourished in eighteenth-century Europe. Peter Forsaith has begun to deepen our understanding of Wesleyan iconography through careful examination of the portrayals of the personnel in the revival, especially the Wesleys.

Some Wesleyan-related materials cry out for further study and comment. The manuscript journals of William Seward, Methodism's first 'martyr,' will hopefully be made available to the public soon for careful perusal. George Whitefield's biography has been done many times, but a careful study of his relationship to the Wesleys remains a desideratum. Samuel Wesley's sermons will hopefully appear in print in the near future, which will flesh out not only the understanding of Samuel's thought but perhaps of his theological influence on his sons. And one body of material that represents no shortage of material still awaits major examination – the anti-Methodist literature of the eighteenth century. Some of these topics have eluded the careful researcher for lack of sources, such as the life of the Wesley family at Epworth and the schooling of the Wesley children, but more information is coming to light every year.

These are only a few of the areas that continue to provide food for thought among the people called Methodists. Many other specific topics are still open for continued investigation. Some people think that the lives of the Wesleys or the rise of Methodism is a field that has been 'done.' Not so! Not only are new materials, such as letters, constantly coming to light, providing new insights on particular situations in their stories, but there is some truth in the idea that every generation needs to retell the story for itself, on its own terms, in its own vocabulary, answering its own questions. New methods of research, such as the electronic media, make it possible for the researcher in this generation to gather information that was nearly impossible for previous generations to recover and consider. New questions arise as society continues to press forward and confronts new issues, such as those related to gender and race that have arisen in the last half century. Old materials bear re-examination in the light of new situations. The Wesleys can always be considered important to the beginnings of Methodism and to developments in eighteenth-century British history, but the nature of that influence will continue to present important questions to examine in each generation.

Approaches to Areas Requiring Attention

Each of these areas demands that the best methods relative to that field should be used to look at the Wesleys' role in that area. Several suggestions of methods and procedures have already been made in the discussion above, but some obvious general comments bear repeating in this regard.

1. Let the Wesleys be themselves rather than reflections of present-day perspectives and issues. Many people have a tendency to read their own prejudices back into the Wesleys, using the Wesleyan writings very selectively to prove their own point(s). Very few people would agree with every point of view of these two eighteenth-century parsons – there is nothing wrong with disagreeing with the Wesleys or explaining Wesleyan ideas and actions that are tied to an out-of-date perspective or questionable views, such as a belief in the reality of witchcraft or a dated view of the role of women in society. Many of their ideas and actions are indeed ahead of their time, and there is no need to bolster up their images artificially in some areas and ignore others.
2. Examine the views of the opponents and detractors of the Wesleys. A well-rounded view of the Methodist leaders takes into account the anti-Methodist literature of the time as well as the apologetic work of the Wesleys' friends. Both extremes present views that are not totally consistent with reality, but a good judge does not simply listen to the defense lawyers and ignore the prosecutors – both sides must be examined critically in order to come up with a credible view of the people, events, and ideas of the time.
3. Rely primarily on the writings of that day in trying to recreate and understand the sense of the times, but do not accept primary sources uncritically just because they come from the period under examination. Many times, conflicts of information or points of view must be resolved, and additional material from the period itself can often do that. Also, there are now resources from that period that have not been widely available to previous generations. These materials, whether they are government documents, prison records, newspaper accounts, private diaries, or other new material, are very helpful in reconsidering some issues that have previously lacked sufficient data to answer some of the obvious questions that arise. Some computer sources, such as Eighteenth Century Collections Online (ECCO) make available a wide range of publications from the period that most scholars could not possibly examine thoroughly in previous generations.
4. Use secondary sources carefully and critically. The best authors acknowledge their biases, which allow the reader to weigh the evidence independently. It is best to allow the conclusions to emerge from the primary material, rather than to try to prove a preconceived hypothesis or put secondary authors into some sort of contest to see which one has the best points of view. Monographic studies can provide useful

expertise in examining particular issues, but should be used critically within the context of other material from the period itself. The hardest task sometimes is to allow the period to speak for itself – to allow the period to present its own views clearly, rather than to read present perspectives back into the past which often leads to selective proof-texting from the primary material in order to prove a current point of view from the Wesleys' writings.

For Further Reading

The indispensable resources for the study of John and Charles Wesley are the recent editions of their works. For John, the *Bicentennial Edition of the Works of John Wesley* has published about half of the proposed thirty-four volumes and contains not only a reliable critical text (with variant readings from eighteenth-century editions) but also significant introductions and useful annotations, which have not been part of previous editions.[15] The indispensible bibliographic work of Frank Baker that undergirds the editorial project can be found in his *Union Catalog of the Publications of John and Charles Wesley*.[16] For Charles, there is no 'Works' project as such, but new editions have appeared of his *Journal*,[17] many of his *Sermons*,[18] and most of his previously unpublished poetry.[19] His letters and journal letters are presently in preparation for publication. For both brothers, many of their unpublished manuscript materials are now available online at the Duke Divinity School Center for Studies in the Methodist Tradition web site.[20]

Researchers should also take seriously the materials that the Wesleys read, based on references in their writings such as the diaries and journals.[21] This approach is essential to any modern understanding of the way the Wesleys went about doing their work. A good indication of what John Wesley felt was important from these 'borrowed' and abridged resources, as well as what parts of them could easily be edited out, can be seen in the wealth of Wesleyan editorial work that appeared in his fifty-volume *Christian Library* and the fourteen volumes of the *Arminian Magazine* that appeared in his lifetime.

One of the most overlooked primary sources for studying the Wesley brothers is the array of anti-Methodist literature that was produced during their lifetime. These were listed first by Richard Green about a century ago, but more recently listed and analyzed by Donald Kirkham and Clive Field.[22]

Secondary sources on the Wesleys have appeared constantly during the two centuries since his death, but the most useful material has appeared in the last half century. Henry Rack's biographical work, *Reasonable Enthusiast*, presents a wealth of useful information, especially in its third edition.[23] Richard Heitzenrater has produced a study of the rise of Methodism in his *Wesley and the People Called Methodists* and has examined the pitfalls that confront any potential biographer, as well as a survey of the historiography of two centuries of Wesley studies in his *The Elusive Mr. Wesley*, now in a second edition.[24] Two recent studies of John Wesley's theology that present somewhat different perspectives are *Responsible Grace* by Randy Maddox and *The Theology of John Wesley* by Kenneth Collins.[25]

Several recent dissertations have examined important aspects of Wesley's life and thought,[26] such as Adam Zele's on Wesley and America, and Geordan Hammond's on Wesley in Georgia.[27] Several unpublished dissertations from the last several years provide invaluable perspectives on important topics, such as those by Rex Matthews and Thomas Albin.[28]

One excellent source of Wesleyan studies is the Kingswood Books imprint of Abingdon Press, which includes many examples of the best of scholarship on early Methodism. The Center for Studies in the Wesleyan Tradition at the Duke Divinity School is developing a web site that includes a remarkable list of critical materials that will be of interest and assistance to researchers and inquirers in Wesley studies.[29] These two sources are setting the standard for the next generation of research and study of the early development of the Wesleyan movement in the eighteenth century.

2 Theology of John and Charles Wesley

Randy L. Maddox

When 'Methodism' was first identified – and criticized – in eighteenth-century British religious life, the most frequent target was George Whitefield. This reminds us that there was a Calvinist strand of early Methodism that existed in some tension with the strand led by John and Charles Wesley. While a few remnants of Calvinist Methodism can still be found, it is the Wesleyan wing of the movement that flourished and spread across the globe, shaped by the theological contributions of the Wesley brothers. As a result, Methodism today is generally equated with its Wesleyan form and theological emphases.

Historical Background to John and Charles Wesley's Theological Stance

The theological emphases of John and Charles Wesley, including points of divergence from their friend Whitefield, are best understood in light of the theological spectrum of their day. This spectrum was broad due to the history that lay behind it.

The original split of the Church of England from Rome was more over jurisdictional matters than theological concerns. Henry VIII was no champion of Protestant agenda. Through his reign there were mixed influences of moderate Lutheranism and currents of the Reformed tradition with strong continuing Catholic sympathies. When Edward VI was enthroned (1549) the Reformed influences grew stronger, but this was abruptly halted by Edward's death and the ascension of Mary Tudor (1553), who attempted to restore Roman Catholic primacy in England. While Mary's short rule produced several hundred martyrs, it did not accomplish her broader goal. Elizabeth I quickly renewed the autonomy of the Church of England from Rome and provided stability for this status through her extended tenure on the throne (1558–1603).

The Elizabethan church is often described as a *via media* (middle way) between Rome and Geneva (as center of the Reformed tradition). This description may fit when considering issues of church organization and liturgical practice. Its adequacy for capturing the theological tone of this period is less clear. It suggests that the mainstream of the church held to moderating views on central issues like predestination and justification. Recent studies have built a strong case that the majority of church leaders and educated laity in the Elizabethan church were instead solidly Reformed in theological commitments, and stress how this identity carried over through the reign of James I (1603–1625).[1]

When Charles I took the throne in 1625, William Laud and some associates were given key leadership roles in the church. They emphasized episcopal authority, sacramental piety, and the use of liturgy and symbolism in worship, while downplaying or rejecting predestinarian theology. They justified these stances by appeal to a model of the *via media* that now cast Geneva as the antipode to Rome. But for many English clergy and laity their moves appeared to be a covert reversion to 'popery.' Reaction contributed to the outbreak of civil war in 1642 and the subsequent martyrdoms of Laud (1645) and Charles I (1649).

The Commonwealth government that displaced Charles I was dominated by Puritans and set about transforming the Church of England toward a Presbyterian polity and replacing the *Book of Common Prayer* with a Reformed *Directory of Public Worship* and the *Articles of Religion* with the Westminster *Confession of Faith*. These were heady times for Puritans, but short-lived. Continuing political chaos led to the recall of Charles II to the throne in 1660, and soon after the restoration of the church to its prewar standards of doctrine and practice. This was capped by the Act of Uniformity of 1662 which forced approximately 2,000 Puritan clergy out of the established church, effectively ending the dominance which Reformed or Calvinist theological emphases had held within the Church of England for over a century.

This dramatic change left the stream of seventeenth-century theologians who shared the emphases of Laud and supported Charles (hence, known as the 'Caroline divines') as the new centrist position within the Church of England. Since those who remained loyal to prayer-book religion and episcopacy during the interregnum had laid special claim to the title 'Anglican,' this term has come to be reserved by most scholars to designate those *from this period forward* who stand in the stream flowing from the Caroline divines.

One of the deep concerns of the Caroline divines was to demonstrate continuity of their church with the broad Christian tradition, particularly in its primitive form. This led to a distinct flowering of patristics studies and a particular interest in reintroducing many of the Eastern (Greek-writing) Christian theologians who had been relatively neglected in the (Latin) West.[2] Lest this be seen as a turn to antiquarianism, it is important to note that these divines often invoked the example of the early Christian apologists as warrant for equally engaging the Enlightenment emphases on reason and scientific explanation spreading in British culture. Indeed, the most characteristic feature of emerging 'Anglican' theology was its methodological emphasis on the importance of *integrating* consideration of scripture, tradition, and reason – as opposed to the one-sided alternatives of biblicism, traditionalism, or rationalism.

The Caroline divines generally shared Laud's view that the doctrine of unconditional reprobation makes 'the God of all mercies to be the most fierce and unreasonable tyrant in the world.'[3] This placed them in the Arminian camp of the current debates in the Reformed arena, even if their rejection of the Augustinian model of God's unilateral action in salvation drew more from alternative voices in the early church than from Jacob Arminius or other Remonstrants.

The Caroline divines also shared a deep uneasiness with antinomian themes developed by some Reformed writers defending justification by faith *alone*. Jeremy Taylor was particularly prominent in developing an alternative conception of justifying faith, which emphasized the vital connection of true faith with obedience and love. Drawing on the title of his most influential book, *The Rule and Exercises of Holy Living*, those contemporaries who shared Taylor's stress are often designated 'holy living divines.' For some scholars they epitomize the regrettable turn from authentic Reformation theology toward moralism; for others, they represent a long-needed reintroduction of Eastern Christian emphases in spirituality into the Augustinian West.[4]

Toward the end of the reign of Charles II there were mounting calls to broaden the range of accepted doctrinal emphases and liturgical practices within the Church of England, with a goal of reincorporating the Puritans who had been pushed out into (minimally tolerated) dissenting churches in the 1660s. This support crumbled when James II succeeded to the throne in 1685. James had converted to the Roman church and urged to include Roman Catholics in the circle to be embraced – or at least tolerated. For the vast majority of his citizens, including the Anglican bishops, this was too much. The staunchly Reformed William of Orange, who was married to James' daughter Mary (also a Protestant), was encouraged to invade and drove James into exile. William was put on the throne, with support gathered in part by issuing the Act of Toleration in 1689, which granted freedom of worship to all dissenting Trinitarian churches *except* Roman Catholics.

In opting for toleration of the Puritan dissenters (rather than their incorporation), the Anglican stance of the Church of England was solidified. But William's replacement of James II also triggered a rebalancing of this stance. A group of nine bishops and over three hundred clergy refused to take the Oath of Allegiance to William and Mary, on the grounds that they had sworn the same oath to James II, who was still alive, and could not break it. These 'nonjurors'[5] were strong Anglicans, putting particular stress on conformity to the teaching and practice of the early church. Part of their hesitation was the lack of precedent in the early church for supporting a revolution against a reigning sovereign. When they were deprived of their positions in 1689, becoming a splinter tradition that dwindled over the coming century, the Anglican stance of the established church was left less 'primitivist,' and somewhat less 'high-church.'

In contrast with its predecessor, the eighteenth century was void of major political changes that directly shifted theological stances in the Church of England. From the final stage of the Stuart reign under Queen Anne (1702–1714) through the successive Hanoverians (George I, II, and III) the general Anglican commitments of the church remained in place. There was a relative tone of peace and unity within the church. The differences that were present are best understood as varying *tendencies*, rather than as aggressively competing parties.[6]

The most significant divergent tendencies related to the cultural spread of Enlightenment convictions. To be sure, these convictions took more moderate expression in Britain than they did in continental Europe and were generally less antagonistic toward religion.[7] If anything, they reinforced the Arminian and holy living emphases characteristic of Anglicanism. But they also posed challenges for the Anglican emphasis on the unity of Christian tradition, scripture, and reason. In particular, the Enlightenment tendency to question *traditional* authority opened the door to suggestions that later doctrinal formulations (like the doctrine of the Trinity) were not organic developments from scripture but ill-fitting metaphysical impositions upon it. This inclined a growing number of Church of England clergy toward the 'latitudinarian' stance that only the clear teachings of scripture should be considered essential to affirm, placing traditional doctrinal elaborations in the category of nonessential 'opinions.' A much smaller, and more radical, group of deist 'free thinkers,' like John Toland and Matthew Tindal, rejected privileging scripture, turning to 'natural religion' as the normative basis for belief and practice.

One other dynamic in eighteenth-century religious life that must be mentioned is the evangelical revival that bubbled up in continental European pietism, spilled over to Britain, and spread to North America.[8] At the core of this 'religion of the heart' was the concern not to equate Christian identity with mere church affiliation or intellectual affirmation of Christian doctrine. In reaction to their perception of such tendencies, pietists emphasized the importance of a *personal* faith in Christ's atoning work that is evidenced by a specific *experience* of assurance (the 'witness of the Holy Spirit'). They also developed innovative structures and practices to nurture this personal experience of faith.

John and Charles Wesley's Stance within Their Theological Context

The Wesley brothers had connections with most of the currents just surveyed. Their grandfathers on both sides – John Westley (c. 1636–1670) and Samuel Annesley (c. 1620–1696) – were Puritan clergy expelled from the established church when Charles II was recalled. Yet both of the Wesley brothers' parents opted, as young adults, to return to the established church. Samuel and Susanna clearly shared Anglican convictions concerning predestination, holy living, primitivism, high-church spirituality, and the like. Their most famous disagreement was over William of Orange's replacing James II, which Samuel supported while Susanna joined in the nonjuror dissent. Thus John and Charles imbibed classic Anglican sensibilities in their youth, including the deep appreciation for early church doctrine and practice championed by the nonjurors. These commitments were reinforced by their Oxford training, which privileged the writings of the Caroline divines. But they were also exposed to the currents of Enlightenment thought in their academic work. On their trip to Georgia they made contact with the emerging evangelical movement in its Moravian form. This contact facilitated their spiritual renewal in 1738, and the beginnings of the Methodist revival.

Interweaving these influences, the mature theological stance of both John and Charles Wesley was Anglican at its center, shaped by the holy living divines, with overtones of the nonjurors' particular appreciation for the earliest church. It was also permeated throughout by the pietist emphasis on experiencing the empowering work of the Holy Spirit. Grounded in this focus, the brothers shared a notable willingness to draw upon moderate Reformed voices (within the earlier established church and present dissenting traditions) and recent Roman Catholic mystical writers (mainly French and Spanish).[9] Both the focus and the breadth of these commitments are evident in the remnants of the brothers' personal libraries.[10] The core of the collections is composed of Anglican doctrinal standards and the writings of early church fathers. This is surrounded by the works of Caroline divines like Benjamin Calamy, John Pearson, and Robert Sanderson; holy living divines like Richard Allestree and Jeremy Taylor; and eighteenth-century Anglican stalwarts like Francis Atterbury, John Potter, and William Wake. But there is also a solid representation of pietist writers and moderate Puritan voices like Isaac Ambrose, Richard Baxter, and Isaac Watts, along with a sprinkling of Roman Catholic authors. Significantly, the same focus and breadth are evident in the selection of writings that John Wesley recommended to his Methodist people in the fifty-volume *Christian Library* (1749–1755).[11]

This raises the question of how the Wesley brothers conceived the relationship between their focal convictions and their openness to those with differing convictions. John was more articulate on this point than Charles, and a bit more pliant.[12] Prior to their contact with the Moravians, both John and Charles were ardent defenders of the high-church Anglican stance on most issues. This fervor was redirected as they embraced the pietist emphasis on personal assurance of God's love as the heart of 'real' Christianity. John once expressed this new emphasis in the contrast that 'orthodoxy, or right opinions, is, at best, but a very slender part of religion.'[13] When questioned, he denied that he was dismissing all concern for doctrine in Christian life; he was only stressing that Christian life involved more than *mere* affirmation of correct doctrine. But over time John sketched a hierarchy of significance among theological claims that overlapped somewhat with latitudinarian emphases. He affirmed that there are core doctrinal convictions, central to scripture and the early creeds (Trinity, incarnation, human sin, atonement, etc.), that are essential to Christian life and constitutive of Christian identity. Those who deny these convictions place themselves outside the Christian fold. But he was quick to insist that there is room for legitimate variation of 'opinion' in philosophical articulation of these core doctrines.[14] Moreover, there are a number of theological debates that are less clearly defined in scripture and the creeds, and are, correspondingly, less pivotal to authentic Christian life. In the sermon 'Catholic Spirit,' John encouraged his readers to allow for alternative 'opinions' on these debates while maintaining Christian fellowship with all who agree on the 'main branches of Christian doctrine.'[15] As a specific case in point, while he staunchly rejected unconditional predestination, John Wesley usually classed this difference with Whitefield and the Calvinist wing of the Methodist revival as a matter of 'opinion' that should not rupture their cooperation in ministry.[16]

Forms of John and Charles Wesley's Theological Activity

The Anglican setting of John and Charles Wesley is reflected in the dominant forms of their theological activity.[17] Through the second millennium, as specialized academic institutions took over the task of training clergy, it became common in western Christianity to identify serious theological activity with the curricular forms in this new setting – compendiums, *summae*, systematic theologies, apologetic treatises, and the like. This stood in some contrast with the early church, where theology was centered in the pastoral task of guiding the formation of Christian belief and character in believers, and the most prized forms were materials like hymns, liturgies, catechetical orations, and spiritual discipline manuals. When Henry VIII severed the continental oversight of the Church of England, the leadership he put in place turned to the early church for normative guidance. Embracing the earlier precedent, they privileged the theological forms of liturgies (the *Book of Common Prayer*) and catechetical sermons (the *Homilies*), alongside the *Articles of Religion*.

Likewise, manuals for clergy candidates in the Church of England, including the one that John Wesley read before his ordination, typically stressed that 'theology is doubtless a *practical science*' and located its focal task in the work of pastoral theologians (or 'divines') guiding Christian communities.[18] Thus, John and Charles Wesley naturally understood their role as shepherds of a renewal movement within the church to be the work of divines. They were also readily drawn to exercise this task through forms likely to impact the range of believers.

One form that they prized was hymnody. John's early *Collections of Psalms and Hymns* (1737, 1738, 1741) were among the first to introduce congregational hymns into formal Anglican worship.[19] While Charles soon proved the more gifted creator of hymns and other religious verse, John's appreciation for the formative power of this genre led to publishing a series of hymnbooks for Methodist (and broader) worship, including the definitive 1780 *Collection of Hymns for the People Called Methodists* that he characterized as a 'little body of experimental and practical divinity.'[20] Charles complemented John's broader volumes with booklets of hymns on each of the major Christian festivals, as well as collections for use in family worship, etc.

Preaching was another prominent activity of both brothers. They valued sermons for more than just their motivational impact, viewing them as significant means of shaping the faith and actions of believers. After all, they inherited from their father the Anglican privileging of sermons as a key way for pastoral theologians to convey to their congregations 'the whole body of divinity.'[21] This was surely John's goal in publishing the volumes of his *Sermons on Several Occasions* as models for his lay preachers and to benefit the larger Methodist family.

Early church and Anglican precedent also help to explain the amount of time that John devoted to producing other practical-theological materials for the movement – such as recrafting the liturgy in the *Book of Common Prayer* to provide the *Sunday Service* for his followers in North America after they won independence from the British crown and established church, gathering selective *Explanatory Notes* to guide lay readers through the Old and New Testaments, and republishing numerous abridgments of his favorite devotional and catechetical materials by other authors. Isabel Rivers has even argued that John's *Journal* may be the most important work of 'practical divinity' in the eighteenth century.[22]

This latter valuation points toward an important distinction. Eighteenth-century English authors typically identified three genres of theology: (1) practical divinity, focused on nurturing and forming believers; (2) doctrinal or speculative divinity, concerned with articulation and defense of specific doctrines as normative; and (3) controversial divinity, devoted to criticizing on rational, historical, or scriptural grounds the beliefs and practices of rival groups. There is obvious overlap between the concerns of each genre, but their focal purpose drew the varying genres toward different literary forms. Practical divinity found a natural home in 'first-order' forms used in Christian worship and devotional practice – liturgy, catechisms, prayer guides, and the like. The other two genres were more often expressed in essays, tracts, and monographs.

The majority of the Wesley brothers' publications fit within the focus and literary forms of practical divinity. John repeatedly defended this preference by a quote from the early church, 'God made practical divinity necessary; the devil, controversial.'[23] Both John and Charles recognized that the formative task of pastoral theologians required attention at times to normative and apologetic concerns. Charles typically remained in lyrical mode when addressing these concerns, as in his satirical attack on unconditional election in *Hymns of God's Everlasting Love* (1741–1742). It is hard to imagine singing many of these in corporate worship and few found their way into John's collections. John more conventionally adopted tracts or essays when focused on normative or apologetic concerns. Some of his essays were book-length, with *The Doctrine of Original Sin* (1757) being the longest monograph he ever published.

Shared Convictions of John and Charles Wesley's Theology

What characteristic theological convictions are found in this range of materials from the hands of John and Charles Wesley? A comprehensive survey is beyond the scope of this chapter.[24] But a general orientation will aid readers in preparing for further study. The brothers shared broad areas of agreement on theological matters. Thus, hymns of Charles are often the best illustrations of points that John makes in sermons. But there were also some points of tension. We will highlight central shared convictions before touching on the most prominent tensions.

To begin with theological method, the brothers strongly endorsed the Protestant emphasis on the primacy of scripture. Indeed, they placed study of scripture at the heart of Christian life. John encouraged Methodists to read both the Old and New Testament daily, providing them with the *Explanatory Notes*; while Charles adopted a routine of writing reflective hymns on passages of scripture (a type of lyrical *lectio divina*). But the brothers rejected any suggestion that theology could be based on scripture *alone*. In good Anglican fashion, they valued the insights of tradition in interpreting scripture, and frequently appealed to both reason and experience in defending a theological stance.

This means that inquiry into John or Charles Wesley's convictions on a theological issue should always begin by noting what they shared in common with broader Christian tradition and their Anglican peers. Too much focus on their distinctive claims is likely to overlook central assumed convictions, and thereby distort the claims it highlights. The precedent of the brothers is more promising. They typically endorsed the Anglican standards, and then highlighted their concern by appeal to the standards. A good example is John's publication (encouraged by Charles) of an extract from the *Homilies* early in the evangelical revival to defend their embrace of the pietist emphasis on assurance of one's saving relationship to Christ. The extract placed in italics every insistence in the selected homilies that defined faith as including a *sure trust and confidence* in God's mercy.[25]

In this same vein, the Wesley brothers typically rejected attempts to define Methodism by its distinctive doctrines, emphasizing instead a distinctive concern for spiritual life.[26] At most, they were willing to concede that Methodists placed special emphasis upon certain traditional doctrines, particularly in the area of soteriology. Their characteristic concern in this area was to reclaim a more holistic account of the human problem and of God's salvific response.

On one front this meant defending the universal reality of human spiritual need in the face of idealized accounts of human nature by some Enlightenment thinkers. John's *Doctrine of Original Sin* (1757) was devoted to this concern. Characteristically, the treatise focuses less on debates over inherited guilt, or the modes of transmitting depravity, than on demonstrating the shared human experience of spiritual infirmity and bondage. Imagery of spiritual infirmity permeates Charles' hymns as well.

Turning the focus around, the Wesleys were equally concerned to reject depictions of depravity as the final word about humanity. As good Anglicans, convinced that 'God's mercy is over all God's works' (Ps. 145:9), they insisted that God reaches out in love to all persons in their fallen condition. Through that encounter, which they termed 'prevenient grace,'[27] God awakens sufficient awareness and upholds sufficient volitional integrity that we can *either* responsively embrace God's deeper salvific work in our lives *or* culpably resist it.

This brings us to the brothers' dominant soteriological concern – countering the tendency of many to restrict the present benefits of salvation largely to forensic justification. As John put it, 'By salvation I mean, not barely (according to the vulgar notion) deliverance from hell, or going to heaven, but a present deliverance from sin, a restoration of the soul to its primitive health.'[28] Both John and Charles placed sanctification at the center of soteriology, valuing justification as the doorway into this larger focus. They called their Methodist followers to 'holiness of heart and life' nurtured in the full range of the 'means of grace.' One of their enduring contributions was emphasis on the many ways in which the Lord's Supper sustains Christian life, epitomized in the 1745 collection of *Hymns on the Lord's Supper*.[29]

Given the coherence of the Christian worldview, these focal concerns in soteriology were reflected in characteristic emphases within the other loci of theology. For example, both John and Charles present God's reigning attribute as love – in specific contrast with sovereignty. They also placed strong emphasis on the responsive relationship between God and humanity, which opened the door for some later Wesleyans to question atemporal models of God's existence.[30]

The Wesley brothers stood with the Anglican Articles of Religion in affirming the two natures of Christ and the role of Christ's death in satisfying God's justice. But several scholars have noted how Charles' hymns in particular offer a rich range of images for appreciating that Christ's death not only atoned for guilt, but freed us from slavery to sin, convinced us of God's wondrous love, and renewed us in the divine image.[31] Their broader soteriological concerns also led the brothers to emphasize relating to Christ 'in all his offices' – not just as the priest who atones for guilt, but also as the prophet who teaches the ways in which we are to live, and as the king who oversees the restoration of wholeness in our lives.

Moving to pneumatology, the Wesley brothers focused more attention on the work of the Holy Spirit than was common in their Anglican setting. It began with stress on the assurance of God's pardoning love, or the 'witness of the Spirit,' which evokes and empowers a believer's responsive love for God and neighbor. They then emphasized how this 'new birth' makes possible the journey of sanctification, or growth in the 'fruit of the Spirit.' Add to this John's particular concern to reclaim (within the western tradition) the 'gifts of the Spirit,' like the gift of preaching, for laymen and women. The combination of emphases led a contemporary opponent to characterize their movement as 'Montanus revived.'[32] More recently, scholars are prone to see this recovered emphasis on the work of the Spirit as a significant contribution to the renewal of Trinitarian theology in Anglicanism.[33]

Divergences between John and Charles Wesley

The shared convictions of the Wesley brothers were substantial and broad ranging, contributing to the coherence of their movement. But there were some areas of divergence in view which found echoes in the broader movement. One prominent difference concerned the potential of a split between Methodists and the Church of England. Charles was clearly the stronger 'Church Methodist.'[34] He was committed to the revival of *The Church of England*, while John was more committed to the *revival* of The Church of England. This difference played over into their disagreements on other topics, such as the use of lay preachers.

Some differences between the brothers may have reflected their personalities. John was generally healthy and optimistic in outlook, while Charles endured significant physical suffering and was frequently melancholy.[35] This possibly contributed to their divergence on the question of whether suffering was integral to spiritual growth. Charles readily spoke of the 'sad necessity of pain' for growth in holiness, while John consistently rejected such causal connection.[36] On this point Charles stands closer to the classic spiritual emphasis on the 'dark night of the soul.'

Moving beyond the relative contribution of suffering, John and Charles diverged sharply in the aftermath of the perfectionist controversy of the 1760s over the stress they had earlier placed on attaining *entire* sanctification, or 'Christian Perfection,' in this life. While John continued for some time to encourage hope that one could enter into this experience soon after justification, Charles increasingly ridiculed such hope and discouraged anyone from testifying to the experience.[37] The possibilities, limits, and dynamics of sanctification have been central to Methodist proclamation and debate ever since.

One other divergence is worthy of note. John Wesley's optimism about the transformative impact of the Spirit in individual lives led him to embrace an early form of postmillennialism in his later years. This move was reflected in his encouragement of the Methodist people to get involved not just in works of mercy, but also in the work of social transformation.[38] By contrast, Charles took on the apocalyptic tones of premillennialism in the midst of natural disasters and wars during the 1750s, then retreated to the eschatological agnosticism typical of amillennialism in his later years.[39]

Reception and Transmission of Wesleyan Theology in Methodism

The theological contributions of John and Charles Wesley played a significant formative role in the early development of Methodism. They also continue to hold some type of *normative* status in most bodies of world Methodism. This role goes back to the 'model deed,' which was adopted in 1763, in response to Calvinist Methodist preachers using preaching houses that John Wesley had built to turn audiences against Arminian theology. The deed restricted the pulpit in these chapels to persons who preached in accordance with the four volumes of John's *Sermons* currently in print (1746–1760) and his *Explanatory Notes upon the New Testament* (1755). This set a precedent for Methodists in the Wesleyan wing of the movement that their theological teaching should emulate both the Wesley brothers' embrace of the core doctrines of classic Christianity and characteristic Wesleyan emphases within these doctrines.

This precedent was formalized when the remnants of the Methodist societies in North America were gathered after the Revolutionary War and organized as the Methodist Episcopal Church in 1784. John sent over for the new church an abridged set of the Articles of Religion of the Church of England to serve as the affirmation of core Christian doctrine. He also expected them to continue preaching in accordance with his *Sermons* and *Notes*. Although the two sides of this expectation are not formally adopted in every current branch of the Methodist family of churches, the general expectation remains.[40]

When attention turns from formal expectations to the realities of practice, it is arguable that the continuity of Wesleyan themes in Methodist theology is due more to the popularity of some of Charles' hymns than to John's doctrinal publications.[41] After John's death, Methodists in England tended to align with the dissenting traditions. This was even more the case in North America where the main peers surrounding Methodism were Congregationalists, Presbyterians, and Baptists. In these peer settings, theological standards were generally conceived on the model of John Calvin's *Institutes*. They made clear that John Wesley's *Sermons* did not measure up! This pushed Methodists to develop scholastic compendiums of theology. These compendiums were generally conservative in scope and much more Protestant in tone than Wesley's precedent. Indeed, the compendiums rarely cited either of the Wesleys, and then almost exclusively in the section on soteriology. The most prominent example is Richard Watson's *Theological Institutes* (1823–1824), the standard theology text in Methodist circles for over fifty years.

Toward the end of the nineteenth century, Methodist theologians in both England and North America were interacting more with currents in their culture. They also turned attention to the new theological trends being championed in Germany. This resulted, by the turn of the century, in a stream of 'modernist' or 'liberal' Methodist theologies. Mixed within this stream were concerns for cultural apologetics, for undergirding the Social Gospel, and for addressing the challenge of the historical and natural sciences. Many of these agenda resonated with Wesleyan emphases and there was the occasional attempt to claim John Wesley as a forerunner. The more common tendency was to ignore his writings as products of an outmoded age.

In the mid-twentieth century, the optimism of liberal theology was subject to critique by the movement known as Neo-orthodoxy. Methodists who resonated with this critique, but who were less comfortable with the one-sided alternatives being championed, began to reclaim the Wesley brothers' soteriological balance. A landmark in this renewed theological interest was the volume on *John Wesley* that Albert C. Outler published in 1964 as part of Oxford University Press Library of Protestant Thought. It sold more copies than any other volume in the series, demonstrating growing interest in Wesleyan theology in Methodist circles and beyond.

This interest fueled the growth of Wesley Studies as a scholarly field through the second half of the twentieth century. The Oxford Institute of Methodist

Theological Studies began gathering scholars for periodic conferences in 1958, with the Wesleys as a frequent focus of attention. A new scholarly journal on *Methodist History* was launched in 1962. The Wesleyan Theological Society was formed in 1965, issuing its own *Wesleyan Theological Journal*. A Wesleyan Studies Group was organized at the American Academy of Religion in 1982. In 1988 Abingdon Press launched the Kingswood Book series, dedicated to Wesleyan and Methodist scholarship. The Charles Wesley Society was added to the mix in 1990. Chairs of Wesley Studies have been established at universities such as Duke, Southern Methodist and Vanderbilt, as well as several research centers.[42]

This growing scholarly interest has been paralleled in many of the denominations in the Methodist family by increased expectation of studying the theological writings of the Wesley brothers in ministerial education.

Growing Edges in Studying the Theology of John and Charles Wesley

As scholarship on the theology of the Wesley brothers developed, some interpretive issues emerged. Most of these are finding resolution. For example, there is now broad agreement about the need to take their Anglican stance seriously, avoiding readings that lean too heavily in either a Protestant or Catholic (East or West) direction. Similarly, the importance of studying the range of the brothers' writings, not just those given 'official' status in Methodist settings, is generally acknowledged. Finally, most scholars concur on the need to recognize – but not exaggerate – the transitions in John Wesley's thought between his early writings (1733–1738), his middle writings (1738–1765), and his most mature theological works (1765–1791).[43]

In recent decades, about ten books or dissertations and several journal articles have appeared annually on John and Charles Wesley. At their best, these embrace at least the first half of the task that Albert Outler articulated for 'Phase III' of Wesley Studies in 1985, namely analyzing the Wesley brothers on various topics with a broad and nuanced sense of their context and their sources.[44] A perusal of recent dissertations will notice several focal themes.[45] There has been significant interest, for example, in clarifying John Wesley's epistemology, showing that his 'empiricism' is grounded in the Aristotelian logical tradition at Oxford and stands in some tension with John Locke.[46] Another topic of high interest has been John's grounding of the holy life in the 'tempers' or 'affections,' exploring resonance with the model of a 'virtue ethic' in Aquinas and others.[47]

While focus on John still predominates in theological studies, there are promising signs that Charles is receiving more scholarly consideration. A fitting exemplar is the insightful contextual analysis of the theme of suffering in

Charles' hymns, which shows how his hymns helped early Methodists make sense of and draw spiritual benefit from the suffering that they endured.[48]

Returning to John, the range of topics being considered has broadened in recent years. For example, there has been attention to the theological dimensions of his interest in medicine and the natural sciences.[49] Likewise, suggestions of the significance of his theological account of conversion and sanctification for psychology have led to a series of interdisciplinary articles, and even the creation of The Society for the Study of Psychology and Wesleyan Theology.[50]

As this suggests, many of the recent studies are building on careful contextual study with exploration of the second half of Outler's vision for Phase III, that is, continuing the trajectory that John and Charles began, addressing new issues in light of their characteristic convictions and concerns.

Editions of John and Charles Wesley's Theological Writings

The long standard, and still broadly used, collection of John Wesley's *Works* was edited by Thomas Jackson, and released in 1829–1831. There are many limitations to this edition. In the first place, it is not complete. Not only was Jackson unaware of some of John's writings, he omitted portions that he thought reflected badly on Wesley. For example, in the setting after Methodism had separated from the Church of England, Jackson omitted items where Wesley stressed his connection to the Anglican Church (such as the extract from the *Homilies*). Secondly, Jackson is not consistent in which edition of various Wesley publications he prints, nor does he indicate variants between editions. Thirdly, Jackson only rarely indicates the sources from which Wesley drew many of his publications. Finally, Jackson's edition provides little introductory material or annotations to set Wesley's writings in context.

One of the key moments in Wesley Studies was the launch in 1960 of the Wesley Works Editorial Project, dedicated to producing the first critical edition of John Wesley's writings.[51] It addresses all of the shortcomings of the Jackson edition, and much more. As of this writing, sixteen of the projected thirty-five volumes are in print as *The Bicentennial Edition of the Works of John Wesley*. They have become the standard text for scholarly study of John Wesley.

Until the *Bicentennial Edition* is complete, however, it will be necessary for students to draw as well on the Jackson edition, as well as other resources listed in the select bibliography below. Readers should be aware that there is a CD-ROM version of the major sections of the *Bicentennial Edition* that are in print.[52] For convenience, this CD-ROM also includes the complete Jackson edition. The Jackson edition is also available online in several locations.[53]

The situation is somewhat similar regarding Charles Wesley's works. Once again, Thomas Jackson issued *The Journal of Charles Wesley* (1849), a two-volume set that included a selection of private letters and poems. This was soon complimented by a thirteen-volume set of *The Poetical Works of John and Charles Wesley* (1868–1872), edited by George Osborn. Both works have significant limitations. Fortunately, students have a growing set of scholarly editions as alternatives. The select bibliography lists print editions of Charles' sermons, his manuscript journal (in more complete and accurate form than in Jackson), and the poetry that Charles left in manuscript which Osborn omitted. Print editions of all of Charles' letters are in process.[54] In addition, readers should note the project to make all of Charles' poetry available online in annotated edition at the Center for Studies in the Wesleyan Tradition.[55]

For Further Reading

John Wesley's Works

The Bicentennial Edition of the Works of John Wesley. Frank Baker and Richard P. Heitzenrater, general eds. Nashville: Abingdon, 1984ff. [Volumes 7, 11, 25, and 26 appeared first as the *Oxford Edition of The Works of John Wesley*. Oxford: Clarendon, 1975–1983].

A Christian Library: Consisting of Extracts from and Abridgments of the Choicest Pieces of Practical Divinity Which have been Published in the English Tongue. 50 vols. Bristol: Farley, 1749–1755.

Explanatory Notes upon the New Testament. 2 vols. 3rd ed. Bristol: Graham and Pine, 1760–1762 (many later reprints).

Explanatory Notes upon the Old Testament. 3 vols. Bristol: Pine, 1765; reprint ed., Salem, OH: Schmul, 1975.

John Wesley's Prayer Book: The Sunday Service of the Methodists in North America. James F. White, ed. Akron, Ohio: OSL Publications, 1995.

The Letters of the Rev. John Wesley, A.M. 8 vols. John Telford, ed. London: Epworth, 1931.

A Survey of the Wisdom of God in the Creation, or A Compendium of Natural Philosophy. 4th ed. London: J. Paramore, 1784.

The Works of John Wesley. 14 vols. 3rd ed. Thomas Jackson, ed. London: J. Mason, 1829–1831; reprint ed., Grand Rapids, MI: Baker, 1979.

Charles Wesley's Works

The Manuscript Journal of the Rev. Charles Wesley, M.A. 2 vols. S. T. Kimbrough Jr. and Kenneth G. C. Newport, eds. Nashville: Kingswood Books, 2008.

The Sermons of Charles Wesley: A Critical Edition with Introduction and Notes. Kenneth G. C. Newport, ed. New York: Oxford University Press, 2001.

The Unpublished Poetry of Charles Wesley. 3 vols. S. T. Kimbrough, Jr. and Oliver A. Beckerlegge, eds. Nashville, TN: Kingswood Books, 1988–1992.

Introductory and Survey Studies

Abraham, William J. *Wesley for Armchair Theologians*. Louisville: Westminster John Knox, 2005.

Collins, Kenneth Joseph. *The Theology of John Wesley: Holy Love and the Shape of Grace*. Nashville: Abingdon, 2007.

Maddox, Randy L. *Responsible Grace: John Wesley's Practical Theology*. Nashville: Kingswood Books, 1994.

Rattenbury, J. [John] Ernest. *The Evangelical Doctrines of Charles Wesley's Hymns*. London: Epworth, 1941.

3 Hymnody of Charles Wesley

S T Kimbrough, Jr.

Eighteenth-century England was a formative period for English-language hymnody. Isaac Watts (1674–1748), who wrote over six hundred hymns, is often called the 'father of English hymnody.' Standing within the Nonconformist tradition, he produced two especially important volumes, *Hymns and Spiritual Songs* (1707–1709) and *Horae Lyricae* (1706–1709), which moved beyond traditional psalm singing to a freer, if not paraphrastic, formulation of metrical verse, and was relatively easy to sing. Like the Wesleys, who would follow him and build, to some extent, upon his model, Watts was a student of Greek, Hebrew, and Latin and was able to convey superbly the sense of scriptural passages in his lyricism.

John and Charles Wesley had a deep appreciation for Watts' achievements. Many of his hymns were included in the first publication issued under both their names, *Hymns and Sacred Poems* (1739). The Wesley brothers were, however, very different from Watts in that they were loyal priests of the Church of England. Watts, the nonconformist, did not write hymns for the Christian year or draw on the language of the liturgy in the way the Wesleys did. Watts tended toward a singular evangelical focus rooted in the scriptures, while the Wesleys combined a high church emphasis with an evangelical one rooted in the scriptures, the liturgies of the Church of England, and the Christian year, yet their hymns reached far beyond their own denomination.

While Watts set the tone and established a pattern for English-language evangelical hymnody, the Wesleys united evangelical hymnody and the liturgical and devotional life of the established church.

To understand Charles Wesley as a poet, it is important to review briefly his familial poetical heritage, for it helped shape his poetical gifts. His father, Samuel, an Anglican priest, was an erudite classicist and poet. His first poetical publication was *Maggots* (1685), a series of rather immature poems on somewhat superficial subjects, e.g., 'On the Grunting of a Hog.' Nevertheless, his composition in Hudibrastics and Pindarics indicated much more than a superficial knowledge of poetical structure. His second volume of poetry was titled *Life of Our Blessed Lord and Saviour* (1693), a series of heroic couplets in epic style. The preface to this volume bore the title 'Essay on Heroic Poetry' and provides considerable insight into Samuel Wesley's erudition, particularly his acquaintance with Aristotle, Horace, Homer, Balzac, Rapin, Philo, Josephus, Boyle, Cowley, Virgil, Spenser, Milton, Dryden, and many others.

In 1695 he published *Elegies*, which mourned the deaths of Queen Mary II and Archbishop Tillotson. In addition to *An Epistle to a Friend Concerning Poetry* (1700), Samuel Wesley published four more volumes of poetry. A number of Samuel and Susanna (his wife) Wesley's nineteen children were greatly influenced by this wealth of classical and poetical knowledge. Of the ten surviving children, seven girls and three boys, the eldest son Samuel, also an Anglican priest, was a gifted poet and satirist, as revealed in his volume *Poems on Several Occasions* published in 1736, just three years before his death. We know that Charles Wesley was an admirer of Samuel's poetry and on occasion, when his brother was headmaster of Tiverton School, would visit Samuel and copy his verse. All three of the surviving brothers, Samuel, John, and Charles, were excellent students of the classics, mastered Greek, Hebrew, and Latin, and became gifted poets. Their sister, Mehetabel, affectionately known as Hetty, who also became a published poet, could read the Greek New Testament when she was only eight years old. John also mastered German and demonstrated his own poetical gifts by translating many German hymns into eloquent English verse. John's and Charles' knowledge of Latin was so advanced that they could easily converse in the language.

It is fair to say that Charles Wesley was surrounded by poetical and classical influences in his own family, which played a significant role in his own development as a poet. It is reported, however, that his mother once warned him that he should never attempt to make a living as a poet. That was, of course, never his goal.

During his university years at Oxford, Charles combined an ongoing interest in the classics and poetry by writing metrical paraphrases of some of the Latin poets, such as Ovid, Virgil, Juvenal, and Horace, of which a few examples survive. Through such discipline his gifts in the use of meter, rhyme, assonance, alliteration, and other poetical characteristics were honed. Here is one example from Horace's *Satires* (I.iii.107–110).[1]

> *Fuit ante Helenam mulier*[2] *teterrima belli*
> *Causa: Sed ignotis perierunt mortibus omnes*[3]
> *Quos Venerem incertum rapientes, more ferarum,*
> *Viribus editior caedebat, ut in grege taurus.*

> Full many a war has been for woman wag'd,[4]
> Ere half the world in Helen's cause engag'd;
> But unrecorded in historic verse,
> Obscurely died those savage ravishers:

> Who, like brute beasts, the female bore away,
> Till some superior brute re-seiz'd the prey.
> As a wild bull, his rival bull o'erthrown,
> Claims the whole subject-herd, and reigns alone.

While at Oxford University, Charles deepened his knowledge of Greek, Hebrew, and Latin, thus garnering a superb knowledge of the content and meaning of the scriptures. In addition, not only at Oxford, but throughout his life, Charles' knowledge of biblical poetry, i.e., primarily the Psalms, was greatly enhanced through the regular use of the *Book of Common Prayer*[5] Psalter (Coverdale translation of 1535) in public worship and private devotions.

The Literary Context of Charles Wesley's Verse

Wesley's hymnody is often read as a sacred literary corpus in isolation, but nothing could do greater injustice to his work. Literary critics have also made a great mistake by considering hymn literature as unworthy of careful study. Charles Wesley is a man of his times whose hymns emerge from his education and literary influences of the period. Donald Davie has rightly observed in his book *A Gathered Church: The Literature of the English Dissenting Interest, 1700–1930*:

> One looks for a long time before finding any attempt to place Charles Wesley, or Isaac Watts either, in relation to the more secular poetry of their times – in relation to Pope, or Thomson, or Gray or Goldsmith. One consequence is that the eighteenth century is thought to have produced little *lyric* poetry, whereas the eighteenth-century lyric is to be found in the hymn books just as surely as seventeenth-century lyric is in George Herbert's *Temple*. The dependence of line after line of Wesley on the precedent of Matthew Prior has been duly noted, but no one has explored the significance, stylistically and historically, of this surprising connection with the suave and frequently improper author of 'Henry and Emma.'[6]

One of the earliest significant attempts to explore literary influences on Charles Wesley is the work of Henry Bett, *The Hymns of Methodism*.[7] Of particular interest is his concluding chapter 'The Hymns and the Poets.' Bett traces the influences of Virgil's *Aeneid*, Edward Young's *Night Thoughts*, Homer's *Illiad*, John Milton's *Paradise Lost*, and recollections in Wesley's poetry of William Shakespeare, John Dryden, Matthew Prior, and others.

An extremely important volume, *Hymns Unbidden*, by Martha Winburn England and John Sparrow was published by the New York Public Library in 1966.[8] England's contributions to the volume include a series of erudite chapters comparing the work of Wesley with that of his contemporary William Blake, as well as with that of John Milton. Her literary analysis is exemplary for all students of the Wesleys. She is able to see beyond details to the larger strokes of continuity and discontinuity, particularly in her study of Wesley's *Hymns for the Nation*, in 1782:

> What *Hymns for the Nation* has in common with Blake is belligerence, exuberance, excess.[9] . . . Wesley and Blake are comparable in arrogance, vulgarity, and excess. These traits of enthusiasm poetry entered into all their poetic successes and can be seen with greatest clarity in their poetic failures.[10] . . . Their poetry is prophetic and evangelical, the messages are intensely personal and aimed at reformation of the social order. They meant to bring about an inner change, in the heart, the imagination, and hoped that social changes would come about as a result.[11]

Fortunately, in more recent times others have explored in depth the rich literary sources from which Wesley draws and which shape his diction, style, meters, phraseology, imagery, and grammar. In *A Collection of Hymns for the Use of the People Called Methodists*, volume 7 of the series *The Works of John Wesley* (1983), James Dale addressed 'The Literary Setting of Wesley's Hymns'[12] with a strong emphasis on the Wesleys' reliance on works of James Thomson, John Milton, Alexander Pope, John Dryden, and others. These influences are not merely of diction and poetical structure, for as Dale avers, 'even a passing acquaintance with the verse of Dryden and Pope, of Johnson and Gray, makes clear that reason and emotion can coexist, that strong feeling gains in intensity when it is given controlled and concise utterance.'[13] Most certainly the coexistence of reason and emotion play a vital role in the thought and theology of Charles Wesley and is reflected in his hymns.

One of the most helpful recent discussions titled 'The Hymns of Charles Wesley and the Poetic Tradition' by J. R. Watson appeared as chapter 21 in the collection of essays *Charles Wesley, Life, Literature and Legacy*, edited by Kenneth G. C. Newport and Ted A. Campbell.[14] Watson makes a convincing case for the strong influence of Greek and Latin poets on Charles Wesley. His discussion of the importance of Ovid's *Metapmorphoses* is particularly valuable for understanding some of Wesley's *Hymns on the Lord's Supper*, an influence generally overlooked by students and teachers of that important volume.

Watson has eloquently summarized Wesley's assimilation and articulation of a vast array of literary influences.

> The idea of the text as a tissue of quotations has an obvious application to Charles Wesley's hymns. His choice of culture-centres comes from his

education, his reading, his memory, his understanding and appreciation, his critical sense, his personal needs. He takes them into his hymns, and then sends them out, filled with their accumulated meaning, for the readers and singers to take in to themselves: the words come down to us from Charles Wesley's many sources, but enriched by him. They are from different places – the Bible, the Prayer Book, other poets, such as Herbert, Matthew Prior, Elizabeth Singer Rowe, Samuel Wesley – but the very fact that Charles Wesley has used them gives them a new lustre. His hymns shine with words he has transformed.[15]

James Dale illustrates[16] beautifully what Watson avers by exploring words, phrases, and concepts, which Wesley borrows and/or appropriates from Elizabeth Singer Rowe in his well-known hymn 'Christ whose glory fills the skies.' The line, 'Visit then this soul of mine,' Dale sees as a virtual quotation of Rowe's line 'O! visit then thy servant, Lord' from a poem of Rowe that John Wesley included in *Moral and Sacred Poems* (1744). Dale notes further the quotation by Charles Wesley in his *Hymns Occasioned by an Earthquake* (1750) of the phrase 'amaranthine bowers' from Rowe's poem 'On Heaven': '. . . those blest shades, and amaranthine bowers.'[17]

It is clear from the hitherto unpublished poetry[18] of Charles Wesley that he was capable of writing secular verse that would have stood on its own among the poets of his time. For example, he composed Alexandrine verse, and wrote in heroic epic style 'The American War,'[19] a poem of 615 octosyllabic lines of rhyming couplets with occasional rhyming triplets. He addressed a variety of subjects, such as, music, contemporary events, patriotism, and political ideas. Yet, he chose not to publish such verse. 'He chose instead,' as Kenneth D. Shields appropriately states, 'to employ his considerable talents to serve his Lord as a priest and evangel of His Word. In his pursuit of Christian Perfection, he rejected . . . the pursuit of a literary reputation.'[20] He chose to be a sacred poet, a purpose to which God had called him. While all of his sacred verse by no means reaches heights of literary eloquence, much of his lyricism does and it deserves to stand among the best poets of his time and their works.

Charles Wesley's Sacred Poetry

It is not by chance that John and Charles Wesley selected the title *Hymns and Sacred Poems* for their first joint publication in 1739, and for two succeeding volumes in 1740 and 1742, and that Charles used the same title for a two-volume work he published as the sole author in 1749. In the 1739 volume John included sacred poems by a number of authors that were not written specifically as hymns for use in worship. Throughout his career as a poet of religious verse, Charles would also write much non-hymnic poetry, such as, *An Epistle to the Reverend Mr. John Wesley* (1755), *An Epistle to the Reverend Mr. George Whitefield* (1771), and *An Elegy on the late Reverend George Whitefield MA* (1771). He wrote numerous sacred poems on the occasion of the deaths of individuals.

It should be added that Charles did not necessarily intend all of the poems he wrote in hymnic style to be sung. An example from the second edition (1756) of *Hymns occasioned by the Earthquake*, March 8, 1750 (London, 1750) will suffice to illustrate this point. A hymn titled 'An Hymn upon the pouring out of the Seventh Vial, Rev. xvi, xvii, &c. Occasioned by the Destruction of Lisbon,' is added at the conclusion of Part I. It follows the heading 'To which are added An Hymn for the English in America, and another for the Year 1756.' It is very clear from Part 2 of the poem on Lisbon that Charles would not have intended for it to be sung in the Methodist societies, as illustrated by stanza 3:

> Then let the thundering trumpet sound;[21]
>   The latest lightning glare;
> The mountains melt; the solid ground
>   Dissolve as liquid air;
> The huge celestial bodies roll,
>   Amid that general fire,
> And shrivel as a parchment scroll,
>   And all in smoke expire!

Sources of the Wesley's Hymns
Having established that Charles Wesley's poetry and style of writing were greatly influenced by the Latin and Greek classics and a number of British poets, we turn now to the sources which shaped the content and theology of his hymns: the Thirty-Nine Articles of Religion, *The Book of Common Prayer*, the Holy Scriptures, the early Church Fathers, other religious sources, and contemporary events.

Thirty-Nine Articles of Religion of the Church of England
Unquestionably, Charles Wesley was a man educated and nurtured within the life, liturgy, and beliefs of the Church of England. Hence, it is not surprising that this rich ecclesiastical heritage surfaces quite often in his sacred poetry. J. R. Watson has explored the importance of understanding the Thirty-Nine Articles of Religion of the Church of England as the fulcrum of the theological ideas one encounters in Wesley's hymns.[22] It is not so much a question of direct quotation from the Thirty-Nine Articles, as it is Wesley's ability to convey in his verse their theological perspectives and

posture. For example, as the theological matrix of Wesley's thought in a stanza of 'Hark! How all the Welkin rings,' Watson quotes the following passage from Article II, 'Of the Word or Son of God, which was made very Man':[23]

> The Son, which is the Word of the Father, begotten from everlasting of the Father, the very and eternal God, and of one substance with the Father, took Man's nature in the womb of the blessed Virgin, of her substance: so that two whole and perfect Natures, that is to say the Godhead and Manhood, were joined together in one Person, never to be divided, whereof is one Christ, very God, and very Man.

Wesley affirms this in these words:

> Christ, by highest heaven adored,[24]
> Christ, the everlasting Lord,
> Late in time behold him come,
> Offspring of a virgin's womb.
> Veiled in flesh the Godhead see!
> Hail the incarnate Deity!

The Book of Common Prayer (1662)
A number of scholars have explored the influence of the language, metaphors, images, and ideas of the *BCP* on Charles Wesley's hymns. He attended Westminster School, adjacent to Westminster Abbey, where he experienced the daily offices and eucharistic liturgy of the *BCP*. While there are many examples of the presence of the *BCP* imprimatur on Wesley's hymns, perhaps this is nowhere clearer than in the volume *Hymns on the Lord's Supper*[25] published jointly by John and Charles Wesley in 1745. It is generally concluded that John wrote the preface to the volume based on Daniel Brevint's treatise, *On the Christian Sacrament and Sacrifice, by way of discourse, meditation, and prayer upon the nature, parts, and blessings of the Holy Communion* (1672), and that Charles wrote the hymns.

Some of the eucharistic hymns are metrical versions of passages from the *BCP* liturgy such as 'Lord, and God of heavenly powers,' which is preceded with the words of the *BCP* liturgical Preface to the Sanctus: 'Therefore with angels and archangels':

> Lord, and God of heavenly powers,[26]
> Theirs – yet oh! benignly ours;
> Glorious King, let earth proclaim,
> Worms attempt to chant thy name.

> Thee to laud in songs divine,
> Angels and Arch-angels join;
> We with them our voices raise,
> Echoing thy eternal praise.
>
> Holy, holy, holy Lord,
> Live by heaven and earth adored!
> Full of thee they ever cry
> Glory be to God most high!

Another example is the hymn 'Glory be to God on high,' a metrical paraphrase of the *Gloria in excelsis Deo*, which Wesley prefaces in his text with the words, 'Glory be to God on high, and on earth peace, etc.' The first three stanzas of the seven-stanza hymn suffice to illustrate the influence of the language of the liturgy:

> Glory be to God on high,[27]
> God whose glory fills the sky;
> Peace on earth to man forgiven,
> Man the well-beloved of heaven!
>
> Sovereign Father, heavenly King,
> Thee we now presume to sing,
> Glad thine attributes confess,
> Glorious all and numberless.
>
> Hail by all thy works adored,
> Hail the everlasting Lord!
> Thee with thankful hearts we prove,
> Lord of power, and God of love.

The hymn 'Meet and right it is to sing,' another metrical paraphrase of the Preface and Sanctus, reveals Wesley's reliance on the words, imagery, and language of the eucharistic rite.

Hymn Number 7, 'Jesu, show us thy salvation,' in *Hymns for Our Lord's Resurrection* (1746) is based on The Great Litany, which, in Wesley's time would have been read regularly at the Eucharist. The following portion of the liturgical text precedes Wesley's metrical paraphrase.

> By the Mystery of thy holy Incarnation; by thy holy nativity and
> circumcision; by thy baptism, fasting, and temptation; by thine agony,
> and bloody sweat; by thy cross and passion; by thy precious death and

burial; by thy glorious resurrection and ascension; and by the coming of
the Holy Ghost, good Lord, deliver us.

The first stanza illustrates what Wesley accomplishes throughout the nine-stanza poem, namely, the eloquent lyrical rendering of the language and imagery of the liturgical text.

> Jesu, show us thy salvation,[28]
>   (In thy strength we strive with thee)
> By thy Mystic Incarnation,
>   By thy pure nativity,
> Save us Thou, our New-Creator,
>   Into all our Souls impart,
> Thy divine unsinning nature,
>   Form thyself within our heart.

One must hasten to add, however, that is not merely Wesley's repetition of *BCP* language imagery, and theology that is of importance. It is his further development of all three. He enriches the affirmations of the Great Litany by introducing the Pauline idea of new creation and not only deliverance but the formation of the divine nature within the human heart. This is for Wesley the evangelical focus of deliverance. J. R. Watson rightly asserts:

> ... the significant and creative element of Charles Wesley's hymnody is his ability to take a familiar phrase or idea from the Bible or the Prayer Book and transform it, to use it in a way which 'de-familiarises' it or gives it new and unexpected meaning. It is not, therefore, the actual repetition or seizure of a phrase which is important, but the felicitous development of it.[29]

Wesley's hymns are filled with phrases and echoes of the *BCP*, such as the Order for Morning Prayer, diverse collects, the Order for the Service of Holy Communion, and the *BCP* Psalter. What is truly extraordinary is his ability to appropriate this material to Christian meaning and living, and this he most often does by the turn of an artful poetical phrase or line.

Robin Leaver superbly summarizes Wesley's use of the *BCP*:

> Charles Wesley's many allusions to the Book of Common Prayer are not mere quotation but rather sophisticated recreations of Prayer Book imagery, theologically understood and poetically expressed. It is witness to a man who was not only aware of the verbal content of the Anglican book of worship but who had also imbibed its basic thought-forms and images to form an essential part of his creative genius.[30]

Holy Scripture

The Holy Scriptures are the primary motivation of most of Charles Wesley's sacred verse. He has literally consumed its content and spirit through his reading of it in Hebrew, Greek, Latin, and English. He lived and breathed its words, imagery, metaphors, similes, phraseology, stories, and parables. He saw within himself the potential for the full spectrum of emotions that he found there. The English of the Authorized Version (AV) was normative biblical language for him and often made its way into his poetical lines, yet his knowledge of Hebrew and Greek often provided him correctives for the AV's English translation. 'He sometimes corrected errors of translation in the Authorized Version and even anticipated the emendations of the revisers.'[31] Frank Baker has averred, 'His [Charles Wesley's] verse is an enormous sponge filled to saturation with Bible words, Bible similes, Bible metaphors, Bible stories, Bible ideas.'[32] J. Ernest Rattenbury makes yet a stronger claim, 'A skilful man, if the Bible were lost, might extract much of it from Wesley's hymns. They contain the Bible in solution. . . . His language was the language of Israel. His complete mastery of the Holy Scriptures was really amazing.'[33]

Two volumes superbly illustrate how line after line of Charles Wesley's poetry reflects his saturation with the language and content of the scriptures. In *A Collection of Hymns for the Use of the People Called Methodists* (1780), volume 7 in the series, The Works of John Wesley, one of the editors, Oliver A. Beckerlegge, provided a very helpful tool for the study of Charles Wesley's hymns, namely the marginal scriptural references which indicate Wesley's use of biblical language, imagery, figures of speech, metaphors, etc., as well as scriptural quotations and allusions. Similarly, in *The Wesley Hymns: As a Guide to Scriptural Teaching*[34] John Lawson has selected 53 Wesley's hymns and suggested biblical references for almost every line of poetry. Lawson's marginal scriptural references are more prolific than Beckerlegge's and some of them fall short of certainty. Nevertheless, they remind the reader of how skilled Wesley was in weaving together multiple threads of the scriptures throughout his poetry.

Wesley is unquestionably a master at creating scriptural hymns. Very early in his published poetry he often prefaces a poem with a specific biblical passage on which it is based. At other times, while he does not cite a passage, it is clear that the background is biblical. This occurs in numerous publications from the Wesley brothers' first joint publication, *Hymns and Sacred Poems* (1739), onward.[35]

In addition to his use of typology and allegory,[36] Wesley had a special gift in paraphrasing entire passages. His paraphrases often integrate textual content and language with personal experience. He is able to internalize the scriptural moment. For example, in *Hymns and Sacred Poems* (1749), in a poem titled

'Desiring to Love' Wesley eloquently paraphrases and appropriates Peter's response to Jesus' question in John 21:15, 'Simon, son of Jonas, lovest thou me more than these? He saith unto him, Yea, Lord; thou knowest that I love thee.' Wesley responded:

> O that with humbled Peter I[37]
> Could weep, believe, and thrice reply
>   My faithfulness to prove,
> Thou know'st (for all to thee is known),
> Thou know'st, O Lord, and thou alone,
>   Thou know'st that thee I love!

During his latter years Wesley devoted much time to the composition of metrical paraphrases of the Psalms. Much of this material remained unpublished at his death and some of the paraphrases were published posthumously in the *Arminian Magazine*.

In 1762 Charles Wesley published a two-volume lyrical commentary on the Bible, *Short Hymns on Select Passages of the Holy Scriptures*,[38] beginning with the Book of Genesis and continuing through the Revelation of John. In this and succeeding works his scripture hymns are more closely reasoned. At times these hymns can be somewhat pedantic, but at others, particularly in *Short Hymns*, Wesley rises to the heights of lyrical eloquence of his earlier verse.

Short Hymns is a lyrical commentary[39] on the entire Bible, which may be seen as somewhat of a counterpart to his brother John's *Explanatory Notes upon the New Testament*. Below is a tabulation of Charles' productivity in *Short Hymns*:

Vol. Nr.	Nr. of Poems	Lines of Poetry	Stanzas
1 (Old Testament)	1,160	10,903	1,241
2 (Old Testament)	318	3,320	446
3 (New Testament)	871	8,912	1,306
Totals	2,349	23,135	2,993

As impressive as these figures are, this is less than half of the biblical poetry Charles composed from 1762 onward. Much of it was left unpublished at his death, for example, hundreds of poems in *MS Scripture Hymns 1783* were not put in print. Though some unpublished poems appeared posthumously in the *Arminian Magazine*, still over 1,200 hymns and poems were unpublished until the three volumes of *The Unpublished Poetry of Charles Wesley*[40] appeared in 1988, 1990, and 1992.

What do we learn about Charles Wesley's biblical interpretation in *Short Hymns*? While he has the utmost confidence in the authority of Holy Scripture and in the knowledge of it as sufficient to the salvation of humankind, he is not a literalist in the strict sense. While he has utmost confidence that the promises of the Bible will indeed be fulfilled according to 'the Word' (e.g., the return of Christ), he wrote:

> Thy word in the bare *literal* sense,[41]
>   Tho' read ten thousand times, and read,
>   Can never of itself dispense
>   The saving power which wakes the dead;
>
> The meaning *spiritual* and true
>   The learn'd expositor may give,
>   But cannot give the virtue too,
>   Or bid his own dead spirit live.

First and foremost, as this poem makes clear, Wesley is concerned with what the scriptures mean. There are various levels of understanding: literal, spiritual, and experiential. This three-dimensional aspect of his interpretation surfaces time and again in his hymns and poems.

In his preface to *Short Hymns*, Charles expresses his debt in biblical interpretation to three scholars: Matthew Henry, Dr. Gell, and Bengelius. Matthew Henry's commentary was well known and widely read. Gell, a London biblical scholar, produced an 'Amended Translation' of the Pentateuch with which Charles had apparently become acquainted, since he associates his debt to Gell with the Pentateuch. Charles had become familiar with the work of Bengelius, a Lutheran scholar, while assisting his brother John with *Explanatory Notes upon the New Testament*, due to John's strong reliance on Bengelius' work. Charles also makes clear in the preface that he has written these two volumes of hymns in order to rectify certain wrong ideas about holiness and perfection. He is no protagonist of instantaneous perfection, as numerous satirical poems throughout both volumes make clear.

Short Hymns illustrates Wesley's ongoing interest in translation. Though he usually quotes texts from the AV immediately prior to every poem, often [Heb.] and [Gk.] appear indicating what he considers to be the appropriate translation of the Hebrew or Greek word or phrase. In the section on the Psalms, though he does not indicate it in the printed text, he often quotes from the *BCP* Psalter instead of the AV.

As important as *Short Hymns* is for insight into the scriptures and into

Charles Wesley's biblical interpretation, it would be misleading to ignore other aspects of his biblical interpretation in his hymnody. He is often at his best in biblical narrative poems, though few of these survive in contemporary hymnody. For example, in his lyrical interpretation of Jesus' encounter with the woman of Canaan in Matthew 15, he intertwines and personalizes reality, symbol, and allegory.

> 1. Lord, regard my earnest cry,[42]
> A postsherd of the earth,
> A poor guilty worm am I,
> A Canaanite by birth:
> Save me from this tyranny,
> From all the power of Satan save,
> Mercy, mercy upon me,
> Thou Son of David have.
>
> 2. Still Thou answerest not a word
> To my repeated prayer;
> Hear thine own disciples, Lord,
> Who in my sorrows share;
> O let them prevail with thee
> To grant the blessing which I crave:
> Mercy, mercy upon me.
> Thou Son of David have.
>
> 3. Send, O send me now away,
> By granting my request,
> Still I follow thee, and pray,
> And will not let thee rest;
> Ever crying after thee,
> Till thou my helplessness relieve,
> Mercy, mercy upon me
> Thou Son of David have.
>
> 4. To the sheep of Israel's fold,
> Thou in thy flesh wast sent,
> But the gentiles now behold
> In thee their covenant.
> See me then, with pity see,
> A sinner, whom thou cam'st to save;
> Mercy, mercy upon me
> Thou Son of David have.

5. Still to thee, my God, I come,
And mercy I implore,
   Thee (but how shall I presume)
Thee trembling I adore,
   Dare not stand before thy face,
But lowly at thy feet I fall,
   Help me, Jesu, show thy grace:
Thy grace is free for all.

6. Still I cannot part with thee,
I will not let thee go,
   Mercy, mercy unto me,
O Son of David show,
   Vilest of the sinful race,
On thee importunate I call,
   Help me, Jesu, show thy grace:
Thy grace is free for all.

7. Nothing am I in thy sight,
   Nothing have I to plead;
   Unto dogs it is not right
To cast the children's bread:
   Yet the dogs the crumbs may eat,
That from their Master's table fall,
   Let the fragments be my meat:
Thy grace is free for all.

8. Give me, Lord, the victory,
My heart's desire fulfil,
   Let it now be done to me
According to thy will;
   Give me living bread to eat,
And say, in answer to my call,
   'Canaanite, thy faith is great,
My grace is free for all.'

9. If thy grace for all is free,
Thy call *now* let *me* hear,
   Show this token upon me,
And bring salvation near;
   Now the gracious word repeat,
The word of healing to my soul,

> 'Canaanite, thy faith is great,
> Thy faith has made thee whole.'

It is fascinating how Wesley's poetic imagination deals with the hidden meaning of this biblical story, which has troubled interpreters for many generations. While some might accuse him of psychologizing the story by moving the reader to the inmost thoughts of the Canaanite woman, he sees beyond the things in the story which have troubled interpreters: calling the woman *kunavria* (in Greek a diminuitive for dog), Jesus' silence or lack of response to her, acknowledging faith in a Gentile, and the exclusivity of his response, 'I was sent *only* to the lost sheep of Israel' (Matthew 15:24). Through poetic and theological imagination, Wesley tells the story in the first person from the perspective of the woman. He wants the reader to feel and sense her plight.

If the Matthew 15 story has been seen by many as evidence of the tension between Jews and Gentiles in the New Testament period, Wesley is able to see beyond this to the woman herself: her humility and desire for mercy, the triumph of faith, and the universality of God's grace and covenant. Ever the evangelical poet-priest, he focuses on the person, God's universal grace, and the importance of faith.

Fathers of the Early Church
Nicholas Lossky has made a convincing case for the strong influence of the Early Fathers of the Church and patristic theology through Wesley's reading of Lancelot Andrewes, particularly his *Preces Privatae*. While one might labor to find numerous quotations of the Early Fathers in Charles Wesley's poetry, his theology exudes the spirit of much of their theology. Lossky avers:

> Here in poetical form, we find an expression of the Church's experience of God. Much of the theology is of the school of Andrewes. It is a trinitarian theology, with a Christology inseparable from pneumatalogy. As for the divine dispensation, Charles Wesley insists many times on the fact that Christ 'died for all' and that grace is offered to all. The poetical form, often magnificent, is also something that links Charles Wesley with Orthodox practice: the non-Greek Orthodox should never forget that in the original, most of our Syro-Byzantine hymnography is in rhythmic poetry (most of the time untranslatable).[43]

We do not have the same kind of bibliographical evidence of the Early Fathers in the writings of Charles that one finds in his brother John's writings, though most certainly Charles had read John's *A Plain Account of Genuine Christianity* where the following are mentioned: Clemens Romanus, Ignatius,

Polycarp, Justin Martyr, Irenaeus, Origin, Clemens Alexandrinus, Cyprian, Macarius, and Ephrem Syrus. Furthermore, in the brothers' first joint publication *Hymns and Sacred Poems* (1739), their appreciation of one of the Fathers just cited was expressed by the inclusion of a poem titled 'On Clemens Alexandrinus's Description of a Perfect Christian.'[44] While John may have agreed with the spirit of the poem, Charles probably identified more strongly with the imagery of a long desert struggle toward holiness, as expressed in stanza one:

>Here from afar the finish'd height
>   Of holiness is seen:
>But O what heavy tracts of toil,
>   What deserts lie between?

Peter Bouteneff finds resonances of Gregory of Nyssa in Charles' poetry. The 'themes of salvation as restoration, and as change and movement from glory to glory,'[45] are evident in these words:

>Finish then thy new creation,[46]
>   Pure and spotless let us be;
>Let us see thy great salvation
>   Perfectly restored in thee;
>
>Changed from glory into glory,
>   Till in heaven we take our place,
>Till we cast our crowns before thee,
>   Lost in wonder, love and praise.

One matter of theological concern that surfaces time and again in Charles Wesley's poetry in concert with many of the Early Fathers of the Church is *theosis*. A. M. Allchin addressed this eloquently in a chapter on Charles Wesley in his important study *Participation in God: A Forgotten Strand in Anglican Tradition*.[47] Wesley understood that, as Bishop Kallistos Ware says, 'God's Incarnation opens the way to man's deification.'[48] Wesley emphasized this a number of times in *Hymns for the Nativity of our Lord* (1745). Stanza 2 of Hymn 14 reads:

>2. The Creator of all[49]
>   To repair our sad Fall,
>   From his Heav'n stoops down,
>Lays hold of our Nature, and joins to his own.

Stanzas 5 and 8 of Hymn 8 give even stronger voice to this emphasis:

> 5. Made flesh for our sake,[50]
>   That we might partake
>   The Nature Divine,
>   And again in his image, his holiness shine.
>
>   . . .
>
> 8. And while we are here
>   Our King shall appear,
>   His Spirit impart,
>   And form his full image of love in our heart.

Wesley's understanding of *theosis* is intimately bound to Holy Communion. 'It is a means of grace by which the Incarnation is imparted to the life of the Christian and by which and through which God makes divine. Here . . . Charles Wesley stands close to Ephrem Cyrus for whom Holy Communion was the cradle of *theosis*.'[51] This is clear from many passages in Wesley's *Hymns on the Lord's Supper*:

> What streams of sweetness from the bowl[52]
> Surprize and deluge all my soul,
>   Sweetness which is, and makes Divine,
> Surely from God's right-hand they flow,
> From thence deriv'd to earth below,
>   To cheer us with immortal wine.

Perhaps more familiar are the lines from two additional eucharistic hymns:

> Christ in us; in him we see[53]
> Fulness of the Deity,
> Beam of the Eternal Beam;
> Life Divine we taste in him.

> Who thy mysterious supper share,[54]
>   Here at thy table fed,
> Many, and yet but One we are,
>   One undivided Bread.

> One with the Living Bread Divine,
>   Which now by faith we eat,
> Our hearts, and minds, and spirits join,
>   And all in Jesus meet.

Other Religious Sources

It has already been made clear in this discussion that Charles Wesley drew from multiple sources of his education and knowledge to create the sacred verse that would change, with his brother John's editorial assistance, the course of English-language hymnody.[55] It has also been stated that it was not Charles' intention that all of his poems written in hymnic style be sung. There are two major examples of his use of other religious sources, more specifically both are theological treatises, as the subject and theological substance of his writing. They illustrate that poetry was the means whereby Charles worked through theological issues. He sounds the depths of theological reflection in lyrical language, in spite of the fact that his sacred poetry is often labeled 'doxological.'

The first example is *Hymns on the Lord's Supper* published in 1745 under the names of both brothers. The primary literary source for this publication was Daniel Brevint's *On the Christian Sacrament and Sacrifice* (1672).[56] *Hymns on the Lord's Supper* follows in large measure the outline of an abridged version of Brevint's volume that serves as an introduction to the volume, written most probably by John. As the title suggests, Brevint addressed Holy Communion as a sacrament (the first five sections of the treatise) and as a sacrifice (the last three sections). John Wesley reduced or compressed Brevint's eight sections into five: (1) 'As it is a Memorial of the Suffering and Death of Christ,' (2) 'As it is a Sign and Means of Grace,' (3) 'The Sacrament as a Pledge of Heaven,' (4) 'Concerning the Sacrifice of our Persons,' (5) 'The Holy Eucharist as it implies Sacrifice.' The Wesleys then added an additional section, (6) 'After the Sacrament.' In the hymns Charles Wesley essentially follows thematically the five sections, expounding and often expanding Brevint's theological emphases and ideas: Section 1 – Hymns 1–27; Section 2 – Hymns 28–92; Section 3 – Hymns 93–115; Section 4 – 116–127; Section 5 – 128–157. Section 6 – Hymns 158–166. Some of the more closely reasoned hymns are so packed full with biblical imagery and metaphors from line to line that they were most probably not intended for congregational singing. For example, in a rehearsal of some aspects of salvation history Wesley composed the following words for stanza 2 of Hymn 61, 'Thou God of boundless power and grace':

> Let but thy ark the walls surround,[57]
> Let but the Rams-horn Trumpets sound,
>   The city boasts its height no more,
> Its bulwarks are at once o'erthrown,
> Its massy walls by air blown down,
>   They fall before Almighty power.
> Jordan at thy command shall heal
> The sore disease incurable,

> And wash out all the leper's stains;
> Or oil the med-cine shall supply,
> Or cloths, or shadows passing by,
>   If so thy sovereign will ordains.

Nevertheless, there are numerous texts of Charles Wesley in *Hymns on the Lord's Supper* that are composed with such eloquence, combining depth of perception with human experience, that they cry out to be sung.

> 1. Author of life divine,[58]
>   Who hast a table spread,
>   Furnish'd with mystic wine
>   And everlasting Bread,
>   Preserve the life thyself hast given,
>   And feed, and train us up for heaven.
>
> 2. Our needy souls sustain
>   With fresh supplies of love,
>   Till all thy life we gain,
>   And all thy fullness prove,
>   And strength'ned by thy perfect grace,
>   Behold without a veil thy face.

The hymns in Section 6, 'After the Sacrament,' are more doxological in nature, including paraphrases of the *Sanctus* and the *Gloria*.

The second example of Charles Wesley's specific use of a religious source for his hymns and poems is evident in his *Hymns on the Trinity* (1767).[59] As with *Hymns on the Lord's Supper*, he responds to a prose theological treatise in poetry. This time his subject involves a poetical appropriation of William Jones's treatise, *The Catholic Doctrine of the Trinity, proved by above an hundred short and clear arguments, expressed in terms of the Holy Scripture* (1756).

There are two parts to *Hymns on the Trinity*. In Part 1 (Hymns 1–136) Wesley works his way carefully through Jones' treatise: 'Hymns on the Divinity of Christ' (Hymns 1–57), 'The Divinity of the Holy Ghost' (Hymns 58–86), 'The *Plurality* and *Trinity* of Persons' (Hymns 87–109), 'The Trinity in Unity' (Hymns 110–136). Just as Jones based most of his discussion on the strength of argument from Holy Scripture, in Hymns 1–136 Wesley prefaced almost every lyric with a passage of the scriptures. Once again, his closely reasoned verse reflects his wrestling with the meaning and understanding of the Trinity, but at times the lyric is more for reflection than singing. He packed so much into the first stanza of Hymn 42, which is based on 1 Corinthians 11:3, 'The head of Christ is God,' that it is difficult to imagine these lines in congregational song.

> The Partner of our flesh and blood,[60]
> As man, inferior is to God:
> The lower part of Christ, the heel
> Was bruised, and did our sorrows feel;
> But though he would his life resign,
> His part superior is divine,
> And doth, beyond the reach of pain,
> God over all for ever reign.

What happens with Jones' treatise is precisely what happens with Brevint's treatise in *Hymns on the Lord's Supper*. Wesley transformed the prose apologetic into what Wilma Quantrille calls 'lyrical theological discourse.'[61] The result is often the language of praise and thanksgiving. Though Wesley followed Jones very closely in the concluding Part 2, 'Hymns and Prayers to the Trinity,' hymns newly numbered 1–52, he transcended Jones' treatise and moved to the realm of experience. The link between knowledge and practice is experience in worship, private devotion, and daily living. So important is the aspect of articulating the mystery of the Trinity in song that for the first 24 hymns in Part 2 Wesley prescribed the 24 tunes of John Lampe's in *Hymns on the Great Festivals* (1746) to be sung with the hymns so designated.

Here is an eloquent example of how Wesley moved from the glory of God to the human experience of goodness and love:

> Make thy goodness pass before me,[62]
>   Glorious God thyself proclaim,
> To my first estate restore me,
>   Re-imprest with thy new name,
> In the likeness of my Maker
>   Re-begotten from above,
> Of thy holiness partaker,
>   Fill'd with all the life of love.

Knowledge of God without the experience of the 'life of love' is for Wesley unthinkable.

Contemporary Events
One of the early examples of Charles Wesley's writing hymns in response to contemporary events is the booklet *Hymns for Times of Trouble and Persecution* (1744). The period of time immediately before and after the Jacobite Revolution of 1745 resulted in grave difficulties for the Methodists. The mob violence directed against them resulted in destruction of property and often physical injury. Their loyalty to the British Crown was questioned and they were often

labeled papist and Jacobites. Charles responded to this chaos with a call to the faithful to stand firm in their faith:

> The waves of the sea have lift up their voice,[63]
> Sore troubled that we in Jesus rejoice;
> The floods they are roaring, but Jesus is here,
> While we are adoring, he always is near.
>
> Men, devils engage, the billows arise,
> And horribly rage, and threaten the skies:
> Their fury shall never our stedfastness shock,
> The weakest believer is built on a rock.

By and large the language of the hymns in this booklet is general in nature, although four prayers in the first section indicate the Wesley brothers' allegiance to King George II. Three prayers are titled 'A Prayer for His Majesty King George' and another 'For the King and the Royal Family.'

Three other examples suffice to underscore Charles Wesley's lyrical and theological response to contemporary events. (1) A day of public thanksgiving was declared by the government in response to defeat of rebels in the Battle of Culloden (April 16, 1746) in which supporters of the Stuart takeover of the throne were defeated. For this event Wesley published seven hymns in *Hymns for the Public Thanksgiving-Day, October 9, 1746*.[64] Stanza one of hymn Number 2 reads:

> Thanks be to God, the God of Power,[65]
> Who shelter'd us in Danger's Hour,
> The God of Truth, who heard the Prayer,
> Let all his Faithfulness declare,
> Who sent us Succours from above,
> Let all adore the God of Love.

(2) The little booklet *Hymns occasioned by the Earthquake, March 8, 1750*,[66] was published in two separate parts with the first including six hymns and second including 13. These texts were motivated by the Lisbon earthquake of 1755.

(3) During the summer of 1759, a frenzy of public fear broke out over the threat of a French invasion of England. News of the French successes in the Seven Years War had spread, but it was genuinely believed that the French had built boats specifically for an invasion. Due to several defeats of the French, the invasion was never undertaken. Nevertheless in the face of the public panic Charles wrote *Hymns on the Expected Invasion*.[67]

Hymns for the Church

It is remarkable that, in spite of the fact that Charles Wesley wrote so many of his hymns directly out of the life and context of the Church of England, hymn singing was forbidden in that church until 1821, thirty-three years after his death. In other words, he created a liturgical art form for which his own church had no place in its worship during his lifetime. His output was phenomenal. He wrote some 9,000 hymns, sacred and secular poems. At his death the secular material was left unpublished, as well as hundreds of stanzas of sacred verse. One often reads that he wrote 6,500 hymns. While he indeed composed over 6,000 texts, which may be called hymns, by no means were all of them intended for singing.

Wesley has become one of the most important English-language hymn writers of all time, whose hymns enrich the lives of worshiping Christians across most denominational lines. He wrote for the worshiping community, and for the corporate and individual devotional life of Christians.

Holy Communion

While the literary sources of the Wesley's volume *Hymns on the Lord's Supper* have been addressed above, it must be emphasized that the hymns of this collection are some of the most important ever composed by Charles. This book of hymns remains today perhaps the most important ecclesiastical and ecumenical Wesley document. It gives voice to the centrality and constancy of the Eucharist in the life of the church as a community of faith and for the individual Christian.

Three stanzas from the concluding hymn of *Hymns on the Lord's Supper* reveal the Wesley's hope for the church through its regular observance of the Eucharist to become a community of love.

> Happy the saints of former days[68]
>   Who first continued in the Word,
> A simple lowly race,
>   True followers of their Lamb-like Lord.
>   . . .
> From house to house they broke the bread
>   Impregnated with life divine,
> And drank the Spirit of their Head
>   Transmitted with the sacred wine.
>   . . .
> O what a flame of sacred love
>   Was kindled by the altar's fire!
> They liv'd on earth like those above,
>   Glad rivals of the heavenly choir.

Hymns for the Christian Year

Before Charles Wesley began publishing collections of hymns for specific feast days and seasons of the church year, he composed such hymns for the first joint collection of the brothers, *Hymns and Sacred Poems* (1739), which included: 'Hark! how all the welkin rings' (titled 'Hymn for Christmas-Day'), 'Christ the Lord is risen today' (titled 'Hymn for Easter-Day), and 'Hail the day that sees him rise' (titled 'Hymn for Ascension-Day').

In 1745 he published *Hymns for the Nativity of our Lord*, followed in 1746 with *Hymns for Our Lord's Resurrection*, *Hymns for Ascension-Day*, and *Hymns of Petition and Thanksgiving for the Promise of the Father* (or *Hymns for Whitsunday*). That same year the volume, *Hymns on the Great Festivals*, with the tunes composed by John F. Lampe was published with three hymns 'On the Nativity,' four hymns 'On the Crucifixion,' three hymns 'On the Resurrection,' three hymns 'On the Ascension,' three hymns 'On Whitsunday,' one hymn 'On the Trinity,' and additional hymns on the themes of faith, love, and death.

Hymns for Christian Experience

As one sees from the outline of *A Collection of Hymns for the Use of the People Called Methodist* (1780), which is organized according to the Christian's pilgrimage from repentance and new birth in Christ through life and its vicissitudes to triumphant death and resurrection, Wesley touched on an amazingly broad spectrum of Christian experience from conversion to the daily faith journey. His hymns are marked by a strong sense of the experience of the Holy Trinity revealed on earth in the person of Jesus Christ and the guidance of the Holy Spirit. Hymns such as 'And can it be that I should gain an interest in the Savior's blood' and 'Where shall my wondering soul begin' chart a deep inner quest for a life of enduring meaning in following Christ and his example.

It is difficult to come to the conclusion of a Wesley hymn without encountering the word 'love,' which for him is the key to human experience and existence. 'Love divine, all loves excelling' is not an illusive dream for Wesley; it is a lived reality. One reason many of his hymns continue to have meaning is that he raised questions people are ever asking: Who am I? Why do I exist? What shall I do with my life for it to have its greatest meaning? Who is God? How can God be known?

He wrote also for a broad spectrum of society. He addressed the poor and marginalized, prisoners, murderers. He visited prisons and ate with the poor. He prayed:

> Thy mind throughout my life be shown,[69]
> While listening to the sufferer's cry,
> The widow's and the orphan's groan,

On mercy's wings I swiftly fly
The poor and helpless to relieve,
My life, my all for them to give.

He wrote a hymn stanza that begins 'Help us to make the poor our friends.' At the same time he circulated among some of English aristocracy. By no means is Charles Wesley all things to all people, but he grasped the breadth of human experience and eloquently addressed it in his hymns. This is why his hymns endure.

The State of Charles Wesley Studies

One owes a debt to a number of twentieth-century scholars for their distinguished contributions to Charles Wesley studies, particularly John Telford, J. Ernest Rattenbury, Frank Baker, and Oliver A. Beckerlegge. The 1983 publication of a critical edition of *A Collection of Hymns for the Use of the People Called Methodists*, volume 7 in The Works of John Wesley series, was a major step forward. Since the organization of the Charles Wesley Society (CWS) in 1990 and the establishment of its scholarly journal, *Proceedings of the Charles Wesley Society*, and its annual meeting, there has been an ever-increasing repertory of scholars whose publications have enriched the field. The organizational meeting of the CWS resulted in a volume, *Charles Wesley: Poet and Theologian*,[70] which provides an excellent overview of the state of Charles Wesley studies in 1990. The most complete bibliography has been prepared by Donald A. Bullen and published in the volume *Charles Wesley: Life, Literature and Legacy*.[71]

An ongoing problem has been the availability of Charles Wesley's literature, prose, and poetry. The CWS initiated a program to publish facsimile reprints of first editions with critical introductions and indices, which has resulted thus far in eight reprints.[72] Fortunately, his hitherto unpublished poems are now in print,[73] and there are new editions of his sermons[74] and of his manuscript journal.[75] In the latter all of Wesley's shorthand passages have been deciphered.

There is still a desperate need for an edition of Charles Wesley's letters, since over six hundred of them remain unpublished. A publication of the letters and a separate group of letters, known as 'journal letters' because of their style, should be forthcoming in the near future. Until the letters are published it will remain impossible to write a comprehensive biography of Charles Wesley. There is also an enduring need for adequate indexing of his poetry. The website (http://www.divinity.duke.edu/wesleyan/texts/) made available by the Center for Studies in the Wesleyan Tradition of The Divinity School of Duke University is a marvelous contribution to the accessibility of Wesley poetry. The online collection provides a standard source for scholarly study and citation of the poetical works of John and Charles Wesley.

There is an ongoing need for the cross-referencing of materials and for adequate indexing of all publications. It may be said, however, that one is better prepared today to study the works of Charles Wesley than ever before.

For Further Reading

Kimbrough, S T, Jr. and Kenneth G. C. Newport, eds. *The Manuscript Journal of the Reverend Charles Wesley, M.A.* 2 vols. Nashville, TN: Abingdon/Kingswood, 2007–2008.

Lloyd, Gareth. *Charles Wesley and the Struggle for Methodist Identity.* New York: Oxford University Press, 2007.

Newport, Kenneth G. C. *The Sermons of Charles Wesley: A Critical Edition with Introduction and Notes.* New York: Oxford University Press, 2001.

Newport, Kenneth G. C. and Ted A. Campbell, eds. *Charles Wesley: Life, Literature & Legacy.* Peterborough: Epworth, 2007.

Stevick, Daniel B. *The Altar's Fire: Charles Wesley's Hymns on the Lord's Supper, 1745 Introduction and Exposition.* Peterborough: Epworth, 2004.

Tyson, John R. *Assist Me to Proclaim: The Life and Hymns of Charles Wesley.* Grand Rapids, MI: Eerdmans, 2007.

Authority and the 'Wesleyan Quadrilateral'

Ted A. Campbell

'Wesleyan Quadrilateral' is a term that has been used since the early 1970s to describe the use of scripture, tradition, reason, and experience as sources and guidelines for Christian theological and moral reflection in Methodist or Wesleyan communities. The word 'quadrilateral' (without 'Wesleyan') appeared in a statement of 'Our Theological Task' adopted by the United Methodist Church (UMC) in 1972, a statement that was significantly revised in 1988.[1] Discussion of the 'Wesleyan quadrilateral' has become a focal point since 1972 for the larger discussion of theological authority in the United Methodist Church and in other Wesleyan and Methodist communities. This essay will consider the larger issue of sources of religious authority as well as particular matters related to the definition of the 'Wesleyan quadrilateral.'

Evolution of the Concept of the Wesleyan Quadrilateral

The study of the Wesleyan quadrilateral and related issues about the authority of scripture in relation to other sources and norms of theology has developed as a result of a substantial revival of Wesleyan studies since the 1960s. Prior to that time, the only substantial, critical account of the interrelated religious authorities underlying John Wesley's thought was a little-known German dissertation by Stanley Frost, whose work on *Die Autoritätslehre in den Werken John Wesleys* ('Teaching on Authority in the Works of John Wesley') was published in 1938. Frost described a variety of sources of authority in Wesley, emphasising that it was the primal authority of God that underlay all expressions of theological authority, including that of the Holy Scriptures.[2] It is unfortunate that Frost's work has remained unstudied, since his notion of the authority of God underlying all other grounds of authority could provide a way to integrate the various approaches that have been provided in the discussion of sources and norms of authority.

    Colin Williams' influential book *John Wesley's Theology Today* (1960) offered a consideration of 'Authority and Experience' early on and divided this discussion into five subcategories that foreshadowed the development of the

'Wesleyan quadrilateral': the first two subcategories had to do with the authority of scripture, and the subsequent subcategories dealt with experience, reason, and tradition. Williams understood 'tradition' as denoting developments beyond the time of the New Testament scriptures, for example, traditions about orders of ministry and the liturgy of the church.[3] Williams' categories would provide a basic framework for the discussion of the Wesleyan quadrilateral in the decades that followed.

Williams' four categories appeared in a discussion of 'The Wesleyan Concept of Authority' in a 1970 interim report of United Methodism's Theological Study Commission on Doctrine and Doctrinal Standards presented to the specially called General Conference of the newly organized denomination that met in St. Louis that year.[4] The Commission, chaired by Prof. Albert C. Outler of Southern Methodist University, had been authorized by the denomination's uniting conference in 1968 to examine and make recommendations concerning the church's doctrinal statements, especially since the new church inherited distinct doctrinal statements from the former Evangelical United Brethren Church (EUB) and the former Methodist Church. The interim report of 1970 signalled the Commission's intention to develop a contemporary statement of faith rather than replacing the inherited statements. Its discussion of 'The Wesleyan Concept of Authority' is an entirely historical, that is, non-normative, account of John Wesley's understanding of religious authority which appeared in a sequence of sections dealing with a variety of sources for authority in the traditions of the Methodist and the EUB churches. In describing John Wesley's views, the report noted that:

> In this quadrilateral of 'standards,' Scripture stands foremost without a rival. Tradition is the distillate of the formative experiences of the People of God in their wrestlings with problems of biblical interpretation. 'Experience' ('the inner witness of the Spirit') is the name for that vital transit from the objective focus of faith to its subjective center – from 'dead faith' (correct belief) to 'living faith' that justifies and saves. And reason is the referee of the terms in which all this is expressed. Any insight, therefore, that is a disclosure from Scripture, illumined by tradition, realized in experience, and confirmed by reason is as fully authoritative as men may hope for in this life.[5]

A few features stand out in this account. The final authority of scripture, consistent with John Wesley's own views, was unambiguously asserted. Also consistent with John Wesley's views was its claim that 'experience' was to be understood primarily as religious experience, 'the inner witness of the Spirit.' More problematically, however, Wesley was understood in this account as holding a notion of 'tradition' answering to the way in which Williams and

Outler had become familiar with the term in contemporary ecumenical circles, that is, as a positive indication of the work of God through the history of the Christian community, especially in the period after the New Testament. Perhaps most importantly, in this account the 'quadrilateral' was understood to be 'Wesleyan' in that it was utilized as a way of summarizing John Wesley's own views of authority in Christian communities.

By the time the notion of the quadrilateral appeared in the statement on 'Our Theological Task' adopted by the 1972 General Conference of the UMC, however, several things had changed in the description of the quadrilateral. Most importantly, the discussion of the quadrilateral in the 1972 statement was no longer couched as a discussion of John Wesley's understanding of authority, but was instead given as a discussion of 'Doctrinal Guidelines in the United Methodist Church.' The elements of the quadrilateral were not attributed to John Wesley; they appeared as guidelines for contemporary theological reflection in the church.[6]

Although members of the Theological Study Commission intended to assert the primacy of scripture among other authorities, the 1972 statement was vulnerable to the charge that it held the four elements of the quadrilateral to be equally authoritative; thus some critics claimed that the problem with the quadrilateral was that it was an 'equilateral.' A critical pair of sentences stated that 'There is a primacy that goes with Scripture, as the constitutive witness to the biblical wellsprings of our faith. In practice, however, theological reflection may find its point of departure in tradition, "experience," or rational analysis.'[7] This was significantly different than 'Scripture stands foremost without a rival' in the earlier interim report. The second sentence did not strictly contradict the first; it simply claimed that a 'point of departure' could be found in the other elements of the quadrilateral besides scripture. The construction of the sentences, especially the use of the transitional 'However' ('There is a primacy that goes with Scripture ... However ...') lent the impression that the second sentence seriously qualified the claim to scriptural primacy in the first sentence.

The understanding of 'tradition' was significantly changed in the 1972 document. The formulation adopted in 1972 reflected the precise language of the Montreal 1963 Faith and Order statement on 'Scripture, Tradition, and traditions,' a document that Outler himself had helped to shape,[8] and the 1972 UMC document made explicit reference to 'contemporary Faith and Order discussions of "Tradition and Traditions." ' The 1972 statement identified three senses of 'tradition': tradition as process, tradition as reflecting the diversity (and division) of the churches, and then a 'transcendent' sense:

> In a third sense, however, 'the Christian tradition' may be spoken of transcendentally: as the history of that environment of grace in and by

which all Christians live, which is the continuance through time and space of God's self-giving love in Jesus Christ. It is in this transcendent sense of *tradition* that Christians, who have been isolated from one another by various barriers of schism, race and rivalries may recognize one another as Christians together.[9]

This 'transcendent' sense of tradition answered to what the Montreal Faith and Order Conference called 'Tradition,' with a capital 'T,' although the Montreal statement was bolder, referring to 'Tradition' in this sense as 'the Gospel itself.' 'The Christian tradition' was understood as coming both prior to, as well as subsequent to, the New Testament.

Although the definition of 'reason' in the 1972 statement remained focused on 'rational analysis,' the section on 'experience' was expanded to include reference to communal as well as individual experience in addition to the distinctly Wesleyan sense of experience as the assurance of divine pardon.[10] Moreover, the 1972 statement made the claim that 'In this task of reappraising and applying the gospel, theological pluralism should be recognized as a principle.' The Commission drafters seem to have understood 'theological pluralism' to denote a healthy dialogue framed by a given Christian theological inheritance, but the term 'pluralism' was to take on broader meanings in subsequent years, specifically, when it came to be associated with inter-religious dialogue and with forms of conceptual relativism associated with postmodern culture from the 1980s.

The 1972 statement was adopted by an overwhelming majority of the UMC General Conference of that year, and the idea of the 'Wesleyan quadrilateral' came to be understood as a distinctly Wesleyan and Methodist contribution to Christian thought, often attributed in popular church culture to John Wesley himself, perhaps reflecting the suggestion made by Colin Williams and the 1970 draft statement. The quadrilateral became a staple of United Methodist theological work: Dennis M. Campbell, for example, utilized it in 1982 as a framework for the investigation of Christian approaches to professional ethics.[11]

By the early 1980s, however, the statement of 'Our Theological Task,' and its assertion of the quadrilateral, in particular, had come under fire from many, especially conservatives, within the UMC. Jerry L. Walls wrote on *The Problem of Pluralism* in 1986.[12] Ted A. Campbell questioned whether the quadrilateral as formulated in the UMC could be attributed directly to John Wesley,[13] and others expressed growing unease with the weakness of the statement's claims about biblical authority. The 1984 UMC General Conference authorized a new Theological Study Commission to consider revising the earlier statement, and the denomination's 1988 General Conference adopted a revised statement offered by the Commission.

When it was adopted in 1988, the primary significance of the revised statement was understood to be its clear assertion of the primacy of scripture among the elements of the quadrilateral. The first sentence under the topic of scripture in the revised statement claims that 'United Methodists share with other Christians the conviction that Scripture is the primary source and criterion for Christian doctrine.'[14] The section on the quadrilateral concludes with a statement that 'In theological reflection, the resources of tradition, experience, and reason are integral to our study of Scripture without displacing Scripture's primacy for faith and practice.'[15]

The 1988 document also made other important revisions that have not been as widely acknowledged. It removed references in the earlier document that claimed that historic UM doctrinal statements should not 'be construed literally and juridically.'[16] This statement appeared to contradict the restrictive rules of the denomination's constitution, which maintain a legally ('juridically') protected status for the Articles of Religion, the General Rules, and the Confession of Faith. This would bear on the issue of the scope or intent of doctrinal change intended by the quadrilateral and the statement of 'Our Theological Task.' Moreover, the 1988 statement made an important distinction between 'theology' and 'doctrine,' where the latter represents the church's consistent teachings and the former ('theology') can denote ongoing attempts at the application of theological insights to new situations and reappropriating the insights affirmed in communally sanctioned doctrinal standards.[17]

Moreover, the 1988 revision significantly altered the statement on tradition in the document, removing the references to the 'transcendent' meaning of tradition that had come from the Montreal Faith and Order statement of 1963. This left the 1988 statement with a sense of tradition more as an appendage to the Christian faith, referring to material subsequent to scripture, and without the very strong sense of Montreal 1963 or of the earlier 1972 statement about the 'transcendent' meaning of tradition. To be fair, the preface to the UM doctrinal standards in the 1988 *Book of Discipline* (and subsequent *Disciplines*) does refer to 'the apostolic witness to Jesus Christ as Savior and Lord, which is the source and measure of all valid Christian teaching.'[18] This claim suggests the transcendent meaning of 'tradition' as it had been expressed earlier, because the core meaning of Tradition (capital 'T') was 'the apostolic witness to Jesus Christ.' But in the revised UM doctrinal statement, it was detached from the category of 'tradition.'

Discussion of the Wesleyan quadrilateral and related issues of authority has not abated since the 1988 revision. William J. Abraham has argued that the quadrilateral offers only a methodology for theological reflection, but not a means of affirming the substance of historical doctrinal claims.[19] Others have cautiously advocated positive approaches to affirming the Wesleyan quadrilateral. Wesleyan evangelical theologian Donald Thorsen has explored the quadrilateral as a resource for evangelical Christians, especially for those of the Wesleyan-Holiness tradition.[20] W. Stephen Gunter and a group of United Methodist scholars, including Ted A. Campbell, Rebekah L. Miles, Scott J. Jones, and Randy L. Maddox have explored the relevance of the quadrilateral for theological renewal in the United Methodist Church.[21]

The UMC statement of the Wesleyan quadrilateral has also influenced other Methodist churches and the World Methodist Council. A similar, though briefer, statement, including a reference to the role of tradition, experience, and reason in the interpretation of scripture, was adopted by the Methodist Church in India in the 1970s or earlier 1980s.[22] The basic idea was also expressed in the statement of 'Wesleyan Essentials of Christian Faith' adopted by the World Methodist Council in 1996: 'Methodists acknowledge that scriptural reflection is influenced by the processes of reason, tradition and experience, while aware that Scripture is the primary source and criteria of Christian doctrine.'[23]

Issues Associated with the Wesleyan Quadrilateral

We now turn to a consideration of some particular issues related to the Wesleyan quadrilateral and the broader issues of authority in Wesleyan and Methodist churches.

The first issue is simply the historical question of whether, or in what sense, John Wesley could be considered the author or originator of the so-called Wesleyan quadrilateral. There are some grounds in Wesley's writings for such a claim. Two passages in Wesley's works, in particular, should be considered. (1) Wesley's doctrinal treatise on 'Original Sin' (1756) was formally titled 'The Doctrine of Original Sin, according to Scripture, Reason, and Experience.'[24] (2) The preface to the first collected edition of Wesley's works (1771) has the following statement: 'So that in this edition I present to serious and candid men my last and maturest thoughts, agreeable, I hope, to Scripture, reason, and Christian antiquity.'[25] If one were to place these two statements together, and made the further assumption that 'Christian antiquity' was understood to be an element of Christian 'tradition,' then one might be able at least to interpolate a 'quadrilateral' of authorities named by Wesley. Albert Outler made just such an interpolation in claiming that the quadrilateral was derived from John Wesley.[26]

But the assumption that Wesley himself understood 'Christian antiquity' to be an element of 'tradition' is highly problematic because, in the first place, the term 'tradition' was a negatively weighted term in Wesley's culture, and he himself did not utilize the term in the positive sense in which it is used in describing the 'Wesleyan' quadrilateral. Furthermore, regardless of how the term 'tradition' was utilized by Wesley, there does not seem to be a corresponding concept in his thought that would designate the continuity of God's work through the history of Christian communities. As Outler himself pointed out, Protestants had come to a renewed and positive sense of Christian tradition only in the 1950s and 1960s,[27] and it is not appropriate to expect such a concept in the thought of Wesley. For this reason, Scott J. Jones proposed that we might think of a group of five authorities in Wesley's work, including scripture, the early Church ('Christian antiquity'), the Church of England, and then reason and experience.[28] But even here, one could not claim that Wesley himself saw these five sources of authority as somehow linked together as a systematic means of evaluating theological claims. Perhaps it would be better to claim that the Wesleyan quadrilateral is a fruitful contemporary means of evaluating theological and moral claims, grounded in both the Wesleyan inheritance and in ecumenical insights such as the renewed sense of 'tradition' that has prevailed since the 1950s and 1960s.

A second issue in the discussion of the Wesleyan quadrilateral has been the issue of the authority of scripture. As indicated above, the 1988 revision of the UMC statement about the quadrilateral made clear the primary authority of the scriptures and in doing so better accounted for the status of scripture in historic doctrinal standards including the Articles of Religion inherited from the Methodist Church and the Confession of Faith inherited from the Evangelical United Brethren Church. This revision also made clear that the internal authority of the scripture is grounded in their conveyance of 'the apostolic faith,' the gospel message that lies at the core of Christian belief.

The issue of biblical authority in relation to other authorities was examined critically by Scott J. Jones in his study of *John Wesley's Conception and Use of Scripture* (1995). Jones showed that John Wesley shared a common conviction from the culture of the Reformation according to which there is a central core or meaning of scripture as a whole, typically described as the 'analogy of faith' (Romans 12:6). Based on Wesley's comment on this passage in the *Explanatory Notes upon the New Testament* and other documents, Jones showed that Wesley held 'the analogy of faith' (and thus the central meaning of scripture as a whole) to lie in a core of beliefs about the 'way of salvation': Wesley's own definition of the 'analogy of faith' was 'the general tenor of . . .' the scriptures, '. . . that grand scheme of doctrine which is delivered [in the scriptures], touching original sin, justification by faith, and present, inward salvation.'[29] Jones thus exposed a critical element in understanding Wesley's view of biblical authority that had been overlooked in earlier scholarship: he showed that the 'analogy of faith' functioned for Wesley as a norm within scripture that should guide the proper understanding of scripture as a whole.

Building on Jones' discovery of Wesley's understanding of this central norm within scripture, we might observe that, unlike other Protestant theologians, Wesley defined the 'analogy' of faith almost entirely with reference to the believer's appropriation of the work of Christ, specifically, in conviction of sin, justification, and sanctification. That is to say, Wesley's definition focuses on what has been called the *fides qua creditur*, the 'faith by which [something] is believed.' Other Protestant theologians defined the 'analogy of faith' with reference to the objective facts of Christ's work on behalf of humankind, that is to say, the *fides quae creditur*, the 'faith that is believed.' Thus the Reformed theologian Guillaume du Buc (Bucanus) of Lausanne defined the 'analogy of faith' as 'the constant and unchanging sense of Scripture expounded in open [or clear] passages of Scripture and agreeing with the Apostles' Creed, the Decalogue, and the Lord's Prayer.'[30] In this sense, the 'analogy of faith' denotes what in the patristic tradition had been called the 'rule of faith' involving the narrative of Christ's work embedded in the ancient creeds, which continued to norm the church's understanding of the scriptures. We might say, then, that Wesley's understanding of the central meaning of scripture needs to be balanced by an ecumenical perspective that emphasizes the objective work of Christ in addition to a believer's appropriation of the work of Christ. This would comport well with the claim in the 1972 version of the quadrilateral that the 'transcendent' sense of Christian tradition involves the Gospel itself, or the repeated claims of the 1988 revision of the quadrilateral statement that the 'apostolic faith' underlies the scriptures and is the internal ground of the scripture's meaning.

These considerations lead us to a third issue related to the Wesleyan quadrilateral, and that has to do with the use of 'tradition' as a source and norm for authority. As we have seen above, the term 'tradition' and the conceptions of tradition used in the Wesleyan quadrilateral cannot be claimed as a direct inheritance from John Wesley or earlier strands of Wesleyan doctrine or theology. It was a central contribution of the Faith and Order work of the 1950s and 1960s in which Albert C. Outler was centrally involved. It was natural for Outler as well as Colin Williams (also a participant in Faith and Order dialogues) to see Wesley's appeals to 'Christian antiquity' and to the Church of England as presaging this twentieth-century ecumenical reappropriation of Christian tradition. One can even make the case that in some ways John Wesley appealed positively to medieval precedents for Methodist work such as the Dominican use of lay preachers or his concern for the poor as bearing the image of Christ.[31] But whatever Wesleyan precedents might be claimed for it, the conception of tradition that appears in the quadrilateral should be fairly represented as a twentieth-century development, and in this respect it may be important to recognize that neither the 1972 nor the 1988 version of the statement on 'Our Theological Task' attributed the quadrilateral or its conception of tradition directly to John Wesley.

Authority and the 'Wesleyan Quadrilateral'

As indicated above, a critical transition occurred in the understandings of tradition expressed between the 1972 and 1988 versions of the Wesleyan quadrilateral. The 1972 version called directly upon the Montreal 1963 definition of 'tradition' as encompassing 'the Gospel itself,' which precedes scripture and which, as the heart of 'the apostolic faith,' norms the meaning of the scriptures. This sense of tradition is far less clear in the 1988 revision, which on the whole views tradition as embracing positively valued material from the history of the Christian community subsequent to the time of the New Testament. Neither of these senses of tradition could be justified by appeal to Wesley, but a case can be made that the 'transcendent' sense of tradition ('Tradition,' with capital 'T,' as described at Montreal) can be seen as the 'rule of faith' that is embedded in scripture (e.g., I Corinthians 15:1–4) and which norms the meaning of scripture. The 1988 revision of 'Our Theological Task' speaks of 'the apostolic faith' in just this way, although it does not identify this as tradition in any sense: 'the apostolic witness to Jesus as Savior and Lord, which is the source and measure of all valid Christian teaching.'[32] Recognition of one sense of Christian tradition that embraces this central meaning of apostolic witness (*kerygma*) might be a way of seeing Christian scripture and Christian tradition as interlocking authorities, both of which have the apostolic message at their core.

Fourth, although it has not been a contentious issue, the use of reason as a source and norm of theological and moral reflection is another issue that has to be considered in relation to the Wesleyan quadrilateral. A number of scholars have examined Wesley's own use of philosophical traditions. Henry D. Rack and D. W. Bebbington have both reflected on the ways in which John Wesley reflected the general culture of the Enlightenment.[33] Frederick Dreyer, Gregory Clapper, and Richard Brantley have all pointed to Wesley's utilization of Lockean concepts (such as 'simple ideas') to explain the epistemological status of religious experiences.[34] None of these maintained straightforwardly that Wesley simply acquiesced in Locke's empirical epistemology. In Rack's words, 'Wesley was certainly a Lockeian, though not quite a wholehearted one,'[35] since Wesley's claim to religious experience as a valid source of knowledge contradicted Locke's central claim to knowledge based solely on sense experience. In fact, Rex Dale Matthews' 1986 Harvard dissertation on ' "Religion and Reason Joined": A Study in the Theology of John Wesley' examined this concept in detail, showing that Wesley's 'transcendental empiricism' in fact had Aristotelian roots – though sometimes expressed in Lockean language. Wesley thus provided a critical account of religious experience including his emphasis on the 'witness of the Holy Spirit.'[36]

The assertion of reason as a source and criterion of theological and moral reflection in the Wesleyan quadrilateral (both in the 1972 and 1988 versions of it) relied little on Wesley's own epistemological views and emphasized the role of reason as a divinely given tool for understanding what has been revealed in scripture and, to a lesser extent, by tradition and the experience of the divine. Rebekah L. Miles has developed this conception of 'the instrumental role of reason,' emphasizing the limits of reason, both according to Wesley and in contemporary epistemological reflection. This prompted Miles to caution Wesleyans against thinking that 'reason' can somehow function by itself as a source or criterion of theological or moral claims, stressing that reason always functions in an 'instrumental' role as it helps clarify truths that we have in the first place from God, whether we have come to know these truths by way of scripture, tradition, or our own experience.[37]

This leads to a fifth issue related to the Wesleyan quadrilateral – the appeal to experience as a source and criterion for Christian theological and moral reflection. From what has been said in the previous paragraphs, one can see that in Wesley's own thought, reason and experience could hardly be separated, since he understood experience (religious experience as well as sense experience) as a critical ground of human knowledge. The 1970 interim report that first laid out the Wesleyan quadrilateral as a doctrinal proposal for the UMC considered experience only as an historical category describing John Wesley's views. Appropriate to this setting, it dwelt on Wesley's understanding of such religious experiences as conviction of sin and assurance of pardon. The versions of the document on 'Our Theological Task' approved by the 1972 and 1988 General Conferences of the UMC also referred to the Wesleyan emphasis on personal religious experience, but the 1972 statement opened up the possibility of other realms of human experience, since the believer's 'mindset' will be changed in such a way that all of their experiences ('the empirical sciences, the arts, philosophy, and culture in general') become ways of knowing the divine, and the knowledge of the divine affects all other avenues of knowledge.[38] Developing this notion of experience as an element of the Wesleyan quadrilateral, Randy L. Maddox has made the case that experience cannot be separated from tradition, since tradition can denote 'seasoned wisdom,' the knowledge gained by a community through reflection on its own experience.[39]

A sixth and final issue related to the Wesleyan quadrilateral, perhaps an overarching or framing issue, has to do with its status in relation to other doctrinal claims made by Wesleyan churches and specifically by the United Methodist Church. William J. Abraham has raised this issue most passionately, arguing that the quadrilateral has deflected United Methodism from making specific theological claims and leading the church instead to a generalized avowal of four theological criteria so broadly stated that almost nothing in the known universe could be excluded from them.[40] There can be little doubt that some United Methodists took the statement of 'Our Theological

Task' as taking priority over historic statements of doctrine, and in fact the version of this statement approved by the 1972 General Conference did indeed pass judgment on the earlier doctrinal standards by claiming that they were 'not to be construed literally and juridically,'[41] although this language was removed in the 1988 revision.[42]

A different reading of the work of the Theological Study Commission (1968–1972) would be that it presupposed the historic doctrines and practices defined in the UMC's Confession of Faith, its Articles of Religion, and its General Rules, all of which were protected by the restrictive rules in the denomination's constitution.[43] On this reading, the purpose or intent of the quadrilateral was not to call into question historic Christian teachings or distinctively Methodist teachings, but rather to offer criteria for reflection on new issues that had not been dealt with in the doctrinal and moral documents that the UMC inherited from the Evangelical United Brethren and the Methodist Church. In favor of this reading is the preface entitled 'The Gospel in a New Age' at the beginning of the 1972 statement of 'Our Theological Task,' a preface that calls Christians to 'proclaim and live out the eternal gospel in an age of catastrophic perils and soaring hopes.'[44] Also consistent with this interpretation of the 1972 statement is its own explicit restatement of historic Christian doctrines (such as the doctrine of the Trinity) and of distinctive Wesleyan teachings, a statement that was expanded in the 1988 revision of the statement.[45]

In his work on Wesley's teachings about authority, Stanley Frost suggested in the 1930s that we should consider all forms of authority as expressions of the authority of God. It is possible to see at least three elements of the Wesleyan quadrilateral as interlocking expressions of divine authority, specifically conveying the central Christian belief in the work of God in Jesus Christ. The gospel that lies at the heart of the apostolic faith, the belief 'that Christ died for our sins in accordance with the scriptures, and that he was buried, and that he was raised on the third day in accordance with the scriptures' (I Corinthians 15:3b–4) is the heart and nucleus of the Christian tradition (or 'Tradition'), the apostolic faith that is 'the source and measure of all valid Christian teaching.'[46] It is the inner norm that shaped the canon of Christian scripture in the first place and continues to shape its interpretation in the half-year liturgical sequence involving Advent, Christmas, Epiphany, Lent, and Easter. It is the faith that was handed on in the forms of baptismal profession that evolved into the historic creeds and the faith that is proclaimed in the celebration of the Lord's Supper ('Christ has died. Christ is risen. Christ will come again.') and in faithful Christian preaching.[47] The Wesleyan tradition has insisted that it is the same faith that shapes believers' experience of divine grace given through the work of God in Jesus Christ, by the present power of the Holy Spirit. Thus the content of Christian tradition, Christian scripture, and Christian experience can be understood as interlocking means by which the one gospel of Jesus Christ is known and proclaimed in Christian communities. Reason, as Rex Dale Matthews and Rebekah L. Miles have pointed out, serves an ancillary or instrumental role as a divinely given capacity by which individuals and communities understand this common faith and experience.

For Further Reading

Abraham, William J. *Waking from Doctrinal Amnesia: The Healing of Doctrine in the United Methodist Church*. Nashville, TN: Abingdon, 1995.

Gunter, W. Stephen, Scott J. Jones, Ted A. Campbell, Rebekah L. Miles, Randy L. Maddox. *Wesley and the Quadrilateral: Renewing the Conversation*. Nashville, TN: Abingdon, 1997.

Thorsen, Donald A. D. *The Wesleyan Quadrilateral: Scripture, Tradition, Reason & Experience as a Model of Evangelical Theology*. Grand Rapids, MI: Zondervan, 1990.

5
Methodism in the UK and Ireland

Martin Wellings

Methodism began in Great Britain and much of its early development and distinctive identity was inevitably shaped by its British (or, more specifically, English) context. Although by the time of the first Methodist Oecumenical Conference in 1881 American Methodism was far more numerous than its British counterpart, the American promoters and advocates of the conference were keen for it to take place in London, at the City Road Chapel opened by John Wesley in 1778.[1] British Methodism therefore holds an inescapable chronological priority in the history of world Methodism and it has also often been accorded a courteous priority of esteem, being regarded still as the 'mother church' by Methodists from many parts of the globe.[2] The story of the origins and development of Methodism in what is now the United Kingdom and the Republic of Ireland, therefore, is the story, first, of an eighteenth-century movement which gave birth to the whole Methodist enterprise and then of a nineteenth-century church whose influence reached out across the world through the missionary endeavors of the various British Connexions within and beyond the British Empire. The twentieth-century story, marked by the quest for reunion within Methodism, by the ecumenical pilgrimage in England and by the challenge of secularization, is more specific to Britain and Ireland, but the broad issues exemplified by this narrative play out in different ways in many other parts of the world also.

The interpretation of Methodism's story by the writing of its history is almost as old as the Methodist movement itself. Indeed, narrative was a fundamental component of the Evangelical Revival even before Wesley's Aldersgate Street experience. From John Wesley's defense of the Oxford Holy Club in his letter to Richard Morgan and the serial publication, from 1740 until 1791, of his carefully crafted *Journal* onwards, apologists and detractors, hagiographers and imitators, enthusiasts and alarmists, and psychologists of all kinds, have debated Methodist origins and have sometimes also considered the movement's subsequent development. The historiographical field is wide, and ever-expanding, enriched in more recent times by the insights of economic, social, cultural, literary, and feminist historians, and influenced by the changing fashions and passions of the academy and the church. In reviewing the origins and development of Methodism in the United Kingdom and Ireland the present chapter can claim to offer no more than an outline of the salient features, painted with an inevitably broad brush, and drawing attention to trends and opportunities in contemporary research.[3]

The Wesleys' Methodism and the Evangelical Revival, 1730–1791

The weight of interest in British and international scholarship has always rested on Methodism's formative years in the eighteenth century. The period of the Wesley brothers and the Holy Club, of the rise and development of their particular brand of Methodism within the broader setting of the Evangelical Revival, and of the evolution of Methodism from spiritual experience to religious movement has preoccupied Methodists and fascinated historians. The attraction of something new and controversial may in part account for this; moreover, the origins represent the part of Methodist history shared by all strands of the movement across the world and a considerable contribution to Wesley studies has been made by scholars from North America. As a result, eighteenth-century Methodist history has been well studied and has benefitted from an international community of scholarship.

For much of the last 270 years, early Methodist history has been read principally through a biographical lens and presented as a narrative structured around the life of John Wesley. Wesley has attracted the attention of innumerable biographers, but in the last quarter century Methodist history has been particularly well served by the publication of several critical studies based on close and insightful reading of hitherto inaccessible primary sources. Notable in this regard have been the books of Richard Heitzenrater and Henry Rack, informed and supported by the massive ongoing project for a new critical edition of Wesley's works.[4]

Alongside scholarly biographies of Wesley may be set several other significant developments which shed light on Methodist origins. First, the study of evangelicalism has burgeoned since the 1980s, with contributions from British, American, and Canadian scholars. The Wesleys' Methodism is increasingly seen not in isolation, but as part of a transcontinental and transatlantic phenomenon. The structures, networks, and experiences of the first Methodists can fruitfully be compared, and sometimes contrasted, with those of other evangelicals.[5] Second, Methodist history has also benefitted from work on the social, economic, and intellectual context of eighteenth-century England, particularly as historians of Methodism have drawn on these insights and engaged more fully with mainstream historiography. Third, after generations of neglect, the eighteenth-century Church of England has attracted new research, leading to a reappraisal of Methodism's roots and to a reassessment of its place in the religious life of English society in this period.⁶ Fourth, it has been recognized that there is more to Methodism than John Wesley, so fresh attention has been paid to Charles Wesley and to other leaders, and also to the experience of grassroots Methodists, both women and men. The result of all this work has been to add both breadth and depth to the picture of early Methodism. Instead of the caricature of a single heroic leader revitalizing a moribund church and saving a nation from revolution, a richer understanding has emerged of a whole movement interacting with its contexts and experiencing all-too-human tensions and growing pains.

Four principal areas of current interest and further study may be identified. The first is the condition of religion in England in the first half of the eighteenth century. Methodist, evangelical and Tractarian commentators have united in denigrating the Church of England in this period, thus justifying the rise of Methodism, the development of the Evangelical party in the national church and the campaign for reform waged by the Oxford Movement from the 1830s. At the same time, it has been assumed that the Protestant Dissenting denominations were declining numerically and collapsing into apathy and heterodoxy until renewed by the Evangelical Revival. The indications are that these interpretations are too simplistic, and that further work on Church and Dissent will continue to reveal a much more diverse picture, with energetic bishops and conscientious clergy alongside the more familiar figures of time-servers and opportunists. In turn, this opens up scope for investigation into the continuity between Dissent and Methodism or the religious societies and Methodism, and poses questions about Methodism's impact and appeal in a context of lively lay piety.⁷

Second, there is more to be done in integrating the Wesleys' Methodism into the picture of international evangelicalism. This task embraces the intellectual background, including the relationship between Methodism and Pietism.⁸ It also draws in the network of personal contacts and publications which spread news of the revival between Britain and North America. Teasing out the relationships between John and Charles Wesley, George Whitefield, Howell Harris, John Fletcher, the Countess of Huntingdon, and other leaders still offers scope for further research, as does the exploration of evangelical experiences and sensibilities through the narratives of hitherto overlooked individuals.⁹

Third, in recent years Charles Wesley has begun to emerge from his brother's shadow and to claim a place in the history of Methodism beyond that of prolific hymn writer. Until the present century this work has been hampered by a lack of accessible primary sources, but with new editions of his sermons, journals, and letters available or soon to be published, and with new critical biographies appearing, a reassessment of Charles Wesley is in process and with it a re-evaluation of Methodist origins.¹⁰ A small note of caution may be entered here, lest a proper appreciation of Charles Wesley should be thought to require the denigration of John; it should be possible to produce a fuller picture of Charles without succumbing to the temptation to caricature his elder brother.

Fourth, work is called for on the composition of the Methodist movement, on who were 'the people called Methodists.' Popular Methodist history has tended to focus on the leaders and on exemplary figures; 'history from below' encourages paying attention to ordinary people. It is likely that the majority of early Methodists were women, and this insight needs to be appropriated and worked out. A couple of generations ago Leslie Church published several studies of 'the Methodist people,' and this theme is ripe for revisiting.[11]

Many of the tasks facing the study of Methodist origins and early developments have already been mapped out and are already engaging the attention of historians. Work continues to catalogue the Methodist collections at the John Rylands University Library of Manchester and to promote their use. As primary sources are identified and published (for instance, the Charles Wesley letters), and as local studies of Church of England dioceses and parishes continue to accumulate, there will be further opportunities both to pursue research in detail and to assimilate fresh insights into the broad picture of eighteenth-century Methodism. Perhaps it is the synthesis which is most needed now, an account of the Wesleys' Methodism which has its foundations in up-to-date research but which can present a persuasive overview of the movement in its setting in eighteenth-century Britain, analyzing the origins and appeal of Methodism and its place within the wider mosaic of contemporary religious life.

Growth and Division in British Methodism, 1791–1857

At John Wesley's funeral at the City Road Chapel in March 1791, when the officiating clergyman reached the sentence in the burial service, 'Forasmuch as it hath pleased Almighty God to take unto Himself the soul of our dear brother,' he substituted 'our dear father' and the congregation dissolved into tears.[12] The veneration of Wesley, established before his death, continued well into the nineteenth century, shaping not only the writing of Methodist history by generations of devout Wesleyans, but also the mindset of the Connexion's leaders and ministers, resolved to preserve the doctrine, discipline, and ethos bequeathed by 'our venerable Founder.' The sense of bereavement was profound, but the wider impact on Methodism and Methodist history was also deeply significant.

For Methodist historians, 1791 marks the point at which the stories of British and American Methodism diverge. The date is in fact largely artificial. Francis Asbury was charting his own course well before Wesley's death, and his references to 'our old daddy' were noticeably less respectful than the language of his British counterparts. Since the Christmas Conference of 1784 the American Connexion had been constitutionally independent of the British Conference. Although the relationship between British and American Methodism has been described as 'only fraternal,' however, transatlantic links and influences remained much more important than has often been recognized.[13] It remains the case that historians of Methodism have tended to take Wesley's death as a convenient boundary marker, and scholars whose principal focus of interest is American Methodism pay little attention to British developments after the 1790s or very early 1800s. One consequence of this is that nineteenth-century British Methodist history is far less studied than the period of the Wesleys.

John Wesley's death also ushered in an era of unprecedented growth and tension in the British Methodist movement. There were unresolved contradictions within the Wesleys' Methodism: whether the Methodists were part of the Church of England, or really Dissenters[14]; whether the Connexion was an autocracy, an oligarchy, or a democracy; whether Methodism had an affinity with campaigns for social and political reform, or stood with conservative forces in church and state. These contradictions re-emerged after 1791, in the turbulent conditions of a protracted war with Revolutionary and Napoleonic France, and in years of postwar economic and social dislocation, and political upheaval. The leaders of British Methodism found themselves trying to conserve Wesley's legacy, to handle astonishing numerical growth, and to deal with challenging political and social pressures. Fervent and effective evangelism marched hand-in-hand with the creation of new institutions and structures to manage and control a Connexion far larger than anything Wesley had known. The choices and decisions of this period shaped the Wesleyan[15] Connexion of the Victorian era, but also determined which Methodists would remain within Wesleyanism and which would find a spiritual home elsewhere.

Four areas of investigation have engaged historians in this period. First, there has been discussion of the gradual separation of Methodism from the Church of England. Unlike 'Old Dissent,' expelled in 1662, or the Countess of Huntingdon's Connexion, which formally seceded in 1783, Methodism established its separate ecclesial identity very gradually and rather reluctantly, and with considerable scope for local variation. The impact of the Oxford Movement in the 1830s was important, both in raising Wesleyan suspicions of the Established Church, and in influencing the changing pastoral priorities of local parish priests which made it difficult for Methodists to continue to belong to both 'church' and 'chapel.'[16] It is clear, however, that the picture remained untidy for several generations, with Wesleyan Methodists in particular retaining an affinity for their parish church and recoiling from 'the dissidence of Dissent.'

Second, the evolution of the Wesleyan Connexion and its structures and ministry have been explored, notably by John Bowmer and David Hempton.[17] The figure of Jabez Bunting looms large in this story, although Bunting should be seen as one, albeit the ablest and most prominent, of a number of leaders who sought to organize Methodism, place its finances on a firm footing, and prevent phenomenal growth toppling over into bankruptcy or anarchy. There is an institutional aspect to this account, investigating bodies like the Wesleyan Methodist Missionary Society and the Theological Institution and tracing the creation of Wesleyan schools. There is also the ideological aspect of the articulation of a theology of the 'pastoral office' which gave sole authority to the Conference and to the preachers (ministers).

Third, the many divisions which occurred in this period have attracted historians. Primitive Methodism, the largest of the non-Wesleyan groups, has proved the most popular, perhaps because of its associations with the poor and its roots in revival, rather than unedifying Connexional feuds.[18] Other groups, like the Independent Methodists and the Tent Methodists, have also found their historians.[19]

Fourth, the relationship between Methodism, industrialization, and revolution has continued to stimulate debate, as historians have reacted to the work and reputation of Elie Halévy and E. P. Thompson. Hempton discusses this theme in Methodist historiography in his *The Religion of the People*, subjecting Thompson's 'pungent Marxist interpretation' to a searching critique and paying tribute to the work of W. R. Ward.[20] Uncomfortable as the Thompson thesis may be for Methodists, it has a continuing resonance in popular historiography and demands attention.

Two broad areas in need of further research may be identified. The first is local, and comprises the different strands of late eighteenth- and early nineteenth-century Methodism, especially in its non-Wesleyan forms. There is still plenty of work to be done on Primitive Methodism, and on the smaller Connexions: Bible Christians, New Connexion, and Free Methodists of various kinds. Since the reunion of British Methodism in 1932 reference to these traditions has been discouraged, almost as a throwback to an unhappy past. The larger, wealthier, older, and better-organized Wesleyan Connexion, with fuller records and established institutions, has attracted more historians, and the sheer variety of nineteenth-century Methodism remains to be explored more fully.[21] This requires local investigation and painstaking work in local archives. The same is true of the relationship between Methodists and the Church of England in this period, if we wish to move beyond official pronouncements at national level to the reality on the ground.

Complementing this local focus is a wide-angled attention to British Methodism in a broader context. Methodism's particular place within the world of evangelical Protestantism has often been overlooked, and there is scope for remedying that neglect.²² The evangelical world, moreover, was self-consciously transatlantic, and the links connecting Methodists in Britain and North America would repay further study. David Hempton has done much to encourage this perspective and to suggest potential lines of inquiry and interpretation.²³ This opportunity needs to be developed further, looking at contacts, networks, institutions, the sharing of ideas, and the effects of emigration from, and travel between, the Old World and the New.

Sources for this work are available in local record offices in Britain, which are the principal repository for the papers of British Methodist churches and circuits. Further material may be found in the rich archives of the British Methodist Church, located at the John Rylands University Library at Manchester. Printed sources, in newspapers and periodicals, are also held in the Rylands Library, in the British Library in London and, in the case of local newspapers, which flourished in the nineteenth century, in local studies libraries in major British towns and cities.

British Methodism in the Heyday of Nonconformity, 1857–1918

British society underwent massive changes between the 1850s and the end of the First World War. The population increased steadily, and shifted from a rural to an urban majority; a majority, too, dwelling in large rather than small towns. Participation in the political process was widened through a broader franchise and a new framework of local government; state or civic regulation of trade, health, housing, and education steadily increased; accelerating imperial expansion brought Britain the largest overseas empire the world had ever seen. There was a revolution in communications, and the combination of the railways and rising levels of literacy brought the first mass circulation newspapers to complement the development of mass membership political parties and a burgeoning trade union movement. In the world's first modern urban industrial society affluence and squalor coexisted at the poles of the class spectrum, while social elevation (at best) and respectability (at least) became the aims of the lower-middle and working classes. For the first time since the Enlightenment, moreover, powerful ideological challenges were launched to traditional Christian assumptions: from scientific materialism, fueled by Darwinian evolution, from militant secularism, and from new critical readings of the Bible. For all the churches, visible numerical success and apparent social influence marched alongside unsettling questions about method and message.

Three major themes have dominated the study of Methodist history in this period. The first has been Methodism's fulfillment of its calling as a missionary movement in the face of a rapidly increasing urban population with a wide range of social needs. Work has been done on the evangelistic enterprises of the Connexions, from revivals to chapel building to the creation of institutions to minister to the urban poor, notably deaconess orders, settlements and Thomas Bowman Stephenson's National Children's Home and Orphanage.[24] The so-called Forward Movement, associated with Hugh Price Hughes, has come to symbolize aggressive evangelism allied to social concern, and to represent a willingness to reform Connexional structures and alter cherished ways of working, like the three-year ministerial itinerancy, for the sake of missionary effectiveness.[25]

Second, and again associated with Hughes, the ecclesial trajectory of Methodism in this era has attracted attention. From a mediating position between the Church of England and Dissent earlier in the century, Methodism developed a greater church consciousness and an identity as a 'Free Church,' expressed from the 1890s in membership of local and national Free Church councils and congresses. For some, this was a step on the way to a wider ecumenism; for others it represented a conviction that Methodism might replace Anglicanism as the religious expression of the British Empire. Linked with this was the attempt to exercise political influence and to promote a reforming agenda, sometimes characterized as the outworking of the 'Nonconformist Conscience.' The issue of temperance has attracted particular attention,[26] but there have also been studies of other social topics and of the differences of emphasis and approach between Methodism and Old Dissent.[27]

Third, Methodist missions across the world grew and flourished in the second half of the nineteenth century.[28] Study of missions and of home organization of auxiliaries and publications sustaining the work overseas has been an important theme for historical study, albeit sometimes undertaken almost in isolation from the agenda of domestic historiography. There are obvious links here to the growing and sometimes contentious fields of imperial and colonial history.[29]

At the time of this writing, work is continuing on the history of Methodist missions, with the intention of producing a multi-authored study which can replace the monumental, but now outdated achievement of G. G. Findlay and W. W. Holdsworth, published as long ago as 1924. The enterprise now in hand has made very clear the size and complexity of the task, and it may be suggested that there will be plenty more for scholars to do, both in studying the growth and development of Methodist missions on many continents and in exploring the place of the Missionary Society in Methodist life in Great Britain. The challenge of an international and interdisciplinary project of this kind is considerable, but Methodism has an excellent resource in its Missionary Society archives, now housed at the School of Oriental and African Studies of the University of London. Clearly, missionary history needs to be undertaken in collaboration with partners elsewhere in the world church, in Connexions and denominations which are now autonomous.

Methodism in the UK and Ireland

Turning to Home Missions, the effectiveness of the Victorian Church, regardless of denomination, continues to preoccupy researchers. Was Methodism in its various branches succumbing to institutional inertia? Had the fires of revival burned out? Had routine and respectability taken the place of spiritual fervor? Were sincere efforts still being made to communicate the gospel, but with decreasing success in an anonymous urban society? Or has the demise of the Victorian Church been exaggerated? Local studies, using local records and newspapers, offer opportunities for reconstructing the priorities, programs and place of Methodist congregations in villages, suburbs, towns, and cities in this period. There are plenty of generalizations about chapel life, whether glowing accounts in denominational newspapers or theories of creeping secularization on the part of modern historians, but these need to be tested and evaluated through local studies.

Local detail is also a potentially fruitful avenue of approach to the 'thick study' of congregations.[30] The discipline of congregational studies has developed relatively recently as a tool for pastoral ministry, but it also offers opportunities for historians to attempt to reconstruct the life of a congregation in the past. Late Victorian churches were exceptionally rich in diverse activities and associations, through which they engaged with a substantial proportion of the population. The place of faith, of church, and of Christian associations as part of the fabric of British society in the late Victorian and Edwardian era is a suggestive topic for historical investigation.[31]

Considered overall, late Victorian Methodism in Great Britain remains surprisingly understudied.[32] With the exception of a few modern biographies, a small number of monographs,[33] and a few unpublished doctoral and other theses, the field for further investigation is wide open. To give just a flavor of the opportunities, the Central Halls have yet to find their historian. The Forward Movement and the endeavor to commend the gospel in an urban setting, rural Methodism in its relationship with the Church of England and its response to agricultural boom and depression, Methodism in its engagement with Victorian high culture (whether literary, architectural, or visual), and the whole history of the non-Wesleyan Connexions remains largely untold. Compared to the energy expended on the eighteenth century, this more recent period has been woefully neglected by serious historians, and there is considerable scope both for study in detail of localities or topics for a more comprehensive overview. The archival sources in Manchester, London, and local record offices, are extensive, as are the printed sources in newspapers, periodicals, and books, and perhaps this has been a deterrent to those overwhelmed by the sheer volume of materials to master. The challenge to historians of British Methodism is to address this gap, and to do so in dialogue with the flourishing studies of Victorian church and Victorian society going forward in the academy. It is worth mentioning too that growing popular enthusiasm for genealogy has meant that sources for local history like census returns, trade directories, school records, and maps, as well as baptism and marriage registers, are much more readily available in searchable forms than was previously the case.

British Methodism in the Twentieth Century

The twentieth century witnessed the steady marginalization of Methodism in Great Britain. In 1900 Methodism was by far the largest Free Church denomination and in the dreams of Hugh Price Hughes and Sir Robert Perks it was well placed to supplant Anglicanism as the authentic religious expression of the British Empire. The opening of Westminster Central Hall, opposite Westminster Abbey and close to the Houses of Parliament, in 1912 symbolized Wesleyan triumphalism and confidence in the Edwardian Indian summer of Nonconformity; the Hall itself was the most visible outcome of the Twentieth Century Fund's appeal for 'a million guineas from a million Methodists.' By 1912, however, there was already anxiety about fluctuating membership statistics, the challenge of aggressive Roman and Anglo-Catholicism, and the task of mission to an increasing complex society – more literate, more affluent, more aware of the rival Utopias promised by Socialism or leisure.[34] Although after twenty years of tortuous negotiations, the project for home reunion bore fruit in 1932 with the reconciliation of the Wesleyan, Primitive, and United Methodist Connexions, Methodist union failed to release the hoped-for energy and enthusiasm for mission, partly because of intractable local difficulties in restructuring circuits and closing redundant chapels and partly because of the dislocation caused by the Second World War. After a decade of modest progress and new initiatives in the 1950s Methodism was hit hard by the social revolution of the 1960s. The last forty years of the century saw collapsing membership and ebbing confidence across the Connexion, neither of which were allayed by bouts of reorganization of the central structures of the church. Through this period there was a continuing commitment to ecumenism, usually focused on reunion with the Church of England. At the same time the theological identity of British Methodism evolved from a liberal evangelical consensus to an open acceptance of pluralism with a corresponding broadening of ethical options.

Declining numbers, evaporating influence, and diminishing vitality have made Methodism in the twentieth century far less interesting to historians in general than was the case in the eighteenth and nineteenth centuries. If religion as a whole is sometimes downplayed or even overlooked altogether in general and social histories of this period, it is not surprising that historians are inclined to consider Methodism only as one among a number of shrinking enclaves in a secularized and secularizing society.[35] For those who are

Methodism in the UK and Ireland

prepared to accept that religion still has a place in the modern world, resurgent evangelicalism and Islam attract more attention and interest. When Methodism does feature, it appears as part of a wider picture, for instance as one strand in Ian Machin's study of the political influence and social priorities of the churches in the twentieth century and as an aspect of David Bebbington's broad survey of evangelicalism.[36] It naturally has a place in overviews of British or English Christianity, for example in the works of Adrian Hastings and Callum Brown, but not as a major protagonist.[37] The only full-scale book on an entirely Methodist theme emerging from the academy in recent years is Michael Hughes' investigation of Methodist attitudes to peace and war in the twentieth century.[38]

For historians working within Methodism, reunion and ecumenism have provoked investigation. Several scholars have explored negotiations leading up to the creation of the Methodist Church of Great Britain in 1932, and some have analyzed the effectiveness, or otherwise, of reunion in subsequent decades.[39] Anglican–Methodist discussions, and wider ecumenical relationships, have also been considered.[40] Beyond this, and with very few exceptions,[41] Methodist history in the twentieth century has been largely confined to accounts of institutions and to biographical studies of a few prominent individuals.[42]

Two areas of continuing activity may be identified in contemporary scholarship. The first, the preoccupation of many historians and sociologists, is secularization. The attempt to map, to understand, and to explain the place of religion in modern society has generated a vast literature, and has provoked fierce debate around theories and methodologies.[43] Among the competing models are those which claim that modern urban and industrial society is inimical to religious faith and practice, and which trace the decline of Christianity in Britain back to the nineteenth century; those which posit a change in the expression of faith to 'believing without belonging'; and, most recently, those which locate the significant changes in mindset to the 1960s and which deduce a catastrophic and irreversible decline in Christian adherence from that period.[44] As the debate continues, historians are engaged in testing the models against empirical data and in comparative studies to see to what extent Britain may be regarded as typical.

The second area of activity is the study of fundamentalism. The perceived links between religious extremism, political instability in volatile parts of the world and international terrorism have generated interest in and funding for the investigation of faith and its various expressions. Among the outcomes of this development have been projects to explore the relationship between Methodism, evangelicalism, and fundamentalism in the twentieth century.

Both secularization and fundamentalism offer opportunities for the study of twentieth-century British Methodist history. However, as with the nineteenth century, there is a vast area of uncharted territory to be explored beyond these currently fashionable topics. In common with other evangelical denominations, for example, nineteenth-century Methodism was active in social and philanthropic work, and in education. These extensive programs were largely superseded by state provision in the twentieth century, but in the last quarter of the century the voluntary sector once again became a provider of social care and of faith-based schooling. The story of Methodism's engagement with this evolving situation has still to be told in the investigation of schools and education policy, teacher training, caring agencies linked to urban churches, national structures of Home Missions and Mission alongside the Poor,[45] the work of the National Children's Home, and of Methodist Homes for the Aged. There is scope, too, for a history of Methodist youth work, and work with university and college students, an aspect of Methodist mission that expanded enormously with the extension of higher education in the 1950s and 1960s and the changing social patters after the Second World War. Turning overseas, the policies of the Methodist Missionary Society (MMS) in the post-1945 era of retreat from empire certainly warrant investigation. Methodist missionaries were engaged in the liberation struggles in Northern Rhodesia (now Zambia) and Southern Rhodesia (now Zimbabwe), and the MMS oversaw the transition from Overseas Districts to autonomous churches in former colonies. Moreover, one element in an increasingly multicultural British society is the presence of citizens of New Commonwealth origin in the United Kingdom, and their experience has included both racism within the church and the renewal of struggling urban congregations through the arrival of Methodists from other parts of the world. As with the nineteenth century, archival and printed sources for these subjects are extensive, with the principal Connexional collections being housed in Manchester (domestic records) and London (overseas records).

Methodism in Ireland

Methodism in Ireland is being treated separately in this essay for three reasons. First, since 1752 there has been a separate Conference in Ireland, and although the President of the British Conference has presided at its sessions and there has been a frequent interchange of personnel, Ireland constitutes in Methodist terms a different Connexion.[46] Second, since 1922 a large part of the island of Ireland has been a separate political jurisdiction from the United Kingdom, achieving a large measure of independence as the Irish Free State in 1922 and then full autonomy and statehood toward the end of the following decade. Third, the social and ecclesiastical history of Ireland is very different from that of Great Britain, particularly of England, where the Wesleys' Methodism made the greatest and most enduring impact.[47]

Methodism in the UK and Ireland

John Wesley visited Ireland for the first time in 1747. He made twenty subsequent visits, crossing for the final time in 1789. Wesley found a country with an established and episcopally governed Protestant church, a significant Presbyterian minority, principally in the north of the island, and a majority Roman Catholic population. Much of the country was rural, with parliament and administration based in Dublin. Over the next three-quarters of a century, through the rising of the United Irishmen in 1798 and the Act of Union of 1804, Methodism established itself in Ireland, experiencing phases of extraordinary growth and what David Hempton has called 'pulses of revival.'[48] Growth was localized, linked to social and economic conditions in particular regions of the country, and to the political atmosphere, as well as to the message and methods of the preachers. As in England, women played a key role in the spread of the movement, and the resolution of tensions between revivalism and institutional order in favor of the latter in the era of Bunting's ascendancy did not ultimately favor the Methodist cause. Massive economic distress in the prefamine years of the 1840s and in subsequent decades also adversely affected the Connexion and set a pattern of emigration which produced a wide Irish Methodist diaspora. Irish Methodists played leading roles as ministers and lay leaders in British and North American Methodism, and exercised an influence as missionaries out of all proportion to their size as a community. In the late nineteenth and early twentieth centuries the Connexion weathered the political storms around Home Rule and the creation of the Free State. During the so-called 'Troubles' in the North in the last third of the century Methodists were sometimes able to mediate between Unionist and Nationalist communities otherwise divided on religious, political, and ethnic lines. After many years in which Ireland, whether North or South, seemed very different from Britain, the turn of the twenty-first century saw the dawn of peace in the North and rapid economic development stimulating cultural change in the Republic, as a hitherto apparently traditional Roman Catholic society gave way to a modern secular state.[49]

Much writing about Irish Methodism has emerged from the denomination and has comprised a faithful narrative of events rather than a critical analysis of context and causation. The standard history of Methodism in Ireland is still the three-volume work by C. H. Crookshank, published in 1885–1888; it finishes in 1859, with a volume by Richard Lee Cole added in 1960 to cover the next century. Seminal work by David Hempton has brought a new depth of analysis and has opened up fresh areas of investigation, particularly in relating the Irish Methodist story to the world of transatlantic revivalism and to the broader history of the country.[50] The Irish diaspora has found its historian in Norman Taggart, who has worked on the leading nineteenth-century Irish Methodist William Arthur, and on the place of the Irish in world Methodism.[51]

In general terms, therefore, Irish Methodist history is open to further scholarly research. David Hempton's essay, 'Methodism in Irish Society, 1770–1830,' points the way, and draws attention to the wealth of resources held in the collection of the Wesley Historical Society in Ireland at Edgehill College, Belfast. There is considerable scope for the integration of the Methodist story with the social and economic texture of particular communities, to see where, why, and how Methodism experienced success or failure. The influence of Methodist styles and methods on other denominations in Ireland might also be explored: whether and to what extent Methodist evangelicalism affected the Church of Ireland or the Presbyterians, and how far it contributed to that pan-evangelical Protestant 'crusade' which itself provoked a Catholic backlash in the 1820s. Methodist relations with Roman Catholics also call for examination. Contemporary Methodists are proud of John Wesley's, *Letter to a Roman Catholic*, and of his sermons, 'Catholic Spirit' and 'A Caution against Bigotry,' but are less keen to remember his ambivalent attitude to Lord George Gordon and the Protestant Association.[52] The effect of the Irish dimension on British Methodist attitudes to Roman Catholic emancipation and to Irish immigration in mid-Victorian Britain might be considered, as might the level of involvement of Irish Methodists in the debates over Home Rule in the late nineteenth century and in the structures and politics of Unionism into the twentieth century.

Conclusion

The first phase of the development of Methodism in the United Kingdom and Ireland is a story shared by Methodists across the world because it recounts the rise of Methodism itself in eighteenth-century England. This story has become almost a founding myth, cherished and retold in many places and cultures. Therefore, it behooves Methodists to pay attention to this particular historical episode and to understand the birth of Methodism in its original context.

Many of the structures and patterns laid down by the Wesleys proved remarkably enduring. Most significant of all, perhaps, were Charles Wesley's hymns, which still find a place in Methodist hymnals more than two centuries later. The vocabulary of preacher and circuit, conference and class, have also survived to shape subsequent expressions of Methodism. The theology of Methodism – 'our doctrines' – comprising the cluster of emphases which constitute the Wesleys' evangelical Arminianism have also remained at the heart of world Methodism, giving Methodists a particular family resemblance within the broader evangelical community.

Beyond the eighteenth century the British story becomes more localized, although the expression of Methodism in an industrial society, in an expanding (and then contracting) empire, and in the face of secularization offers points of comparison with experiences elsewhere. The global reach of David Hempton's, *Methodism: Empire of the Spirit*, encourages such comparisons, and reminds us that the twenty-first century is not the first era to take a world-wide perspective. After all, the first Oecumenical Conference met in 1881 and it might be argued that transatlantic connections between the branches of Methodism were stronger in the early nineteenth century than they are today.[53]

The survey of historical writing on British Methodism presented here leads to a number of obvious conclusions. First, the weight of scholarship rests heavily on the eighteenth century. Later periods have been significantly overlooked and the opportunities for primary research on Methodist institutions, individuals, and activities are considerable.

Second, there is a need to make connections in the study of British Methodist history. In the past much of the work was done by Methodists, sometimes for apologetic or hagiographical reasons. In more recent times Methodism has engaged the attention of historians from other backgrounds. This has opened up opportunities for fruitful dialogue between church and the academy. Methodism has been more firmly located in a social and political context. Another series of connections has come with the development of the history of evangelicalism, and yet another with the greater awareness of European and transatlantic influences.

Third, immersion in local materials is a vital part of the historian's task. The fluctuating state of Methodism in Ireland in the late eighteenth century illustrates the influence of particular local circumstances and conditions which can only be uncovered with patient attention to primary sources.

Fourth, a synthesis of research is called for. A multi-authored history of the Methodist Church in Great Britain appeared between 1965 and 1988. Arguably, the first volume was out of date before the third volume was published in 1983.[54] A new history is urgently needed.

The materials for work on Methodism in the United Kingdom and Ireland are extensive and ever-improving. It is hoped that the Wesley Works Project will soon deliver a complete critical edition of Wesley's works. In the meantime considerable progress has been made in supplying the scholarly community with the works of Charles Wesley. The principal archives of British Methodism, housed in the John Rylands University Library, Manchester, and the School of Oriental and African Studies in London, are accessible and gradually being catalogued. Local (city and county) record offices hold rich deposits of local Methodist records in places which facilitate the study of Methodism in local context. The Wesley Historical Society's *Proceedings* and conferences sponsored by the World Methodist Historical Society and by the Association of Denominational Historical Societies and Cognate Libraries assist in disseminating the fruits of research. The tools for pursuing the study of the origins and development of Methodism in the United Kingdom and Ireland lie ready at hand. It is hoped that they will be effectively used.

For Further Reading

Cooney, Dudley Levistone. *The Methodists in Ireland: A Short History*. Dublin: Blackrock, The Columba Press, 2001.

Davies, Rupert, A. Raymond George, and Gordon Rupp, eds. *A History of the Methodist Church in Great Britain*, 4 vols. London: Epworth Press, 1965–1988.

Kendall, H. B. *The History of the Primitive Methodist Church*. London: E. Dalton, 1906.

Taggart, Norman W. *The Irish in World Methodism, 1760–1900*. London: Epworth, 1986.

Townsend, W. J., H. B. Workman, and George Eayrs, eds. *A New History of Methodism*. London: Hodder and Stoughton, 1909.

Vickers, John A., ed. *A Dictionary of Methodism in Britain and Ireland*. Peterborough: Epworth, 2000.

6 Methodism in North America[1]

Russell E. Richey

One might begin the narrative of American Methodism in various places. With the home life of Susanna and Samuel Wesley and with the formative experiences shared there by sons John and Charles. With John and Charles Wesley's missionary misadventures in Georgia in the 1730s, but through which they came into formative contact with Moravians. With John's and Charles' May 1738 conversion experiences. With the Great Awakening and the grand itinerant George Whitefield's multiple triumphant American tours and his modeling of aggressive evangelistic itinerant preaching. With 'spontaneous' colonial evangelical beginnings in the 1750s and 1760s – Robert Strawbridge in Maryland, Philip William Otterbein and Martin Boehm in the middle colonies, and Barbara Heck, Philip Embury, and Thomas Webb in New York. With the roots that these several evangelical movements shared with European Pietism.

Pietism

Each starting point accents particular aspects of movements which converged in American Methodism. By accenting a shared Pietism, we point to importing dynamic and diffuse European and British forms of spirituality, belief and practice, *and* to both creation of new patterns and transformation of imported ones. The subset of these renewal impulses, which we will collectively here term Methodist, from the start crossed lines of race, language, nationality, and class, and made space for creative contributions from women as well as men. Full credit for some of the creativity, as for instance that of African American women and men, now proves hard to document. Only the asides of itinerants' journals capture their vibrant, full-orbed enthusiasm for preaching that affirmed their full humanity and dignity before God. Such contributions from below – from the poor, the enslaved, the marginal, the laity – Pietism made possible.

By 'Pietism' we point to similarity in practices, beliefs, mores, and communal structures among reformers in very different contexts – the

Lutheran Pietist pioneers, Johann Arndt (1555–1621), Philipp Jakob Spener (1635–1705), and August Hermann Francke (1663–1727), late English and colonial Puritanism, the Moravians, Catholic Jansenism, British evangelicalism (including Methodism), and the North American revivalism of the First and Second Great Awakenings. These loosely related renewal efforts reacted against formalism in religious practice, scholasticizing of doctrine, secularizing policies by states and nations, and class distinctions within religious communities. Positively, these movements affirmed the capacity of laity (women and men), when their hearts had been renewed by the Holy Spirit and their lives turned around by conversion, to live as obedient, disciplined, and faithful Christians. To so equip and empower laity, Pietism generated small groups for Bible-reading, hymn-singing, witness, mutual support, and discipline. From ministers Pietism expected vibrant, heart-touching preaching, from laity the willingness to testify to new life in Christ, from everyone obedience to Scripture's moral dictates. Accenting biblical literacy, Pietist movements put a premium on programs and publications by which children and adults could be educated and nurtured in the faith. Accenting the Great Commission as well as the Great Commandment, these renewal efforts began the Protestant missionary endeavor.

Where they prospered, these renewal efforts challenged religious, social, and political authority that settled for formal, notional, legal, or outward religiosity and repudiated, as worldly, compromises of religion with status, wealth, power, display, and prerogative. This prophetic principle, a source of its appeal to the marginalized, powerless, enslaved, and voiceless, naturally elicited counter-reactions from those critiqued. The counter-cultural impulse in Pietism did not, by and large, lead to Puritan-like organized political or military endeavor. It warred instead against spiritual principalities and powers that distorted Christian life – individual, interpersonal, and familial. It focused its strongly communal and reformist instincts into small groups, the conventicles, the *collegia pietatis*, by which soldiers of Christ might be equipped and kingdoms not of this world might be ushered in. Wesley put his signature on Pietism by knitting renewal, revival, and communalism into connectional order.

Beginnings

Philip William Otterbein (1726–1813) led such spiritual reordering as a German Reformed pastor from his arrival in 1752 until his death. Educated at the Reformed university at Herborn, Germany, Otterbein brought to the colonies and to pastorates in Pennsylvania and Maryland, a salvation-oriented, practical, confessional, and covenantal Pietism shaped by the Heidelberg Catechism. Itinerating widely throughout German-speaking communities in the middle colonies, Otterbein identified, recruited, nurtured, trained, mentored, ordered, and deployed other like-minded preachers. A 1785 'Constitution' for his Evangelical Reformed Church of Baltimore spelled out expectations for the cadre of preachers and communities aligned with him – discipline, class meetings, itinerancy, repudiation of predestination, and recognition that persons can fall from grace. In 1767, on one of his itinerations, Otterbein attended a several day 'great meeting,' then common among German-speaking communities and one of many roots of the later camp meetings. There he met and embraced Martin Boehm (1725–1812), a Swiss-German Mennonite then also itinerating, conducting what may only be termed revivals, and exercising a ministry of oversight. A farmer, selected by lot to preach, Boehm's expansive revivalism threatened Mennonite leadership and led to his expulsion. Otterbein experienced similar tensions with the Reformed Coetus (synod). By 1789 the two were convening a conference of like-minded preachers from the two communions, and an 1800 conference formalized the creation of the United Brethren in Christ (UB), electing Otterbein and Boehm as bishops. The mantle then passed to George Adam Geeting (1741–1812) and Christian Newcomer (1749–1830), later Andrew Zeller (1755–1839), the latter two to be elected bishops.

The migration of Wesleyans[2] to the colonies produced similar efforts to improvise and experiment, in effect, to chart a rapid path from colonial to postcolonial status. The official statement of Methodist beginnings, which prefacing the *Discipline* from 1787 through much of the nineteenth century, succinctly captured that indigenizing pattern. 'What was the Rise of Methodism, so called, in America?'

> *Answ.* During the Space of thirty Years past, certain Persons, Members of the Society, emigrated from England and Ireland, and settled in various Parts of this Country. About twenty Years ago, Philip Embury, a local Preacher from Ireland, began to preach in the City of New-York, and formed a Society of his own Countrymen and the Citizens. About the same Time, Robert Strawbridge, a local Preacher from Ireland, settled in Frederick County, in the State of Maryland, and preaching there formed some Societies. In 1769, Richard Boardman and Joseph Pilmoor, came to New-York; who were the first regular Methodist Preachers on the Continent. In the latter End of the Year 1771, Francis Asbury and Richard Wright, of the same Order, came over.[3]

The *Discipline* in similar fashion Americanized what had been the mission statement for the British movement. To the query, 'What may we reasonably believe to be God's Design, in raising up the Preachers called Methodists?' The British Methodist 'Large Minutes' had answered, 'To reform the Nation, particularly the Church, and to spread scriptural holiness over the land.' The American answer refocused the mission in expansive geographical terms and warranted it with colonial evangelistic successes already achieved:

> To reform the Continent, and spread scripture Holiness over these Lands. As a Proof hereof, we have seen in the Course of fifteen Years a great a glorious Work of God, from New-York through the Jersies, Pennsylvania, Maryland, Virginia, North and South Carolina, even to Georgia.[4]

Neither John and Charles Wesley's mission to Georgia nor the multiple, dramatic itinerations of the Calvinist Methodist George Whitefield up and down the eastern seaboard figured in the Methodist Episcopal Church's self-presentation. The official narrative neglected the role of women, for example Elizabeth Strawbridge in forming a Methodist class and Barbara Heck in pressuring her cousin Philip Embury to begin preaching. The Hecks and Emburys played foundational roles as well in taking Methodism to Upper Canada in their migration north with other loyalists during the American Revolution.[5] Overlooked as well was the African American response to, appropriation of, and improvisation with, the Methodist message. Black preacher Jacob Toogood was one of a number of Strawbridge converts who would exercise ministerial leadership. So, too, the first five auditors in New York included a servant, Betty. African Americans constituted half of the early converts of one-eyed Captain Thomas Webb, who gained notoriety initially by preaching in his scarlet regimentals and later by collaborating with British troops. From very early in the movement, Methodism preached an egalitarian gospel, affirmed the full human dignity of African Americans, and spoke forthrightly and courageously against slavery. The biracial character and key role of women in American Methodism figure prominently in reports to John Wesley on the status of American Methodism.

Actors in these spontaneous beginnings, of course, drew upon what they had grasped of 'the imperatives of Wesleyan Methodism – missionary drive, cross-denominational appeal, enthusiastic preaching, and household recruitment of followers.'[6] As John Wesley responded to pleas to send over leadership, his deputized assistants for America pressured these scattered startups to conform to the practices and studied limitations that Wesley imposed through the 'Large Minutes,' the movement's quasi-constitution. Exercising such authority, Francis Asbury (1745–1816)[7] and Thomas Rankin fought tendencies of the colonial Methodists to connive their way to ecclesial self-sufficiency. The first conference, convened by Rankin in 1773, implicitly referenced and explicitly countered such tendencies. The ten preachers pledging to honor Wesley's authority and 'the doctrine and discipline of the Methodists, as contained in the [Large] Minutes,' committed themselves to avoid administering the sacraments and to refrain from publishing Wesley's books without explicit authorization. The first restraint, aimed at Strawbridge, would sustain the presumption that they were, as the Wesleys insisted, a reform movement within Anglicanism. The second aimed at another preacher who had immigrated on his own, Robert Williams, secured Wesley's authority.

Revolutionary Crisis

It was one thing in England to claim to be part of the Church where parish churches dotted the landscape, infants were routinely baptized therein, and church membership became thereby a birthright. It was quite another where the Church of England was established in but a few of the colonies, even there inadequately staffed, and where but a very few priests like Devereaux Jarratt, Anglican priest of Bath, Virginia, welcomed Methodist efforts at renewal.

The pretense of remaining within the Church became increasingly difficult as relations between the colonies and Britain deteriorated, Anglican priests and members fled home or to Canada, and much of the leadership sent by Wesley (except Asbury) returned as well. Wesley's outspoken support of the crown and active collaboration with the British troops on the part of a few Methodists like Webb made the Methodist cause difficult.[8] A few, including itinerant Freeborn Garrettson (1752–1827), suffered threats, beatings, and imprisonment. Methodists, including other preachers, located themselves along the entire spectrum of stances with regard to the Revolution – from patriot military service, to noncombatant participation, to pacifism, to neutrality, to loyalism, to fleeing and thereby exporting Methodism to British North America (Canada). Ironically, patriot Garrettson would later play a role in consolidating Methodist order among the loyalists who relocated to the Maritimes during the Revolution.[9]

The Revolutionary crisis produced in 1779 the first Methodist schism, graphically illustrating the tension between fidelity to Wesley, Wesleyan protocols, and renewal-within commitments, *and* the independent, indigenizing, experimental spontaneity that the Pietist spirit unleashed. Manuscript versions of the Minutes indicate that for the prior two years the preachers had been debating contingency plans for functioning, in effect, as an independent church. What was the presenting symbolic and substantive issue? Making the sacraments of baptism and communion available in a war torn society in which the Church of England no longer really existed. The regularly called conference for 1779 in Fluvanna County (VA), recognizing that 'the Episcopal Establishment is now dissolved,' acted on that planning. It convened under emergency leadership, established a presbytery of preachers to celebrate the sacraments, ordained and appointed, and sketched very minimalist guidelines for administering baptism and the Lord's Supper. A year later, the Fluvanna conference yielded to Wesleyan loyalists led by Asbury. Meeting as a reunited body in 1781, the preachers recommitted to remain in connection with Mr. Wesley, 'to preach the old Methodist doctrine, and strictly enforce the discipline, as contained in the *Notes, Sermons*, and *Minutes* published by Mr. Wesley.'[10]

Wesley's further provisioning on such foundations came in 1784 when for American service he ordained his then chief assistant, the priest and lawyer Thomas Coke (1747–1814),[11] as superintendent, and ordained future bishop Richard Whatcoat (1736–1806) and Thomas Vasey as elders. He sent the three, along with revision of the Anglican liturgies in *The Book of Common Prayer*, misleadingly titled *The Sunday Service of the Methodists in North America*. Included in the latter, with Articles of Religion, a lectionary, and orders for baptism, communion, matrimony, burial, morning and evening prayer, and a Sunday service, were orders for *ordaining* deacons, elders, and superintendents. Setting aside Asbury was among Wesley's instructions, but not the election of superintendents by preachers in conference. But Asbury insisted on election, turning conversations with Coke at a quarterly meeting at Barratt's Chapel in Delaware into the preparatory session for a called conference. The latter gathering in Baltimore, known thereafter as the Christmas Conference, elected both superintendents and codified that practice in *Minutes of Several Conversations between the Rev. Thomas Coke, Ll.D. the Rev. Francis Asbury and Others at a Conference . . . in the Year 1784. Composing a Form of Discipline.* Coke *ordained* Asbury deacon, elder, and superintendent on successive days; in the latter service, at least, Otterbein participated, laying his hands on Asbury as well.

Wesley made no special provisions in 1784 for order and oversight of the Methodists who had scattered to Canada during the Revolution. He did encourage William Black who had emerged as a Methodist leader in the Maritimes to attend the Christmas Conference. That body responded by sending Garrettson[12] and James O. Cromwell back to Canada with Black. In 1787 Wesley did envision more substantive support for Canadian Methodism, sending Coke over again with instructions to call another 'General Conference of all our preachers in the United States, to meet at Baltimore on 1 May 1787.' He specified further that Whatcoat be appointed superintendent with Asbury and that Garrettson be superintendent for British North America. The United States Methodists heeded neither of Wesley's personnel directives nor did they return Garrettson to Canada. Abandoned by the Americans, Black appealed in 1800 to the British conference for ministerial support in the Maritimes. That same year the Methodist Episcopal Church (MEC) did respond to overtures from Methodist pioneers in Lower Canada (Ontario and Quebec) and sent missionaries, among them Nathan Bangs (1778–1862). American support for

Methodist efforts in Upper Canada came easier and strong leadership emerged, notably William Case and Henry Ryan. Missionary expansion across Canada by the British conference and deterioration in Canadian–American relations, preeminently during the War of 1812, let the 1820 MEC general conference begin the process of disengagement. Canadian Methodism would thereafter create its own rich synthesis of British and American ecclesial patterns and in the twentieth century leaven the United Church of Canada created in 1925.[13]

Biracial and Engendered

The Christmas Conference, apparently attended by African Americans Harry Hosier and future African Methodist Episcopal bishop Richard Allen (1760–1831), adopted 'Methodist Episcopal Church' as a name for the new denomination, revised the 'Large Minutes' into the aforementioned *Discipline*, and included therein remarkable strictures against slavery. In 1780, the American Methodists had already gone on record against slave-holding:

> Quest. 16. Ought not this conference to require those travelling Preachers who hold slaves, to give promises, to set them free?
>
> Ans. Yes.
>
> Quest. 17. Does this conference acknowledge that slavery is contrary to the laws of God, man and nature, and hurtful to society, contrary to the dictates of conscience and pure religion, and doing that which we would not others should do to us and ours? – Do we pass our disapprobation on all our friends who keep slaves, and advise their freedom?
>
> Ans. Yes.[14]

The first *Discipline* extended those strictures to members, as far as permitted by state law, and specified dates by which slaves of certain ages were to be manumitted, concluding with the stipulation that infants were to be freed at their birth. The Christmas Conference also specified that black classes should have white leadership. The 1796 General Conference acted to permit the ordination of African American deacons, but refused to include the provision in the *Discipline* and further extended exceptions for manumission recognizing laws governing slavery and the circumstances of the case. By 1804, the church curried slaveholder favor by publishing two *Disciplines*, moving the legislation against slavery to the *Discipline's* very end and simply omitting it from a version printed for circulation in the South.

While at that point American Methodism proved incapable of winning the war against slavery and racism, it had mounted a serious assault. In many places it preached antislavery. In Delaware and Maryland it convinced many owners to free their slaves. It embraced African Americans as children of God and invited them into membership. And it permitted some exercise of leadership and self-government (both of the latter on a highly limited basis). This egalitarianism, though imperfect, produced significant response as the following membership statistics indicate:

Year	White	African American
1786	18,791	1,890
1796	45,384	11,280
1806	103,313	27,257

Early Methodism was a biracial movement. While it proved unable to sustain and/or live into its antislavery witness and lost leaders and members to the African Union, African Methodist Episcopal, and African Methodist Episcopal Zion independence movements, the MEC retained significant numbers who continued, and continue in United Methodism, to sustain hope in Methodism's egalitarian promise.[15]

As Methodism lived into 1784's formalization of ecclesial authority, it circumscribed official roles permitted to women as well. Decreasingly permitted to be class leaders, women found voice and influence informally. They testified within the family, in women's classes, in love feasts. They wrote to one another and to kin. A few turned their struggles into spiritual autobiography, emulating those made prototypical for Methodism in Wesley's publications. American Methodist women read and then echoed the *Account of the Experience of Mrs. Hester Ann Rogers*, republished by American Methodists as early as 1804, and among the best selling items in a fast growing and expanding network of circuit-riding booksellers. American women spoke their own concerns and testified about their religious experience through *The Methodist Quarterly Review*, the *Christian Advocates*, and eventually the *Ladies Repository*. In these media, that quite literally created the first national reading public, women heard about and from each other. Informal 'offices' emerged – spiritual exemplars, intercessors for their families, priestesses at the family altar, organizers of familial order, and prophets in their own right as wives of itinerants, sometimes even co-itinerants.

Some women, widows especially, opened their homes to the itinerants, making them into regular bed-and-breakfast stops on the two-, four- or six-week circuits. Young preachers, still maturing, looked to these women for spiritual counsel. They named them and other women whose leadership roles remained informal, 'mothers in Israel.' More formal offices, albeit carefully circumscribed, emerged when the church established in 1819 the Methodist Missionary Society and its Women's Auxiliary. Other renewal and reform voluntary societies followed in this pattern – organized nationally with conference and local auxiliaries and with parallel denominational (male) and separate women's structures. Despite the church's conviction that God did not work in such fashion, women nevertheless heard calls to preach, some of whom, like Fanny Newell and Jarena Lee, found breaches in denominational resolve. By the 1840s, through the Tuesday Meetings for the Promotion of Holiness established by her sister, Sarah Worrall Lankford, and later on the camp meeting and assembly circuit, Phoebe Palmer (1807–1874) demonstrated how women could expand 'women's sphere' to encompass the entire church, to shatter the shackles of domesticity, to claim a transatlantic hearing, and to revive and transform Methodism's signature holiness doctrine. In 1859, Palmer took advantage of her pulpit to remind the church of the scriptural promise that her daughters as well as her sons would prophesy. A century would be required for episcopal Methodism to heed Palmer's call and authorize full conference membership and elders orders to women, but within two decades, women like Anna Oliver (1840–1892) and Anna Howard Shaw (1847–1919), would gain sufficient recognition of their gifts and grace for preaching to test denominational constraints and Shaw to receive ordination from the Methodist Protestants.[16]

Differentiation, Division and Constitution-Making

With roots in fissiparous revivalistic Pietism, with its mandate to evangelize the continent, and its Wesleyan instinct to invite all into fellowship, Methodism breached lines of race, class, ethnicity, and language. One of the large minorities in the new nation was German-speaking. Competing with the United Brethren for this population in Pennsylvania, Maryland, and Virginia was a movement that began with closer ties to the MEC. Its leader and first bishop, Jacob Albright (1759–1808) initially enjoyed especially close associations. Catechized Lutheran, but converted by Methodists, Albright embraced the latter's discipline, order, practices, and doctrine and was licensed as an exhorter. Itinerating in the mid-1790s through German-speaking communities and insisting that salvation came through a renewed heart not traditions, liturgies, and catechisms, he experienced conflict with the Lutherans, Reformed, and Mennonites. The Lutherans expelled him in 1797. Albright gathered converts into classes, held camp meetings, and raised up others to preach. An 1803 conference of class leaders recognized Albright as leader, ordained him, commissioned two other preachers as associates, and constituted itself a society. Its first regular annual conference in 1807, near Kleinfeltersville, PA brought together five itinerant preachers, three local preachers, and twenty class leaders, adopted the name *Neuformirten Methodisten Conferenz* (Newly formed Methodist Conference), and elected and ordained Albright as bishop. It also requested that he prepare a German translation of the MEC *Discipline*, 'for the instruction and edification of the societies' and appoint the preachers to their circuits. Albright licensed several preachers, selected George Miller (1774–1816) to be his chief assistant, presided at the first Communion service, and began to baptize. Although determined to travel widely, Albright's health failed and he died the next year.

Miller undertook the production of a *Discipline* and Articles of Faith, drawing upon Dr. Ignatius Römer's rendering of the Methodist doctrine and discipline, a translation which had been undertaken for the UB. The 1809 annual conference adopted Miller's *Discipline* and authorized a catechism, hymnal, handbook of faith and practice, and biography of Albright. Until its first general conference (1816), the movement identified itself as *Die sogenannten Albrechts* and *Die sogenannten Albrechtsleute*.[17] From the start the Evangelical Association (EA) entertained hopes for unity either with the UB or with the MEC. Overtures about the possibility of becoming the German conference of the MEC went nowhere, in part because of Asbury's insistence on the EA's adoption of English.

Matters of unity and division, often focused in struggles over policy, power, and authority, and invariably involving Asbury or his successors in the itinerant general superintendency, continued through Methodism's first century. Conflict yielded important constitutional and polity developments. The Fluvanna schism and beginnings of African Methodism have already been noted. Another serious division occurred as the church's rapid expansion and growth stressed its decision-making in conference. In 1788 alone Methodism added 11,481 members and nineteen circuits, bringing its total to 37,354 (including 6,545 African Americans). With eighty-five circuits, including new circuits in South Carolina, western Pennsylvania, Kentucky, (West) Virginia, Ohio, New York, and Georgia, multiple conferences were required as well – six were appointed for 1788, but seven were held according to Jesse Lee. The next year the bishops appointed eleven conferences. To that point, the bishop or bishops had carried issues whose adjudication required assent – as for instance changes in the *Discipline* – from one conference to the next, leaving resolution of the matter to Baltimore. To improve on that cumbersome process, Coke and Asbury proposed the creation of a council and further proposed that it be composed of themselves plus those whom they appointed to oversee the circuits, the presiding elders (PEs). Lee, who exercised that office, traveled as assistant to Asbury and was nearly elected bishop himself, viewed the council as 'entirely new, and exceedingly dangerous.' Although they approved it in conference ballots, the preachers soon recognized, he reported, that 'the whole of the council were to consist of the bishops, and a few other men of their own choice or appointing.'[18]

The council, Asbury plus ten presiding elders, convened twice in 1789 and again in 1790 and showed by its deliberations the value of a central body authorized to make decisions for the connection. However, opposition to it grew. Among others concerned over this consolidation and shifting of power from conference(s) to the bishops was James O'Kelly (c. 1735–1826), participating in the first, but boycotting the second council. He, Lee, and others pressed for a plenary. Asbury consented and the first general conference met in 1792.

General conference claimed the right to legislate for the church, specifically to revise the *Discipline* – two-thirds majority being required for new actions or total rescission of existing legislation, but only a majority to amend. It established itself as a permanent body and decided to convene again in four years in a conference 'to which, all the preachers in full connection were at liberty to come.' That plenary definition of itself, its claim to a future, and its assumption of authority provided what Asbury had sought through the Council, namely a politically competent and sovereign center to the movement.

Sovereignty focused consensus-making. It also served as platform for conflict. On day two of the 1792 general conference, O'Kelly moved that preachers 'injured' by their appointment have the 'liberty to appeal to the conference' and the right, if the appeal was sustained, to another appointment. Lee reported, 'There never had been a subject before us that so fully called forth all the strength of the preachers. A large majority of them appeared at first to be in favor of the motion.'[19] O'Kelly's motion eventually failed. He walked out to establish the Republican Methodists. As rationale for the new denomination, O'Kelly claimed Scripture and democracy, enunciating an apologetic which reforming-cause-after-reforming-cause would echo for a century. By appeal to scripture alone, the liberties of people and preacher, resolve against tyrannical authority of bishop or king, vigilance in defense of freedom, anti-slavery, rejection of appointed presiding elders, and explicit attack on Asbury, O'Kelly drew together the radical Pietist impulse to rid religious practice of anything not explicitly mentioned in scripture and the equally radical language of republican Whiggery, the ideology of the Revolution. In staunching the bleeding of adherents to O'Kelly's banner, countering his effective rhetoric, and answering his intemperate publications, Asbury and the MEC argued for unity, developed a Methodist apologetic, and laid the foundations for Methodist constitutional theory. Asbury did so by editing and publishing, in Wesley-like fashion, *The Causes, Evils, and Cures of Heart and Church Divisions; Extracted from the Works of Mr. Richard Baxter and Mr. Jeremiah Burroughs*. At the direction of the 1796 General Conference, Asbury and Coke collaborated in an annotated version of the *Discipline* annotated on scriptural and Wesleyan principles.[20] In terms still relevant to this day, the bishops defended Methodist episcopacy as the bedrock of itinerancy and connectionalism, presiding elders as providentially given extensions of these principles, and the entire Methodist Episcopal system as apostolic. Nicholas Snethen, another traveling companion for Asbury, his 'silver trumpet,' contributed several refutations of O'Kelly.[21]

The defense countered another important, albeit short-lived schism, which began also in 1792 around William Hammett in Charleston, South Carolina, enunciated its loyalty to primitive Wesleyanism, critiqued episcopacy and Asbury in print, and took the name Primitive Methodism. Ordained by Wesley in 1786 for service in British America, Hammett had accompanied Coke on the latter's second voyage over, had served effectively in the West Indies, and in ill health, had been brought to Charleston in 1791 by Coke. Refused an appointment, Hammett established churches there and in Savannah, Georgetown (SC), and Wilmington (NC), the latter an African American congregation. At the northern reaches of the denomination (New York, New England, Canada), a group of 'Reformed Methodists,' led by Pliny Brett who itinerated from 1805 to 1812, sought church government and local authority more akin to that established in New England Congregationalism. They protested episcopacy, emphasized the attainability of entire sanctification, repudiated war and slavery, organized in 1814 at a convention in Vermont, and later affiliated with the Methodist Protestants. Yet another body of Primitive Methodists, developed around the eccentric figure of Lorenzo Dow (1777–1834), exported American-style camp meeting revivalism to Britain after 1805, and imported the export as a distinct denomination, beginning in 1829. The Primitives, also critics of established MEC order, developed strength in Pennsylvania and especially in Canada.

Growth and Reform

If some conflict and division came from overt challenge to authority and order, others occurred naturally as Methodism exploded west and south. Laity and leaders moved with the expanding frontier, found Methodist compatriots, and formed classes. Itinerants arrived almost immediately to knit classes into circuits. And the bishops called or appointed conferences with traveling difficulties and the appointment process in mind. The number of ill-defined annual conferences in the still small movement swelled to seventeen in 1792 and nineteen in 1793. To rectify the chaos, the 1796 general conference specified boundaries for six annual conferences.

Annual conferences marched westward with the overall American settlement. So, after reducing the number of conferences in the interest of communication, efficiency, and fraternal authority, the preachers in general conference assembled authorized their increase as the church exploded west, north, and south. Six in 1796, seven in 1800, nine in 1812, eleven in 1816, twelve in 1820, along with three provisos, seventeen in 1824, twenty-two in 1832, and twenty-nine in 1836, including 'an annual conference on the western coast of Africa, to be denominated the Liberian Mission Annual Conference.'

The establishment of conference boundaries made them belonging, membership, and socio-political units and so made their representation in general conference critical. By custom convening in Baltimore, general conferences came to be numerically overwhelmed and dominated by the two nearby annual conferences, Baltimore and Philadelphia. Such disproportions remained though attendance initially permitted to all conference members, was reduced to those in full connection and (after 1800) to those who had traveled four years. Even so members from nearby conferences attended in larger numbers and those from distant southern and western conferences did not. In 1804, Philadelphia sent forty-one, Baltimore twenty-nine, and the other five conferences together only one more than Philadelphia. Lee proposed a system of delegation. It failed, but came back in 1808 as a petition endorsed by the four more distant conferences – New York, South Carolina, New England, and Western.

Under Bishop Asbury's guidance the 1808 general conference established a committee of two persons from each conference to deal with what had become a contentious issue, establishing a constitution. Drafting was further delegated to Joshua Soule, Ezekiel Cooper, and Philip Bruce, the first two of whom produced proposals. Cooper envisioned a decentralized connectional structure, essentially which pertains today, with a bishop for each conference, but with elected presiding elders. Soule (1781–1867) proposed a delegated general conference and limitation of its legislative power in several crucial areas. These 'Restrictive Rules' prohibited alteration of the plan of an 'itinerant general superintendency' or modification of 'our present existing and established standards of doctrine.' After considerable debate, the testing of alternatives, and a compromise permitting seniority as an alternative mode of representation, Soule's version passed. That general conference elected to the episcopacy a representative of the West and the first American-born, William McKendree (1757–1835). Four years later, McKendree delivered what would thereafter be the agenda-setting address, a surprise to the failing Asbury, but a means for the bishops to regain a determinative voice, a voice denied them by the new Constitution's construal of them as presiders, not members.

The 1808 Constitution resolved one concern about representation, but it did not settle the matter of presiding elders. Leaders who had exercised the office pressed for election – Cooper and Lee in 1808, Lee and Nicholas Snethen in 1812, Nathan Bangs in 1816. That general conference, its mood dominated by Asbury's death and ceremonial reinterment in Eutaw Street Church,

Baltimore, functioned in crisis state. It received a petition on yet another democratic front – from local preachers for representation, a role in the administration of discipline, and opportunities for salary. It elected Enoch George and Robert Richford Roberts to the episcopacy; condemned pew rental as a funding device; worried over Methodist slippage on discipline, dress, sacramental practice, and doctrine; selected Joshua Soule as book editor; authorized the publication of the *Methodist Magazine* (which appeared two years later), and established the Course of Study. The following quadrennium saw the 1819 formation of the Methodist Missionary Society. A movement that had understood itself as youthful frontier revival confronted signs of maturation. Increasingly, the church invested in the nurture of its members, preeminently through the Sunday school and the colleges which it spread across the land.

In the Episcopal Address to the 1820 general conference, McKendree deemed 1808 to have settled governmental and constitutional issues. 'It is presumed,' he asserted, 'that no radical change can be made for the better at present.'[22] Undeterred by this admonition, Timothy Merritt of New England and Beverly Waugh of Maryland again moved for an elective presiding eldership before general conference. John Emory (1789–1835), a lawyer by training and future bishop, attempted a consensus – episcopal nomination and conference election of presiding elders. Soule, elected to the episcopacy while the matter was under consideration, but not yet consecrated, tendered his resignation in a stinging challenge to the constitutionality of the measure just passed. In another speech, McKendree concurred with the Constitution's author, pronouncing the legislation unconstitutional and himself 'under no obligation to enforce or to enjoin it on others to do so.'[23] Stunned, general conference accepted Soule's resignation and suspended the legislation.

Over the following quadrennium, McKendree sought concurrence in his construal. Seven conferences complied, but the older five northern and eastern did not. And the contest – reflecting democratic impulses of the Jacksonian era and concerns over actual and potential abuse of power and authority by bishops and presiding elders – broadened to embrace other stakeholders. Laity weighed in, especially in Methodism's urban strongholds: Baltimore, Philadelphia, and New York. Among them, William Stockton (1785–1860), a New Jersey (later Philadelphia) printer, founded in 1821 an important medium in broadening the reform cause, the *Wesleyan Repository and Religious Intelligencer*. It yielded in 1824 to the Baltimore periodical, *The Mutual Rights of Ministers and Members of the Methodist Episcopal Church*, which in turn became the serial of a new denomination.[24] The papers pressed not only for the election of presiding elders, but also for the rights of local preachers, for lay representation, for procedural reform in church trials, for checks on episcopal tyranny – in short, the reform of the church.

A bitter 1824 General Conference passed sixty-three to sixty-one a resolution deeming the suspended PE legislation unconstitutional. Similar close votes reelected the constitutionalist Soule and the reformer Elijah Hedding to the episcopacy. Rejecting petitions for representation of laity and local preachers as well, general conference instructed the PEs to explain to the church's members why no change in 'the present order of our Church Government' was wanted or needed.[25] While general conference sat, seventeen of its members joined other reformers to establish the Baltimore Union Society, the foundation of a new denomination.[26] In two years, the reform cause had spread sufficiently to call a convention. Bishops, PEs, and annual conferences sought to suppress the movement with censures, denials of appointment, and suspensions of preachers. The *Christian Advocate* and the reform papers exchanged highly intemperate charges. Among the key reform spokespersons was Irish-born Alexander McCaine (1768?–1856) whose establishment credentials included service as a PE and secretary of the 1820 general Conference, but who had trained for the Anglican priesthood and been converted under the schismatic William Hammett. His 1827 *History and Mystery of Methodist Episcopacy* charged conspiracy and argued that 'monarchical' episcopal government had not been intended by Wesley, but surreptitiously introduced and imposed 'under the sanction of Mr. Wesley's name.'[27] Immediate responses came from John Emory and Thomas Bond.[28]

The 1828 MEC general conference, showing no patience for democratic reform, declared the (suspended) PE legislation void, dismissed memorials from the reformers' convention (rejecting lay representation), confirmed suspensions, and offered relief from these decisions only if the union societies were dissolved and *Mutual Rights* suspended. It also initiated the first amendment of the Constitution, refining amendment of the Restrictive Rules from concurrence 'of all the annual conferences' to a majority of three-fourths of the members of annual conferences.

In response, reformers met in Baltimore in a second general convention of Methodist Reformers, laid plans for a third convention, drafted protocols for a new denomination, and deputized agents, including Snethen and McCaine, to travel on behalf of the cause. The 1830 General Convention birthed the Methodist Protestant Church, with twelve annual conferences, authorized *Mutual Rights* as an official church weekly, elected the Rev. Francis Waters, of Baltimore, president and named William S. Stockton, of Philadelphia, one of its secretaries. Its *Constitution and Discipline* spelled out the reform agenda – an elective superintendency, lay representation, the president's stationing preachers but subject to revision by an annual conference committee. Local preachers, however, were not granted conference membership, nor were women. Denying 'colored' persons membership in General Conference, it permitted each annual conference to form its own rules 'for the admission and government of coloured members within its district; and to make for them such terms of suffrage as the conferences respectively may deem roper.'

Divisions over Slavery and Race

Slavery and race figured prominently in five subsequent divisions, those launching the Wesleyan (1843), Free (1860) and Colored (1870) Methodist churches, in the division, north and south of the MEC, and in the MEC's establishment of black annual conferences (1864). The 1830s saw strident sectionalism in society, politics, and the churches. A new anti-slavery movement emerged, lacking the careful staging of manumissions to which early Methodism had committed itself. Instead, the immediatism of William Lloyd Garrison set the tone. Abolitionists pronounced slavery evil and slaveholders sinners. Few supported violence as the way to overthrow the institution. Increasingly, however, southerners took all opposition to slavery to be of a piece. Fears of slave conspiracies and slave insurrections, such as those associated with Methodist Denmark Vesey in Charleston in 1822 and of millenarian Nat Turner in Virginia in 1831, reinforced slaveholder and southern support for its peculiar institution. As abolition found traction in Methodism, especially in New England, southern Methodists recoiled in defense, appropriated the 'doctrine' of the spirituality of the church, insisted that slaveholding was not a moral evil, and in a few cases published biblical and theological justifications of slavery.

Constructively, southern Methodists sought to curb slavery's worst abuses and to Christianize the slave. Led by slaveholding preacher, later editor, and still later bishop, William Capers (1790–1855) of South Carolina, southerners created in 1829 a mission to the slaves. Drawing on his experience as superintendent of the Creek Nation mission in Georgia and Alabama, Capers fashioned a plantation mission evangelism on slaveholder terms. Southerners also supported another missionary venture, embraced by the denomination as a whole, namely, colonization. A Liberian mission would Christianize Africa and allow freed slaves to 'return' home, the latter an option offered to the young slave acquired in marriage by Bishop James O. Andrew.

The MEC's media and leadership, well practiced in divisive apologetics from the contest with the reformers, began to tilt along sectional lines. The *Christian Advocate and Journal* (New York) and *The Methodist Magazine* (MQR), ostensibly the national paper and magazine actually competed for attention with six regional papers, the *Western Christian Advocate* (Cincinnati), *Zion's Herald* (Boston), the *Pittsburgh Christian Advocate*, and three southern papers – the *Southwestern Christian Advocate* (Nashville), the *Richmond Christian Advocate*, and the *Southern Christian Advocate* (Charleston). The bishops, ostensibly itinerant *general* superintendents, elected in the politicized atmosphere of the

Methodist Reform movement, Robert Richford Roberts and Enoch George, elected in 1816, and Joshua Soule and Elijah Hedding elected in 1824, developed regional commitments. George and Hedding worked Philadelphia and north, Roberts and Soule, Baltimore and south.[29]

In the New England Conference (MEC), La Roy Sunderland (1804–1885) and Orange Scott (1800–1847) preached abolitionism in camp meetings, quarterly conferences, rallies, letters, petitions, and elections. They attacked colonization, the church's acquiescence in slavery, and editors' suppression of antislavery, particularly Nathan Bangs, editor of the *Christian Advocate* (New York) after 1834. Gaining weekly access to *Zion's Herald*, Scott and company charged that Bangs did 'apologize for the crimes of the enslavers of the human species and attempt to justify the system' and set forth a vigorous Methodist case against slavery, including a reprinting of Wesley's condemnation. In May 1834, abolitionists established a New England Wesleyan Anti-Slavery Society. In the New England Conference, abolitionists gained six of the seven delegates to the following general conference. They failed to pass antislavery resolutions, the questions not being put by the presiding bishop, Elijah Hedding, but did beat back motions of censure on their activities.

Countering the abolitionists at this stage, along with Bishops Hedding and Emory (elected 1832) were other annual conferences and key members of the church's intelligentsia, including theologian Daniel D. Whedon (1808–1885), Wesleyan University president Wilbur Fisk (1792–1839), and Abel Stevens (1815–1897), later to edit *Zion's Herald* and the *Christian Advocate*. The 1836 general conference followed suit, acted to muffle the antislavery cause and censured two delegates for abolitionist activity. Considerably more antislavery activity, organization, and production – memorials, resolutions, and legislation on slavery, elections of general conference delegate 'slates,' trials and other 'political' use of the annual reviews of character – anticipated the 1840 general conference. Nevertheless dominated by southerners and northern conservatives, the 1840 General Conference elected conservative editors for the three northern papers and passed a highly symbolic motion proposed by Emory College president Ignatius A. Few: '*Resolved*, That it is inexpedient and unjustifiable for any preacher among us to permit colored persons to give testimony against white persons, in any state where they are denied that privilege in trials at law.' The bishops refused to bring into general conference a petition by Baltimore African American Methodists protesting the latter action.

Conceding defeat, Scott and Sunderland led a withdrawal to form yet another Methodist body, the Wesleyan Methodist Connection. Meeting in an organizing convention in 1843, holding a general conference in 1844, the new church pledged itself to Wesleyanism, holiness, and antislavery. Naming its paper, the *True Wesleyan*, it continued its prophetic witness, 'The

M. E. Church, is not only a slaveholding, but a slavery defending, Church.' By 1844 when the MEC general conference convened in New York, continuing defections to the Wesleyans, already 15,000, helped stimulate antislavery resolve across the North. 'Whole conferences,' reported Abel Stevens, 'which once rejected antislavery resolutions now sustain them with scarce a dissent, and it cannot be doubted that soon, very soon, all our northern conferences will be of one mind on the subject.'[30] Southern conferences and papers intensified their defenses, proclaimed slavery to be no moral evil, insisted that the institution itself lay beyond the church's purview, proposed the election of a slaveholding bishop, and prepared for division over slaveholding Bishop James O. Andrew, should that be necessary.

In the 1844 general conference, the first to be covered daily by the *Christian Advocate*,[31] the centrists, representing the Baltimore Conference, tilted toward antislavery. Month-long debates focused on the Bishop Andrew's slaveholding, the relation of general conference and episcopacy, and related constitutional issues. The decisive motion, proposed by Ohio delegates, deemed that slaveholding would 'greatly embarrass' a bishop's 'exercise of the office as an itinerant General Superintendent, if not in some places entirely prevent it,' and called for Andrew to 'desist from the exercise of this office so long as this impediment remains.'[32] The motion passed and a Committee of Nine on the Division of the Church was instructed to plan an amicable division. It recommended measures to assure peaceful delineation of a geographical boundary in the church and to divide property. A key provision, an enabling constitutional revision of one of the restrictive articles, required three-fourths majorities in annual conferences – assured that the debates and acrimony of general conference would roil the following annual conferences.

Ecclesial warfare began before closure with posturing declarations by both northern and southern sections. After adjournment, the delegates from the slaveholding states met, called a convention to be held in Louisville, May 1, 1845, for the annual conferences 'within the slaveholding States,' explaining the call in terms of slavery, 'The opinions and purposes of the Church in the North on the subject of slavery, are in direct conflict with those of the South.' Ecclesial war then followed, especially pitched along the line of division and the property issue (publishing assets) eventually decided by the nation's Supreme Court. To hold its circuits along the border the northern church again muted its abolitionist rhetoric until tested by another antislavery movement. Free Methodists protested slavery, championed holiness, and sought recovery of the church's witness to the poor. When Civil War began, both the MEC and the Methodist Episcopal Church, South (MECS) endorsed their respective crusades. During the war, responding to petitions by African American leaders and resolutions by their white annual conferences, the MEC in 1864 authorized the formation of black conferences. Delaware and

Washington organized first conference, to be followed by others as the northern church evangelized in the postwar south. The MECS, in turn, encouraged its African American membership into a separate denomination, the Colored (now Christian) Methodist Church in 1870.

Reorganization and Unifications

If fission characterized Methodism's first century, fusion themed its second, culminating in the tripartite union (MP, MEC, and MECS) that created the Methodist Church in 1939, the uniting of the Evangelical and United Brethren churches in 1946, and the merging of these two into the United Methodist Church in 1968. To be sure, further late nineteenth-century division occurred, notably in both the Evangelical and United Brethren churches and in yet another effort to reclaim Methodism's piety and holiness commitments. The latter, an outworking of Phoebe Palmer's Tuesday Meetings for the Promotion of Holiness and the National Camp Meeting Association for the Promotion of Holiness eventuated in the formation of the Church of the Nazarene and later in the various Pentecostal movements. So, too, missions abroad and domestically yielded within Methodism conference lines drawn along lines of language, ethnicity, and race.

In consolidation, preeminently for missions, the MEC led the way, profiting from its highly successful experience in mobilizing material, theological, pastoral chaplaincy, and nursing support for the Civil War effort. Immediately thereafter, in 1866, it launched the first connection-wide modern capital campaign, seeking to raise two million dollars for ten mission projects, some specific, some for general purposes (a connectional fund for the various church institutions). By 1868, this Centenary cause had raised $8,709,498, with more to come, for seminaries, colleges, and missions, all benefitting from the church's largesse. Four years later, the MEC restructured itself, making what had been voluntary associations for missions, education, publishing, Sunday school, and church extension into agencies accountable to general conference. Over the next twenty years, Methodism underwent an organizational revolution, culminating in the establishment on a connectional level of its accrediting agency, the University Senate, and in the refashioning of local Methodism with modern Sunday schools in complex Akron-plan church facilities.

Appropriating corporate patterns of organization and finance, episcopal Methodism also found it imperative to capitalize on lay talent. The southern church led, here, resolving to permit lay representation in both annual and general conferences in 1866 and seating laymen four years later. The MEC followed in 1868 but for general conference only. The UB and EA permitted laity in annual conferences in 1872 and 1903 and in general conferences in 1889 and 1907. Led by Frances Willard (1839–1898), women campaigned to be included in these deliberative bodies, having created and led robust missionary organizations, for example, the Ladies' and Pastors' Christian Union, the Woman's Christian Temperance Union, educational institutions, Sunday schools, and the deaconess order. Theological schools for the latter – the MEC Chicago Training School (1885) and MECS Scarritt Bible and Training School (1893) – capped off what amounted to a shadow, female denomination. Telling victories in women's long campaign for inclusion came in 1956 with full ordination and conference membership, and twenty years later the election to the episcopacy of Marjorie Matthews (1916–1986). In building for service, mission, and witness, women undertook their own organizational revolution and also led the church in the appropriation and institutionalization of the Social Gospel. The MEC also adapted the Social Gospel through city missionary societies, institutional churches, the Methodist Federation for Social Service (1908), the Social Creed (1908), support for organized labor, and in witness against lynchings and segregation.

However, denominational consolidation and full inclusion worked at cross-purposes for African Americans as well as for women. Efforts to heal the rupture of 1844 began after the Civil War, a significant step being the August 1876 meeting of a Joint Commission on Fraternal Relations, three clergy and two laypersons from each northern and southern church at Cape May, NJ. Participation in world Methodist gatherings, joint celebrations and projects, including a common hymnal, and further unity explorations followed. A key stage, the 1916–1920 negotiations of the fifty member Joint Commission on Unification[33], outlined the plans approved eventually in the 1939 union – a Judicial Council, several regional white and one black jurisdictional conferences, and the jurisdictional election of bishops. A Council of Bishops would be added to the unity agenda in subsequent negotiations. Participating in these racially tense conversations and exchanges were two African American delegates, one of whom, editor of the *Southwestern Christian Advocate*, Robert Jones (1872–1960), was among the first two elected to the episcopacy (in other than an African missionary status). Black Methodists overwhelmingly opposed the legislation that established the 1939 union, both in the MEC 1936 general conference and in the conference-level endorsement process. Over their opposition and that of leadership of Methodist women, the new Methodist Church institutionalized segregation on a national basis with an all-black Central Jurisdiction. Ironically, by that point American Methodism was ending its century-and-a-half language specific conferences – German, Spanish, Swedish, Norwegian, Danish, Japanese, Chinese – the result of long-term trends of Anglicization and World War I paranoia over German collaborators. Symbolizing an end to language particularity and bridging their theological and political differences, the Evangelical and United Brethren churches united in 1946.

Caucus and Cause

American Methodists led in the post-World-War-II era, in a 'Crusade for a New World Order' and in cooperative and ecumenical creations to that end – the world, national, state, and local councils of churches and the Consultation on Church Union (now Churches Uniting In Christ) – as they had in world missionary, faith and order, life and work, and Methodist conferences and organizations for over half a century.[34] In a quest for church unity to heal Christ's broken body and witness more effectively on local, national, and world bases, the several Methodist Pietist families and their eleven million members came together in 1968 to form the United Methodist Church. Among commitments that the EUB extracted from the Methodists was ending the scandal of the Central Jurisdiction.

The 1968 union ended racial-ethnic conference structures for mission and ministry just as American society opened to new waves of immigration. Furthermore, a century of black efforts to live and work within a segregated order had produced strong networks, infrastructure, communication systems, women's organizations, and support initiatives (especially for black colleges). With racism an unfinished agenda, Black Methodists for Church Renewal formed as the Central Jurisdiction disappeared. Just two years prior Charles Keysor had sounded the alarm that led to the formation of Good News, laying foundations for a network of conservative–evangelical caucuses.[35] Over the next decade an array of ethnic, racial, gender, and advocacy caucuses emerged. The church embraced this new day, with important 1972 innovations in the *Discipline*, two long sections, Parts II and III, 'Doctrine and Doctrinal Statements and the General Rules' and 'Social Principles.' The latter included and explicated 'Our Social Creed.' The former, which held together the doctrinal emphases and standards of the two churches, featured a significant statement on 'Our Theological Task' which situated the new church as a pilgrim people in a crisis-ridden world, equipped it with a new hermeneutic (the Quadrilateral), and understood itself to be appropriately theologically pluralistic and doctrinally diverse.[36] Advocacy could not have had a better platform.

Advocacy was hardly new. Indeed, from the 1760s, Methodist voices had raised racial and gendered concerns. And particularity, however organizationally expressed, had always expressed itself in piety (prayer, hymn-singing, witnessing) and in nurture (catechizing, teaching, forming disciples). Over its two centuries, however, the relative emphases on piety, nurture, and advocacy shifted. Early Methodism in its two languages and various ethnic missions had put the emphasis on piety, conversion, and evangelism – the work of classes and revivalistic itinerancy. Its signature? The camp meeting. Post-Civil War Methodism had put the emphasis on nurture, worship, the family, and Christianizing the culture – the work of station churches and

Methodist colleges. Its signature? The international Sunday school lesson. After 1968, Methodism put the emphasis on cause and concern. Its signature? The caucus.

To be sure, much momentum lay behind the premium on such advocacy and prophetic utterance, indeed a half century's worth. Late nineteenth- and twentieth-century Methodism had invested heavily in building city churches – central city initially, suburban later. And it had structured itself with connectional agencies and corresponding conference and local committees to deal with the possibilities and problems of urban industrial America.[37] It had embraced the social gospel, featured social concerns in seminary curricula, and dedicated itself to various causes. Its great work had been temperance and prohibition, liquor then thought to be key to crime, poverty, ignorance, abuse, unemployment, corruption, and conflict. But on industrial conflict, immigration, labor, war and peace, race, prohibition, political corruption – the major problems of the day – Methodism took stands and did so through its boards and by conference and general conference resolutions. The latter continued after 1968. Indeed, the church's utterances on the problems of the day grew longer and longer. Previously issued separately or partially incorporated in the *Discipline*, they now were issued in a *Book of Resolutions*.

A common format might suggest prophetic unanimity across the church. Increasingly, the church's common resolve fragmented into separate concerns of caucus and cause, sometimes reinforced by new connectional agencies and divided along cultural war lines. The church's corporate structure – its councils, boards, commissions and agencies, and especially the General Council on Ministries – became targets for critique, especially from Good News and its network of caucuses. General conference sessions roiled in contests over theological and social issues, homosexuality and abortion particularly, notwithstanding a 1988 rewriting of Part II of the *Discipline* and efforts at 'holy conferencing.'

Amid the cacophony, a new unitive voice sought a hearing. The Council of Bishops, initially after its formation in 1939 a social fraternity, began to focus its work and the church's attention on major issues, beginning with its 1986 pastoral letter *In Defense of Creation: the Nuclear Crisis and a Just Peace*, the first of a number of episcopal teaching efforts. The bishops made especially strong attempts to reorient United Methodism to its global nature, to the task of disciple-making, and to stemming hemorrhaging membership losses. At this writing, the Council of Bishop's effort to lead the church from advocacy to structural reform remains only partially tested. The church's story remains that of piety giving way to nurture, giving way to advocacy.

For Further Reading

Hempton, David. *Methodism: Empire of the Spirit*. New Haven and London: Yale University Press, 2005.

Matthews, Rex D. *Timetables of History for Students of Methodism*. Nashville: Abingdon Press, 2007.

Schmidt, Jean Miller. *Grace Sufficient: A History of Women in American Methodism 1760–1939*. Nashville: Abingdon Press, 1999.

Semple, Neil. *The Lord's Dominion: The History of Canadian Methodism*. Montreal & Kingston: McGill-Queen's University Press, 1996.

Wigger, John H. *Taking Heaven By Storm: Methodism and the Rise of Popular Christianity in America*. New York and Oxford: Oxford University Press, 1998.

7 Methodist Missions/ Missiology

Norman E. Thomas

'I look upon all the world as my parish' said John Wesley in 1739 when denied freedom to preach in Anglican churches. 'Why not be a missionary?' was D. T. Niles' challenge in 1962 – not only to fellow Methodists in Ceylon, but to all Christians. These two phrases epitomize mission(s) from a Wesleyan/Methodist perspective.[1]

Earlier essays on this topic focused on the mission history of USA and British Methodism.[2] The present reality is that today all 107 member bodies of the World Methodist Council (WMC) – both Methodist and united churches – engage in mission. It would take a book to write all those mission histories.

Instead, we will seek answers to the question: 'Where have Methodists made distinctive contributions in each historic period?' The hope is that once introduced to examples of creativity in mission by Methodists, we will be motivated to learn of others.

Founders, 1703–1791

The cultural seedbed of Methodism in the eighteenth century was both the Enlightenment and Pietism. Enlightenment thinkers believed that persons and cultures everywhere can progress. Pietism provided the corrective that it is God who gives humans freedom to change, that individuals can experience personal salvation, and that converted persons will proclaim the gospel redemption to all.

John Wesley (1703–1791)[3]

From pietistic Moravians, Wesley received both the assurance of salvation and a model for nurturing both inquirers and followers through small groups. He inspired his followers to 'spread scriptural holiness' by word and deed. He would have all Christian workers 'devoted to God' and 'breathing the whole spirit of missionaries.'

Wesley encouraged Methodists to lead in missions. Nathaniel Gilbert (c. 1721–1774), a distinguished Antigua lawyer and Speaker of the House of

Assembly, influenced by Wesley's preaching in 1758, returned to Antigua to encourage slaves to embrace Christianity through Methodist societies. In 1769 Wesley appointed Richard Broadman and Joseph Pilmoor to be lay preachers in the American colonies, and Thomas Coke (1747–1814) and Francis Asbury (1745–1816) in 1784 to superintend the work there. Wesley formed a management committee for Methodist missions in 1790 shortly before his death.

Thomas Coke (1747–1814)

Coke has rightly been called 'the father of Methodist missions.' Appointed to superintend Methodist work in North America, he convened the organizing conference in Baltimore in 1784 and consecrated Asbury as superintendent following Wesley's instruction. Through eight subsequent visits to the growing church in the USA, Coke symbolized the unity of Methodists on both sides of the Atlantic.

Coke intended to establish missionaries in Nova Scotia in 1786, but a storm forced an alternative landing in Antigua, West Indies. Thrilled on finding Methodism already established there by Gilbert, Coke extended the work in subsequent years to other islands in that region. As the head of the first management committee for Methodist missions, and later as its president from 1804, Coke led in establishing new missions in Sierra Leone, Nova Scotia, Ireland, and France. He also organized work among 70,000 French war prisoners held in England during the Napoleonic Wars. Coke died in 1814 en route to India, leading a band of Methodist preachers for India.

Francis Asbury (1745–1816)

Between 1769 and 1774 twelve British Methodist preachers journeyed as missionaries to the American colonies, including Francis Asbury in 1771. Only Asbury remained after the colonies won their independence, becoming the leader and shaper of Methodism in the USA.

For Asbury, as for Wesley, ministry by nature was to be missionary. In 1813, toward the end of his life, he described 'the apostolic order of things in the first century' church, and then claimed that 'an apostolical form of church government was established in America in 1784.'[4] Asbury made normative the itinerant traveling pattern of Methodist ministry. For him the terms 'preacher' and 'missionary' were interchangeable.

Asbury modeled the normative pattern of early Methodist ministry – the circuit rider on horseback who sought out converts in the remotest settlements of the frontier. Never married, Asbury traveled incessantly for forty-five years, covering an estimated 300,000 miles on horseback and preaching over 16,000 sermons. He never returned to England, but crossed the Appalachian

Mountains more than sixty times to preach and guide Methodists on the frontier. His was an apostolic urgency to present the gospel to all persons, including Native and African Americans. The movement with 13,740 members upon his arrival in 1771 was to grow under his leadership to 214,235 members and 695 traveling preachers upon his death in 1816.

Pioneers, 1792–1858

Three factors nurtured the flowering of Protestant missions in the nineteenth century: exploration, colonialism, and revivals. Explorers, like missionary David Livingstone (1813–1873), provided knowledge of other people and cultures. First chartered companies, then European colonies, opened opportunities for new mission fields. Enthusiasm for evangelization and missions arose during the Second Great Awakening in the USA as well as in England, and continental Europe. Those whose faith was revived were moved to advance education, mission, and moral reform.

Church Extension

Methodist growth in the USA during this period was phenomenal. In 1776 Methodists were the smallest Protestant denomination with barely 2,000–3,000 members. By 1830, there were 158,000 white, 15,000 black, and 2,000 Native American members. By the 1840s there were more Methodist churches in the USA than federal post offices! By 1850 Methodists had become the largest Protestant group with 1,324,000 members. At least one scholar has called this period the 'Methodist Age' in US Christianity, during which human freedom, warm-hearted emotion, and romantic perfectionism carried the day.[5]

The Methodist ministry was both flexible and effective. It was easy for a young person with a vibrant faith and preaching gifts to begin as a class leader, become a lay preacher, and with proven ability be trained and promoted to be a circuit rider and ordained pastor. Not until 1839 was the first seminary education for pastors begun at the Newbury Biblical Institute in Newbury, Vermont – the forerunner of Boston University.

From its earliest days in North America Methodist policy was to create a church, not simply a mission. Methodist work was organized into circuits knitting together the people called Methodists in a geographic area, even where there were no church buildings. The entire church was missionary to its core. In a new territory the Methodist circuit rider might preach every day wherever people could be reached – in cabins, fields, or under a tree. Those who responded were invited to weekly class meetings – groups usually from twelve to fifteen with a designated leader. New converts of ability could be leaders with little delay, with training to follow. Often there would be twenty to thirty classes in a circuit – each meeting for Bible reading, prayer, and mutual support and encouragement. Seven-day-a-week ministry was essential.

Even before Methodism formed a denominational missionary society, individual Methodists launched cross-cultural missions. African American John Stewart (1786–1823), on his own initiative, began work among the Wyandotts of Ohio in 1816 – the first known Methodist missionary to Native Americans. His example inspired the formation of the Methodist Missionary Society (MMS) in 1820.

Methodists sent missionaries beyond what was then the western frontier in North America. Jason Lee (1803–1845), born near present-day Quebec, Canada, was converted during a Wesleyan Methodist revival in 1826. Four years later he led a pioneer missionary party westward and preached the first Protestant sermon west of the Rocky Mountains in 1834 near present-day Pocatello, Idaho. His mission to Native Americans in the Willamette Valley included founding the Indian Manual Labor Training School, the forerunner of Willamette University.

Opening New Fields
As in the Caribbean, many of the founders of Methodism in Africa were African in ancestry. Those who introduced Christianity in much of Oceania were Pacific Islanders.

West Africa
Methodists were the pioneer 1,100 settlers in Sierra Leone in 1792, who had come to Christ when plantation slaves or soldiers, or as squatters or farmers in Nova Scotia. British Methodist missionary George Warren (d. 1812), upon arrival in Sierra Leone from England in 1812, found a 200-member Methodist society organized there. Daniel Coker (c. 1780–1846), a founder of the AME in 1816, became the first African American missionary to Africa. He was sent to Sierra Leone by his church in 1820 and organized the first overseas branch of the AME on shipboard. He became an official of the Sierra Leone colony, working throughout his life as a government administrator and church organizer. When a church split occurred he became superintendent of the independent West African Methodist Church.

Methodism began in the Gold Coast/Ghana with a Christian study group known as the Cape Coast Bible Band. They were graduates of the school established in 1822 in memory of Philip Quaque (1741–1816), the first African to be an Anglican priest, who had labored there for fifty years. It was these Fante Christians, traveling inland to trade, who carried the faith to the interior.

Thomas Birch Freeman (1809–1890), son of a freed slave and English mother, was the most outstanding and effective early Methodist missionary to West Africa. Where others died, he survived for fifty-two years. By his friendliness, courtesy, and respect for African traditions, Freeman developed promising relationships with chiefs of the dominant Ashanti tribe in Ghana. It was his conviction that the church would grow only as Africans came to Christ and with joy witnessed and spread the faith.

In 1842 Yorubas, who had been freed from slavery and accepted Christ in Sierra Leone, made their way back to their homeland and asked the Wesleyan mission for help. Freeman and William de Graft, a Fante pastor/missionary, established Methodist missions first at Badger, and later at Lagos and Abeokuta. From there Methodism spread north and west of the River Niger in the next generation. Freeman had similar success in founding Methodism in Benin in 1843. In Dahomey, however, where he placed a preacher at Ouidah, he could not persuade the chief to abandon a slaving economy, nor a mission organization to underwrite the work.

Australasia
Samuel Leigh (1785–1852) pioneered Wesleyan Methodist missions in Australia and New Zealand. With the blessing of the governor, Leigh revitalized a tiny existing Methodist society upon arrival in Sydney in 1815, formed Bible classes in four towns, and ministered at fifteen preaching places in the district. In failing health in 1819, he accepted an invitation from Samuel Marsden (1764–1838) of the Church Missionary Society to join him in ministry to the indigenous Maoris of New Zealand – a generation before white settlement there.

Pacific Islands
John Thomas (1796–1881) was the pioneer Wesleyan Methodist missionary to Tonga in 1822 and remained there in ministry for twenty-five years. Before his arrival the high chief Taufa'ahau Tupou (1797–1893) had heard of Christianity and engaged a teacher, Pita Vi, a Tongan chief and convert. It was Thomas who baptized and named the high chief 'George' in 1834. Four years later the Tongan Revival occurred with thousands becoming Methodist Christians. In 1845 Tupou was crowned king of all Tonga by Thomas, and the Wesleyan Church became the state church with the king as its head. He sent his own missionaries to Samoa to start the Wesleyan Methodist Church there. John Williams (1796–1839) of the London Missionary Society (LMS) visited in 1830 and 1832 leaving islanders to work as evangelists and church planters. By 1837 almost every village had an LMS or Wesleyan chapel with more than 20,000 – half the population – under Christian instruction.

From Tonga, Methodism spread to Fiji where three Tahitian teachers of the

LMS had introduced Christianity in 1830. David Cargill (1809–1843) and William Cross (1797–1842) and their Tongan assistants arrived in 1835 and began to preach. They were reinforced in 1839 by Tongan Joeli Bulu (c. 1810–1877), who settled there and became one of the most venerated leaders of Methodism in Fiji, and John Hunt (1811–1848), a gifted linguist who translated the entire New Testament. It was his Bible reading and prayer that moved the warrior Varani to give himself to Christ – one of the factors that led to a Pentecostal-style revival on the island of Viwa and the conversion of Fiji's greatest chief Thakombau in 1854.

Other Fields
In 1813 Thomas Coke, then elderly, offered to the Conference his remaining fortune of £6,000 to establish a British Methodist mission to the East. This commitment, and the story of Coke's heroic death, stirred Methodism to support foreign missions as never before. Within ten years of his death 111 Methodist missionaries were at work in West and South Africa, Ceylon, India, the West Indies, Australia, New Zealand, and the islands of the Pacific. Often unofficial Methodist lay preachers preceded them – often soldiers on overseas placement during the Napoleonic Wars. Response by both soldiers and native people led to appeals for the Conference to send ministers and chaplains. The British Methodist Missionary Society (MMS), founded in 1818, was an integral part of the Methodist Church (MCUK) to be supported by every local Methodist, since to be a member of the church was to be also a member of the MMS.

John Boggs was the earliest commissioned AME missionary to reach Africa, serving briefly in Liberia in 1824. Melville Beveridge Cox (1799–1833), the first MEC missionary, served there just four months before dying of malaria. His words, 'Let a thousand fall before Africa be given up,' induced many others to volunteer for missionary service.

Although the slavery issue split US Methodism into separate churches, north and south, in 1844, they continued to cooperate well in new mission fields in China and Argentina (1847), Germany (1849), and India (1856). Two of the first missionaries to China of the Methodist Episcopal Church, South (MECS) inspired others to missionary giving and service in the south, much as Melville Cox had done a generation earlier in the north. James William Lambuth (1830–1892) and his wife Mary McClellan Lambuth (1832–1894) felt called to serve in China. Mary's note in the collection basket, 'I give five dollars and myself for work in China,' later inspired women to support her educational work there. James was called 'the Jesus man' because he traveled widely preaching to the peasants. Following the Civil War, he functioned as head of the southern church's mission in China for two decades, and in 1885 moved to Japan to found the mission there.[6]

Women in Mission

Women were major supporters of missions in the first half of the nineteenth century. It is the judgment of Wade Barclay, historian of Methodist missions, that, 'Missions were one of the chief means of opening up to the women of the American churches increased opportunity for participation in church and community life.'[7] Mary W. Mason organized the Female Mite Society of New York, to be succeeded in 1819 by the New York Female Missionary and Bible Society – the first women's auxiliary for the MMS. The latter was formed initially to provide support for missionary Ann Wilkins (1806–1857) in Liberia. It was the model for Methodist women's organizations to support missions, especially work among women and children. Wilkins served as a teacher from 1837 to 1857, and founded The Millsburg Female Academy – the first US Methodist girls' school overseas. A noted scholar called her 'the most effective missionary in early-twentieth-century Liberia.'[8]

The Ladies' China Missionary Society, formed in Baltimore, Maryland, in 1849, was the most successful of the Methodist women's auxiliaries. It supported the first three single women missionaries sent to Foochow, China, in 1858 to begin the first Methodist girls boarding school in China. By 1860 the MEC had sent out thirty-one single women missionaries, several of them funded exclusively by women's groups.

Expansion and Colonialism, 1858–1914

Stephen Neill, in his now-classic history of Christian missions, called 1858–1914 'The Heyday of Colonialism.'[9] He begins with 1858 – the year treaties opened the interior of China to Christian missions – and ends with the onset of World War I. But China was not the only country or continent undergoing change in 1858. In that year British colonial rule replaced East Asia Company governance in India, Roman Catholics reopened their mission in Japan, and David Livingstone inspired formation of new missions to Central Africa.

In 1857 a third Awakening began in the USA as Methodists, Baptists, and Presbyterians began meeting to pray for revival and awakening. Within six months 10,000 businessmen were meeting daily to pray in 150 different groups. Dwight L. Moody (1837–1899) began his Christian work in evangelism in 1858 and started the first of many Sunday schools formed at his initiative. Prayer for revival spread to the British Isles with a great revival sweeping Wales in two years. William Booth (1829–1912), a Wesleyan Methodist preacher, began work as a full-time evangelist. The Christian mission founded in East London in 1865 became the Salvation Army in 1878.

Wesleyan/Holiness Missions

The third Awakening among some Methodists led to a renewed emphasis on 'scriptural holiness,' principally in the USA and England. It became known as the 'Holiness Movement.' Common to holiness groups was the belief that a Christian could and should undergo a second crisis experience through which to receive the Holy Spirit more fully than at conversion, and to grow to a new level of holiness or sanctification in life. Some like William Taylor (1821–1902) remained within Methodist denominations. Others split in the USA to form the Wesleyan Church (1843), the Free Methodist Church (1860), and the Church of the Nazarene (1908). Beginning in 1901 the Pentecostal Movement, also tracing its roots to John Wesley, emerged from the broader holiness movement.

The Wesleyan Church in the USA began its mission work in Sierra Leone in 1889, and later worked in Colombia, Japan, Haiti, Puerto Rico, Honduras, Mexico, and the Philippines. Free Methodists worked first in India's Maharashtra State in 1881, with later success in the central Congo (where it merged with the Congo Gospel Mission), Japan, Brazil, the Philippines, Egypt, Mozambique, South Africa, and Paraguay. The Church of the Nazarene mission program began with leadership by Hiram Farnham Reynolds (1854–1938). Their focus was on mission in India, South Africa, Swaziland, Korea, Brazil, and China, including the overseas Chinese Diaspora.

Many mission pioneers of Wesleyan-Holiness persuasion began independent ministries and later formed strong churches and mission societies. Charles Elmer (1864–1924) and Lettie Burd Cowman (1870–1960) were converted in a Methodist church, but went to Japan in 1901 as independent missionaries. A distinctive feature of their ministry was the Every Creature Crusade (1912–1918) to reach every Japanese home with the gospel of Jesus Christ. They established the Oriental Missionary Society, now OMS International.

Expansion

Self-supporting Missions

William Taylor was first appointed a MEC missionary to California in 1849. He ministered there without salary to Native Americans, Chinese immigrants, the sick, and the poor. He not only wrote about the Pauline methods of missionary work, but also put them into practice in his own ministry and in the churches he helped establish. In South India (1870–1875) he established MEC churches that were self-supporting, self-propagating, and self-governing, arguing that these new churches should be recognized as equals to those of the sending MEC in the USA. He tested his three-self principles in Latin America (1877–1896) supported not by the Methodist board, but increasingly by Holiness leaders and congregations. His solo effort introduced the

MEC in Peru, Chile, Panama, and Belize. As missionary bishop for Africa (1884–1896), Taylor established self-supporting churches in Liberia, Sierra Leone, Angola, Mozambique, and the Congo. More than any other person Taylor was responsible for the extension of the MEC beyond the USA and Europe, and his influence spread broadly. His revivalist message and activity strengthened Wesleyan Methodism in Austria, New Zealand, Ceylon (Sri Lanka), South Africa, and throughout the Caribbean. He was the primary mission theorist for Holiness missionaries, and later for Pentecostals.

Walter Russell Lambuth (1854–1921) was Taylor's counterpart in the MECS in expansion of the church's mission into new fields. Son of the founders of that denomination's missions in China, he worked there as a doctor (1877–1885) – founding an opium treatment center in Shanghai and beginning what became Rockefeller Hospital in Peking. In 1887 he founded the MECS mission in Japan with his parents. As secretary of his church's board of missions (1892–1910), Lambuth began missions in Cuba and Korea. Elected bishop in 1910 for the church in Brazil and Africa, Lambuth traveled to the Belgian Congo in partnership with John Wesley Gilbert (1864–1923) of the Colored (now Christian) Methodist Episcopal Church (CME), the first African American archaeologist. Lambuth founded missions there, and later to Russians and Koreans in Siberia and Manchuria.

Melanesia and Micronesia
In 1857 Australian Methodists re-entered Samoa, a field from which Methodists had withdrawn to avoid competition with the larger LMS. In 1860 they sent George Brown (1835–1917), a gifted linguist and ethnographer. Under his sensitive leadership the Methodist Church there, in proportion to its size, became the strongest and most active of Methodist churches in the Pacific Islands. In 1875 Brown sailed from Samoa to New Britain – the only European among a team of devoted South Sea island missionaries. This was the beginning of a great movement of Methodist missionaries from Fiji, Samoa, and Tonga that continued strongly for fifty years. As general secretary of the mission board in Australia (1887–1908), Brown worked to give more autonomy to the older churches of Tonga, Fiji, and Samoa.[10]

Mass Movements

India
James Mills Thoburn (1836–1922) entered the ministry of the MEC in 1858 and was sent to India to join William Butler (1818–1899) who had founded the work there in 1856. It was Thoburn who insisted that the mission reach the entire country. Later, as first missionary bishop for India and Malaya, he presided over a period of rapid church growth, with mass movements of

converts into membership. Thoburn also initiated MEC work in Burma (1879), Singapore (1885), and the Philippines (1899).

West Africa
William Wade Harris (c. 1860–1929), a 'born Methodist,' became a lay preacher in his native Liberia under Methodist influences. Dismissed by the Episcopal (US) mission, he experienced an anointing of the Spirit when in prison, and emerged to become the most successful missionary West Africa has known. Working independently, he baptized as many as 120,000 in one year, beginning in the Ivory Coast. West African Methodism dates its beginning not from the first British missionary in 1924, but from what Harris began in 1914. Similarly, the Methodist mission in the Gold Coast (Ghana) experienced a mass revival movement in the 1920s through the preaching of Kwame Sampson Oppong (c. 1884–1965), when 20,000 came under Methodist care within five or six years.

African American initiatives
After earlier abortive efforts, the permanent work of the AME Church in Sierra Leone began in 1886 with the appointment of John Richard Frederick to serve there. He was the first AME missionary to work extensively with indigenous Africans rather than the black settler community. Together with Presbyterian Edward Blyden (1832–1912) and Anglican James 'Holy' Johnson (c. 1836–1917), Frederick founded the Dress Reform Society that succeeded in making traditional African attire fashionable. Sarah Gorham (1832–1894), the first AME commissioned woman missionary, worked among Temne women and girls in Liberia, and established the Sarah Gorham Mission School providing both religious and industrial training.

The African Methodist Episcopal Zion Church (AMEZ) sent Andrew Cartwright as its first missionary to Liberia in 1876. John Bryan Small (d. 1915), a native of Barbados, in the next generation became the AMEZ's most effective missionary in West Africa. Elected bishop to Africa, the West Indies, and three home conferences in 1896, Small excelled in training indigenous African church leaders, especially in the Gold Coast (Ghana).

Bible Translation
Scholars are reassessing the inextricable connection between Bible translation and the empowerment of people and their cultures. Lamin Sanneh writes, 'in spite of nationalist reaction against vestiges of colonial rule, thanks to its vernacular translation, Christianity has become too local to consign to the colonial limbo.'[11]

One dramatic case of the importance of Bible translation in mission comes from northeast India. Welsh Calvinist Methodists introduced Christianity to the Khasi people as early as 1841. After fifty years of labor, however, they could count only 2,147 communicant members and about 10,000 affiliated Christians. In the church's jubilee year, 1891, the Bible was finally translated and disseminated. Progress thereafter was rapid, life in the hills transformed, and in wide areas the entire population became Christian.

In 1884 Yi Su-Jong, who was in Tokyo translating the Bible into Korean, asked the churches in the USA to send missionaries. The Korean Bible, translated and printed in Japan, was already in the hands of the first Methodist missionary from the USA, when Henry Gerhard Appenzeller (1858–1902), arrived in 1885 to assist in further translation work in cooperation with Koreans and Presbyterian missionaries. Inquirers were taught *Hangul* (the Korean alphabet) and read the Bible in their own language. It was the church that affirmed Korean culture when Japan, the colonial power (1904–1945) tried to impose its language and culture. The 1907 revival and speed with which Christianity was accepted, must be seen in this perspective.

Education

India
Isabella Thoburn (1840–1901) was recruited by her brother James to serve in India, but began the work as a single woman with support only by women. The boarding school for girls that she founded in 1870 became in 1886 Lucknow Woman's College – the first Christian college for women in Asia.

China
Frank Dunlap Gamewell (1857–1950) served the MEC as a teacher in China, acting president of the future Yenching University, executive secretary of the Educational Association of China, and then as an associate general secretary of the mission board in New York. Mary Porter Gamewell (1848–1906), his first wife, in 1872 opened the pioneer school for girls in Peking – the forerunner of a great educational movement for girls that gained recognition and promotion by the Chinese government after 1900.

Korea
Mary F. Scranton (1832–1909) was a pioneer missionary of the MEC in Korea. Upon her arrival in 1885 she emphasized evangelistic and educational work among women. Starting with one female student in 1886, she founded Ehwa Haktang (Institute) in Seoul – the first school for girls in Korea that later became Ehwa Women's University. With support from the queen she expanded the work to many regions including Soowon and Inchon. Her vision was to lead Korean women out of secluded lives based on Korean tradition into

Methodist Missions/Missiology

modern education and cross-cultural mission. She served as first chairperson of the Korean Women's Conference for Methodist Women.

Medical

Women in China, much of India, and in Muslim countries did not permit examination and care by male doctors. To meet this need the women's missionary societies gave priority to the support and sending of women doctors when openings for medical training were available to them. In 1869 Clara Swain (1834–1910) sailed for India with Isabella Thoburn. She was the first woman medical missionary sent by any society or board. Swamped by women patients, she began the next year teaching fourteen orphan young women to be her assistants. She opened a dispensary at Bareilly in 1873 and in 1874 the hospital that later bore her name. The work grew under her leadership to include a nursing school, large hospital, rural outreach, and other departments. In 1885 Swain helped the British viceroy's wife to develop the plan initiating the National Medical Association for Supplying Female Aid to the Women of India. In the same year she left the employment of the Women's Foreign Missionary Society (WFMS) to become physician to women in the domain of the rajah of Khetri, thereby opening up a large area controlled by a Muslim prince to Christian witness and modern medicine.

Lucinda L. Coombs (*c.* 1849–1919), like Swain a graduate of the Women's Medical College in Philadelphia, went to China in 1873 as the first female medical missionary of any denomination in that country. Supported by the WFMS, in 1875 she opened the first women's hospital in China. Fruits of her pioneer work included the later founding of medical schools for Chinese women, better hygiene and medical care, and greater openness to the gospel by women who received loving care by Coombs and others.

William Benton Scranton (1856–1922) was the Methodist pioneer of medical missions in Korea. He entered Korea at the invitation of Presbyterian Horace Newton Allen (1858–1932), the first resident Protestant missionary in that country, who had been given permission by the king to open a hospital. In addition to his medical practice, Scranton was active in evangelism and church planting, and a Bible translator. He resigned from the Methodist mission in 1907 to engage in medical education under the Korean government.

Women in Mission

Prior to 1858 only missionary wives served in British Methodist overseas missions. In that year women in London broke through that barrier and formed The Ladies Committee for the Amelioration of the Conditions of Women in heathen countries. At a period when Florence Nightingale was a national hero, a breakthrough was made and 'Women's Work' was accepted as a necessity rather than a novelty.

The appeal by two missionary wives that only women can reach women in India motivated Methodist women in Boston to form the WFMS of the MEC in 1869. Forty-five women in seventeen states were named vice-presidents providing denomination-wide leadership. Their goal was to set up a society cooperating with the MMS but independent and equal to it – a status only achieved after much struggle in 1884. The women sent Isabella Thoburn as their first missionary to India. The Women's Missionary Society (WMS) of the MECS, organized in 1878, had similar origins in a local initiative in Nashville, Tennessee, in 1873 led by Margaret Lavinia Kelley, later called 'the mother of Foreign Missions.'[12]

The two missionaries sent by the WFMS to China in 1872, Maria Brown and Mary Porter, decided that if they were able to begin a school, they would require that the girls unbind their feet. Foot binding was so entrenched as a social norm that of 150 applicants for free schooling in the first two years only seven were enrolled. The women firmly adhered to their principles, believing that opposition to foot binding was intrinsic to mission among women in China. By the 1880s progressive Chinese joined the crusade that accelerated until Chinese law forbade the practice in 1907.

Methodists did not form women's missionary orders as did their Roman Catholic counterparts. The closest parallel was the deaconess movement. Its purpose was to revive the ancient ministry of Christian women to persons in both physical and spiritual need. Although Lutherans brought the concept to the USA from Germany, it was Methodists who developed the movement. As early as 1871 Methodist women adapted the idea in East Asia. 'Bible Women' were employed first in Foochow, China, to travel to rural villages to evangelize and perform acts of mercy. By 1900 special training schools for them developed in China with forty-eight enrolled in the Wesleyan Training School for Women in Canton, and twenty-eight in the MEC's school in Foochow. Later Bible Women became an important ministry in Korean Methodism. Back in the USA, by 1887 women began to be licensed as missionary deaconesses and wore a distinctive uniform. In subsequent years even more were recruited and supported as home missionaries in the USA.

The ecumenical Women's Missionary Movement celebrated its centennial in 1910. In the official history Helen Barrett Montgomery lauded the WFMS of the MEC as 'the greatest Woman's Missionary Society of the country' because it was not merely an auxiliary of the denominational board of missions. Not only did it send and support its own missionaries, but it pioneered among all denominations in opening the first women's hospitals and colleges in Asia. She rated it to be 'the most powerful women's mission organization of the 19th and early 20th centuries.'[13]

From Mission to Church, 1914–2010

Kenneth Scott Latourette titled the final volume of his monumental history of world Christianity 'Advance through Storm.'[14] He maintained that for the church the twentieth century really began in 1914 with the outbreak of the Great War. Buffeted by two world wars, economic depression, and the onslaught of secularism, historic churches declined in Europe, and the numbers of their cross-cultural missionaries shrank. Some scholars, upon the virtual end of colonialism, predicted the end of Christian missions.

But Christian churches around the world, including Methodists, rebounded with renewed vigor and mission outreach. By 1990 a majority of Christians were in the global South – Africa, Asia, Latin America, and the Pacific Islands. Of the seventy-one member churches of the World Methodist Council in 2009, only twelve (or their predecessor bodies) existed as autonomous churches in 1914. All the churches of world Methodism are in mission and have stories to tell.

Evangelization

Much vital evangelization by churches of the Wesleyan tradition took place as they embraced five elements from their Wesleyan heritage: a passion to present Jesus Christ as Savior, conviction of the active working of the Holy Spirit, a radical holiness vision, a broad ecumenism, and a passion for social justice. In each they were connected to wider streams of vital Christianity than their Wesleyan heritage: the passion for presenting Christ of evangelicals, the vital worship of the charismatic and Pentecostal movements, the Holiness tradition, the ecumenical movement, and the struggle of people for liberation and social justice.

In combining these many flowing streams E. Stanley Jones (1884–1973) was the most influential Methodist missionary, mission theorist, and evangelist of the twentieth century. Converted and educated within the Wesleyan/Holiness tradition, Jones served as an ordained Methodist minister in India (1907–1930). It was Christ who was the focal point of Jones' evangelism – not Christianity. In presenting Christ to persons of other faiths in India, he introduced methods that were a natural part of Indian societies including Round Table conferences for sharing religious experience and understanding, and *ashrams*.

Appointed 'evangelist-at-large for India and the world' in 1930, Jones extended his evangelistic work to six continents, including ten visits to post-war Japan where tens of thousands registered their decisions for Christ. Based in the USA after 1944, he spoke out against racism in society and churches, and for Christian unity and world peace.

Common Witness

Methodists, with passion for mission and commitment to common witness with other Christians, have provided strong leadership in the ecumenical movement. John R. Mott (1865–1955) has been called 'the leading Protestant ecumenical and missionary statesman of the world during the first half of the twentieth century.'[15] Formed as a youth in the Wesleyan/Holiness tradition, Mott was profoundly influenced as a young man by Dwight L. Moody as a YMCA secretary and later as its general secretary (1915–1931). One of the first to sign the Student Volunteer Movement (SVM) pledge, God willing, 'to become a foreign missionary,' Mott enlisted over 20,000 missionary volunteers through SVM conferences by 1951 with a call for the 'evangelization of the world in this generation.' He led in the formation of the World Student Christian Federation (WSCF) in 1895, and served as its general secretary (1895–1920) and chairman (1920–1928).

A Methodist layman, Mott can be rightly called the father of the World Council of Churches (WCC). He was a leader in each of the movements (faith and order, life and work, and missions) that led to its formation. Mott teamed with J. H. Oldham (1874–1969) both in leading the World Missionary Conference (Edinburgh, 1910), and the International Missionary Council (IMC) in 1921 which he chaired from 1928 to 1946. Through the IMC Mott promoted global cooperation in missions, national and regional mission conferences that were the forerunners of later councils of churches, and a pattern of representative leadership from churches of the north and south, east and west, that became normative for the ecumenical movement. Honored for his promotion of world peace and global justice, Mott was awarded the Nobel Peace Prize in 1946. Having chaired the provisional committee of the WCC through the war years, he was named its honorary president at the inaugural assembly (Amsterdam, 1948).

Methodists have carried well the multiple legacies of John R. Mott in combining evangelistic passion with ecumenical witness and social justice concerns. D. T. Niles (1908–1970) of Ceylon/Sri Lanka was instrumental in founding the East Asia Christian Conference (EACC), headed the Methodist Church of Ceylon, and served the WCC successively as chairman of the Youth Department, executive secretary of the Department of Evangelism, and one of the six world presidents. Philip A. Potter (*b*. 1921) brought a West Indian perspective to his ministry as a Methodist missionary in Haiti, staff member of the MMS in London, and successively youth secretary, director of the Commission on World Mission and Evangelism (CWME), and general secretary (1972–1984) of the WCC. Emilio Castro (*b*. 1927) served as president of the Ecumenical Methodist Church of Uruguay, and the WCC as CWME director (1973–1983) and as general secretary (1985–1992). Mortimer Arias (*b*. 1924), a Uruguayan Methodist minister, was Methodist bishop of Bolivia.

There he produced the 'Bolivian Theses on Evangelization in Latin America,' a document that so cogently presented evangelism as biblical, holistic, liberating, and conscientizing that leaders both of the WCC and of the Lausanne Movement embraced it. Ghanaian Methodist Mercy Amba Oduyoye (b. 1934) served as youth director of the WCC (1967–1973), president of the WSCF, deputy general secretary of the WCC (1987–1994), and president of the Ecumenical Association of Third World Theologians.

Within the growing world fellowship of churches sharing the Wesleyan heritage, new possibilities for common witness and mission have evolved. Partnership became the operative principle between autonomous churches. In some countries organic union with churches of other confessional families became important for more effective witness and service. Notable was the entry of daughter churches of British Methodism into the Church of South India (1947), and those connected to both British and Australian Methodism into the Church of North India (1970).

The Evangelical United Brethren Church (EUB) developed a distinctive ecumenical pattern of relating to churches outside the USA. While the US Methodist Church, prior to 1968, continued to relate overseas churches organically to it, the EUB church encouraged the formation of autonomous united churches such as the United Church of Christ in the Philippines.[16]

Cambodia is a striking affirmation of the potential for common mission by Methodists. The work began through ministry to refugees from the genocide perpetuated by Pol Pot's regime in the 1970s. In the 1980s Methodists from the USA, Korea, Singapore, the Chinese diaspora, France, and Switzerland worked independently in community rehabilitation and building faith communities. The missionaries included overseas Cambodians returning to their country of birth to share their faith. Cooperation began in the 1990s that led to the establishment of a united Methodist mission in 2002 and later an autonomous Methodist Church of Cambodia. A Bible school founded by the Korean Methodist Church in 2000, but supported by all partners, provides training for the more than 160 pastors serving in this growing church.

Women in Mission

The beginning of the twentieth century were years of increased pressure on women's mission societies in the USA to integrate with the general church boards. Such mergers began in the MECS in 1910, with most other Protestant denominations following suit in the 1920s. Only the MEC women retained their independence and initiative. That is why Dana Robert judged that 'the most powerful woman's missionary agency in the twentieth century was the WFMS of the MEC.'[17]

This uniqueness among mainline Protestant churches in the USA continued upon the formation of the Methodist Church (MC) in 1939 uniting the MEC,

MECS, and Methodist Protestant Church. Women had equal representation with men in board decision-making, apart from the bishops. Uniquely among Protestant boards, the Women's Division retained authority to select fields of labor, accept, train, commission, and support missionaries of their choice, and to buy and sell property. Giving by local women's societies was channeled directly into this division rather than to the general board. This structure carried over to the United Methodist Church (UMC) upon its formation in 1968, with periodic return to the earlier priority to support ministries to women and children – both in the USA and overseas.

Methodist women kept the issue of world peace before the church. Central was the contribution of Evelyn Riley Nicholson (1873–1967), the president of the WFMS from 1921 to 1940. She wrote study books on world peace and authored the 1924 resolution adopted by the MEC General Conference that the church has a responsibility to educate for peace. To strengthen this ecumenical imperative, Nicholson contributed to the first ecumenical study of the role of women in the churches.[18]

It was Helen Kim (1899–1970) of Korea who in 1923 first proposed creation of an international organization of Christian women to promote peace and justice along the lines of the League of Nations. Her dream was fulfilled by the founding of the World Federation of Methodist Women in 1939 by participants from twenty-seven nations, with Evelyn Nicholson as its first president.

For fifty years Kim personified Methodist global commitments to education for women and ecumenism in missions. Her PhD (Columbia University, 1931) was the first earned by a Korean woman. From 1918 to 1970 she served her Ewha alma mater successively as teacher, professor, dean, first Korean president, president emeritus, and chair of its board of trustees. She led Ehwa from college to university status in 1939 despite the difficulties of Japanese occupation. Under her leadership Ehwa grew to be the largest women's university in Asia. She attended over fifty international conferences as a speaker, and served over thirty institutions and organizations in various capacities including the IMC and WCC, and as ambassador-at-large for Korea.

Majority World Missions
Korean Methodism shares in the remarkable leadership by Koreans in twenty-first century mission. From just ninety-three career missionaries of all denominations sent in 1979, the total grew to almost 15,000 in 2006. Among them were more than hundred Korean Methodists serving in forty-three countries including Russia, Sri Lanka, the Philippines, and Malaysia. The multiplicity of Methodist sending bodies included three mission societies and numerous local churches. The Methodist seminary in Moscow, begun in 1995, was built on the foundation of Korean Methodist mission to Russia.

Increasingly 'reverse mission' is revitalizing the former sending churches of Methodism. In the 1970s the MMS in Great Britain became the Overseas Division of the British Methodist Church. Its program of 'World Church in Britain Partnership' facilitates coworkers from other countries serving in various ministries in Britain.

Relief and Development
Upon the end of World War II in 1945, Methodists in most countries directed much of their mission giving and program to the tasks of relief and rebuilding. In 1948 US Methodists adopted a ministry of relief called the Advance for Christ and His Church. In its first year the Methodist Committee on Overseas Relief sent food, clothing, and medicine to thirty-two countries. In addition the new Crusade Scholar program provided scholarships and support for some three hundred in higher education that year – the largest number from China, but others from every continent. In the years that followed the MC helped to resettle 15,000 refugees in the USA.

In the next twenty-five years Methodists responded in mission to varied food and refugee crises such as that created by the war in Biafra (1967–1970). The United Methodist Committee on Relief worked with minimal staff to channel millions of dollars plus material aid through Church World Service of the National Council of Churches. When the 1976 General Conference voted to make World Hunger a missional priority, the means to deliver aid was well established.

The Methodist Relief and Development Fund (MRDF) since 1985 has been British Methodism's agency to help some of the most vulnerable people in the world. In 2009 the MRDF supported more than forty-three local, community-based organizations (NGOs, or development offices of Methodist churches) in twenty-one of the poorest countries in Africa, Asia, and Latin America, assisting individuals and communities to transform their lives and become more self-sufficient. The goal is to seek positive change in the whole of human life, especially of the poor.

MRDF chose to partner in transformational development with a voluntary, non-profit organization in India seeking to empower Dalit and tribal communities in South Orissa. Established in 1992, Rural Educational Activities for Development (READ), led by Ms. Manjulata Sahu, took up the struggle of women against violence and oppression, and for social justice and gender equality. Working for long-term development, READ helps women entrepreneurs with microloans and facilitate marketing through cooperatives. It educates concerning HIV/AIDS and human trafficking. It organizes non-formal education for Dalit and tribal children, and seeks to empower ethnic groups about socio-political rights, economic self reliance, and cultural independence.

Liberation and Justice

During the 1960s Methodists in many countries added to priorities for autonomy and development a passion for liberation and justice. Individual Methodists frequently led national struggles against oppressive rulers and violations of human rights.

Ralph Edward Dodge (1907–2008) served as bishop for Rhodesia/Zimbabwe from 1956 to 1968. He helped the MC to move to black leadership, and from being a compliant partner with colonial white rule to become a strong advocate of social change. Although expelled by the Ian Smith regime in 1964, Dodge passed the mantle to another leader passionate for justice – Abel Tendekai Muzorewa (*b*. 1925) who went on to lead the United African National Council (1972) and served as a president of the transition government that gained independence for Zimbabwe.[19]

Dodge was but one of those missionaries described during the 1960s as 'the new breed – liberal, practical, secular Christians who have extended the church beyond the stained-glass window into the world' who 'may well represent a rebirth of true Christianity.'[20] Another was Colin Morris (*b*. 1929), British Methodist missionary to Zambia, who worked closely with that nation's first president, Kenneth Kaunda, and served as first president of the United Church of Zambia in 1965.

Methodist Theology of Mission

The sources common to all in the Methodist family are to be found in scripture, in the Articles of Religion, in John Wesley's sermons, and in Methodist hymnody. To these since 1921 can be added agreed positions of the IMC and WCC.

Few denominations have developed their own theologies of mission. The UMC and its predecessor bodies are an exception. In 1956 the WCC asked member churches to participate in a study of the theology of mission. In response, the MC mission board held annual consultations of theologians, mission professors, and mission board executives, including British Methodist theologians, to discuss questions given as related to the problems and perspectives of the MC in mission.

From 1981 to 1984 the UMC mission board carried out a major restructure – the centerpiece of which was to be a theologically grounded mission statement. The board held a series of mission theology conferences – not only in the USA, but also with global mission partners in Africa, Asia, Latin America, and Europe. The WCC's major statement, *Mission and Evangelism: An Ecumenical Affirmation* (1982), served as a common resource. The finished document, 'Theology of Mission Statement: Partnership in God's Mission,' received wide circulation. Simultaneously, the 1984 General Conference authorized a church-wide commission to prepare a denominational statement. Its final document, entitled *Grace upon Grace – The Mission Statement of the United Methodist Church*, that drew heavily upon Wesley's theology, was approved for church-wide study in 1988. Mission board staff met annually with Methodist professors of mission to continue these conversations.[21]

Methodist Leadership in Mission Associations

Methodist missiologists,[22] unlike world Lutherans, have not established a confessional association for mission studies. Instead, they have chosen to participate and lead in ecumenical bodies at international, regional, and national levels. Two, out of the many, have made major contributions.

Gerald H. Anderson (*b*. 1930), Methodist missiologist, was instrumental, together with Ralph Winter (*b*. 1924), in forming the American Society of Missiology in 1972 to supplement the efforts of the Association of Professors of Mission to advance mission studies in North America. In the same year Anderson participated in the inaugural meeting of the International Association for Mission Studies, served on its first executive committee and later a three-year term as its president. From 1976 to 2000, as director of the Overseas Ministries Study Center located in New Haven, Connecticut, and as editor of the *International Bulletin of Missionary Research*, Anderson promoted studies on global mission including those by and about Methodists.

Andrew F. Walls (*b*. 1928), the Scottish Methodist historian of mission, was secretary of the Scottish Institute of Missionary Studies and of the Society for African Church History, and president of the British Association for the Study of Religions. In 1982 he developed the Centre for the Study of Christianity in the Non-Western World housed initially in Aberdeen and since 1987 at the University of Edinburgh. Walls founded and edited several periodicals: *Sierra Leone Bulletin of Religion*, *Bulletin of the Society for African Church History*, *West African Religion*, and the *Journal of Religion in Africa*. For many years he compiled the quarterly bibliography in the *International Review of Mission* – the most comprehensive in the field for both books and periodical articles.

Conclusion

It is Andrew Walls' judgment that 'the great issues of twenty-first century Christianity are likely to be ecumenical' and that they will be 'about how African and Indian and Chinese and Korean and Hispanic and North American and European Christians can together make real the life of the body of Christ.'[23] That life includes the stories of Christian witness in word and deed by each community of faith, and by the members of each as salt and life in the world. The kaleidoscope of such narratives and local histories, gathered on six continents, will be the ongoing history of the people called Methodists in mission.

For Further Reading

Anderson, Gerald H., ed. *Biographical Dictionary of Christian Missions*. Grand Rapids, MI: Eerdmans, 1998.

Anderson, Gerald H., Robert T. Coote, Norman A. Horner, and James M. Phillips, eds. *Mission Legacies: Biographical Studies of Leaders of the Modern Missionary Movement*. Maryknoll, NY: Orbis, 1994.

Barclay, Wade Crawford and J. Tremayne Copplestone. *History of Methodist Missions*. 4 vols. New York: Board of Missions (or General Board of Global Ministries), 1949–1973.

Cole, Charles E., ed. United Methodist History of Mission. 6 vols. New York: General Board of Global Ministries of the United Methodist Church, 2003–2005.

Robert, Dana and Douglas D. Tzan. 'Traditions and Transitions in Mission' in *The Oxford Handbook of Methodist Studies*, ed. William J. Abraham and James E. Kirby. Oxford: Oxford University Press, 2009: 431–448.

8 Methodism in Africa

John Wesley Z. Kurewa

On 29 November 1758 at Wandsworth, England, John Wesley baptized two Africans who were slaves belonging to Nathaniel Gilbert (d. 1774). Gilbert had recently arrived from Antigua.[1] Wesley commented on the two persons baptized, 'One of these is deeply convinced of sin; the other rejoices in God her Saviour and is the first African Christian I have known.'[2] Little did he know that Methodism would find Africa a fertile continent for his brand of Christianity!

Today, Methodism is found in all the regions of Africa that include West Africa, Southern Africa, East Africa, and even North Africa. This essay examines the origin of Methodism in various African countries, most of which emerged from the missionary efforts of British and American Methodist denominations.

The main objectives of the essay include: (1) identifying where Methodism in Africa has been engaged in evangelizing; (2) examining the origin and impact of the Methodist churches which were formed from this evangelization; (3) exploring the cultural and social challenges these churches have encountered; and (4) assessing the extent to which the churches of the Methodist tradition are participants in the growing Christian community on the African continent.

This study considers African Methodism on a regional basis, beginning with West Africa, then Southern Africa, East Africa, and North Africa. It has been limited by scant library literature and unproductive attempts to gather information from some of the Methodist denominations which have ministries on the continent. Uncovering descriptions of the origin and early history of Methodism in the countries mentioned has proven considerably less difficult than information on more recent historical development.

Methodism in West Africa

British and American Methodism came to Africa through freed slaves who settled in Sierra Leone and Liberia. We consider below the genesis and something of the development of Methodism in Sierra Leone, Benin, Gambia, Ghana, Liberia, Nigeria, Ivory Coast, and Togo.

Sierra Leone

Three groups of settlers arrived in Freetown in the late eighteenth century. The first party arrived from England in 1787. The second included approximately 1,200 from Nova Scotia in 1792.³ In the second contingent were Christians representing dissenting denominations.⁴ According to Elizabeth Isichei, they landed, '. . . Bibles in hand, singing a [Charles Wesley] hymn: "The Day of Jubilee is come; Return ye ransomed sinners home." '⁵ The third group of settlers, numbering about five hundred from Jamaica, arrived in 1800.⁶ The members of these three groups faced disappointment and suffering. So many of them died that it became customary for them to ask one another every morning, 'How many died last night?'⁷ Nevertheless, Christian religion defined their identity.

The British Methodist leader Thomas Coke (1747–1816) sent the first team of missionaries to Sierra Leone in 1796. He dispatched them with a special mission, 'to civilize the Fulani, to carry out community development work among them.'⁸ Coke also sent George Warren (d. 1812) and three schoolmasters to Freetown in 1811. In 1859 the Methodist Church in Sierra Leone was admitted into the British United Methodist Free Churches⁹ and by 1880 the membership of this church was approximately 6,000 and continued to grow.¹⁰ On 21 January 1967 the Methodist Church in Sierra Leone was established as an autonomous community of Christian believers governed by a conference which meets annually. At first, this church concentrated its ministry in and around Freetown, but gradually moved into the interior. Its program included not only evangelization, but education, health care, and community development.

The West African Methodist Church was born in the midst of conflict between the Nova Scotians who settled in Freetown and those rescued from slave ships on the high seas. In an 1844 sermon preached at the Rawdon Street Chapel, Anthony O'Connor rebuked the Nova Scotians for their belittling attitudes toward the those liberated from the slave ships. As a result of O'Connor's diatribe and other factors, approximately 2,000 people from several congregations in Freetown and surrounding villages forged the West African Methodist Church.¹¹ This church employs elements of both Methodist and Anglican traditions.

United Methodist presence in Sierra Leone traces its roots to the missionary work of the Church of the United Brethren in 1855 by W. J. Shuey, D. C. Kumler, and D. K. Flickinger. Health problems among the missionaries hampered the work, but it was supported by an African chief Chaulker and his family. An African American pastor, Joseph Gomer and his wife Mary were sent by the United Brethren in 1871 to evangelize and teach in the nascent Sierra Leone mission. The Gomers are recognized as the persons most responsible for establishing the United Brethren mission in Sierra

Leone.[12] The mission was especially successful in establishing schools at Shenge, Bompetoke, and elsewhere. Despite attacks on mission stations by native people in 1898 resulting in the deaths of missionaries and indigenous leaders, the Sierra Leone work continued and grew significantly. In 1968 the Sierra Leone mission became affiliated with the United Methodist Church; in 1973 it attained autonomy and elected its first indigenous bishop, Benjamin A. Carew.[13]

Benin
The Protestant Methodist Church Benin (*Eglise Protestante Methodiste du Benin*) originated with the work of British Wesleyan Methodist Thomas Birch Freeman (1809–1890) who in 1843 pioneered missionary ministry not only in Ghana and western Nigeria, but in Dahomey (Benin) and Togo. While Methodism spread very slowly, it has recently opened successful work in north Benin. Its ministries include evangelism and church planting, education, medical work, and a theological college which also serves Ivory Coast and Togo.

The Gambia
In response to a request from the Governor of Gambia, to send missionaries to Africa, the Wesleyan Methodist Missionary Society sent John Morgan (1792–1872) as the first preacher to the Gambia. Morgan and John Baker, who had been working in Sierra Leone, established the initial mission station in the capital, Banjul. The Gambian work showed signs of growth despite being located in a large Muslim population. The Methodist population has never been large, but work among the Gambians has been important in education, agriculture, and medical work in addition to its evangelistic emphasis. Gambian Methodism maintained a close relationship with British Methodism and achieved autonomy in May 2009.

Ghana
Methodism in Ghana originated from a Bible study group formed in 1831. Desiring to train young Africans for colonial administration, Charles McCarthy, the Governor of Sierra Leone who also supervised the British forts in Ghana, established a school at Cape Coast Castle. The school's African headmaster, Joseph Smith, who was a devoted Christian, organized the group to study scripture.[14]

Smith's group petitioned the Anglican Bishop of London to send a teacher to assist them. It was the Methodists who responded by sending Joseph R. Dunwell (1806–1835) who arrived in Ghana 1 January 1835. Not accustomed to the climate, Dunwell died six months later.[15] The mission work initiated by Dunwell influenced some in the Fante area who became Christian and carried their new faith inland. These Fante Christians made a substantial contribution to inaugurate a mission to the Asante, their traditional inland enemies.[16]

Thomas Birch Freeman, the Wesleyan Methodist missionary born of an English mother and African father, arrived at Cape Coast with his wife in 1838 to strengthen the mission work. Freeman's wife died after only six months. In spite of the hardships he faced, Freeman entered Kumasi, the Ashanti capital in April 1839 and successfully established new mission stations in the area.[17] Within two years Methodist membership in the region increased to one hundred; five schools were opened.[18] Methodist evangelization of the Fante area resulted in a number of converts who were scattered in small congregations and by 1896 there were more than 7,000 Methodists in Ghana.[19]

Freeman emphasized the use of indigenous converts who spread the gospel and planted new churches. While there were three European missionaries in 1885, there were already fifteen ordained African pastors and more than a hundred 'catechists' and evangelists.[20] By 1919 Methodist work had spread extensively over southern Ghana. A revival in 1920 led by Sampson Opon, an illiterate lay preacher, is believed to have transformed Asante Methodism; approximately 10,000 were baptized within two years and mission stations increased from nine to more than seventy.[21]

By the early twenty-first century the Methodist Church Ghana was one of the largest Christian bodies in the country. Since 1961 it has been autonomous. It maintains schools and medical work, and participates with other denominations in the Christian Council of Ghana.[22]

The African Methodist Episcopal Zion Church (AMEZ) has been organized in Ghana since the late nineteenth century. John Bryan Small (1845–1915), elected a bishop by the AMEZ in 1896, was largely responsible for introducing Zion Methodism at Johnsonville, possibly in 1887.[23] In 1898 he authorized Thomas Freeman, who had resigned from the Methodist Church on disciplinary grounds, to organize the AMEZ in Ghana. Freeman formed what became the first AMEZ congregation in Ghana 'at Keta, Volta Region, and later the same year at Cape Coast.'[24] Encouraging indigenous leadership, as early as 1898 Bishop Small recruited African young men to receive education in the USA.[25] James Emman Kwegyri Aggrey (1875–1927), popularly known as Aggrey of Africa and born within the AMEZ Ghana mission field, was a beneficiary of this educational program. Other beneficiaries of the program were Kwame Nkrumah of Ghana, A. B. Xuma, and J. R. Rathebe from South Africa, John Chilembwe, Daniel Malekebu, and Hastings Banda from Malawi, and many others.[26] The AMEZ was the first denomination consciously to promote trained leadership for the continent of Africa. The denomination continues its evangelistic and social action ministries in its two Ghana conferences.

Liberia

Liberia was founded as an American colony in Africa, although there are divergent opinions about justifying the choice of Liberia as the location for settlement. The African Methodist Episcopal Church (AME) originated in Africa through freed African slaves. Among the settlers who arrived in Liberia in 1822 was Daniel Coker (1780–1846), an AME clergyman, who traveled to Liberia as a missionary.[27] Before landing in Africa, Coker organized those who were Methodists into a society. Their landing on Liberian soil marked the introduction of both American Methodism and the AME to Liberia.

Denominational missionary efforts were organized into a missionary society by the Methodist Episcopal Church (MEC) in 1819. These efforts were largely inspired by the work of John Stewart (d. 1823), a 'black man, the son of free and pious Baptists in Virginia,[who] was converted through Methodist preaching at Marietta, Ohio, in 1816. [Stewart] evangelized the Wyandots. . . . The church was roused [by his work], and by him [was] led into missions.'[28] Stewart's ministry laid the groundwork for MEC missionary endeavors in both domestic and overseas missions work.

At the general conference held in Philadelphia in May 1832, MEC Bishops William McKendree, Elijah Hedding, and Joshua Soule approved Melville Cox (1799–1833) as Methodist Episcopal (ME) missionary to Africa. Already suffering tuberculosis, Cox was commissioned for a Liberian ministry. His conversation with a friend before embarking for the African continent is revealing, 'If I die in Africa you must come and write my epitaph,' Cox told him. 'I will,' the friend replied, 'but what will I write?' 'Write,' Cox said, 'Let a thousand fall before Africa be given up.'[29] Cox arrived in Liberia in February 1833. 'Africa was the first [foreign] field [of the MEC mission society], [and] Cox was the first missionary of the Society.'[30] Cox worked hard in organizing the MEC in Liberia. A number of conferences were organized, and Articles of Religion and General Rules adopted according to the American *Discipline*.[31] Cox died 21 July 1833. Methodist ministry continued after his death, some of it under the supervision of a medical missionary named Goshen who arrived in 1836. In 1868 the Liberian mission became the Liberian Annual Conference.

Bishop William Taylor (1821–1902), energetic evangelist and church organizer, became the first resident MEC missionary bishop to Africa from 1884 to 1896. Taylor is said to have confided to his successor, Bishop Joseph C. Hartzell (1842–1928), who served in Liberia from 1896 to 1916, that he was disappointed with the results of his 'self-supporting' missions among the Liberian people. It appears that Taylor's supervision of the Liberian mission was weak. For example, educational work in Monrovia remained at the primary school level with one teacher. Many young children attended schools of other denominations with the result that they left Methodism.[32]

Hartzell attempted to revitalize the Liberian work by recruiting African American missionaries; he succeeded in enlisting twenty-one. Alexander P. Camphor (1865–1919) and his wife were among the recruits. Camphor, formerly a professor of mathematics at New Orleans University, effectively served as President of the College of West Africa in Monrovia from 1897 to 1907. He observed that the Liberian church did not exhibit significant improvement or growth under African American leadership. Camphor, however, had a vision that the future of the Liberian church depended on indigenous people, not those from the USA. Thus, in 1903 he proposed that the church move outside Monrovia, where it had minimal support, to the interior of the country where it would find a place among 'strong and promising indigenous tribes.'[33] Camphor also informed Bishop Hartzell and the MEC mission board that if his dream of a vibrant Liberian church was not fulfilled he would not return to Africa after his furlough in 1907.[34] Camphor's return to Liberia was initially blocked by Bishop Isaiah B. Scott (1854–1931), but after he and Camphor reconciled, the mission board did not have sufficient funds to support Camphor's return. Bishop Scott visited the Liberian interior more than either Bishops Taylor or Hartzell. The indigenous people 'begged him for teachers and preachers.'[35] New missions were opened at various distances from the coast and Liberian Methodism grew modestly between 1908 and 1916.

One of the aims of the AMEZ was to Christianize Africa and develop their homeland for Christ.[36] Andrew Cartwright, born a slave, persuaded the AMEZ to support him in a mission to Liberia. Upon his arrival in Africa, Cartwright settled at Brewerville where on 7 February 1878 he organized the AMEZ work and in 1886 extended the mission to Cape Palmas. Through the labors of an African pastor Drybauld Taylor and others an AMEZ annual conference was inaugurated in 1910. AMEZ presence and ministries continue in Liberia.

Nigeria

Thomas Birch Freeman and William de Graft, a Fante Christian, are credited with the introduction of British Wesleyan Methodism to Nigeria. Freeman and de Graft traveled to Yorubaland in 1842. Shodeke, chief of Abeokuta in Yorubaland, invited representatives of three major religious groups – African religionists, Christians, and Muslims – to present their views so that he could determine what he considered the true religion. The chief chose Christianity. Freeman and de Graft thereafter enjoyed a warm reception from the chief and his people. Freeman returned to Ghana while de Graft and his wife remained in Badagry where they founded a Methodist mission station and ministered to Methodist immigrants from Sierra Leone.[37] The number of Methodists in Badagry increased and from Badagry Methodism spread to various parts of the country west of the River Niger and to the north.[38] The expansion of Wesleyan Methodism in western Nigeria until about 1910 was successful and was primarily spread through the use of laity in evangelizing, especially around Lagos, Ibadan, and Ilesha.[39] Similarly, the Home Missionary Committee of the Primitive Methodist Church (PMC), having already sent missionaries to the Spanish island of Fernando Po, where they faced several major problems, responded favorably 'to the invitation from JaJa of Apobo in the Oil Rivers, southeastern Nigeria, asking them to enter Opobo.'[40] In 1893 the first Primitive Methodist mission station was opened at Archibongon with Marcus Brown as minister in charge.[41] The discovery of bituminous coal in the district of Enugu, which resulted in the construction of a railroad enabled the PMC to establish churches at most of the railroad junctions including Orim, Abani, Uzuakoli, Umuahia, and Aba.[42]

While Wesleyan Methodism was established in West Nigeria, Primitive Methodism was important in East Nigeria. Eventually, there were two Methodist districts, one on the western side of the River Niger and the other on the eastern side. In 1962 the two districts merged and constituted the Conference of the Methodist Church Nigeria with seven districts. In 1976 the Methodist Church in Nigeria adopted an episcopal system of government. Presently, the church has a strong ministry in the social and economic welfare of the Nigerian people with a reported membership exceeding 2,000,000.[43]

What is now United Methodism was introduced to Nigeria through the mission of the Evangelical Association/Church (EAC). German missionary Karl Kumm and some friends from Sheffield, England, 'founded a British Sudan Pioneer Mission with the sole aim of bringing the gospel to the people of Adamawa and all the Upper Benue.'[44] Later, Kumm traveled to Nigeria in July 1904, and after leaving Nigeria the following year visited a number of western countries to speak about Africa. In the USA Kumm recruited C. W. Guinter, a United Evangelical Church pastor, who arrived in Wukari in 1906. Guinter opened mission stations in Kona and Mumuye in 1918 and 1920, respectively.[45] By December 1923 Guinter, other missionaries, and indigenous leaders successfully opened Evangelical United Brethren work among the Kulungu people.[46] Between 1923 and 1945 additional indigenous preachers employed evangelistic meetings, began new places of worship, and offered primary school education.[47]

The name 'Ekan-Muri Church' was used for the Evangelical United Brethren Church in Nigeria because 'prior to 1926, Nigeria was known as Muri, a province of Britain.'[48] In the 1970s the church experienced a schism that led to a number of missionaries leaving, some of the nationals losing their positions in the church, and some church members joining other denominations. In 1978 the Church Council 'adopted the name "The United Methodist Church" after it was resolved that the church would be a conference in the

UMC and not an affiliated autonomous denomination as suggested by the missionaries.'[49]

Ivory Coast (*Côte d'Ivoire*)
Methodism in the Ivory Coast traces its origins to William Wade 'Prophet' Harris (c. 1860–1929) who preached in the area around 1913–1915. In 1923 British Methodist missionary William J. Platt (1893–1993) began the formal organization of Methodism with ties to the British Methodist Church. In 1985 the church became autonomous and took the name Protestant Methodist Church of the Ivory Coast. In 2004, after mutual negotiations, the Ivory Coast denomination united with the United Methodist Church taking approximately 750,000 members into the UMC.

Togo
Thomas Birch Freeman visited Togo in 1843 and gained the favor of local chiefs including the King of Anecho who granted permission to preaching the gospel and the establishment of schools. While the Protestant Methodist Church Togo was an independent district of the British Methodist Church, the church became autonomous in 1999.

Methodism in Southern Africa

Both British and American Methodism engaged actively in mission work in Southern Africa.

South Africa
Methodist presence in South Africa began in 1806 when a group of soldiers held worship and formed a society in 1806.[50] Wesleyan Methodist missionary Barnabas Shaw (1788–1857) arrived in 1816. He was sent to Cape Town with instructions to minister to the indigenous people.[51] Shaw began work in Namaqualand and founded a base at Leliefontein about 300 miles north of Cape Town in Chief Nama's area. Nama must have also been known as Chief Kama of Ciskei near whose village Wesleyville was established. Shaw founded other mission stations including Mount Coke (1824), Butterworth (1827), Morley (1829), Clarksbury (1830), Buntingville (1835), Shawbury (1839), and later Maclear, Fletcherville, and Tsitsana.[52] A number of lay preachers with Shaw ministered to the white population which settled at Salem and Grahamstown in the eastern district of the Cape Colony and by 1844 there were eighteen Wesleyan churches in the area.[53] Similarly, Wesleyan Methodism entered the Natal Colony through a minister who accompanied British troops in 1842. The church also spread into the Orange Free State where two congregations were formed by 1872. From 1881 to 1885 Methodism

also grew in the Transvaal, largely because of the area's gold rush. From South Africa Wesleyan Methodism expanded to Botswana, Lesotho, Namibia, Mozambique, Swaziland, and Zimbabwe.

Methodism's largest church in South Africa and one of the nation's prominent Protestant denominations is the Methodist Church of Southern Africa which spread among all the racial groups of the nation including Whites, Africans, and Asians. In spite of serious schisms which began as early as 1884 and lasted until at least 1978, the church grew. Ministries of the denomination, especially in the apartheid era emphasized evangelism, social justice (including dismantling of the apartheid system), education, and health care.[54]

As the AME grew in the USA, it extended its presence into western Africa and later into South Africa (1896). In 1892 a group of black Christians in Pretoria called themselves 'Ethiopians,' drawing their identity from the biblical text, 'Envoys will come from Egypt; Cush [Ethiopia] will submit herself to God' (Ps. 68:31). The 'Ethiopians' were led by Mangena Mokone who withdrew from affiliation with the Wesleyan Methodist Missionary Society. In 1896 this group of black Christians was formally incorporated as the African Methodist Episcopal Church.[55]

United Methodism in South Africa was established through the efforts and contacts made with its Mozambique Annual Conference which operated mission work in the Transvaal through the ministry of Joseph M. Mahlatsi and Ben Thunyiswa. United Methodism is concentrated in the Eastern Cape and Western Cape provinces.

Angola
David Livingstone (1813–1873) traveled through Angola in 1854 and prayed that the church might gain a rich harvest of souls there. One year later Methodist missionary Bishop William Taylor was inspired to evangelize the interior of the African continent including Angola.

Taylor, accompanied by forty-two missionaries landed in Angola on 20 March 1885. Most of the missionaries, which included men, women, and children, died within months of their arrival. The first Methodist mission station, St. Paul de Luanda, was established in Luanda, the capital city, later that year. Other inland stations were founded at Dondo, Nhanguepepo, Pungo Andongo, Malanje, and other places. A Congo Mission Conference was formed and held its first session in June 1897. This action forced the reorganization of the Angola mission and a reduction in the number of mission stations. Bishop Joseph Hartzell decided to close some of the inland mission work, but retained mission stations in Luanda, Pungo Andongo, and Malanje.[56]

As Angolan Methodism expanded from 1902 to 1919, The Mission Conference of Angola was formed which in 1948 became the Angola Annual Conference.[57] The history of Angolan Methodism reflects a long-lasting struggle, especially during the colonial rule of the Portuguese. Going back to 1898, the missionaries in Angola felt that they had not won sufficient converts and nurtured them as full-fledged Christian disciples. They were discouraged as there were only thirty-six church members, 'hardly more than double the number of missionaries.'[58] This prompted the missionaries to engage in theological reflection regarding the task of evangelization. One missionary, Amos Withey, began to explicate David Livingstone's philosophy, 'that the pioneer missionary's criterion of success should not be "the conversion of a few souls, however valuable they may be," but the diffusion of a general knowledge of Christianity throughout the world.'[59] Withey urged his colleagues not to despair over the small numbers of conversions by quoting Livingstone, 'It was enough for the missionary simply to have been faithful in preaching Christ, just as Paul preached faithfully though his message was not accepted; yet God's cause moved forward.'[60] That is the sort of theological orientation in which United Methodism in Angola has developed to the present. Retired United Methodist Bishop Emilio J. M. de Carvalho, the first indigenous bishop, often emphasized the importance and role of class meetings in teaching and practicing the faith among United Methodists in the process of evangelizing Angola. As a result, new congregations have multiplied through preaching and teaching the Christian faith, and the organization of class meetings.

Zambia

Three British Primitive Methodist (PM) missionaries, Henry Buckenham (1844–1896), John Smith (1840–1915), and his son Edwin Smith (1876–1957) went to Zambia in 1874.[61] In 1897 two African evangelist-teachers, Robert Maolosi and James Tozzo and their wives joined the PM missionary enterprise. Apart from speaking several languages, including English and Dutch, the two Africans could make bricks, quarry and cut stone, and were builders; this made them significant contributors to the development of the mission.[62] In 1916 the PM established Kafue Training Institute. This school became attractive and effective in training African leaders so that the London Missionary Society and the Wesleyans employed it to educate their students.[63]

The Wesleyan Methodist Church (WM) entered Zambia through the invitation of Cikala who had become a Christian while working in the mines of South Africa. Cikala was passionately devoted to having the gospel preached to his people. His Zambian home was Ilala where the heart of David Livingstone lies buried. After Cikala's brother became a tribal chief, Cikala returned to Zambia and the two brothers shared a vision to invite missionaries to start a mission in their homeland. Cikala visited John White (1866–1933), then chairman of the WM in Harare, Zimbabwe. Although White visited Zambia in 1909, it was not until 1912 that Henry Loveness and three unnamed African evangelists opened a mission in Zambia. By the time of this team's arrival in Zambia, Cikala, who had constructed a small church building there, had died. His brother, Chief Mbosha, received the team warmly and the first worship service was held at Cikala's village with the whole community attending.⁶⁴ The passion and work of Cikala marked the beginning of WM presence in Zambia.

When the PM and WM united to form the Methodist Church (MC) on 20 September 1932, the PM and WM in Zambia united into one district of the MC. On 16 January 1965 at the Mindolo Church, the MC in Zambia joined with other denominations to become the United Church of Zambia, the largest Protestant Church in the country.

Democratic Republic of Congo
Methodism came to the Congo on two fronts: first, the central Congo, and second the southern Congo.

ME Bishop William Taylor established eleven mission stations in 1886. Fifty-eight missionaries were recruited for the work, but by 1896 only five missionaries were engaged in the ministry.⁶⁵

In February 1912 Bishop Walter R. Lambuth (1854–1921) of the MEC, South, and John Wesley Gilbert (1865–1923), Colored MEC leader, visited Chief Wembo-Nyama in the Central Congo and were received graciously.⁶⁶ Lambuth opened the Wembo-Nyama Mission on 12 February 1914 with emphases on evangelism, medical care, education, and industrial training.⁶⁷ In December 1931 the area missionaries invited Gilbert Ridout to conduct a revival at the Wembo-Nyama mission. It drew many people and a large number of clergy and laity received baptism and power of the Holy Spirit.⁶⁸ By 1935 there was a marked increase in the number of Atetera preachers and church members. It is not surprising that revivalism and mass evangelistic meetings have become the pattern and practice that Methodism in the Congo has been employed throughout recent years.

In the southern Congo, John M. Springer (1873–1963), ME missionary in Zimbabwe, believed that he had a divine vision to start missionary work in the southern Congo.⁶⁹ On 18 July 1910 Springer and his wife Helen arrived at the Congo copper mining camp of Kansanshi and by 1 October he moved to Kalulua. Herman Heinkel, former missionary colleague in Zimbabwe, joined the Springers.⁷⁰ Together they began work among the Lunda people at Musumba (Kapanga) and Kambove. Two Africans, Jacob Maweni and Kayeka Mutembo, joined the effort. Mutembo, son of a former chief, had been stolen as a boy by African slave traders from Angola. After his conversion to Christianity, Mutembo prayed for a missionary to be sent to his Lunda people. Mutembo believed that the appointment of the Springers to work among the Lunda was the answer to his prayer. In 1914 Springer opened a church in Lubumbashi with Christians from Malawi and others from Angola.

Springer went north of Lubumbashi in 1917 where he was joined by Kaluwashi, a Luba, and other Christians from Angola. Springer established important mission stations: Kabongo among the Luba people; the Kapanga mission to the Balunda; and the Kapongo mission to the Baluba. Lubumbashi and Kambove were considered white men's towns and attracted a variety of ethnic groups and nationalities.[71] Other significant mission stations inaugurated were Sandoa and Kinda-Kanene.[72]

Springer, who relocated to Zimbabwe, was elected Bishop for Africa in 1936. Upon his return to the Congo in 1937, his long-time friend Joseph Ellis sold a farm to Springer in exchange for a life annuity [of] $100 a month. Springer took title to the farm in his own name in March 1938.[73] Later the mission took ownership of the farm on which the Congo Institute – Mulungwishi was developed with various programs for boys and girls.[74] Today, Mulungwishi offers degree programs. The United Methodist Church in the Democratic Republic of Congo has grown rapidly. Since 1988 it has been designated United Methodism's Congo Central Conference and is composed of several annual conferences.

Mozambique
After British Wesleyan Methodism had spread from the Cape Province to the Natal and Transvaal Provinces of South Africa, Robert Mashaba (c. 1861–1939) introduced Wesleyan Methodism to Mozambique in 1855.[75] Mashaba, who was Mozambican, occasionally traveled to South Africa to sell animal skins. Later he enrolled in school and became a Christian. Upon his return to Mozambique, Mashaba began preaching in his Ronga language and translated the Bible into Ronga. He opened a school where he taught Ronga and English; this made him a prominent and influential citizen in Maputo.[76] The school was a major factor leading to Mashaba's persecution, arrest, and imprisonment without trial for six months by the Portuguese colonial government on the Cape Verde Islands. Upon his release, Mashaba returned to Mozambique and carried on a ministry among his people.[77]

After the American Board of Commissioners for Foreign Missions made its intention known to relocate its work from Inhambane, Mozambique to Gazaland, Zimbabwe, William Taylor negotiated to secure the Inhambane mission. Erwin Richards and his wife, former missionaries of the American Board, who were on furlough in America, agreed to work with the Methodists. Richards tendered his resignation to the American Board in June 1890.[78] On Christmas Eve 1890 William Taylor commissioned the Richards as missionaries. They proceeded immediately to East Africa.[79] The Inhambane Mission, secured by the MEC, included three main mission stations: Gikuki, Kambini, and Makondwenti.

In 1918, Sikobele, a leading pastor-teacher, with the support of a few clergy and laity, broke away from the ME. He wrote to Frank Mason North

(1850–1935), the mission board secretary in New York, stating that he was breaking away because of two missionaries, Terril and Keys, whom he accused of 'not letting Africans work freely.... They have not brothership with native [Africans].... When [the] Bishop come[s] they will not let us have freedom to be [with] or talk to him....'[80] The missionaries interpreted Sikobele's behavior as the influence of 'Ethiopianism.'

Tizore Navess, 'one of the foremost Mozambican pioneers of the Methodist Church,'[81] like Sikabele was dissatisfied with the ME mission in his country. He created an Inhambane branch of the African National Congress which was formed in Maputo along the lines of the African National Congress in South Africa.[82] Navess, who is said to have 'preached so often about Moses and his liberation of Israel, ... [began to take seriously] the political consequences of his own message.'[83] He adopted a nationalist position, for he had a vision of a free Mozambique. In spite of difficult circumstances, Navess 'continued faithfully to pastor his ME flock at Mocodoene.'[84]

His ordination was delayed until 1921 when he was admitted 'on trial' and three years later was received as a full member of the annual conference.[85]

Mozambique in the midst of political and economic struggle experienced a very difficult period from the 1960s through the 1980s. Fortunately, the United Methodist Church (UMC), the successor to the ME, was aware of what was needed in the Mozambican church. By looking back, they understood the vision of the pioneer African preachers, Sikobele and Navess, who anticipated a free Mozambique. Likewise, in 1964, Escrivao Zunuze, who was elected the first indigenous bishop of the UMC in Mozambique, prepared the church for a new era by embarking on new programs of evangelization which emphasized the Africanization of the church including emphases on youth work, home missions, stewardship, leadership training, projects for healthier living, and new attitudes toward traditional values.[86] The Maputo episcopal area now consists of two annual conferences.

Zimbabwe

The first Wesleyan Methodist missionaries, Owen Watkins (1842–1915) and Isaac Shimmin, arrived at Fort Salisbury on 9 September 1891. The British South Africa Company ceded land to the Methodists to begin missionary work in several locations including Fort Salisbury (1891), Hartley (1891), Epworth (1892), Nenguwo [Waddilove] (1892), and Kwenda (1892). Additional mission stations were opened later in Bulawayo and elsewhere. George H. Eva and eight African evangelists and teachers – among them Joseph Ramushu, Mudumeni Moleli, Samuel Tutani, Wellington Belisi, and James Anta – arrived from Transvaal and Cape Colony in August 1892. Moleli and Anta were martyred during the Shona uprising of 1896–1897.[87]

Wesleyan Methodist missions always included evangelism and planting new churches, education (industrial and ministerial training), and translation of the Bible into vernacular languages. The Wesleyan Methodist work became autonomous in 1977, becoming the Methodist Church in Zimbabwe (MCZ) under the presidency of Andrew Ndhlela.[88] MCZ is one of the largest denominations in the country with sizeable membership in Matabeleland and Mashonaland. Among its important educational mission stations are Wadillove and Tegwani.

The African Methodist Church in Zimbabwe (AMCZ) was founded by Dr. K. Nemapare who had been ordained in the MCZ. Failing to persuade the MCZ to establish itself in Masvingo, his home area, Nemapare decided to break away to form the AMCZ in 1947. Ngezi Mission in the Chirumanzu area, thirty kilometers from Mvuma, a small mining town, became his first mission station and headquarters for his church's evangelization. Congregations were founded in cities such as Bulawayo, Harare, and Gweru. While the AMCZ considers itself an indigenous independent church, liturgically and theologically it is not much different from the MCZ.[89]

ME Bishop Joseph C. Hartzell arrived in Mutare on 10 December 1897 and entered into negotiations with the British South Africa Company to take over the old site of Mutare to inaugurate a mission station. On 21 March 1898 the request was granted.

Between 1897 and 1921 the ME engaged in an intensive missionary thrust in Zimbabwe, establishing mission stations and outstations. If the missionaries were the planners and strategists, the African pastor-teachers were the basic workers, founding almost all of the outstations. First, Old Mutare Mission, which is sixteen kilometers north of Mutare was established in 1898. Morris Ehnes and his wife, having arrived in October 1898, were appointed to Mutare where they opened both school and church work among the Europeans. The Reids, missionary husband and wife, who arrived at the same time as the Ehnes, were appointed to the Old Mutare Mission. Second, Mutambara Mission, situated about seventy-five kilometers south of Mutare was established in 1905 at the invitation of Chief Mutambara. Stephen Tiki and John Mazonya were the first episcopal appointees to the mission in 1905 and 1907, respectively. Third, Murehwa Mission northeast of Harare was opened in 1908 or 1909. This mission site was formerly occupied by a trading station; after the death of the trader, ownership of the site and building reverted to the government which offered the site with all its buildings to the ME. Dr. Samuel Gurney was appointed to Murehwa in 1911 with an African assistant Job Tamutsa (or Tsiga). Fourth, Mutoko Mission, about sixty-five kilometers north of Murehwa was established early in 1911 when the government gave an old police camp, which contained several brick buildings, to the ME to start mission work in the area. James Apiri was the first appointee to Mutoko. Fifth, Nyadire Mission, forty kilometers north of Murehwa was opened in 1922.

Samuel Gurney and L. E. Tull were the first episcopal appointments. From the outset, the emphasis of the work at Nyadire has been medical treatment. Other mission stations which emerged at a later date included Nyamuzume in the Mutoko area, and Lydia Chimonyo in the Mutambara area. Several outstations were founded near the major mission stations.

Programs of the MEC and its successors have emphasized evangelism and planting new churches according to comity agreements, especially in the eastern and northeastern regions of the country. In the 1950s, however, expansion largely ignored comity agreements as the church aggressively followed its members to the major cities, suburbs, and towns. Another major program has been education; several high schools, including Hartzell and Murehwa, are highly respected among the best schools in the nation. Finally, Nyadire and Mutambara mission hospitals stand tall among denominational sister institutions; they not only provide medical care, but also nurses' training.

The years 1921 to 1945 were a period of reflection for the predecessors of United Methodism in considering religious, cultural, and social issues such as African religion, patterns and practices of marriage, community and social life, schismatic movements, and other important developments. The rise of ordained indigenous ministry in 1921 and strengthening class meetings came as measures to meet some of the challenges mentioned above. Since 1945 the church has been more sensitive to the reality that is no longer a missionary church, but a church in mission. This period has brought its own challenges: African nationalism and the struggle for political liberation; the search for genuine peace and economic development; the rise of urban population; theological understanding of mission and the role of the church amidst political conflict; Christian stewardship; and the shift of power from the mission stations to urban churches. Two annual conferences presently compose the Harare episcopal area.

United Methodism boasts the founding of Africa University in Old Mutare in 1992. Beginning with forty students, its student body now numbers approximately 2,000. Agriculture and Natural Resources, Education, Health Sciences, Humanities and Social Sciences, Management and Administration, Theology, and the Institute of Peace, Leadership, and Governance are the principal programs of the university. Since 1994 thousands of graduates from across Africa have been employed in their home countries in government, business, agriculture, church, and a multiplicity of other vocations.

Methodism in East Africa

Kenya

United Methodist Free Churches, a British Methodist denomination, sent a team of missionaries to Kenya in 1861. They arrived in Mombasa in 1862 and began their work.⁹⁰ This group included Johann Ludwig Krapf, a German; Thomas Wakefield (1836–1901) and James Woolner from England; and two Swiss church leaders, S. Elliker and J. F. Graf. The missionaries immediately encountered the common cultural issue of the region, namely, female initiation which included circumcision, which resulted in permanent mutilation and affected women's health and reproduction. At the beginning, the missionaries employed confrontational strategy to deal with the problem, but by the 1930s the church adopted a more tolerant attitude.⁹¹

By 1912 a Methodist mission was opened in Meru through the efforts of Reginald T. Worthington (1880–1933), J. B. Griffiths, and Kenyan Christians from the coast. That mission produced a young Kenyan named Philip M'noti who was ordained in 1934 and later became a chief. One of the missionaries described him as follows:

> Philip Inoti developed into manhood, proud of his colour and his race. He had given his friendship to a white man and his loyalty to Christ, but he neglected none of the steps [by] which a Meru boy develops into full citizenship of his tribe; he reverenced the traditions of his ancestors, never despising them even when they had outlived their usefulness for him; he maintained his respect for the tribal sanctions that through the generations had maintained the integrity and preserved the unity of his people. He never felt that in order to be a Christian he must cease to be a Meru. Nationality and Christianity were never to him opposing and exclusive loyalties.⁹²

Over the years the Kenyan Methodist Church has emphasized: evangelism and new church starts with expansion in north Kenya, the Masai area, Uganda, and Tanzania; educational work which includes 130 schools and four agricultural training centers; youth polytechnics and a number of women's development projects; and an ecumenical theological school, St. Paul's United Theological College in Limuru, which is also the site of Kenya Methodist University. The Methodist Church in Kenya utilizes an episcopal form of government and is divided into several synods.

Burundi, Kenya, Rwanda, Sudan, Tanzania, and Uganda
The East Africa Annual Conference of the United Methodist Church includes Methodist work in Burundi, Kenya, Rwanda, Sudan, Tanzania, and Uganda. United Methodism entered East Africa in a variety of ways. For example, in Burundi, Methodism is the product of the World Gospel Mission (WGM) in Africa which was begun in Egypt in 1875.⁹³ The first WGM missionary to Burundi was John Wesley Haley who established the first mission station in 1937 at Kayero, southeast of Burundi, and within a short time had a network

of twenty-one mission stations.[94] The Burundi mission program included evangelism and planting new churches, education, and health care. Mass evangelism was a predominant method of the WGM. Church growth occurred from the 1950s to the late 1960s. Unfortunately, ethnic conflicts in 1969 and 1972 disrupted the life of the church in the Great Lakes region of the country. This ethnic conflict not only resulted in large loss of life, but led many to migrate to neighboring countries of the Great Lakes Region. According to Jean Ntahorturi, it was in the refugee camps that new Christian communities were born. She claims, 'In new Methodist communities in Kenya and Uganda, people became Christians because they were called by next of kin.'[95] Thus, United Methodist communities emerged through the refugee camps. Following the expulsion of missionaries from the Great Lakes region in 1981, the WGM changed its name to the Evangelical Episcopal Church (EE). The EE under the leadership of Alfred Ndoricimpa entered into negotiations with the United Methodist Church and became an annual conference by action of the 1984 United Methodist General Conference held in Baltimore.[96]

Methodism in North Africa

Methodism was introduced to North Africa by French Methodists as early as 1886.[97] An American Methodist delegation attending the World Sunday School Convention in Rome in 1907 also visited Algiers, became interested in establishing a mission there, and launched cooperative work with the French in 1908.[98] Methodists formed a North Africa Provisional Conference in 1928 which was reorganized into a district of the Swiss Annual Conference in 1973.[99]

Concluding Comments and Suggestions

In researching and writing this essay a number of conclusions were discovered and/or confirmed as follows:

1. Many of the missionaries from Europe, Great Britain, and America risked health and life in answering the call to engage in ministry on the African continent. The hazards of travel and illnesses unique to Africa often posed devastating results for the missionaries.
2. Training and employing indigenous evangelists, teachers, and laypeople contributed to the growth of Methodism among the African populace.
3. Delaying the ordination of African preachers in the countries of Southern Africa, unlike West Africa, may have contributed to schismatic movements which disrupted Methodism's advance.

4. In every country where Methodism has been established, it has struggled with various cultural and social issues. In the missionary venture, therefore, there has always existed a need to become aware of the African context in which mission takes place, that is, African culture, religion, and traditional values.
5. The evangelization program of early missionaries included not only the presentation of the gospel, but also education, medical care, and industrial or practical training.
6. Never to be forgotten is the role of ex-slaves from Britain, Canada, and the United States who introduced Methodism to many of the areas of Africa, especially West Africa.
7. While churches in Africa of the British Methodist tradition have endeavored to become autonomous bodies, those of the American tradition have tended to remain more closely related to their parent denominational bodies.
8. Churches of the British Methodist tradition in Africa have increasingly adopted an episcopal form of polity.
9. Methodism on the African continent has demonstrated phenomenal growth. While Methodism in Europe and North America has numerically declined, African Methodism continues to grow, in some cases at a phenomenal rate.

A few recommendations are also in order.

1. The churches of Methodist traditions in Africa possess a rich unwritten history. There is a critical need for scholarly research and writing on African Methodism on a national, regional, and continental basis. This work demands adequate funding in order for the researcher to gather documentary evidence as well as to conduct oral history interviews.
2. More research is required on the participation of Methodist bishops and other leaders in African partisan politics.
3. There is a very great need to establish an African Methodist Studies Center with a systematic attempt to create a Methodist archives for the continent. One such attempt has already begun at Africa University in Zimbabwe where an archives has been created to support the historical and theological research of students and faculty.

For Further Reading

Angell, Stephen W. and Anthony B. Pinn, eds. *Social Protest Thought in the African Methodist Episcopal Church*. Knoxville: University of Tennessee Press, 2000, especially Chapter 4.

Barclay, Wade Crawford and J. Tremayne Copplestone. *History of Methodist Missions*. 4 vols. New York: Board of Missions and Church Extension, Board of Global Ministries, especially vols. 3 and 4.
Campbell, James T. *Songs of Zion: The African Methodist Episcopal Church in the United States and South Africa*. New York: Oxford University Press, 1995, especially Chapter 8.
Davies, Rupert, A. Raymond George, Gordon Rupp, eds. *A History of the Methodist Church in Great Britain*. London: Epworth Press, 1983, especially vol. 3.
Isichei, Elizabeth. *A History of Christianity in Africa: From Antiquity to the Present*. Grand Rapids, MI: Eerdmans, 1995.
United Methodist History of Mission, 6 vols. New York: General Board of Global Ministries of the United Methodist Church, 2003–2005.

9 Methodism in Asia and the Pacific

Luther J. Oconer

Philip Jenkins' cogent account on the shift of Christianity's 'center of gravity' to the 'global south,' in his seminal *The Next Christendom: the Coming of Global Christianity* (2002), has essentially confirmed what missiologists have been saying for sometime.[1] Accordingly, if we agree with Jenkins' thesis, it would not be difficult to acknowledge that Methodism's 'center of gravity' has also shifted to the 'global south' as well. We can safely say that while much of 'northern' Methodism has become, for the most part, staid, Methodism still maintains its vibrancy and growth in Asia, Latin America, and Africa. Hence, in this essay we endeavor to identify four themes to explain the origins and development of Methodism in the Asia and Pacific regions to help us discern why the energy that once sustained it in the British Isles and the American frontier, is now to be found, albeit in translated forms, in those parts of the globe.[2]

For its origins, first we need to look intrinsically at the two movements – factors within British and American Methodism – to identify what created the missionary impulse to the countries examined in this study. Second, we need to look extrinsically to investigate the intersection of Methodist missionary impulse with empire to see how the encounters helped shape, in variegated ways, Methodist work in the two regions. The second part of the essay deals with development. We divide it into two main recurring themes – close to the character of both early British and American Methodism – which stood out in this survey of the development and growth of the different Methodisms. The first theme is the 'social religion' dimension of Methodism, which when applied to missions emphasizes 'civilizing' educational and medical work; the second is the 'heart religion' facet or the revivalistic essence of Asian Methodisms. Robbie H. Goh's *Sparks of Grace: the Story of Methodism in Asia* (2005) was a noble attempt to understand, among other factors, the development of Asian Methodism through the looking glass of 'social mechanisms,' and its social impact in light of 'context sensitive assessment.'[3] It is not necessary to reiterate what Goh has already effectively done. We will, however, take a more functional approach in this section to help ourselves recognize in broad strokes how Methodism grew and how Methodist identities were formed in the two regions.

Finally, given the scope of the task at hand, this essay will only look at the two largest branches of Methodism across the Atlantic from each other which had a significant presence in the region. For British Methodism, we will mainly examine the work of the Wesleyan Methodists, and for its American counterpart, the work of the Methodist Episcopal Church. While we recognize diversities, and the uniqueness of the Methodist Episcopal Church, South (MECS), Methodist Protestant Church, Church of the United Brethren in Christ, and Canadian Methodist Church, as well as other British Methodist denominations, it is hoped that the patterns established by the two transatlantic Methodisms will at least do justice to the important role of missions in other Methodist churches in the two regions.

Rise of Methodist Denominational Identity and Initial Steps

The beginnings of Methodist missions in Asia and the Pacific came as a consequence of an emerging denominational identity and pride among British Methodists or what noted missiologist and Scottish Methodist Andrew Walls has described as Methodism's transition from being a 'national mission' to being a 'church.'[4] This was exemplified through the rise of the Wesleyan Missionary Society (WMS), which was initially launched as a local society within the Leeds District at the Old Chapel in Leeds on 6 October 1813 by leading Methodists such as Jabez Bunting, the society's 'organizing hand' who became the autocratic leader of Wesleyan Methodism. The mission society, which was intended to centralize and formalize missionary funding and deployments, was the fruition of mounting efforts among Wesleyans to rival other missionary societies like the Calvinistic nonconformist London Missionary Society (LMS), which since its establishment in 1794 had siphoned interest in missions resources from Methodist chapels, and the Anglican evangelicals' Church Missionary Society (CMS) formed in 1799.[5] Most importantly, also providing early inspiration, if not exigency, for the birth of the movement were the piecemeal and somewhat chaotic attempts made by Thomas Coke, who hitherto had made Methodist overseas missions his 'private domain.'[6] The revered 'Father of Methodist missions,' who in the years after John Wesley's death up to 1813 had already led Methodist expansion (with Wesley's blessing) in a number of islands in the West Indies and West Africa, and had dreamt of reaching India. Incidentally, shortly after the Leeds meeting, Coke, weakened by age, along with a band of six British and Irish Methodists, sailed for Ceylon (present-day Sri Lanka), a gateway for western trade in the region. While Coke died en route to the island, his dream remained alive in those who accompanied him. The disheartened surviving missionaries, despite difficulties, were able to proceed with their work soon after their arrival on 29 June 1814, and, consequently, just as Coke had hoped, helped make Ceylon a launching pad for Methodist work in India.[7] In 1817, Irish Methodist James Lynch, one of those who originally sailed with Coke and now connected with the Ceylon mission in Jaffna, reached Negapatnam, a coastal town on the southern tip of India near Ceylon.[8] From Ceylon, missionary W. R. Winston reached Upper Burma (now Myanmar) in 1887.[9] Concurrent with the work of the WMS in the East Indies was its push to Australia with the arrival of Samuel Leigh in New South Wales in 1815. From Australia, Leigh began to establish the foundations of Methodism in the Pacific island country of Aotearoa, or New Zealand, in 1821. From Australia, Methodism also secured footholds in the 'Friendly Islands' of the Kingdom of Tonga in 1826, which eventually paved the way for its entrance to the neighboring islands of Samoa (1827) and Fiji (1835).[10] In 1851, British Methodist George Piercy began work in Hong Kong.[11]

While it was not until after more than three decades that Wesley's American progeny first sent their own missionaries to the region, their entrance into Asia was not without similarity to their British counterparts. For years since its founding in 1784, the Methodist Episcopal Church (MEC), a product of British and Irish Methodist missions among migrants in the American colonies, had always been regarded as a missionary church in light of its phenomenal advance along the eastern seaboard.[12] However, its missionary nature was significantly altered with the establishment of its very own Missionary Society (MSMEC) in 1819, which, as Russell Richey has convincingly argued, occasioned the MEC's shift from being 'less of a mission than a body having missions.'[13] The formation of the society, however, was unlike that of the Wesleyan Methodists, but only because it initially addressed domestic concerns, particularly the sending of missionaries among Native Americans and among the burgeoning migrant populations westward. Methodist migration to Liberia and Latin America, nevertheless, enlarged the range of the MSMEC in the 1830s from that of domestic to overseas endeavors.[14] By the time the MEC gained national prominence and influence in the 1840s, however, becoming the largest Protestant denomination in the country, it was well positioned for expansion beyond the Pacific Ocean. Reminiscent of its British predecessor, American Methodist ambitions in Asia seem to have heralded its rise from the fringe to important social status. On 4 September 1847, just three years after the bitter split between northern and southern episcopal Methodism, Judson D. Collins and Moses C. White (with his wife Jane Isabel Altwater), landed in Foochow (now Fuzhou), one of the five treaty ports in China.[15] China not only became the MEC's passageway to East Asia, but also provided ample experience for the denomination that helped prepare its entry into Japan in 1873, and neighboring Korea in 1885. In addition to East Asia, American Methodists also set their sights on South Asia. On 25 September 1856, barely forty years after James Lynch landed in Negapatnam, Irish Methodist William Butler of the MEC's New England Conference and a former associate of Lynch in Ireland, landed in Calcutta with his wife Clementina Rowe Butler, and two of their children.[16] From India, American Methodists eventually inched their way to Lower Burma in 1873, Pakistan in 1879, Singapore and Malaysia in 1885, the Philippines in 1899, and Indonesia 1905.[17]

On the Coattails of Empire and Colonialism: Benefits, Paradox, and Disadvantages

While both British and American Methodist missions in Asia essentially emerged from an era of denominational growth and self-awareness, it cannot be denied that they came at a time when their respective governments had already muscled their way into the region. Given the differences between the two transatlantic Methodist branches that planted missions in Asia and the Pacific, it is safe to say that there is no single pattern that can be established to encompass the contours of interactions by these two 'Methodisms,' which were unique in their own right, with the variegated manifestations of empire and the resultant indigenous reaction to them from country to country. We can argue, though, that despite the complexities, such interaction can perhaps best be discerned by focusing mainly on the impact the different colonial settings had on the various Methodist mission projects in the region.

It is important to note that the formation of the WMS itself and the sending of its first delegation to Ceylon in 1813 followed the lifting of prohibitions to missionary activity by the British East India Company, the entity granted exclusive charter by the British crown to oversee trade in the East Indies.[18] British Methodist work in India, and, to a lesser degree, in China mainly capitalized on and benefited from strides made by these secular entities of the British Empire. By the time James Lynch arrived in South India in 1817, the East India Company, with its Indian conscripts or *sepoys*, had not only wrested control in most parts of the country (which by that time included Bangladesh and Pakistan) from local princes and European rivals, but also for a century secured key trading ports in the country such as Madras (now Chennai), Bombay (now Mumbai), and Calcutta (now Kolkata). It was in Madras, for example, where Methodism made its 'first advance.' It was there Lynch found a society of twelve 'serious persons' who had already read John Wesley's and John Fletcher's works apparently under the guidance of a Methodist soldier who was once stationed in the area.[19] Hence, the consequence of empire made it possible for Wesleyan missionaries to establish quickly a toehold among British and English-speaking Europeans already in the country.

A different dynamic, however, emerged in Australasia, most particularly in

New Zealand, where the official entrance of Methodist missions in 1821 coincided with a nascent European colonization which resulted in the increasing exploitation and dislocation of the existing Maori population. While WMS missionaries, with their CMS counterparts, protested colonial expansion and lobbied for Maori rights, they did little to question British hegemony in the island. The creation of the Treaty of Waitangi in 1840, which the missionaries helped to negotiate and draft seems to illustrate this paradox. Although the treaty, controversial to this day, guaranteed some degree of rights to the different Maori tribes, it effectively granted British sovereignty over their land.[20] Methodist missionaries in Asia and the Pacific, as the New Zealand mission demonstrated, were not ready to repudiate the empire which helped create for them the very milieu that enabled them to do their mission work in the first place, even though they fared far better than most of their compatriots as far as their relationships with indigenous populations were concerned. Simply put, their work provided an ethical and benevolent face to the imperial and colonial projects with which they came to cross paths.[21]

American Methodism's first forays into Asia cannot be separated from the fact that they also benefited from the ever-expanding grasp of the British crown and an emerging American commercial empire. We must remember that its arrival in China came just two years after the British East India Company-initiated first 'opium war' (1839–1842) and its consequent 'unequal treaties' of Nanking, which forced the largest East Asian nation to open five treaty ports to western trade and to cede Hong Kong to the British. The United States also forced the 'unequal' Treaty of Wanghia in 1844, which allowed the erection of American churches in the treaty ports. In consequence, it was no accident that three years later, the MEC, partly as a result of increasing requests by American Methodists, sent its first missionaries to Foochow, one of the treaty ports, as the base to establish their work in the country. Escalating antiforeigner feeling occasioned by the lopsided policies forced upon China, in addition to a host of other factors, made MEC's work during its early years in the country extremely difficult. Missionary reliance on American consuls did not help, but created further resentment which took the form of violent persecution of both missionaries and their converts.[22] It was only ten years later (1857) that the MEC baptized Ting Ang, its first Chinese convert, at the Iongtau Street Chapel which is located just outside the Foochow city walls. In 1877 after three painstaking decades, its Foochow annual conference was established.[23]

American Methodism was slow, however, to follow its government's first commercial imperialist venture in the region, namely on the island nation of Japan. Methodists did not immediately seize the opportunities created by 'unequal' treaties agreed upon by the once isolationist nation under the duress of United States' gunboat diplomacy, despite the missionary zeal it generated among Methodists back home. It was, however, not until 1 June 1873, twenty years after Commodore Matthew C. Perry's arrival, that MEC missionary and former China mission superintendent Robert S. Maclay arrived in Yokohama. His arrival coincided with the easing of official prohibitions of Christianity and increasing Japanese receptivity to western ways – in stark contrast to the antiforeign resentment he and his former colleagues encountered in China. Such conditions allowed Methodism to produce its first Japanese converts just a year after Maclay's arrival.[24]

In Korea, the dynamic was much different, however, since it was the Japanese navy that scored the first 'unequal' treaty with the East Asian nation in 1876 and forced it out of isolation. The Americans soon negotiated their own treaty in Chemulpo in 1882 which accorded the United States a 'most favored nation' status and allowed for Korean migration to the United States. Since the United States declared neutrality concerning religious affairs in the country, American missionaries, unlike in China, could not ask for protection from the United States legation. Thus, the MEC was left to adopt what Wade Barclay has called an 'indirect missionary approach' policy through education and medical work by its missionaries Dr. William B. Scranton, his mother Mary F. Scranton of the Woman's Foreign Missionary Society (WFMS), and Henry G. Appenzeller in 1885. Despite restrictions, especially to public preaching, and barriers brought about by language and culture, the confidence-building measures employed by the mission quickly assisted them to gain solid ground. After only more than a year, the mission was able to report more than a hundred adherents. Methodist Episcopal Church, South missionaries adopted a similar strategy after their arrival in 1896.[25]

The Philippines also deserves mention. It was the only country in Asia annexed by the United States. MEC work in the Philippines began with the arrival of Bishop James M. Thoburn in Manila on 28 February 1899, just five months after the Treaty of Paris, which essentially transferred Philippine sovereignty from Spain to the United States.[26] Although Thoburn intended to grow MEC work in the Philippines initially around American soldiers and expatriates who were already in the country, Filipinos entered the picture much earlier than he anticipated. Since Spanish Roman Catholic hegemony had been disestablished by the new political regime, there were hundreds of Filipinos, angered by years of friar injustice and meddling in the socio-political life of the country, who found disestablishment a positive development. Hence, among them, there were those who were eager to exercise their newly found religious freedom. Hence, when Thoburn returned exactly a year later, more than six hundred Filipinos had already adopted Methodism – and this happened even before the first regular MEC and WFMS missionaries arrived. Although Philippine Methodism would experience unparalleled growth in its early years, it carried with it the stigma of American imperialism, not enhanced by the lack of missionary support for Philippine independence, an issue which also caused dissension within Methodist ranks and probably slowed its progress in later years.[27]

Agents of 'Civilization' and Social Change

After discussing the origins of Methodism in Asia and the Pacific in the first two sections, we can explore its development. This development is related to identifying missions as an agent of 'civilization.' This pattern seems to be significant with most Methodist missionaries who went to the region as they wittingly or unwittingly carried with them what they strongly believed to be 'blessings' of western society to supplement their chief objective of bringing the gospel unto the ends of the earth. For years, medical and educational work were the tools of choice by Methodists to reach the masses. Medical work, according to William Scranton of the MEC Korean mission, was an implement 'for plowing up prejudices, and opening a custom-ridden country' so that the 'the preacher will find a ready soil.' He added that the school, 'is our harrow to smooth and dress the ground.'[28] While missionaries saw them as measures to lead people to Christ, Methodist medical and educational work also planted seeds for social transformation in the communities they served.

When Coke's party of newly appointed WMS missionaries landed in Ceylon in June 1814, they came not only to propagate the Methodist brand of Christianity, with its own set of values and spiritual culture, but also to engage in educational work. This first came to fruition in 1817 through the founding of the Jaffna English School located in the central district of Jaffna in northern Ceylon. In 1832, Peter Percival, who was known for his work on the Tamil version of the Bible, renamed the school the Jaffna Central School (now, Jaffna Central College). Six years later, the mission operated a total of seventy-seven schools, including several girls' schools, throughout the country. Methodist colleges of repute would later emerge in southern Ceylon, namely, Wesley College in Colombo (1874), Richmond College in Galle (1876), and Kingswood College in Kandy (1891).[29] Similar educational pursuits also accompanied Wesleyan Methodist missions in South India, which, by 1832 had begun to focus greater attention on the lower caste Hindu population rather than conveniently cater to an existing English-speaking Protestant European constituency and higher caste Brahmins.[30]

Another effective WMS instrument in South India was medical work, which was mostly undertaken by the Women's Auxiliary (WA) of the WMS in the 1880s and carried what Dana Robert would call the missiological concept of 'Woman's Work for Woman.' Because of the seclusion of females in some Asian cultures like India, the healing ministry of the WA allowed Indian women to be treated by female health practitioners and their associates, since women could be turned away from other hospitals because of age-old gender discrimination, and because women themselves were unwilling to be treated by males. By the 1920s, the WA operated nine hospitals in the Madras, Hyderabad, and Mysore Districts, and twelve dispensaries in south India.[31] It must be remembered, however, that WA medical work in India was preceded and may well have been inspired by the groundbreaking medical and education work of WFMS missionary Clara A. Swain in north India, about which more will be said later.

A similar pattern can also be found among American Methodists. By the time American Methodists sent their first missionaries to China, both educational and medical missions had been tried and tested by their British counterparts and other American Protestant mission boards who had been sending missionaries to overseas fields before the Methodists. Therefore, when Judson D. Collins, and Moses C. White and his wife arrived in Foochow on 30 September 1847, even though there were no MEC precedents by which to be guided in the mission to China, it was apparent that the mission board expected them to employ mission strategies which had proven successful in other places. Accordingly, the board instructed them to engage in medical and educational work. In fact, White was chosen because he had some medical training in the United States. Soon after the missionaries' arrival, White, an Oneida, New York native, began visiting sick, and after five months opened a dispensary where he received patients and dispensed medicines without cost.[32] White established a blueprint for American Methodist mission that would not only be replicated by a long line of MEC and WFMS medical missionaries who would later arrive in China, but would also be utilized in other stations throughout Asia. Medical work did plow the ground, to use Scranton's analogy, in China as it enabled the MEC mission to gain entry to other locations, for example Tientsin (now Tianjin), which is located south of Peking (now Beijing). WFMS medical missionary Leona Howard developed such a close friendship with one of her patients, Lady Li Hung-Chang, the wife of the Viceroy of Tientsin, that it opened that large city to MEC work in a manner 'such as never occurred before in China,' her superintendent wrote.[33] In addition to aiding the expansion of its ministry, MEC medical work also provided medical training among indigenous women to enable them to engage in 'Woman's Work for Woman.' On 1 March 1870, Clara Swain began training women in Bareilly, north India – sixteen orphanage girls and three women attended – to staff what would later become the Woman's Hospital and Medical School (now Clara Swain Hospital).[34] It is not exaggerating to say that the medical ministry of Methodist women missionaries, as their concern for Indian women's health and for medical training illustrates, contributed to women's empowerment and advocacy for women's rights in the region.

As far as educational work was concerned the MEC's China mission provides a good starting point as well. As White directed his efforts to the ministry of healing, Judson D. Collins, superintended educational work. He hired a Chinese teacher, and on 28 February 1848 opened a school for boys in a room next to the missionaries' home. Eight boys came on the first day in what could well be the MEC's first school in Asia. The daily regimen included reading the Lord's Prayer in the vernacular, memorizing Chinese classics in the morning, and Christian books in the afternoon.[35] Such humble beginnings paved the way for hundreds of day schools for boys and girls as MEC work spread from Foochow to other parts of China. From these schools would emerge great institutions of learning such as Nanking University, founded in 1889, which merged with other schools to form what is today Nanjing University.[36] We must also note that the China day schools not only brought free education to the poor, but also affected changes in Chinese society. For example, the refusal of WFMS missionary Anna B. Sears, principal of the girls' boarding school in Peking, to admit girls with bound feet was influential. It was said that even parents from rural districts abandoned the age-old practice to prepare their daughters for the highly regarded school.[37] Without a doubt, Methodist educational work not only validated the underprivileged's right to education, but also showed that Methodists were serious about enlarging the sphere of women and mitigating the oppressive practices against them. Other institutions of learning in the region which were established by Methodists to bear testimony to the same spirit of empowering women included Lucknow Woman's College (now Isabella Thoburn College), founded by WFMS pioneer Isabella Thoburn in Lucknow, India (1886),[38] and Ehwa Hakdang or 'Pear Flower School' (now Ehwa Women's University) organized by Mary F. Scranton in Seoul, South Korea.[39]

Heart Religion: Holiness Revivalism and the Struggle against Nominal Christianity

Although we have demonstrated that Methodism in Asia and the Pacific developed as a social religion through educational and medical work, it emphasized the same heart religion which not only endeared it to its followers, but also set it apart from other Protestants in its original countries. We must remember that Methodism itself was a reaction to the 'nominal' Christianity or Anglicanism of Wesley's day and that Methodist societies were designed to make 'real Christians' out of those who desired to 'flee from the wrath to come.'[40] Wesley's soteriology extends the Protestant Reformation's call for justification with a postconversion experience of holiness or sanctification that he qualified as either instantaneous or as a process. Consequently, Methodists for decades emphasized an experience of holiness, or at least set higher moral standards as benchmarks for true conversion. This quest for real Christianity was also accompanied by Methodist enthusiasm expressed through noisy and emotionally charged revivals which ritualized conversion and sought the entrance of the already-Christians into a higher plane of Christian experience. The appeal of heart revivalism was not lost among Methodists for years and contributed to its vibrancy and growth in the British Isles and on the American frontier where it was often highlighted in camp meetings. By the time Methodists launched into Asia and the Pacific, it was natural that they carried the revivalistic paradigm with them. But how did heart religion with its overarching concern for Christian experience and moral quality find application in the mission field where nominal Christianity or the need for revival seemed not yet ready to exist in the first place?[41]

First, it would be helpful to note that holiness experience helped encourage Methodist missionary volunteerism in both sides of the Atlantic. By the time British and American Methodists began sending missionaries to Asia, Wesley's teaching on entire sanctification or the 'second blessing' still persisted as the ultimate objective for most Methodists on both sides of the Atlantic. For example, John Hunt, future WMS missionary to Fiji, yearned to attain the experience in 1836 while studying at the Wesleyan Theological Institution in Hoxton, London. He was eventually 'cleansed from all sin' when a revival broke out at the institution about a month later. Hunt later carried the same emphasis in his work in Fiji by seeking the conversion of Fijians to Christianity, 'not in name, but in power.'[42] For American Methodists, the quest for Methodism's *grand depositum* had already taken a more concerted phase with the rise of the Holiness movement, a movement which reemphasized Wesley's doctrine of sanctification. Efforts by holiness revivalists to articulate the doctrine throughout the nineteenth century, nevertheless, was modified and later Pentecostalized into expressions like 'baptism of the Holy Spirit' and 'Spirit-filled life' and a gamut of other associated terms mostly inspired by the non-perfectionist Keswick holiness movement, a Reformed offshoot of the Wesleyan Holiness movement.[43] Holiness revivalism eventually intersected with the Methodist missionary impulse. Dana L. Robert has convincingly argued that holiness revivalism was the fuel that enabled WFMS missionaries to volunteer and engage in mission work. It was, in fact, through ubiquitous holiness revival rituals woven into the annual WFMS branch or district gatherings that a number of women who testified to experiencing the 'second blessing' also consecrated their lives for missionary service. Some 'sanctified' WFMS missionaries 'disseminated holiness concerns on the mission field into the 1920s, if not longer.'[44] The role of the Holiness movement was further supplemented by the Holiness/Pentecostal campus revivalism of the Student Volunteer Movement (SVM) in the recruitment of Methodist college students for later appointment by Methodist mission boards.[45] A perusal of the SVM's statistics from 1906 to 1913 reveal that thirty percent of the more than 17,000 men and women who signed SVM pledge cards and sailed to Asian fields were North American and Canadian Methodists – the largest number was in 1910 with almost half the total (seventy-five out of one hundred sixty) claiming Methodist allegiance.[46]

Secondly, holiness revivals found ready application in colonial settings where there was already an existing English-speaking population. A good example was the MEC work in India which benefited from the work of the famed MEC evangelist William Taylor who came at the invitation of James M. Thoburn. Upon his arrival in 1870, Taylor began unprecedented revival campaigns initially within the MEC mission areas of north India, and then southward to the provinces beyond the famed Ganges River, albeit to the utter disregard of existing comity agreements and much to the embarrassment of the MECMS.[47] Not surprisingly, Taylor's holiness revivalism, which specialized in the conversion of the 'already-converted,' largely found success among European and British 'nominal Christians,' mostly Anglicans who would later form the bulk of MEC membership in what was to become the South India Conference in 1876.[48] Another example was the Philippines where the MEC mission's revival work in its early years was largely directed among American soldiers to address the growing vice and immorality among them which had been a cause of embarrassment.[49] For this special work, Bishop Thoburn assigned a Woman's Christian Temperance Union evangelist, WFMS missionary Cornelia C. Moots of Bay City, Michigan. Moots' holiness and Pentecost-themed revivalism in Manila resulted in a number of successful 'conversions' among the already-Christian 'soldier boys.'[50]

Finally, holiness revivalism found further application as antidote to the lack of zeal among indigenous Asian and Pacific Methodists, mostly those who were previously baptized *en masse* through 'mass movement' evangelization after their chiefs or leaders embraced Christianity. This was the premise behind the 'Tongan Pentecost,' for example, which began through the preaching of Tongan Methodist preacher 'Aisea Vovole in 'Utui on 23 July 1834 and resulted not only in spontaneous confessions and bitter cries for mercy, but also in the 'baptism of the Holy Spirit' of about a thousand Tongans in the island chain of Vava'u, including King Tafau'ahau (George Topou I) and Queen Lupepau'u. While the revival was largely made possible by indigenous efforts, it is interesting to note that it also came as an answer to the earnest prayers of WMS missionaries in the islands for an 'outpouring of the Holy Ghost' to address the lack of real Christianity among their Tongan converts.[51] Similarly, when John Hunt began preaching holiness in Viwa, Fiji in 1845, a revival broke out among many converts who in Hunt's words had been previously 'careless and useless.' Spontaneous emotional outbursts and physical manifestations accompanied the revival so that business in the island was suspended for several days.[52]

In India, the MEC also saw phenomenal growth through its successful mass movements among the *dalits* or lower caste groups, made possible by the conversion of village caste leaders.⁵³ The lack of true conversion among these groups had always raised concerns.⁵⁴ This was, however, checked by the prevalence of holiness revival culture in the warp and woof of MEC life in India. In fact, the denomination had designated a number of camp meeting sites or Christian *melas*, as they commonly called them in India, for the promotion of holiness, and hosted annually the interdenominational *Dasehra* gathering in Lucknow – the flagship of holiness promotion in north India among missionaries, indigenous workers, and converts seeking revival.⁵⁵ In 1905, the mission experienced a 'Jubilee Revival' which began among Bengali girls and boys in Asansol in north India and accompanied by speaking in tongues. This was an outgrowth of the Great Indian Revival of 1905–1907 which first occurred in Khassia Hills, Assam Province, and later at Pandita Ramabai's Mukti mission in Kedgaon.⁵⁶

In the Philippines, a similar mass movement of people shifting their allegiance from the 'Romish Church' to Methodism made missionaries uneasy about the lack of membership commitment that accompanied it. One missionary, for instance, even complained in 1901 that 'the social life of the convert is beset with difficulties. Smoking is a universal habit. Women, men, and children all smoke,' and that one affluent member continued to maintain his cockfighting business. Similar observations compelled the mission to shift from its anti-Roman Catholic emphasis to fight against sin and immorality, and launched a holiness and Pentecostal revival culture which lasted for decades, thereby making the MEC the most revivalistic Protestant denomination in the country.⁵⁷ Methodism's quest for real Christianity and its consequent holiness and Holy Spirit-themed revivalism would also take place in other Methodist Asian fields. It would also figure prominently within both the MEC and MECS mission in Korea through the interdenominational 'Korean Revival' in Pyongyang in 1907,⁵⁸ and the MEC mission during the 'Hinghwa Pentecost' in Hinghwa (now Putian) and in Fookien (now Fujian), China in 1909–1913. It was during the revival that the young John Sung was converted. Later to become the evangelist of the Hinghwa Conference of the Methodist Church in China, Sung led spectacular Pentecostal type revivals in China, and among the Chinese diaspora in Taiwan and Southeast Asia in the 1930s.⁵⁹

Summary and Conclusion

Methodism in Asia and the Pacific emerged as a consequence of Methodist denominational self-awareness or its shift from being a 'national mission' to becoming a 'church.' Its presence in the two regions, without a doubt, not only helped herald Methodism's rise from the fringe to higher social status, but also demonstrated that, like other denominations, it too was capable of organizing for missions and sending resources to distant lands. But we also noted that the rise of Methodist identity and pride and its resultant missionary zeal to reach Asians and Pacific islanders also coincided with the expanding grasp of the British Empire and the nascent commercial imperialism of the United States. We have demonstrated, nonetheless, that Methodism's relationship with both empire and colonialism is fraught with paradox, complex and varied from country to country and hence, simply to indict it as generally guilty of conspiring with British and American imperialism would be difficult, if not inaccurate.

Despite the uniqueness of varied Asian and Pacific settings, Methodism nevertheless, developed in a manner that generally still reflected the main motifs of Methodist development in its country of origin. The social implications of educational and medical work, while qualifying as 'civilizing' tools that may have wittingly or unwittingly brought an ethical and benevolent face to the colonialist and imperialist projects of western powers, also helped present Methodism as a social religion – a religion that concerned itself not only to benefit the underprivileged, but also to empower the helpless. Asian and Pacific Methodists have faithfully carried and expanded this legacy as part of their identity as evidenced by the persistence of medical and educational institutions originally established by missionaries. These institutions continue to stand as living testaments of Asian and Pacific Methodism's role in nation building and social change.

While it is true that Asian and Pacific Methodism developed as a social religion, we would be doing a disservice by not acknowledging that it also, as it was in the development of British and American Methodism, developed a religion of the heart identity. It remained faithful to Wesley's original intent of a Methodism that was vibrant and that was continually at odds with nominal Christianity. As we have demonstrated, Methodist heart religion and the holiness revivalism that accompanied it did find a place in the two regions, although it may, at first glance, appear not to have a place in non-Christian settings. First, holiness revivalism with its emphasis on spiritual empowerment was essential to Methodist missionary recruitment on both sides of the Atlantic and, therefore, it would not be implausible to see why missionaries expected to promote them in the field. Second, the consequence of empire and colonialism also prepared a ready English-speaking audience for Methodist revival work. It was usually among European or American 'nominal Christians' that Methodism was able to establish its first congregations, most specifically in occupied lands. Finally, the nature of mass movement conversions in the field did create a perceived nominal Christianity backdrop, which, consequently, necessitated vigorous holiness promotion among indigenous converts. Undeniably, periodic holiness revivals ingrained in the spiritual culture of Asian and Pacific Methodists helped ensure not only their vitality but also their growth through the years.

For Further Reading

Barclay, Wade Crawford. *Methodist Episcopal Church, 1845–1939: Widening Horizons, 1845–1895*. History of Methodist Missions. Vol. 3. New York: Board of Missions and Church Extension of the Methodist Church, 1957.

Copplestone, J. Tremayne. *Twentieth-Century Perspectives, the Methodist Episcopal Church, 1896–1939*. History of Methodist Missions. Vol. 4. New York: United Methodist Church, 1973.

Findlay, George G., and William W. Holdsworth. *The History of the Wesleyan Methodist Missionary Society*. 5 vols. London: Epworth Press, 1921–1925.

Goh, Robbie B. H. *Sparks of Grace: The Story of Methodism in Asia*. Singapore: Methodist Church in Singapore, 2003.

Hempton, David. *Methodism: Empire of the Spirit*. New Haven: Yale University Press, 2005.

Oconer, Luther J. 'The Culto Pentecostal Story: Holiness Revivalism and the Making of Philippine Methodist Identity, 1899–1965.' PhD diss., Drew University, 2009.

Robert, Dana L. *American Women in Mission: A Social History of Their Thought and Practice*. The Modern Mission Era, 1792–1992. Macon, GA: Mercer University Press, 1996.

Walls, Andrew F. 'Methodists, Missions and Pacific Christianity: A New Chapter in Christian History' in Peter Lineham, ed. *Weaving the Unfinished Mats: Wesley's Legacy-Conflict, Confusion and Challenge in the South Pacific*, 9–32. Auckland, New Zealand: Wesley Historical Society, 2007.

Wood, Alfred H. *Overseas Mission of the Australian Methodist Church*. Vol. 1. Melbourne: Aldersgate Press, 1975.

10 Methodism in Northern and Continental Europe[1]

Ulrike Schuler

It is challenging to focus on Christianity in Europe, especially Methodism, because the continent is enormously diverse. Although it is the world's second smallest continent[2] with a population density of about 700,000,000 in a relatively small area, Europe includes forty-eight nations, twenty-three official languages, more than a hundred spoken languages, and innumerable dialects. The geographic area called 'Europe' has changed over the centuries and is not clearly defined. To the north and west Europe is bordered by the Arctic and North Atlantic Oceans, and to the south the Mediterranean Sea. To the east there is no clear natural division from the continental mass of Asia – though the Ural Mountains are often cited.

Over the past two centuries, the time period addressed in this chapter, national boundaries within Europe have changed because of war or political circumstances. Even the names of several nations have been altered. An example in the recent past is the fall of the Soviet Union in 1991. Whole books could be written about specific European countries, each with specific historical, social, political, economic, and religious developments. Currently, 'Europe' is considered the coalescence of those states that identify themselves in the historical and cultural traditions rooted in Greece and Rome.

Europe occupies a prominent place in the western world since it is usually considered the birthplace of western culture. Its influence has extended to other continents through colonialism, the slave trade, Christian missions, and other forces. Europe has also played an important role in the history of the Christian church – its organization, theology, and doctrine. The three basic traditions of Christianity – Roman Catholic, Eastern Orthodox, and Protestant – were born and developed in the geographic and cultural boundaries of Europe. The strong awareness that in God's world order the coherence of a commonwealth can only be thought and guaranteed in its religious unity led to the social model of the 'Corpus Christianum' which was adamantly defended for centuries. This forced a long tradition of interplay of church and state fighting for dominance in the West while in the Eastern Orthodox hemisphere a hierarchical form of government, the so-called 'Caesaropapism,' with a clear understanding of the church's subsidiary role was instituted. Those established relationships were significant when – following the Enlightenment – the demands for a separation of church and state increasingly took shape in European countries. The call for the abolition of established churches as well as freedom of faith, conscience, and creed led in the nineteenth and twentieth centuries to a variety of constitutional systems in European countries. For example, France and Portugal have a complete separation of state and church (laicism). Germany, Italy, and Spain have a kind of partnership or cooperation in public affairs with a system of agreements with churches (a concordat with the Roman Catholic Church or with Protestant churches). A 'unity system' where the head of state is also the head of the church, exists in Norway, Denmark, and England (up to the year 2000 that was also the case with Sweden). Separation of church and state has also led to the suppression of religious practice. The strongest of that type was realized in Albania where from 1968 to 1990 state atheism was in effect.

Europe was not only the scene of major Christian expansion, but also witnessed some of history's most brutal religious persecutions. These include medieval Inquisition, Protestant campaigns against the Anabaptists during the Reformation era, anti-Semitism of the pogroms, and Christian complicity in the Holocaust. All these resonate in Europeans' thinking and acting.

A number of developments were exceptionally important for the unfolding of Christianity in more recent centuries. Among the most significant were the Enlightenment, the Industrial Revolution, two world wars followed by the Cold War (and Iron Curtain), the fall of the Soviet empire, and the creation of the European Union. Each of them left its mark on the Christian faith and European churches including Methodism. An important development for the churches is the influence of the confessional 'mixture'[3] that arose mainly after World War II and forced the churches to become more knowledgeable about each other and gave rise to a growing ecumenicity.

When the Soviet Union collapsed, a number of middle and eastern European countries became independent.[4] From the 1990s on all of them became members of the European Union,[5] a cooperative of sovereign nations committed to freedom, security, participatory democracy, justice, and solidarity. Europe is now in the early stages of growing together and recognizing that its religious identity is defined by three lines of tradition: Greek-Roman antiquity, the Jewish-Christian tradition with a Latin and Orthodox imprint, and the Enlightenment. In the light of all those different aspects[6] as the context we turn to Methodist missions that brought Christianity in a transformed form back to the 'cradle of the Reformation' – trying to support renewal and reform, and dedicated to continuing the reformation which Pietism advocated.

Methodist Missions to European Countries[7]

The beginning of Methodism's influence on old traditional Europe extends from the late eighteenth century to the middle of the nineteenth century. During that period Methodist missions must be recognized in the light of renewal movements that influenced different parts of Europe as a late extension of Pietism, followed by revivalism, the Holiness Movement, and Pentecostalism.

General Description of Methodist Missions to Europe

Methodism in Europe began with people sharing stories of faith with each other. Migrants, sailors, soldiers, travellers, and others who had been touched by Methodist people on their journeys outside of Europe, primarily to Great Britain and the USA, and who had been transformed by the Methodist message, eagerly talked about the gospel which revolutionized their lives. As others were drawn by this faith-sharing, small informal Methodist gatherings were sometimes formed. The official beginning of a mission among those interested, by a Methodist mission board or conference followed much later, sometimes several decades later. Often the local people supported small Methodist gatherings until denominational officials offered formal support and supervised further organization.

Methodist missions to Europe were also linked to migration. People immigrated to Great Britain and the USA for a variety of reasons. They came into contact with Methodists in those countries, were converted, and reported this back home (or in some cases actually took their newly found faith back to their native lands). Recognizing the potential of church growth among European immigrants, Methodists in the USA organized foreign language annual conferences. These annual conferences were an important factor in the spread of Methodism in Europe by initiating missions, providing financial support, and nurturing personal contacts with family and friends 'back home.' For decades there developed communication between European Methodists in Britain and the USA and those in their home countries through European-language books, periodicals, letters and personal contacts. At first the main concern of Methodist missions was to support the renewal of the established Protestant state churches in Europe.[8]

Where the Orthodox Church was strong in Europe the situation was very different. In Bulgaria, for example, the Ottoman Sultan officially sanctioned an autonomous Bulgarian Orthodox Church in 1849. He also invited other confessions for ministry.[9] While Methodism's first expressed mission effort (1857) was to enliven the Orthodox Church, the (Islamic) government's motivation was much more to destabilize the Orthodox Church as well as to provide for

Christian plurality.[10] That situation provoked strong Orthodox resistance that precluded the idea of cooperation with other churches. In areas where Orthodox churches were strong it was difficult to extend the Methodist mission and to establish its brand of Protestantism as 'genuine Christianity.'

Different still were missions to countries where Roman Catholicism was dominant. In those countries Methodism encountered strong and aggressive opposition in its attempt to break the Catholic stronghold[11] and to bring the Reformation to completion.

Numerically the greatest success of Methodist mission occurred in the German-speaking countries and Scandinavia.[12] Yet, Methodist congregations were organized all over Europe. Typically, the organizational strategy included forming classes, Sunday schools, translating and publishing a Methodist hymnbook and Discipline, and establishing a periodical.[13] Later, in some places a publishing house[14] was founded, a training center for circuit preachers instituted,[15] and deaconess 'mother houses' created.[16] Nursing care facilities, hospitals, children's schools, and other social institutions followed.[17]

The Methodist objective was to spread social holiness across the continent and within this mandate Methodist missions deliberately supported the very poor in rural and urban areas with educational and other social service ministries. Those missions were extremely expensive. The need for financial support of these missions existed for decades – often up to the present.

The policy of British Methodists was to delay the initiation of more mission projects than they were able to support financially. Their mission philosophy also included departing from a mission-field as soon as it could become fully autonomous which was often possible with the cooperation of other denominations. Financial support of its European missions supported by Methodists in the USA was generally significant not only from congregational giving, but sometimes through the large generous gifts of individuals. It was not rare, however, for mission projects to be abruptly abandoned because of financial exigency. Such situations caused deep disappointment to those who were involved in these ministries and those who benefitted from them. They nurtured a sense of abandonment.

United States Methodism organizationally created an international connectional structure by integrating mission-fields while giving them increasing administrative and financial accountability. Typically, a 'Mission Conference' was formed. If the work developed to become approximately twenty-five ordained ministers (the benchmark was boosted to thirty-five in the twentieth century) the mission conference became an 'Annual Conference' with the same responsibilities (rights and duties) as annual conferences in the USA. They also instituted an intermediate step, a 'Provisional Conference,' (minimum ten ordained ministers) for those locations where a mission conference was not possible.[18]

Responding to its international expansion and a growing self-understanding as an international church,[19] and counteracting world-wide national tendencies aiming for autonomy at the turn of the nineteenth to the twentieth century,[20] 'Central Conferences' were created beyond the USA in 1884 by the MEC general conference. Central conferences today perform basically the same functions as the UMC's jurisdictional conferences. Delegates elected by annual conferences normally gather every four years to elect bishops, choose persons to serve on denominational boards and agencies, and conduct other routine business. After appropriate meetings and discussion,[21] a European Central Conference of the Methodist Episcopal Church (MEC) was founded in 1911.[22] Nine years later the 1920 general conference decided to divide the European Central Conference into three. As result of political circumstances and the UMC union in 1968 the country composition of the European Central Conferences changed several times.[23] The current three central conferences in Europe are: the Northern Europe and Eurasia Central Conference, the Central and Southern Europe Central Conference, and the Germany Central Conference.[24]

The Evangelical Association (EA)[25] had a similar structural arrangement: In 1922 a Central Conference for Europe was organized. It included all the EA's European missions in Germany and Switzerland, dividing it into three annual conferences: North-German, South-German, and Switzerland.[26]

Overview of Anglo-American Methodist Missions to Europe

British Methodist Missions[27]

The chronological beginning of Wesleyan Methodist (WM) mission from Great Britain to Europe originated and developed as follows: (* = catholic territories; first date, beginning by a lay person; date in parentheses, responsibility for the mission adopted by a mission society).

Gibraltar*	1769	*British soldiers*	(1808)
France*	1790/1791	*tradesman*	(1818)
Belgium*		*British soldier/lay preacher*	(1816)
Spain*	ca. 1825	*missionary from Gibraltar/propagating the Bible*	(1854/1868)
Sweden	1809	*manufacturer*	(1826)
Germany	1830	*returning emigrant*	(1859)
Switzerland	1840	*Minister from Great Britain, having begun in France (=> French-speaking Switzerland)*	
Austria*	1870	*preacher from Germany*	
Italy*	1861	*converted catholic priest*	(1861)
Portugal*		*lay person*	(1871)

Methodism in Northern and Continental Europe

Methodism's spread from Great Britain to the European continent was very simple in its beginnings; it was connected to individuals and their Christian experience. Sometimes the work initiated by individuals faded away when there were no successors to carry on mission work. Because of Methodism's self-understanding as a renewal movement within the Anglican Church John Wesley did not encourage missions abroad. Extensive mission work was mainly organized by others, Thomas Coke being the early leader in this endeavor.

In the first half of the nineteenth century Wesleyan Methodism as a reform movement within the Anglican Church changed and Methodism was increasingly turned out. That also influenced the approach to missions abroad which, especially in Protestant areas, was considered extremely inappropriate with overtones of proselytism. At the same time an anti-Catholic disposition grew among WMs which encouraged them to consider mission to Catholic areas.[28] British Wesleyan Methodists were sceptical about evangelizing in Protestant regions, but repeated requests to send a Methodist preacher for a growing mission work started by a lay person forced them to argue for this work as a springboard into traditional Catholic territories.[29]

An example of this is the start of the WM mission to Germany in 1830 by Christoph Gottlob Müller,[30] a butcher and German immigrant who was converted in a Methodist congregation in London. After a long correspondence with relatives and friends in his hometown of Winnenden in Wuerttemberg he went back as a lay preacher, spoke in pietistic meetings and founded classes.[31] He repeatedly asked the WM mission society for support. Modest annual funding was finally approved by the society after considerable correspondence. After Müller's death in 1858, the mission board sent an official superintendent, John Lyth.[32] In 1863 Lyth published the periodical *Der Sonntagsgast*, a hymnal (*Die Zionsharfe*), and a Sunday school song book. Also in 1863 the first chapel was built in Prevorst. Lyth trained the first German Methodist ministers and campaigned for religious freedom against Lutheran restrictions. Not until the arrival of Lyth's successor, John Cook Barratt,[33] was a Methodist society formally organized in 1865. Under Barratt's leadership German Methodism began to grow. Classes were formed, Sunday schools founded, a *Discipline* and a periodical (*Methodist Herald*) published, a training center for preachers established in Waiblingen/Wuerttemberg,[34] and a deaconess facility (Martha-Maria-Verein Nürnberg) planted in Nürnberg/Bavaria in 1889. Barratt also applied for the status of an incorporated society (Verein) according to newly enacted laws in the Kingdom of Württemberg[35] and in Bavaria.[36]

As mentioned previously, the main WM strategy was to encourage the mission to become independent from the mission board as soon as possible for organizational and financial reasons. In 1897 the mission work of the WM in Germany and Austria was formally combined with the mission work of the MEC in Germany.[37] In other European countries WM mission work was also transferred into MEC missions. Transfer to the MEC also happened in 1852 with the France-Switzerland Conference, in 1898 with the mission among the Portuguese on Madeira, in 1900 with the French-speaking mission in Lausanne/Switzerland, and in 1946 in with the mission in Italy.

In other countries some Methodist societies founded by the British WMs became autonomous as in Belgium, Portugal, and Spain. Some went into a communion with other Protestant churches. In Belgium WMs went into the Eglise Protestante de Belgique in 1963, which after further unions with two Reformed churches became the Eglise Protestante Unie de Belgique in 1978. In Spain the WMs merged in 1955 with an existing union which had been founded in 1869, the Iglesia Evangélica Española. In Italy the United Methodists merged with the Waldensians in 1979 to form the Chiesa Evangelica Valdese.

Missions from the USA
In addition to what has already been said about the origin of Methodist beginnings in Europe being 'narrative,' it must be noted that the mission also arose out of a situation peculiar to the USA. In the nineteenth century there was extensive immigration to the North America from Europe[38] as people fled revolutions, wars, and pogroms.[39] Americans drew their own conclusions from the experiences of those immigrants. Revolution, many believed, meant opposing God's established order and showed the distance between the people and God, and the need to continue reforms that began with the Reformation. Church periodicals regularly outlined the main problems – the spiritual situation that followed the Enlightenment and the onset of liberal theology. Furthermore, letters were published from 'positive' ministers including the 'impromptu' by Johann Hinrich Wichern[40] concerning the need for home missions given the social circumstances created by the Industrial Revolution. All this information heightened the desire of American Methodists to support missions to the people of Europe, whether in the USA or on the continent.

Methodist Episcopal Church Missions
As a result of the large influx of immigrants arriving in the USA, domestic MEC missions were first initiated in their native languages.[41] These foreign language missions later played an important role when supporting mission work in the immigrants' native countries. There was thus a dynamic interdependence between home and foreign missions. This work was also substantially supported by the Women's Foreign Missionary Society, founded in 1869.

Mainly driven by the Scandinavian immigrants and of special importance is the *Bethel Ship* mission. It was located in the New York harbor, Brooklyn, Pier 11. The ship was appropriately named 'John Wesley.' The *Bethel Ship* mission functioned from 1845 to 1876.[42] It was heavily influenced by the Holiness movement (see below) and focused on immigrants who regularly arrived in the port and were in danger of being defrauded in their new homeland and forced into financial dependence after arrival by unscrupulous villains. In some cases that had already been perpetrated by those, including would-be employers who paid the immigrants' passage to the USA in exchange for cheap labor after their journey from Europe. Several converted at the *Bethel Ship* mission – mainly sailors – returned to Scandinavia and began to evangelize in Sweden, Denmark, Norway, and Finland. From Finland this evangelism spread to Russia.

The Swedish missionary Olaf Gustaf Hedstrøm[43] supervised the evangelical and social service work of the *Bethel Ship* mission. He was a pioneer of the Scandinavian mission in the USA as well as in Sweden where he effectively preached on a visit in 1863. He also assisted the Norwegian sailor Ole Peter Petersen[44] to find Christ and to be led into the ministry. Peterson became the pioneer missionary to Norway as well as a minister to Norwegian immigrants in the USA.

The founder of Methodism in Denmark was Christian Willerup,[45] a Dane who had emigrated to the USA, converted, and was ordained in the MEC in 1850. He served for a short time at the *Bethel Ship* where he met Ole Peter Petersen and Olaf Gustaf Hedström. After having had an appointment in Cambridge, Wisconsin, Willerup was appointed superintendent for all ministries in the Scandinavian countries (Norway, Sweden, and Denmark[46]). He and his family arrived in Copenhagen in 1856 and stayed there briefly. He was later sent by the mission board to support Ole Peter Peterson in Norway. Willerup lived and worked in Norway for two years during which three congregations were founded. In 1858 he returned to Copenhagen, Denmark, where he held the first Methodist service. A congregation was founded there in 1859.[47]

The counterpart to the *Bethel Ship* mission was the German mission which strategically began in Bremen in 1849.[48] Bremen was the chief port of embarkation to the USA. It was also one of the few cities in Germany that possessed a constitution guaranteeing full religious freedom. So, Bremen offered a unique opportunity to evangelize emigrants. Letters from Germany to American Methodists requesting support, articles in periodicals describing Methodist prospects in Germany, and a visit and report by the German-American Methodist leader Wilhelm Nast[49] in 1844 encouraged Methodist work among the Germans. After the German Revolution of 1848 and the launching of religious liberty[50] Ludwig Sigismund Jacoby[51] started mission work in Bremen in 1849 with the support of the German-speaking conference of the MEC and the denomination's mission board. Under his supervision the mission broadened rapidly and strategically. Jacoby founded the Traktathaus Bremen (publishing house) and published a periodical, *Der Evangelist*. In 1858 Jacoby established a seminary for Methodist ministers (Bremer Missionsanstalt) and became its director until 1868.

Before leaving Bremen for America some became Methodists as a result of the mission work in Germany. Others, such as Ernst Gottfried Mann,[52] instead of departing for the west, went back to spread the gospel as Methodist preachers in their homeland. Mann returned to the Palatinate, caused an awakening in that area and founded the 'Pirmasens and Alsace mission.' He became a circuit minister and was the first of the MEC appointed to Lausanne, Switzerland in 1856 after he had suffered persecution and punishment in Alsace for preaching despite official prohibition.[53] From Bremen, therefore, the MEC mission work expanded into other German areas.[54]

Independent of the Bremen mission, in another part of Germany, namely Thuringia and Saxony, a mission was started by the witness of a returning emigrant from the USA, Erhard Friedrich Wunderlich.[55] In 1865 this work was integrated into the MEC mission.

The following is a chronological the list of the MEC missions in the particular European countries.[56]

Sweden	1833	Converted sailors (Bethel Ship)	(1854)
Norway	1849	Sailors (Bethel Ship)	(1853)
Germany	1840	Correspondence of immigrants	(1849)
	1850	Returning emigrant (in Thuringia/ Saxony)	(1865)
Switzerland[57]	1856	Preachers from Germany	(1886)
Denmark	1857	Returning emigrant	(1858)
Bulgaria		Request off the American Board[58]	(1857)
Finland	1859/80	Laypersons (Bethel Ship)	(1880)
France/Alsace	1855/68	Contact to German speaking people in German-speaking Alsace	
Macedonia[59]	1867	American Board	(1921)
Italy*		Decision of the mission board	(1871)
		Decision of an Italian Annual Conference of the MEC in the USA to open a mission in Trieste (at that time Austria)	(1898)
Serbia[60]		Contact with German settlers in the South of Austria-Hungary (today North Serbia)	(1899)

Evangelical Association Missions
The largest immigrant population to the USA came from Germany. The two German-speaking denominations, the Evangelical Association (EA) and the Church of the United Brethren in Christ (UBC), had retained a strong German identity. The UBC opened several English-speaking annual conferences, but that was not normal for the EA in the USA which had only a few until after World War I.[61] Members of both denominations kept in touch with relatives and friends in Germany. Through these contacts and through their church periodicals Members were well informed about social, political, and religious developments in their homeland.[62]

The EA celebrated its fiftieth anniversary in 1850. Their denomination's general conference minutes and denominational periodical reported that the American members of the EA desired to express their thanks to their homeland and the land of Reformation. They thoughtfully considered all the information received regarding the situation in Germany as well as Wichern's well-known 'impromptu.' In 1850 major financial campaign was begun to send two missionaries to Germany.[63] As a result of the campaign, Conrad Link[64] was dispatched as the first official EA missionary to Germany. The mission joined with a class meeting organized by Sebastian Kurz,[65] a returning immigrant from the USA to Germany who wrote about his work in the periodical (*Evangelischer Botschafter*), and asked for EA support in 1846. The main mission goal of what followed was not the founding of a new church, but the support of orthodox theology, ministry, and renewal in Protestant churches which already existed. Those involved in the mission were clearly aware that theirs could only be a humble contribution to much needed wider mission work.[66] They joined with the mission taking place in those areas that already had strong pietistic development, that is, the kingdom of Württemberg which was mainly a rural area. Even so, the EA mission soon gained ground in cities.[67] By 1911 they had established congregations in twenty-eight of forty-one principal German cities.[68] The key features of the EA mission were evangelism, education and medical treatment (in a time when it was not compulsory for the state to provide medical care).

In 1865 after a long period of negotiation and chicanery by the state churches, an EA annual conference was organized under the direction of Bishop John J. Escher as Deutschland-Konferenz der Evangelischen Gemeinschaft. Nine preachers for Württemberg, Baden, and Switzerland were appointed. The mission work spread largely through personal connections with friends and family. It spread from Germany to Switzerland in 1866, to Alsace-Lorraine in 1868, and to East Prussia in 1895. From its churches in East Prussia, the EA began a mission to the German-speaking people in Latvia in 1911. All mission work in Europe was exclusively in German and conducted by German people; in that manner the EA mission differed from the mission philosophy of the MEC.

Listed here are the EA missions in Europe with chronological detail.

Germany		Letter connections of emigrants with relatives and friends	(1850)
Switzerland		Personal contacts between Germans and people in the German speaking-Switzerland	(1866)
Alsace-Lorraine[69]	1865	Personal contacts between Germans and people in Alsace-Lorraine; relatives	(1868)
East Prussia[70]		Personal connections, also from immigrants in the USA, expending to West-Prussia and Pomerania	(1895)
Latvia		Ministers from East-Prussia	(1911)

It should be mentioned that beginning with the initial meeting of the Ecumenical Methodist Conference in London in 1881 delegates of the MEC, EA, and WM also held regular meetings on their common work in Germany. Among other actions they agreed not to begin a mission in a German region if another Methodist church already had started mission work.[71]

Church of the United Brethren in Christ Mission
The UBC began a mission in Germany in 1869. Unlike other Methodist missions to Europe, the intention of the UBC general conference was to learn more about Germans because of shrinking German conferences in the USA.[72] There was also an expectation to enlist ministers in Germany for the German-speaking conferences in the USA. These expectations arose by observing the MEC and EA missions and the interdependence between their German-speaking home missions and missions abroad.

The UBC mission in Germany was opened by Christian Bischoff,[73] a former butcher, innkeeper, and cattle-dealer who emigrated to the USA, converted in the UBC, and was sent back to Germany as lay preacher. He started preaching in Naila, Franconia – a Catholic area without religious liberty. The mission extended north to Thuringia, Saxony, Pomerania, and Posen. The mission was not as prosperous as anticipated. Although a publishing house and book store was founded in Zeitz, the mission remained small and was finally integrated into the MEC's German mission in 1905.

Methodist Episcopal Church, South (MECS) Mission
World War I left an extraordinary amount of destruction in European countries which was only exceeded by that which remained after World War II.

The Methodist churches in the USA and Great Britain immediately started an impressive wide-ranging relief campaign.

The Episcopal Methodist churches (MEC and MECS) prepared to celebrate the centenary of their foreign mission work in 1919. The MEC's goal for this 'Centenary Movement' was to raise $40 million over five years to expand its mission outreach and to spend more than $3 million to enlarge mission work in Europe.[74] In consultation with the MEC, the MECS decided to help with reconstructing postwar Europe. They already supported European foreign-language annual conferences in the USA and had received requests for widening their missions in Europe. For example, Czech ministers and students urged them not to forget Bohemia and Moravia[75] which, they argued, was the cradle of Moravianism which led to John Wesley's conversion to living faith. Therefore, materially supporting that territory was a way of giving thanks for its contribution to Methodism's origin.[76]

As a part of the Centenary Movement, the MECS wanted to extend its current mission fields and open new missions. In cooperation with the MEC, which at that time had missions in seventeen European countries, both churches cooperatively sent a committee to Europe to study the social and religious situation. Upon the return of the MECS representatives, their denomination decided in 1920 to start missions in Poland,[77] Czechoslovakia,[78] and Belgium.[79]

With enormous effort mission work was initiated in Poland. A building with eight floors was constructed as a church center with a chapel, apartments, a flourishing language school, and a soup kitchen which daily served about 2,600 students and workers. A pharmacy and medical clinic was also established. Between 1922 and 1925 ten schools were opened as well as a Bible school.[80]

A similar initiative shaped the mission to Belgium beginning in 1922. Among the facilities built were an orphan house, a boarding school for girls, a headquarters building with book store and a Bible house, a center from which colporteurs could distribute Bibles and Christian literature, a hospital and nurse's training school, and a Bible school that also provided theological training for ministers.[81]

Help for the mission in Czechoslovakia was not as forthcoming as in Poland and Belgium. Nevertheless, the mission fed a hundred students daily. With the Red Cross social work among very poor children and refugees from Russia was undertaken. A successful tent evangelism was promoted. A publishing house distributed tracts among the population and a Bible school offered Bible study, theological education, and an English-language class.[82]

Those who energetically and financially initiated MECS missions found that their labors had to be curtailed or abandoned when the goals of the Centenary

Movement were not achieved and funds were lacking. Furthermore, the global economy crisis in the late 1920s exacerbated the problem. The same fate occurred to the projects that were enthusiastically started by the MEC.

After the union of the MEC, MECS, and Methodist Protestant Church in 1939, the MEC and MECS missions were more modestly continued by the Methodist Church (MC).

Turning Points in European Methodism in the Twentieth Century

Influence of the Holiness Movement

The Holiness movement that reached European shores and inland in the last quarter of the nineteenth century focussed on a central Methodist tenet, namely the holy life. This movement was critically viewed by the European churches of the Reformation who generally viewed holiness with scepticism. Furthermore, even in Methodist churches the Wesleyan holiness doctrine had lost theological stature at the time the Holiness movement evolved. Not until the Holiness movement was underway was holiness doctrine again recognized as a spiritually inspiring feature of Methodism. After a period of uncritically embracing holiness doctrine and of exaggerating the doctrine of Christian perfection, and an intense period of schismatic activity, Methodist churches on the whole chose to distance themselves from the Holiness movement and began to work on a rigorous, theologically based definition of scriptural 'justification, holiness and Christian perfection.'[83] Sympathic writings by supporters of the Holiness movement, for example, EA bishops William W. Orwig, and John J. Escher encouraged a new interpretation in the 1902 EA *Discipline*. There followed subsequent work by other writers and theologians.[84]

When the Methodist societies on the European continent are considered, the Holiness movement only seems to have affected Germany, Switzerland, and Scandinavia. When it appeared it was at first trans-confessional as a result of the Anglo-Saxon-German relationship as were the societies that were established at the same time (like the Evangelical Alliance).[85]

Looking at **Germany** and **Switzerland** there were different holiness society meetings involving Methodists in 1874–1875 under the leadership of Robert Pearsall Smith. Very clearly an increasingly ambivalent situation arose: Methodists were very well informed about the Holiness movement in the USA and England, following the reports that were published in periodicals in the USA and Germany. They were touched by it and naturally worked, in some cases leading to large revival-like gatherings. German Methodist minister and hymn writer Ernst Gebhardt with Robert Pearsall Smith became the musicians of large holiness assemblies. More and more conflicts arose from the criticism and suspicion by state church clergy. It is important to remember that at that time Methodism's legal situation was uncertain. As mentioned before, religious freedom was given in some German territories. In the 1870s MEC, EA, and WM made use of their rights, after the conflicts[86] with the state churches continued. In that tense situation there was considerable suspicion that Methodists sought to benefit from the dissolution of the state church by stabilizing and consolidating their own community from those initially raised by Lutheran ministers and congregations. In fact Methodists did express a hope of greater acceptance and recognition by representatives of the state church as the holiness emphasis became more accepted and they certainly hoped for missiological cooperation.

Based on overly enthusiastic and exaggerated reports of experiences of Christian perfection, and the recognizable schismatic impact of the Holiness movement (including the Pentecostal movements), Methodists in Germany increasingly dissociated themselves from the whole movement deliberately and distinctively. This was necessary because German Methodists were generally identified with the Holiness movement through their doctrines. However, they wanted to protect themselves and their important ministry from the criticism of Lutheran theologians and clergy. These combined efforts weakened a holistic understanding of 'holiness' including 'social holiness' in Germany.[87]

Methodist churches in the USA and **Scandinavia,** however, absorbed this holiness impulse. The mission in Scandinavia was directly affected by the holiness movement through the *Bethel Ship* mission.[88] During the following years there emerged a distinctive social work under the influence of the Holiness movement.

In **Denmark**, Methodists engaged in social holiness projects with problem drinkers using the model of the Methodist Central Halls in Great Britain which were centers for homeless, unemployed, and chronically poverty-stricken people. Dansk Methodists developed a comprehensive program of social work: treatment for alcoholism, a children's home for sick mothers and small children, a home for elderly and poor persons, provision for basic needs support such as food, clothes, shelter, and health care, an office for adoptions, an orphanage, and a holiday home in the country for boys and girls. There work also gave rise to a temperance movement that sought to influence secular society.

In **Norway** the Holiness movement influenced Methodism and the secular women's movement. Women argued for the right to preach and were successful in the campaign for the women's suffrage. Furthermore, Methodists advocated for religious tolerance, temperance, and religious education. Leaders of trade unions, temperance organizations, and the labor party were members of Methodist churches which leads us to remember the powerful social–political dedication at the beginnings of the Methodist movement.

In Norway a Pentecostal movement evolved inside the MEC guided by superintendent Thomas Ball Barratt[89] who was influenced by the movement in Los Angeles. Barratt was finally suspended by the Norwegian Annual Conference. He later relinquished his certificate of ordination. Barratt went on to work as an independent evangelist, becoming the 'father' of the Norwegian Pentecostal movement.[90]

Two World Wars, 1914–1918, 1939–1945
Both World Wars left their marks all over Europe with enormous death and destruction. People suffered (physically and mentally). There was massive damage to buildings, infrastructure, and cultural identity. Many felt hopeless and feared the future. The collapse of European society cannot be painted darkly enough to describe the situation that people – guilty or through no fault of their own – experienced. Empires and kingdoms collapsed while new republics and states advanced.

Methodism made no general study of the European situation, although the Methodist mission organizations and the denominational general conferences (EA, EUBC, and MC) tried to take stock. In the UMC archives in Madison, New Jersey, is a very large photograph collection. Many of those photographs were taken in European countries after the wars to promote fund raising to support immediate relief programs and to convey the desperate circumstances of European Methodists and their neighbors.

After World War I help came directly and less bureaucratically than after World War II when many different agencies first had to be authorized by the USA government and had to work with the occupying armies. Both periods need more careful research.

Perhaps this is a good place to offer a few general conclusions. At the end of World War II, the EA and MC experienced severe interruption in their European work – the death or imprisonment of preachers and church members, and major damage or complete destruction of buildings.[91] This devastation produced a crisis. Should the denominational work in Europe continue? Would the devastating effects of the conflict allow reconstruction? The EA and MC in Europe was again deeply dependent on their parent churches.

Support was provided by the churches in the USA, Switzerland, and even Scandinavia – shipments of food, clothing, kitchen utensils, and bicycles for routine travel. Donated spare parts and raw materials could be sold to raise funds for the reconstruction of churches, schools, and hospitals. In some cases complete wooden churches with furniture were sent to be constructed on appropriate plots. Changing state laws made it necessary to transfer monetary donations directly.

This material help came under an evangelistic-mission program that started in both denominations prior to the end of the war: the Kingdom Advance program of the Evangelical United Brethren Church (EUBC),[92] and the Crusade for Christ program of the Methodist Church (MC).

In 1945 there was in Germany in addition to the Methodist programs a relief organization founded by the churches called Hilfswerk der Evangelischen Kirchen. It was the first time that free churches were officially included in the work of the main Protestant church[93] in Germany. This was not because of the increased interest of free churches, but was something that resulted from ecumenical initiatives in the USA where, among others, Methodist churches as main-line denominations were able to give advice on how to cooperate with other free churches in Germany. It also arose out of consideration of the future help that could be delivered by the free churches in the USA.[94] How this worked in other European countries is question open to further examination.

After World War II an awareness of the larger European Methodist community emerged. A conference of European Methodist churches was held in 1950 to coordinate mission work and other collective concerns. In the 1990s a European Commission on Mission was formed in which British Methodists were also involved. A European Methodist Youth Council was created in 1970 and composed of the autonomous churches of south Europe. In 1966 the Council of European Central Conferences (MC) met and invited the British Methodists as observers. In 1990 a Fund for Mission in Europe was established with the collaboration of the British. After years of consultative working the European Methodist Council expanded in 1993 by including the autonomous Methodist churches in Europe – the British Conference, the Irish Conference, the Methodist Church in Portugal, the Opera for the Evangelical Methodist Churches in Italy, the Spanish Evangelical Church, and the Church of the Nazarene. The goal was to develop a stronger Methodist witness in Europe by building connections, coordinating mission and ecumenical projects, engaging in theological studies, and giving financial support for mission in Europe.

Finally, an association of United Methodist Theological Schools in Europe was organized in 1999.[95] Its stated intention was to support an interchange of professors, organize joint conferences, exchange information, cooperate in a Doctor of Ministry program, and form a corporate effort for accreditation and theological education in Europe. It is agreed that the deans of all the theological schools meet every other year and the professors every fourth year to coordinate Methodist theological education on Europe.

Since financial support from the UMC general conference has been lacking, some of the east European theological schools have experienced difficulty. A newly designed collective European theological education was started with the founding of the European Methodist E-Academy in February 2008.

Ecumenical Concerns and Participation
While being one of the European minority churches,[96] the Methodist churches in Europe are considered a 'bridge' between former state churches and the free churches. In this function Methodists are highly esteemed. On the one hand, this situation is explained by Methodism's connectional church structure. The majority of free churches are organized congregationally which hinders closer authoritative agreements with other churches as well as their participation in ecumenical dialogues.[97] Furthermore, Methodists also practice an ecumenical spirit that allows them to be among the founding members of all the principal European ecumenical institutions including the World Council of Churches (1948), the Conference of European Churches (1964), the Community of Protestant Churches in Europe (1973), as well as – on the level of free churches – the 'Free Church Association' that is organized at the federal state level.

Methodists have a long tradition of quality educational work. In recent decades more and more Methodist theologians have been recognized and accepted in scholarly theological dialogues.[98] Methodist work in evangelism, education, and social service is also well known. In spite of its small size Methodism operates a large number of hospitals, health care institutions, residences for the elderly, child care services, and other community facilities.

European Methodist Historical Organizations and Archives

Following the mandates of the *Book of Discipline of the United Methodist Church*[99] most European annual conferences attempted to establish commissions on archives and history. For various reasons historical commission cannot be organized in all European countries, but there are at least basic efforts to pay attention to the importance of history and its documentation. The longest continuing historical work and publishing by a European historical society is the German one that was established by the central conference of the German-speaking areas (Austria, Switzerland, and Germany) in 1927.[100]

Historical Organizations

European Historical Commissions
The Methodist Church in Great Britain has had the Wesley Historical Society[101] for decades. In 1979 a Historical Commission on the European mainland was founded as a section of the World Methodist Historical Society, an affiliated organization of the World Methodist Council. Each UMC European central conference is represented on the Historical Commission by two delegates. The commission generally meets every other year. The commission's purpose is to

build a network by sharing information about what is being done regarding historical research in the various European countries, to discuss historical matters that are of interest to all these regions, and to initiate special research to be shared at a European historical conference.

Since European Methodists are a minority in Europe and the pool of Methodist historians is very small, the annual conferences are an important component in choosing persons who are experts as well as others who have a vital interest in history to work together on specific issues which may be presented at the historical conference. These conferences and the historical research presented at them encourage others to recognize the importance of history and the establishment of archives in their geographical area.

The European Historical Commission was a UMC structure. Recently, however, a broader recognition of denominational Methodism in Europe has prompted the Historical Commission to involve other Methodist denominations and to work more closely with the British Wesley Historical Society. This wider understanding of European Methodism hopefully will become reality for the first time at the European Historical Conference held in 2010 in Budapest, Hungary. The topic for the conference was 'Methodism in Europe after World War II (1945–1965).' It is also interesting to note that international Methodist historical interests in the UMC since the 1990s with representation from Europe on the denomination's General Commission on Archives and History. Also two European vice-presidents serve on the executive committee of the World Methodist Historical Society.

Methodist Libraries and Archival Depositories

Except for Scandinavia, Germany, and Switzerland, continental European Methodist archives collections are in their infancy. Two archive workshops were conducted in 2001 and 2004 by the UMC's general commission to motivate those European Methodists who did not have an archive to establish one and to organize it according to professional guidelines.[102]

Below is a list of known European Methodist archives:

North European and Eurasia Central Conference (UMC)
Denmark: Located in Copenhagen; well organized and constantly updated.
Norway: Located in Oslo; well organized and constantly updated.
Sweden: Located in Gothenburg. In addition to cooperating with the Gothenburg archives, the annual conference also directed local congregations in the cities where their congregations are located to integrate Methodist historical material with the local city's municipal historical archives. The result is Methodist resources are spread across the country.
Finland: Located in Helsinki and Helsingfors.

Central German Conference (UMC)
Central archives in Reutlingen, located at the School of Theology; very well organized; books and other resources are electronic catalogued.

There are also archives in the three Annual Conferences (North German Conference in Hamburg; South German Conference in Stuttgart; East German Conference in Zwickau). They are all linked to Reutlingen by the same archive computer program. The German Board of Global Mission in Wuppertal and the deaconess mother-houses maintain their own, mostly very well organized archives (Bethesda Wuppertal, Bethanien Hamburg/Frankfurt am Main, and Martha-Maria Nürnberg).

Middle and South European Central Conference (UMC)

Bulgaria:	Located in Sofia; unorganized.
France:	on the way to being organized in the Taborkapelle in Mulhouse.
Macedonia:	Valuable documents are preserved in Strumica, others in Austria.
Austria:	Located in Vienna; well organized.
Switzerland:	Located in Zurich; the inventory is currently catalogued in the Zurich and Lausanne libraries; catalogue available on the internet.
Serbia:	District archives located in Novi Sad; central archives planned for Kisac.
Slovakia:	Collection of resources from 1993 to the present in Bratislava with older documents in Prague.
Czech Republic:	Located in Praha (for the time prior to 1993 with the material of Slovakia after 1993 for the Czech Republic)
Hungary:	Located in Obuda in Budapest; well organized and catalogued.

Conclusion and Important Questions

The rationale for all Methodist mission is soteriological and ecclesiological. It arises out of a concrete theological focus on a holistic holiness doctrine supported by a connexional church structure. Both doctrine and structure create a deep understanding of the oneness of the church as Christ's body, rooted in work of the Trinitarian God. They place humanity in a vital, living, ongoing relationship with God, in a perpetual covenant with God and other people. The combination of Methodist theology and ecclesiology can open a dialogue which is trans-confessional and multicultural; this seems ideally suited to the European reality.

The Methodist way of living is continually confronted with other theologies, traditions, and cultures. This inevitably leads to conflict. Methodism has to co-exist with and appreciate the reality of other scriptural concepts of what it means to be the church. It has to find a creative ways to work and coexist with other churches as something always new and dynamic by reflecting scripturally on its own actions in each new situation.

Methodism in continental Europe went through several phases. New emphases and structures were sought in each new context, sometimes without careful reflection on more traditional ones. Whenever scriptural reflection was undertaken, erroneous trends could be recognized and sometimes partly corrected. So, class meetings as centers of Methodist missions were understood as communities to live and learn. Spiritual living and learning belonged to a discipline, and the truths of faith were acquired through musical and poetic form by the singing of hymns. Christian publications and a Christian education program for all ages and for responsible members were developed alongside social service work undertaken by either individuals or institutions. All of this formed a part of the life-changing process which the believer adopts in becoming Methodist.

The desire 'to spread scriptural holiness across the nation' with other faithful people must always become concrete in each new context. Reversals and frustrations never justify either weakening or discarding mission. History shows that the cooperative ecumenical missionary work developed in the twentieth century could progress and develop.

In Europe, the Methodist churches created their own distinctive organizational structures: some chose autonomy; some joined in church unions with other confessions; still others stayed in a world-wide connection of one church, working together so that the experience of God's grace could become more widely and convincingly known.

Beside these conclusions there are numerous questions to ponder. Their answers could help to verify what has already been said.

First, there is the need for more basic Methodist historical research in all European countries. This is made difficult because of the loss of written sources destroyed during war or dangerous state anti-religious policies which forced the church to work underground and discouraged documenting decisions and developments (as happened mainly under communistic rule). A systematic world-wide search for notes in periodicals as well as a network of Methodist archives to share sources should be mandated. Furthermore, local oral history projects could retrieve information which is in jeopardy of being lost.

United Methodism's connectional structure may assist us to focus on important questions that could be explored in complex European contexts.

A variety of questions are listed here in three categories: church, special groups, and projects.

1. Church
   - What is the meaning of Methodist connectionalism in the context of globalization, migration, reconciliation, international understanding, and building democracy?
   - How can an international church help to prevent national arrogance and international isolation as well as function as a safeguard against exploitation?
   - Can a connectional church structure facilitate reconciliation after political conflict or war? How did Methodism act strategically after both world wars?
   - Can Methodism, if it critically reflects its specific historical and theological roots, be life giving and inspiring in increasingly secular contexts?
   - How did Methodism's connectional structure stand the test in various decades and national contexts of being boundary crossing, supranational, and balancing poor and prosperous congregations?
2. Special church groups
   - How did women advance global mission work through mission societies, female missionaries, the deaconess movement, and otherwise?
   - What role did 'Bibelfrauen' (Bible women) play in Italy, Spain, Bulgaria, Macedonia, and other countries in the spread of the gospel (and Methodism)?
   - Did youth groups and organizations such as the Epworth League influence adult organizations to modernize and/or adapt to contemporary questions?
   - What role did/do international youth meetings and festivals play to support a special Methodist identity?
   - How did Methodists from the USA and Europe exert influence on the development of the ecumenical movement?
3. Church projects (branches)
   - What were the different mission strategies of British and American Methodism and how did they fare in different political, confessional, and cultural contexts?
   - What role did/does educational work play in Methodism, for example, major school projects that were started in the beginnings of the MEC and WM missions in Italy, Spain, Portugal, Bulgaria, Yugoslavia, and Macedonia?
   - Why was the model of the Central Halls not adopted on the

European mainland when it was so successful in Great Britain and Scandinavia?
- What is special about Methodist theological education?
- What is the relationship between the Methodist Churches in Europe and Pentecostalism?
- Does the successful scholarly teamwork of Roman Catholic and Methodist theologians, as well as the on-going dialogue between the Roman-catholic Church and the World Methodist Council, change the local circumstances of Methodist congregations in a mainly Catholic context?
- How did/do Methodist churches in European countries deal with non-Christian religions?

For Further Reading

Behney, J. Bruce and Paul H. Eller. *The History of the Evangelical United Brethren Church*. Nashville: Abingdon, 1979.

Hecker, Friedrich, Vilém Schneeberger, and Karl Zehrer. *Methodismus in Osteuropa: Polen – Tschechoslowakei – Ungarn*. Stuttgart, 2004 [EmKM 51].

Nuelson, John. *Geschichte des Methodismus von den Anfängen bis zur Gegenwart*. Bremen, 1929.

O'Malley, J. Steven. *'On the Journey Home' The History of Mission of the Evangelical United Brethren Church, 1946–1968*. The United Methodist History of Mission. New York: General Board of Global Ministries, The United Methodist Church, 2003.

Schuler, Ulrike. *Die Evangelische Gemeinschaft. Missionarische Aufbrüche in gesellschaftspolitischen Umbrüchen*. Stuttgart, 1998 [emk studien 1].

Stephens, Peter. *Methodism in Europe*. Peterborough, UK: Methodist Publishing House, 1998.

Streiff, Patrick Ph. *Der Methodismus in Europa im 19. und 20. Jahrhundert*. Stuttgart, 2003 [EmKG.M 50]. [English version: Streiff, Patrick Ph.. *Methodism in Europe: 19th and 20th century*. Tallinn/Estonia, 2004]

Streiff, Patrick Ph. (ed.). Der europäische Methodismus um die Wende vom 19. zum 20. Jahrhundert. Referat der historischen Konferenz der EmK in Europa vom 10. bis 15. August 2004 in Tallinn, Estland. Stuttgart 2005 [EmKG.M 52].

11 Methodism in Russia and the Baltics: Old and New Beginnings

Rüdiger R. Minor

History of Methodism in Russia and the Baltic Countries

Russia and the Baltic countries have been closely linked for more than two hundred years. This began with Russia's westward expansion under the Romanoff Tsars, notably Peter I, up to Baltic independence at the end of the Soviet era with a short break between the two world wars. While Russia controlled the Baltic countries, they were a means of entry for western ideas and achievements into Russia, thereby creating an interesting cultural mix of mutual fertilization. St. Petersburg, Peter's artificial capital, is a witness to this special atmosphere. Built with western technology by hundreds of Russian workers, who perished in hard labor, St. Petersburg has been a city with a western design and a Russian soul. So far as the religious scene is concerned, St. Petersburg's main avenue, Newski Prospect, offers a vivid illustration. Beside the Russian Orthodox 'Kazan Cathedral' there are the leading churches of the Lutheran, Roman Catholic, and Armenian denominations. The close vicinity of Finland, for more than one hundred years under the Russian crown, adds to this unique cultural setting. Therefore, it may be natural that Methodism's first contact with Russia happened in St. Petersburg which became the starting point and support center for the spread of Methodist groups in the area. In Soviet times Baltic Methodism attempted to keep contact with Russia and the remnant of its adherents there. For decades the Estonian Methodist Church was the only remnant of Methodism in the area. Since Methodism in Russia and the Baltic states have been linked for many years, they are treated together in this essay.

The one hundred twenty years of Methodism's history in this area's history[1] can be divided into four phases: (1) Methodist beginnings in Tsarist Russia; (2) the Russian revolution and the time between the two world wars; (3) Methodism in the Soviet Union; and (4) rebuilding Methodism after the demise of the Soviet power. We deal with each of these phases in the pages that follow.

Methodist Beginnings up to the Russian Revolution

St. Petersburg and Vicinity

St. Petersburg Methodism from its start in the 1880s to the end of World War I is usually understood in close connection with northern European and especially Finnish Methodists. Swedish-speaking people in St. Petersburg provided the first connection with Methodism in the early 1880s. Rev. Bengt A. Carlson established a 'Methodist society' there in 1889, consisting of a group of elderly Swedes. When in 1907 Finnish pastor Hjalmar Salmi, a native of St. Petersburg, was appointed, his ministry focused on the Finnish-speaking population in the villages of 'Ingermanland,' east of the city. Two congregations were formed in the villages of Handrovo and Sigalovo.[2] The beginning of St. Petersburg Methodism in Swedish and Finnish circles gives witness to a number of interesting characteristics: interdependence with Scandinavian (and later central European) Methodism, and the 'international' composition of the population in and around St. Petersburg. In 1907, Methodist Episcopal clergyman Dr. George A. Simons was appointed superintendent of the Finland and St. Petersburg Mission. The son of a German Methodist preacher in the United States, Simons soon discovered and cultivated contacts in the large German population of St. Petersburg, but also reached out to other language groups. The 'First Methodist Episcopal Society' held services in Russian, Finnish, Swedish, German, English, and Estonian. The Finnish population in and around St. Petersburg together with Germans represented the major number of followers. Historically, there have been many bicultural persons in St. Petersburg. Among the Methodists we could name such outstanding persons like Hjalmar Salmi, or Julius Hecker, St. Petersburg-born German. The Methodist monthly for Russia *Khristianski Pobornik* (Christian Advocate) in 1910 gives a list of names of persons preparing for the ministry, most of them of double national heritage.[3] It remains an open question, how strong the influence on and participation of Russians has been. In a report, given at the 1912 general conference of the Methodist Episcopal Church in Minneapolis, Minnesota, Simons spoke of predominance of the Russian element among the membership of the church.[4]

The arrival of Sister Anna Eklund and other Methodist deaconesses in 1908 added an important dimension to the Methodist mission in St. Petersburg including a ministry to the sick, poor, and especially to children. Besides offering home care, the deaconesses were active in several hospitals of the city and in military hospitals during World War I. Even more important was relief work especially for children. A children's home was established in Handrovo, one of the village churches in Ingermanland.[5]

Methodism was not the first Protestant group in St. Petersburg. Historic Protestantism in Russia, dating back to the sixteenth century was strongly related to ethnic groups that were traditionally Protestant (Germans, Scandinavians, Fins, Latvians, and Estonians). The same was true of other confessions, for example, Roman Catholics (Poles, Lithuanians) and Muslims (Tatars, Caucasian nations). Those groups enjoyed some freedom to exercise their religion, though with the condition that they would not seek to minister to ethnic Russians. For them the Russian Orthodox Church was the one and only religion. It was not until April 1905 that Tsar Nicolas II allowed Russians to leave Orthodoxy.[6] St. Petersburg became the center of the Russian evangelical movement.[7] Methodists were actively involved in this movement. According to available evidence, however, there seems to be less emphasis on Methodist participation in the wider evangelical milieu in St. Petersburg than in other localities.[8] There is a need to widen the horizon and to recognize a notably strong influence of an 'Alliance' spirit that has been present throughout European Methodism and which also had an impact on the Russian empire.[9]

A crucial matter for Methodists throughout the Tsarist era in Russia has been the development of religious freedom in Russia. Methodism was influenced by the changes of Russian attitudes toward religious freedom and tolerance. Salmi, who began his ministry in St. Petersburg, received official permission 'to hold religious meetings.'[10] It was not until June 1909 that the First Methodist Episcopal Church in St. Petersburg was registered by the Department of Spiritual Affairs of Foreign Confessions.[11] Police maintained surveillance of the Methodist congregation. Files in the archives of the Ministry of Interior (MDI) – so far awaiting closer research – contain reports by police officers, present at Methodist meetings (for some time required by law) as well as reports about arrests of Methodists (many of Finnish nationality) for holding Sunday School in (Finnish) villages near St. Petersburg. Copies of *Khristianski Pobornik* collected in the St. Petersburg public library show signs of critical reading by government officials, for example, *Khristianski Pobornik*, August 1910 pages 163–172, which contains a comprehensive report about the mission with many handwritten marginal remarks and comments by local officers.

There was little Methodist sympathy or appreciation for the Orthodox Church. Dunstan rightly asserts that Simons held a negative view of Orthodoxy.[12] In *Khristianski Pobornik*, there is a striking absence of references to Russian Orthodoxy as well as to Russian spirituality and Christian philosophy even in articles written by Russians. An article on 'God-seekers' does not even mention Russian literature, although it was the era of Dostoyevsky, Tolstoy, and other important Russian writers.[13]

The acquisition of a building in St. Petersburg in 1914 – on Vassili Ostrov (Island), a prestigious quarter of the city – was important for the stabilization of Methodist work.[14] It was dedicated in March 1915 and remained the center of Methodist activities even through the time of the revolution up to the final closure of the Methodist work by the Russian authorities in 1931.[15]

Baltic Countries

About the same time as Methodism came to St. Petersburg, Methodist work began in the Baltic countries. A spiritual awakening in a suburb of the city of Kaunas, **Lithuania**, brought the formation of meetings for preaching and prayer led by laypersons. The members were German Lutherans, and in the early stages these meetings were welcomed by the Lutheran clergy. Conflicts, however, arose with neighbors who took offense at the evangelical nature of the meetings. Their complaints also estranged the pastor. Being spiritually orphaned, the group came into contact with German Methodists in Königsberg, eastern Prussia in 1900. Upon their invitation, Georg Durdis was appointed pastor by the North German Annual Conference in 1905. He soon began work in other places in Lithuania. Since Lithuania was part of the Russian empire, administration was transferred to the superintendent in St. Petersburg. George Simons was able to support the mission in dealing with Russian bureaucracy. The first Methodist prayer house in the Russian empire was erected in Kybartay in 1909 and a church in Kaunas in 1911.[16]

Close proximity to German East Prussia was also important for Methodist origins in **Latvia**. This is especially true for the mission of the Evangelische Gemeinschaft,[17] which was present in that country. Upon an invitation to Riga in 1908, a German pastor, Reinhold Barchet, was appointed in 1911. Riga was viewed as the door to further work in Russia and among Russians. At the same time that Durdis was sent to Riga, the Methodist Episcopal Church started its Riga ministry. Since the majority of members of both churches in the two countries were German, the work suffered a number of problems and substantial losses during World War I.

Contact with the mission in St. Petersburg brought Methodism to **Estonia**. Two friends, Vassili Täht and Karl Kuum, began a lay preaching movement on the island of Saaremaa in 1907. Täht was a colporteur of the British and Foreign Bible Society and had met Simons in St. Petersburg. Kuum was a Moravian lay preacher. Despite opposition of the Lutheran state church, Methodism grew and meetings were held in several places. In 1910 the first Methodist congregations were formed on the island, soon to be followed by others in major Estonian cities (Tallinn and Tartu). These beginnings were clearly motivated by a desire for a more intensive spiritual life that attempted to avoid sectarian tendencies and drew on an evangelical spirit.[18] The work in Estonia was clearly marked by the leading role of indigenous people from the start.

While the work in the different areas seems to have been loosely knit, relationships of the parts of the Russian empire and Baltic states (including Finland) were mostly through the connectional structure of the Methodism which formed a mission conference and later districts. The personnel policy of the appointive system was important. It sustained the mission work through the selection and deployment of leaders sent to various places, thus building connections. Subsequently, there was strong emphasis on the linguistic ability of preachers. To what degree this was accomplished is an open question. George Simons reported, 'There are spoken more then forty languages and dialects in Russia. For this need, our church has a sufficient number of linguists and co-workers, dedicated to the Lord; however, the organization of a proper seminary is advisable in Russia.'[19] The dream of a seminary was not realized and there seems to be no real recruitment and leadership of indigenous leadership, especially Russian. While the appointive system produced a mobile ministry, it obviously did not develop a strong relationship to an area or territory. Heavy emphasis was placed on the central leadership of the church. Visits of bishops and other leaders were regularly mentioned and celebrated in *Khristianski Pobornik*. Superintendent George Simons and Anna Eklund, head of the deaconesses, were outstanding leaders who gave their utmost. But apparently, there were no other leaders with them.[20]

The Russian Revolution and the Time between the Two World Wars

The revolution of 1917 put Methodism in Russia on a roller coaster. The February revolution and the provisional government were enthusiastically welcomed by George Simons. It seemed that the time had come when even Russia would subscribe to the principles of western society so dear to Methodist leadership. The Bolshevist October revolution, however, was viewed negatively from the beginning. Methodists were not alone in this judgment. The dissolution of the Russian empire and its re-formation as the Soviet Union was achieved in a protracted and often cruel struggle between the Communist government and forces of the old regime, often supported by foreign powers. After the stereotype pro- or anti-Soviet historiography of the twentieth century, only now is awareness growing about the wavering loyalties between the front lines of 'Reds' and 'Whites.'[21] There was polarization in the churches, too, most of all in the Russian Orthodox Church, which for several years suffered a schism between the supporters of Patriarch Tikhon and reformist groups of the 'Living Church.'[22]

For the Baltic countries, however, the end of the Russian empire opened the possibility of new development for freedom and self-determination with new possibilities for the end of national churches. Although the time between the two world wars was an interlude, for Methodism it provided circumstances for growth and meaningful ministry.

Russian Methodism in St. Petersburg and the Western Part of the Country
In the course of the anti-church measures of the Soviet government, Methodists lost ownership of their building, though they were able to use it, paying

a fee to the government as was the case with all religious buildings. Religious activities were increasingly restricted. However, worship life and for sometime even social activities were able to continue. In October 1918, the United States government ordered all of its citizens to leave Russia. George Simons left for Finland and later settled in Riga, Latvia. Until relieved by Bishop John L. Nuelsen from his duty as the leader for Russia in 1922, Simons directed the work from abroad, including making trips to Russia. Power in the country was transferred to Sister Anna, who led church and charitable activities. In 1920–1921 Russia was severely hit by famine. Methodists in the West sent relief supplies and Sister Anna, the Angel of Petrograd, distributed them among the poor. Her incredible workload and dedication was admirable. Clearly, while anti-Bolshevist in her convictions, Eklund did her best to continue the church's mission. She watched over the church 'like a lion.'

Despite hardships, bureaucratic harassment, inflated prices and fees, life in Russian Methodism was not only maintained, but new places and people were reached, and the hope of further progress was nurtured. The mid-1920s was a time of relative freedom and prosperity in the Soviet Union. The 'New Economic Policy' (NEP) had revoked some of the harshest measures of economic and political oppression in order to revive Russian life which had severely suffered from world and civil wars. There was also a reprieve for religious life.[23] While in the Russian Orthodox Church it was the time of fierce striving between the competing groups, other churches enjoyed new possibilities. The government let this happen under the assumption that these churches provided welcome competition to the Orthodox. Baptists and other Protestant groups were able to organize and issue publications.[24]

Sister Anna Eklund reported new work in Novgorod and a chapel purchased in Jablonitzy.[25] She worked tirelessly to support evangelistic and social ministry as well as the maintenance of the Methodist building in Leningrad. She was supported by people of Leningrad and elsewhere.

Methodists abroad and the leadership of the Methodist Episcopal Church were supportive of the Russian mission and followed its development with great interest. At the same time, they tried to support Russia and the Russian church on a wider scale. Methodist bishops Nuelsen and Edgar Blake established relationships with the leadership of the Russian Orthodox Church, which was at that time represented by the 'Living Church.'[26] Nuelsen was the more active, bearing responsibility for the Russian work over a longer period, though Blake attended the 1923 'Sobor' (National Council) of the Russian Orthodox Church that was dominated by reformers. He promised support, especially with the reestablishment of theological education. Though he carefully abstained from taking sides, controversy arose among Methodists in the United States and in the wider public about Methodists supporting the

Bolshevist regime. Bishop Nuelsen was hopeful that the Methodist Episcopal Church would bring substantial social, educational, and theological support to the Russia work through its Centenary Fund. He frequently visited Russia and established contacts with church and government officials. However, there were problems with the immediate leadership of Methodist work in Russia. George Simons had made several strong anti-Bolshevist statements and had used his influence accordingly even after the bishop had relieved him from responsibility for the mission. It was Dr. Julius F. Hecker, the native of St. Petersburg mentioned earlier, later a Methodist pastor in the United States and active in relief work for Russians during and after World War I, who became Bishop Nuelsen's contact in Russia. Though not in an officially appointed position, Hecker lived in Moscow and maintained close relations in church and society.[27] Mindful of the faults and deficiencies of Russian Orthodoxy in Tsarist times and critical of the reactionary position of the 'patriarchal' faction, Hecker longed for a genuine renewal of Russian Christianity which he thought possible in the new Russia.[28] Hecker was actively involved in the reestablishment of theological schools in Moscow and St. Petersburg which were financed by the Methodist church. Preaching in Moscow and Leningrad, he supported the Methodist mission and the ministry of Sister Anna, although he never became the leader of Russian Methodism.

Nuelsen's great plans for the renewal of Russian Christianity were not fulfilled for two reasons: (1) the tightening of antireligious measures and legislation in the Soviet Union that culminated in the law of 1929 prohibiting all activities beside worship services in a few churches or prayer houses, and (2) the drying up of financial support through Methodist agencies and membership. There is almost no information regarding what happened to the Methodist churches, their members, pastors, preachers, and other workers, after the Soviet authorities prohibited further work.

In retrospect, we are left with conflicting stories and memories. To a certain degree superintendent George Simons and Sister Anna Eklund maintained a fiercely anti-Bolshevist position, while persons like Julius Hecker and bishops Nuelsen and Blake sought rapprochement with the new power. The tension between confrontation and attempts at cooperation, persecution, and high hopes for Methodism in a post-Tsarist Russia, grand planning outside the country and struggling of the work in the country to survive, finally led to the withering away of the Methodist presence. All this resulted in one of the most contradictory epochs in Methodist history.

Baltic Countries – the Blooming of Methodism

The end of the Russian empire and the restitution of the Polish state led to the definition of new borders in northern central Europe. Methodism in the three

Baltic countries continued to exist in close connection and indigenous work was strengthened.

With the eventual relocation of headquarters from St. Petersburg to Riga, **Latvia** became the center of Baltic Methodism. There were several congregations in Riga as well as a theological training institute for future pastors which prepared them for study at one of the Methodism's European seminaries. While work among Germans continued and even a Russian-speaking congregation in Riga, there was substantial growth among the Latvian population. A young man in Liepaja, Alfred Freiberg, had grown up in the evangelical 'Alliance' climate, provided by the Latvian 'Blue Cross,' the Moravian Church, and other free churches. It should be noticed that the organized temperance movement of the Blue Cross had been helpful at the beginnings of the Methodist church as well as the Evangelische Gemeinschaft in Latvia even in Tsarist times. Freiberg developed and maintained a close relationship to superintendent Simons and other Methodist leaders in 1911. He did not, however, organize Methodist groups since he worked as a Moravian preacher. In 1921, he and his congregation joined the Methodist Church, marking the beginning of indigenous Latvian Methodism.[29] Soon Latvians became the majority group in the denomination, and most of the pastors were of Latvian nationality. By contrast, the work in the three congregations of the Evangelische Gemeinschaft continued to be basically a German mission, though an indigenous pastor was appointed to them.

The time between the two world wars was the blossoming period also for the Methodist Church in **Lithuania**. Indigenous Lithuanian Methodism was established in 1923 with a church in Birzai. Lithuanian pastors were trained in the theological institute in Riga and the seminary in Frankfurt/Main. The majority German congregations had strong ties to German Methodism, especially in the area of church music. The Lithuanian capital Vilnius belonged to the part of the country that was subject to Poland between 1922 and 1939. For this time it was served by the Polish mission of the Methodist Episcopal Church, South, and became the mother congregation of work among Belarusians.[30]

Methodist work in **Estonia** enjoyed continuous growth with the establishment of churches in all of the major cities and the typical Methodist structure of circuits, that is, several congregations served by one appointed pastor. While Methodism was basically an evangelical movement in its beginnings, social and educational ministries later became its trademark.[31] Unlike the mission in other Baltic states, it has been indigenous from the very beginning, drawing on active laypersons who became preachers and pastors. Estonian students went to the training institute in Riga and to the Frankfurt seminary, which for the time between the wars became the intellectual and spiritual center of the Methodist Episcopal Church in continental Europe.

Toward the end of the period between the wars, problems arose with Hitler's policy of repatriating Germans. The churches in Latvia and Lithuania lost many members, though some of them returned for a short period during World War II when German troops occupied the Baltic countries. The definitive blow came when advancing Soviet troops brought a return of Russian influence and power. Churches were closed, property confiscated, and a huge exodus of members led to the complete dissolution of Methodist work in Lithuania and Latvia. All Lithuanian pastors fled to the West as did the majority of Latvian pastors. Those who remained joined Baptist or Lutheran congregations. Estonian Methodism was more resistant and only in Estonia did ministry survive even through Soviet times. It paid a high price, however, with the martyrdom of leaders and laypersons.

Mission of the Methodist Episcopal Church, South in the Russian Far East and Belarus

An important development, though connected to the events in mainland Russia, is the rise and demise of Methodism in the Russian Far East and in the present territories of Ukraine and Belarus (at that time Poland and Slovakia/Hungary).

Since the late nineteenth century, large crowds of ethnic Koreans migrated to the Russian Far East as well as to Chinese Manchuria, among them a substantial number of Methodists. As the Korean Methodists felt a responsibility for their fellow believers abroad, Bishop Walter R. Lambuth of the Methodist Episcopal Church, South, saw an opportunity to inaugurate a Methodist mission to Russia's Far East. Beginning in 1920, churches were soon established among Koreans in Vladivostok, Nikolsk-Ussurijsk in the Russian Far East, Harbin in Manchuria, and places along the Transsiberian railroad. Korean pastors were appointed and work among children and youth was supported by lay helpers. American missionaries went on mission trips with Korean pastors. Buildings were acquired or newly built in Nikolsk, Vladivostok, and Harbin. To lead the work among Russians, American missionaries were sent to Harbin and Vladivostok. Rev. J. O. J. Taylor opened a mission office in Vladivostok in 1921; he and his family were later joined by Rev. George Erwin with his family. In the turmoil of the Russian Civil War with its constantly changing borderlines, peaceful times as well as atrocities on both sides, this city was for several years a stronghold of the anti-Communist 'White' forces supported by international troops. The fledgling Methodist mission enjoyed good relations with the ruling forces.[32] Churches functioned in Korean and Russian, schools were opened, and social work established. Korean contacts usually took the lead. However, this time of prosperity came to an abrupt halt, as the 'Red' forces of the 'Far Eastern

Republic' retook Vladivostok in October 1922. Foreign troops left the city with most of the international population and missionaries. The Taylor family left for Harbin, Manchuria in February 1923 as did many Russian Methodists. It seems that most of the Koreans stayed. Soon the same prohibitions were enforced by the Communist rulers as in the European areas: church buildings were nationalized; schools and social work closed or put under state control. For a fee, churches could continue the use of buildings for worship purposes only, and were restricted even in this.[33] The Russian work in Vladivostok continued for some time under lay leadership, while the mission among Russians in the Far East was concentrated in Harbin. Korean Methodist churches continued to function for awhile under many hardships. The Vladivostok congregation had use of the church building up to the late 1920s.[34] It was still used by Korean Protestant groups in the early 1930s, which brings us close to the forced removal of Koreans from the Far East by Stalin in 1937. It can be correctly observed that the Korean presence and witness in the Russian Far East formed the context for the missionary intermezzo of the American church.

Harbin, Manchuria, became the center for Russian expatriates in the Far East. Methodist work there was blooming with several churches in the city and along the Chinese section of the Transsiberian railway. Several schools and medical centers were established, and women's work was started. All those ministries were financed by the Centenary Fund for Mission of the Methodist Episcopal Church, South which supported a large missional expansion of the church's work. Churches were pastored by American missionaries and Russian converts, for whom a theological institute was founded. Among the Russian pastors was N. J. Poysti,[35] who once was one of George Simons' coworkers in St. Petersburg. Working for the YMCA, Poysti and his family were forced to move eastward during the Civil War. He introduced the Harbin mission to the publications of the Russia Mission of the Methodist Episcopal Church in St. Petersburg, even publishing a *Khristianski Pobornik* for Far East Russian Methodists.

Financial problems and doubts about the future of a mission to an expatriate community, led to the decision by the mission board of the Methodist Episcopal Church, South to discontinue the work in Harbin, much to the chagrin of the Russian members and the missionaries.[36]

Two female missionaries in Harbin were sent to the other mission enterprise of the Methodist Episcopal Church, South in the territory of the former Russian empire, Belarus (White Russia). In the painful process of re-establishing the Polish state after World War I, the western part of Belarus (Little White Russia) together with a part of Lithuania had come to Poland, where the Methodist Episcopal Church, South had started a relief mission in 1921. The Lithuanian capital Vilnius, then known as Vilna, under Polish administration was also viewed as the center of Belarusian life, especially since Minsk, the capital of Belarus, was under the Soviets.[37] The Methodist mission started relief work in 1924, especially supporting the school system. Female missionaries were sent to lead a girls' boarding school and also took part in the evangelizing mission among Byelorussians despite language problems. Jan Witt, pastor in Vilna, 1928–1932, actively promoted work in the Belarusian language, both in Vilnius and in towns and villages in western Belarus. The use of the Belarusian language in preaching and singing proved especially attractive. There were at least two centers of Belarusian work besides Vilna: villages around Srednie Siolo and Dereczyn (both in western Belarus). Ernst Nausner, a German who had lived in Russia, started a holistic ministry of evangelism and social work in three villages around Srednie Siolo (west of Minsk).[38] Jan Piotrowski, a Belarusian student at the Polish Methodist seminary in Klarysew (near Warsaw) was a local preacher in Dereczyn (about 100 km east of Polish Byalistok), 1932–1936. Although serving later in Warsaw and eventually in Vilna, Dereczyn continued to promote the church's work in the Belarusian language, even editing a small church newspaper. Belarusians as an ethnic minority felt discriminated against both in Poland and Russia. Religiously, some of the national leaders looked at Protestantism as an alternative to (Russian) Orthodoxy and (Polish) Catholicism. The recapturing of western Belarus by Soviet forces in 1939 brought an end to Methodist endeavors. Some memory of them, however, remained during Soviet times.[39]

Methodism in the Soviet Union

As described above, coming under Soviet power resulted finally in the end of Methodist work. Estonia was the only exception, but at a heavy price. The two waves of Soviet occupation at the beginning of World War II (German Russian 'Hitler–Stalin Pact' on the division of Poland and the Baltic countries)[40] and at its end (reintegration of Baltic countries into the Russian – now Soviet – empire) brought persecution, detainment, confiscation of property, trials, and severe verdicts including capital punishment. The first prominent victim was the superintendent and long-time leader, Martin Prikask, who was arrested in July 1941 and accused of anti-Soviet activities. His pastoral work was disparaged. With forced 'confessions,' Prikask was sentenced to death and shot in a Siberian camp in September 1942. By 1945 one-third of Estonian pastors lost their lives, and membership was reduced from 1,300 to around 700. As in Latvia and Lithuania, strong pressure was exerted by the Soviet authorities on the Methodist church to join other Protestant denominations, preferably the Baptists.[41] There were several reasons for the resilience of Estonian Methodism compared to other Baltic countries.[42] As mentioned earlier, it had the most homogeneous indigenous leadership. It had also become financially self-sufficient in the prewar period. However, the most important factor seems to have been the leadership which did not leave the country and showed a high degree of commitment and strength in the conflict with the authorities. The outstanding figure was Rev. Alexander Kuum, pastor of the Tallinn congregation for more than thirty years and superintendent from 1962 to 1974. From 1952 to 1956 he was a prisoner in a Siberian labor camp. When released he was more energetic and dedicated to his congregation. Under his evangelistic and pastoral ministry the Tallinn congregation grew to become the largest Methodist congregation on the European continent (1,166 members in 1971). The growth of Methodism was completely contrary to Communist predictions and beliefs. The journal *Nauka i Religia* (*Science and Religion*), the leading publication of Soviet atheism, devoted several articles in the 1960s and 1970s to this strange phenomenon.[43] Besides strong biblical preaching, an openness to new forms of evangelism including elements of youth culture and pop-music, and creative ways to circumvent restrictions imposed by the authorities contributed to this success. It should also be noted that Methodism's public worship and its official organization provided shelter for people from other traditions who were unable to work openly. Controversies and loss of membership to charismatic groups in the 1980s weakened the Methodist witness resulting in some decline of numbers.

For years, Estonian Methodism was separated from other Methodist churches. In 1962, Bishop Odd Hagen, episcopal leader of the Northern Europe Central Conference of the United Methodist Church, was able to visit this part of his flock for the first time. Other Methodists from Europe as well as the United States followed, and Estonian Methodist leaders were finally able to travel. Connections to the West resulted in moral and other support. Publicity in the West also served as a shield against pressure from the state.

Estonian Methodism played an important role in representing Methodism to churches and society in the Soviet Union. It shaped an appreciation for Methodism and its contacts to other areas prepared the ground for the later renewal of Methodist work. It provided protection for the only remnant of the mission of the Methodist Episcopal Church, South in southwest Ukraine in and near the city of Uzhgorod which was in the border-triangle of Ukraine, Slovakia, and Hungary. An evangelical movement among the rural population there joined the Methodist mission to Czechoslovakia initiated by the Methodist Episcopal Church, South after World War I. In the course of territorial changes before World War II, the area became a part of Hungary, and a pastor was appointed by the Hungarian Methodist Church. After annexation by Soviet Ukraine in 1945 the church building was confiscated and Methodist work was prohibited. Despite oppression by the Soviet authorities, a lay preacher, Ivan Vuksta, gathered a small congregation that finally joined the Tallinn church (though 1,800 km away).

Estonian Methodism has represented the Soviet Union to Methodists in the West.[44] It is by way of the unbroken tradition of Methodism in Estonia that Methodists in Russia and the Baltic countries receive their historic identity.[45]

Rebuilding Methodism after the Demise of Soviet Power

Russia and the 'Commonwealth of Independent States'

Changes in Soviet society under the leadership of Gorbachev's Perestroika (reorganization) provided space for new beginnings of Methodism through the 1980s and 1990s. A new law on freedom of conscience and religion was passed in 1990. By action of the presidents of Russia, Ukraine, and Belarus, the Soviet Union was dissolved at New Year 1992 and replaced by a loose confederation of states, the Commonwealth of Independent States (CIS).

Methodist activities were characterized by spontaneous 'grassroots' activities, triggered by contacts with various parts of the worldwide Methodist movement. Vladislav Spektorov, a student from the city of Samara (1,000 km east of Moscow on the Volga River) committed to the Christian faith in the Methodist church in Tallinn in the mid-1980s. As he took part in the lay training program there, he later began biblical lectures in his hometown, ironically under the auspices of an organization that had propagated scientific atheism. New converts organized and legally registered a Methodist church. Korean Methodists from Korea and the United States living in Moscow organized a Bible study group that from its genesis prayed for spiritual renewal in Russia. In 1990 a Methodist Church was registered under the leadership of Rev. Cho Young Cheul, a Korean pastor from the New York Annual Conference of the United Methodist Church. Rev. Dwight Ramsey, a Methodist pastor from Shreveport, Louisiana, took part in a city friendship program that brought him to Sverdlovsk in the Ural Mountains. He met with the Baptist church there, and found a group of people, interested in Methodism. Under the leadership of Lydia Istomina, they started a church in 1990 in the city which had been renamed Yekaterinburg. Early in 1991, Bishop J. Woodrow Hearn and General Secretary Randolph Nugent of the United Methodist General Board of Global Ministries traveled to Moscow for conversations with the Russian Orthodox Church about possible support and cooperation. The most visible outcome of this effort was providing food for Moscow in the winter 1991–1992. Chris Hena, a physician from Liberia, was sent as medical missionary to Moscow. The General Board of Global Ministries as the main mission arm of the UMC together with the Council of Bishops and the European parts of the UMC discussed goals and strategies for the renewed commitment in Russia. In fall 1991 the Council of Bishops appointed Bishop Ruediger Minor, bishop in East Germany since 1986 and acquainted with the situation in wider Soviet empire, as the episcopal coordinator for ministries in

Methodism in Russia and the Baltics: Old and New Beginnings

Russia. The 1992 UMC general conference established an episcopal area for the countries of the former Soviet Union which was officially launched in Moscow in August 1998. It is obvious that there have been many people involved in this effort. Most important of all have been persons deeply touched by the gospel and eager to share it. There were also self-appointed missionaries, the agencies of the UMC, and interested ecumenical partners. From the outset, the strategic planning led to restructuring the work in Russia and other countries of the former Soviet Union. Awareness of indigenous culture and spirituality, an emphasis on the whole gospel of word and deed, ecumenical cooperation, and United Methodist connectionalism have been critical to the renewed organization of Methodism in Russia. A Joint Task Force on Extended Mission to the Commonwealth of Independent States[46] brought together representatives from the General Board of Global Ministries, the European Council of the UMC, and the annual conferences in Russia's neighboring countries.

Empowering indigenous persons in positions of responsibility and the role of women in ministry have been trademarks of United Methodism in Russia. Leadership for new groups and churches was found locally among the newly converted persons, many of them women. First training seminars for lay leaders were held in 1992, then a course of study was launched in 1993, and in 1995 the Russia United Methodist Theological Seminary was opened in Moscow.

The renewed work of Methodism in Russia from its inception had both a spontaneous and an institutional component. Coordination of both (not competition) has been an important part of United Methodist success in Russia. United Methodist connectionalism has been an indispensable element in the Russian work from its inception. In a new model of participatory mission (the 'Russia Initiative'),[47] it has avoided domination in favor of self-determination. New churches have been formed by outreach from existing churches through contacts established by 'partner churches' to areas in Russia where no Methodist work previously existed and by the appointment of pastors to strategic places.

Methodism in Russia from its launching was interested in connection and cooperation with other churches and movements. Conversations with the Russian Orthodox Church, held in Moscow in 1993 and 1994, were a form of 'Church diplomacy' without influence on the grassroots. Relationship to other Protestant groups has grown on various levels. The ministry of local United Methodist churches has gained appreciation, even the acceptance of Methodist women pastors by Baptists and Pentecostals. Initiatives of leadership of several denominations led to the formation of a Protestant Evangelical Alliance as a forum for spiritual encounter with elements of political representation.

There is an emerging face of Methodism in Russia, though the movement is still fairly young. Methodists in the Eurasia area share an evangelical zeal with their European sisters and brothers, offering Christ's personal invitation. They experience it in the church as the communion of saints through lands and times. Therefore, common worship is important because it reflects the corporate experience of the church. In that way, Methodists discover their spiritual roots in the Methodist tradition inherited from American and European expressions and the spirituality of the Eastern Church in thought, prayer, and worship as well as indigenous religious customs. The result is the discovery of a striking consonance of Methodist and Russian thought and a worship style and hymnody that reflect this multifaceted heritage.[48]

Beginning on a small scale in three centers (Moscow, Samara, and Yekaterinburg), within a decade the work spread over a large area from the former German eastern Prussia (Kaliningrad region) to the Russian Far East (Vladivostok) from the north of Russia to the southern countries (former Soviet republics) of Ukraine, Moldova, and Belarus; and to Central Asia (Kazakhstan, Kyrgyzstan, and Uzbekistan). While widely spread out, it includes all the areas of the old Russian empire where Methodism was active before Soviet power (northwest Russia around St. Petersburg, the Far East, central Siberia, western Ukraine, and Belarus).

Renewal in the Baltic Countries
In 1990 and 1991 the Baltic countries regained their independence from the Soviet Union.

Under the leadership of Rev. Olaf Pärnamets, the church in **Estonia** happily welcomed the new possibilities and with renewed vigor embraced programs of evangelism, social work, church development, and theological education. Many of these activities were not new. They had been accomplished only on a smaller scale and often under cover during the Soviet regime. The two most visible projects are the Baltic Mission Centre, a large multipurpose building in the center of Tallinn. It houses worship for the Tallinn Methodist Church, replacing the church building that was destroyed at the end of World War II. During the Soviet time, Methodists worshiped in the Seventh-day Adventist church building. Support from Methodists worldwide made the construction of the Mission Centre possible. The building also houses the Baltic Theological Seminary. With its interdenominational student population, it became the largest Methodist seminary in Europe.

In Liepaja in **Latvia**, a group of Methodists joined the Lutheran church because the Soviet authorities closed Methodist work at the end of World War II. The congregation maintained some of the spiritual vitality and memories of its former Methodist activities. With the help of expatriate Latvian Methodists, the displaced Methodists explored possibilities of renewal. Under the leadership of Rev. Arijs Viksna, a former Lutheran pastor from

Liepaja, property in Riga and other places was reclaimed, congregations reestablished, and vibrant social work was developed with special emphasis on help for mothers and children.

Research conducted by United Methodism's GBGM with the help of expatriate Lithuanian Methodists, discovered the vestiges of Methodist work in **Lithuania**. The church in Kaunas became the center for a renewed mission. The church's building, dating back to Tsarist times, was reclaimed and restored. The same was possible in other places. In a nation with a traditionally strong Catholic presence, Methodist work centers on evangelization and social work, especially rehabilitation for persons with addictions and chemical dependency.

Within the highly secularized post-Soviet society, Methodist ministries in Russia, the other CIS countries, and the Baltic nations bear the marks of a 'post-Christian' church – a small, but highly motivated membership, whose outreach and social influence is stronger than immediate results of evangelization. It receives strong and highly needed support from United Methodism in the United States and Europe.

For Further Reading

Barclay, Wade Crawford and J. Tremayne Copplestone. *History of Methodist Missions Series*. 4 vols. New York: Board of Missions and Church Extension, 1949–1973.

Kimbrough, S T, Jr. *Methodism in Russia & the Baltic States. History and Renewal*. Nashville: Abingdon Press, 1995. Russian enlarged edition, Yekaterinburg, Ural University, 2003.

Kimbrough, S T, Jr. *A Pictorial Panorama of Early Russia Methodism 1889–1931*. Madison, NJ: General Commission on Archives and History. The United Methodist Church, 2009.

Nikitin, Arkhimandrit Avgustin Nikitin. *Metodizm i Pravoslavie (Methodism and Orthodoxy)*. St. Petersburg: Svetoch, 2001.

Sledge, Robert W. *'Five Dollars and Myself': The History of Mission of the Methodist Episcopal Church, South, 1845–1939*. New York: General Board of Global Ministries, The United Methodist Church, 2005.

Streiff, Patrick Ph. *Der Methodismus in Europa im 19 und 20 Jahrhundert (Methodism in Europe: 19th and 20th Century)*. Frankfurt: EmK Geschichte – Monografien Band 50. Studiengemeinschaft für Geschichte der Evangelisch-methodistischen Kirche, 2003. English edition, Tallinn: Baltic Methodist Theological Seminary, 2005.

12 Methodism in Latin America and the Caribbean

Paulo Ayres Mattos

Throughout Latin America and the Caribbean there are many varied evidences of Methodism's presence in small villages and big cities, large churches and small chapels, small parish schools and big universities. When we talk about Methodism in those two regions of the Americas, our conversation must always be about different types of Methodism since Latin American and Caribbean Methodism are diverse. The rich varieties of Methodism in Latin America and the Caribbean islands and their contributions to the church of Jesus Christ around the world must be recognized and affirmed with joy and thanksgiving. Methodists in Latin America and the Caribbean have many reasons to be grateful for the testimony of those women and men who, transformed by God's grace, have become agents of transformation by God's love manifested in Jesus Christ in the power of the Holy Spirit.

The present state of research on Latin American and Caribbean Methodism deserves serious concern from those that acknowledge the importance of history for understanding the worldwide Christian mission. The fact that most Latin American and Caribbean Methodist churches have not created and developed appropriate policies and structures for preserving the memory of their past, which has significantly affected research on Latin American and Caribbean Methodist history and theology. Church historians and archivists often report that important documents have been treated as expendable and have been lost or destroyed, particularly at the local church level. Furthermore, conference archives at the national or regional level are not adequately organized and administered because resources – principally financial – are not available for the task. These problems impede research on Methodism in Latin America and the Caribbean. The churches' disregard for the importance of history and preserving historical records at all levels makes serious research on the history and theology of Latin American and Caribbean Methodism extremely difficult.

Methodism in Latin America and the Caribbean

Although Methodist historians and theologians in Mexico, Peru, Chile, Argentina, and Brazil have published the results of historical research in books and journals, it must be admitted that systematic research and writing about Methodism reflecting the nature and mission of the Wesleyan movement in that area of the world is waiting to be produced.

It is important to observe that a large amount of historical material on the missionary work of Methodists in Latin America is deposited at the Archives and History Center of the United Methodist Church in Madison, New Jersey. Much of the research on Latin American Methodism has depended on materials there.

In spite of these difficulties, this chapter is an attempt to do justice to the enormous diversity of 'Methodisms' in Central and South America as well as in the Caribbean islands. The first section gives a historical survey of the establishment and development of Methodism in the different regions of the Americas. The second section describes the process and context of the autonomy of Latin American and Caribbean churches in the 1960s. The third section considers the formation of Council of the Evangelical Methodist Churches in Latin America (CIEMAL) in 1969 and the importance of the connectional work of this body of Latin American and Caribbean Methodism. There follows a section that describes the emergence of new Methodist churches established in Latin America after the missionary era and another that recognizes the presence of other Methodist expressions in both regions. The final section analyzes the meaning of the Methodist presence and witness in Latin America and the Caribbean.

Establishment and Development of Methodism in the Caribbean and Latin America

Even when missionary outreach beyond the British islands was not part of John Wesley's evangelical commitment to spread scriptural holiness over the land, *'mainline Methodism'*[1] arrived in the Caribbean in the eighteenth century, even before it was organized in North America in the 1760s. John Wesley was involved in the very beginning of the Methodist work in Antigua and later Thomas Coke became one of the major supporters of Methodist missions in the West Indies.

Caribbean Methodism originated in 1759 when Nathaniel Gilbert, converted during a visit to John Wesley in England with his family and two African slaves, returned to his home in Antigua and began Methodist meetings on his plantation, preaching particularly to his African slaves and forming a Methodist society. After Gilbert's death in 1774, this society was held together under the leadership of two black women, Mary Alley and Sophia Campbell.

In 1778 John Baxter, a government shipwright and Methodist local preacher, went to Antigua and with Wesley's approval began to preach and lead the society organized by Gilbert. Baxter was ordained a few years later and appointed to Antigua by the Methodist Episcopal Church. Late in 1786, Thomas Coke's vessel, sailing from England to Nova Scotia with three other British preachers including William Warrener, was driven far off course by a storm, and landed in Antigua. Coke organized Baxter's work as a circuit and placed Warrener in charge. Coke's recently published journal demonstrates his special interest in the Methodist work in the Caribbean and reports on his regular visitations to the churches there.

During the nineteenth century and in the first half of the twentieth century, under the auspices of British Methodism, Caribbean Methodism developed especially among African people and their descendents. It spread not only over the islands, but also to Central and South American countries including Costa Rica, Panama, and Guyana, in which over time English-speaking Caribbean migrant workers took up residence.

Most of the Methodist Churches in Latin America and in Spanish-speaking Caribbean countries have their roots in the missionary work of American Methodists. When the Missionary Society of the Methodist Episcopal Church officially organized in 1819, American Methodism considered Latin America a missionary priority. In 1825, Nathan Bangs, a major leader in the development of North American Methodism in the first half of the nineteenth century, informed the Missionary Society board that he knew a 'person ready to enlist as South America missionary.' This announcement moved the board members to adopt a resolution that 'if any opening should occur for a mission to South America, and a suitable person should offer, the Board deem it very desirable that such a mission should be established.'[2]

Twelve years after the organization of the Methodist Missionary Society, an anonymous Methodist living in Buenos Aires wrote a letter to Methodist leaders in New York informing them of the organization of a Methodist class in that South American city and requesting a missionary to assist the newly organized small congregation. The Society took three years to answer the request, finally sending Fountain E. Pitts on an exploratory journey to check missionary opportunities in Argentina, Uruguay, and Brazil. After a six-month visit to those countries, Pitts reported to the Society in 1836 and strongly recommended sending missionaries to establish Methodist work in Rio de Janeiro, Montevideo, and Buenos Aires. The Society accepted Pitts' recommendations in 1836 sending Justin Spaulding[3] to Rio de Janeiro and John Dempster[4] to Buenos Aires. Soon class meetings, societies, and Sunday schools appeared in Rio de Janeiro, Montevideo, and Buenos Aires.[5] Unfortunately, financial troubles in the United States, fatal health problems encountered by missionary families, and fierce opposition from Catholic clergy against the Methodists forced the Mission Society to discontinue work in Brazil,

Uruguay, and Argentina in the early 1840s, recalling its personnel from those countries.[6]

Notwithstanding, the Methodist congregation in Buenos Aires decided to assume the financial support of William H. Norris,[7] a Methodist minister who arrived in Montevideo in 1839 and was appointed by the Society to organize Methodist work. In 1843, Argentinean Methodism constructed the first Methodist church building in Latin America.[8] When in 1844 division came to episcopal Methodism in the United States, Latin American Methodism was reduced to the congregation in Buenos Aires, which remains active to this day.

The second half of the nineteenth century saw Methodist missions established and consolidated in Latin American countries by the two major branches of North American episcopal Methodism, with the exception of Guatemala, Honduras, El Salvador, and Nicaragua in Central America, and Colombia, Venezuela, the Guyanas, and Ecuador in South America. From historical and geographical points of view, the establishment and development of Latin American and the Spanish-speaking Caribbean missionary work of American Methodism concentrated most of its resources around six major regional areas: Argentina, Uruguay, and Paraguay; Brazil; Mexico; the Andean region; the Spanish-speaking Caribbean; and Central America.

Strong leadership was provided by missionary pioneers between 1760 and 1885 including Nathaniel Gilbert in Antigua in 1760, Daniel Kidder[9] (Brazil, 1838), Junius E. Newman[10] (southern Brazil, 1866), Thomas Wood[11] (Argentina, Uruguay, Peru, 1870), Alejandro Hernandez[12] (México, 1871), William Butler[13] (Mexico, 1873), Bishop John C. Keener[14] (Mexico, 1873), J. J. Ransom[15] (southern Brazil, 1876), Bishop William Taylor[16] (Chile, Bolivia, Peru, Brazil, Panama, 1877), Ira and Adelaide LaFetra[17] (Chile, 1878), Francisco Penzotti[18] (Bolivia, Peru, Panama, Costa Rica, 1879), Justus Nelson[19] (northern Brazil, 1880), Martha Watts[20] (southern Brazil, 1881), Enrique B. Someillan[21] (Cuba, 1883), João Correa[22] (Uruguay, southern Brazil, 1885), Carmén Chacón[23] (southern Brazil, 1885), and H. C. Tucker[24] (southern Brazil, 1886). Much of this missionary work was clear evidence of the deep commitment of northern and southern episcopal Methodist people and by the end of the nineteenth century Methodist churches, schools, and clinics were founded in various Latin American and Caribbean countries.

Later, in the first half of the twentieth century, with the growth of the Methodist missions and development of indigenous leadership, annual conferences were formed which provided ecclesial structures for the Methodist ministry established in Latin America. Although North American mission boards still controlled much of the decision-making power, their missionaries and indigenous leaders sometimes were dissatisfied and disagreed with control exercised so far from the mission field. The Congress on Christian Work in Latin America held in Panama in February 1916 was in many ways a clear manifestation of disagreements between the workers in the mission field and their mission boards.[25]

These tense relations created a favorable atmosphere for the development of demands among indigenous leaders, particularly in Mexico and Brazil. The missionary work sponsored and supported by North American Methodists grew rapidly in both countries. The 'three self' philosophy of the missionary movement – self-governing, self-supporting, and self-propagating – motivated Mexican and Brazilian Methodists to develop nationalist movements that agitated for the autonomy of their churches in the 1920s. Strong pressures from their indigenous leadership demanded from the two branches of North American episcopal Methodism ecclesiastical policies and structures that could respond to missionary challenges in the context of national uniqueness. As a consequence of nationalist movements, the Methodist churches in Mexico and Brazil became autonomous in 1930. Their autonomy did not sever connectional links with North American Methodism, but their relationships were carried on in a different and more mature manner. The autonomous Mexican and Brazilian Methodist churches maintained a strong association with their parent bodies before and after the 1939 union of northern and southern episcopal Methodisms, which with the Methodist Protestant Church, formed the Methodist Church.

Another dimension of the Methodist missions in Latin America was its participation in the cooperative missionary work developed by different Protestant denominations. The missionary conferences that followed the 1916 Panama Congress, Montevideo in 1925, and Havana 1929, emphasized missionary cooperation instead of competition among the different denominations involved in Latin America and the Caribbean, including the establishment of 'united evangelical churches.' Methodism in the Dominican Republic became part of the Dominican Evangelical Church in 1920. A similar development took place in Puerto Rico when the mission of the former Church of the United Brethren in Christ (an antecedent of the Evangelical United Brethren Church which merged with the Methodist Church in 1968), organized with other Protestant missions to become the United Evangelical Church of Puerto Rico in 1933. A comparable process took place in Ecuador when Methodists participated in the formation of the United Evangelical Church of Ecuador, in 1965.

Autonomy in Latin American and Caribbean Methodism in the Second Half of the Twentieth Century

In the 1960s ecumenical discussions regarding new missionary paradigms, ongoing decolonization procedures around the world, increasing nationalist ideologies throughout Latin America (particularly after the Cuban Revolution in 1959), and consolidation of a stronger national lay and clergy leadership, imposed on Latin American Methodists the necessity of a deep and radical revision of their missionary philosophy and structures. The Commission on the Structure of Methodism Overseas (COSMOS), a committee established by the Board of Missions of the Methodist Church, sponsored negotiations between North American and Latin American Methodists on new relationships and structures. In the case of Methodism in Cuba, because of political and economic restrictions imposed by the United States government against Fidel Castro's regime in the context of the Cold War, in 1964 Cuban Methodists seriously considered the matter of autonomy before COSMOS conversations reached consensus about it. The Methodist Church in Cuba became autonomous in 1968. All other Methodist churches under the Latin American Methodist Central Conference, after the formation of United Methodism in 1968, also became autonomous in the following years.

British-related Methodism in the Caribbean followed a similar track, although in a different context. The end of the European colonialism in the region in the 1960s and the growth and consolidation of Caribbean Methodism throughout the twentieth century led the Caribbean districts of the British Methodist Church to form the autonomous Methodist Church in the Caribbean and the Americas (MCCA) in 1967.

The case of Puerto Rican Methodism was distinct because of Puerto Rico's unique relationship with the United States. The Methodist Church in Puerto Rico remained part of the United Methodist Church until 1994 when it became autonomous.

As in the case of Brazilian and Mexican Methodism, the establishment of newly autonomous Methodist churches in Latin America and the Caribbean did not result in disconnecting their relationship to United Methodism or the Methodist Church in Great Britain. On the contrary, Methodism in the three Americas and the Caribbean has retained close partnerships with their former parent churches in several areas of mutual mission, keeping strong ties with their United Methodist and British Methodist families.

Council of Evangelical Methodist Churches in Latin America and the Caribbean

Newly autonomous churches and the elimination of the Methodist Church's Latin American Central Conference threatened the connectional ties that had historically held together Latin American Methodism. Therefore, the autonomous Methodist churches in Argentina, Bolivia, Costa Rica, Chile, Panama, Peru, and Ecuador, with the encouragement and support of the older autonomous Methodist churches of Mexico, Brazil, and Cuba, decided to stay together through the work of the Council of the Evangelical Methodist

Churches in Latin America (CIEMAL). Those churches officially organized CIEMAL in Santiago, Chile, in 1969. Years later, the Dominican Evangelical Church, the United Evangelical Church of Ecuador, the Methodist Church in the Caribbean and the Americas, the Primitive Methodist Church of Guatemala (a former mission of the American Primitive Methodist Church), and the Methodist Church of Puerto Rico also joined CIEMAL. Today CIEMAL (with the words 'and the Caribbean' added to its full name) includes among its member churches recently organized Methodist denominations not related to the missionary efforts of traditional mainline Methodism. That is the case of the Methodist Church in Colombia, established through the efforts of CIEMAL, and the Evangelical Methodist Community of Paraguay which was organized through the outreach of Brazilian Methodist lay people resident in Paraguay.

The main objective of CIEMAL is to express the connectional relationship and witness of the Methodist churches in Latin America and the Caribbean in their commitment to serve the peoples in those areas. CIEMAL develops its objectives through programs which include: 'New Church Development and Evangelism' (ELADE – Latin American School of Evangelism); 'Young Adults in Mission' (Jóven in Misión); 'Basic Community Health Care-HIV-Aids'; and 'Children, Youth, and Family.' Besides these four regional programs, CIEMAL develops jointly with the General Board of Global Ministries of the United Methodist Church a program titled 'Encounter with Christ' that seeks to motivate churches and individuals in North America to become partners in mission with Methodism in Latin America and the Caribbean.

Emergence of New Methodist Churches in Latin American in Recent Decades

Latin American Methodists have witnessed the new development of *emerging churches* (not to be confused with a North American movement with similar name) that are seeking connectional support from CIEMAL and the General Board of Global Ministries of the United Methodist Church in their commitment to adhere to Methodist tradition. Some of these churches, originating from other denominational traditions, have become aware of Methodism's rich spiritual heritage and have manifested a strong desire to embrace Wesleyan spiritual disciplines, theological doctrines, and practices. Others have resulted from the work of Latin American immigrants in the United States who joined United Methodist congregations during their time in North America and, returning to their home country, have started Methodist work without institutional connection to other Christian groups in the country. This has been the case of the Methodist work in El Salvador, where a few faithful United Methodists are struggling to organize a new Methodist denomination there. In Nicaragua, an Argentinean lay resident in Managua in 1991 began Methodist work which culminated in the organization of the Evangelical Methodist Church of Nicaragua. It may also be the case that in different areas of the same country Christian groups discover John Wesley's teaching and practices, and are prompted to develop religious and social ministries, soon forming Methodist congregations. These groups may decide to establish a Methodist church inviting CIEMAL to assist them in their efforts to assume the Wesleyan identity. That has been the case of a new Methodist church emerging in Venezuela.

In other countries, evangelical groups already organized in small communities in different regions of the same country, as in the case of Colombia, having discovered Methodism, decided to request CIEMAL and the General Board of Global Ministries of the United Methodist Church for information in order to organize according to Methodist principles and polity. Now, after a long, difficult, and turbulent process of formation, there is a Methodist Church organized in Colombia, already affiliated with CIEMAL. In Honduras, where MCCA was already working with the English-speaking population, Methodist work among the Spanish-speaking people is the result of a planned program supported by the General Board of Global Ministries of the United Methodist Church. These newly emerging Methodist churches are both a challenge and a source of hope for the future of Latin American and Caribbean Methodism.

Other Expressions of the Methodist Presence in Latin America

In 2009 'Mainline Methodism' in Latin America and the Caribbean numbered approximately 550,000 members. However, it is not the only expression of the Wesleyan presence in Latin America and the Caribbean. *Holiness Methodism* also has a substantial presence in many parts of both regions. In every country of Central and South America, as well as the Caribbean, the Church of the Nazarene has engaged in missionary work for many years. In some countries, the Nazarenes have the largest membership among the churches of the Wesleyan tradition, for example, Guatemala, Haiti, Peru, and Bolivia. According to the 2006 *World Methodist Council Handbook of Information*, Nazarene membership in Latin America almost matched the membership of the Methodist churches which originated from mainline North American Methodism. Other Holiness churches, such as the Wesleyan and the Free Methodist denominations, despite small membership in most places, are present in several Latin American and Caribbean countries. The Salvation Army is another Holiness Methodist presence in Latin America and the Caribbean, notwithstanding its small membership; in countries like Brazil it enjoys enormous respect from the larger Brazilian society because of its moral integrity and the impact of its programs serving the poor.

African American Methodism is present mostly in the Caribbean region and in Guyana. The African Methodist Episcopal Church has the largest membership among the American black missions in the region and has sponsored mission work in the Caribbean since 1824. The African Methodist Episcopal Zion Church and the Christian Methodist Church, in much more modest numbers, are also present in some Caribbean countries and in Guyana.

Among the Methodists present in South America, Chile's *Pentecostal Methodism* represents the most successful development of Wesleyanism in Latin America. It was born from a Pentecostal revival under the leadership of the Rev. Willis Collins Hoover, a North American Methodist missionary, with strong roots in the Methodist Holiness movement. A revival developed in 1909 when Hoover was serving churches in Valparaiso. Criticized by other missionaries, Hoover and his Pentecostal followers were expelled from the Methodist Episcopal Church in 1909 and a new denomination, the Pentecostal Methodist Church (*Iglesia Metodista Pentecostal*), was organized in the same year. In 1932, a power struggle among Pentecostal Methodists resulted in the formation of the Pentecostal Evangelical Church (*Iglesia Evangélica Pentecostal*). Even though Chilean Pentecostal Methodism suffered other divisions over the decades, it has experienced extraordinary growth, being the main Pentecostal denomination related to historic Methodism and the principal expression of the Chilean Protestantism. Although Pentecostal Methodism in Chile accepted some of the teachings and practices of the 1906–1913 Azusa Street (Los Angeles) Pentecostal revival, Chilean Pentecostalism is doctrinally and structurally very close to historic Methodism. Therefore, both Chilean Pentecostal churches, according to José Míguez Bonino, in spite of being 'strongly engaged in their culture – in song, methods of expansion, language, and so on – [still retain] the connectional organization, ministerial order, and the sacramental life (including infant baptism) of the Methodist tradition.' The membership of Chilean Pentecostal Methodism is estimated to be more than 2,000,000.

There are other denominations of Wesleyan Pentecostalism in Latin America – for instance, in Brazil, the National Wesleyan Church, a division within the Brazilian Methodist Church, and in Costa Rica, the Pentecostal Methodist Church, but they are without the same kind of growth and importance as Chilean Pentecostal Methodism.

Meaning of the Methodist Presence and Witness in Latin America and the Caribbean

Doctrinally and structurally, Methodist work developed by different Methodist denominations has more similarities than differences. Even in the case of Chilean Pentecostalism with its emphasis on the speaking in tongues as the evidence of Holy Spirit baptism, there is a demonstrated loyalty to Methodist doctrine and structure; this represents its unity with other forms of Latin American Methodism.

According the World Methodist Council, Methodism in Latin American and Caribbean in the early twenty-first century had a membership of more than 2,000,000 people.[26] As Míguez Bonino reminds us, 'it is not terribly important to assess the numerical force of Wesleyan churches in Latin America. . . . But the influence of the Wesleyan awakenings has penetrated Latin American Protestantism much more broadly than this official presence suggests.'

Methodists on the continent, since missionary times, have significantly participated in the developments of the Latin American and the Caribbean Protestant world. In the congresses on Christian Work in Panama in 1916, Montevideo in 1925, and Havana in 1929, Methodist contributions were fundamentally important for Protestant cooperation across the continent. Methodists have assumed the same kind of commitment to Christian unity and witness in the celebration of the 1949, 1961, and 1969 Latin American Evangelical Conferences (CELA – *Conferencia Evangélica Latino-Americana*). Another Methodist contribution to Latin American Protestantism was its participation in the establishment of the Evangelical Theological Seminaries in Argentina, Chile, Costa Rica, Mexico, Cuba, and Puerto Rico. A major contribution of the Latin American and Caribbean Methodism to Christianity has been its ecumenical commitment.

Outstanding leadership by Methodists in Latin America and the Caribbean offered to a variety of ecumenical organizations has enriched the worldwide ecumenical movement. This leadership has included: Gonzalo Báez-Camargo (theologian, Mexico), César Dacorso Filho (bishop and ecumenical leader, Brazil), Sante Uberto Barbieri (bishop and ecumenical leader, Brazil/ Argentina/ Bolivia), Otilia Chaves (world Methodist women's leader, Brazil), Dame Nita Burrow (ecumenical leader, Caribbean), Federico Pagura (bishop and ecumenical leader, Argentina), Philip Potter (ecumenical leader, Caribbean), Eunice Weaver (social health activist, Brazil), Emilio Castro (world ecumenical leader, Uruguay), José Míguez Bonino (theologian, Argentina), Mortimer Arias (bishop and theologian, Uruguay/Bolivia), Julio de Santa Ana (theologian, Uruguay), Justo Gonzales (theologian, Cuba, United States), Elza Tamez (theologian, México, Costa Rica, Colombia), Beatriz Ferrari (ecumenical leader, Uruguay), Nellie Ritchie (bishop and ecumenical leader, Argentina), and Almir Maia (educator, Brazil). These persons have served, or are serving Methodist and ecumenical organizations in their own countries in the Caribbean or Latin America, and around the world with outstanding dedication and competence.

In the context of ecumenical relationships as expressions of the catholic spirit of the Wesleyan movement, Methodist historians and theologians in

Latin America have been active participants in the Oxford Institute of Methodist Theological Studies where they have engaged in developing fresh interpretations of Wesleyan theology and have offered world Methodism a Latin American perspective on it. Four conferences on Latin American Wesleyan studies have been convened in San José (Costa Rica), Piracicaba (Brazil), São Bernardo (Brazil), and Buenos Aires (Argentina). As part of the theological praxis of Latin American Methodists, Wesleyan study centers have been established in different countries including Brazil and Argentina.

It is also important to observe that many Latin American and Caribbean Methodist women and men have effectively contributed to building a more democratic, free, and just society. Despite an individualistic theology that permeates the life of many Methodist congregations across Latin America and the Caribbean, which reinforces an otherworldly escapism, they have struggled within a context of constant and brutal violations of the human rights to implement the social principles of historic Methodism. The most recent examples come from the Methodist churches of Peru and Bolivia where two Methodist indigenous women, the Bolivian Casimira Rodriguez Romero[27] and Peruvian María Cleofé Sumire de Conde,[28] have displayed heroic public witness to their faith.

Studies have shown that the establishment of Methodism over the continent, in most cases was deeply influenced by nineteenth-century Anglo-American revivalism within the ideological context of North American 'manifest destiny.' Under such influence, Latin American Methodism is in fact far different from Wesley's social religion in its theological teachings and practices among the poor urban masses of emerging English industrial cities. The Methodist message preached and lived in many places in Latin America has had a strong individualist emphasis on personal conversion characteristic of rural North American Methodism. In fact, Latin American Methodism lacked, and still lacks, the communitarian discipline proper to the pursuit of the holiness of heart and life – personal *and* social – practiced by Wesleyan societies and class meetings in eighteenth-century industrial Great Britain. As a direct consequence of this kind of individualistic and subjectivist salvation, sanctification preached and understood by the Methodists has had a very legalistic and moralistic emphasis. Unfortunately, unlike the earliest Methodists, most Latin American Methodists do not practice 'works of mercy,' for example, attending the needs of the poor through schools, day care and community centers, hospitals and health clinics, and orphanages, as a fundamental component of their soteriology. They give them a minor place in their evangelistic outreach and 'works of piety' spirituality.

A consequence of self-absorbed spirituality, with little concern for transforming Latin American society, an unfortunate characteristic of Latin American and the Caribbean Methodism is the weak numerical strength of the different Wesleyan churches throughout these areas, except for the enormous growth of Chilean Pentecostal Methodism. When compared with other regions of the world, the numerical growth of Methodism in Latin America is deeply frustrating. For example, different from Methodism in Africa, Latin American Methodism, since its beginning, faced difficulties that impaired its growth and consolidation. Robert J. Harman, in an unpublished paper presented at a consultation in Panama in 2007 between CIEMAL churches and the mission agency of the United Methodist Church, noted that the Methodist missionary optimism that characterized the outreach efforts in other parts of the world did not work well in Latin America. Major obstacles not present in Africa or Asia created powerful barriers impeding the development of Methodist missions across the continent. Harman observes that the prevailing Roman Catholic culture was the first and foremost challenge to such missionary progress. People sent by Methodist missionary agencies to work in Latin America, deeply influenced by the anti-Catholicism prevalent among North American Protestant churches, believing in the superiority of Protestantism over other religions including Roman Catholicism, had to face surprisingly strong opposition to their work. Harman analyzed the impact of such difficulties as follows:

> Confident in their North American experience gained during Methodism's remarkable westward march across the continent, they were soon beset by the staunch opposition of Catholic hierarchy, fanatical believers, and protective state policies. What they failed to comprehend was that 'new space' [Africa or Asia] was easier to conquer than 'old space' [Latin America]. This was not only true for the practice of religion, but other cultural influences as well. They relied heavily upon the English language in their offerings of worship and educational opportunities and failed to penetrate deeply held indigenous values. Their efforts did not experience overwhelming results, but barely established toehold in the countries they poured out their hearts and labor.[29]

In spite of these limitations, Latin American and Caribbean Methodist churches are characterized by their emphasis on personal evangelism, education, and social work.

- Across Latin American and the Caribbean lands, the people called Methodists are consistently spreading Wesley's message that God's grace is free for all and in all, and many are accepting Jesus Christ as Lord and Savior. In some countries, the churches are developing strong ministries with and by indigenous people in places like Argentina, Chile, Bolivia,

Brazil, and Guatemala. In other countries, such as Cuba, Methodism is experiencing numerical growth among young people. Therefore, in recent decades, most Methodist churches, with the support of CIEMAL and the World Methodist Council, are attempting to make evangelism a major priority in their missionary programs with effective relevance for people in their own cultural context.

- Education remains a major contribution that Methodist denominations have offered their societies. In many communities, especially in the early twentieth century, Methodist day schools provided the only education available to the poor in communities where Methodism had established churches. Presently and unfortunately, however, most of those schools have given way to large institutions, like colleges and universities serving mostly the middle and upper classes. It must be observed again, however, that Methodism has been able to found theological schools, many of them through ecumenical partnerships. Furthermore, Christian education through Sunday schools and other educational ventures receives important attention in most Latin American and Caribbean churches.
- Social work with the poor continues to be a major concern of Latin American Methodists, even without connection to Wesleyan spiritual discipline. Methodist churches through their own social programs, or in cooperation with CIEMAL, or ecumenically with other Christian churches, are involved in various programs to improve human dignity among women, children, youth, the elderly, indigenous peoples, afro-descendents, and other marginalized and exploited groups in their local communities.
- As previously noted, it is also important to underscore the courageous witness in the name of the gospel given by several Methodist people, lay and clerical, at local and national levels, often through ecumenical cooperation, in defense of human rights. Methodists committed to the struggle for human dignity in different Latin American and Caribbean countries have given eloquent witness, many times in very dangerous circumstances, as in those countries where there were repressive and violent military dictatorships between the 1970s and 1990s.

Finally, Latin American and Caribbean Methodism are facing a period of great challenge and opportunity. Among the areas that demand theological reflection and action are ecclesiology, mission and evangelism, worship and spiritual formation, personal and social holiness, religious freedom, ecumenism, and inter-religious dialogue, neo-pentecostalism and new religious movements, poverty, racial and gender abuse and violence, human sexuality, sustainable economic development, environmental justice, participatory democracy, and human rights. Within and outside the churches these challenges call for reflection and witness of the Methodist people of Latin America and the Caribbean. It is again a time to proclaim together with our spiritual father John Wesley, 'the world is our parish.'

The following information on Latin American and Caribbean Methodist churches is derived from the *World Methodist Council Handbook of Information* (2007). Further information is available in the most recent World Methodist Council handbooks.

- Caribbean and Central America region
  Official name: The Methodist Church in the Caribbean and the Americas (MCCA)
  Year of missionary beginnings: 1760
  Year of autonomy: 1967
  Ecclesiastical System: connectional/presidential

- Argentina
  Official name: Iglesia Evangelica Metodista
  Year of missionary beginnings: 1836
  Year of autonomy: 1969
  Ecclesiastical System: connectional/episcopal (one active bishop).

- Brazil
  Official name: Igreja Metodista
  Years of missionary beginnings: (1836) 1866
  Year of autonomy: 1930
  Ecclesiastical System: connectional/episcopal (eight active bishops).

- Mexico
  Official name: Iglesia Metodista de Mexico
  Year of missionary beginnings: 1871
  Year of autonomy: 1930
  Ecclesiastical System: connectional/Episcopal (six active bishops).

- Uruguay
  Official name: Iglesia Metodista en el Uruguay (IMU)
  Year of missionary beginnings: (1838) 1878
  Year of autonomy: 1968
  Ecclesiastical System: connectional/presidential.

- Chile
  Official name: Iglesia Metodista de Chile
  Year of missionary beginnings: 1878
  Year of autonomy: 1969.

- Cuba
  Official name: Iglesia Metodista en Cuba
  Year of missionary beginnings: 1883
  Year of autonomy: 1964
  Ecclesiastical System: connectional/episcopal (one active bishop).

- Peru
  Official name: Iglesia Metodista del Peru
  Year of missionary beginnings: (18770)1889[AQ]
  Year of autonomy: 1970.

- Puerto Rico
  Official name: Iglesia Metodista de Puerto Rico
  Year of missionary beginnings: 1900
  Year of autonomy: 1992
  Ecclesiastical System: connectional/episcopal (one active bishop).

- Bolivia
  Official name: Iglesia Evangelica Metodista en Bolivia
  Year of missionary beginnings: 1906
  Year of autonomy: 1969
  Ecclesiastical System: connectional/episcopal (one active bishop).

- Panama
  Official name: Iglesia Evangelica Metodista de Panama
  Year of missionary beginnings: 1906
  Year of autonomy: 1970
  Ecclesiastical System: connectional/episcopal (one active bishop).

- Costa Rica
  Official name: Iglesia Evangelica Metodista de Costa Rica
  Year of missionary beginnings: 1917
  Year of autonomy: 1973
  Ecclesiastical System: connectional/episcopal (one active bishop).

- Dominican Republic
  Official name: Iglesia Evangelica Dominicana
  Year of missionary beginnings: 1920 (a Methodist, United Brethren, Presbyterian, and Moravian joint missionary initiative: *'the oldest piece of cooperative denominational work in the world.'*)
  Year of autonomy: 1992
  Ecclesiastical System: connectional/presidential.

- Guatemala
  Official name: Iglesia Evangelica Nacional Metodista Primitiva de Guatemala
  Year of missionary beginnings: 1924 (a missionary initiative of the Primitive Methodist Church in the USA.)
  Year of autonomy: 1973
  Ecclesiastical System: connectional/presidential.

- Ecuador
  Official name: Iglesia Evangelica Metodista Unida del Ecuador
  Year of missionary beginnings: 1965 (as United Evangelical Church of Ecuador, an ecumenical work with the participation of the Presbyterian Church, the Church of the Brethren, the United Church of Christ, and the Methodist Church. In 1988, the UEC General Assembly decided to adopt a Methodist identity.)
  Ecclesiastical System: connectional/Episcopal (one active bishop).

- Nicaragua
  Official name: Iglesia Metodista de Nicaragua
  Year of missionary beginnings: 1985
  Year of autonomy: 1985
  Ecclesiastical System: connectional/presidential.

- Paraguay
  Official name: Comunidad Evangelica Metodista del Paraguay
  Year of missionary beginnings: 1886: first beginning; 1988: second beginning
  Year of autonomy: 1986
  Ecclesiastical System: connectional/Episcopal.

- Colombia
  Official name: Iglesia Colombiana Metodista
  Year of beginnings: (1981) 1996
  Ecclesiastical System: connectional/episcopal (one active bishop).

For Further Reading

Barclay, Wade Crawford. *History of Methodist Missions*. 3 vols. New York: Board of Missions, The Methodist Church. 1949–1957.

Bucke, E. Stevens, ed. *The History of American Methodism*. 3 vols. Nashville: Abingdon Press, 1964.

Cole, Charles E., ed. *Christian Mission in the Third Millennium*. New York: General Board of Global Ministries, The United Methodist Church, 2004.

Committee on Cooperation in Latin America, '*Christian Work In Latin America – Survey and Occupation, Message and Method Education*' [Panama Congress

Report], Vol. 1. New York: Missionary Education Movement in the United States and Canada, 1917.

Miguez Bonino, José. 'Methodism and Latin American Liberation Movements,' in Joerg Rieger and John J. Vincent, eds. *Methodist and Radical: Rejuvenating a Tradition*. Nashville: Kingswood Books, 2003.

Miguez Bonino, José. 'Wesley in Latin America: A Theological and Historical Reflection,' in Randy L Maddox, ed. *Re-thinking Wesley's Theology for Contemporary Methodism*. Nashville: Kingswood Books, 1998.

The United Methodist History of Mission Series. 6 vols. New York: General Board of Global Ministries, The United Methodist Church, 2003–2005.

13 Evangelism in the Methodist Tradition

Paul Wesley Chilcote

Evangelism involves 'efforts to communicate and celebrate the redeeming and reconciling love of God as revealed in Jesus Christ to [all] persons, ... to invite persons to commit their lives to Christ and to his church; and to enable persons to live as Christian disciples in the world.'[1] The historical foundations of this missional practice in the Methodist tradition can be understood only in the context of the evangelical revival that arose from within the Church of England in the eighteenth century as a movement of spiritual renewal.[2] Six primary emphases of early Methodism constitute a Wesleyan paradigm of renewal – the rediscoveries of the living Word, saving faith, holistic spirituality, accountable discipleship, formative worship, and missional vocation. While many of these characteristics can be found in other movements of renewal in the history of the church, they combined in the Wesleyan revival with unusual effect. Certainly, the ecclesial and cultural context shaped Methodist evangelism, particularly at a time when inertia within the church seemed to be oriented in the direction of institutional preservation. John and Charles Wesley recaptured a vision of the church rooted in God's transforming power and mission in the world, and manifest in practices that sought solidarity with those who stood on the periphery of society. The overview of the history and development of evangelism in the Methodist tradition that follows includes an exploration of a Wesleyan theology of evangelism and its attendant practices, and an attempt to navigate the complex and shifting paradigms related to evangelism in the evolution of Methodism following the deaths of its founders to the present time.

A Wesleyan Theology of Evangelism

John and Charles Wesley were unquestionably two of the greatest evangelists of their day. The evangelistic practices of the Wesleys and of the Methodist societies they founded reflect their understanding of God's character. The God they had come to know in Christ was a 'missionary God' – a God who always reaches out, whose grace is active and working to save and restore all creation. They attempted to reclaim mission as the church's reason for being and evangelism as the heart of that mission in the world.[3] The holistic vision of mission and evangelism that they developed refused to separate faith and works, personal salvation and social action, physical and spiritual needs. The constitutive dimensions of that vision included a trinitarian foundation, a holistic soteriology, a missional ecclesiology, and an inclusive ministry.

A Trinitarian Foundation
A Wesleyan theology of evangelism begins with God and two Christian doctrines, in particular, the doctrine of creation and the doctrine of the incarnation. The Wesleys viewed God's act of creation as a sheer act of grace, motivated by nothing other than God's loving nature. Incarnation – the act by which God took on human flesh in the person of Jesus of Nazareth – demonstrated the same missionary character. In the fullness of time, God entered into human history and manifest love supremely through Jesus Christ. The God of the Wesleys reached out to create all things, to redeem all things, and to restore all things in Christ. God's mission, God's evangelistic activity, God's proclamation and embodiment of good news, began in creation, continues through redemption, and stretches out toward the consummation of all things in Christ.

This description of God's evangelistic character reflects God's triune nature as well. Not only did this trinitarian framework elevate the relational dynamic in evangelism, it also shaped a holistic vision of evangelistic practice. The Wesleys' vision of evangelism was concerned with the forgiveness of sins, emphasizing what God has done *for* humankind in Christ. But evangelism in the Wesleyan spirit also celebrated what God is doing *in* the faithful through the presence of the Holy Spirit. They believed that disciples of Jesus were not only saved from sin, they were also saved into a life of love. Charles Wesley used a powerful image to communicate this understanding of the Christian life and the concomitant call to be 'gospel-bearers.' He described the Christian as a 'transcript of the Trinity.' The triune God is known through people in whom the essence of God radiates through those who have become the bearers of God's good news about the love of Christ for all.

A Holistic Soteriology
One of the most distinctive characteristics of the Wesleys' doctrine of salvation was their emphasis upon the integral nature of faith and works. They proclaimed and lived a gospel of God's free grace received by faith *and* worked out in love. In his sermon, 'Upon our Lord's Sermon on the Mount V,' John Wesley argued:

> And when we say, 'Believe, and thou shalt be saved,' we do not mean, 'Believe, and thou shalt step from sin to heaven, without any holiness

coming between, faith supplying the place of holiness;' but, believe and thou shalt be holy; believe in the Lord Jesus, and thou shalt have peace and power together.' (III.9)

This holistic conception of redemption rested on two simple premises. First, the biblical conception of salvation by grace through faith provides the proper foundation for the Christian life. Secondly, the purpose of a life reclaimed by faith alone is the restoration of God's image (love) in the life of the believer. Faith, in other words, is a means to love's end. The phrase 'faith working by love leading to holiness of heart and life' summarizes the Wesleyan understanding of salvation.

For the Wesleys, therefore, faith in Christ was not the goal of the Christian life; rather, the goal was to love God and others with Christ-like love. The Wesleyan conception of God's grace as *relationship* made it possible to hold the means (faith) and the end (holiness or love) together. Always initiated from God's side, the Wesleys reconceived salvation as a dynamic, relational process, the purpose of which was healing and the restoration of wholeness in all people. John Wesley painted a portrait of this therapeutic vision of the Christian life in his Sermon 43, 'The Scripture Way of Salvation.' He spoke of 'justification by grace through faith' as a *relative* change in one's status before God. But he placed equal emphasis on the *real* change that takes place in the hearts, lives, and loves of the faithful as they become new creatures in Christ. Rather than viewing salvation as a static act of God at some demonstrable point of time ('once saved, always saved'), he understood salvation as a *process* that begins with justification (faith), but continues thereafter as the transformed person grows in grace toward entire sanctification (active love rooted in holy intention) as a flying goal. Moreover, they always characterized this goal by the twin dimensions of holiness of heart (internal) or love of God (a vertical dimension) and holiness of life (external) or love of neighbor (a horizontal dimension). It is not too difficult to see how this holistic soteriology shaped the evangelistic practice of the early Methodists. The teleological orientation of their doctrine of salvation – with its goal of perfect love – necessitated a theology of evangelism that refused to separate faith, as the means, from love, as the end, of a process of restoration.

A Missional Ecclesiology
The Wesleys rediscovered a missional ecclesiology, seeking to reclaim participation in God's mission as the primary reason for the being of the church. They believed that there was a necessary connection in the life of the Christian community between evangelism and mission. It is not too much to say that all three concepts taken together – church, evangelism, and mission – defined early Methodism. The Wesleys believed that the church was not called to live

for itself; rather, it was called to give itself for the life of the world in imitation of Christ. The church of Wesley's England had exchanged this missional vocation for maintenance. It had become distant from and irrelevant to the world it was called to serve, needing desperately to reclaim its true identity as God's agent of shalom in the world. Two concomitant principles undergirded this vision: (1) the community of faith makes disciples who bear witness to the gospel, and (2) the church functions itself as evangelist. The Wesleys firmly believed that God raised up the people called Methodists particularly for the task of resuscitating a missional, evangel-bearing church.

The early Methodists, therefore, viewed themselves as disciples ('learners'), gathered together in a pilgrim community in order to learn how to love. Then God sent them out ('apostles') to serve the present age by sharing that love with others. They embraced this vocation, not because of what they had done, but because they knew themselves to be God's own people, formed by and for God's purpose and grace. In this vision of the church, evangelism and mission were inseparable, but distinct. 'Offering Christ,' to use Wesley's own terminology, involves both word and deed, both proclamation and action; it connected the gospel to the world. The Wesleys defined the church as an alternative mission community and the Methodist people reclaimed this mission-church model in their own time.

An Inclusive Ministry
The understanding that God commissioned all believers to be evangelists resonated with this missional vision. The Wesleys encouraged and empowered all of their followers to become effective evangelists in the normal round of their ordinary lives, inculcating a vision of evangelism as the perennial privilege and task of the whole church. They employed a vast network of itinerant preacher-evangelists, including women, to further this mission. Mary Bosanquet, for example, both preached the good news of God's love and established an orphanage/school for the most destitute in London, bearing witness to that love of God for all people. Methodists believed and taught that nothing proclaimed Christ more fully than an authentic Christian life and that love could never be coerced. Ideally, no means or methods of evangelism were employed, therefore, that were antithetical to its loving end. In this regard, John Wesley offered the following suggestions in his *Advice to the People called Methodists*:

> Above all, stand fast in obedient faith, faith in the God of pardoning mercy, in the God and Father of our Lord Jesus Christ, who hath loved *you*, and given himself for you. Ascribe to him all the good you find in yourself, all your peace, and joy, and love, all your power to do and suffer his will, through the Spirit of the living God. . . . Abhor every approach, in any kind

or degree, to the spirit of *persecution*. If you cannot *reason* or *persuade* a man into the truth, never attempt to *force* him into it. If love will not compel him to come in, leave him to God, the Judge of all. (*WJW(B)*, 9: 129–130)

Wesleyan Evangelistic Practice

The holistic paradigm for evangelism developed by the Wesleys can be described as an interdependent network of missional practices that included faithful preaching, inspirational singing, accountable discipleship, authentic worship, and incarnational service.[4]

Faithful Preaching

There can be no question that the Wesleys defined evangelism in terms of verbal proclamation. While his published sermons are really more like theological essays for the purpose of teaching, the urgency of an invitation characterized John Wesley's extemporaneous preaching. Eyewitness accounts of these events stress the word 'now' time and time again. Wesley's persistent theme was simply, '*Now* is the day of salvation.' In the *Conference Minutes of 1744*, he asked the question, 'What is the best method of preaching?' His fourfold response was simple and clear: '(1) to invite, (2) to convince, (3) to offer Christ, (4) to build up, and to do this (in some measure) in every sermon.' As we have already seen, the central message was that of universal love to all made known to us in Jesus Christ. Evangelism in the Wesleyan spirit is nothing less than wooing God's children back into God's loving embrace.

It is noteworthy that the Wesleys launched the Methodist movement, not at the time of their 'conversions' in 1738, so much as with their 'field preaching' in 1739. Instead of waiting for the people to come to them, the Wesleys took the message of God's unconditional love to the people where they were. The importance of this action cannot be overestimated. In time, an army of itinerant preachers carried the message of the gospel to every corner of England, and beyond. The primary content of their preaching is aptly summarized in the so-called 'four alls:' all need to be saved; all can be saved; all can know they are saved; all can be saved to the uttermost. But their preaching addressed the social evils of their day with equal force. Personal salvation and participation in God's inbreaking reign characterized their evangelistic preaching.

Inspirational Singing

The Methodist movement was born in song. Early Methodists found their true identity as the children of God through singing, and the hymns of Charles Wesley, in particular, shaped their self-understanding and practice. The leaders of the movement recognized the potency of congregational singing as a legitimate medium of theology. The hymns functioned both as a communal confession of faith and a common catechism for the faith – embodying the fullness of the gospel. The hymns constituted, as John Wesley would suggest in his preface to the 1780 *Collection of Hymns for the Use of the People Called Methodists*, 'A Little Body of Experimental and Practical Divinity.' The lyrical theology of Charles Wesley both transformed and formed the singer. With regard to the theology of evangelism communicated through the hymns, four themes pervade the Wesleyan corpus: the nature of God's unconditional love, the all-sufficiency of God's grace, the all-embracing nature of inclusive community, and the missional vision of God's people.

Tore Meistad examined the missiological orientation of Wesley's hymns.[5] He concluded that Charles grounded his vision of missional evangelism on the creating, atoning, life-giving Triune God, universal redemption and the person in corporate perspective, salvation conceived as the new creation, love as the manifestation of God's presence, and the messianic kingdom symbolized in the year of Jubilee. One of the most popular of Wesley's hymns, 'O for a thousand tongues to sing,' reflects the evangelistic thrust of this vision. Not only does the hymn celebrate the personal experience of salvation, understood primarily as forgiveness of sin, but it elaborates the concept of salvation and the Methodist mission theologically, articulating a conception of evangelism actualized through the discipleship of those committed to the reign of God. Other hymns, such as, 'Blow Ye the Trumpet, Blow,' pull together Wesley's missional motifs, describing the evangelistic mission of the messianic people in terms of economic justice and human liberation. It is not too much to claim that the early Methodist people sang and discovered their essential identity as gospel-bearers and experienced the inclusivity of the community of faith through the very act of singing together.

Accountable Discipleship (Small Groups)
Despite the centrality of verbal proclamation to evangelistic practice in the evangelical revival, the Wesleys believed that evangelism was much more than simply preaching the gospel. The ministry of small groups figured just as prominently in the Methodist structure. It would even be valid to claim that evangelism took place more fully in the intimacy of the small group than in the anonymity of the crowd at major preaching events. John Wesley emphasized this principle in a journal entry of 25 August 1763, 'I was more convinced than ever that the preaching like an apostle, without joining together those that are awakened and training them up in the ways of God, is only begetting children for the murderer' (*WJW(B)*, 13:424). The definitive organisms of early Methodism were the small group meetings (classes and bands). These intimate circles of accountable discipleship functioned as potent cells for the promotion of inward and outward holiness. In these small groups dedicated people learned what it meant to find redemption in Christ,

to grow in Christ, to plumb the depths of God's love for them all together, and to live out that love in their daily lives. On the basis of his detailed study of the early Methodist societies, Tom Albin has argued that most of the early Methodist people were converted, not in response to preaching, but as a consequence of personal relationships with other Christians in the intimacy of small groups. This context proved the most fertile ground for the sharing and nurture of faith. In small groups, faith was born and awakened sinners were encouraged to grow in grace so as to be channels of love for others. They came to understand their true vocation, and that of the church as the whole people of God, as a summons to enter a particular, revolutionary path of self-sacrificing love for the world.

Authentic Worship (Eucharist)
It is interesting that John Wesley's first definition of the Methodists revolved around worship. 'A society,' he wrote in his *General Rules*, 'is no other than a company of men [and women] having the form and seeking the power of godliness, united in order to pray together, to receive the word of exhortation, and to watch over one another in love, that they may help each other to work out their salvation' (*WJW(B)*, 9: 69). He described authentic worship as a communal act that looks upward and inward, a profoundly relational and transformational experience that reveals the fullness of the gospel and calls for response. He believed, therefore, that worship ought to engage the whole person – heart, head, and hands. The central purpose of worship, as Wesley would have argued, is to present the whole gospel to the whole person; evangelism defines both its content and its character.

The Wesleyan revival was an evangelical reawakening, but it was also a sacramental or eucharistic revival. The Wesleys believed that their sacramental practice – their frequent celebration of the Lord's Supper – was in every way as evangelistic as their preaching, singing, or interaction with one another in the context of small groups. There was a certain sense in which the sacrament of Holy Communion brought all of these practices together in one great sign-act of love. If evangelism has to do with heralding the good news, bearing witness to God's love, and servanthood in the life of the world, then the sacrament is the supreme place where the community embodies this action on behalf of the world. Whereas in preaching words become the instruments of proclamation, in the sacrament God's grace becomes tangible. All are offered the bread of life. When asked to define evangelism, the great Sri Lankan Methodist, D. T. Niles, responded by saying it is one hungry beggar showing another hungry beggar where to find bread.

The sacrament embodies a holistic gospel. The Lord's Supper memorializes the passion of Christ. It is a remembrance in the sense of *anamnesis*, that is, calling the event of Christ's self-sacrifice to mind in such a way as to make it real in the present. The eucharist celebrates the presence of the living Christ as a sign and means of grace in which God offers mercy, forgiveness, and love to those who receive Christ by faith. Holy Communion anticipates the Heavenly Banquet to come in which God unites all of God's children in one great feast of love. The Wesleys employed these various dimensions in an effort to communicate the expansive nature of God's good news and to offer it effectively and fully to all who participate in the meal. The sacrament functions as a converting as well as a confirming ordinance. In this sign-act of love, the past, present, and future – faith, hope, and love – are compressed, as it were, into a timeless, communal act of praise. Moreover, the sacrament forms the church into a community of evangelism that reaches out to preach, teach, baptize, and make new disciples of Christ, shaping the church for its mission of partnering with God in the redemption of the world. As followers of the One who ate with sinners and reached out to the marginalized, the church intentionally concerns itself about those who are absent from Christ's Table – those who feel unworthy, the poor, the unconverted, victims of prejudice, and others who are oppressed or neglected.

Incarnational Service
To the verbal proclamation of the gospel, the intimacy of small groups, the singing and sacramental fellowship of early Methodist societies, the witness of loving service to others must be added, an outward holiness that also defined Methodist evangelism. Familiar words from the pen of Charles Wesley strike this diaconal chord:

> A charge to keep I have,
>   A God to glorify,
> A never-dying soul to save,
>   And fit it for the sky;
> To serve the present age,
>   My calling to fulfil;
> O may it all my powers engage
>   To do my Master's will. (WJW(B), 7: 465)

Unlike some forms of evangelism, the goal of which would seem to be the redemption of one's own soul, the ultimate goal of a Wesleyan approach was the redemption of the other and the world. The 'charge to keep' for the Christian, in other words, is to glorify God, and believers glorify God most fully by becoming the servants of all. The primary question for the early Methodist was not, 'Am I saved?' The ultimate question was, 'For what purpose am I saved?' For the Wesleys, the answer was clear. The neighbor was the goal of redemption, just as the life, death, and resurrection of Christ were oriented toward the salvation of all humanity. The self-giving love of Christ became the goal, purpose, and style of the Christian life and evangelistic witness. The genuine Christian was the one who embraced the mission of Jesus in humility and servanthood.

St. Paul's word to the Roman Christians, 'to present your bodies as a living sacrifice' (12:1), provided the foundation upon which the Methodists built this *kenotic*, self-sacrificial vision of life. With regard to this Christian oblation, the Wesleys clarified three points in particular. First, the Spirit makes personal self-sacrifice possible; to live as Christ lived means to be filled with the Holy Spirit. Second, the offering was holistic, involving both soul and body; the Wesleys guard against any false separation of the spiritual from the physical in the life of the believer. Third, self-sacrifice, while an act of obedience and compliance, roots the believer in love; self-giving love and God are one. They also went to great lengths to specify the two-fold character of Christian service as integral to Christian evangelism. First, the servant offers to others what he or she has freely received from God. Christ-like servants engage in evangelism – offering God's grace to all in both word and deed. Second, to have the mind of Christ, to be a gospel-bearer, entails the care of the poor. The early Methodist people took this 'call to serve the present age' with utmost seriousness. They lived out their lives in solidarity with those people who were shut out, neglected, and thrown away. In his hymns, Charles Wesley memorialized those persons who realized this lofty ideal in their lives, who befriended the least in their communities through incarnational acts of mercy and service.

Methodists sought to proclaim and embody the whole gospel for the whole person throughout the whole world through this holistic network of missional practices.

Developments within Methodism

Following the deaths of John and Charles Wesley at the end of the eighteenth century, monumental changes swept through Methodism both in its original setting in Britain, where the movement of renewal faced the challenge of institutional consolidation, and particularly in the unique cultural context of the New World. Two critical paradigm shifts during the nineteenth century redirected much of the thought and practice of evangelism away from the holistic design of the original Wesleyan model. A rising tide of concern about evangelism in a shrinking globe, fueled in large measure by the Protestant missionary movement, characterized the first half of the twentieth century, and a critical decade of reflection on mission and evangelism (1972–1982) set the agenda for efforts to rethink evangelism during the closing decades of the millennium. An agenda for further reflection and research spins quite naturally out of the challenging discoveries and exciting developments of the twentieth century and affords a unique opportunity for the renewal of an authentic vision for Methodist evangelism.

Shifting Paradigms in the Nineteenth Century
The holistic model of evangelism that characterized the early Methodist movement is unfamiliar to most Methodists today. Two monumental paradigm shifts that occurred over the course of the nineteenth century shaped popular thought about evangelism in directions antithetical to the synthetic approach of the Wesleys and continue to influence attitudes about evangelism around the world. First, the revivalist milieu of the American frontier led to a shift from holiness of heart and life as the goal of the Christian life for Methodists to the experience of conversion as the defining event of redemption. The goal of evangelism shifted from authentic discipleship to conversion. This paradigm shift led directly to the second. The holistic vision of the Wesleys also deteriorated under the weight of a radical individualism that tended to separate personal salvation from social action. If the goal of evangelism was securing eternal security in heaven for the individual, then it is not difficult to see how attention would be shifted away from the concerns of this world and active engagement in Christ's rule over human history. The effect was similar to that of a conversion-fixated theology of evangelism; the status of the individual before God became more important than the establishment of communities of faith committed to the reign of God in this world. The primary instrument in these changes was the Second Great Awakening and its camp meeting revivalism. The impact of this phenomenon was so powerful that many today assume the conception and practice of evangelism in the Second Great Awakening to be normative.

Certainly, there were efforts to maintain a more dynamic theology of evangelism in Methodism that held means and ends, personal and social aspects of redemption together. Studies are beginning to demonstrate how the practice of evangelism among Methodist women, in particular, promoted a more holistic vision. In Britain, one of the great champions of holistic evangelism was Hugh Price Hughes. He believed that Methodism would fail in its primary mission unless evangelistic zeal was harnessed to social responsibility. J. Ernest Rattenbury maintained this legacy, serving for many years at the great Kingsway Hall of the West London Mission, one of the chief centers of evangelism in Britain. He articulated a vision counter to the truncated conceptions of evangelism that tended to dominate nineteenth-century Methodism:

> We must preach the whole gospel of personal salvation and social service, and whatever it means, have no fear of giving actual expression to love of the neighbour. It is imperative that social service should not be substituted

for evangelical religion, as it sometimes has been, but be shown to be one of its integral characteristics . . . the gospel of salvation must be preached not only as a gospel of personal redemption, but also of social reconstruction, if we are to reach this age, and if, indeed, we are to preach the whole gospel of the New Testament.[6]

Donald Lord Soper and William Sangster, two of the greatest Methodist preachers and evangelists of the twentieth century, stand in this same line of succession, both having served in the great central halls of English Methodism.

Early Twentieth-Century Developments

The twentieth century witnessed a birth of renewed interest in evangelism and Methodists stood very much at the forefront of these developments. A Methodist layman, John R. Mott, presided at the World Missionary Conference held in Edinburgh in 1910 which launched the modern ecumenical movement. His best-known book, *The Evangelization of the World in this Generation*, not only set the theme of the Edinburgh conference, but became a widespread missionary slogan of that day. He assumed that the West was a reasonably homogenous, fully evangelized world, a 'home church' from which to carry the gospel to the non-Christian world. This attitude would be challenged in significant ways over the course of the century. The establishment of the World Council of Churches (WCC) in 1948 fanned the evangelistic flame that had been kindled at the outset of the century, and much of the interest in and controversy about evangelism revolved around the evolution of this conciliar Protestant movement and its counterpart, the International Missionary Council. The global Methodist community provided three of the six WCC General Secretaries, Philip A. Potter of Dominica, Emilio Castro of Uruguay, and Sam Kobia of Kenya, all of whom shaped the dialogue concerning evangelism, particularly in the postcolonial era.

On the American scene, one of the most significant developments at this time was the establishment in 1949 of the Foundation for Evangelism, the purpose of which was to enlarge and extend the work of the General Board of Evangelism of the Methodist Church. Harry Denman, who had headed the board since Methodist union in 1939, both inspired and directed this new support structure. At the fortieth anniversary banquet of 1989, commemorating both the life of Denman and the contribution of the Foundation to the advancement of evangelism, Bishop Earl G. Hunt recognized the distinguished evangelists of that generation in the Methodist world. Included in this impressive list of influential thinkers, church leaders, and practitioners were Mary McLeod Bethune, Violetta Cavallero, Bishop Ralph Spalding Cushman, Harry Denman, E. Stanley Jones, Helen Kim, John R. Mott, Daniel Thambyrajah Niles, Albert C. Outler, Mortimer Arias, Donald English, and Sir Alan Walker.

The partial list of the forty scholars and practitioners of evangelism gives some sense of the breadth and depth of the Methodist contribution to global conversations related to mission and evangelism throughout this fertile period of inquiry.

A series of important events following World War II fractured the Methodist (and wider) community into two fairly distinctive schools of thought. The decade of the 1960s proved tumultuous in every imaginable way. With regard to matters related to evangelism, it witnessed the birth of a parallel movement among evangelical Protestants contradistinguished from that of the ecumenically minded conciliar community. Billy Graham had become an icon of revivalistic evangelism during these years, and he and other evangelical leaders began to consolidate the energy of this movement. The first World Congress on Evangelism in Berlin in 1966 echoed the concerns of Edinburgh 1910 for global evangelization, but the participants distanced themselves significantly from the socio-political concerns of the WCC. The stage was set for a confrontation between evangelicals who emphasized personal salvation in Christ and conciliar Protestants who increasingly elevated God's work in the redemption of the social order. Over the course of the decade a classic fissure developed along the fault line of evangelism and Methodists became embroiled in these debates.

A Critical Decade of Missiological Reflection and Debate (1972–1982)
The world mission conference of the WCC, held in Bangkok in 1972–1973, fanned the flame of controversy into white heat. Concerned about the complicity of the church with regard to colonial exploitation and injustice, sensitive to emerging postcolonial contextual theologies, and cognizant of the importance of cultural identity, the delegates proposed a temporary 'moratorium' of Euro-American mission activity. The evangelicals countered with the International Congress on World Evangelization (LCWE), held in Lausanne, Switzerland in 1974. The Lausanne Covenant, the first of three monumental declarations on evangelism in the final decades of the twentieth century, disassociated itself from the ecumenical agenda and emphasized the necessity of world evangelism. The congress established the Lausanne Committee for World Evangelization which, in fact, became the essential mouthpiece of this movement of evangelistic renewal. Robert E. Coleman, a United Methodist and founding member of the LCWE, played a major role in the shaping of this movement. Even by this time, his *Master Plan of Evangelism* (1963) had become well established as a classic work and exerted wide influence around the globe. For more than forty years, this program of evangelism patterned after the ministry of Jesus has challenged and instructed over three million readers.

Ironically, although Lausanne helped to delineate two opposing camps within the Protestant community (and within global Methodism) and their competing theologies of evangelism, it also marked the beginning of rapprochement. That conciliatory spirit surfaced in surprising ways, not among Protestants, but between the Protestant and Roman Catholic communities by virtue of the Second Vatican Council. During this same period, Catholic Christians were engaged in creative conversations about evangelism that would completely reorient their thinking. This dialogue came to a climax in the second evangelistic declaration of enduring significance from this era *Evangelii Nuntiandi* (Evangelization in the Modern World), promulgated by Pope Paul VI in 1975. This statement confirmed that evangelism constitutes the essential mission of the church, but also declared the need for the re-evangelization of the church. The declaration also claimed the witness of authentic Christian lives to be the primary means of evangelism.

In 1971, Albert Outler had anticipated much of this spirit in his Denman Lectures, entitled *Evangelism in the Wesleyan Spirit*, in which he sought not only to reorient Methodist thinking about evangelism around the evangelical ethos of its founders, but also embraced the new spirit of ecumenical consensus that was beginning to surface. In the same year, the World Methodist Conference established a new division for World Methodist Evangelism, calling upon all Methodists to:

1. Affirm the relevancy and adequacy of the Christian faith for this age.
2. Initiate a worldwide mission and evangelism offensive.
3. Lead persons into a personal experience of Jesus Christ as Lord and Savior.
4. Encourage within the Methodist Movement a sense of unity of the entire Christian Church and a sense of global consciousness.
5. Stimulate new strategies of ministries to persons and society.
6. Give mutual encouragement to the Body of Christ.

Bishop Gerald Ensley gave leadership to this new development and Sir Alan Walker served as the first full-time World Director of Evangelism from 1978 to 1988. Dr. H. Eddie Fox has served in this capacity since 1989 and as Executive Director (1992) of the World Methodist Evangelism Institute. Often referred to as the 'best-known Methodist evangelist in the world,' he is responsible for leading sixteen regional secretaries of world evangelism in developing indigenous evangelism on every continent.

In 1982 the WCC published *Mission and Evangelism – An Ecumenical Affirmation*, the third landmark declaration of critical import in the development of a theology of evangelism during this period. This affirmation remains the fundamental text on mission and evangelism for the WCC and has been very influential with regard to the shaping of Methodist thought and practice. It seeks to establish a balance between the proclamation of the gospel and the prophetic challenge to manifest God's just purposes in human history. It is a convergence document characterized by commitment to evangelism as the heart of mission, personal conversion to Christ as the foundation of the Christian life, solidarity with the victims of unjust social and economic systems, and witness to the reign of God through word and deed. While significant differences still exist between evangelical and ecumenical theologians and practitioners of evangelism (even within the Methodist family), the chasm between them has narrowed significantly and the distinctions tend to be more matters of emphasis than of substance.

Rethinking Evangelism at the Close of the Millennium
As the study of evangelism advanced along these fronts, visionaries within academia began to consider the importance of these developments for theological education. Prior to the critical decade of missiological reflection (1972–1982), few Methodist seminaries had faculty dedicated to the study of evangelism. Responding to what they perceived as a critical need, denominational agencies, such as the Foundation for Evangelism, attempted to support the ministry of evangelism in both the church and the academy. Within a decade of its inception in 1949, the Foundation had established two endowed chairs of evangelism in high profile United Methodist seminaries. But these positions remained anomalies until the 1980s, when the vision to establish positions of evangelism in all the denominational centers of ministerial training became a passionate goal of the leadership. Today the Foundation supports Chairs of Evangelism in fifteen United Methodist institutions on three continents.

In a parallel effort to bring increased legitimacy to the discipline of evangelism in the life of the academy, in 1973 a small group of scholars established the Academy for Evangelism in Theological Education. The purpose of the Academy was to facilitate the teaching of evangelism, to share pedagogical ideas and methods, to develop new resources, to examine new trends in the discipline, and to foster scholarly research in evangelism and related concerns. Likewise, the American Society for Church Growth, focusing its attention more particularly on the nature, function, and health of Christian churches, employs the insights of social and behavioral sciences in its effort to resource the evangelistic mission of the church. George G. Hunter III, founding Dean of the E. Stanley Jones School of World Mission and Evangelism at Asbury Theological Seminary, was central to all of these developments. Few Methodists have published more in the area of evangelism. Nearly all of Hunter's books touch on evangelism and church growth in one way or another, from *Rethinking Evangelism* (1971) to *Radical Outreach* (2003). Hunter's passion has been to help the church rediscover 'apostolic ministry' as its main business. Several of his books, in particular, *How to Reach Secular People* (1992), *Church for the Unchurched* (1996), *The Celtic Way of Evangelism* (2000), and *Radical Outreach* (2003), all stress the importance of attending to and adapting the lived gospel in dynamic ways to historical and cultural contexts. Christian authenticity forms the center of his conception of vital evangelistic practice.

Much of the recent discussion concerning evangelism has related to the conspicuous neglect of the reign of God. Mortimer Arias brought 'kingdom issues' front and center in his groundbreaking study *Announcing the Reign of God* (1984). In this work, which may be the most important treatment of the subject in the last fifty years, he marshals biblical resources to demonstrate the crucial relevance of Jesus' core teaching for the manner and aim of mission and evangelism today. A second significant contribution is the classic study of William Abraham entitled *The Logic of Evangelism* (1989). Over against reductionist tendencies that view evangelism simply as verbal proclamation or simply as engagement in ministries of justice, he describes the dynamic process of evangelism as 'a polymorphous ministry aimed at initiating people into the kingdom of God' (95). Concerned that evangelism not slips back into a 'mind-set of technique,' Bishop Earl Hunt, through the Foundation for Evangelism, invited fifty Methodist scholars and leaders to a symposium on 'Theology and Evangelism in the Wesleyan Heritage.' Participants represented Africa, Asia, Europe, and the Americas, the conference being one of the first serious efforts to present a global platform for evangelism from a specifically Methodist perspective. James Logan edited the papers and published them under the title of the conference in 1994. The following year, the Foundation sponsored a second 'evangelism conference' at Wesley Theological Seminary, this time gathering together nearly twenty bishops of the United Methodist Church. The publication from this symposium, entitled *Christ for the World* (1996), remains the only effort of this body's episcopal leaders to deal exclusively with the theme of evangelism.

By the end of the twentieth century, re-conceiving evangelism as a dynamic practice that engages the whole people of God, many Methodists were beginning to embrace evangelism as a critical aspect of the *missio Dei*. A number of authors contributed significantly to these developments, exploring evangelism through the lens of 'ecclesial practice.' Maxie Dunnam devoted his Denman Lectures (1992) to the theme of *Congregational Evangelism*. Inspired by Dunnam's concept of the 'congregation as evangelist' and the earlier pioneering work of Eddie Fox and George Morris related to 'the personal evangelism of the whole people of God' in their classic guide *Faith Sharing* (1986), Roger Swanson and Shirley Clement developed their vision of *The Faith-Sharing Congregation* (1999) in which a network of practices within the community of faith functions as a profound evangelistic nexus. In similar fashion, the studies of Ron Crandall, *The Contagious Witness* (1999), and, *Witness* (2001), emphasize the holistic character of evangelism in the context of a body of Christian believers. In *Contemporary Worship for the 21st Century: Worship or Evangelism?* (1994) Dan Benedict and Craig Miller bring their keen insight concerning contemporary culture to bear upon questions related to the interface of good liturgical practice and evangelistic ministry. Just as evangelism is the heart of the church's mission, so evangelism is the core of all ecclesial practices. If practices of worship, discipleship, or pastoral care are pursued without an evangelistic orientation – namely an intentional proclamation and embodiment of the gospel of Jesus Christ – then such practices not only lose their motivation and power, but arguably cease to function as Christian practices altogether.

Six recent volumes merit particular attention. Walter Klaiber's *Call and Response* (1997) is undoubtedly the most thorough biblical theology of evangelism within the Methodist tradition. He examines both the rich variety of New Testament images related to evangelism and the significance, nature, and necessity of conversion. In *Evangelistic Love of God and Neighbor* (2003) Scott Jones builds upon the earlier work of Abraham, defining evangelism as 'that set of loving, intentional activities governed by the goal of initiating persons into Christian discipleship in response to the reign of God' (18). The book surveys the more recent serious study of evangelism and develops a constructive proposal that roots evangelistic practice in God's unconditional love. Perhaps the most rigorous and challenging new argument for postliberal evangelism rooted in a robust ecclesiology comes from Bryan Stone, a work entitled *Evangelism after Christendom* (2006). Stone's central argument is that the prevailing model of evangelism, built upon the crumbling foundations of the Enlightenment, is inadequate and must be replaced by an engagement with 'the actual lived habits of the very church which invites the world around to consider its habituated gospel.' In *The Mystic Way of Evangelism* (2008) Elaine Heath affords a unique approach to evangelism, revisioning the task of making disciples from the perspective of Christian mysticism. Paul W. Chilcote and Laceye C. Warner gather into a single volume some of the most groundbreaking essays on evangelism in the last quarter century in *The Study of Evangelism* (2008) including incisive statements by Methodist scholars.

From varied perspectives around the world, Methodist scholars and practitioners have developed definitions and built theologies of evangelism that refuse the old dichotomies separating mission from evangelism – the gift of personal salvation from the call to live in and for God's just and peaceable rule. Evangelism emerges as a complex set of formational practices at the heart of God's mission for the church in the world. Despite the monumental achievements of the past quarter century, in particular, with regard to the theology and practice of evangelism in the Methodist tradition, much work remains to be done. Several of the trajectories that have been set demand further attention: the shift from evangelistic techniques to the theological foundations of evangelism; from hagiographical studies of evangelists to more robust examinations of ecclesiology; from fixation on soteriology to wider missiological perspectives; and from 'either/or' to 'both/and' ways of thinking that are more in line with the Wesleyan ethos. Three areas, however, merit particular attention.

An Agenda for Further Research

First, the contribution of women to the evangelistic ministry of the church is a much neglected area of study. Paul W. Chilcote brought attention to the place and role of women as evangelists in several studies related to the early Methodist movement, *She Offered Them Christ* (1993), *Her Own Story* (2001), and *Early Methodist Spirituality* (2007). In similar fashion, in *Turn the Pulpit Loose* (2004) Priscilla Pope-Levison weaves together the narratives of American women evangelists, including Methodists such as Jerena Lee. In *Saving Women* (2007) Laceye Warner demonstrates how Methodist women (and others) not only preached the gospel, but embodied it in their own lives. This only represents the beginning stages of a movement to unearth the legacy of women who bore authentic witness to the gospel in word and deed throughout the history of Methodism.

Second, little has been written up to this point in Methodist circles concerning the seismic cultural shift from modern to postmodern culture in the western world and the ramifications with regard to evangelism. Attention to western secular culture pervades the work of George Hunter. Bryan Stone has provided his own critique of and response to contemporary cultural shifts. Leonard Sweet offers a fresh perspective in *The Gospel According to Starbucks* (2007). In response to a postmodern context, Sweet demonstrates how Christianity must move beyond rational, logical apologetics, and find ways of showing people that it can offer 'symbols and meaningful engagement,' particularly through an EPIC, an alliterative paradigm emphasizing experience, participation, image, and connection. More Methodist voices, however, need to be added to the growing number of scholars concerned about this pressing issue.

Third, there is a serious dearth of material exploring contextual issues related to evangelistic theology and practice from global perspectives. Despite the truly global nature of contemporary Methodism and the amazing growth of Methodism beyond the boundaries of a collapsing Christendom, western concerns still dominate the literature. In his many discussions of evangelism in a Latin American milieu, Mortimer Arias has argued for a paradigm of contextualization that reflects the dialectic relationship between gospel and culture, calling for a 'prophetic contextualization' that is conflictive, engaged, and emancipatory. Hwa Yung has explored strategic issues related to mission and evangelism from a Malaysian perspective. Building upon the 'clash of civilizations' theory of Samuel Huntington, he advocates a vision of evangelization sensitive to issues of indigenization, holism, contextualization, and the potential synergy between western and Asian forms of the Christian faith. In the African context, John W. Z. Kurewa stands in the vanguard of a rising generation of Methodist historians and theologians concerned about evangelism. In his book *Drumbeats of Salvation in Africa* (2007), Kurewa develops a concept of evangelism sensitive to the heritage and practices of his Shona culture. Recently, Paul Chilcote has solicited a group of international contributors for a project entitled *Making Disciples in a World Parish: Global Perspectives on Mission/Evangelism* in which he hopes to provide a window into the 'best' evangelistic practices of the Methodist family around the world. In a global community of faith, the voices of the whole world must be heard.

A Renewed Wesleyan Vision

Six principles drawn from the legacy of holistic evangelism within the Methodist tradition and discussions concerning its practice in the global community today provide a platform to help contemporary Methodists grapple with the privilege of making disciples for the transformation of the world:

> First, evangelism is a vital part of something larger than itself, namely, the *missio Dei*. While evangelism is but one part of God's larger mission in the world, it is the essence – the heart – of all Christian mission.
>
> Second, although the goal of evangelism is conversion, often experienced in crisis moments in the lives of individuals, evangelism is a process. . . .
>
> Third, evangelism is concerned with discipling people in Christ. The primary purpose of evangelism is not growing churches or recruiting members (although both may be its consequence). God forms people into authentic disciples of Jesus, and we participate in that process through evangelism.
>
> Fourth, evangelism is oriented toward the reign of God. The ultimate goal toward which evangelism moves is the realization of God's reign in human life. While not unconcerned with the salvation of the individual in and through Christ, initiating persons into an alternative community of God's people who give themselves for the life of the world is its proper end. We embrace a 'holistic' vision of evangelism that affirms both personal salvation and social justice.
>
> Fifth, evangelism is a missional practice of the whole people of God. Evangelism is not simply an activity, it is a set of practices – a habituated way of being in community. While some persons may be particularly gifted as evangelists within the community of faith, God claims all of God's

Evangelism in the Methodist Tradition

children as 'evangel bearers' for the purpose of God's mission of shalom in the world.

Sixth, evangelism is inescapably contextual. Just as all Christianity is contextual, the culture of the practitioner shapes the practice of evangelism and the culture of those evangelized determines the nature of the relationship and the practice. Evangelism, in other words, engages the Christian community in a complex inter-relational dynamic in both intra- and cross-cultural experiences of evangel-sharing.[7]

For Further Reading

Chilcote, Paul W. and Laceye C. Warner, eds. *The Study of Evangelism: Exploring a Missional Practice of the Church.* Grand Rapids: Eerdmans, 2008.

Hunter, George G. *Radical Outreach: The Recovery of Apostolic Ministry and Evangelism.* Nashville: Abingdon Press, 2002.

Klaiber, Walter. *Call and Response: Biblical Foundations of a Theology of Evangelism.* Nashville: Abingdon Press, 1997.

Kurewa, John W. Z. *Drumbeats of Salvation in Africa: A Study of Biblical, Historical & Theological Foundations for the Ministry of Evangelism.* Mutare, Zimbabwe: Africa University, 2007.

Logan, James C., ed. *Theology and Evangelism in the Wesleyan Heritage.* Nashville: Kingswood Books, 1994.

14 Methodist Worship

Karen B. Westerfield Tucker

Ritual Texts

For generations, the study of Christian liturgy and worship has focused primarily upon the texts mandated or approved for use in the different Christian communions. Research generally takes three principal forms. In the first case, philological investigation exposes the origins and longevity of specific words and phrases in ritual texts. Then second: through a comparative methodology, a ritual text or a part thereof is examined in relation to the structure (*ordo*) and contents of other texts – within a particular denomination or broad ecclesiastical tradition, across one or many denominations or confessions (ecumenical), with non-Christian traditions (e.g., Jewish ritual texts and rabbinic material), or with some combination of the previous three. A third approach is to scrutinize the instructions for liturgical events that are embedded in ritual texts as means of determining matters – sometimes controversial – related to performance. These rubrics may then be contrasted with explicit or implied rules pertaining to worship that are laid out in registers of canon law or contained in theological treatises.

The Sunday Service of the Methodists (1784) and Its Derivatives

Methodist scholars, certainly since the late nineteenth century, have engaged in text-based liturgical research that utilizes one or more of these three principal forms. One liturgical book in particular has been the subject of considerable analysis by Methodists (and others): the revision of the 1662 *Book of Common Prayer* made by John Wesley in 1784 under the title *The Sunday Service of the Methodists in North America. With Other Occasional Services*.[1] Although Wesley identified in his personal diary for 5 March 1736 that he dabbled with revision of the Prayer Book, and in the essay 'Ought We to Separate from the Church of England?' of 1755 he criticized the Prayer Book's inclusion of certain components, it was only at the end of his life that he undertook a full revision with the stated purpose of supplying the Methodist people in America with a 'rational' and 'scriptural' resource for worship. After Wesley excised much of the 1662 book's contents, what remained, in addition to a limited number of instructions, tables, and proper collects, were amended rites for

Morning and Evening Prayer, the Lord's Supper, adult and infant baptism, matrimony, communion of the sick, burial of the dead, and ordination (of deacons, 'elders,' and 'superintendants' [sic]). Wesley's revision was not the only one of its time, for dozens of alternatives had been proposed since the issuance of the 1662 edition, some designed to recover texts and practices associated with Christian antiquity, others concerned to edit out what was perceived as nonscriptural material, and still others determined to go in a more Unitarian direction.[2] The connection of Wesley's product with these other revisions has not been fully investigated; yet some comparative work has revealed that certain decisions for omission taken by Wesley are shared with other revisers (e.g., the dropping of the Athanasian Creed) while other deletions are apparently unique to Wesley (e.g., the elimination of the giving away of the bride in the marriage rite).

Study of the 1784 *Sunday Service* has not been without challenges, as can be seen by an examination of relevant articles contained in the *Proceedings of the Wesley Historical Society* from the 1940s and 1950s, and by the proliferation of dissertations and theses in the second half of the twentieth century that consider some aspect of Wesley's revision. One notable and ongoing problem has been the question of Wesley's intent in regard to the use of the manual acts (the celebrant's gestures) at the consecratory prayer in the communion rite and the postbaptismal signing of the cross in the rite for infants. Two versions of the 1784 book exist: one with the manual acts and signation; the other without either. Which was Wesley's original design, and which might be the preference of Thomas Coke, an Anglican priest set apart by Wesley as 'Superintendent,' who had transported copies of the *Sunday Service* loose-leaf to America and who Wesley later claimed had made alterations to the text without his knowledge? Unfortunately on this matter – and it is the case with the entire revision – Wesley provided no rationale for the choices he made; scholars have typically turned to his journal, letters, sermons, and other writings to glean possible explanations, and many have found them in Wesley's sympathies for the Puritan wing of the Church of England that sought the removal of supposedly 'Romish' and unscriptural liturgical texts and practices.[3] In regard to the two versions of 1784, a clue may possibly be found in later editions of the *Sunday Service* overseen by Wesley (1786, 1788, 1790, and likely 1792), which retain the manual acts but not the signation.

These subsequent editions of the *Sunday Service*, with versions designated for North America, Britain, and 'His Majesty's Dominions' – the North American form omitting the references to royalty included in the other two – helped to ensure the importance of Wesley's abridgment as a foundational liturgical resource for Methodism worldwide even though its reception was not the same in every place. The founding 'Christmas' Conference (1784) of the Methodist Episcopal Church in the United States adopted Wesley's revision as their 'prayer-book,' though its Sunday-specific material was little used and short lived principally because of an overwhelming preference for a more informal and extemporaneous worship style. A year after Wesley's death, the young denomination in 1792 laid aside the collects, lectionary, Wesley's abbreviated psalter, Morning and Evening Prayer, Litany, and the Communion of the Sick. The Order for the Administration of the Lord's Supper – which Wesley expected to be used every Lord's Day – received significant adjustments: the ante-communion was deleted (from the opening 'Our Father' up to the sentences said during the collection of alms; the omission included rubrics for scripture reading and sermon), though the Collect for Purity ('Almighty God, unto whom all hearts be open') was kept and relocated; and certain prayers in the parts of the rite that remained were eliminated or modified. The Prayer Book's rich liturgical texts for Sunday were then reduced to a few rubrics in the section 'Of Public Worship' in the church's *Discipline* that advised the inclusion of singing, prayer, preaching, and scripture reading on the Lord's Day – what had, in fact, constituted the peculiarly Methodist Sunday supplement to the expected attendance at the liturgy from the Prayer Book in the local Church of England parish, though many Methodists in the colonies had ignored this guidance. These minimal rubrics for Sunday were retained when, as the result of theological, social, and/or political dissatisfaction, new Methodist denominations in the United States were established. In later years a few attempts were made to restore Wesley's rich liturgical diet for Sunday morning – one of the earliest was by English Methodist immigrant Thomas O. Summers for the Methodist Episcopal Church, South in 1867[4] though by the late nineteenth century worship in the several American Methodist and Wesleyan denominations had developed their own liturgical trajectories. However, the residue of Wesley's Sunday plan may be seen in the early twenty-first century in a few official texts such as that of the African Methodist Episcopal Church.

Whereas the liturgical materials for Sunday inherited from Wesley were, for the most part, abandoned by Methodists/Wesleyans in the United States, a connection with Wesley's *Urtext* was mostly kept with the rites for baptism, marriage, funeral/burial, and ordination into the twentieth and twenty-first centuries. All these rites underwent alteration in different periods to different degrees and in different directions by the various denominations. Methodists in the holiness tradition held liturgical views typically unlike those in the more liberal streams of Methodism, and each group's rites (or lack of certain rites) reflected their own theological and social perspectives. For example, the rites for baptism received particular scrutiny in most of the denominations because of questions that arose concerning baptismal regeneration (especially in the late eighteenth and early nineteenth centuries) and original sin (the twentieth century); and after the mid-nineteenth century, some groups claimed that a bishop was more properly 'consecrated' than ordained, but did not significantly readjust the ritual text for ordination.

The reception of the *Sunday Service* was generally more positive in Britain and 'His Majesty's Dominions,' the latter referring to regions of Methodist mission in North America still loyal to the crown, which included Nova Scotia, Newfoundland, and the (British) West Indies. These Methodists were more culturally and liturgically accommodated to the contents and ethos of the *Book of Common Prayer* and to the Church of England's typical Sunday format of Morning Prayer followed by the ante-communion. Even so, some Methodists regarded Wesley's handiwork as a weak imitation and objected to his deletion of material such as the Athanasian and Nicene Creeds, the sanctoral calendar, and certain of the Psalms. Wesley himself, even after the production of the *Sunday Service*, pressed for the use of parts of the Prayer Book in Methodist worship when the hour of service conflicted with worship in the Anglican parish, lest the Methodists 'be prejudiced against it, if they heard none but extemporary prayer.'[5] Other Methodists, however, sought a more radical approach to Lord's Day worship such as the Methodist Episcopal Church had undertaken, and were equally heavy-handed in their abridgement of the occasional rites.

During the nineteenth century, the practice of some Methodist/Wesleyan denominations in Britain and particularly what became known as the Wesleyan Methodist Connexion, was to take their liturgical materials from the Established Church's Prayer Book. However, Wesley's *Sunday Service* was not forgotten, for from 1792 to 1910, approximately thirty editions of the book were published in Britain under the title *The Sunday Service of the Methodists*, though the rites included and the wording of the contents varied. The sacramental texts from the *Sunday Service* also appeared in separate books between 1839 and 1881, and after 1848 sometimes included the rites of marriage, burial, and ordination as well. Two 'specialized' collections also drew upon the contents of the *Sunday Service: The Sunday Morning Service of the Methodists* (1812); and *Selections from the Sunday Service of the Methodists; Designed for the use of Sunday-Scholars on the Morning of the Lord's Day* (1838, 1842). Although these books reportedly were little used, they continued to be published – the publication run for the 1910 book was evidently 1,000 copies.[6] After the demise of books published under Wesley's title, portions of the contents survived in subsequent service books, though sometimes in a form more akin to the 1662 Prayer Book than to the *Sunday Service*.

Comparative studies, mostly in doctoral dissertations, have been undertaken to track the omissions and/or additions made to succeeding revisions of liturgical texts derived originally from Wesley's *Sunday Service*. This research, usually of a particular Methodist denomination or cluster of denominations, is generally restricted to either the American or the British family tree. The work done in 1926 by Nolan B. Harmon on the rites of communion, baptism, marriage, burial, and ordination of the two largest episcopal Methodist denominations in the United States has been quite important to later scholars (though it was ignored when it was published) even though it is incomplete, contains inaccuracies, and is now dated. Harmon (later a bishop of the Methodist Episcopal Church, South) took up the methodology embraced by F. E. Brightman in his *The English Rite*,[7] which placed in parallel columns the Prayer Book rites of 1549, 1552, and 1661 alongside the sources taken by Thomas Cranmer for the 1549 book. In *The Rites and Ritual of Episcopal Methodism*,[8] Harmon included columns containing the sources for 1549 and the texts of 1661, and added a column each for Wesley's *Sunday Service*, the 1844 Methodist Episcopal Church rite (just prior to the fracture that would create the Methodist Episcopal Church, South), the post-1844 rites of the Methodist Episcopal Church (using the rites of 1924 as the basis), and the rites of the Methodist Episcopal Church, South (with the rites of 1922). Harmon's research not only brought to light the precise lineage of the liturgical texts used by two denominations in the 1920s, it had the added benefit of connecting Methodism liturgically with the church catholic at a time of growing ecumenical interest and engagement. Thus when Methodists used the Collect for Purity at the Lord's Supper, they were reminded of their Anglican roots, but also of their linkage to the medieval Sarum Use of the Catholic Church in England from which Cranmer had borrowed the collect.

Another type of comparative work is in the early stages at the start of the twenty-first century. If the liturgical texts derived from the *Sunday Service* in the United States and Britain are considered as the first wave, these texts would constitute the second wave. During the nineteenth and early twentieth centuries, Methodist missionaries from Britain and America took with them into the field the liturgical texts they knew, which were then received or adapted or abandoned. A new generation of scholars resident in the countries to which those missionaries were sent has been engaging in comparative work with those imported texts that may be traced back to the *Sunday Service* with a view to understanding liturgical development in their own contexts; Korean scholars have been especially productive in this endeavor.[9] Particularly complex are those places that were influenced by both British and American liturgical streams, as is the case in parts of Africa and Asia.

Transmission of the liturgical texts into other languages and cultures did not take place only outside the borders of Britain and the United States. In the former, English-language liturgical books needed translation into Welsh. In the case of the latter, Methodist liturgical texts were printed in non-English languages such as German, Danish, and Swedish during the late nineteenth and early twentieth centuries in order to accommodate large immigrant communities. Scholars have yet to analyze those texts in comparison with the English-language denominational texts of the same vintage to determine what types of cultural readjustment other than language may have occurred.

Another important form of scholarship helps to shed light on the history of development of *Sunday Service*-derived liturgical texts, provides a theological interpretation for those texts, and gives insight into the ritual practices and problems of a particular period: the ritual commentary. An early example of this genre is the 'explanatory notes' on the *Discipline* made by Bishops Thomas Coke and Francis Asbury and published in 1798. Essentially a rubrical study since no complete ritual texts were printed in this version of the *Discipline* (they were contained in a section of 'Sacramental Services, etc.' later renamed the 'Ritual'), it nonetheless presented brief comments on the Conference-approved decisions related to public worship, preaching, singing, baptism, communion, marriage, and the decorum expected in church buildings. Addressing what apparently was an increasing neglect in the expected reading of at least one chapter from the Bible during public worship both on Sunday morning and afternoon, the bishops wrote:

> Our church insists on the reading of the Scriptures in the congregation, and gives directions accordingly. This is of the utmost consequence, and we trust will be most sacredly observed by all our ministers and preachers. A peculiar blessing accompanies the public reading as well as preaching the word of God to attentive, believing souls. And in these days of infidelity, nothing should be omitted, which may lead the people to the love of the holy bible.[10]

Over time, commentaries became more elaborate and substantial as teaching texts and reference works. Two notable examples from the United States are *Commentary on the Ritual of the Methodist Episcopal Church, South* (1873) by Thomas O. Summers[11] and *History of the Ritual of the Methodist Episcopal Church* (1900) by R. J. Cooke.[12] Summers provided a running commentary at the foot of the approved 'Ritual' of his denomination, whereas Cooke supplied chiefly a narrative of ritual history from the English Reformation to 1900, only part of which directly interpreted his current 'Ritual.'

Other Sources for Methodist Texts
Not all officially published resources for Methodist and Wesleyan worship used Wesley's *Sunday Service* as a template or a guide. This was particularly true of books produced by some denominations on both sides of the Atlantic that at their creation shied away from print resources for worship out of concern that such 'formalism' or 'ritualism' might inhibit the free movement of the Spirit. It was also true for a few denominations of British or American

missionary origins that became ecclesiastically independent and sought to articulate their own liturgical voice.

Even those denominations that kept ties to Wesley's *Urtext* at some point added material from other sources, including texts newly composed as well as material borrowed from service books of other denominations and from single-author collections of prayers. The Methodist Protestant Church in the United States included among the occasional services in its *Constitution and Discipline*, from the group's founding in 1830 through to 1877, a set of instructions entitled 'Visitation of the Sick' – material not contained in either the *Sunday Service* or in the collection of services printed by the Methodist Episcopal Church out of which the denomination developed. Comparison with other 'directory'-style instructions from the early nineteenth century reveal that the material was taken almost verbatim from the 'Directory for the Worship of God' approved by the General Assembly of the Presbyterian Church in the United States in 1821. Reasons for this Presbyterian dependency are unknown, though a Methodist Protestant historian noted in 1849 that his denomination was grateful for Presbyterian support during the years prior to 1830.[13]

Identification of sources usually requires careful sleuthing, for many, if not most, Methodist/Wesleyan liturgical books produced in the nineteenth century, and a large percentage in the early twentieth century, did not specify from whom or from what the particular materials were borrowed. For those that declared their sources fully or partially as well as those that did not, when sources can be pinpointed, questions may be raised as to the rationale for specific selections or choices taken. Following the union of the Wesleyans, Primitive Methodists, and United Methodists, the first official service book constructed by the new Methodist Church of Great Britain, entitled *The Book of Offices* (1936), declared its indebtedness with a bibliographic shorthand, but with enough information to suggest the apparent desire of the book's editors to appease both 'Prayer Book' and 'Free' liturgical camps:

> Thanks for the use of Prayers are due to Dr. W. E. Orchard; to the Editor and Messrs. J. M. Dent and Sons, Ltd., publisher of *The Free Church Book of Common Prayer*; for extracts from the Prayer Book as proposed in 1928 reprinted in this publication by permission of the Prayer Book Copyright Committee on the Central Board of Finance of the Church of England; to the General Council of the United Church of Canada.[14]

In the United States, the *Book of Worship for Church and Home* (1945) published by the Methodist Church – the body formed by the merger in 1939 of the Methodist Episcopal Church, Methodist Episcopal Church, South, and the Methodist Protestant Church – furnished two full pages of acknowledgments, revealing surprising sources that perhaps hint also at the denomination's nonliturgical agendas. Among the titles: two prayer collections by John Wallace Suter (Dean of Washington National Cathedral [Episcopal Church] in the year of the book's publication); Walter Rauschenbusch's *Prayers of the Social Awakening* (1909); *The Union Prayerbook for Jewish Worship* (1918 and 1940) of the Central Conference of American Rabbis; and the Methodist Church in Great Britain's *Book of Offices*. But there was also unattributed material contained therein as well.

From the mid-twentieth century onward, numerous Methodist/Wesleyan denominations drew upon an influential source broader than a single book: the Liturgical Movement that sparked the reforms hammered out at the Second Vatican Council, which, in turn, inspired ritual revision among many Protestant denominations worldwide. With the recovery across the western churches of early Christian praxis that remembered and gave thanks for the one who was made known in 'the scriptures' and in the 'breaking of the bread' (Luke 24:27, 32, 35), and with the rediscovery of the strong eucharistic piety characteristic of the early Wesleyan movement, Methodists in many places exchanged the usual Sunday preaching service or service of the word for a normative pattern of 'word and table' whether or not the sacrament was actually observed. Thus the order of Sunday worship outlined in the worship books of many denominations inspired by the Liturgical Movement – Methodist/Wesleyan and others – looked quite similar. Although differences in specific content remained, there was often shared material, for example, the inclusion of an epiclesis or invocation of the Spirit in the communion liturgy that was evident in many early Christian texts and still retained in the rites of the Orthodox churches, but largely lost in the West. Similarities exist in the occasional rites as well.

In an ecumenical age, these adjustments in parallel were significant. But for some denominations in the Wesleyan tradition, these changes brought the final severance with the array of rites in Wesley's *Sunday Service*. This break is most noticeable in the two worship books produced by the Methodist Church in Great Britain after their initial one of 1936, and particularly in the Lord's Supper rite: the liturgy of 1936 kept connection with the Prayer Book and *Sunday Service* texts; the *Methodist Service Book* (1975) included the 1936 rite as well as a new form based on the ecumenical liturgical consensus; and the seasonally based texts in the *Methodist Worship Book* (1999) bear little resemblance to the historic Anglican/Wesleyan material. The same disjuncture is evident in the *Book of Worship* (1992) of the United Methodist Church – the denomination created in 1968 by the merger of the Methodist Church with the Evangelical United Brethren. The identification of textual sources post-Vatican II has become increasingly more complicated as the pool of materials from which borrowing may occur is both wider and deeper, aided by the instant accessibility of information on the internet.

Descriptive Primary Sources

Although the analysis of authorized ritual texts has been and remains the mainstay for liturgical research, in recent decades the attention of liturgical scholars has broadened to include other sources in recognition that official ritual texts printed in worship books usually do not provide full information about a liturgical event's performance. To go 'beyond the text' means to examine other sources helpful in painting a more complete picture of the practices of a liturgical tradition, such as ecclesiastical legislation related to worship, resources for liturgical instruction (clergy and lay), essays and books on liturgical theology, ritual commentaries, and the descriptive reports of individuals.

The need for research beyond the ritual text is not a new concept for those who have studied Methodist as well as other 'free' church worship, for most Methodists/Wesleyans have never worshiped exclusively 'by the book.' Indeed, in the uniquely 'Methodist' worship of the eighteenth century that included scripture reading, sermons and/or exhortations, hymn singing, and extemporaneous prayers, written texts generally were not used except for the Bible and the words published in the hymn collections produced by John and Charles Wesley. A full account of the styles and types of worship held among eighteenth-century British and Irish Methodists, therefore, can only be amassed by reading descriptions in the journals, diaries, letters, tracts, and published articles of Methodism's adherents and detractors, as well as worship-related guidelines in the Minutes of Conference prepared by those leaders in 'connection' with John Wesley. A case in point: the recollection of Silas Told, which illustrates one of the many types of sources from which reports about Methodist worship may be gleaned, in this instance a published spiritual and pastoral autobiography. Told quite unintentionally reveals valuable information about the space, leadership, content, and ethos of worship, and about the worshipers themselves:

> In one of these recluse parts of the Foundry sat three or four old women, one of whom appeared in the attitude of an unmoveable statue, with her apron over her face, nor was she uncovered during the whole time of divine service. The enemy of souls immediately suggested that she was an hypocrite. My friend, Mr. Greaves, stood close behind me, to prevent my going out . . . to which I was strongly tempted, and had it not been for the multitude of people assembled together, so early in the morning as between four and five o'clock, and the striking consideration of such profound seriousness, which evidently appeared in the countenance of almost every person there, I must certainly have given way to the temptation, and thereby have lost the greatest blessing I ever experienced

before. I tarried there a full half hour before the service began, during which my mind was sorely disturbed with many strange notions, as I had been so strongly attached to the church of England. Exactly at five o'clock a general whisper was conveyed through the congregation, and 'Here he comes! Here he comes!' was repeated with the utmost pleasure. I was filled with curiosity to see his person, which, when I beheld, I much despised. The enemy of souls, who is never unprepared to hinder the salvation of individuals, suggested, that he was some farmer's son, who, not able to support himself, was making a penny in this low and ignoble manner. He passed through the congregation into the temporary pulpit, and having his robes on, I expected he would have begun with the Church service; but, to my astonishment, the introduction to his preaching was the singing an hymn, with which I was almost enraptured; but his extemporary prayer was quite unpleasant, as I thought it savoured too much of the Dissenter's mode of worship, which at that time my prejudice could not abide. After which he took his text in the second chapter, of the first epistle general of St. John, twelve and thirteen verses. 'I write unto you, little children, because your sins are forgiven you, &c.' The enemy struck a deadly blow at me, and in that moment suggested, that he was a Papist, as he dwelt so much on forgiveness of sins; and although I had read this portion of Scripture many times before, yet I never understood that we were to know our sins forgiven on earth; supposing that it referred only to those to whom the apostle was then writing, especially as I had never heard this doctrine preached in the church. However, my prejudice quickly abated, through the excellent wisdom with which Mr. Wesley spoke: This clearly elucidated the subject, and proved the point. I then plainly saw I could never be saved without knowing my sins were forgiven me; and in the midst of his sermon the Spirit of God sealed the truth of every word upon my heart. At the close of the discourse, however strange it may appear, a small still voice entered my left ear, with these words, 'This is the truth!' and instantly I felt it in my heart; and for five and thirty years I have never once doubted of those truths and doctrines received amongst us, viz. 'Of salvation by that faith productive of good works.'[15]

Like all personal accounts, Told's narrative contains biases and perhaps distorted or faulty recollection which need to be taken into consideration when piecing together the practices of a certain time period.

Eyewitness records are essential for reconstructing the content and practices of worship in all areas where Methodism was planted since many of the Methodist denominations lacked liturgical texts or rubrics for guidance, and those that had them often believed themselves at liberty to depart from them. Descriptions of Sunday worship and weekday prayer (private, domestic, and public) are the most numerous of all the accounts of Methodist worship that are preserved, particularly if the records of sermon topics and preaching texts are included. The British Wesleyan Joseph Nightingale included a portrayal of public worship in an 1807 publication of a series of letters that reflected upon Methodism in general. His report was not without value judgment; and it is quite interesting that one of his critiques echoes the complaint of Bishops Asbury and Coke in their explanatory note (cited above):

> The mode of conducting divine worship among the Methodists is of all others the most regular and simple. If their plan be defective in any point, it is in not having the scriptures read to the people. This certainly ought never to be dispensed with. In every other respect, it is impressive and engaging in the highest degree.
>
> Here is no pomp; no idle parade; no vain shew of unmeaning ceremonies, nor irksome of tedious liturgies; all is simple and intelligible, agreeable to the easy decorum and decent order of a Christian temple, and a spiritual worship. It is not the least of its recommendations, that, although musical instruments are not generally permitted in a Methodist chapel to divert the attention from the inward contemplation of divine and spiritual pleasures, the charms of vocal melody warm the zeal, and animate the spirits, of the numerous worshippers. Hence it is, in a great degree, that the meeting-houses of Methodists are always so well attended by hearers. Thousands, I make no doubt, repair to the meeting, as well as to the church, 'Not for the worship, but the music there.'
>
> Public worship is begun by singing; the hymns being given out, line by line, by the preacher. After singing follows prayer; then singing again; to which succeeds an extempore sermon; after this another hymn is sung; and the service is finally concluded by prayer, and the customary benediction. The whole service usually lasts about an hour in the morning; at noon, and in the evening, about an hour and a half. This, however, depends much upon the prudence, the zeal, the modesty, or the loquacity, of the preacher. I have known the congregation kept in pain more than two hours. This service of the Wesleyans is, however, upon the whole, shorter and more simple than that of the Whitefieldians, or Calvinists, whose preachers are usually extremely tiresome.[16]

Because first-hand accounts may reveal popular and local customs, their use is especially beneficial when examining occasional services such as weddings and funerals. Custom largely shaped the structure and content of the special services of worship that, from the beginning of the Methodist movement, reinforced Methodist identity – love feast (in imitation of the early Christian agapé),[17] watch night (the Methodist equivalent of a vigil), and covenant renewal. In 1780 Wesley published *Directions for Renewing Our Covenant with God* which eventually went through at least nineteen editions (and variations) in Britain;[18] there is no direct evidence of the use of Wesley's text in America. The action of covenanting, though it occurred among Methodists in America and their missionary offshoots, was not as popular as it was in the British line. The Americans made much more of the love feast (particularly at their quarterly meetings) and the watch night, the latter shifting from its original monthly practice in conjunction with the full moon to an annual observance linked with New Year's Eve. The improvisatory character of an American congregation's gathering on New Year's Eve of 1829 is recounted in an unpublished diary kept by clergyman George Coles:

> At 8 o'clock began the watchnight. I commenced the services by giving out, 'Thou Judge of quick and dead,' with as much solemnity of voice, attitude and look as I could command: it was well sung by a good choir, and numerous congregation in the old tune called 'Aylesbury.' After this I made a long prayer, and then gave out 'Lo, he comes with clouds descending,' which was well sung. I then preached a long sermon on the 11th & 12th verses of the 20th Chapter of Revelation. After this we had singing and prayers, and some exhortation such as it was, for there was not a regular exhorter, nor a preacher of any kind, present besides myself. One of my *volunteer* exhorters made a very crooked piece of work of it; and his singing set the whole house in an uproar of laughter from which I found it rather difficult to recover them. I then dismissed them.[19]

Although love feast, watch night, and covenant renewal were key Methodist events well into the nineteenth century, their practice gradually declined, though they persist in some places in the twenty-first century. The same general trend of demise and limited continuation is also true for the once extremely popular camp meeting and its special forms of worship as well as for the worship associated with the extended revival meeting.

While eyewitness accounts are extremely beneficial for the study of Methodist worship, they do represent a limited perspective, for most are recorded by clergy or by the Methodist lay preachers – in other words, predominantly the male leadership. It is unusual to find descriptions of worship by laymen who were not active church leaders, and rarer still to find sustained recollections by women, though occasionally there are passing comments that are gems, like those recorded by Mississippi native and teenager Maria Dyer Davies in her personal diary dated 1853: 'Wednesday. We have been to church again, but I could not feel interested. Mr. Finley preached, was not in the spirit, thought his sermon not good. The church seemed cold.'[20] With the loss of the discipline of journal and diary-keeping in the early twentieth century, a major source for discerning Methodist worship practices was also lost. Yet at roughly the same time, a new source with a different type of information emerged with the advent of mimeograph: the worship leaflet/service order/worship bulletin; and the church newsletter.

Other sources yield information about worship practices for the patient reader willing to hunt. Sermons may reference worship matters in passing, as may church or secular newspapers and journals (local, regional, and national). Records of general church debates in official proceedings may reveal the pressing liturgical issues of a particular time, such as questions regarding the appropriateness of playing certain musical instruments in Sunday morning worship; altering a word in an ecumenical creed (out of concern about the 'catholic' in the 'holy *catholic* and apostolic church'); using grape juice instead of wine for Holy Communion; giving rings to both bride and groom; providing a ritual text to address infant death or stillbirth or miscarriage. Even essays or books that address the subject of worship disclose (overtly or subtly) what is happening liturgically at the time of writing when an author argues for what should be kept, introduced, modified or rejected. J. Ernest Rattenbury exposed current practices in his published perception of the state of worship in British Methodism in 1936,[21] and John Bishop did the same fourteen years later.[22]

Examination of some sources bears unexpected fruits. For example, plans of preaching assignments for clusters of congregations ('circuits' or 'stations') under the responsibility of several preachers or ministers – such plans were introduced in the eighteenth century and still are used in parts of the British line, but they did not survive long in America – often indicated when the Lord's Supper was to be celebrated and where. In one study of American urban station plans from the late eighteenth and early-nineteenth centuries, it was discovered that Methodists in a particular city might be able to receive the sacrament multiple times each month, thereby challenging a long-held assumption of American eucharistic indifference.[23]

At the beginning of the twenty-first century, research of Methodist worship requires an innovative use of the descriptive sources that may be available given the range of styles and materials drawn upon in a given congregation and across a denomination. Orders of service, songs, and prayers flashed on screens may mean that there is only one complete copy of a text or plan for a liturgical event, likely electronic, which may or may not be saved for future reference. The presence of multiple leaders for a given service of worship may in some cases result in the absence of a centrally formalized plan. Of course, it is highly unlikely that a descriptive prose reflection will be produced to place flesh on the bare bones of an outline. Other methods, some yet to be conceived, will be required to analyze emerging trends in Methodist worship.

Song: Text and Tune

An investigation of the sung music of Christian worship involves three components: the text (poetry); the music (melody and harmony); and the marriage of text and music. A song text is literature and may be assessed and analyzed as such; but it is also, as sacred poetry, a theological statement, grounded in scripture and Christian tradition, and nuanced by the cultural context and spiritual circumstance of the author. Likewise, the music may be judged according to the rules of music theory and analysis; but because it is music set with words for worship, it has a particular function: to work together with the text to convey, in a lively manner, Christian truths. Because tunes are often not exclusively fixed to certain texts, the dynamics of this partnership between text and tune are regularly overlooked in liturgical scholarship.

It has been said that Methodism was born in song, and indeed it was a hymn book – the seventy-four page *Collection of Psalms and Hymns* of 1737, known also as the 'Charles-town Hymnal' – that was the first published 'Methodist' liturgical book. Although (surprisingly) John Wesley did not include rubrics for singing in his *Sunday Service*, the presence of song at Methodist gatherings was of singular importance, as Joseph Nightingale observed in 1807, and has continued to be such. When the question of what makes Methodist worship uniquely Methodist is asked, singing – and especially singing the hymns of Charles Wesley – would be an answer affirmed by Methodists/Wesleyans worldwide.

The earliest of the hymn collections produced by John Wesley or in collaboration with his brother Charles borrowed sacred poetry and psalm paraphrases from other authors, principally George Herbert and Isaac Watts. Later Methodists inherited this propensity to exploit what was believed to be the best and most suitable material available. Nevertheless, Charles soon became the main contributor to numerous hymn books, pamphlets, and tracts produced for the Methodists on topics that took account of fundamental Christian teaching (e.g., the Trinity), the way of salvation (the *via salutis*), the festivals of the liturgical year, the Christian sacraments, and natural and political phenomena. Selections from the smaller collections fed into larger compilations, among them: *A Collection of Hymns for the Use of the People Called Methodists* (1780), which, expanded by supplements in 1831 and again in 1876, was printed for British Methodist worship until it was replaced in 1904; and *A Collection of Psalms and Hymns for the Lord's Day* (1784), a slight abridgment of a 1741 collection, which was sent to America along with Wesley's *Sunday Service*, but had only a short life there. Some of the texts in these eighteenth-century collections persist in the hymnic vocabulary of twenty-first-century congregations: for example, 'And can it be, that I should gain,' 'Depth of mercy, can there be,' 'Love divine, all loves excelling,' and 'Thou hidden source of calm repose.'

Because the majority of these early Methodist hymn books were printed without the benefit of musical notation, separate books were produced from which the Methodist communities were expected to draw their tunes. Two books contained melody only and in a variety of meters: *A Collection of Tunes, Set to Music, As They Are Commonly Sung at the Foundery* (1742); and *Select Hymns with Tunes Annext: Designed Chiefly for the Use of the People Called Methodists* (1761), which incorporated John Wesley's 'Directions for Singing' in the section of tunes entitled *Sacred Melody*. A third book, *Sacred Harmony, or A Choice Collection of Psalm and Hymn Tunes in Two or Three Parts for the Voice, Harpsichord & Organ* (1780), was John Wesley's concession to popular musical forms against his own stated preference (at least where worship was concerned) for unaccompanied, unison singing. The tunes in these books, borrowed and original, can be traced to sources both churchly (e.g., metrical psalms, German chorales, and other hymn tune collections) and popular (e.g., folk tunes and the music of the theater) – and this precedent for a diversity of sources for tunes would continue for later generations, though sometimes not without controversy. The 'marriage' of a particular text and tune was arranged by the song leader or by the custom of the local community. With a 1786 printing of the *Collection of Hymns* (1780), Wesley named a tune for each text, likely recommending what had become the most commonly used associations.[24] But until the late nineteenth century when technical advancements enabled the printing of multiple stanzas with a tune (often in four-part harmonization), thereby fixing a certain melody with particular text, there was generally fluidity in the relationship between text and tune.

Study of the hymns, songs, and tunes used within the Methodist family is complicated by the diversity of types of books produced and the degree of authority (if any) a book carried. A denomination, for example, through its legislative processes might authorize a book which would carry the imprimatur of that denomination, but whose use would not necessarily be required (though its adoption in a local congregation might be strongly urged). In some denominations, such as book of texts might, in addition to being a source for songs during worship, function also as theological textbook for ministers-in-training who would be instructed by individual hymn texts and by the theological system underlying the organizational structure of the book as a whole (e.g., the *via salutis*). Some books might be approved for use but not carry the denomination's imprimatur. Other books might be printed by a denominational press and be the product of an individual Methodist author. Still other books might come from publishers and authors unaffiliated with a Methodist group, but find a place with the Methodist people. Economic and social as well as theological and musical factors often governed which books were used in a particular community or home. Determining what was used – and where – requires recourse to the kinds of descriptive primary documents necessary to reconstruct broader liturgical practices.

Within the above categories could be found numerous collections for public Sunday worship, family and 'social' worship, and private devotions – and, at least in the nineteenth century, single volumes were produced that contained resources for each of these different circumstances. Additional types of collections were available for Sunday schools, children and youth, revivals, and camp meetings (to name a few), and to address social issues of concern, such as abolition and temperance. A task ahead is to identify the lineage and interconnections of these various resources, explore the theological suppositions of the texts contained therein, and expose the contexts in which collections developed and were used.

In each generation, the creative spirit that inspired Charles Wesley's poetry has rested upon Methodists young and old, male and female. Among them may be named Ann Griffiths, Fanny Crosby, Charles Albert Tindley; and in the late twentieth and early twenty-first centuries, D. T. Niles (Sri Lanka), Fred Pratt Green (England), Pablo Sosa (Argentina), Tomas Boström (Sweden) and Ludmila Garbuzova (Russia). Methodist tune-smiths have likewise been stirred, and among the most recent vintage may be numbered Swee Hong Lim (Singapore) and Patrick Matsikinyiri (Zimbabwe). The inculturation of musical forms and the setting of old texts (e.g., Charles Wesley to a Chinese melody) as well as the composition of new texts in languages other than English make the musicality of Methodism a rich area for ongoing inquiry.

Expanding Methodologies

As scholars recognized the necessity of research beyond the ritual text, fresh questions started to be asked about the meanings of a liturgical event – the words, the actions, the setting/space, the event as a whole, the dynamics of its leadership, the complexities of its reception, its implicit and explicit theology, its social ramifications, etc. New questions necessitated the application of methodologies not previously applied in liturgical studies, many of which drew from social science disciplines such as anthropology, ritual studies, psychology, pastoral care, sociology of religion, and congregational studies. The literary products of these new engagements began to emerge in the late 1980s. Joining them were other innovative approaches inspired by general academic trends; these included interests in postmodern critique, contextualization, semiotics, and literary theories (especially reader–response).

At the conclusion of the first decade of the twenty-first century, studies of Methodist liturgy have only started to utilize these different approaches. Methods from congregational studies and from the discipline of practical theology are, among the new types, most often found, and these are taken up in dissertations and theses that examine a single congregation as a 'case study.' The diversity of Methodist worship presented in a case study format is highlighted in two publications produced by the Alban Institute – one focusing on United Methodist and African Methodist Episcopal Zion congregations in the greater Boston (Massachusetts) area; the other concentrating on four ethnically varied United Methodist congregations in the Dallas (Texas) area.[25]

Ultimately a thorough study of Methodist worship needs to integrate and synthesize methodologies in order to add as many pieces to the mosaic as possible. Initial research has been done for Britain and the United States,[26] but much more work is necessary to expose the global liturgical texts and practices of John Wesley's spiritual descendants.

For Further Reading

Chapman, David M. *Born in Song: Methodist Worship in Britain*. Warrington: Church in the Market Place Publications, 2006.

Ruth, Lester. *A Little Heaven Below: Worship at Early Methodist Quarterly Meetings*. Nashville: Kingswood Books, 2000.

Westerfield Tucker, Karen B. *American Methodist Worship*. New York: Oxford University Press, 2001.

Westerfield Tucker, Karen B., ed. *The Sunday Service of the Methodists: Twentieth-century Worship in Worldwide Methodism*. Nashville: Kingswood Books, 1996.

15 Methodism and the Sacraments

Laurence Hull Stookey

Reformation Roots of Methodism's Sacramental Perspective

To know where we are, it is necessary to see where we have been. With reference to the sacraments, the primary data are liturgical texts (with rubrics) and any official undergirding statements of faith, in this case pertinent articles of religion.

Methodists are the heirs of those who at the Reformation changed the medieval status of sacraments, largely in one of three ways.

First, most Protestants reduced the number of sacraments from the traditional seven to two (baptism and eucharist) while retaining in a nonsacramental status some form of the other five practices (confirmation, penance, marriage, ordination, and last rites). This was the strategy of Lutherans and Calvinists. When Henry VIII ousted Catholic teachers of theology at Oxford and Cambridge, Archbishop Thomas Cranmer brought from the Continent those Protestant thinkers of various stripes whom he could persuade to cross the English Channel. Thus, Anglicanism, from which Methodism came, held together somewhat differing positions within the one Church of England. However, the Puritans (who were never able to get as much non-Roman 'purity' as they sought) ultimately willingly left or were ejected from Anglicanism. Still, always within the Church of England there was the insistence that a sacrament is a means of grace, a sturdy and reliable sign of divine goodness. Water, bread, and wine are not vague reminders of shadowy events locked away in New Testament times; rather, they are reliable indicators of God's work in our midst.

Secondly, other Protestants reduced the status of all seven liturgical practices by jettisoning the term 'sacrament' in favor of 'ordinance.' Those who preferred the word ordinance stressed that the actions of sacramental washing in baptism and eating in the eucharist were to be retained in a reformed church because in Matthew 28:19 and 1 Corinthians 11:24b, respectively, Jesus clearly 'ordered' the church to do these. But for the other five rites these reformers could find no such warrant in the New Testament. In one modified form or another, these Protestants retained all seven practices, but counted none to be sacraments, and only two were to be continued in obedience to Christ's direct order to the church. This was the option popular among Zwinglians, Baptists, and other 'free church' groups. For them, baptism and the Lord's Supper were not strong signs, but mere symbols (in a weak sense of that term), or reminders that aid us in obeying the commands of Jesus.

Thirdly, a few groups, such as the Society of Friends, abolished entirely the sacramental principle and its resulting rites. To this day devout Quakers may assert that they do indeed observe baptism and the supper of the Lord, but only inwardly, in spirit, in the thoughts of the heart, without the outward rites and the need for liturgical forms, ordained clergy, or even water, bread, and wine.

Early Methodism's Reliance on Anglican Understandings of Sacraments

At its founding, Methodism followed Anglicanism, but from time to time, like the mother church, developed an affinity for Zwinglianism – in practice even if not in official doctrine. Nevertheless, the Methodist acceptance of its Church of England sacramental heritage is revealed by comparing the opening words of three parallel articles of religion, as follows:

Anglican Article XXV: 'Of the Sacraments'
Sacraments ordained of Christ be not only badges or tokens of Christian men's profession, but rather they be certain sure witnesses, and effectual signs of grace, and God's good will toward us, by which he doth work invisibly in us, and doth not only quicken, but also strengthen and confirm our Faith in him.

Methodist Article XVI: 'Of the Sacraments'
Sacraments ordained of Christ are not only badges or tokens of Christian men's profession, but rather they are certain signs of grace, and God's good will toward us, by which he doth work invisibly in us, and doth not only quicken but also strengthen and confirm our faith in him.

Evangelical United Brethren Article VI: 'The Sacraments'
We believe the Sacraments, ordained by Christ, are symbols and pledges of the Christian's profession and of God's love toward us. They are means of grace by which God works invisibly in us, quickening, strengthening and confirming our faith in him.[1]

The evidence of the conflict between those Protestants who linked ordinances with sacraments and those who instead detached ordinances and did not go beyond them is found in the original Anglican Article (above) with its grammatical contrast of 'not only ... but rather.' Baptism and eucharist are 'not only badges or tokens of Christian men's profession,' (Anglican and Methodist). They are not merely 'symbols and pledges of the Christian's profession' (Evangelical United Brethren, henceforth, EUB). They are that, but they are also 'certain sure witnesses and effectual signs of grace' (Anglican), or 'certain signs of grace and of God's good will toward us' (Methodist), or of 'God's love toward us' (EUB). Thereby, they not only 'quicken but also strengthen and confirm our faith.' All affirm, with slight grammatical modifications in EUB, that God doth work 'invisibly in us.' The EUB adds that they are 'means of grace,' a point agreed on in other sources by both Anglicans and Methodists.

Sacraments are thus seen as being 'from above.' That is, they are divine acts directed toward humanity as a way of ultimately sanctifying us. Ordinances are seen to be 'from below.' They are human acts directed from believers toward God as a way of giving testimony to the world. Or, to put it another way, sacraments are primarily God's word to us, a kind of enacted sermon; while ordinances are primarily our word to God, a kind of enacted creed. Ironically, the churches that prefer the 'ordinance only' position are largely either anticreedal or lukewarm toward creedal statements.

Sacraments stress divine initiative in a way that ordinances do not, and in a way quite congenial to Methodist emphasis on prevenient grace. But whether considered sacraments or ordinances only, both viewpoints insist upon the need for growth in grace as Christian disciples. Both groups deny anything implying a magical character or an automatic impartation of saving grace without both faith, and good works flowing forth from that grace. Sacraments are the gateway to, but not an absolute guarantee of, sanctification. On this point sacramentalists often feel misunderstood or even misrepresented by the nonsacramental churches. In particular, the frequent charge that sacramental Christianity places no emphasis on personal commitment is quite wrong.

Related matters may be enhanced and clarified by turning now to a look at each sacrament separately.

Baptism: the Sacrament of Christian Initiation

When viewed as an ordinance only, baptism is an expression of human faith in God, a form of public declaration before the world. Therefore, it is normally open only to those who can make an original or agreed upon statement of faith, preferably in the presence of the congregation of Christian people. Submission to baptism openly declares each believer's possession of faith and hence is often called 'the baptism of believers.'

Infants and children are therefore precluded from baptism until they reach an 'age of accountability,' a rather imprecise term almost never assigned to a specific number of years. But certainly the candidate for baptism is to be old enough to distinguish between sin and grace, and to reject the one while embracing the other.

When viewed as a sacrament, baptism is seen as entrance into a holy covenant between God, the church, and those being baptized. If truly sacramental, it is a very ecclesial rite in contrast to the ordinance only position, which may be quite individualistic – concerned more with the eternal salvation of the individual's soul than with the lifelong ministry of the whole congregation in the present world. Precisely because of this, the focus is as much upon the worshipping assembly, and the larger church beyond it, as it is on the candidates. Therefore, infants and young children are seen to be legitimate candidates, for the necessary statement of faith is the faith of the congregation as a whole, not solely that of the candidate. On this point even Zwingli affirmed infant baptism.

Because God is the initiator of and principal actor in the baptismal covenant, we need to understand, insofar as possible, what it is we believe God is doing. Throughout the middle ages, it was taken for granted that in baptism God is eradicating the stain of original sin. It was believed that until this stain is removed, even an infant who has not yet committed sinful acts ('actual sin') could be barred from heaven due to the guilt passed on from Adam and Eve. Such an infant could be consigned forever to 'limbo' – a place not of active punishment but of nothingness, rather akin to the Hebrew conception of Sheol. So unpleasant was this prospect that infants were baptized as soon as possible, usually on a weekday without the presence of the congregation, and certainly without the child's mother who, according the medical practices of that day, would be confined to bed for some time.

The hardy Augustinian doctrine of original sin has been greatly modified over the centuries. Most Methodists have long felt unfriendly to such an interpretation. Unfortunately, John Wesley retained a rather sturdy understanding of original guilt. He was devoted to a treatise on baptism written by his father Samuel, and both father and son accepted medieval teaching, the practice of which traditionally assumed two stages: (1) baptism in infancy removes original sin and (2) but actual sin is removed through the sacrament of penance, with confession to God though the priest and absolution to the penitent from God, also through the priest.

John Wesley significantly altered the second step. New Testament teaching insisted that we are saved by grace through faith alone. Compensatory acts prescribed by the priest after confession must not lead anyone to believe that salvation comes through good works. So Wesley's second step was not penance and absolution, but the conversion of the heart, the new birth, the birth from above. He taught that baptism is indeed salvific for guilt inherited from

Adam and Eve. But the sacramental effect of regeneration is short-lived because we readily sin away baptismal grace and have nothing sufficient to cover the active sin in which we are willing participants. Then, the necessary second step becomes this: that through conversion, with its subsequent lifelong journey toward sanctification, we are granted divine forgiveness for the sins for which we are accountable. Wesley tended to define sin rather tightly, as the willful transgression of a known law.

The changing views of sin across the past several centuries are discovered by examining the rites themselves. The traditional introductory sentence in rites of baptism both for infants and adults began with these words from the prayer books of the Church of England: 'Forasmuch as all men are conceived and born in sin, and that our Saviour Christ saith, "None can enter into the kingdom of God, except he be regenerate and born anew of water and of the Holy Ghost...."' This did not square well with Enlightenment thinking. Indeed to the rationalists it was sheer superstitious poppycock. Along came Charles Darwin, whose teaching about evolution seemed to dispense with Adam and Eve, whether understood literally or emblematically. There followed Sigmund Freud, whose views convinced even deeply pious people, that sin is merely neurotic imagining.

Along the way in the United States the opening sentence of the official baptismal rites was altered to fit the current scene. By 1916 the Methodist Episcopal Church substituted terms that seemed to remove the scandal of sin by altering the words used in previous centuries to this: 'Forasmuch as God in his great mercy hath entered into covenant relation with man, wherein he hath included children as partakers of its gracious benefits....'

When the Methodist Episcopal Church, the Methodist Episcopal Church, South, and the Methodist Protestant Church reunited in 1939 the new joint liturgy included a form for the baptism of infants, introduced as follows: 'Forasmuch as all men are heirs of life eternal and subjects of the saving grace of the Holy Spirit, and that our Saviour Christ saith: "Suffer the little children to come unto me...."' Mention of sin was gone. The closest the introductory words of this rite came to defining the work of God had to do with 'saving grace,' but there is little clue about what it is we need to be saved from. Instead the focus is placed on pious parents or other adult sponsors who present infants at the font. Nor is there much hint of a covenanted community through which God might be at work in the world. Indeed the words 'all men are heirs of life eternal' suggest a doctrine of universal salvation. In the mid-1930s, World War I had ravaged Europe, the Great Depression was in full swing, and Hitler was firmly ensconced in the Third Reich, but all seemed rosy to American Methodism, whose cheery face shone brightly.

By the mid-1960s a new generation had arisen with a less optimistic view of the world and of human nature. In the Methodist Church the service of baptism for children (1964) began with this address to the congregation:

> Dearly beloved, Baptism is an outward and visible sign of the grace of the Lord Jesus Christ, through which grace we become partakers of his righteousness and heirs of eternal life. Those receiving the Sacrament are thereby marked as Christian disciples, and initiated into the fellowship of Christ's holy Church.
>
> *The Methodist Hymnal* (Nashville: Methodist Publishing House, 1964), 828.

But the Methodist rite for the baptism of adults, also approved in 1964, again harkened back to the mid-sixteenth century Anglican prayer books (1549, 1552, and 1559) with this warrant for administering the sacrament: 'Dearly beloved, forasmuch as all men have sinned and fallen short of the glory of God, and our Savior Christ said, "Unless one is born of water and the Spirit, he cannot enter the kingdom of God,. . . ."' It is clear that the followers of Karl Barth and Reinhold Niebuhr had made inroads into American Methodist optimism.

Finally, the 1989 United Methodist Hymnal (the first joint work following the Methodist-EUB merger) more firmly rooted the United Methodist Church in historic covenant theology. Happily, it restored to the service the ancient baptismal affirmation commonly (if incorrectly) called 'The Apostles' Creed.' Also recovered was a form of thanksgiving over the water (popularly known as 'the flood prayer' because of its imagery from the flood of Noah's day). Both of these elements had been missing since Wesley; for reasons best known to him, he deleted them in his 1784 prayer book revision for American Methodists. Wesley's editing of earlier texts is always something of a puzzle. Did he simply want to shorten a received liturgy? Was he responding to theological objections from the Puritan wing of the church or some other interest group in his day? Did he have deep objections of his own to the official rites of the Church of England? Or was he a born abridger who altered almost everything that came across his desk? Usually it is impossible to know.

Certainly we can say about revised baptismal rites in our time that congregational participation is greatly increased. Methodists have made a conscious and concerted effort to merge the historic Anglican tradition and the ecumenical understandings of our day as expressed in the World Council of Church's *Baptism, Eucharist, and Ministry*.[2]

Baptism is increasingly seen as a rite once administered to an individual within the company of a congregation committed to nurturing lifelong commitment within that person. If the candidate is an infant, child, or someone unable to articulate the faith (whether due to age or a developmental disability), if and when the impediment is removed it is appropriate for the person to make a public affirmation of faith in the rite known as confirmation. Confirmation is not needed for those who at their baptism have been able to make their own profession of faith. Baptism is not to be regarded as being incomplete until followed by confirmation, but each individual should make for himself or herself an affirmation of faith in the presence of the congregation.

Methodists historically do not rebaptize unless the ecumenical formula was not used or another major impediment calls into question the adequacy of an earlier rite. When questions arise of a very grievous nature, there is the possibility of conditional baptism using the words 'If you are not already baptized, I baptize you in the name, etc.'

For a fuller understanding of official statements on Anglican-Methodist teaching see Anglican Article XXVII and Methodist Article XVII, both titled 'Of Baptism.'

Eucharist: the Sacrament of Strengthening Disciples for Service

If the Wesleyan movement was not noteworthy in its renewed understanding of the meaning of baptism, the early Methodists made up for it in their zeal for and understanding of the eucharist. More commonly referred to by Methodists as 'Holy Communion' or simply as 'Communion,' the sacrament has also long been known as 'the Lord's Supper.' Increasingly it is known as 'the eucharist,' first because that is a very ancient designation, and also because of its denotation of thanksgiving by the whole church as one way of escaping tendencies in the past to think of the sacrament as severely individualistic and often somewhat dour. So inward looking has the sacrament become that at times it takes on the solemnity of a funeral rather than the joy of our preparation for partaking of the great feast of heaven. A literal translation of the word 'eucharist' is 'good gift' or 'good grace.' And such it is to be.

Until mid-1960s, in most sectors of Methodism there was one denominationally approved 'prayer of consecration' as it was then termed, now more likely called 'The Great Thanksgiving.' Within this prayer until recently there were two defects. First, like most such prayers in the western church (but not among the Eastern Orthodox) there was no 'epiclesis' – a calling upon the Holy Spirit to make the bread and wine 'to be for us the body and blood of Christ' in order that we, the communicants, in turn may be 'the body of Christ for the world.' Secondly, in the older forms of the consecratory prayer we were exhorted to 'do this' 'in remembrance of his death and Passion.' This latter phrase always seemed to put these two events in the wrong order. Did Jesus not suffer before his death? Or, are we supposed to remember, as someone has said, 'that he suffers until the end of time for the sins of his people'? Or, had some editor or author unknowingly engaged in a case of *hysteron proteron*? The answer is not clear.

But what is not said in the old prayers is as much to be noted as what is said. In 1964 the Methodist Church opened the door a bit both by changing the order of suffering and death and by introducing the resurrection. 'In remembrance of His death and Passion' happily became 'in remembrance of his passion, death, and resurrection.' For the church in our time, that facilitated a return to the kind of eucharistic services observed in early Methodism: rites done frequently, joyously, with large crowds joining together for the feast.

When we find Mr. Wesley reporting that on certain occasions many hundreds, even thousands, had gathered together for a sacramental occasion, we are inclined to accuse Father John of inflating attendance statistics, as preachers still are wont to do – until we discover the objective report of one participant who recorded that on a certain occasion we 'sipped away' thirty-five bottles of wine.[3] Truly that would require a vast crowd.

For the theological foundations that undergirded early Methodist devotion to the supper of the Lord, we need only read John Wesley's sermon 'On the Duty of Constant Communion,'[4] in which he argued for the difference between constant communion and what he regarded as merely frequent communion.

But the great testimony to early Methodist eucharistic devotion is the 1745 volume by Charles (with some contributions from John, but we cannot always say which) of 166 eucharistic poems.[5] This volume was a devotional reader and prayer book before its texts came to be set to music for use by those in the Methodist societies. It is unlikely that anyone else in the history of the Christian Church has ever published for congregational use 166 poems on the meaning of the eucharist. The collection reveals the Anglican synthesis of the continental Reformation. Some texts clearly reflect either Lutheran or Calvinist influences. And still other poems can seem to show the influence of Zwinglianism without in any way suggesting the abolition of the sacramental foundation of Anglicanism.

When writing 'O the Depth of Love Divine,' Charles Wesley may well have had open to Book Four of Calvin's *Institutes of the Christian Religion*. This is a remarkable doctrinal hymn, intended to be meditated upon after reception of the sacrament. In the first stanza and the opening half of the second, Wesley seems to agree with the Zwinglians that none 'can say how bread and wine God into man conveys.' If not even 'the wisest mortal' can present a readily acceptable explanation of the sacramental presence of the Lord; surely such a presence is not to be affirmed (Zwinglianism). But the final sentence of stanza two reveals the true Wesleyan sentiment, to be grasped after the communicant has pondered the experience of partaking of the bread and wine, for 'these the virtue did convey, yet still remain the same.'

Then in stanza three there is a wonderful theological joke. The poem moves back to the question of 'Ask the Father's wisdom how' feeble elements can bestow a divine power. 'The Father's wisdom' is none other than Christ himself (1 Corinthians 1:25), through whom the virtue (or power) came. In other words, if you wish to explain the eucharistic presence, ask Jesus how. He is the one who told us to 'do this.' And the joke is: He is not going to tell you how. Then the elaborating and evocative final line of stanza three: 'Angels round our altars bow to search it out in vain.' If the angels cannot define the eucharistic presence of the Lord, how can we ever hope to grasp it?

The summation is that 'these [elements we consumed] the virtue did convey, yet still remain the same.' Thus the Roman explanation of transubstantiation, the Lutheran counter-explanation of the ubiquity of Christ's risen body, and bare nonexplanation of Zwinglianism are all swept away, and we are left alone with Calvin – a lawyer who could logically explain anything at all until he came to the sacrament. There he had to confess that what he could not understand he had nevertheless experienced at the holy table – and that with great joy. So the final stanza affirms that 'the grace' of the sacrament is 'sure and real,' but 'the manner' is left 'unknown,' a mystery fathomable only to the God who has willed it to be a means of grace. To us it is given to 'taste the heavenly powers,' and we are to seek nothing further. God blesses us through the sacrament; our appropriate response is not to explain, but 'to wonder and adore.'

If all other eucharistic hymns by the Wesleys were lost, this single four-stanza text would enable us to understand the eucharistic fervor of the Methodist revival and to see how much we have lost by reducing the sacrament into what someone has called 'a mere audiovisual aid.' But does not the poem just cited align entirely with John Calvin's confession: 'If anyone should ask me how this [sense of the presence of Christ at the table] takes place, I shall not be ashamed to confess that it is a secret too lofty for either my mind to comprehend or my words to declare. And to speak more plainly, I rather experience than understand it.'[7]

The Wesleyan hymns (of which there are more than the 166 of 1745) do occasionally refer to 'the real presence' of Christ in the eucharist, but only rarely so. That phrase is fraught with difficulties. The issue is: What stands in contrast to 'the real presence'? Dom Gregory Dix unfairly ridiculed certain Protestants, who he said believed in 'the real absence' of Christ. Certainly not! So where is the contrast – 'the unreal presence'? That is hardly a better solution. The deeper problem is that today we tend to think that the opposites are 'real' and 'not real, fleeting, spectral.' But the root Latin word from which we get 'real' is '*res*,' meaning 'the thing.' The question then becomes, 'How is Christ present in the things of bread and wine?' Or is he not? If not, is he dependably present in some other way in fulfillment of his own promises?

What seems more congenial to Methodism is to see the presence of Christ not so much in the bread and wine themselves (though these are necessary for the service), but in the actions of taking, giving thanks, breaking, and sharing. These actions are reported in the New Testament narratives not only in the upper room on Thursday evening, but also in the accounts of the feeding of the thousands, the revelation of Jesus to two disciples at Emmaus, and other New Testament passages including what likely is the oldest literarily, 1 Corinthians 11:23–26. From this could be developed a theology of 'the active presence of Christ' rather than the 'real' or thing-oriented presence.

All of this leads us to a central concern, that the eucharistic means of grace is intended to nourish us inwardly, so we may grow in our own active service to the world in God's name. The active presence of Christ is revealed in the eucharist not to honor us, let alone to entertain us, but to shape us, to form us, to empower us as active disciples.

The water of baptism denotes spiritual birth and washing. The bread and wine denote spiritual nutrition and formation as God's people, fed and prepared to serve God at every opportunity. We may well borrow these words from Eucharistic Rite II, Prayer C, of the Episcopal Church in the United States: 'Deliver us from the presumption of coming to this Table for solace only, and not for strength; for pardon only, and not for renewal. Let the grace of this Holy Communion make us one body, one spirit in Christ, that we may worthily serve the world in his name.'[8] Christ is actively present in the eucharist in ways we may be unable to discern, let alone fathom. But this much is clear: Christ is actively present so that we may be more actively present in the mission of the church to the world.

For official statements on Anglican-Methodist teaching on the eucharist, see:

Anglican Article	XXVIII – Of the Lord's Supper.
	XXIX – Of the Wicked, which eat not the Body of Christ. . . .
	XXX – Of both kinds.
	XXXI – Of the one Oblation of Christ finished upon the Cross
Methodist Article	XVIII – Of the Lord's Supper
	XIX – Of Both Kinds
	XX – Of the One Oblation of Christ, Finished upon the Cross
EUB Article	VIII – Reconciliation Through Christ

Formally adopted Articles of Religion reveal official teachings, but may not as accurately tell us about informal sources, doctrines, and practices. They do not inform us, for example, that Martin Boehm brought into the United Brethren movement influences from the Mennonites in which Martin was a bishop, but from which he was excommunicated. Boehm's associate, Philip William Otterbein, was a Reformed pastor. The founder of the Evangelical

Association, Jacob Albright, was baptized and confirmed Lutheran. Thus, the German-speaking antecedents of United Methodism had a more variegated and complicated sacramental heritage than might be imagined by reading the EUB Articles.

Nor can formal Articles express the richness of eucharistic theology in the first century of Methodism, but the comparative paucity of the baptismal theology which John Wesley held, in part out of respect for a volume on baptism by his father Samuel.

Finally, there are always elusive influences that are felt, often without precise documentation. The Pentecostal movement, Billy Graham crusades, tele-evangelists, and mega-churches – all of these have altered traditional sacramental piety for good or ill, more by subtle forces than by deliberate design. Hence, the truth of the barb that, 'Methodists are sacramental chameleons who take on the coloration of whatever is the dominant religious landscape.' In Texas, where Baptists predominate, Methodists may have baptismal pools in their houses of worship. In Minnesota, where Lutherans predominate, Methodists may hold confirmation classes that last for a year or two rather than the more usual six to twelve weeks. Beliefs and practices taken for granted in one congregation may be held differently in a neighboring parish of the same branch of Methodism, thus defying any attempts that would impose uniformity.

Practical Questions and Implications Growing out of Our History and Theology

We turn now to examine certain understandings that come less from articles of religion or from the rites directly, but from the experience of differing practices, many of which are due for new forms of interpretation or total reconsideration.

Baptism

Although not all churches that practice baptism accept the baptism of certain other churches (because of mode of administration, age of the candidate, variance of the baptismal formula, or ecclesial issues of faith or order), it is still true that baptism is not a denominational act but an ecumenical one. Therefore whatever matters can be brought into alignment should be, and where this is not possible the points of disagreement and divergence should be set forth as clearly and consistently as possible. Here and in the case of other pertinent issues, the World Council of Churches *Baptism, Eucharist, and Ministry* should be given due consideration.[9] Indeed it is long overdue for all of the sacramental churches to hold a joint consultation to discuss the viability of using a common baptismal rite as a sign to the world of a basic unity despite the many divisions so evident to outsiders.

The Baptismal Formula. Methodists normally accept all baptisms done in good faith and 'In the name of the Father, and of the Son, and of the Holy Spirit [or, Ghost].' When substitutions for the historic formula are employed (e.g., 'In the name of the Creator, Redeemer, and Sustainer') the efficacy of the baptism may well be called into question even by other trinitarian churches. The least perilous alteration seems to be by addition rather than deletion or substitution. That is, at the close of the trinitarian formula the administrator adds: 'the God who is the mother of us all.' More discussion and much negotiation are needed to reach agreement even among all sacramental Protestants, let alone by Orthodox and Roman bodies.

Dealing with those whom we consider unbaptized is also a thorny issue, particularly in the instances of the Salvation Army and the Religious Society of Friends. But before the Army came into existence, John Wesley certainly baptized Quakers. Still more questionable is the baptismal practice of the Latter Day Saints; the United Methodist Church specifically does not recognize Mormon baptism.

The Orthodox use the passive voice for the formula, thereby implying that Christ himself is the administrator: 'NAME is baptized in the name of the Father,' etc. Evangelical Lutherans allow this as an option and there is no reason for Methodists to see this as an impediment to mutual recognition. Indeed, given our affinity for Orthodox theology in other areas, when making revisions to the baptismal rite Methodists might consider whether the passive voice is an option for us also.

The Baptismal Water. The water of baptism should be fresh and plentiful. In many recent liturgies it is made clear that if baptism is done at a font (rather than a river or a pool for immersion) the filling of the font just before the prayer of thanksgiving over the water should be both visually and audibly evident to all. The sacraments are designed to reveal to us that God works through the ordinary things of life, enabling us to find divine activity through their use. Baptism should not be done with water imported from the Jordan River, nor should tourists at the Jordan make a fetish of its water by engaging there in baptism itself, let alone submitting to 'rebaptism' there, which action is an impossibility since the covenant promises of God neither expire nor give themselves to repetition. If someone insists on being baptized with the same water used by Jesus, point out that given the laws of evaporation and condensation, as much of Jesus' baptismal water now resides in any river on earth as in that particular stream. Nor should water from any source be bottled up after the baptismal rites and taken home as a souvenir or for use in some superstitious way.

Mode and Age. Although these are separable issues they are often bound together. Baptists and their kin insist on immersion after a candidate has come to 'the age of accountability.' The Orthodox baptize infants by immersion.

Mennonites baptize believers only, but they do this by pouring water over them. Some immersionists insist on a backward movement of the body, resembling the burial and resurrection of Christ, but some baptize forward. In general, it is best to let the mode of actual burial in a culture determine the practice.

Related is the matter of a single or a triple [trine] application of water. However, rarely will the receiving church consider a prior baptism unacceptable over this issue. Indeed, some Baptists will not question either the mode or age for administration when receiving a person into fellowship even though an unbaptized person must be immersed, and that as a believer, not an infant.

Methodists have long practiced baptism largely by sprinkling, but this matter surely needs reexamination. Major sacramental churches (including the most recent rites of American Episcopalians and Evangelical Lutherans) specify in the rubrics that water is to be administered by pouring or immersion. Both have important symbolic connotations. Immersion centers us on the death and rising of Jesus. Pouring calls to remembrance the power poured out upon the church by the Holy Spirit on the Day of Pentecost and thereafter. Sprinkling has no clear New Testament symbolic reference. Some find scriptural warrant in Ezekiel 36:25 and Numbers 8:7. But both of these are actions of renewal of the covenant with God, not of initiation into it. And the Numbers passage pertains to the cleansing of those who are to be Levitical priests, not laity in general.

It can be argued that for Christians, sprinkling should be reserved for acts of personal or corporate reaffirmation (including confirmation). Thus, a small amount of water calls to mind the much greater baptismal waters, whether administered earlier by immersion or pouring. Furthermore, in all circumstances the amount of water used at baptism should be sufficient in quantity to signify the great generosity of God toward us. This is particularly true at the baptism of infants or young children, in order that the Methodist emphasis on prevenient grace may be evident in the sacramental action.

Chrismation. The Protestant reformers so fully rebelled against the papacy as to deride anointing oils as being 'the Pope's grease.' By now we (who absolutely love to quote Psalm 23:5b) should have enough distance from the sixteenth century to separate out the chaff from the wheat of Reformation polemics and exaggeration. Culturally, chrism may not have for us the appeal it had in the early centuries of the church: to beautify the body after bathing. But theologically oil has great meaning, for 'christos' refers to the anointed one (Christ) who shares with us a messianic mission in the world. A cross traced with olive oil on the forehead of someone who has just come out of the waters of baptism can significantly enhance the meaning of initiation into Christ's holy church.

Proper Administrators of Baptism. Usually it is assumed that the administrators of baptism are those ordained to the ministry. This restriction does help to set right practices that arose out of previous theological misunderstandings or even superstition. In the pre-Reformation period it was believed that so great was the threat to the eternal well-being of an unbaptized person that anyone willing to perform the rite in good conscience could do so. To take the extreme: a person dying in the Sahara desert, lacking water, could be baptized by the pouring of sand, and said sand could even be administered by a Muslim who knew the proper formula and intended not to make fun of Christian practice but who willingly would engage in the practice for good reason. Even to this day, in some hospitals, pediatric nurses are taught how to administer baptism to a dying infant, without necessarily having consulted the parents or even without telling them after the fact that their child has been so baptized (presumably to escape damnation at the hands of ungracious deity).

For such reasons the administrators of baptism have come under the control of ecclesiastical law, sometimes with a vengeance. Historically, deacons were given the right to baptize as a part of their ministry. But Methodists have gone back and forth on this one. At the time of the EUB–Methodist merger (1968) the EUBs did not have deacons. And when the finished legislation came into being, Methodist deacons discovered that they could no longer baptize, but had permission only to assist the elders. This is a matter that deserves reconsideration within United Methodism.

In the Congregation of the People of God. Throughout much of our history, Methodists have seen nothing wrong with baptisms conducted privately in a family home on Thursday evening or even at a country club on Saturday afternoon with a cocktail hour for close friends following. But increasingly we have become aware that baptism is not a covenant between two parties (the candidate and God), but a covenant involving also the entire congregation. It is to be observed in the midst of a congregational service to persons who have had previous instruction. Our Methodist rites generally include promises the laity make by way of assuming their responsibility for the ongoing nurture of the newly baptized. When the congregation is not present, who is to make (and later to keep) promises on their behalf?

In Methodism, as elsewhere, the past half-century has seen great changes in our understanding of baptism. A recycled set of superstitious ideas and questionable practices has given way to rich and empowering rites. The texts of the rite are full of biblical allusions, and are centered in the conviction that baptism is a lifelong event, administered only once to each person, but with enduring promises from a faithful God to those who hold sacrosanct their own promises to God.

The extent to which this understanding has taken hold, among the clergy at least, can be anecdotally illustrated. A pastor reported a phone call from someone he did not know who wanted a grandchild baptized in private and with no religious commitment from parents or grandparents evident. As the pastor carefully went over the church's rather different expectations, the caller became increasingly distant and then hostile, and just before slamming down the receiver on the pastor the caller bellowed: 'What is going on with you Methodists anyhow? You are the fifth pastor I have phoned and I get exactly the same brush-off each time!' May we suspect that the caller then went on to test out a sixth pastor?

Greater efforts need to be taken to educate the laity concerning how the congregation may best live out its commitments to those who have received baptism or wish to be baptized.

Eucharist

A number of issues also arise about the practical implications of our theology for eucharistic practice.

Consecration from a distance. We seem to know that ordained (or otherwise authorized) persons are to preside at the supper, but it is not clear that we know why. Certain magical powers seem to accrue to the accredited persons, such that they (but no one else) can make sacred the bread and wine. It is still true in sectors of Methodism that those who are not approved to preside at the eucharist are told by their ecclesiastical supervisors to bring the bread and wine to the telephone before the Sunday service so that an ordained or licensed person can say the prescribed words on Saturday evening, and thus the elements may be distributed the next morning, without a certified person being present. This totally misses the point.

Intentionally or not, we suggest that certain people have the power to change bread and wine from something to something else. That makes sense if you firmly believe in transubstantiation. But we do not. Particularly if we believe in the active presence of Christ, the Lord is to be especially evident in the action of the eucharist, not in the elements as such. But the person who says the words over the phone is invisible to the congregation and in no way is seen as standing in the stead of Jesus.

Eucharist and Ecclesiology. Should we not make the most of the polity we proudly possess? Why in Methodism is an ordained pastor no longer a member of a local congregation, but is instead a member of an Annual Conference? Because the ordained are the connecting link between each local congregation and the larger church. The ordained or properly certified persons stand at the holy table in the stead of Christ, but also as representatives of the connectional system. Even though it may happen subconsciously, when the congregation sees a flesh-and-blood pastor take bread and cup, give thanks over bread and cup, break the bread, and distribute the bread and cup, spiritually that congregation is intended to see Christ in their midst doing here and now what he did long ago on the hillsides, in the upper room, at Emmaus, and beside the sea.

The church does not ordain so it can call down upon certain people magical powers from heaven. The church ordains because anyone who is going to stand in the stead of Christ first needs to be well instructed and examined by the larger body of the church. That person must have, and be able to communicate to others, a healthy vision of the link and yet the distance between the parish church and the church catholic. There is necessarily a gate which is the entrance for those who are being authorized, but there is also an exit for any deemed no longer fit to stand in Christ's place and to do the things he did at table.

Anyone who doubts this phenomenon has not lived through an unhappy time such as this: with or without justification, a pastor has been accused of actions deemed unsuitable, but has not yet been transferred out of that appointment or dismissed from office. In such an instance a significant number of laity will absent themselves from church saying, 'I simply cannot bring myself to take communion from *that* person.' Without having heard the formula *in persona Christi* such persons intuitively know that whoever presides at the Lord's table in some mysterious way stands there in the stead of Christ.

Those who are approved to stand in that place should constantly be aware of the awesome responsibility of their office. Their task is not magically to change bread and wine into something else; their task is to help make communicants aware that the eternal Christ is in our midst to bless what we bring to the table and to enable us to take away more than we brought.

Nature and Disposition of Remaining Elements. At the Lord's Supper we do as fully as practicable what Jesus did. It seems certain that he took bread (possibly barley bread rather than wheat) and the cup (filled with fermented wine, not grape juice). Unfermented wine was not even a possibility before the perfecting of pasteurization in the latter part of the nineteenth century. The church has learned to make accommodations necessary for practical or cultural reasons – grape juice for alcoholic priests, rice cakes for those suffering with severe allergic reactions to gluten. Usually common sense dictates how to resolve such problems.

But a differing set of problems arose during the great missionary expansion period of the church. When evangelizing a Pacific island where both wheat and grapes are unknown, must communicants be faced with strange foods imported from the United States because these are believed to be 'closer to what Jesus used'? Or, is it more appropriate to use native foods such as sake wine and rice cakes? The missionaries disagreed over this one. But is this not the sacramental principle: that God, the maker of all things, seeks to give heightened meaning to the ordinary such that what we take for granted before the service begins means far more to us after the service ends? If the serving of grape juice or grape wine and leavened whole wheat bread is regarded as something irregular and even unacceptable in a particular setting, how is God going to heighten the 'ordinary'?

Methodism and the Sacraments

This does not suggest that on a church youth retreat, pizza and cola may be used instead of the usual elements. Teenagers in most cultures now know what bread and grape juice are, and they are not apt to ask in the manner of Exodus 15:16: 'Manna?' (What is this?) Substitutions should be made only when justified by unusual circumstances.

More important is this: to focus exclusively on the eucharistic elements (the things) rather than on the actions of the Lord raises questions also about what to do with the remaining elements at the close of the service. Shall the unconsumed bread and wine be consumed, and if so by whom? By the clergy, in full view of the congregation, or in private? By the laity who prepared the elements, who then consume them out of sight in a private room? By anyone in the congregation who wishes to come forward? Or shall we dispose of the remaining elements in the trash can or septic system, or by taking them out-of-doors so the wine can nourish the earth and so birds and squirrels can feast? Or do the Romans have it right after all, that the remaining wine is to be drunk by the presider, while unleavened bread is to be retained for purposes of adoration or to be eaten at a later time by communicants, including the sick and shut-ins?

Does it make more sense for us as Methodists to center our hearts on Christ's action in our midst rather than to debate about the exact nature of the things Christ uses to communicate with us? Can each congregation find reverent ways in which to use the remaining elements without suggesting that these are permanently holy in and of themselves?

Who May Communicate? Some churches have steadfast laws forbidding reception by anyone outside of that particular local church or denomination. Some have a set age after which reception may be observed. Others are less rigid, but do assume that reception is for the baptized only. Methodists tend not to see what baptism has to do with communion. We often suppose that anyone with good intentions can receive. While the communion of newly baptized infants is practiced in Eastern Orthodoxy, Methodists generally have not taken to this, but have gone so far as to see that (as is true in the Roman Church) regular communion may commence at around age nine or ten, with the sacrament of confirmation following later. Some Methodists may lower that age to five or six in the awareness that children feel excluded when they are forbidden to eat food being served. This matter of who may receive merits further study among Methodists.

'Take Away Communion.' Presumably, to allow more services to be held in the same building on Sunday morning, some have experimented with this practice: after the Great Thanksgiving, servers of the elements go to a number of stations, including all exit doors. Worshippers who are in a hurry go to one of these exit locations, take the bread and cup, and hasten to their cars in the parking lot without ever returning to their seats in the congregation. This is

frequently a practice at Catholic Mass, but much to the chagrin and dismay of those in charge of the service. What they have discovered about a practice that once introduced seems impossible to abolish, may be a source of valuable learning for Methodists.

Communion of Shut-Ins. Although it is admirable for the pastor to visit shut-ins, taking communion to them, this often results in hurried visits by a harried pastor. It also does nothing to strengthen the bond between members regularly in attendance and members unable to attend at all. Congregations can find ways for shut-ins (or hospital patients) to have communion from the congregational Lord's table brought to them on communion Sundays by teams of laity who engage in this ministry on a rotating basis.

Into the Future

Both the testimony of the church catholic and the willing devotion of the early Methodists to the observance of the sacraments should move us to a deeper study and practice than we currently have. The historic infrequency (typically four times a year) of the eucharist did not grow out of a Zwinglian fear of frequent reception. It grew out of a lack of ordained clergy and John Wesley's conviction that although laity might be given authority to preach weekly, they should not so readily be granted the right to baptize or to preside at the font and at the holy table. That should be reserved for the ordained, even though they were usually on the scene only four times a year to conduct quarterly conferences.

The witness of our sacramental legacy should compel us to reform, not because we are antiquarians who think what is old is always the best, but because our history bears witness to the power of the sacraments when coupled with preaching and teaching that are biblical in content, evangelical in spirit, and catholic in breadth.

For Further Reading

Felton, Gayle Carlton. *By Water and the Spirit*. Nashville: Discipleship Resources, 1998.
Felton, Gayle Carlton. *This Holy Mystery*. Nashville: Discipleship Resources, 2000.
Stamm, Mark W. *Sacraments and Discipleship*. Nashville: Abingdon, 2001.
Stookey, Laurence H. *Baptism: Christ's Act in the Church*. Nashville: Abingdon Press, 1982.
Stookey, Laurence H. *Eucharist: Christ's Feast with the Church*. Nashville: Abingdon Press, 1993.
Wainwright, Geoffrey. *Eucharist and Eschatology*. 2nd ed. London: Epworth, 1978.
White, James F. *Sacraments as God's Self-Giving*. Nashville: Abingdon, 1983.

16 Spirituality in the Methodist Tradition

Thomas R. Albin

> The soul and the body make a man; the spirit and discipline make a Christian.[1]

The Methodist understanding and experience of the Christian life is grounded in the ministry and leadership of John and Charles Wesley. Together, the brothers found their way into a unique synthesis of theology, practice, and structure that proved extraordinarily effective in helping others to know, love, and serve God and their neighbors.

Christian Spirituality

The term, spirituality, has become increasingly popular in the study of religion. It has no direct equivalent in scripture and did not emerge as a well-defined branch of theology until the seventeenth century when Giovanni Scaramelli, S. J. (1687–1752), established 'ascetical and mystical theology as a science of the spiritual life.'[2] It derives from one of the classifications habitual to the Church of Rome, and formulated by M. l'Abbe Pourrat in his *La Spiritualité Chrétienne* wherein 'dogmatic' and 'moral' theology are understood to provide the basis for 'spiritual' theology which is the greatest of all. Spiritual theology is above them because it is a branch of the science which deals, not with abstract statements of faith (doctrine) and objective laws of conduct (ethics), but with the life in Christ itself, the reality of that union with him, which all traditions in some form would assert as the meaning of our salvation.[3]

Since Vatican II, there has been significant work done by a wide range of ecumenical scholars to establish the study of spirituality as an academic discipline in its own right. Within the last few decades large multi-volume works,[4] extensive dictionaries,[5] and numerous single volumes have been produced to examine the whole range of Christian spirituality.[6] Numerous articles on the topic have appeared in existing periodicals, new journals have been created[7] and new academic forums have been established.[8]

Christian spirituality, at the most basic level, may be defined as the lived experience of human beings in relationship with God. Christian spirituality is 'life in the Spirit.'[9] It is an intimate relationship with God that is both personal and ecclesial.

The twenty-first century understanding of Christian spirituality differs significantly from that which preceded it in the modern period. Today spirituality is a holistic involvement of the person in a spiritual quest that involves the body as well as the spirit, gender and social location as well as human nature, emotion as well as mind and will, relationships with others as well as with God, socio-political commitment as well as prayer and spiritual practices.[10] This new understanding involves self-transcendence, an openness to the infinite that does not deny the particularity of the individual, but subverts any tendency to reduce spirituality to a purely private or narcissistic quest for one's own self-realization. This view affirms 'the necessity of the *community context and the commitment to social transformation* [in] contrast with the overly individualistic understanding of spirituality encountered in many manuals from the eighteenth to the twentieth century.'[11] Through all of this, there has developed a general consensus about core issues in the study of spirituality. Christian spirituality is no longer emerging as an academic discipline; it has clearly arrived. The material object of this study is *spirituality as desire and practice*, an existential phenomenon arising from a deliberate way of living in relation to God and an authentic desire for growth. The formal object of this field of study is *religious experience*; the focus is on Christian faith as the experience of the concrete believing subject(s). Therefore, the study of spirituality studies is not simply Christian faith but *the lived experience of Christian faith*.[12]

Sandra M. Schneiders identified three general approaches to the study of Christian spirituality. The first, the historical approach, has always allowed for specializations in subject matter. Scholars of spirituality have utilized the tools and methods of the historian in significant and helpful ways. Second, the theological approach to the study of spirituality, has a complex history involving the Orthodox, Protestant, Anglican, and Roman Catholic perspectives. The Orthodox tradition has maintained the synthesis of theology and spirituality that characterized the pre-medieval common tradition. After the western church was divided by the Protestant Reformation, the more Reformed traditions were suspicious of any forms of 'mysticism' not clearly grounded in scripture. They preferred to speak of 'piety' and daily practices of Bible reading and prayer. The Anglican tradition preferred the term 'devotion' to that of piety and would affirm more of the inner life nurtured by the *Book of Common Prayer*. The Roman Catholic tradition incorporated the study of spirituality into the university curriculum as a sub-discipline within theology – which in turn helped to give rise to the current development of spirituality as an academic discipline. The third and most recent approach to the study of spirituality is the anthropological approach. This approach is rooted in the recognition that spirituality is a constitutive dimension of human nature; human beings have both the capacity and desire for self-transcendence toward an ultimate value. Building on the historical and theological approaches, the anthropologist also utilizes the non-theological disciplines of psychology, linguistics, art, and hermeneutics. Schneiders concludes her survey by stating, 'Experience strongly suggests that these three approaches are not mutually exclusive or competing.'[13]

The Emergence of Methodism and a Distinctive Methodist Spirituality

The Methodist movement that emerged in the lives and the ministries of John and Charles Wesley must be understood within the larger context of the Christian heritage of England,[14] the widespread sources of the evangelical revival independent of any contact with the Wesleys,[15] and the family home, the Epworth rectory. The theological and spiritual environment of the Wesley home was a unique blend of Anglican spirituality, both High Church and Puritan based on the 'love of God' more than the 'faith in Christ' tradition of continental Protestantism.[16] Genuine concern for 'inward religion' was shared by both Samuel and Susanna Wesley as well as numerous spiritual writers they valued (e.g., Henry Scougal's *The Life of God in the Soul of Man*, the *Pensées* of Blaise Pascal, *The Imitation of Christ*, and *The Life of Monsieur de Renty*).

From their family home, John and Charles Wesley understood that the lived experience of faith was directly related to God's activity in creation. Humankind was created in the image of God (*imago Dei*) and God breathed into them the breath of life (the Hebrew term, *ruach*). The first man and the first woman enjoyed unhindered communication, friendship, and relationship with God. After the fall, the image of God, although marred and effaced, continued in human beings, and the restoration of that image and relationship was the essential aim of God in salvation. With Irenaeus (d. 190) and the writers of the Eastern Church, the Wesley brothers understood the goal of salvation to be the restitution of the *imago Dei* and the relationship with God as distinct from a spirituality focused on salvation as conversion and escape from hell. The Wesleyan view of salvation was made possible by faith in Jesus Christ alone, the Second Adam, 'Who did, through His transcendent love, become what we are that He might bring us to be what He is Himself.'[17] The aim of the Christian life is nothing less than a life-transformed; it is all the mind of Christ, the life of God in soul. In order for this to become a reality, required were a conversion of the mind, a conversion of the will, a conversion of the heart, and a community of other believers mature enough to assist the new born Christian in the process of spiritual growth and maturity.[18] Through their extensive Oxford reading which encompassed more than 684 different titles, the name of John Norris appears most frequently. Norris wove together the strands of moralism, mysticism, and rationalism in a theology of holiness and happiness that the Wesley brothers found philosophically and existentially attractive. He appealed to the heart and provided spiritual motivation for the reader to live a holy life, affirming that 'the Design of the Christian Dispensation is to perfect Holiness, to advance the interest of the Divine Life, to elevate us in the utmost Degree of Moral Perfection our Nature is here capable of, and, as far as possible, to make us Partakers of the Divine.'[19]

The entire spiritual journey depends upon divine initiative, the grace of God at work in ways which are initially imperceptible (prevenient grace), then felt in the yearning of the heart (convincing grace) until one experiences saving faith or the new birth (justifying grace), followed by the conscious journey toward spiritual maturity or spiritual adulthood (sanctifying grace) and active engagement in God's mission to reach as many other people as possible. Thoroughly grounded in the two biblical commandments of love for God and love for neighbor (which the Wesley brothers summarize in the phrases 'works of piety' and 'works of mercy'), the spiritual life involves the intentional practice of the 'means of grace.' While there is an individual or personal dimension of Methodist spirituality, the means of grace were also to be practiced in the family, in small groups, and in the gathered congregation.

The Centrality of Prayer

John and Charles Wesley's first publication was *A Collection of Forms of Prayer for Every Day in the Week* (1733) based on a 170-page manuscript prayer manual developed from 1727 to 1733.[20] The published volume consists of morning and evening prayers for each day of the week including 'Something of Deprecation, Petition, Thanksgiving and Intercession.' It included, 'in the Course of Petitions for the Week, the whole Scheme of our Christian Duty.'[21] For each day, as a part of evening prayer, there are questions for reflection related to essential spiritual virtues: Sunday was focused on the love of God, Monday on love of neighbor, Tuesday on humility, Wednesday mortification, Thursday resignation and meekness, Friday returned to the theme of mortification, and Saturday focused on thankfulness. Readers learned to pray by praying significant prayers and received spiritual guidance to give 'the whole heart and the whole life to God.'[22]

John and Charles Wesley understood that prayer is to the spiritual life, what oxygen is to the body. One's spiritual life would soon be extinguished without the breathings of prayer to inspire and give it motion. They were convinced that the person born of God,

> feels 'the love of God shed abroad in his heart by the Holy Ghost which is given unto him.' . . . he is alive to God through Jesus Christ. . . . God is

continually breathing, as it were, upon his soul, and his soul is breathing unto God. Grace is descending into his heart, and prayer and praise ascending to heaven. And by this intercourse between God and man, this fellowship with the Father and the Son, as by a kind of spiritual respiration, the life of God in the soul is sustained: and the child of God grows up, till he comes to 'the full measure of the stature of Christ.'[23]

Prayer, according to the Wesleys, 'is the lifting up of the heart to God: all words of prayer, without this are mere hypocrisy. Whenever therefore thou attemptest to pray, see that it be thy one design to commune with God, to lift up thy heart to him, to pour out thy soul before him.'[24] Prayer is the foundation for everything else in the spiritual life because 'God does nothing but in answer to prayer; and even they who have been converted to God without praying for it themselves, (which is exceeding rare,) were not without the prayers of others. Every new victory which a soul gains is the effect of a new prayer.'[25]

For those unable to read and those who felt inadequate to form words in prayer, they learned that 'a continual desire is a continual prayer'; therefore, any person, from the youngest child to the most elderly adult is capable of praying in this manner.[26] The aim was to pray as Jesus prayed in order to live as Jesus lived – between the mountain of prayer and ministry to the multitude of people in need. In the words of Charles Wesley:

> How happy, gracious Lord, are we!
> Divinely drawn to follow thee;
> Whose hours divided are.
> Betwixt the mount and multitude:
> Our day is spent in doing good;
> Our night in praise and prayer.[27]

A Clear Vision

The aim of the Christian life is union with God. John Wesley's sermon before the University in 1733 made it clear that participation in the divine life is the essence of Christian existence:

> One thing shall ye desire for its own sake – the fruition of him that is all in all. One happiness shall ye propose to your souls, even an union with him that made them, the having 'fellowship with the Father and the Son,'[28]

The Clear Path

John Wesley's sermon 'The Scripture Way of Salvation' clearly expresses the Methodist understanding that salvation is 'the entire work of God, from the first drawings of grace on the soul till it is consummated in glory.' Justification by grace through faith is pardon, a *relative* change in one's status before God, and in that same instant the process of sanctification begins. The spiritual new birth is analogous to the physical birth of a child. There is a real as well as a relative change because one is 'born from above,' 'born of the Spirit.' Drawing on the wisdom of Macarius, John Wesley warns the new born Christian that sin may appear to be entirely removed; however, it can and often does return. The gradual work of sanctification enables one to begin to walk in the Spirit, to learn to mortify the deeds of the flesh and willfully abstain from evil. The believer must 'go on to perfection,' that is, spiritual maturity. Sanctification is a *real* change that takes place in the hearts and lives of those who become new creatures in Christ. Spiritual maturity or full salvation is the ultimate goal of the spiritual life; the means of grace are pathways to that goal.[29]

The Means of Grace
The means of grace are spiritual practices or activities that connect the believer to God in Christ through the gracious activity of the Holy Spirit. John and Charles Wesley instructed their followers to 'use' all the means of grace in order to grow in their relationship with God and neighbor. These included the 'instituted' means of grace identified explicitly in scripture (worship, prayer, searching the scriptures, fasting, and spiritual conversation) and the 'prudential' means of grace implicit in the Bible (intentional spiritual practices such as keeping a spiritual journal, participating in small groups for spiritual instruction and reproof, and some form of leadership development). These means were directly connected to the Methodist understanding that 'the Spirit and discipline make a Christian.' In Methodism there is a dual emphasis on helping Christians experience the empowering presence of God and being formed in the character of God.[30]

The Wesleys were also careful to distinguish between spiritual practices that were a 'means' to an authentic relationship with God and the false understanding that treated spiritual disciplines as a goal, or 'end' in themselves:

> . . . in using all means, seek God alone. In and through every outward thing, look singly to the *power* of His Spirit, and the *merits* of His Son. Beware you do not stick in the *work* itself; if you do, it is all lost labor. Nothing short of God can satisfy your soul.[31]

Methodist spirituality and practice made it clear that the means of grace are appropriate for use at any and every stage of the spiritual journey. Regardless of whether one has a small interest in spiritual things, or is spiritually awakened and convinced of the need for God, or born again and growing in grace, or spiritually mature, using all the means of grace continues to be essential. Every person created in the image of God is capable of an eternal relationship with God, a relationship where the potential for spiritual growth has no end.[32]

An Intentional Community

The centrality of the Methodist small groups cannot be overlooked or neglected. From their earliest days in Oxford, the Wesley brothers learned the value of having spiritual friends and companions who shared the same desire for God and a willingness to engage in intentional spiritual exercises to help form and transform one into the image and likeness of Christ.

The Methodist small group structures began in the early years of the Oxford period (1729–1730). These groups were comprised of university students who gathered to pray, study scripture, read books of spiritual guidance, and engage in spiritual conversation. They held each other accountable for keeping a spiritual journal, and regular participation in public worship and the sacrament of the Lord's Supper. In August 1730, at the behest of one of the group's members, William Morgan, Jr., the Wesleys began visiting inmates at the local prison. This experience transformed their lives. Until this time the focus of the Holy Club was on 'works of piety'; now spiritual practice expanded to include what they would later describe as 'works of mercy' (i.e., ministry with the poor, sick, and imprisoned). This launched them into active involvement in social justice and local mission beyond the university. This change was powerful and permanent; it connected love for God (expressed in acts of devotion, study, worship, prayer, and praise) with love for neighbor (in acts of compassion, witness, and social justice).

The first Methodist **band** meeting was formed in London in May 1738, a joint venture with the Moravians. The rules for the bands were published in December 1738 and bear the distinctive touch of the Wesley brothers. These Christians were joined with others who had an equal desire to grow in grace and who shared a common situation in life. There were separate groups for married women, married men, single women, and single men. There were even bands for children and youth, with boys and girls meeting in separate bands.[33]

Before joining a band, personal experience of justifying grace and saving faith was required. Thus, some degree of spiritual maturity was presupposed and the spiritual guidance offered by the leader could focus on deeper understanding and experience of the Christian life.

The **select band** (or **select society**) was first mentioned in John Wesley's diary entry for Wednesday, 20 May 1741, 4:00 p.m. in Bristol.[34] It was the place where Christians of maturing faith could support one another in the understanding, experience, and practice of sanctifying grace. This small group setting helped men and women 'to *press after perfection*; to exercise their every grace, and improve every talent they have received; and to incite them to love one another more and to watch more carefully over each other . . .'[35] It also provided spiritual care for the movement's leaders, including the Wesleys themselves. Within this circle of servant leaders, every member had

> . . . an equal liberty of speaking, there being none greater or less than another. . . . I often found the advantage of such a free conversation, and that, 'in a multitude of counselors there is safety.'[36]

Unlike the male and female bands for new believers, the select band included everyone actively engaged in this stage of the spiritual journey; men and women, married and single – all met together.

By 1743 the basic structure of the Methodist United Society had emerged. This structure organized the disparate small groups for people at different stages on their spiritual journey into a cohesive system for Christian formation. For every significant theological understanding, there was now a small group structure to help people understand doctrine, experience the Spirit, and participate in a community of other believers who could help them learn to live a disciplined Christian life. For those who were seeking God, there was a *trial band*; for those convinced of sin and willing to engage actively in the process of repentance and seeking a new life there was the *class meeting*; for those who had been born again by grace through faith in Christ alone there was the *band meeting*; and for those who had been filled with the love and spirit of God there was the *select band*.[37]

The foundation for being admitted to a Methodist society was a significant commitment to a simple rule of life, similar to the rule established in the monastic tradition. However, this rule was designed for ordinary people of the working class and required one to have a sponsor, a full member of the society, to accompany them and oversee their progress on their spiritual journey. Anyone who had a sincere desire for salvation and a willingness to engage in an intentional Christian community was welcome:

> There is only one condition previously required of those who desire admission into these societies: 'a desire to flee from the wrath to come, and to be saved from their sins.' But **wherever this is really fixed in the soul it will be shown by its fruits**. It is therefore expected of all who continue therein that they should . . . evidence their desire of salvation, First, By doing no harm . . . Secondly, By doing good . . . Thirdly, By attending upon all the ordinances of God.[38]

The pastoral wisdom linking sincere desire with concrete behavior is unmistakable.

Having become a member of the Methodist society, one not only participated in a small group setting to provide understanding, experience, and community on the path to spiritual maturity, but also participated in large group experiences for spiritual nurture as well. The *Watch-nights, love feasts, covenant renewal services, letter days,* and *prayer meetings* were occasions for lay people to share their Christian lives with one another by means of these gatherings of the faithful. These special assemblies were open to all society members. Visitors were allowed, but only with the permission of the presiding preacher. These special occasions provided additional opportunities for Methodists to share their struggles, pray for one another, share faith stories, sing hymns, and experience the presence of God.

The Power of Music
Every small group and large group setting for spiritual experience included music appropriate to the occasion. Early Methodists found their true identity as the children of God through singing and the hymns of Charles Wesley, in particular, shaped their self-understanding and practice. Hymns functioned both as a communal confession of faith and a common catechism – embodying the fullness of the gospel. Charles Wesley's skill as a poet and spiritual guide helped to form and transform the singer. In the 1780 *Collection of Hymns for the use of the People Called Methodists*, John Wesley suggested that this volume contains 'all the important truths of our most holy religion . . . and this is done in regular order . . . according to the experience of real Christians. So that this book is in effect a little body of experimental and practical divinity.'[39]

Nineteenth-Century Methodist Spirituality

After the death of Charles Wesley in 1788 and John Wesley in 1791, the spiritual vitality of the Methodist movement continued. The evangelical passion for reaching as many people as possible resulted in numerical growth in the Methodist societies in England, Ireland, Scotland, Wales, North America, and in a variety of mission settings around the world. The experience of God in prayer, worship, and small groups continued to transform the hearts and lives of ordinary people. However, unresolved issues related to ecclesiology and the sacraments created stress and division. The transition from a movement raised up by God to spread scriptural holiness across the land into an ecclesiastical body responsible for all the functions of a local congregation was not easy in Britain or North America. Perhaps if the British Methodist Plan of Pacification (1795) had not been so anxious to avoid the appearance of rivalry to the Established Church it would not have prohibited the celebration of the

Lord's Supper during church hours. This matter, and his strident advocacy for lay representation at annual conference meetings, led to the expulsion of Alexander Kilham from the Wesleyan Methodist movement and the formation of the Methodist New Connection in 1797.

The fabric of the Wesleyan movement continued to unravel under the stresses of revivalism. The spiritual energy of the camp meeting movement in the USA and the Cane Ridge revival of 1801 in Kentucky spread to Britain by means of the American evangelist, Lorenzo Dow. At the invitation of Daniel Shubotham, Dow participated in the historic gathering at Mow Cop in Staffordshire with Hugh Borne and William Clowes. The Wesleyan Methodists were not able to adapt to the changing context and the result was the separation of the Primitive Methodists in 1811 and the Bible Christians in 1815. The holistic vision and pattern of Methodist spiritual formation gave way to the dramatic events of the camp meeting and the enthusiasm of the revival. Some of these problems were a natural consequence of John Wesley's own ambiguous relationship with the Established Church and issues of church order. The divisions were about ecclesiology, not spirituality.

In North America, the emphasis on holiness of heart and life gained significant attention. Combined with American enthusiasm and the instantaneous nature of religious experience in revivalism, the Holiness Movement came to emphasize the 'second blessing' or 'second work of grace' and minimize the Wesley brothers' equal commitment to the progressive nature of sanctification and 'growth in grace.' The early efforts of Phoebe Palmer, a doctor's wife in New York City, were blessed with dramatic responses to her preaching and her writing. Her work among the poverty-stricken in lower Manhattan and the establishment of mission stations embodied the Wesleys' own concern for the bodies and the souls of their neighbors. The spread of the Holiness Movement across the USA was aided by camp meetings, revivals, the call to abolish slavery, social reform, and the feeling among many Methodists that Methodism had strayed from the original teachings of the Wesleys.

With the onset of the Civil War, the Holiness Movement gained converts to Methodism on both side of the battle line. After the Civil War the flames of revival increased resulting in the creation of the National Camp Meeting Association for the Promotion of Holiness in 1867. At the turn of the century, the movement quickly spread beyond Methodism's confines.

Methodist spirituality in the nineteenth century continued to stress the importance of the family. Marriage was a spiritual partnership between two committed Christians. It was not good to be unequally yoked with unbelievers; there were strong warnings against marriage to someone who was not a member of the church and an active participant in the means of grace. Husbands and wives were strongly encouraged to pray together. When expecting a child, prayer for the unborn was also encouraged in the hope that when the child was of age, he or she would gladly enter into a personal relationship with Jesus Christ and share the faith of his or her parents. Sabbath observance was expected and supported by sermons, stories, and hymns.

Mission was another core value of nineteenth-century Methodism. The spiritual journals and stories of those who answered the call of God to service in foreign mission settings are both inspiring and humbling. These heroic men and women, and their families, knew the cost of sacrifice. It would be a mistake to limit the discussion to any branch of the now fissiparous Methodism from other Protestant and Roman Catholic missions equally active during this period. These faithful missionary Christians actively obeyed Christ's command to lay down their lives, to take up the cross, and to be his witnesses in India, Africa, Asia, and South America. Their ministry and mission must not be judged by the values and standards of another age.

The final fifty years of the nineteenth century was an era of great preachers and 'Methodist spirituality was undoubtedly influenced by the cult of the pulpit.'[40] Great preaching houses were built in cities with sufficient population and thousands came to hear the word proclaimed. Methodist worship, on both sides of the Atlantic Ocean, moved far beyond the meeting of the United Society and became indistinguishable from that of other Protestant denominations. The sermon became the primary place for the work of evangelism and the Christian instruction of believers. The voices of class leaders, band leaders, and the members of the select society were supplanted by the voice of the trained preacher.

Twentieth-Century Methodist Spirituality

The twentieth century was marked by the continued influence of revivalism, the Holiness Movement, the rise of Pentecostalism, liberalism, the ecumenical movement, and the New Age movement (which engaged in spiritual practices without the guidance of any specific world religion, Christian or non-Christian). In North America, the Modernist–Fundamentalist controversies that began among the Presbyterians during the early decades of the century soon spread to Methodism and the other mainline Protestant denominations.

Revivalism and the Holiness Movement came to be embodied in institutions and structures during the first half of the twentieth century. In Britain, Cliff College became the central location and Samuel Chadwick (1860–1932) emerged as one of the key leaders. Chadwick believed that earnest prayer, living testimony, impassioned enthusiasm, and intense spirituality would enable Methodism to spread scriptural holiness throughout the land, evangelize the world, and reform the nation. He encouraged Franciscan-type 'trekkers' in 1926 who journeyed out on special evangelistic missions. In response to the more Calvinistic orientation of the Keswick Convention, Chadwick initiated the Southport Convention in order to meet the spiritual needs of people and bring the Wesleyan theological perspective to the masses (focusing on the eradication of inbred sin and imparted holiness, rather than the Keswick teaching of sin repressed and holiness imputed). In the USA, revivalism and the Holiness Movement found a home in the First Church of the Nazarene (1895 in Los Angeles), the Brethren in Christ (1910) and Henry Clay Morrison's participation in the founding of Asbury Theological Seminary (1923). In addition, American evangelicals like Billy Graham and Tony Campolo found significant support among the people called Methodists.

The rise of Pentecostalism in North America has a close affinity with Methodist theology of holiness, the practice of prayer, and a high view of scripture. In 1901, at the Bible College founded by Charles Parham in Kansas, students reading Acts 2 experienced a supernatural outpouring of the Holy Spirit that included speaking in an unknown tongue. Their witness spread quickly and provided the catalyst for the experience of the African American, William J. Seymour, and the Azusa Street Revival of 1906 in Los Angeles. Subsequently, the Holiness Movement divided into those who affirmed the Pentecostal theology and experience and those who did not. In time, the classic Pentecostal teaching that the ability to speak in 'tongues' was the initial and only reliable evidence of the person having been filled with the Holy Spirit, gave birth to the charismatic or neo-Pentecostal movement of the 1960s. Charismatic teaching affirmed that the presence of the Holy Spirit could be expressed through any of the spiritual gifts recorded in the Bible, with 'tongues' being one of many authentic manifestations. From its beginning, the ecumenical charismatic renewal has exerted a continuing influence upon mainline Christian bodies, both Protestant and Roman Catholic. A 1972 study by the American pollster George Gallup indicated that approximately 18 percent of United Methodists identified with the movement. In 1976 the UMC general conference approved an extensive set of guidelines regarding *The United Methodist Church and the Charismatic Movement*.[41] The document provided guidance for clergy and laity, and suggested appropriate ways to listen, learn, examine, and test the experience of other Christians – those who have had a Charismatic experience and those who have not. New organizations were formed to help Methodists integrate their newfound spiritual experiences with the ongoing life of the church. In North America, the United Methodist Renewal Services Fellowship was formed in 1978 to provide a fellowship for charismatics and received official approval as an affiliate organization of the United Methodist Church.

Liberalism was both a natural progression of modern thought and a negative response to revivalism, the holiness tradition, and Pentecostalism. Many Methodists were unhappy with the excesses they perceived in aggressive evangelicalism and the uncontrolled enthusiasm of Pentecostal services. The

British reaction can be seen in the works of Newton Flew, W. R. Maltby, J. Alexander Findlay, and Leslie Weatherhead. These more liberal clergy drew their spirituality from the synoptic gospels and the cross. According to Findlay, 'The only Pentecost which can really turn the world upside down is the Pentecost that shall follow a new vision of Calvary.'[42]

During the 1960s many Methodists in the USA lost confidence in revivalism, orthodox Christianity, and traditional methods of spirituality resulting in more radical expressions of theology and experience. Those inclined toward mysticism moved in the direction of eastern religions or the New Age movement. Those who favored social activism moved toward the 'Jesus People' movement or into Christian communities dedicated to mission and evangelism. Those inclined to philosophy found the work of Albert North Whitehead (1861–1947) and 'Process Theology' of value (e.g., Charles Hartshorne, Schubert M. Ogden, John B. Cobb, Jr., and W. Norman Pittenger). Those who preferred an ecumenical approach supported the work of the Consultation on Common Texts to develop common versions of key liturgical texts (e.g., the Gloria Patri, Creed, and Lord's Prayer); however, this work was soon taken up by an international body which became known as the International Consultation on English Texts (ICET). Those who preferred more historic and formal forms of worship endorsed programs for liturgical renewal.

The ecumenical movement enjoyed early success in the late nineteenth and early twentieth centuries. It gathered together diverse members of the Christian tradition – mainline Protestants, the Orthodox, some Pentecostals, Independents, and charismatic congregations. Although Roman Catholicism has not been as active as many Protestant denominations, it has maintained direct contact through official observers and representatives. The World Council of Churches (1948) and the National Council of Churches (1950) in the USA are the two most influential ecumenical organizations. Among Methodists, one must include the World Methodist Council (1881) and The Upper Room (1935) in this stream of Methodist ecumenical spirituality. The core practices of the 'ecumenical' churches and organizations include some form of daily prayer, regular participation in worship, significant commitment to ecumenical cooperation, and a willingness to engage in actions intended to bring social justice and the reign of God. The Upper Room Academy for Spiritual Formation is one example of an ecumenical undertaking designed to support people on their inward journey of Christian growth in order to sustain the outward journey of Christian discipleship.

In the final decades of the twentieth century, postmodern philosophy and theology in the northern and western hemispheres made room for renewed conversation about the Christian experience of God; for example, Morton Kelsey's work, *Encounter with God: A Theology of Christian Experience*, and Kenneth Leech, *Experiencing God: Theology as Spirituality*. There was also a growing interest in world religions and the possibility of dialogue on a more universal experience of God.

Within the larger context of spiritual formation for clergy in North America, the Association of Theological Schools came to the decision to make explicit the expectation that all of its 252 members would attend to this matter in the graduate training of students from 1996 onward. The new accreditation guidelines made it clear that 'Personal and Spiritual Formation' shall be provided so 'the student may grow in personal faith, emotional maturity, moral integrity, and public witness.'[43]

An Agenda for Future Research

The nature and limits of the classical disciplines of Bible, history, theology, pastoral care, worship, and anthropology must be acknowledged and understood for every discipline loses sight of that which is beyond its focus and its tools can only yield the result for which they were designed. The interdisciplinary study of Christian spirituality goes between and through established disciplines to bring together a larger understanding of the lived experience of Christian faith and life in the Spirit. The 'self-implicating' nature of this work must be acknowledged. For some students drawn to the study of Christian spirituality, there is a personal desire to experience for themselves more of the divine life as they gain insight into the spiritual lives of others. For other students who approach Christian spirituality as an academic discipline rather than a faith they call their own 'it is nonetheless self-implicating for them in the way that every great human endeavor invites – even compels – us to engage questions of authenticity and meaning, of purpose and commitment.'[44]

There is growing interest in Christian spiritual formation and Methodist spirituality. While there are significant primary source documents and studies of the spirituality of John Wesley,[45] less attention has been paid to Charles Wesley, the cofounder of the movement. With the exception of his hymns, Charles' role in the origin of the evangelical revival and the development of early Methodist spirituality has been largely neglected. Little original research had been done and almost no new ground broken since the anonymous publication of the *Sermons by the Late Charles Wesley* (1816), Thomas Jackson's volumes on Charles Wesley's *Life* (2 vols., 1841) and *Journals* (2 vols., 1849), and George Osborn's publication of *The Poetical Works of John and Charles Wesley* (13 vols., 1868–1872). It was almost a century before Frank Baker's volumes on Charles' manuscript letters and unpublished verse contributed new primary source information.[46] Since 1983 and the publication of the critical edition of the 1780 *Collection of Hymns for the Use of the People Called Methodists*, new fields of study have been opened through the publication of

Charles' shorthand manuscript sermons, journal, and religious verse.[47] In 1989 the Charles Wesley Society was formed and gave rise to significant new academic conversation and the publication of a new journal, *The Proceedings of the Charles Wesley Society*. The recent publication of a complete and critical edition of all Charles Wesley's sermons in 2001 and a two-volume critical edition of *The Manuscript Journal of the Reverend Charles Wesley, M.A.* (2008) have significantly advanced the literature needed to understand the spirituality of the youngest Wesley brother and cofounder of the Methodist movement.[48] However, the publication of the 600 known Charles Wesley letters is yet to be completed.

It is indeed fortunate that Methodist spirituality may also be studied from the perspective of the early Methodist people. In the first years of the evangelical revival, John and Charles Wesley requested that their followers write notes and letters of thanksgiving describing what God had done in their hearts and lives. These manuscript sources were largely unnoticed, existing in manuscript form alone until 1980.[49] The 1982 'Wesleyan Spirituality and Faith Development Working Group' at the Seventh Oxford Institute of Methodist Theological Studies meeting at Keble College chaired by James W. Fowler opened the door to a broader discussion and awareness of the early Methodist sources.[50] Paul W. Chilcote's 1984 doctoral dissertation entitled, 'John Wesley and the Women Preachers of Early Methodism' provided important new primary source documents and significant insights into the spirituality of Methodist women.[51] Also worthy of note is Lester Ruth, *Early Methodist Life and Spirituality: A Reader* (2005).[52] Another important study was published by D. Bruce Hindmarsh in 2005 and includes manuscript conversion accounts of eighteenth-century Methodists, Moravians, and Presbyterians.[53] The Hindmarsh volume contains useful insight into the literary genre of spiritual autobiography and provides interpretive tools for analysis.

What is needed is a larger conceptual framework that links the historic disciplines of history, theology, worship, pastoral care, and anthropology with a transformational paradigm similar to the threefold pattern suggested above (understanding, spiritual experience, and living community). There is also the challenge of primary source documents, particularly in those cultural contexts that deny education and expression for women, minorities, and the poor.

Enduring Qualities of Wesleyan Spirituality

There are important and enduring qualities of Wesleyan spirituality that provide help for contemporary Methodists engaged in Christian life, the mission of God, and the study of Methodist spirituality:

First, the human desire for a deep, personal, spiritual relationship with the living God made possible by grace.

Second, the work of spiritual formation and transformation is the work of the triune God. God, the Holy Spirit, forms people into authentic disciples of Jesus Christ.

Third, the goal of spiritual formation is scriptural holiness, holiness of heart and life; the holiness and happiness intended by God in creation.

Fourth, the process of Methodist spiritual formation is unending; because God is infinite, the opportunity to grow in love and grace is infinite as well.

Fifth, the context for spiritual formation is personal, incarnate, and contextual; it involves the individual, the family, the Christian community, and active engagement in God's mission in the world.

Sixth, the basic elements of spiritual formation and transformation at every stage of the spiritual journey involve understanding (doctrine), experience (Spirit) and community (discipline).

Seventh, the scope of spiritual formation is the whole people of God. It is not for the spiritual elite. Every Christian is called to grow up into every way into Christ who is the head of the body.

Eighth, the fruit of spiritual formation is manifest in the fruit of the Spirit as described in Galatians 5:22–23, 'love, joy, peace, patience, kindness, goodness, faithfulness, gentleness and self-control.'

Ninth, the works of piety (love for God) are inextricably linked to the works of mercy (love for neighbor); therefore, the spiritual life is always mystical and missional.

Tenth, spiritual formation in the Wesleyan tradition involves the voluntary acceptance of a rule of life, an intentional plan and practice to engage all the means of grace.

For Further Reading

Chilcote, Paul W. *Her Own Story: Autobiographical Portraits of Early Methodist Women*. Nashville: Kingswood, 2001.

Collins, Kenneth J., ed. *Exploring Christian Spirituality: An Ecumenical Reader*. Grand Rapids, MI: Baker Books, 2000.

Davies, Rupert, A. Raymond George, and Gordon Rupp, eds. *A History of the Methodist Church in Great Britian*. 4 vols. London: Epworth, 1965–1988.

Hindmarsh, D. Bruce. *The Evangelical Conversion Narrative: Spiritual Autobiography in Early Modern England*. Oxford: Oxford University Press, 2005.

Holder, Arthur, ed. *The Blackwell Companion to Christian Spirituality*. Malden, MA: Blackwell Publishing, 2005.

McGrath, Alister E. *Christian Spirituality*. Malden, MA: Blackwell Publishers, 1999.

Sheldrake, Philip, ed. *The New Westminster Dictionary of Christian Spirituality*. Louisville, KY: Westminster/John Knox Press, 2005.

Tyson, John R., ed. *Invitation to Christian Spirituality: An Ecumenical Anthology*. New York: Oxford University Press, 1999.

Wakefield, Gordon S. *Methodist Spirituality*. Peterborough: Epworth Press, 1999.

17 Social Ethics in the Methodist Tradition

Manfred Marquardt

Since its beginning one of the essential marks of Methodism is accepting responsibility for what God has entrusted to human beings. Their divine calling is to be 'good stewards' of God's creation and caring neighbors of their fellow humans. Ethical teaching and practice grow out of faith in God as loving Creator and Redeemer whose grace is working for and in all human beings. For Wesley, faith works through love (Galatians 5:6). Faithful to the gospel mandate faith is 'productive of all good works.'[1]

John Wesley's Seminal Contribution to Social Ethics

At the beginning of the Methodist movement, there was no developed ethical theory as a guide to life according to God's calling. John Wesley had been taught by his parents to lead a holy life in obedience to God's commandments which included personal piety, doing good, and avoiding evil. The student religious society in Oxford called the 'Holy Club' or 'Methodists' was one group among many who tried to lead lives following strict rules, spending time together in 'reading the Scriptures, and provoking one another to love and to good works.' They felt 'an earnest desire to live according to (the) rules [of holy living and dying], and to flee from the wrath to come.'[2] The motivation for doing good works changed after the Wesley brothers received an assurance of being saved by grace through faith alone: the experience and discernment of God's unconditional love provided a more reliable and fertile ground for creative, down-to-earth ethical engagement, while ministry to and life with the poor and needy remained the strongest component of their Christian life and practice.

Ministry with the Poor

During his ministry with the poor, John Wesley developed a number of crucial tenets diametrically opposed to common opinions: poverty is neither a divine decree nor punishment; all people, including the poor, are created in God's image and, therefore, of the same dignity as the rich and the noble; all are souls for whom Christ died. By grounding the dignity of the poor in God's love, Wesley intended to alter the attitude toward the poor and to create a willingness to improve their general situation. His creativity in defeating poverty became manifest in many practical schemes including medical care and dispensaries for the poor, a book on easy natural treatments for minor diseases, loan societies for those who had fallen victim to unscrupulous moneylenders, and provisions for finding work for the poor. These and similar projects were meant to serve two purposes – to provide immediate assistance and to motivate others to use their resources, however small, to serve those in need.

Methodist ministry for and with the poor extended beyond individual service. Wesley regarded poverty as an evil to be eliminated. Far from idealizing poverty, he recognized its life-damaging effects and requested that riches be used to alleviate the burdens of the poor, offering them an opportunity to earn their livings and feed their families. For this purpose he started analyzing the causes of poverty, knowing that the poor are not to be blamed in general for their situation (e.g., because they are lazy). In his tract 'Thoughts on the Present Scarcity of Provisions'[3] he attempted to answer two questions: 'First, Why are thousands of people starving, perishing for want, in every part of the nation?' and 'What remedy is there for this sore evil, many thousand poor people are starving?'

While no statistics and little research results were available, Wesley published his insights, noting the persons and institutions to be held accountable. He openly challenged the wealthy upper class, blaming those who lived luxuriously but who ignored the needs of their neighbors, and stressed the responsibility of the political powers for a legal system that needed immediate changes to protect the poor. His personal knowledge of the living conditions of the poor was complemented by general economic and political observations and proposals for solving the crucial problems of the impoverished. Although he was not a professional economist and his analyses or suggestions for improvement may seem too simplistic, Wesley was a fearless commentator on the problem of poverty who sought to put into action what love for people dictated following the commandments of Christ.

Social Obligations of Income and Property

Wesley's ethic accents people's obligation rightfully to manage all they possess. God, the true creator and owner of material possessions, has committed them to human hands. Property ownership implies a social obligation to be fulfilled according to one's particular status in light of the needs of his or her neighbors independent of their nation, race, gender, or (lower) status.

Logically, it is not surprising that money, in Wesley's view, is not evil in itself; it can be used as an instrument for doing good in the hands of those who are ready to share what God has entrusted to them.[4] Since its use has far-reaching consequences – which is much more obvious in the globalized world of the twenty-first century, but was also true in biblical times and Wesley's day – knowing how to use it properly is of highest importance especially for those who have more than necessary for their normal subsistence.

But in Wesley's opinion neither is money good in itself, nor is striving after it for the sake of becoming rich something to be desired. He found this judgment confirmed by longtime observations of Methodists who grew rich and 'nine in ten of these decreased in grace in the same proportion as they increased in wealth.'[5] They had willingly observed the first two rules concerning the use of money: 'Earn as much as you can,' and 'save as much as you can,' that is, don't waste it in luxurious living, but had forgotten the third: 'Give as much as you can' to serve people in need. Methodists (and others) had failed to be good stewards in using money as an instrument for doing good; the evil consequences of this failure included both deprivation of the poor and damage to the Christian character of people of substance who refused to give to those in need. God's grace is to be received in faith and to be turned into works of love (Galatians 5:6). Heaping up earthly wealth and possessions instead of sharing with the poor most often results in the loss of grace.

Therefore, Wesley continued to teach his people to share their mostly modest living with those in dire need. Since the initiation of the first 'class' in Bristol, sharing a penny (or more, if possible) with the poor was a spiritual obligation life of Methodists, an exercise in loving one's neighbor as oneself. Wesley set an example by limiting his own personal expenses to a constantly frugal amount during his whole life.

Struggle against Slavery
The most critical social issue which confronted Wesley was slavery. England was one of the world's major slave traders; more than fifty percent of the enslaved Africans (those who had survived transport on British ships) were sold in its markets, the largest being London, Liverpool, and Bristol;[6] together with Spain, England's trade supplied slaves for the Atlantic colonies.[7] Royal privilege, state laws, and international agreements supported the slave trade; economic and political factors had made it a widely accepted and rarely disputed way of gaining wealth. Even the church denied that this practice should be criticized as incompatible with Christian teaching.

One of the reasons for this position may have been the lack of biblical statements condemning slavery; most scriptural references treat it as a non-contentious element of the social order, albeit which may need some regulation, for example, the Israelites should allow the impoverished to serve as hired laborers, but not as slaves, or to be sold as slaves (Leviticus 25:39, 42). Paul relativized social structures for those who live 'in Christ,' where 'there is

Social Ethics in the Methodist Tradition

no longer slave or free' (Galatians 3:28), but recommended that a baptized slave 'even if (he) can gain freedom, make use of (his) present condition now more than ever' (1 Corinthians 7:21). For many centuries of Christian history the paradoxical acceptance of slavery as a part of the divine order of the world and the unconditional oneness of all Christians in Christ seemed self-evident. Calixt I, a former slave, became bishop of Rome in the third century, and Thomas Aquinas taught that humans are *per se* (essentially, as created by God) free and only *per accidens* (accidentally) slaves; slavery was seen as a consequence of the Fall, but nonetheless as a necessary part of the social order. Even church leaders owned slaves, and only a small number of Anglican clergy criticized brutal treatment of slaves and advocated emancipation of Christian slaves – with little or no success.

During his time in Georgia, where slavery was not permitted, Wesley had personal contact with slaves in the neighboring colonies of Virginia and South Carolina and offered them pastoral service. His general attitude toward slavery remained unchanged until he read books written by one of the first American abolitionists, Anthony Benezet. Benezet's family were French Huguenots who had fled to England, where Anthony joined the Society of Friends in London. In 1731, the Benezets migrated to Pennsylvania where Anthony became a teacher and founder of schools for Blacks. Wesley was deeply touched by Benezet's reports about atrocities regarding the capture, transport, and sale of black Africans, and by their suffering on the slave ships, in slave markets, and on plantations in North America. He determined to fight against the evil of slavery regardless of its long history, public acceptance, and its alleged economic necessity. In his very last letter, dictated on his deathbed, Wesley wrote to William Wilberforce, a young member of the English Parliament and protagonist of abolition: 'O be not weary of well doing! Go on, in the name of God and in the power of His might, till even American slavery (the vilest that ever saw the sun) shall vanish away before it.' One reason for this harsh judgment was 'a law in all our colonies that the oath of a black against a white goes for nothing.'[8] In his earlier years, Wesley had denounced similar injustice: 'Suppose a great man ... does wrong to his poor neighbour. What will you do? ... Without money you can have no more law; poverty alone utterly shuts out justice.'[9] If there were no law and no justice in the case of slavery, Wesley's judgment was, 'What villainy is this!'[10]

Seventeen years before his letter to Wilberforce in 1774, Wesley published *Thoughts Upon Slavery*,[11] detailing his public condemnation of the evils of the slavery and the slave trade. It is a short tract worth careful study today. A close examination of the text helps us to understand the nature of Wesley's ethical argument which led him, an old man, to change his own attitude and moved him to become a fervent supporter of the early antislavery movement.

The Methodist Episcopal Church in the middle of the nineteenth century experienced its deepest division because of irreconcilable positions on the issue of slavery. It seemed that there were always 'reasonable arguments' for keeping (black) slaves brought forward by (white) slave owners, in order to justify this criminal abuse of human persons as private property.[12] To this day, the fate of human rights still depends on economic and political interests as well as cultural traditions and religious beliefs that allegedly are justified by, or even based on what is considered 'the will of God.' Some of them obviously contradict the teachings of Jesus and the gospel of grace.

War and Peace

As some forms of slavery have changed, but still exist in our time, the problem of war has not been solved. Therefore, examining Wesley's views on war and peace may be useful for forming a Methodist position for our times.

During the first annual conference held in 1744, the question was asked: 'Is it lawful to bear arms?' and answered: 'We incline to think it is: 1. Because there is no command against it in the New Testament, 2. Because Cornelius, a soldier, is commended there.'[13] This cautious formulation seems to indicate that there were different positions among those attending and that John Wesley himself was well aware of the weakness of the argument – an *argumentum e silentio* – which favored permission to bear weapons. Yet, in March 1756, Wesley the conservative Anglican and defender of the monarchy volunteered to raise a company of soldiers to defend the king and country against an imminent invasion in March 1756 in the wake of the Seven Years' War.[14] There is no report that King George II or his most notable minister Sir Robert Walpole took advantage of the offer.

Only eight months later, Wesley published his treatise on *The Doctrine of Original Sin According to Scripture, Reason, and Experience*[15] starting with an analysis of the past and present state of humanity 'with regard to knowledge and virtue.' The focus of the second chapter was on the question, 'Are men in general now wise and virtuous?' After surveying continents and non-Christian religions with mostly negative judgments on human nature Wesley finally commented on Christian countries – Orthodox, Roman Catholic, and Protestant – with words of stinging reproach: 'There is war in the world! war between men! war between Christians! I mean, between those that bear the name of Christ, and profess to "walk as he also walked." ' Can war be reconciled with religion, or 'to any degree of reason or common sense'?[16] The 'reasons' produced by those who go to war are highly dubious and insolent.

The strongest part of Wesley's statement on 'war among men' is his reflective description of the war just started by European states against one another at that time. 'Consider the thing itself!' That is, strangely enough, omitted even today. Look at war and its realities rather than at the censured media reports! Wesley looked at what was happening: 'Here are forty thousand men gathered together on this plain. What are they going to do? See, there are thirty or forty thousand more at a little distance. And these are going to shoot them through the head or body, to stab them, or split their skulls, and send most of their souls into everlasting fire, as fast as they possibly can. Why so? What harm have they done to them? O none at all! They do not so much as know them. But a man, who is King of France, has a quarrel with another man, who is King of England. So these Frenchmen are to kill as many of these Englishmen as they can, to prove the King of France is in the right.'

One may blame Wesley for having simplified the complex prehistory of any war. Nonetheless, he puts the finger to the decisive question of the reason for recurring to arms. The classical term for this criterion is *causa belli* ('the cause of war'). Human beings are called, and are able, to reflect and to choose before initiating such a momentous and ethically problematic act. Therefore, Wesley used the metaphor of a court to question the rationality of war in general: 'Now, what an argument is this! What a method of proof! What an amazing way of deciding controversies! What must mankind be, before such a thing as war could ever be known or thought of upon earth?'[17] In Wesley's judgment wars throughout the eighteenth century were a sign of the fallen condition of humanity.

Wesley's conclusions from his observations on the extensive violence in Europe and North America were more than just an exercise of explaining and complaining. In various appeals to reason and pleas for peaceful agreements, he attempted to convince the combatants on both sides to depart from war as a means of resolving their conflicts. Christians are called to be peacemakers through peaceful means, being aware that peacemaking cannot wait until a war is imminent. Peace is more than the absence of war. Consequently, a peacemaker is 'one that as he has opportunity 'does good unto all men'; one that being filled with the love of God and of all mankind cannot confine the expressions of it to his own family, or friends, or acquaintance, or party; or to those of his own opinions; no, nor those who are partakers of like precious faith; but steps over all these narrow bounds that he may do good to every man; that he may some way or other manifest his love to neighbors and strangers, friends and enemies.'[18] Wesley did not become a 'pacifist' in the sense of denying any use of violence, but the longer he lived the more he became devoted to peacemaking 'provoking all, not to enmity and contention, but to love and to good works.'[19]

Human Rights

'Human rights' is not a term used in Wesley's time. This aspect of human experience was commonly referred to as 'natural rights.' When, in the twentieth century, the concept of 'natural law' became an object of great controversy, 'human rights,' including both men and women, became common parlance as in the United Nations' 'Universal Declaration of Human Rights' (1948). Yet, the recognition of human rights and the fight for its general acceptance over against all kinds of discrimination and oppression is reflected much earlier, for example in the first chapter of the Bible where the priestly author wrote: 'So God created humankind in his image, in the image of God he created them; male and female he created them' (Genesis 1:27). And St. Paul, the greatest exegete of the gospel, deepened this biblical belief: 'There is no longer Jew or Greek, there is no longer slave or free, there is no longer male and female; for all of you are one in Christ Jesus' (Galatians 3:28).

In contradiction to this teaching and other philosophical traditions (from the Stoics through the seventeenth-century Enlightenment), Wesley found that human rights were denied to slaves, poor people, women, and Native Americans. In his 'Calm Address to our American Colonies' (1775) he pointed to dark spots on the flag of liberty: The voting system limits the right to vote to propertied white males. 'Are they guaranteeing universal suffrage? No. Will they give the vote to women, or to Indians, or to slaves? No.'[20] The colonists' protest of being treated like slaves by the British government was met by Wesley's question: 'Who then is a slave?' and his answer is: 'Look into America, and you may easily see. See that Negro, fainting under the load, bleeding under the lash! He is a slave,' whereas the colonists are free to go where they want.[21]

It may well be disputed whether the question of women pastors correctly pertains to 'human rights.' If gender is the only reason for justifying an exclusion from following God's call, it does. At one point Wesley, as a loyal Anglican clergyman, had been convinced that both preaching a sermon outside a church building or allowing a woman to fulfill clerical duties, did not comply with God's will. Yet, as the son of an extraordinary mother-teacher, he had been trained to give reasons for his convictions and decisions. Living in a highly patriarchal society, serving as an ordained presbyter in the Church of England, standing in the historic succession of episcopal ordination, and limiting ecclesial authority to men, Wesley's attitude toward women preachers in the Methodist movement was clear and firm; he believed that in addition to the centuries-old divine order, there are statements in the New Testament that women should not teach (1 Timothy 2:12) and should not speak in church (1 Corinthians 14:35).[22]

He learned, however, when it comes to a decision concerning a matter of conscience, to look for a sufficient reason instead of following the conventional pattern. He had accepted women serving as leaders of women's bands or classes, and as spiritual guides, because their ministry proved effective. Yet, when women asked him to authorize them for preaching in societies at first he refused because Paul's directives and the Anglican authorities held a clearly negative view on the matter. Even after Wesley accepted the preaching of laymen because it proved to bear fruit, it took more than twenty years before he acknowledged a woman could receive an 'extraordinary call' and in such extraordinary cases even Paul 'made a few exceptions.'[23] 'Wesley had to admit that God had blessed the work of women leaders ... So he authorized an increasing number of women to preach'[24] and to lead non-sacramental worship services. Long before, a great number of women – with Wesley's permission and encouragement – had been engaged in a wide variety of services within the Methodist social ministry and in leadership positions.

In the course of this almost lifelong learning process, Wesley developed a keen perception and appreciation for the spiritual and intellectual talents in women. His growing awareness of their capacities in many areas led him to repudiate the traditional raising of women 'in such a manner as if they were only designed for agreeable playthings! ... I know not how any women of sense and spirit can submit to it.' He continued by describing the dignity and rights and God-given status of women: 'Let all you that have it in your power assert the right which the God of nature has given you. Yield not to that vile bondage any longer. You, as well as men, are rational creatures. You, like them, were made in the image of God: you are equally candidates for immortality.'[25] This basic statement was not without ethical or even legal consequences; women became more important agents for social improvement and change. The development of Methodism around the world is closely connected with impressive, innovative, and effective contributions of women teachers, nurses, doctors, missionaries, preachers, and leaders in all kinds of social projects and institutions. After Wesley's death, Methodism 'tended to reinforce the idea that the proper sphere of women was domestic rather than public.'[26] The British conference voted to suspend women from preaching as obviously being necessary in view of 'a sufficiency of [male] Preachers, whom God had accredited.'[27] In spite of this and similar decisions by other conferences or bishops, women were invited to preach and proved themselves to be agents for social change in many places, including foreign countries until, in 1956, the Methodist Church in the USA started ordaining and giving full clergy rights to women. Since 1980, a growing number of woman across the world have been elected to the United Methodist episcopacy.[28]

Learning from Wesley

Learning from Wesley cannot be done properly by returning to Wesley. All attempts of this kind have proved to be tendentious interpretations and abstractions from the historical Wesley and the challenges of his time. Learning from him means studying the ways to find grace-based, reasonable, and practical solutions for people's fundamental needs and problems – personal as well as social. Wesley's practical theology and social ethic opened the minds of his friends and followers to those in need and they aim at a life shaped by genuine gospel patterns. This included a clear rational analysis of the particular situation and its complexity, a realistic and grace-based definition of goal, and a viable strategy for the steps necessary for reaching it.

More importantly, Wesley gave evidence to an anthropological and spiritual breeding ground of social awareness and a sense of social responsibility: the experience of a reality transcending and transforming the personal self with a focus on God whose love is working in us, and on others with whom compassion and love need to be shared. It is an element of any living faith in Christ for which Theodore Runyon introduced the term 'orthopathy.'[29] Social ethics in the Wesleyan tradition goes beyond right beliefs (orthodoxy) and good works (orthopraxy) – without reducing their significance for the Christian faith – because it is informed and nurtured by the experience of God's love present in our world and our lives, liberating and encouraging us to look at our neighbors' needs, to analyze the causes of their difficulties, and to search for effective ways to improve their personal as their social living conditions. Orthopraxy, therefore, needs to be rational and teleological, disconnected from traditions, habits, and mindsets that have been hurting, humiliating, and segregating humans who are equally created in the image of God.

In his publications about ethical issues, Wesley shows a surprising optimism in his expectations for eagerness to learn and motivation to act accordingly. His appeals to prison officials, captains of slave ships, land-owners, and politicians sometimes sound naive and illusionary. Methodists have become accustomed to attribute this attitude to Wesley's 'optimism of grace,' his unlimited trust in the power and goodness of God's affection for creation and especially for those created in God's image. Wesley's confidence in social development that would lead to greater justice and respect for human dignity and to growing love of neighbor fit well into eighteenth-century postmillennialism and the Enlightenment ideal of 'noble savages' living on distant continents ready not only to join hands with Christians in working for a better world, but also to teach and to put to shame those who had forsaken authentic Christianity. Wesley's ethical teaching is rooted in 'his eschatological vision of spreading the reign of God in individual lives, social structures, and creation at large.'[30] Because of Christ's continuing and working presence in this age and world, Christians can become agents of change in their immediate vicinity as in the larger society by perceiving the ills, exploring their causes, and searching for appropriate methods of dealing with them.

Wesley's social ethics is theologically grounded in an understanding of God's gracious action in creation and salvation. In God's salvific work, reconciliation and the transformation of human beings are inseparable. Justification is the initiation of a new relationship with God and life lived in the power of

God's grace. Sanctification – the Christian life being lived in love – is not a secondary part in the saving work of God's Spirit. It is its very substance as it becomes effective in human emotions, convictions, attitudes, and actions.

For Wesley, Jesus' words known as the Golden Rule was the central test about how we look at other humans, especially those whom we perceive as different from ourselves, and whether we are prepared to put into practice what we believe: 'In everything do to others as you would have them do to you; for this is the law and the prophets' (Matthew 7:12).

Social Ethics in the Nineteenth and Twentieth Centuries

Throughout the nineteenth century, Methodist churches grew rapidly in Britain, North America, and beyond.[31] It became a middle-class church in many places. The economic status of Methodists tended to increase. Many became respectable citizens, alienated from the everyday problems of the poor and from the rising working class in the expanding industrial areas. Social work was often reduced to individual assistance on a personal and local basis. The faithful were admonished to endure hardships and to assist the impoverished as they could. An exception to this trend were the Primitive Methodists, a major branch of the Wesleyan movement who were active in trade unions from an early stage while mainstream Methodism lacked real commitment to the labor movement.[32] Sadly, different ethical attitudes among Methodists on such issues as racism and segregation, the place of women, and the role of laypeople in the church resulted in schisms. Yet, within local and regional areas, Methodists developed social networks helping people on the margins, respecting human dignity, opening opportunities for making their own ethical choices, and supporting their participation in the democratic processes of decision-making.

The Social Awakening in Europe and North America

The Deaconess Movement
One of the larger projects to bridge the widening gap between the established churches and the growing number of poor people living under worsening labor and housing conditions was the deaconess movement inspired by German Lutheran, Reformed, and Methodist initiatives. Since the 1860s, 'the founding of deaconess institutions after the German models'[33] was strongly advocated by persons who visited places like Hamburg (Johann Hinrich Wichern, 1808–1881) and Kaiserswerth (Theodor Fliedner, 1800–1864). Fliedner and his wife Friederike founded a 'Motherhouse' with three young Methodist women offering professional nurses training; secure living for unmarried women; ministries in hospitals; aid to families; housing for

children; and a spiritual community for the deaconesses themselves. Their work was as broad as there were places of need. The deaconess movement was established in Britain (e.g., by Florence Nightingale) and the USA (e.g., by William Passavant, Isabella Thoburn, Christian and Louise Golder).

The deaconess movement gave unmarried Christian women an opportunity to find a meaningful commitment in social ministry and, thereby, to follow their calling in a time when people's needs were growing rapidly and the ordination of women was still distant dream. At the same time, the movement crossed denominational and geographical borders through personal and institutional cooperation. As a form of a revitalized order of early Christianity (e.g., Phoebe in Romans 16:1), it involved women and (in smaller numbers) men on a remarkably egalitarian basis and opened hearts and minds for a ministry beyond their ecclesial communities. Nonetheless, the immensity of the social problems required a stronger response from the Christian churches as more and more Americans became aware of the social problems rooted in modern capitalism and other areas.

The Social Gospel Movement and Its Impact on Social Ethics in Methodism
The response to the growing social problems challenging the churches was the 'Social Gospel' movement which arose in the latter part of the nineteenth century. It was a social-reform movement prominent especially among Protestant churches of industrialized North America and was a turning point for Protestant social ethics which brought about a major and lasting change in social awareness and practice that may still be a benchmark for Christians and their churches.

The movement started with persons like Richard Ely (1836–1918), an influential American economist who pleaded for an ethical approach to economics and cooperation with the labor movement, and Washington Gladden (1854–1943), a Congregational minister, who sought to apply 'Christian principles' to social problems. Yet, the roots of the Social Gospel go deep into the history of social movements of the eighteenth and nineteenth centuries. The outstanding leader and theologian of the 'Social Gospel' movement was Walter Rauschenbusch (1861–1918), a Baptist pastor and native German, who tried to cope with the distress of his congregation's location in New York City's lower Manhattan called 'Hell's Kitchen.' Rauschenbusch 'felt alienated from the emotionalism of the American Holiness movement. . . . His understanding of sanctification had more in common with John Wesley than many of his nineteenth-century followers, in that Rauschenbusch understood sanctification more as a process of a holy living, as opposed to a mark of instantaneous conversion or "second blessing." '[34] new model of evangelism should include the consideration of social and economic sins. That was at no surprise for true Wesleyans!

Social Ethics in the Methodist Tradition

Methodists like Frank Mason North (1850–1935), a pastor in New York City and leading mission advocate, and Harry F. Ward (1873–1966), a Methodist pastor in Chicago and seminary professor in Boston and NewYork, were important participants in the Social Gospel movement. Recognizing that the gospel of Jesus had both a salvific and social purpose, they called all Christians, by God's grace, to make the world and the society reflect the kingdom of God. Wesley's understanding of God's Kingdom as a transforming power in the present world, where the least should be heard and considered side by side with the greatest, must be translated into actions like the abolition of child labor, a living wage for all, protection of workers (especially women), a shorter workweek, factory regulation, and support of workers' unions. The power of God's love was seen as mighty enough to reach the hearts of persons and society.

In his familiar hymn 'Where cross the crowded ways of life' (see Matthew 22:9), North urged Jesus, 'the Master from the mountainside' to 'tread the city's streets again,'

> Till all the world shall learn your love
> and follow where your feet have trod,
> till, glorious from your heaven above,
> shall come the city of our God[35]

Wesley's vision of all people living by the power and rule of love and of real Christians leading the way in connection with a common prevailing trust in the unfailing progress of human history created a fertile ground and a source of courage for this movement. Like the eighteenth-century founder of Methodism, the leaders of the Social Gospel movement laid scientific foundations to undergird their program of Christian social reform by including economic and social research as well as an exchange with European social movements and church initiatives in Britain (Birmingham, Liverpool, London), Germany, and Switzerland. The leading persons of this social awakening shared the conviction that a deeper understanding of the interrelatedness of political, economic, social, religious, and cultural factors and rules is essential for a groundbreaking change in the living conditions of the continually increasing poor masses and cannot be replaced by good intentions or a vague inactive 'confidence' in God's providence. A living mature faith, instead, should connect efforts of reasonable analysis of the society's state of affairs (and its complex background), the voice of the prophets, and the gospel of Jesus to discern the ways the Spirit of God will lead his church and its individual followers of Christ.

The 1908 Social Creed of the Methodist Episcopal Church

The birth of the Social Creed of the Methodist Episcopal Church, the first of its kind in history, is closely connected with a small but vibrant initiative by the Methodist Federation for Social Service. Its members, Methodist women and men, were resolved 'to deepen within the Church the sense of social obligation and opportunity, to study social problems from the Christian point of view, to promote social service in the Spirit of Jesus Christ.'[36] Careful preparation of their Social Creed petition to general conference, the openness of the conference to consider it, and an official reception by President Theodore Roosevelt at the White House following its adoption helped to gain public awareness in Methodism and beyond it.

The text of the document adopted by the general conference [37] has a short center section formally known as the 'Social Creed' in addition to an introduction and a concluding section. The introduction expresses the bold belief that 'in the teachings of the New Testament will be found the ultimate solution of all the problems of our social order' as well as the hope that 'when the spirit of Christ shall pervade the hearts of individuals, and when his law of love to God and man shall dominate human society, then the evils which vex our civilization will disappear.' The love commandment and the Golden Rule (Matthew 7:12) are presented as keys for interpreting the scriptures to understand God's will in the context of ethical decisions and actions. The general conference recognized 'the gravity of the social situation' and welcomed 'every indication of a desire to end disputes and hostilities and to find a basis of reconciliation, fraternity, and permanent cooperation' between the employers and the laboring classes as well as competing groups within the Methodist Episcopal Church.

The core of the adopted text includes ten concrete postulations which the Methodist Episcopal Church 'stands for'[38] and one biblical request as the foundation of all others decisions, present or future.

'The Methodist Episcopal Church stands –

- For equal rights and complete justice for all men in all stations of life.
- For the principle of conciliation and arbitration in industrial dissensions.
- For the protection of the worker from dangerous machinery, occupational diseases, injuries, and mortality.
- For the abolition of child labor.
- For such regulation of the conditions of labor for women as shall safeguard the physical and moral health of the community.
- For the suppression of the "sweating system."
- For the gradual and reasonable reduction of the hours of labor to the lowest practical point, with work for all; and for that degree of leisure for all which is the condition, of the highest human life.

- For a release for employment one day in seven.
- For a living wage in every industry. For the highest wage that each industry can afford, and for the most equitable division of the products of industry that can ultimately be devised.
- For the recognition of the Golden Rule and the mind of Christ as the supreme law of society and the sure remedy for all social ills.'

In the final section of the petition the general conference delegates 'gladly recognize the increasing sense of responsibility . . . for these great moral concerns of humanity' and, realizing that this paper could not be but a small strategic step in the right direction, they 'summon all our ministry . . . to [the] patient study of these problems and to the fearless but judicious preaching of the teachings of Jesus in their significance for the moral interests of modern society.' The duty to serve the present age rests on all members of the church within their scope, and all are called 'to seek that kingdom in which God's will shall be done on earth as it is in heaven.'

In December of the same year (1908), the newly founded 'Federal Council of Churches of Christ in America' adopted a similar Social Creed, drafted by Frank North; other churches followed. The turning point in Protestant social ethics, brought about by the Social Gospel movement, became manifest in courageous church documents. In spite of this broad resonance in American Christendom the 'Methodist Federation for Social Service,' their friends, and their actions met distrust and strong opposition from within many congregations and beyond. Today, United Methodism's Methodist Federation for Social Action, its General Board of Church and Society, and other social action organizations encounter similar suspicion and opposition.

After World War I and the ensuing global economic depression the optimism of the Social Gospel began to fade. A response to its overly optimistic expectations and growing pessimism was Reinhold Niebuhr's (1892–1971) 'Christian realism,' pointing to the reality of sin and evil in society and leaving behind naïve moral idealism. He invited American Christians to hear the gospel as it was understood by other people 'living under very different conditions or in other parts of the world'[39] in order to identify their own cultural prejudices. Convinced that love and justice are necessary to ethics, the Christian Realist sees 'the obstacles of self-interest and power that have to be overcome.'

Social Creed and Social Principles of the United Methodist Church
Since 1972 the social teaching of the United Methodist Church has been expressed by two different texts: a new Social Creed and the Social Principles.[40] Furthermore, in 2008 a new poetic Companion Litany to Our Social Creed was added.[41]

The 1972 Social Creed[42] has little in common with its predecessor of 1908; it is a liturgical text of seven sentences, each beginning with 'We.' The first two are a confession of faith in the triune God, the third a confession of sin for misusing God's gifts. Sentences four through eight resonate with the six sections of the 'Social Principles': the natural world, the nurturing community, the social community, the economic community, the political community, and the world community – areas of human life in which social ethics have a central place. The closing sentence of the Creed expresses the belief in the 'final triumph of God's Word' and the acceptance of God's commission 'to manifest the life of the gospel in the world.' There is no mention of the love commandment or the Golden Rule as in the 1908 Social Creed.

Through the Social Principles, which are revised every four years. The document's preface speaks of 'the human issues in the contemporary world from a sound biblical and theological foundation' and calls 'all members of the United Methodist Church to a prayerful, studied dialogue of faith and practice.' A preamble follows with content and language very similar to the Social Creed of 1972.

Each of the six principal sections of the Social Principles opens with a fundamental introduction connecting theological teaching with a short description of specific topics addressing particular subjects. The size of the document has been enlarged from seven pages in 1972 to thirty-five pages in 2008. This expansion represents the growing multiplicity and complexity of social issues as well as the application of deeper biblical and theological insight. One of the most contentious topics in the Social Principles (under the section on the 'Nurturing Community, subsection 'Human Sexuality') is the matter of homosexuality. At question is whether the statement on homosexuality nurtures 'respectful dialogue' in dealing with a widely disputed human problem with a long history in the church. Its discussion during general conferences since 1972 has aroused high public interest, disagreement, and distressing disputes among faithful Methodists. Similar to the struggle over the question of slaveholding in the nineteenth century the homosexual issue moved the denomination close to schism in 2004, a danger not yet averted.

Notwithstanding some inconsistencies of the voluminous text and the often dissimilar situations in countries outside the USA, the Social Principles have helped to keep visible social awareness in Methodist churches around the world. In order to apply their relevance to social debate in different national and cultural contexts, it is necessary to concentrate on principles that are foundational for Methodist social ethics. Freedom of conscience should not be restricted to such questions as civil disobedience or military service. Jesus' love commandment and Golden Rule must still have a prominent place in individual and communal decision-making processes. Enabling Christian believers to identify ethical issues (including sufficient knowledge and available options) and to deal with those issues in a way that is grounded in the gospel is of utmost desirability.

Social Ethics on the Way Through the Twenty-First Century

In many countries across the world, Methodist churches are recognized because of their social, educational, and pastoral work as well as their solidarity with social movements. Social justice is still at the heart of Methodist teaching on public affairs. The responsibility of ethical reflection and teaching is assumed by many Methodist theologians and ethicists. Their contributions to rethinking Wesley's ethics for the present time (e.g., Richard Heitzenrater, Theodore Jennings, Theodore Runyon), articulating essential criteria for social responsibility from a Methodist point of view (e.g., Stanley Hauerwas, Scott Jones, Joerg Rieger, John Vincent), developing concepts of economic and political ethics (e.g., M. Douglas Meeks, Theodore Weber), and integrating liberation theologies into Methodist teaching (e.g., Miguez Bonino, Mercy Oduyoye, Elsa Tamez) are discussed in Methodist academic circles and beyond.

These and other theologians and ethicists are teaching a new appreciation of the Wesleyan way of doing theology and ethics. Our most important tasks at this time seem to be: a fresh examination of where we have been and where we are going, what the word of God and the needs of God's children tell us today; what we stand for, and how we may discharge our moral obligation. God's love has been poured into our hearts and moves us to look at all human beings as created in God's image and destined to live with God and each other. Using the quadrilateral as a tool both in making moral decisions and casting our principles into creative, beneficial actions will empower Methodists to follow the mind of Christ as described in the gospels and made present through the Holy Spirit, to avoid ethical ignorance or laziness and legalistic moralism which have often been a temptation to serious believers. Methodists, accepting God's healing and illuminating grace, open themselves for the working of God's love, turning their faces, minds, and hearts to those 'who need us most.' Stewardship is God's calling and the ethical obligation of all Christians wherever and whenever they have the opportunity and the ability to act in their social contexts, sharing the gift of life in all its dimensions with their fellow creatures.

For Further Reading

Heitzenrater, Richard P., ed. *The Poor and the People Called Methodists: 1729–1999*. Nashville, TN: Abingdon, 2002.

Jennings, Theodore W. *Good News to the Poor: John Wesley's Evangelical Economics*. Nashville, TN: Abingdon, 1990.

Marquardt, Manfred. *John Wesley's Social Ethics: Praxis and Principles.* Nashville, TN: Abingdon, 1991.
Meeks, M. Douglas, ed. *The Portion of the Poor: Good News to the Poor in the Wesleyan Tradition.* Nashville: Kingswood Books, 1995.
Rieger, Joerg and John J. Vincent, eds. *Methodist and Radical: Rejuvenating a Tradition.* Nashville, TN: Kingswood Books, 2003.
Runyon, Theodore, ed. *Sanctification & Liberation: Liberation Theologies in the Light of the Wesleyan Tradition.* Nashville, TN: Kingswood Books, 1981.
Weber, Theodore R. *Politics in the Order of Salvation: New Directions in Wesleyan Political Ethics.* Nashville, TN: Kingswood Books, 1998.

18 Methodism's Polity: History and Contemporary Questions

Thomas Edward Frank

Methodism in the twenty-first century faces some of its most creative and challenging opportunities for shaping the polity for a global church. As Methodism continues its rapid expansion in sub-Saharan Africa and sustains its vitality in Europe, Eurasia, the Philippines, the Americas, and other regions, the movement must address emerging questions of the kind of global communion it will be. These questions with their catholic and ecumenical reach are inseparably related to the practices of Methodist churches in local places and social contexts. A worldwide communion of churches means little apart from the vitality of churches in particular places, and local churches cannot be vital without connection among churches across the world. The relation of global and local, particularly the common discipline that binds local, regional, and world churches in a connectional covenant, will remain the most significant point of tension and promise for the future of Methodism.

Methodism embarks on its political challenges with only a minimal foundation of established scholarship or lively intellectual debate about the distinctly Methodist heritage of polity and possible new forms of governance. The nineteenth century – the era in which independent Methodist bodies became more formally constituted and adumbrated in England and the USA and in which Methodist missions in Asia, Africa, and Latin America began to take more permanent churchly form – was marked by intense exchanges among scholars and church leaders about such polity issues as the authority and organization of conferences, the powers and duties of bishops and the grounding of their authority in apostolicity, the balance of power among clergy and laity, and the oversight and control of agencies for education, publication, mission, and other initiatives.[1]

Similarly, the twentieth century (through the 1960s) produced fervent and often heated debate over polity. The era was marked by political initiatives that achieved a series of organic church unions reshaping Methodism in the USA, Europe, and other regions, and produced Methodism's union with other

Protestant traditions in India, Zambia, and other nations.[2] Methodism in many nations newly independent of colonialism was reorganized from the status of missions of US or European churches into autonomous churches. Methodism addressed persistent divisions of race and gender, abolishing the racially segregated Central Jurisdiction of the Methodist Church in the USA and opening the way for the election of women as conference delegates, ordained clergy, and election and consecration as bishops.[3]

The period since the 1960s, however, has produced a subdued silence of debate on Methodist polity. Few books or articles on polity are published. Only a handful of scholars address the subject. For a large worldwide movement now well into its third century, Methodism is notable for having no network or association of specialists in its canon or church law. By contrast, Roman Catholicism and Anglicanism support active societies of scholars and specialists with over twenty journals published in English. Methodist forms of church discipline lack foundations in political philosophy and ecclesiology that undergird the canon law of those communions. One searches in vain for explanations of the logic of Methodist church law, for substantive discussions of its grounding in scripture and tradition, or for elaboration of constitutive principles that would provide the framework of a new global polity.[4] The kind of focused energy and intellectual investment in polity that was required to produce in the USA a new constitution for the Methodist Episcopal Church in 1900, or church unions and constitutions of the Methodist Protestants, the Methodist Episcopal northern and southern branches, and the Evangelical United Brethren in 1939 and 1968, is simply not apparent in contemporary Methodism.

What the period from 1980 through the first decade of the twenty-first century has brought instead is stagnation, impasse, and resistance in polity development. In England, Sweden, and other nations, sensible plans for Methodism to return to its original status as a society for spiritual renewal and growth within the national church foundered in negotiations. Churches in many nations are conflicted about whether to be autonomous or to seek a formal political covenant with other churches, particularly the largest and wealthiest entity in global Methodism, the United Methodist Church (UMC).

In the USA, fervent but diffuse preoccupation with the smaller size of domestic United Methodism since the 1960s has spawned hundreds of books, articles, conferences, workshops, and consulting firms driven by a passion to recreate and reenergize Methodism as an evangelical movement. Even though membership and participation in all religious traditions in the USA has clearly diminished during the period, marking a distinct social change associated with urbanization, mass media, lower birth rates, and economic prosperity, the UMC has chosen to reverse the trends by adopting forms and styles from contemporary evangelical Protestantism and Pentecostalism.

Since the paradigmatic churches of those movements are independent congregations, often very large (average Sunday attendance over 2,000), with highly visible, usually male, congregationally ordained pastors – some adopting the title of bishop – putting such churches forward as models for Methodist revitalization has set up immediate tensions with Methodist polity and political initiatives of the earlier twentieth century.

Evangelical renewal efforts have generally positioned established polity as a hindrance to the movement of the Spirit. Connectional organization and structures of accountability have been widely viewed as barriers to the evangelical expansion of the church. Reform advocates in the UMC have successfully used general conference procedure to remove or make optional much of the common structure for local churches and annual conferences, a political order created and elaborated in the formation of the new denomination in 1968 and later. Practices of ordination grounded in Methodism's Anglican heritage have given way to an evangelical model of ministry that embraces not only preaching, but administration of the sacraments without ordination. The historic norm of ordained elders serving as the executive session of annual conferences with constitutional powers over conference relations of clergy, constitutional amendments, and election of general conference delegates – a norm reinforced by the adoption of a seminary requirement for ordination in 1956 – has been replaced by a broad definition of 'clergy' that includes the numerous non-ordained pastors appointed to local churches. The most common justification offered for these trends is that spreading the gospel trumps traditional church order.

The evangelical initiative with the broadest political impact in the UMC has been the adoption of a mission statement in 1996. This mission – excerpted from Matthew 28:19 in the phrase 'to make disciples of Jesus Christ' and elaborated by a 2008 amendment 'for the transformation of the world' – is not in the UMC constitution. It has nonetheless emerged as the guiding principle for all church membership, ministry, and action and as the predominant rationale for changes in polity (*Book of Discipline 2008*, para. 120).[5]

The disciple-making slogan was common among American evangelical Protestant denominations in the 1980s, though missiology has since made a distinct turn toward more incarnational understandings of witness and service grounded in biblical passages such as John 20:19–23.[6] The slogan as adopted has no particular origin in the Wesleyan tradition. In fact, the theology of the statement is based on two premises that are arguably out of keeping with Wesleyan doctrine. The first is the assumption that the church needs a mission statement, implying that the church is foremost a self-constituted human organization rather than a gift of God continuous across the centuries from the apostolic church. The second is the instrumentalism that charges the church with the power to 'make disciples,' a power that in Wesleyan theology clearly belongs to the Holy Spirit in the reflected power and glory of the holiness of God.[7]

The mission statement operates as a principle of polity aligned less with ecclesiology than with the production and performance logic of corporate capitalism. The influence of this logic was evident in the adoption of a corporate brand – the cross and flame logo – at the founding of the UMC in 1968; continued through the widespread experiments with a variety of business models such as 'Total Quality Management' to improve the church's productivity (increase in membership); is further advanced by advertising campaigns using an unofficial branding slogan – 'open hearts, open minds, open doors;' and issues in repeated campaigns for revitalization marked by three, five, or seven steps, laws, or practices that will produce more Christians and more churches. Successful 'leadership' in these campaigns marked by increased local church membership is privileged in this paradigm. Performance measures suppress and displace the centrality of a call to ministry affirmed and legitimized through the community of faith in the rite of ordination.

Nonetheless, the UMC has made this mission statement the operative principle of its emerging polity. The productivity logic of the statement overrides established forms and practices of polity. Under the original UMC polity, assembled annual conferences comprised of lay and clergy members had reserved to them regional powers to initiate collective action and make connectional decisions and commitments. This historic power has been diffused by the formation of executive committees or mission councils with broadly permissive authority apart from the assembled conference. The long-held separation of powers between the episcopacy and the conferences carefully delineated in the original UMC polity has given way in many regions to the bishop serving on such councils, even as chair. The principle of separating programmatic and financial decisions, embedded in UMC polity from its inception to prevent control by dominant persons or groups, has been superseded by the creation of entities such as the Connectional Table 'where ministry and money are brought to the same table' with broad and undefined powers of 'stewardship of the mission, ministries, and resources' of the UMC – a polity that under church law lacks proper constitutional structure or authority within the rubrics for general agencies created by the general conference (para. 901, 904).

An astonishing dearth of polity debate has accompanied the decisions that flow from the 1996 mission statement. While the evangelical turn, in corporate mode, is rationalized as a recovery of Wesleyan passion for spreading the gospel, little has been said about how this trend has thrown the Wesleyan synthesis out of balance. Methodism's polity, like its teachings, is an amalgam of Anglican, Catholic, Orthodox, Reformed, Pietist, and evangelical doctrines and practices. Methodism shares its understanding of sacrament and ordination with Anglicanism, its organization of pastoral ministry through an order of itinerating preachers with Catholicism, its theology of growth in the Christian life with early Eastern church fathers and mothers, its impulse to reform the church and nation(s) with the Reformation, its use of small groups for spiritual growth with Pietism, and its reliance on the experience of salvation with evangelicalism.[8]

In the years since the creation of the UMC, the more churchly Anglican elements of Methodist ecclesiology – ordination, sacrament, Trinitarian theology, and tradition as a primary source of authority for practice – have been pushed aside by the evangelical dynamic of Methodist ecclesiology – preaching, conversion through Jesus Christ, mission, and experience as a primary source of authority for practice. The great commandments of Jesus – love of God and neighbor, loving one another – are subsumed under the great commission to go to all nations.

As Methodism moves on into the twenty-first century, its family of churches scattered across all continents and dozens of nations and cultures, the Wesleyan synthesis is once again at stake. Any polity that is created to advance the unity in diversity of Methodism and to constitute the communion of its many regional churches will embody an ecclesiological logic. Whether this polity reflects the complex logic of the whole synthesis or only some aspects of it is an open question that requires the engagement of scholars and leaders in the tradition. Failure to engage these polity questions will create a vacuum in which global Methodism could be reshaped in the paradigm of a multinational business corporation much like the entrepreneurial ventures of television preachers now broadcast worldwide or other global parachurch organizations.[9] A new generation of scholarship probing the range of questions in polity and ecclesiology, from the Wesleyan tradition in its English context to contemporary practices in a multitude of societies, must provide the foundation for this engagement.

Present State of Polity Research and Writing

Polity as the constitution, form of organization, and structure of authority of a nation, institution, or association has been little studied in contemporary Methodist scholarship. The dynamics of the common life of Methodism, by contrast, receive attention in many formats. Focal points of its ministry and mission, such as church growth, prayer and spirituality, new church starts, and programs of missional service, are discussed and advocated in many venues. Methodists amend and add to church law regularly through their legislative conferences, maintaining detailed records of petitions, amendments, conference discussion, and votes. These records, in keeping with the eighteenth century 'Minutes' recorded and published by John Wesley and the early

Methodists, demonstrate on-the-ground Methodist decision-making and offer useful primary source material for the scholar. Few interpretive discussions of conference actions and their implications for polity, however, find their way into print.

Contemporary Methodists, like generations that have gone before, have a predominant disposition for narrative. Methodists are disposed to watch issues unfold, to follow conference discussion, and to imagine how actions mandated on paper will look when carried out by real people in actual communities of faith. This parallels the Methodist attraction to memoir, accounts of spiritual 'journeys,' and other forms of narrative. Today's Methodists come by this disposition honestly; from the earliest conferences and publications, Methodists have given an account of themselves by telling stories of their witness and its effects and results.[10] Every Methodist *Book of Discipline* has described 'the Rise of Methodism,' the distinct purpose of the movement, assured the public of the guidance of the Holy Spirit, and demonstrated that guidance by describing 'the great revival of religion' through the spread of class meetings and preaching places, and the growing influence of Methodist people.[11] Even today one is unlikely to locate an analysis of how ministries are organized, and much more likely to come across a historical narrative of Methodism in a region,[12] or an account of how a conference turned around and invigorated its stagnating ministries.[13]

These otherwise admirable accounts leave unattended most political analysis and interpretation of the church as institution. Only a handful of books fill the gap, providing reference points for understanding Methodist polity.[14] As a consequence, conferences undertake major decisions with reference mainly to narrative (often oral) traditions and without benefit of scholarship that probes the foundations and logics of polity. As a primary example, even though various constitutions have been written in the twentieth century, bringing into being such American church bodies as the Methodist Church and the UMC, no constitutional history of twentieth-century Methodism exists. By contrast, John J. Tigert's classic early twentieth century history of Methodist constitutions in the USA was constructed from close reading of conference minutes, the journals and correspondence of leaders, and the many works on Methodist polity published across the nineteenth century. His book captured the essential logic of American Methodism with thoroughness unmatched by later scholars.

Tigert argued that the two constitutive principles of American Methodism were conference and episcopacy, and that Methodist polity could only be understood through a grasp of those principles and the relation between them. He concluded that Methodist constitutions originated and were grounded in the consent of all the traveling preachers collectively, and that the general conference created in 1792 received its powers from the collective body of itinerants. This principle remains intact, though in modified form in contemporary United Methodism, as all constitutional amendments must be approved by the aggregate votes of all ordained clergy and lay members of annual conferences. He further established that annual conferences, originally for all preachers in the USA, became regional gatherings for the convenience of the itinerant preachers to reduce travel time as the movement grew. That is, the annual conferences were meetings within the connection as a whole and the itinerating preachers constituted one connectional body for ministry and mission.[15]

From this genealogy has grown the chain of conferences – general, jurisdictional or central, annual, and charge – that links UM polity and the practice of conference that typifies Methodism around the world. That is, Methodism makes decisions about ministry and mission in conference, in collective gatherings of ordained and lay leaders. Russell E. Richey explored the nature and history of American annual conferences as the locus of polity, fraternity, and revival in his book on *The Methodist Conference in America: A History*.[16]

Many UMC bishops and other church leaders have advocated the recovery of conference as a means of grace. John Wesley asserted that Christian conference was among the 'instituted' means of grace, those providing a framework for a way of life and growth in the knowledge and love of God.[17] His appeal for conversation, rightly ordered and ministering grace to participants, has transformed many conferences into gatherings of intense encounter, prayer, personal engagement with decisions, and consensus forms of decision-making.[18] The Judicial Council of the UMC has continuously defended the principle of conference, declaring unconstitutional those efforts to reorganize annual conferences with executive bodies empowered to act above and beyond the powers of the gathered conference as a collective group.[19]

Scholarly work drawing themes of conference together to name the principles of conference that distinguish Methodism ecclesiologically has been slim. Russell Richey's *Marks of Methodism: Theology in Ecclesial Practice* is among the few published arguments for the particularly Methodist ecclesiology of connection grounded in conference as the gathering of ministers in covenant.[20] The endurance of conference authority is clear as well in *The Constitutional Practice and Discipline of The Methodist Church* in England, in which the constitutional statement of church government is simple: 'The governing body of the Methodist Church shall be the Conference constituted and meeting annually as provided in this Deed.'[21] Angela Shier-Jones examined the roots of the particular English tradition of conference in a shared rule of life that needs fresh articulation, in her article 'Being Methodical: Theology Within Church Structures.'[22]

The principle of episcopacy received some attention during the peak of ecumenical discussions among American Protestant bodies in the mid-twentieth century. The peculiarity of Methodist episcopacy as a hybrid of ecclesiologies, adopting the life tenure typical of the organic church heritages of Catholicism and Anglicanism while retaining bishops in the order of elder as chief missionary preachers and administrators, was interpreted by Gerald F. Moede in his *The Office of Bishop in Methodism: Its History and Development*.[23] James K. Mathews was one of the few Methodist bishops who attempted a discussion of the ecclesial nature of Methodist episcopacy, arguing that its authority is conciliar and organic.[24] Most bishops have resorted to memoir to show what the practice of episcopacy has actually been like for twentieth-century bishops.[25] More recently, Richey and Frank have explored the historical origins of episcopacy in its uniquely American Methodist form, as well as describing the steady dispersal of the episcopal oversight function (*episkopē*), through connectional bodies.[26]

Episcopacy as understood in the Methodist heritage has been protected as the 'plan of itinerant general superintendency' by the Restrictive Rules of American Methodist constitutions since 1808 (para. 19). This 'plan' entails foremost the bishop's role as pastor of pastors or as head of the order of itinerating preachers. The constitution recognizes that without an itinerant order of ministry under the oversight and presidency of a bishop, Methodism would lose its distinct character.

Issues of ordained ministry and itinerancy in the USA have been explored in numerous works in the late twentieth century, particularly in response to such reforms and trends as the institution of an order of deacon as a terminal ordination, and the challenges of itineracy under contemporary conditions of urbanization and economic prosperity. In part these works arise from the continuous studies of ministry authorized by the general conference, studies which demonstrate how central the organization of ministry – particularly itinerancy – is to the connectional polity of Methodism.[27]

Dennis M. Campbell's *Yoke of Obedience* was among few efforts to articulate a theology of ordained ministry that would honor Methodism's synthesis of ecclesiologies.[28] John E. Harnish's *The Orders of Ministry in The United Methodist Church* identified the logical and practical issues surrounding the ordination of elders and the new diaconate.[29] Jack Seymour and Margaret Ann Crain provided a definitive ecclesiology of the diaconate in their work *A Deacon's Heart: The Ministry of the Deacon in The United Methodist Church*.[30] The state of itinerant ministry has been explored through articles in a volume edited by Donald E. Messer, *Send Me? The Itineracy in Crisis*.[31] The ecclesial grounding for Methodism's practice of appointing some elders to ministries other than local churches or charges – ministry and mission that extends the work of the annual conferences – has been articulated by Russell Richey in *Extension Ministers: Mr. Wesley's True Heirs*.[32]

Since Methodists understand polity primarily as a practice within the living community of faith, one method through which scholarship in polity could be advanced is a keen observation and description of the practices of Methodists in particular places. Ethnographies of congregations and conferences would add much to the picture of how Methodists actually work together, the functional forms of authority to which they defer, and the means of adjudicating conflict. Issues impinging on polity are often explored through survey instruments that record the perceptions and opinions of participants. As issues of diversity in Methodist polity and practice in varied societies come to the forefront, though, instruments of overview and generalization must be complemented by more ethnographic methods that honor local culture and make the distinct appropriations of Methodist practice in various parts of the world more vivid and more accessible.[33]

Polity for the Twenty-first Century: Principles and Possibilities

As Methodist polity is reshaped for a global church, its emerging forms will express principles of communion in the Body of Christ in the world. Some of these principles derive from the nature of polity itself as the governance of a living community. Some principles are originative, carrying forward the distinct character and charism of Methodism from its founding. Some principles have roots in legal traditions of western societies that have profoundly influenced the growing relationships among peoples and nations around the world. Together these principles can guide an emerging polity for a global church.

The Nature of Polity

The English-language term 'polity' derives from the same Greek word *politeia*, as in the more commonly used 'politics.' The Greeks understood *politeia* as the living practices through which the *polis* – the city or the state – sought the common good of the whole community. Aristotle argued that human beings are political by nature, since life together is not possible or sustainable without the practice of working together to create reliable and just structures to govern community life. Aristotle considered the key body in this political process to be the *ekklesia*, the town meeting or assembly in which citizens would propose, argue, contest, and struggle their way toward consensus in how to create a good society.

The adoption of *ekklesia* as the term Christians used to name their own assemblies and the collective life of their assemblies as the church is one of the most striking features of Christian history. Employing this term the early Christians assumed the task of creating a society of ordered life in God the Creator, under the Lordship of Christ, sustained and guided by the Holy Spirit. In a community no longer defined by gender, ethnicity, nationality, or economic and social status, Christians proposed to form a new society that would be a catalytic influence for God's love and justice in the world. Together they would seek the common good of Christian community, that is, ways to exemplify God's intentions for the world in each place.

This political task meant, of course, that from the beginning Christians faced the challenges of unity in diversity. As Christianity spread among languages and cultures, Christian communities became increasingly varied in ways of understanding and practicing the gospel of the Reign of God. All sought grounding for their ways in scripture, and discovered many ways of reading and applying ancient texts as authority for their forms of life. The resulting panoply of Christian polities continues to be a defiance of Christ's prayer that his disciples 'may be one' (John 17:22) and a challenge to the unity in diversity that is the nature of the church.

Originative Principles
Methodism's origins in the eighteenth century as a form of Christian life within an established national church gave it a distinct charism within the panoply of Christian traditions that profoundly shapes the substance of its polity. Methodism derives its distinct charism as a church from its two originative forms of life together. The first was a rule of life, crafted by John Wesley in 1743 as the General Rules of the movement. Inspired by his study of ancient spirituality and monasticism, Wesley intended to offer a framework for growing in the knowledge and love of God in community. This rule of life was developed as a kind of secular monasticism, intended for people living the everyday life of work, home, school, and town; seeking the Christian way of life in covenant with a small group of fellow Christians in mutual prayer, discernment, and admonition under the guidance of a lay class leader.

The General Rules admonished followers to avoid evil and do good, but deliberately did not set forth a proliferation of laws that would lead people into moral perfectionism or works righteousness. The Rules demonstrated that followers could only fulfill a Christian way of life by growing in discernment and judgment of what is good and what is evil in a complex world. This growth came not in solitude or isolation, but in society, that is, in community with others. It would be sustained through the continued practice of the means of grace such as the Lord's Supper, worship, prayer, reading of scripture, and giving to the poor.[34]

The second originative form of life was a disciplined missionary order of preachers bearing the gospel to the town centers and open fields where ordinary folk could hear them. Wesley considered this evangelical preaching an 'extra-ordinary' call beyond the ordered priesthood of the Church of England, a call that could be practiced anywhere in the land regardless of parish boundaries. Hence his expression 'the world is my parish,' that is, his claim that Methodists could preach anywhere in the land because their call was outside ordinary canon law governing the jurisdiction of parishes. Wesley devoted much of his life to calling, educating, guiding, admonishing, and appointing these preachers to their places of service. He called them together in an annual conference beginning in 1744, a meeting in which, like the class meetings for laity, all could grow in their vocation through searching questions of how they were conducting their preaching and teaching and how to make it more effective.

These original Methodist forms of life constituted the connection, which while Wesley was alive meant essentially an immediate connection with him. The connection was personal, sustained by a remarkably dynamic, resourceful, and tireless individual blessed with a charism for synthesizing Christian teaching and making it compelling. Then Methodism faced the challenge that comes to any movement when it grows beyond the grasp of its founder and continues after his death. In nations with national churches in which the whole land is divided into parishes – England, Sweden, Germany, and others – United Methodism still functions in forms very close to its original charisms. The life of piety and preaching deeply shapes United Methodist clergy and laity, and the UMC – while usually a tiny minority in the land – serves as a significant catalyst for effective witness to the Gospel, challenging the majority church itself to become more effective and prodding the social conscience of the nation.

Methodism more broadly, though, was confronted with two questions. The first was how it would govern itself in the absence of the founder. The second was the form it would take as it was compelled to become a church in nations where no national church existed or where accommodation with the national church was not possible.

In the USA, the original charisms of Methodism were absorbed after the organizing conference of 1784 into the project of becoming a national church. Even though the USA had a constitutional barrier to establishment of any one church, Methodists soon became an unofficial church of the nation. By 1850, one third of all church members in the USA were members of the Methodist Episcopal Church.[35] Even today, over 95% of the counties in the USA (smaller regional governments within states) have at least one UMC.[36] Methodism in the USA assumed the mantle of the Church of England in this new national context, becoming a kind of Anglicanism for the common folk. Methodism had bishops without the English episcopal garb, ordination of deacons and elders but with a continuing elevation of preaching over sacrament, catechism with a central emphasis on the living faith experience of lay persons, and clergy meeting in conference along with widespread leadership from laity in national movements of missions and education. Methodism in the USA, like the Church of England, was a broad church, broad enough to encompass camp meetings and cathedrals, revivals and Holy Communion, religion as promise of heaven and religion as social reform, rich and poor, slave and free, urban and rural, and craftsperson and merchant.

The polity of the UMC today is a child of this social history of the church in the USA. UMC polity is rife with assumptions that United Methodism is a church with an established place in society and that society cares how the UMC does things or where the UMC stands on issues. General conference, for example, was born in the US context. Methodism began with a single annual gathering of preachers, just as always was the practice in England. Few English people, John Wesley foremost among them, had any concept of how vast the land of North America really was or the formidable obstacles to travel. Soon the annual gathering was divided in two, then five, and the record of all the actions of these conferences added together was called the 'general conference.' Only in 1792 did all the preachers agree that a general meeting of all preachers was practical only every fourth year, a gathering which came to be called the general conference or conference of all, distinguished from the annual conferences of more finite regions. As the number of traveling preachers grew, this quadrennial assembly became a delegate body, at first one delegate for every five preachers. Over two-hundred years later, the general conference perpetuates the Methodist ethos of governance by delegated conference. It still convenes every four years, constituted by clergy and lay delegates now elected by annual conferences in over fifty nations, with exclusive powers to modify church law.[37]

As Methodism evolves as a global church no longer predominantly American and active in multiple nations and cultures, the movement must decide what form these originative charisms of its heritage will take. The forms of life most central to Methodism's heritage may be distilled into the following principles.

A Common Discipline
The General Rules are well over two-hundred and fifty years old and still offer a basic disposition and practical theology for Methodist people. Yet, they are barely known or studied in today's US churches, nor have they been revised to reflect the reality that the UMC is itself a church and not a movement within the Church of England. For example, this rule of life assumes but is not explicit about the centrality of baptism and Holy Communion as constitutive rites and liturgies of the church. The UMC constitution asserts the sixteenth-century Anglican Articles of Religion as the standard of doctrine for the church, including the theology of the sacraments worked out in the contentiousness with Roman Catholicism that was current at the time (Articles XVI–XIX). The constitution further states only that general conference has the power 'to regulate all matters relating to the form and mode of

worship' and 'to provide' a hymnal and ritual, without offering any additional canon law about what United Methodists believe is central to the church's worship. Methodism must be clearer about its contemporary understanding of the sacraments as well as other means of grace.[38]

Some argue that the Social Principles of the UMC continue the heritage of the General Rules in addressing contemporary ethical and social issues from the standpoint of Christian witness. Yet the Principles are written more as declarations addressed to society and government, leaving unclear whether they are principles by which United Methodists actually shape their daily lives. They are also decidedly American in tone and focus (e.g., beginning 'We, the people called United Methodists') and regularly have to be modified and adapted through translation and adjustments to the situations of societies other than the USA.[39]

The mission statement of the UMC, 'to make disciples of Jesus Christ for the transformation of the world,' has become a rallying cry and organizing principle of Methodist endeavors around the globe. But it is not yet clear what common life and discipline this mission produces. Every church activity 'blesses' and legitimizes itself with the mission statement, but appeal to a common slogan does not generate the needed ecclesiological coherence. More work must be done to connect this mandate with the specifically Methodist heritage of growing in grace and in good judgment of how to respond to and live God's grace, so fundamental to the General Rules.

Governance by Conference
Methodists have always made decisions together in conference. They have gathered, historically as a body of itinerant preachers and then gradually as assemblies of both clergy and laity, to discern what they are called to do and to take action for more effective witness of God's reign. Conferences create agencies, committees, and myriad forms of working groups to carry out the mission they authorize, but the authority to decide the purpose, powers, and limits of such missional bodies remains with the conference itself.

Methodists have never had executive bodies to act on behalf of conferences. No central corporate headquarters, no president, and no executive committee exist in Methodism. No agency is authorized to act beyond the mandate given it by the conference that created it. No Magisterium is authorized to speak for the church beyond what the governing conference has said. This polity has frustrated many leaders over the generations who think the church must not wait for the next conference to act in a particular situation. But this political form is originative to Methodist ecclesiology and to change it would be to create a different church.

That said conference is also a covenant calling and responsibility for those who agree to serve as its constituting members. The courage to make hard decisions or to speak difficult words belongs to each member of a conference; no authority figure can rescue a Methodist from this responsibility. One of the severest tests of Methodist polity in the twenty-first century will be the continued commitment of Methodist people to this political form. In an age of mass media, constant distraction, competing ideologies, individualistic identities, and voices from multiple cultures, conference is a greater challenge than ever. Methodist people will have to step up and answer the call to the work and responsibilities of conference if this form is to thrive.

Itinerant Ministry and General Superintendency
Methodism around the world continues its distinctive form of ministry through the appointment of pastors and other ministers to their places of service. Annual conferences continue as the primary gathering place and locus of church membership for these itinerant ministers who have joined in covenant to serve where sent. Much of the character of the original 'missionary order of preachers' continues, then, undergirded by a theology of subjection to the covenant vow and to God's call to service.

Methodism globally is not of one mind about the superintendency of its ministries, however. The distinctive episcopacy of United Methodism was a child of the geographic and social context of the USA. The nation in early days consisted of scattered port towns up and down the Atlantic coast and farflung interior settlements, with a total population of three million. Annual or quadrennial conferences of preachers would hardly be sufficient to hold together a church with preaching places scattered all across the land. The episcopacy grew up as an essential element in the glue that held Methodism together, not only through the appointment of preachers in annual conferences but also through the perpetual travel and omnipresence of the bishop. Assuming this Wesley-like role of personal connection with early American Methodists was an individual of utterly astonishing stamina and determination, Francis Asbury, who took on the peripatetic itinerant superintendency in perpetual motion, being present in an amazing number of the settlements across the land over a period of forty years.

In the generations since, UM episcopacy has gradually become less definitive of the church's polity and more localized in practice. Twentieth-century American Methodism moved steadily away from defining itself by this office. The historic term 'Episcopal' was dropped from the denominational name of the Methodist Church in 1939. Election of bishops was regionalized in jurisdictions and the 'residential and presidential supervision' exercised by bishops was limited to their jurisdictions (para. 49). The functions of the episcopal office, such as determining what candidates for ministry should study in preparation for ordination, or nominating members of church governing bodies, or acting as a body of judicial review, have been steadily dispersed among conferences, councils, committees, and agencies, leaving bishops in the UMC to serve primarily as chief pastors and preachers. Their only distinct authority lies in ordaining and appointing the pastors and other clergy to their places.[40]

Meanwhile a spectrum of understandings of episcopacy persists across Methodism. In the African Methodist Episcopal Church, for example, not only the term but also the authority of bishops continues and their election is considered determinative of the course and character of the denomination. By contrast, English Methodism has never placed the episcopal role in an office of bishop but has continued the primary Wesleyan language of superintendency.

The Methodist connection can thrive only with durable practices of *episkopē* – oversight (*episkopos*) or superintendency. The oversight function is a constitutional companion principle to conference, and global Methodism has to sort out the separation and balance of power between conference and episcopacy for the thriving of its emerging connection. Conferences hold the power to make the critical decisions on allocating resources to various ministries. However, since conferences exist only when they are meeting, oversight is necessary to help the communion cohere and to hold it faithful to the common life and covenant it has made through its conferences.

Bishops or superintendents play three key roles in this cohesion beyond their appointive powers. (1) They preside in conferences, thus making 'Christian conversation' and conferencing possible for a diverse and multivoiced community of faith. (2) They are present in many times and places, offering the personal bond of trust and mutuality that gives coherence to the widely scattered ministries and mission of Methodism. (3) They provide oversight of connectional work, holding conference agencies accountable for carrying out the mandates given them.[41] Global Methodism must find constructive forms to continue this *episkopē* for a new century.

Constitutional Principles

Polity in western nations has been deeply influenced by legal traditions and practices in civil society. Canon law in continuous development across the centuries adapted terminology, categories, and logics of practice from Roman law – a heritage perpetuated in the continued use of Latin language in Vatican documents today.[42] By parallel, American Methodist bodies constituted themselves as churches at the same time as the writing of national and state constitutions, incorporating such principles as the division of government into legislative, executive, and judicial branches. Western churches, at least since Enlightenment advocacy of human rights, have stood by basic principles such as the right to fair process and a timely trial by a jury of one's peers.[43]

As world Methodism grows in awareness of its common life as a movement and moves toward a shared polity, Methodism must incorporate basic constitutional principles into its polity and practice. These principles, too, are a witness to the love and justice of the reign of God. Many civil societies in which Methodism is active do not fully recognize these principles, making church life organized under human rights an exception, a risk, and a living testimony. Such principles must guide the movement's structures and arrangements of power even as they find local, indigenous forms. Among these some are discussed hereafter.

Reception
Polity is a practice, and practices must take the forms most suitable to local traditions and cultures. Just as the gospel is an oppressive ideology when its message is dictated to a people without finding voice and form in particular languages and cultural ways, so polity is authoritarian when it is not practiced in ways that are understood and accepted by particular communities. Rules of life together must be received, that is, welcomed and adapted by a community; they cannot be imposed.[44]

For Methodism's common discipline to thrive, Methodist leaders must teach and interpret the political heritage and principles distinct to this tradition. Local communities cannot receive what they do not understand, nor can indigenous leaders take roles of authority in a polity the principles of which they do not grasp.

Subsidiarity and Adaptation
The principle of subsidiarity in traditional canon law is a companion to the principle of reception in indigenous cultures and communities. The principle of subsidiarity holds that decisions ought to be taken as close to the locus of action as possible, and that regulations and procedures may be adapted to local needs and context, so that distant governing bodies are not attempting to settle local questions by law or edict. The authority to adapt disciplinary practices to local contexts is already expressed in the UMC through legislation that allows central (non-USA) conferences to 'make such changes and adaptations of the *Book of Discipline* as the special conditions and the mission of the church in the area require' (para. 543.7). Central conferences can also set up their own judicial courts to decide local matters of church law (para. 31.6).

The principle of subsidiarity must be balanced, however, with the principle of a common discipline. Global Methodism must name those tenets, structures, and practices that are constitutive of Methodism and to which all conferences must adhere, in order to define the political space in which local adaptation and decision is legitimate. This balance is necessary for constructing truly collegial relationships among regional conferences around the world.

Church law is good only to the end of the church's effective witness to God's reign in the world. Words on a page are useful only as they guide the church in fulfilling its purpose. Church order marks the living shape of a community engaged with an ever-changing world. This is the perspective that must guide any church leader or community in practicing the covenant of laws, the rules of common life, adopted by the church as a whole.[45]

This overarching perspective must not be used, though, to dismiss church laws that do not seem applicable or useful in a particular situation. Before protesting a church law or refusing to apply it, a local community must first probe its original purpose and grasp the context to which it attempted to respond. This critical investigation may lead to new insights about the purpose of the rule and how it might effectively respond to dynamics of the present situation.

Proportionality

In a covenant of shared mission and mutual obligation, every party to the covenant should give a proportional amount of the human and material resources and carry a proportional amount of the actual costs of advancing the mission. Proportionality must be determined on the basis of fair and open factors and publicly known data. This principle is especially critical given the current economic strength of the USA and other Western nations in contrast to the weak economies and widespread poverty of nations in Africa, Asia, and Latin America. Too much reliance on US resources creates dependency relationships not much different from colonialism. Methodists in other nations are not then empowered by their own contributions to the common work. At the same time, US Methodists have in their hands the resources to have an enormous influence, for example, in providing clergy pensions or materials and labor for building churches in poorer nations. How to determine the factors that constitute proportionality and then achieve it in practice is a daunting challenge for a global church.[46]

Representation

Methodist polity has never been fully participatory in nature; it is more republican than democratic. That is, conferences have always been constituted by an elected membership or delegation, rather than functioning as assemblies with completely open participation. Annual conferences in the UMC by tradition are constructed around the appointments of itinerating clergy. Clergy are members of annual conference, accompanied by a lay member of the conference, one per clergy under appointment from each charge or local church, not necessarily proportional to local church membership numbers. General conference is a delegate assembly with equal numbers of lay and clergy delegates. The size of delegations is determined by a formula based on comparative numbers of church members and clergy in the annual conferences. The principle of fair representation means that formulas for calculating the size of delegations must be clearly and openly stated, and that the opportunity to be elected a delegate must be assured through a fair and open process. In this way, the population of Methodists may be fairly represented by delegates freely chosen and authorized to constitute the governing assemblies.

In the church locally and connectionally, Methodism has always prized the transparency of its programs and finances. Since the earliest conference, church bodies have provided public accounting for decisions taken and funds raised and disbursed. These practices have given clergy and church members the full and equal opportunity to participate as informed members of deliberative bodies. In the USA this transparency has been supported by public laws governing the reporting of all charitable organizations. Yet not all Christian traditions and congregations follow transparent procedures, and in some other nations the control of money is secretive and factional. A global Methodism must assure the public nature of its ministry and mission and the resources required to support them.

Constitutional Rights

The constitution of a worldwide church must be grounded in basic human rights of fair participation and process. Members should have some venue in which their voices can be heard, and an opportunity to elect persons to serve as members or delegates of connectional conferences. Every member should have the right to make a complaint without reprisal. Members should have the right to hear and respond to complaints or charges against them in cases of conflict or challenges to behavior in the church, as well as the right to a church trial by a trial court of one's peers and the right to appeal. These principles have been central to the UMC constitution since 1808 and must remain unchanged (para. 20).

Judiciary

Methodism's polity requires a fair and open judiciary in which questions of constitutionality can be impartially decided within the community of faith. When decisions of church law are made in secret, or by authority figures issuing decrees beyond the scope of their office, the mutual trust of the community is undermined. In the UMC, a Judicial Council decides all matters of the constitutionality of church law, including review of decisions of law by bishops presiding over conferences. Central conferences are empowered to set up judicial courts 'to determine legal questions arising' from the rules and adaptations of the *Discipline* adopted by Central Conferences (para. 31.6).

The respective powers and jurisdictions of the connection-wide and regional judiciaries must be carefully worked out in a global polity.

Connection
Finally, the constitution of a worldwide church must define the nature of connection, differentiating it from ecclesial or corporate hierarchy on the one hand and from local autonomy on the other. The nature of connection as a middle or third way between these poles may be seen in microcosm in the 'model deeds' for local church property in the USA (a term derived from and still current in British Methodism). Such properties are held 'in trust' for the UMC, as places of ministry, teaching, and discipline. They are owned neither by a bishop or annual conference, nor by the local congregation. The trust clause exemplifies the covenant nature of connectionalism by assigning responsibility for maintenance of property and holding the deed to the local church, while keeping the property in trust for the ministry and mission of the whole connection, thus avoiding either hierarchy or local autonomy.

A global constitution must define the basic elements of covenant, conference, trust, accountability, and common mission that comprise the connection. Existing assertions that connectionalism consists of 'a vital web of interactive relationships' (para. 131) or that 'connectionalism is an important part of our identity' (para. 701) will not suffice for defining these elements in a lasting form. Of course, to be effective the constitution of a worldwide church must not be adopted or revised without the consent of the body that creates the constitution, namely, the aggregate of all members of annual conferences worldwide.[47] Here, too, a middle or third way between hierarchical imposition and local independence can be forged through the distinct conference charism of Methodism.

Discernment of Principles
The originative and constitutional principles elaborated above have rarely been articulated as such in Methodist political scholarship. They assume many forms taken for granted, integrated into the everyday life and practice of Methodists. But this lived heritage becomes increasingly weakened and inconsistent with the passing of the generations and the diffusion of Methodism across world cultures. Each culture in which Methodist polity is received brings a unique perspective to the political task. Likewise, each principle brings an essential element to the constitutive task. These principles urgently need study and elaboration in various languages and cultural contexts if they are to be fully integrated into twenty-first-century Methodist life.

Much scholarly work lies ahead, including enriched discussions with other polity traditions and engagement with rapidly changing world conditions. Methodists have often deferred polity questions, dismissing them as less urgent than the pressing need to respond to world poverty and disease or the promise and possibility of offering health care and education to rising generations. These have often surfaced as the driving forces of Methodism, as they were from the first – in Wesley's care for the poor – and across the nineteenth century – in Methodism's building of hospitals and schools across the world – and as they are today – in the four ministry priorities of United Methodism.[48]

Yet, the covenant of common discipline that supports these ministries and missions, and the trust that maintains the covenant, is arguably more essential than it has ever been as Methodism grows more fully into a global communion. Scholarship in polity will be critical in helping Methodism constitute itself for a new century.

For Further Reading

Books of order or discipline of the various Methodist denominations.
Frank, Thomas Edward. *Polity, Practice, and the Mission of The United Methodist Church*. Nashville, TN: Abingdon Press, current edition.

19 Methodism and the Ecumenical Movement

Geoffrey Wainwright

Very broadly speaking, the history of Methodism falls into three phases, corresponding roughly to the eighteenth, nineteenth, and twentieth centuries. Each phase was characterized by a certain ecclesiology or understanding of 'the church,' and each in fact raises certain ecclesiological questions for the theologian. The first historical phase was 'Wesleyan Methodism,' where Methodism existed initially as a 'society' (as John Wesley viewed it) within the Church of England. The second historical phase began with the constitution of the Methodist Episcopal Church in the newly independent USA at the Christmas Conference in Baltimore, 1784, and the gradual separation between Methodism and the Established Church in England that occurred at least from Wesley's death in 1791. The nineteenth century saw, on the one hand, an increasing ecclesiastical self-confidence of Methodism and, on the other hand, a distinct tendency to internal division on several scores, so that the second historical phase may be labeled – with both positive and negative connotations – 'denominational Methodism.' The twentieth century was marked by the healing of several (though not all) earlier fissures within Methodism and even, in some parts of the world, the entry of Methodist bodies into wider ecclesial unions, as well as the engagement of relations with other confessional families where there had been little previous direct contact. This third historical phase may be designated 'ecumenical Methodism,' at least in tendency and aspiration and sometimes in achievement.

Across these phases, the underlying theological question concerns the nature of 'the church' as confessed in the ancient creed, 'We believe . . . in one, holy, catholic, and apostolic church.' What are the identifying marks of that church? Where is that church to be found? What are its constitutive units? Specifically for our purposes, where does Methodism – in its evolving history, present condition, and future prospects – fit into the picture? Does the original schism, if that name may be given to the separation between Methodism and Anglicanism, and then the ongoing nineteenth-century fissiparity within Methodism itself lend support to the critical *Histoire des variations des églises protestantes* of the Roman Catholic Jacques-Bénigne Bossuet (1627–1704)? Or, may the generous grace of God have endowed Methodism with certain gifts that contribute positively to the complexities of Christian history and will one day be recognized within a fully unified 'church' whose shape remains for now a matter of debate and prayer? What will the rest of the twenty-first century bring to world Christianity?

Our account must begin with John Wesley, both for the historical reason that he stands at the origin of Methodism, whose 'principles and practices' he himself saw as representing 'plain, old Christianity,'[1] and for the theological reason that his ecclesiology, marked by tensions as it in fact was, has continued to stamp the traditions that in perhaps variable senses regard him as – under God and in the communion of the saints – their principal founder.

Wesleyan Methodism

John Wesley was an ordained priest in the Church of England. In his irenic *Letter to a Roman Catholic*, written in Dublin in 1749, he sets out the faith of 'a true Protestant' in terms of an expansion upon the Nicene-Constantinopolitan Creed. As precisely to the church:

> I believe that Christ and his Apostles gathered unto himself a church to which he has continually added such as shall be saved; that this catholic (that is, universal) Church, extending to all nations and all ages, is holy in all its members, who have fellowship with God the Father, Son and Holy Ghost; that they have fellowship with the holy angels who constantly minister to these heirs of salvation, and with all the living members of Christ on earth, as well as all who are departed [this life] in his faith and fear.[2]

In this comprehensive sense, there is clearly only 'one church,' and in his late sermon, 'Of the Church' (1785), Wesley delineated on the basis of Ephesians 4 the sevenfold unity by which this one church is characterized within itself and in relation to God:

> The catholic or universal Church is all the persons in the universe whom God hath so called out of the world . . . as to be 'one body,' united by 'one Spirit,' having 'one faith, one hope, one baptism, one God and Father of all, who is above all, and though all, and in them all.' . . . A particular church may consist of any number of members, whether two or three, or two or three millions. But still, whether it be larger or smaller, the same idea is to be preserved. They are one body, and have one Spirit, one Lord, one hope, one faith, one baptism, one God and Father of all.[3]

The 'particularity' of a church is here understood by Wesley purely on a geographical basis, namely, 'the Christians that inhabit one city or town, such as the church of Ephesus, and the rest of the seven churches mentioned in the Revelation,' and even 'the church in the house of Philemon, and that in the house of Nymphas, mentioned in Col. 4:15.' That may be the apostolic case, historically and normatively. Given the geopolitical developments in the intervening centuries, Wesley can also say that 'that part of this great body, of the universal church, which inhabits any one kingdom or nation, we may properly term a "national" church, as the Church of France, the Church of England, the Church of Scotland.' The matter is, however, complicated not only by the rise of the 'nation states' but also by the institutional and confessional divisions that have come to exist between various Christian communities claiming to be 'church' – even while inhabiting the same territory or space.

In that same sermon, 'Of the Church,' Wesley's discussion of Article XIX of the Church of England's Thirty-Nine Articles then needed to become quite differentiated. According to the Article, 'The visible Church of Christ is a congregation of faithful men, in which the pure Word of God is preached, and the sacraments be duly administered.' Taking that definition at face value, it would appear that 'those congregations in which the pure Word of God (a strong expression) is not preached are no parts either of the Church of England or the Church catholic. As neither are those in which the sacraments are not duly administered.' To this, however, Wesley himself then added this commentary:

> I will not dare to defend the accuracy of this definition. I dare not exclude from the Church catholic all those congregations in which any unscriptural doctrines which cannot be affirmed to be 'the pure Word of God' are sometimes, yea, frequently preached. Neither all those congregations in which the sacraments are not 'duly administered'. Certainly if these things are so, the Church of Rome is not so much as a part of the catholic Church; seeing therein neither is 'the pure Word of God' preached nor the sacraments 'duly administered'. Whoever they are that have 'one Spirit, one hope, one Lord, one faith, one God and Father of all', I can easily bear with their holding wrong opinions, yea, and superstitious modes of worship. Nor would I on these accounts scruple still to include them within the pale of the catholic Church. Neither would I have any objection to receive them, if they desired it, as members of the Church of England.[4]

While Wesley seems at first to contemplate the possibility of 'the Church of Rome' as at least 'a part of the catholic Church,' the argument shifts toward recognizing individuals as, in this and perhaps other cases, Christians *despite* their particular ecclesiastical allegiance. He had concluded his *Letter to a*

Roman Catholic with a plea for 'a kind, friendly and Christian behaviour towards each other' and an 'endeavour to help each other on in whatever we are agreed leads to the Kingdom': 'Let us always rejoice to strengthen each other's hands in God.'[5]

How, then, does Wesley view the 'local' church in the narrow sense of that term, and what is the status of its members? In the sermon, 'Of the Church,' he speaks of 'a congregation or body of people united together in the service of God' or 'who assemble themselves together to worship God the Father and his Son Jesus Christ.' And he knows that 'every follower of Christ is obliged, by the very nature of the Christian institution, to be a member of some particular congregation.' Yet in the sermon 'Catholic Spirit' (1750), this is tempered by the recognition, in an historical situation of *dis*-unity, that 'a difference in opinions or modes of worship may prevent an entire external union' among Christians and their respective congregations.[6] Wesley's argument and plea that such differences need not 'prevent our union in affection' is not grounded, be it noted, in 'speculative latitudinarianism' (such as would neglect 'the first elements of the Gospel of Christ' or undercut 'the main branches of Christian doctrine') or in 'practical latitudinarianism': 'The man of a truly catholic spirit' is convinced that his congregation's 'manner of worshiping God is both scriptural and rational,' and 'there he partakes of all the ordinances of God. There he receives the Supper of the Lord. There he pours out his soul in public prayer, and joins in public praise and thanksgiving. There he rejoices to hear the word of reconciliation, the Gospel of the grace of God.'

At its best, the modern ecumenical movement, under the presumed inspiration of the Holy Spirit, has precisely been seeking to restore those conditions of faith and order in which an increasing 'union in affection' may find embodiment in a full, visible unity such as Wesley could not contemplate in his time. Meanwhile, however, we have to account for – and then reckon with – the fact that 'Methodism' itself contributed not only to the spread of 'the gospel' but also to the further institutional fragmentation of 'the church.'

We need first to retrace our steps by looking at the way in which Wesley's energetic concern for the spread of the gospel was attended – however unintentionally – by the threat of ecclesiastical fission. Already from the start of his open-air evangelism in April 1739 Wesley was accused of 'intermeddling in other men's parishes,' provoking his famous response, 'I look upon all the world as my parish'[7]; and again in June 1746, charged with 'breaking or setting aside order, both by preaching in the fields and by using extemporary prayer,' Wesley retorted, 'What is the end of all ecclesiastical order? Is it not to bring souls from the power of Satan to God, and to build them up in his fear and love? Order, then, is so far valuable as it answers these ends; and if it answers them not, it is nothing worth.'[8] Wesley was, in fact,

Methodism and the Ecumenical Movement

regularly accused of fomenting schism, as is reflected in the questions and answers at his first annual conference with his fellow preachers in June 1744:

> Q.7: Do we separate from the Church [of England]?
> A: We conceive not. We hold communion therewith for conscience' sake, by attending both the word preached, and the sacraments administered therein.
>
> . . .
>
> Q.10: Do you not entail a schism on the Church? that is, Is it not probable that your hearers, after your death, will be scattered into all sects and parties; or that they will form themselves into a distinct sect?
> A: We are persuaded the body of our hearers will even after our death remain in the Church, unless they be thrust out. . . . We do, and will do, all we can to prevent those consequences which are supposed likely to happen after our death. But we cannot with a good conscience neglect the present opportunity of saving souls while we live, for fear of consequences which may possibly or probably happen after we are dead.[9]

As the years went by, however, some among the Methodists favored separation from the Church of England, chiefly on the ground of the unworthiness of many ministers in the Established Church and in the conviction that ministerial services could be more suitably provided by Methodist preachers, most of whom were not ordained. From his own angle as an ordained minister of the Church of England, Wesley held that the only reasons that could justify his 'separation' from that institution would be: its imposition of acts that Scripture forbids or its omission of acts that Scripture commands; its denial of liberty to evangelize; its requirement of false doctrine.[10] Wesley did not judge that things had come to such a pass, either for laypeople or for ministers. Indeed, all along he insisted that members of the Methodist Societies – who in their great majority officially belonged to the Church of England – should stay within the Established Church, attending all its ordinances. In a tract published in 1758 and again in 1760, John Wesley – with the passionate support of his brother Charles – advanced a dozen 'reasons against a separation from the Church of England,' and notably argued that such a separation was historically likely to end in sectarianism, with a decline in both holiness and utility, so that it would thwart God's chief design in raising up the Methodists and sending them out, namely, 'to quicken our brethren,' 'the lost sheep of the Church of England.'[11] Wesley stood by those reasons in his sermon of 1787, 'On Attending the Church Service,' just four years before his death.[12]

Nevertheless, the impression could easily be left that, 'Mr. Wesley, like a strong and skilful rower, looked one way, while every stroke of his oar took him in the opposite direction.'[13] For while protesting his fidelity to the Church of England, Wesley acquiesced, or even led, in a series of actions that gradually and almost inevitably increased the autonomy of Methodism over against the Established Church. Frank Baker lists the evidence as the formation of 'independent societies, an itinerant ministry, informal worship and field-preaching, the authorization of lay preachers, the institution of a sacramental community, of a deliberative assembly, the erection of Methodist buildings, and the undertaking of legal proceedings for their security and continuity.'[14] Facing the self-posed question of whether, by all that, 'we [are] not unawares, little by little, sliding into a separation from the Church,' Wesley exclaimed in the Large Minutes (1789), 'O use every means to prevent this!'[15]

By the time of Wesley's death in 1791, and certainly by the time of the Plan of Pacification adopted by the British Conference in 1795, whereby a local majority might allow the Lord's Supper to be administered in the societies by the itinerant preachers with minimal regard to the parochial circumstances in the Established Church, Methodism was irrevocably on its way to 'denominational' existence, even if the 'Wesleyan Connexion' waited until the end of the nineteenth century to assume the name of 'Church.'

Denominational Methodism

The initial circumstances differed between England and North America, but in each case Methodism entered into an autonomous existence. As long as English rule lasted, the transatlantic colonies fell under the ecclesiastical jurisdiction of the Bishop of London. John Wesley unsuccessfully entreated the incumbent to send more priests to the lands across the ocean, where 'for some hundred miles together there is none either to baptize or to administer the Lord's Supper.' When, in 1784, 'by a very uncommon train of providences, many of the provinces of North America [became] totally disjoined from their mother country and erected into independent states,' Wesley – being long convinced that 'bishops and presbyters are the same order and consequently have the same right to ordain' – took it upon himself to 'appoint Dr. Coke and Mr. Francis Asbury to be joint superintendents over our brethren in North America, as also Richard Whatcoat and Thomas Vasey to act as elders among them, by baptizing and administering the Lord's Supper.'[16] The stage was thus set for the American preachers to constitute the Methodist Episcopal Church, wherein Asbury, having had his position confirmed by vote of the Christmas Conference, assumed the title of bishop.

While the Protestant Episcopal Church in the USA found a line of succession that avoided such a rupture with the dominant Anglican understanding, it was the Methodists who moved westward with the frontier until finally it could be reckoned that there was not a single county in the forty-eight contiguous states without at least one Methodist congregation. Thus, Methodism became – in a 'denominational' way that perhaps John Wesley, and certainly Charles, never intended – a vehicle for carrying the Christian faith and life into ever new territories, and even globally as both British and American Methodists engaged in 'overseas missions.'

The crux of the matter for Wesley was 'living faith,' by which he meant a faith active in love toward God and neighbor. In a wide-ranging sermon of 1783 entitled 'The General Spread of the Gospel,'[17] John begins with a lament on the present condition of the world: 'How does darkness, intellectual darkness, ignorance, with vice and misery attendant upon it, cover the face of the earth!' And this not only among 'the heathen,' but among the 'nominally Christian,' whether 'in the Turkish dominions' (where they are 'a proverb of reproach to the Turks themselves') or 'scattered up and down in Asia' or 'under the jurisdiction of the Patriarch of Moscow' or 'in Abyssinia.' With what might perhaps be seen as a fine display of ecumenical even-handedness, Wesley then moved on from the Orthodox of one kind or another to consider 'the Western churches':

> They have abundantly more knowledge; they have more scriptural and more rational modes of worship. Yet two-thirds of them are still involved in the corruptions of the Church of Rome; and most of these are entirely unacquainted with either the theory or practice of religion. And as to those who are called Protestants or Reformed, what acquaintance with it have they? Put Papists and Protestants, French and English together, the bulk of one and of the other nation; and what manner of Christians are they? Are they 'holy, as he that hath called them is holy' [1 Peter 1:15]? Are they filled with 'righteousness, and peace, and joy in the Holy Ghost' [Romans 14:17]? Is there 'that mind in them which was also in Christ Jesus' [Philippians 2:5]? And do they 'walk as Christ also walked' [1 John 2:6]? Nay, they are as far from it as hell is from heaven.

The good news is that the judgment is followed by the promise, for the scriptural text on which Wesley based his sermon is Isaiah 11:9, 'The earth shall be full of the knowledge of the Lord, as the waters cover the sea.' In the rest of this sermon, Wesley goes on to recount – in what might be thought a self-congratulatory way, were everything not ascribed to grace – 'what God has already done' through the Methodist movement, intending this as encouragement to work and pray for the universal coming of God's kingdom:

> Between fifty and sixty years ago God raised up a few young men in the University of Oxford, to testify those grand truths which were then little attended to:

> that without holiness no man shall see the Lord;
> that this holiness is the work of God, who worketh in us both to will and to do;
> that he doth it of his own good pleasure, merely for the merits of Christ;
> that this holiness is the mind that was in Christ, enabling us to walk as Christ also walked;
> that no man can thus be sanctified till he is justified; and
> that we are justified by faith alone.
>
> These great truths they declared on all occasions in private and in public; having no design but to promote the glory of God, and no desire but to save souls from death.

The 'little leaven spread wider and wider': 'More and more saw the truth as it is in Jesus, and received it in the love thereof. More and more "found redemption through the blood of Jesus, even the forgiveness of sins." They were born again of his Spirit, and filled with "righteousness, and peace, and joy in the Holy Ghost." ' The movement extended through Britain and Ireland and 'a few years after, into New York, Pennsylvania, and many other provinces in America, even as high as Newfoundland and Nova Scotia.' And this was but the dawn. Would not the work of God spread 'first through the remaining provinces, then through the isles of North America?' And at the same time, 'from England to Holland,' from there 'to the Protestants in France, to those in Germany, and those in Switzerland. Then to Sweden, Denmark, Russia, and all the other Protestant nations in Europe.' Next to 'countries where Romanists and Protestants live intermixed and familiarly converse with each other.' Then to 'those countries that are merely popish, as Italy, Spain, Portugal.' And gradually 'to all that finally name the name of Christ in the various provinces of Turkey, in Abyssinia, yea, and in the remotest parts, not only of Europe, but of Asia, Africa, and America.' With the increase of holiness, 'the grand stumbling-block being thus happily removed out of the way, namely the lives of the Christians,' then 'the Mahometans will look upon them with other eyes, and begin to give attention to their words,' as will happen also among 'the heathen nations.' Next will come 'those more distant nations with whom the Christians trade': 'The God of love will prepare his messengers and make a way . . . into the deepest recesses of America, and into the interior parts of Africa, yea, into the heart of China and Japan, with the countries adjoining to them.' And even to those nations that 'have no intercourse either by trade or any other means with Christians of any kind, such [as] the inhabitants of the numerous islands in the South Sea,' God will raise up and send preachers. Wesley's vision culminates in a grand peroration to the sermon that anticipates the final triumph and glorification of God.

With hindsight we can of course say that things did not quite work out that way in the intervening period of history, although the eschatological hope remains integral to the Christian faith, whatever may be the modes of its realization. Nevertheless, Wesley's sermon adumbrated certain features of 'mission history' during the following century and a half, and in that history, Methodism played a role that is no less honorable than that of other evangelically motivated bodies in Protestantism and indeed Catholicism. Bearing in mind the 'eschatological reserve' that should qualify all such claims, the role of Methodism in evangelism at home and mission abroad should be part of the evidence when Methodist claims to apostolicity are being evaluated.

Soberly, we nevertheless have to record the splits that occurred among Methodists in the nineteenth century. In Britain the discords concerned church government (beginning with the Methodist New Connexion, 1797) as well as modes of evangelism and styles of worship (Primitive Methodists, 1811; Bible Christians, 1815; United Methodist Free Churches, 1857). The various bodies finally united with the Wesleyan Methodist Church to constitute the Methodist Church of Great Britain in 1932. In the USA, similar issues led to the separate formation of the Methodist Protestant Church (1830) and the Free Methodist Church (1860), while the situation was exacerbated by racial difference and indeed the scandals of slavery. The split of 1844 between the Methodist Episcopal Church and the Methodist Episcopal Church, South remained until 1939, when – joined by the Methodist Protestant Church – they reunited to form 'The Methodist Church,' which would with the inclusion of communities of Germanic origin in 1968 become 'The United Methodist Church.' The African Methodist Episcopal Church (1816), the African Methodist Episcopal Zion Church (1821), and the Christian (originally Colored) Methodist Episcopal Church (1870) continue their autonomous existence.

The last decades of the nineteenth century saw the beginnings of a development that would at least allow Methodists to gain, or regain, a sense of constituting a worldwide 'family' of churches. At American initiative, a first 'Oecumenical Methodist Conference' met in London in 1881,[18] and meetings continued at ten-yearly intervals until the disruption of the Second World War. Thereafter the World Methodist Council (WMC) was constituted. Meeting since 1951 according to a quinquennial rhythm, and held together by very modest continuing structures, the WMC serves study, consultation, and cooperation in several areas of ecclesial life among its seventy-six autonomous denominational member churches ('Methodist, Wesleyan, and related union'). This is the body through which Methodism has conducted theological dialogues with other 'Christian world communions' that became perhaps the most prominent feature of ecumenism at global level in the last decades of the twentieth century.

Ecumenical Methodism

In the twentieth century, the broadly designated ecumenical movement was marked by three features among which there existed, with variations in time and place, different measures of overlap and shifting degrees of prominence. On the lookout for ecclesiological implications, we may deal in turn with: (1) conciliar structures; (2) organically united churches; and (3) bilateral dialogues and relations.

Conciliar Structures

A pioneer here was the American Methodist layman, John R. Mott (1865–1955). Mott played a founding part in the World Student Christian Federation and in the Student Volunteer Movement. Under the headlines of 'that they all may be one' and 'the evangelization of the world in this generation,' these two associations brought together the prayer of Jesus recorded in the Fourth Gospel, that his disciples and those who came to faith through their witness might live in unity in order that the world might come to believe in his own divine mission, *ut unum sint, ut mundus credat* (John 17:21–23). Mott chaired the world missionary conference at Edinburgh in 1910, from which the modern ecumenical movement is conventionally reckoned to date. From 'Edinburgh 1910' sprang both the International Missionary Council (1920) and the Faith and Order movement (first world conference at Lausanne in 1927) and thus, eventually, including also Life and Work interests, the World Council of Churches (inaugural assembly at Amsterdam in 1948, where Mott preached the opening sermon). For the second half of the twentieth century, the World Council of Churches (WCC) epitomized at global level the institutional form taken by the movements which Mott had served in the causes of Christian unity, and of peace and social justice, as well as evangelism and mission, while regional, national, and local 'councils of churches' emerged in roughly corresponding patterns – almost always with Methodist participation.[19]

Especially prominent in the administrative service rendered by Methodists to the WCC at the global level were three general secretaries: Philip A. Potter from the Caribbean (b. 1921, served 1972–1984); Emilio Castro from Uruguay (b. 1927, served 1985–1992); and Samuel Kobia from Kenya (b. 1947, general secretary 2004–2009). Major contributions to the theology of mission and evangelism were made by the Sri Lankan Daniel T. Niles (1908–1970), whose book, *Upon the Earth* (1962), merits special mention. On the faith and order side of things, the Briton Robert Newton Flew (1886–1962) importantly contributed to the study on 'the nature of the church' leading up to the Third World Conference on Faith and Order held at Lund in 1952[20]; and the American Albert C. Outler (1908–1989) helped shape the study on 'Scripture, Tradition, and traditions' at the Fourth World Conference held at Montreal in

1963 which set the hermeneutical parameters for future work in faith and order. At the meeting of the Faith and Order Commission at Lima, Peru, in 1982, Geoffrey Wainwright guided the final formulation of *Baptism, Eucharist and Ministry* (BEM). Having been several decades in the making, and profiting also from the ecumenically oriented 'liturgical movement' of the twentieth century, the BEM document registered and promoted 'convergences' among the churches on its three topics and finally received responses from around 200 denominational churches worldwide, including a most positive evaluation by the Council of Bishops of the United Methodist Church.[21]

One very encouraging outcome from BEM occurred in April 2007. At a service in Magdeburg cathedral, the Evangelisch-methodistische Kirche was among the eleven bodies that declared and enacted the mutual recognition of baptism; the other signatories included the Roman Catholic Bishops' Conference of Germany, the main Protestant bodies (except Baptist), and quite remarkably, the Orthodox Church, and the Ethiopian and Armenian Churches in Germany. The agreed statement on 'Christian Baptism' affirmed:

> Jesus Christ is our salvation. Through him God has overcome the sinner's distance from God (Romans 5:10), in order to make us sons and daughters of God. As participation in the mystery of Christ's death and resurrection, baptism means new birth into Christ. Whoever receives this sacrament and in faith affirms God's love is united with Christ and also with Christ's people from every time and place. As a sign of the unity of all Christians, baptism binds us to Jesus Christ, the foundation of this unity. Despite our different understandings of the Church, we share a basic common understanding of baptism.
>
> Therefore we recognize every baptism performed in accordance with Jesus' command in the name of the Father and the Son and Holy Spirit through the sign of immersion in water or affusion with water, and we rejoice over every person who is baptized. The mutual recognition of baptism is an expression of the bond of unity that is grounded in Jesus Christ (Ephesians 4:4–6). Baptism thus performed is unique and unrepeatable.
>
> We confess with the Lima Document: 'Our one baptism into Christ is a call to the churches to overcome their divisions and visibly manifest their fellowship' (*Baptism, Eucharist and Ministry*, B6).

In fact, 'different understandings of the Church' point to unavoidable questions of ecclesiology: what is the Church, what is the Church for, and where is the Church concretely to be found; what, ecumenically, are the necessary and sufficient conditions of its unity; what is the proper form of that unity.

Ecclesiologically, the World Council of Churches, while constitutionally a 'fellowship of churches,' has never required its members either to modify their own self-understanding or to 'recognize' fully the claims of others to churchly status. In the linguistic terminology of French, it is thus a 'conseil,' not a 'concile'; it has served the purposes of consultation and cooperation, but it could not of itself take doctrinal or institutional decisions that would bind the autonomous 'member churches.' As the formulation eventually ran, the WCC has been an instrument whereby the churches 'call one another to visible unity in one faith and in one Eucharistic fellowship, expressed in worship and common life in Christ, through witness and service to the world, and to advance towards that unity in order that the world may believe' (Harare assembly, 1998). The precise forms of the envisaged 'visible unity' have continued to be matters of debate, although the classic description remains that furnished by the WCC's New Delhi assembly in 1961:

> We believe that the unity we seek which is both God's will and his gift to his Church is being made visible as all in each place who are baptized into Jesus Christ and confess him as Lord and Saviour are brought by the Holy Spirit into one fully committed fellowship, holding the one apostolic faith, preaching the one Gospel, breaking the one bread, joining in common prayer, and having a corporate life reaching out in witness and service to all and who at the same time are united with the whole Christian fellowship in all places and all ages in such wise that ministry and members are accepted by all, and that all can act and speak together as occasion requires for the tasks to which God calls his people.

An emphasis on 'all in each place' has been characteristic of those churches or denominations that have favored the model of 'organic union' and have sought – sometimes successfully – to create 'united churches' in a geographically defined territory. To that phenomenon we now turn.

Church Unions
'Organic union' into 'united churches' was the pattern most favored – sometimes successfully, sometimes not – by Methodist and other ecumenists in the (British) Commonwealth. The explanation may lie in the fact that the English 'free churches' ('dissenters,' 'non-conformists') all had historic relationships, admittedly of varying kinds, with the Established Church of England; and even north of the border, the Church of Scotland, though Presbyterian in polity and Reformed in doctrine, figured in some ways as the social and cultural counterpart to the Church of England.[22]

The first such 'Commonwealth' case was the formation of the United Church of Canada in 1925, where a Methodism of mixed British and American origin entered into a new union with Congregationalists and (a majority of)

Presbyterians. Somewhat similarly in Australia, Methodists in the British tradition joined with Congregationalists and (a majority of) Presbyterians to constitute in 1977 the Uniting Church in that country. While the doctrinal bases of the Canadian and Australian churches were carefully framed in the classic tradition at their founding, the generally more 'liberal' complexion of those bodies as they have developed may not be unconnected with the absence of the more staunchly Calvinist of the Presbyterians (a point to which we shall return).

Meanwhile the Indian sub-continent was the scene of more complex unions involving Methodists and, this time, Anglicans (another point to which we shall have to return). Into the Church of South India (CSI) entered in 1947 the fruits of work by mission bodies originating in the Church of England, the Church of Scotland, the British and Australian Methodist Churches, and various Congregationalist boards. This union appeared to many worldwide as a shining example of multilateral ecumenism. In the area of worship in particular, the CSI had the opportunity to shape a liturgical life that would simultaneously bring together the best inheritances of the constituent traditions, begin to place Christian worship in the context of the local cultures, and put into practice the ideas that were being advocated in the broader liturgical movement for renewal and reform according to scriptural, patristic, and pastoral principles. The most significant and universally influential rite to be developed was the *Order for the Lord's Supper or the Holy Eucharist* (1950). Domestically, this CSI liturgy proved to be a unifying factor in the new church, and after half a century it was reported that 'there are few congregations where this is not the normal Sunday service for the eucharist.'[23] When organic union occurred in North India in 1970, the resultant Church of North India brought together not only Anglicans and Methodists (again those latter of the British and Australian traditions, though not the American) as well as Presbyterians and Congregationalists (from an earlier union), but also (quite remarkably) Baptists (of British origin), the Church of the Brethren in India, and the Disciples of Christ.

In the first half of the twentieth century in England, 'high' Wesleyan Methodists such as John Scott Lidgett (1854–1953) and Robert Newton Flew (1886–1962) had sought – despite tensions – to maintain or restore historic affinity with the Church of England.[24] In a 1946 Cambridge sermon, Dr. Geoffrey Fisher, then Archbishop of Canterbury, invited the 'Free Churches' to consider the possibility of a new structural relationship to the Church of England. After several preparatory steps and much discussion, a two-stage plan was proposed for Anglican–Methodist unity, whereby a thirty-year period of growing together through intercommunion would be followed by full organic union. The plan was approved by the Methodist Conference with practically an eighty percent majority, but was twice blocked – in 1969 and

1972 – by spoiling minorities in the assemblies of the Church of England. The main obstacle, a matter of controversy also in Methodism, was the method and understanding by which British Methodism would 'take episcopacy into its system,' that is, acquire a ministry recognized by the Church of England to be in the 'apostolic succession' it claims for itself. In 1982 a proposed 'covenant' – this time including also the United Reformed Church and the Moravian Church – broke down on largely similar grounds; the same issue imposes restrictions also on the covenant that the Church of England and the Methodist Church finally signed in 2003, even though the two bodies had been collaborating in many 'local ecumenical projects/ partnerships' for several decades. A similar covenantal relationship had been established between the Anglican and Methodist Churches in Ireland a year earlier.

The positive concept of hitherto distinct denominations of differing confessional traditions 'merging' (as the term went) to form a structurally united church had had its supporters in the USA around the middle of the twentieth century. Dating from 1962, the Consultation on Church Union (COCU) – which included the principal Methodist and Presbyterian bodies as well as the Episcopal Church, the Disciples of Christ, and the United Church of Christ – achieved a remarkable agreed statement or 'consensus' on doctrine (1984–1985; revised 1995), but once again matters of polity hindered structural progress, even when the negotiating body came to renounce the aim of 'organizational' unity; thus, the denominational structures would continue in whatever might eventually result from the project reconstituted in 2002 as 'Churches Uniting in Christ.'

Meanwhile the United Methodist Church has entered into various bilateral relationships with other denominational churches in the USA, involving mutual admission to communion even while difficulties remain concerning interchangeabilty of ordained ministry. Thus, with the Episcopal Church, on a basis laid out in *Make Us One with Christ*, there exists since 2006 an agreement of 'interim Eucharistic sharing,' which requires in any 'joint celebration' the use of an 'authorized liturgy' in which 'an ordained United Methodist elder or bishop and an ordained Episcopal priest or bishop stand together at the Lord's Table.' Since 2009 the United Methodist Church enjoys with the Evangelical Lutheran Church in America, on the basis of *Confessing our Faith Together*, a relationship of 'full communion' which provides, under certain circumstances, for the 'interchangeability of ordained clergy.'

Bilateral Dialogues and Relations

It was the official entry, albeit belated, of the Roman Catholic Church into the twentieth-century ecumenical movement – with the conciliar authority of Vatican II's decree *Unitatis Redintegratio* (1964) – that shifted bilateral dialogue into eventual pre-eminence as the method of doctrinal rapprochement. The crucial move from the Roman side may well have been the recognition that other Christians, by virtue of baptism and faith in Christ, were put into 'a certain communion, albeit imperfect, with the Catholic Church,' and that their communities had been used by the Spirit of Christ as 'means of salvation' (*Unitatis Redintegratio*, 3). The Roman Catholic Church decided against membership in the WCC, although since 1968 it has regularly numbered a dozen theologians in the Faith and Order Commission, some of them playing a vital part in the BEM process. Rather, the Catholic Church invited the 'world confessional families' or 'Christian world communions' into dialogue with itself; and these bodies, themselves of various kinds, generally considered it would be important to treat with the world's largest ecclesial community those matters that had been in contention between themselves respectively and it. The bilateral pattern also gained ground between the other bodies, and we shall look, in turn, at how Methodists (through the WMC) have engaged with Anglicans, with the Reformed, with Lutherans, and finally with the Roman Catholic Church.[25]

Methodists and Anglicans
In 1996, an Anglican-Methodist International Commission, in *Sharing in the Apostolic Communion*, was able to formulate an 'agreement in the core of doctrine':

> We believe in God the eternal and undivided Trinity, Father, Son and Holy Spirit; in the work of God as Creator of all that is; in the saving work of our Lord Jesus Christ, true God and truly human; in the sanctifying and liberating work of the Holy Spirit. We recognize the fallenness of humankind and the need for redemption. We believe in the sufficiency of Christ's redemptive work; justification by grace through faith; the Church as the Body of Christ; the sacraments of baptism and the Lord's supper as instituted by Christ; the final judgment; and the hope of eternal life in God's kingdom.

The Commission then proposed that, 'as the basis for growth into fuller communion between Anglicans and Methodists,' the WMC and the Lambeth Conference should 'affirm and recognize' that:

> both Anglicans and Methodists belong to the one, holy, catholic and apostolic Church of Jesus Christ and participate in the apostolic mission of the whole people of God;
> in the churches of our two communions the word of God is authentically preached and the sacraments instituted by Christ are duly administered;
> our churches share in the common confession and heritage of the apostolic faith.

While the WMC, meeting in Rio de Janeiro in 1996, expressed its willingness to join in preparation for such a step, the Anglican bishops at their Lambeth Conference in 1998 were not ready to move toward such a formal 'recognition' of Methodism. The principal obstacle appears to have been the lack by Methodists of historic ministerial succession as understood and claimed by Anglicans.[26]

Methodists and Reformed
Another example from the numerous international bilateral dialogues of the second half of the twentieth century – illustrating another view of the relation between doctrinal agreement and ecclesiology – is provided by that between the WMC and the World Alliance of Reformed Churches. The report *Together in God's Grace* (1987) noted that 'in many places in the world, churches in our two traditions have already entered into close relationship, including both federal and organic unions' (cases in point are Canada, Australia, Zambia, Belgium, and – with Anglicans among other partners – South India and North India). Doctrinally, it was recognized that 'grace has been a principal emphasis in both our traditions': 'From first to last our salvation depends on the comprehensiveness of God's grace as prevenient, as justifying, as sanctifying, as glorifying.' Nevertheless, 'in seeking to preserve this primary truth, our traditions have tended to give different accounts of the appropriation of saving grace, emphasizing on the one [Calvinist] hand God's sovereignty in election, and on the other [Wesleyan], the freedom of human response.' After rehearsing – and even creatively rephrasing – the debate, the report concludes that 'both traditions have gone wrong when they have claimed to know too much about [the] mystery of God's electing grace and of human response.' While 'Wesley and Calvin advocated conflicting ways of holding together what they affirm in common,' their differences 'should not constitute a barrier between our traditions,' but rather be regarded as 'mutually corrective and enriching.' Not only were the earlier twentieth-century unions 'entered after due doctrinal discussions,' but 'there is sufficient agreement in doctrine and practice between our two positions to justify such answers to the Lord's call to unity for the sake of mission and our common praise of God.' Moreover, 'under present conditions, both traditions are increasingly benefiting from our common appropriation of new insights into the gospel granted through theological teaching in this century, through common worship and witness, and through our participation in the wider ecumenical movement.'

Methodists and Lutherans
A dialogue took place between the WMC and the Lutheran World Federation from 1977 until 1984, when it issued in a final report entitled *The Church: Community of Grace*. While recognizing that some topics merited further

exploration (divine providence; the 'two kingdoms'; some aspects of theological anthropology; forms of unity), the Joint Commission concluded that there was sufficient agreement on the authority of the Scriptures, salvation by grace through faith, the Church, the means of grace (Word and sacraments), and mission (evangelization and ethics) for it to be able to recommend the sponsoring churches not only to engage in 'common efforts of witness and service in the world' but also to 'take steps to declare and establish full fellowship of word and sacrament.' This latter step was then achieved in West Germany (1987), East Germany (1990), Austria (1991), Sweden (1993), and Norway (1997).[27]

The international dialogue between Lutherans and Catholics, for its part, reached a highly significant moment with the official signing, at Augsburg on 31 October 1999, of a 'Joint Declaration on the Doctrine of Justification.' In response to a congratulatory message from the WMC, the Lutheran World Federation and the Pontifical Council for Promoting Christian Unity invited Methodists to explore a process by which they, too, could become associated with the achievement so far and the work still to accomplish. A Methodist Statement of Association was formulated, which received approval from the autonomous member churches of the WMC. It expressed gratitude particularly for the Trinitarian approach by which God's work in salvation is explained in the three key paragraphs of the 'Joint Declaration' (15–17). Methodists also affirmed what Roman Catholics and Lutherans now say together on seven historically controversial aspects of the doctrine of justification and considered the 'remaining differences of language, theological elaboration and emphasis' as insufficient cause for division between either party and Methodists. Lutherans and Catholics agreed in turn that Methodism's own 'distinctive profile' on these matters should not be seen as impairing the basic consensus. On the occasion of the meeting of the WMC at Seoul, Korea, in 2006, the solemn signing of an Official Common Affirmation committed the three parties to strive together for the deepening of their common understanding of justification in theological study, teaching, and preaching – and this as part of their pursuit of the full communion and common witness to the world which is the will of Christ for all Christians.[28]

Methodists and Catholics
Ever since the official entry of the Roman Catholic Church into the ecumenical movement with the Second Vatican Council, doctrinal and theological dialogues have been taking place between Methodists and Catholics at the local, regional, and global levels. That the international dialogue takes place between 'the (Roman) Catholic Church' (hereafter RCC) and 'the World Methodist Council' (WMC), points again to what we have seen to be the fundamental issue for ecumenism, namely ecclesiology. The RCC and the WMC

are two different kinds of entity. Simply put: on the one hand, the Roman Catholic Church, according to the Second Vatican Council, understands that the Church *subsists in* the Catholic Church, and is governed by the successor of Peter and by the bishops in communion with him. On the other hand, Methodists are said to 'form a family of churches' which 'claim and cherish [their] true place in the one holy, catholic and apostolic church.' Thus, the RCC makes a close identification of itself with 'the one Church of Jesus Christ,' while Methodism has never had more than a 'denominational' view of itself – though claiming to be 'part of' – 'the Holy Catholic Church,' 'the Church Universal,' 'the Body of Christ' (and committed, since the earliest days of the modern ecumenical movement, to the cause of Christian unity). The crucial questions for the dialogue will, then, concern the sense and ways in which each partner can (come to) recognize the churchly character of the other.

The WMC had accepted the Catholic invitation to have observers present at the Second Vatican Council, and Methodists so attended all four sessions (1962–1965).[29] At its meeting in London in 1966 the WMC enthusiastically voted to accept the subsequent invitation to bilateral dialogue. Since then, the Joint Commission (now composed of eight members on each side) has met four times in each period of five years. Its reports are presented simultaneously to the Holy See (through the Pontifical Council for Promoting Christian Unity) and to the regular meetings of the WMC. At least informally, the reports have become known by the place and year of their presentation to the WMC: Denver (1971), Dublin (1976), Honolulu (1981), Nairobi (1986), Singapore (1991), Rio de Janeiro (1996), Brighton (2001), and Seoul (2006). The sponsoring bodies consider the reports, comment on them, and criticize them, authorize the continuation of the dialogue, and make suggestions for it; but they do not 'adopt' the reports as a doctrinal or practical basis for formal action between the churches.[30]

The first three reports reveal three basic characteristics: they sought a greater degree of mutual acquaintance; they attempted clarification on 'contemporary questions,' that is, secularization, spirituality, and new challenges to Christian life; and they manifested concern for doctrinal themes that were also being tackled in a variety of ecumenical discussions on the sacraments, ministry, and authority. As we shall see, the dialogue between Methodists and Roman Catholics has taken an increasingly sacramental approach toward ecclesiology, although the question of ordination remains delicate. The early reports did, however, lack thematic unity.

Greater thematic coherence started to be achieved in the third round of the dialogue. The Honolulu Report (1981) expounded in remarkably agreed terms – 'with one voice' (7) – the person and work of the Holy Spirit. The doctrinal agreement on the Holy Spirit was pursued into the realms of 'Christian experience' and drew present consequences from them for 'authority in the Church.' It is neatly said that 'the old oppositions of Scripture and Tradition have given way to an understanding which we share, that Scripture in witness to the living tradition from which it arose has a normative role for the total tradition of the Church as it lives and is guided still by the Spirit of Truth' (34). The general pneumatological thrust of the Honolulu Report was then integrated into deliberately and explicitly Trinitarian structures in all the subsequent reflection and writing of the Commission.

'Nairobi 1986' moved tentatively 'Towards a Statement on the Church', treating notably 'the nature of the Church' and reflecting on 'ways of being one Church' (what others called 'models of unity').[31] While recognizing that any ecclesiology 'shaped in a time of division' is unlikely to be entirely satisfactory (22), the report showed interest in an analogy between Wesley's Methodist movement and the rise of 'religious orders, characterized by special forms of life and prayer, work, evangelization, and their own internal organization' – such that, within the Roman Catholic Church, 'the different religious orders, while fully in communion with the Pope and the bishops, relate in different ways to the authority of Pope and bishops.' A hint of broader ecumenical relevance may be contained in the conclusion that 'such relative autonomy has a recognized place within the unity of the Church' (24 b).[32] The Nairobi report even broached the question of 'the Petrine office,' with Methodists considering it 'not inconceivable that at some future date in a restored unity, Roman Catholic and Methodist bishops might be linked in one episcopal college, and that the whole body would recognize some kind of effective leadership and primacy in the bishop of Rome' (62). Meanwhile Catholics and Methodists were 'agreed on the need for an authoritative way of being sure, beyond doubt, concerning God's action insofar as it is crucial for our salvation' (75). Certainly, the Nairobi report designated 'full communion in faith, mission and sacramental life' as the goal for Methodists and Catholics together, and that has remained the case.

It was realized that doctrinal progress would depend on fundamental theological reflection. The next three rounds of the dialogue were devoted precisely to 'The Apostolic Tradition' (Singapore 1991), 'The Word of Life: A Statement on Revelation and Faith' (Rio de Janeiro 1996; cf. 1 John 1:1–3), and 'Speaking the Truth in Love: Teaching Authority among Catholics and Methodists' (Brighton 2001; cf. Ephesians 4:15). These years saw an intense and profound 'exchange of ideas' in a 'dialogue of truth' sustained by an increasing mutual affection between the partners. The level of confidence was now such as to justify a return to the direct theme of ecclesiology. Particularly striking has been the development of a sacramental understanding of the Church. Under the title, 'The Grace Given You in Christ' (cf. 1 Corinthians 1:4), the Seoul report of 2006 declared that in the Church 'the invisible and the visible come together, and the former is made known through the latter. This holding together of the invisible and the visible is essential to our understanding of the Church as Catholics and Methodists. It is rooted in Christ himself, the invisible Word made visible in the flesh, fully divine and fully human' (48; cf. 102). The time had now come, the Joint Commission declared, 'to look one another in the eye, and with love and esteem to acknowledge what we see to be truly of Christ and the Gospel, and thereby *of the Church*, in one another.' The aim of the dialogue partners is to identify 'those elements and endowments that they could [each] suitably receive from, and give to, the other' – and all 'in the service of Christ in the world' (97). Some practical suggestions are made for 'concrete gestures that enter hearts and stir consciences' such as Pope Benedict XVI has declared necessary for ecumenical progress (139).[33]

Whither Now?

The modern ecumenical movement, after a century, faces a task that is still, and perhaps permanently, unfinished. How are Christians and their communities more visibly to embody reconciliation within and among themselves in order to be more credible ambassadors for the God who, in Christ, has reconciled the world to himself (cf. 2 Corinthians 5:17–6:2)? How can they more fully open themselves to the 'Spirit of faith' so that, as they speak out, the grace of God may reach to more and more people and the chorus of thanksgiving increase, and all to God's glory (cf. 2 Corinthians 4:13–15)?

For Methodists the domestic question is that of the structures and instruments that will allow them to maintain and extend in their life and witness what the WMC, meeting at Rio de Janeiro in 1996, discerned as 'Wesleyan essentials of Christian faith':

> Our beliefs: we affirm a vision of the Christian faith, truly evangelical, catholic and reformed, rooted in grace and active in the world. . . .

> Our worship: we worship and give allegiance to the Triune God; we respond in gratitude and praise for God's mighty acts in creation, in history, in our communities, and in our personal lives. . . .

> Our witness: we proclaim Jesus Christ to the world through word, deed and sign. . . .

> Our service: we serve the world in the name of God, believing that our commitment comes to life in our actions, through the power of the Holy Spirit. . . .

Our common life: we share a commitment to Jesus Christ that manifests itself in a common heart and life, binding believers together in a common fellowship and anticipating solidarity within the human family....[34]

Across the full range of ecumenism, Methodists must continue as willing participants in the 'patient and fraternal dialogue' to which Pope John Paul II, in his ecumenical encyclical *Ut Unum Sint* (1996), invited the leaders of other churches and their theologians – in 'the real but imperfect communion existing between us' – as to how the see of Rome might best exercise its claimed and offered 'universal ministry of unity' in historically changing conditions. As the Pope himself said, it will need to be both a dialogue of truth and a dialogue of love, in which there will take place an exchange of gifts as well as an exchange of ideas. A Methodist might even suggest for its agenda the questions that John Wesley, after prayer, treated with the preachers at their very first conference: 'what to teach; how to teach; and what to do, that is how to regulate our doctrine, discipline, and practice.'[35]

For Further Reading

David Carter. *Love Bade Me Welcome: A British Methodist Perspective on the Church*. London: Epworth, 2002.

David M. Chapman. *In Search of the Catholic Spirit: Methodists and Roman Catholics in Dialogue*. Peterborough: Epworth, 2004.

Geoffrey Wainwright. *The Ecumenical Moment: Crisis and Opportunity for the Church*. Grand Rapids, MI: Eerdmans, 1983.

Geoffrey Wainwright. *Methodists in Dialogue*. Nashville, TN: Abingdon/Kingswood, 1995.

20 Methodism and Its Images

Peter Forsaith

'Graven Images'

The Abrahamic religions, and Protestant Christianity in particular, have often been cautious about encouraging the spread of images. The prohibition of the second commandment conveys a continuing fear that the faithful might drink at the mirage, and so be led from truth to falsehood.

Nevertheless, or perhaps because of that caveat, Christendom has evolved a strong artistic tradition whose highlights are not only Ravenna and the Renaissance but embraces the Eastern church and the twentieth-century global ecclesia. Rome remains its epicenter, but while Italian painters and their followers composed biblical scenes, post-Reformation Dutch artists depicted landscapes with huge skies and dark earth, Calvinist visions of the vast majesty of God against the murk of human habitation, punctuated by steeples in the skyline pointing the way to heaven.[1]

So, along with architecture and music, pictures became iconic vehicles for the articulation of the Christian message. The primitive 'chi-rho' symbols in the catacombs, mosaic and fresco decorations in early basilicas, and medieval mural paintings and stained glass were the media of a pre-literate age. Pope Gregory the Great's aphorism, 'Painting can do for the illiterate what writing does for those who read,'[2] carried substantial influence. The Reformation's emphasis on 'the Word' marginalized the image, driving it to a precursor of abstraction. Michelangelo's work is as much a commentary on the text as narrative in itself. Is his 'David' just a beautiful young man or a biblical character, or both? Interpretation is in the eye of the beholder, as much as, say, Dali's 'St. John of the Cross,' Munch's 'The Scream,' or even Caravaggio's 'St. John.'

We may ask whether such art is 'religious,' by which we usually mean, was (or is) the artist a person of faith, is the subject a religious subject, or is the work intended to convey a religious message, or appeal to a religious audience – sometimes all of those? Yet before the nineteenth century, and indeed in some cultures today, the notion of conceptual divisions familiar to Western thought is false. Sectors of human knowledge and interest which we separate were intrinsically holistic. Questions of intent in earlier works of art are non-questions.

The rise of Methodism in eighteenth-century Britain coincided with the 'golden age of the English portrait,'[3] the active careers of its two great luminaries, Sir Joshua Reynolds and Thomas Gainsborough, coinciding almost precisely with that of John Wesley.[4] Indeed, the two phenomena may not be unrelated, as will be suggested later. Yet Methodism has been far from renowned for either patronage or practice of the visual arts, and cultural prohibition has been more its reputation. Thus, a study of Methodism's relation to the fine arts is immediately hampered by a general sense that there is little to say, because little has ever been.

This chapter will endeavor to reach beyond problematic boundaries, and much of it will be spent narrating something of the undercurrents of artistic activity which have persisted in Methodism, though sometimes running deep below the surface. The focus will be on Methodism in Britain partly because this has been this author's area of research, partly because Britain was Methodism's motherland.

It will endeavor to place the Methodist movement in its wider cultural context, and also engage briefly with the theology of esthetics before concluding with some suggestions for further directions and methodology for the topic.

Grace and Space: The Overall Cultural Context of Methodism

Religious movements do not exist in isolation, but a cultural context: it is not just about beliefs and belonging. The experience of what it is to be Methodist engages many senses including the visual. So the arts should be considered in the totality generally associated with Methodism, especially music and architecture. In sketching very briefly something of the development of these areas, a corresponding timeline for the inter-relation of Methodism and art emerges which will apply to later sections.

'Methodism was born in song.'[5] The exquisite religious verse of Charles Wesley, a major literary achievement, together with other compositions, formed the foundation for a dominant musical culture which has typified the movement. Global Methodism has developed in myriad ways, yet its sounds remain its most characteristic feature.

Communal hymnody, a radical departure for the eighteenth-century church, was at the heart of Methodism's early life and probably spread its doctrine as much as sermons. As denominations developed, so did a choral tradition in which performance can subsume participation. Similarly, there may be a tension between spectacle and engagement in an internalized dialogue with works of art.

The design, decoration, and furnishing of its buildings, its three-dimensional face, are arguably its most obvious visual property. While no single architectural style has become characteristic, a trend commensurate with its liturgical diversity, a brief glimpse of architectural history illustrates some areas of commonality.

The first Methodist preaching houses in Britain were basic buildings, though not without an elegance of proportion and detail typical of the eighteenth century. The earliest purpose-built New Room in Bristol (1739, enlarged 1748, and which survives) has a classical simplicity and severity which remains its charm and might be associated with assembly rooms or the theater.[6] Wesley laid down some clear guidelines for both form and function.[7]

Its octagonal 'light,' an overhead multiple window possibly designed to avoid window tax,[8] prefigured Wesley's preference for octagonal designs. Octagons had been used by architects such as Hawksmoor, with a classical reference to the 'Temple of the Winds' in ancient Athens. Wesley was impressed by the Dissenters' octagon in Norwich (1756) as, 'elegant ... and in the highest taste'[9] and a number of octagonal preaching places were built, facilitating an egalitarian layout as well as good acoustics.[10]

Yet in 1778/1779, for the New Chapel in London to replace an adapted munitions factory (the Foundery) he had leased for his metropolitan headquarters since 1739, Wesley reverted to a rectangular 'preaching box.' One notable feature, replicated in a few other locations,[11] was the placing of the communion table in an apse (originally a pagan device to contain the blood or smoke of sacrifice) to the rear of a central pulpit.

Neoclassicism which, in its various languages, governed most building design well into the nineteenth century was largely swept away by the Gothic on the skirts of the Oxford movement in the 1830s and 1840s. Pugin vehemently argued that the classical was pagan, the Gothic truly Christian as it harked back to the medieval.[12] In reality, Gothic owes much to Islamic buildings, but became the architectural language of Europe's medieval cathedrals and abbeys. F. J. Jobson's *Chapel and School Architecture* (1850) swung the Methodists into the ecclesiastical fashion parade.

The worldwide spread of missions in the nineteenth century ensured the global dissemination of both Gothic and Classical architectural styles. The Gibbseian portico with forward spire proved particularly popular in the USA. Methodism's often hybrid architectural preferences have proved resistant to later styles, even in the later twentieth century, new buildings still reflected traditional forms. Frank Lloyd Wright's 'Annie Pfeiffer Chapel' at Florida Southern College is a notable exception.

If stylistic analyses of Methodism's architectural appearance is a largely unexplored field, so are the internal design and workings of Methodist buildings. While there are treatments of Methodist worship, they are largely liturgical studies and rarely pay attention to the layout and furnishing of the buildings in which the services happened. This is hardly surprising; it has already been seen that there is no clear outward architectural style which identifies Methodist buildings, so internally the tradition is diverse.

Cracknell and White note the conflicting tensions in the nineteenth century between revivalism and upwardly mobile respectability, the tension between a movement and a denominational tradition. Each had their architectural needs and buildings were often a compromise, incorporating a formal sanctuary in which 'mahogany Methodism' could 'worship the Lord in the beauty of holiness,' but also contained multipurpose spaces for a variety of communal meetings or education. The flexibility of the latter could be emphasized with an 'Akron Plan' folding screen.[13]

But how were such spaces decorated? Wesley made clear his preference for plainness in most things, and there is a general tendency for Methodist buildings to be – in principle – unadorned. Yet what was often designed as plain later became embellished, particularly by memorials to the deceased. Leading members of congregations (often benefactors), ministers, or military were commemorated by stained glass, wall plaques, or furnishings, often with scant regard for the original design objectives of the space. Beautification was in the eye of the beholder. The walls of Dance's straightforward preaching box at City Road, London, became cluttered with memorials to the great and the good, clear glass replaced with commemorative color. Another plain and elegant Georgian chapel was modified a century later with a complex monumental alabaster pulpit and screens, featuring a profile bust of John Wesley at its center.[14]

Images of the Founder

As in Christianity images of the Christ have predominated, in Methodism likenesses of John Wesley became an iconic preoccupation even during his own lifetime. Posthumously, the evolution of the Wesley image followed some of the tides of artistic fashion and its significance within the denomination has also ebbed and flowed. The middle years of the nineteenth century, for instance, fraught with external challenges, intra-Methodist factionalism, and strong numerical growth, saw an upsurge in scene paintings depicting the founder.

The main initial phase of Methodism's development, from about the 1730s to the close of the eighteenth century, coincided with the most productive period of the 'English school' of portraiture. Indeed, the two can be seen as culturally and conceptually linked to post-Enlightenment developments around the emergence of understandings of the individual 'self.' In art, this was articulated by the dominance of the portrait for the remainder of the century. Representation of the human likeness is perhaps the most enduring artistic form, and as a fashion it has been popular in Britain for generations – in no small way aided by Van Dyke's sumptuous pictures – although largely an elite preoccupation. The eighteenth century, with Britain's commercial growth, saw this percolate down the social scale.

At the same time ideas of personal, over against corporate, human nature gained currency through writings such as those of Hume. The portrait can be considered an artistic embodiment of this while Methodism represented a personalization of religious experience typified by conversion and deathbed narratives.[15] Charles Wesley, whose hymnody was generally worded in the first person, was particularly keen on collecting such narratives.

During John Wesley's lifetime a number of portraits were made of him, by leading as well as homespun artists, reflecting both changes of artistic fashion as well as varying perspectives of Wesley's status. The first authenticated portrait, by J. M. Williams (c.1742),[16] shows Wesley as a Church of England clergyman, robed and holding a Bible or prayer book, with a background of books. Its implications are evident; Wesley was a staunch Anglican clergyman and an academic, his cloth and his books represent his character. Its marked similarity to a portrait of the establishment Bishop Compton of London (1632–1713) may or may not be coincidental.

Yet in the earliest phase of the Evangelical Revival, Wesley was flouting canon law by preaching out-of-doors and without the permission of parish incumbents, as well as propounding 'enthusiastic' doctrines described by Bishop Butler as 'a very horrid thing.' Further, he had abandoned his Oxford responsibilities, preferring the company of 'plain folk' – working people. In short, he was coming to be viewed as forsaking his church and his education and as something of a rebel. This portrait, which Wesley used for decades afterwards, conveyed a message of reassuring conformity. Wesley's resourceful preacher, John Downes (1722–1774), engraved it as a frontispiece to Wesley's *Explanatory Notes upon the New Testament*.[17]

While an actual painted canvas was seen by few, printed engravings were widely circulated. In the eighteenth century, particularly in London, there was a massive and popular print culture.[18] 'Grangerised' albums could be loaned from print shops, and the print shop window served as a kind of public gallery for likenesses of people of note or notoriety. By late eighteenth century, individual prints were bought and displayed in homes by the rising middling sorts, the kind of people who were forming the core of Methodism. From its inception in 1778 the monthly *Arminian Magazine* carried a frontispiece print (usually) of a leading Methodist preacher. These prints were often cut out and framed, or mounted in albums. It is said that in the nineteenth century, the three most popular images found in British homes were Queen Victoria, the Duke of Wellington, and John Wesley.

By the mid-1760s the initial outburst of revivalist fervor was wearing off, more Methodist chapels were starting to be built, and open air evangelism declining. Nathaniel Hone (1766)[19] depicted Wesley in preaching pose out of doors (although this would have been a studio pose against an imagined background). Its implications suggest that outdoor preaching should be normative for Wesley's followers. Although the evidence is scant, it seems as though Wesley was aware of the influence of his image and used it deliberately. The portrait, which now hangs in the National Portrait Gallery, London, was engraved as a frontispiece for Wesley's *Explanatory Notes upon the Old Testament*.[20]

If Sir Joshua Reynolds ever painted a portrait of Wesley it has not survived, although there have been putative claimants. Reynolds 'Sitters' book lists a 'Mr Westley' in March 1755;[21] Wesley's availability for such a sitting was possible. John Wesley twice referred to sitting for Reynolds;[22] in both instances Wesley was critical of Reynolds' slowness, and it is possible that the painting was left unfinished and the canvas later overpainted for reuse.

Two other leading London artists did paint Wesley: John Russell (1772) and George Romney (1789). Russell, who painted Charles Wesley and family, again depicted Wesley in outdoor preaching pose while Romney's straightforward head-and-shoulders pose shows a man in his later eighties still active and alert. The latter was much copied, but while the original has a vigor typical of the artist, copies and prints are more static and stately. Adam Clarke's wife (Mary Cooke) did not think this a 'striking likeness.'[23]

In 1781 a young potter named Enoch Wood modeled what was possibly the best likeness of Wesley: the bust sold many copies. Half a century later, Wood related how, on completion, Wesley asked 'whether it had not a more melancholy expression than he himself.' He therefore resumed his seat and in a few minutes Wood made appropriate adjustments. If evidence is needed that Wesley was concerned about his image, it is here.[24]

Romney's portrait and Wood's bust became controlling images of the founder, especially as they were used by the Methodist painter John Jackson for a portrait frontispiece for the 1827 edition of Wesley's hymns. This picture, although it was not considered a good likeness of Wesley – for one thing, the figure is too bulky – became the most popularly circulated, and influential, image of 'the Founder' through the nineteenth century and beyond.[25]

Images of Wesley on ceramic ware proliferated too. The epicenter of England's pottery industry, Staffordshire, was a Methodist heartland. Love feast cups, statuettes, busts, plates, and pastille burners carried Wesley's likeness, often with texts or other scenes. If the variety and interrelationship of Wesley images is a complex field, so is the world of commemorative 'Wesleyana.'[26]

The last decade of Wesley's life saw the emergence of a taste for profile likenesses, in part driven by the beginnings of phrenology, and ideas that the shape of the cranium indicated personality – a further development of the

Humeian identity of self. A leading proponent of the style was John Kay of Edinburgh, whose (syndicated?) print depicted Wesley with Joseph Cole and Dr. Hamilton in 1790,[27] but a number of other profiles survive including by Butterworth (the last image of Wesley known to have been taken 'from the life,' in Leeds) and, posthumously, by Edridge and Nasmyth – later used for a popular ceramic medallion by Wedgwood. There was also a print of the deceased Wesley 'lying in state,' by W. Ridley.

The same might be said of portraits of monarchs or gods; lifelikeness of the subject is not always the first priority for an iconic image. Early in the eighteenth century, Jonathan Richardson laid down that the portrait should represent the sitter at their best, a view which has hardly faded from fashion. It contrasts with Cromwell's 'warts and all' instruction to Lely.[28] In Wesley's own case, he chose a print for the first *Arminian Magazine* which, though he thought well of it, can hardly represent the man realistically or ideally. It seems a caricature. Similarly, Wesley thought Hamilton's stilted 1788 portrait 'the best that was ever taken.'[29] Wesley's esthetic shortcomings are further noted below.

The London publisher Robert Sayer's[30] posthumous print depicting Wesley's heavenward apotheosis probably mocks Wesley rather than praises him. Sayer issued several hundred such humorous prints, or 'drolls'; in an age of caricature there was often a deliberate ambiguity around seriousness or satire.

For a half-century after his death few new images appeared, besides John Jackson's portrait and a scene painting of Wesley preaching in Ireland by Maria Spilsbury-Taylor. The scene painting, depicting an incident from life or history (so also called 'history paintings'), was an increasingly popular genre from mid-eighteenth century. H. Perlee Parker's 1840, 'A brand plucked as from the burning,' depicting the 1709 fire at Epworth Rectory was the first of a number of 'scene paintings' over the next twenty years.[31]

The verisimilitude of a scene painting matters less than the message it is intended to convey; indeed, in Victorian times the moral message of the picture was its primary purpose. So, while aspects of Parker's picture exhibit artistic license, these are more pronounced with Marshall Claxton's 'Holy Triumph' of Wesley's death. Claxton included those who visited Wesley in his final hours in a spacious scene which does not reflect the small bedroom in his City Road home where Wesley died. Visitors to the house sometimes ask how all those people could have squeezed into that room; it is not principally a realistic depiction, but a visualized deathbed representation of Wesley's immortal apotheosis.

A popular Wesley scene was his preaching from his father's tomb in Epworth churchyard. There are at least three painted versions of this, as well as a number of variant prints.[32] Presenting the artist with elements of a ready composition – the subject active and elevated, a passive crowd, architectural detail, and a rural backdrop – the scene also has symbolic overtones. Standing on his father's tomb Wesley is ambiguously positioned both in respect to his parental heritage and to the Established Church, dutiful son and rebellious child together.

Perhaps the most flagrantly unrealistic scene is that by William Geller of Wesley preaching to twenty-five thousand in Gwennap Pit, Cornwall (1845). Wesley preached in this large hollow in the ground, probably caused by mining subsidence, from 1762. This picture, however, relates more to a popular apocalyptic work by John Martin, 'Joshua commanding the sun to stand still over Gibeon,' than to the West Cornish landscape. Geller had engraved Martin's picture, and the print, with its dire message of divine destructive force, became popular. In his Gwennap Pit picture, Geller construed Wesley as an Old Testament patriarch, replete with dramatized power.

By the later nineteenth century, scene paintings of Wesley were showing closer attention to realistic detail and more of the human, as opposed to heroic, side of the man. Faed (1877) and Bayes (c.1900) showed him with women, a theme to engage scholars a century further on. Lewes (c.1889) painted him meeting George Whitefield in Oxford, while Hatherell (1906), in a powerful monochrome composition, had him preaching at a market cross.[33] Prints of this were used by the Bovril Company for a promotional campaign, perhaps implying the efficacy of beef extract for longevity, health, and achievement, although Wesley was frugal with his diet and vegetarian for part of his life.

William Titcomb, to whose art we shall return, produced two pictures of John Wesley preaching in Bristol, although only one is known to have been worked up into a full-size canvas (1918).[34] In 1788, Wesley preached before the Lord Mayor and Corporation of Bristol, then the second city (and port) of Britain and a center of the slave trade. In dealing with the biblical text of Dives and Lazarus, Wesley preached against slavery.[35] A detail of the picture is the Lord Mayor's black servant peering around his master's ceremonial chair in astonishment.

Intriguingly, while Wesley is often popularly thought of today as on horseback, equestrian images are few and late. None exist before the twentieth century, when the horse was becoming less an everyday mode of transport. Several equestrian statues exist.[36]

So the image of the denominational founder, which has become iconic for the movement, can be shown to have moved through a series of stages in its development and styles in its use. Further, it does not straightforwardly depict the person any more than a head of state on a coin or banknote. Wesley's likeness has so come to typify global denominational identity, it might be fair to ask: is not this a brand?

Pictures of Methodism

Visual depictions of Methodism – before the age of the photograph – are few. Early Methodists were persecuted and despised; their meetings rarely had a public face. A print of Wesley and 446 of his preachers in the new chapel at City Road, London, in 1779 is synthesized and dates from 1822. Fletcher of Madeley, positioned beside the Wesleys, was actually in Switzerland in 1779, and likenesses of the preachers are culled from prints. This is a symbolic scene.

Some contemporary depictions do exist, such as a 1750 print of 'Methodist Preaching at Upper Moorfields' or of George Whitefield's preaching at Leeds in 1749.[37] Philip de Loutherbourg, who apparently accompanied Gainsborough to chapel on Sundays, produced 'A Methodist Preacher' (1777), a rare, if not unique, contemporary painting of outdoor preaching. De Loutherbourg was Garrick's scenery painter and while his works have a realistic basis, they are dramatized and carefully composed. This scene, with its expanse of sky and careful groupings, reflects continental artistic style as de Loutherbourg had trained in Germany and Paris.[38]

De Loutherbourg's realism is tempered by its satirical overtones, which deserve fuller investigation; the preacher is addressing a handful of hearers, while various others stand around to be entertained. It is thus linked to satirical prints of Methodist preaching (which were more numerous), such as Hogarth's 'Enthusiasm Delineated' (and, later, 'Credulity, Superstition and Fanaticism'),[39] as well as the Methodist preacher on the hangman's cart in 'The Idle 'Prentice Executed at Tyburn.' Intriguingly, in the de Loutherbourg picture the preacher's head was later overpainted to appear as Wesley. A traveling pulpit, shown in both the 1750 print and by de Loutherbourg, is similar to that used by Whitefield.[40]

The English caricaturist Thomas Rowlandson (1756–1827) was influenced by de Loutherbourg. His undated satirical drawing 'Methodists filing out' shows a congregation emerging from service. The gowned preacher and elegant chapel (possibly in London) suggest a broader 'Methodist' than Wesley's connexion. In fact most satirical images of Methodist preaching were aimed at George Whitefield and Calvinists. Typical of Rowlandson's amusing caricatures, such works can be significantly informative about the kind of location, crowd, and style of 'Methodist' preaching; the vast crowds of hearers may not have been so vast, nor the faithful or potentially faithful so attentive to preacher or message.

Few, if any, images of Methodist life are known from the nineteenth century, until, among the 'Newlyn School'[41] of artists at the end of the nineteenth century, W. H. Y. Titcomb depicted the religious life of the local people of West Cornwall alongside their work and leisure. An (Anglican) bishop's son, his 'Primitive Methodists at Prayer, St. Ives' (1889), depicts an adult congregation while 'A Mariner's Sunday School' (1891) shows the children. A domestic deathbed scene of an elderly Primitive Methodist woman, 'Piloting her home' (1893), completes the scope of public and private expressions of Methodism. Whether 'The Sunday School Treat' (no date), one of his finest works, depicts Methodists or Anglicans is unclear, it nevertheless illustrates how children were rewarded or encouraged.[42]

The boundary between photography and art is disputed territory. Most photography would hardly claim to be 'art' yet some photographs, and the work of particular photographers, clearly is highly artistic. John Righton, who trained first as a Methodist teacher, photographed Methodist places and scenes and produced postcards for the denomination.[43] Methodism's principal national newspaper from 1861, the *Methodist Recorder*, is not obviously a cultural repository. However, its chief photographer from the 1930s, Edward Tattersall, brought fine artistic, sometimes inspirational, quality to his work.

Methodist Artists

Some artists have been Methodists; some Methodists have been artists. There is a necessary distinction between artists whose Methodism was (or seems) incidental to their practice and those whose faith was the engine which drove their work and life. Yet such a distinction is not absolute and clear. Many artists with Methodist allegiances can be found on a spectrum, a spectrum which can shift with time.

Take, for instance, the successful eighteenth-century portraitist John Russell (1745–1806), although a friend of Charles Wesley he was more closely associated with the Calvinistic side of Methodism – Lady Huntingdon, the Hill brothers, and their circles. While his portrait practice was essentially commercial, and his 'crayons' (pastels) works command good prices today, he had other strings to his bow. His 'fancy pieces,' often moralizing pictures of childhood innocence, are a form of evangelical message.

But more directly related to his beliefs was his interest in, if not obsession with, the moon.[44] Natural philosophy grew out of the evangelical movement, inquiry into the wonder of the divine order in creation. For Russell, the moon was a parable of the church reflecting the light of God to the world; his scientific inquiry had a religious meaning and his lunar pictures were, in effect, portraits of the face of God. The interaction of art and Methodist belief is not straightforward.

Some artists rejected their Methodism; some Methodists rejected their art. In the opening years of the nineteenth century, evangelical attitudes toward cultural pursuits, such as art, music, or theatre, began to harden. Russell's son William was a promising painter who exhibited at the Royal Academy

(1805–1809), but then jettisoned his painting as he believed it contradicted his religion. He became a clergyman. The early nineteenth century painter of nudes William Etty (1787–1849)[45] was raised a Methodist, but abandoned it to pursue his art – as, a century and a half later, did David Hockney (b.1937).[46] Sir Stanley Spencer (1891–1959) had roots in Methodism and while many of his works were religious in theme, his personal beliefs (and lifestyle) seem at least heterodox.[47]

In the USA, the 'foremost portrait painter of his time' John Wesley Jarvis (c.1781–1839) was reputedly Wesley's great-nephew, but hardly noted for a Methodist lifestyle.[48] His contemporary, John Paradise (1783–1833), while more limited in his artistic ability was popular for portraits of Methodist preachers of his time and is now perhaps best known for his 1812 portrait of Francis Asbury.[49]

It is well-nigh impossible to write on Methodism and art without writing of R. A. John Jackson (1778–1831). He has already been mentioned as the painter of the 1827 portrait of Wesley which became the predominant image of 'the founder' during the nineteenth century and after; its spread as a print was global. Although he commenced as a miniaturist in his native Yorkshire, by 1804 he was painting portraits in London and exhibiting at the Royal Academy. His prolific work is a catalogue of the elite of late Georgian England: title and position. He was also a skilled copyist.

Yet, he was not an artist of the first standing. His portraits lack the originality, flair, and technical skill of Reynolds (whom he much admired) or contemporaries such as Lawrence or Raeburn. His work tends to be formulaic and stilted. Perhaps his prodigious output was driven by a dread of debt; like many artists his lifestyle hardly matched his income and after his early death his colleagues collected to support his family. He was thought well of, and John Constable is recorded as paying tribute to Jackson's Christian qualities.[50]

Jackson was a loyal Wesleyan. As well as the synthesized portrait of Wesley and a similar of Fletcher of Madeley, he served the Connexion by providing images of many of its leaders for the engraved prints which fronted each monthly issue of the *Wesleyan Methodist Magazine*, some, but by no means all, of which were worked up as painted canvases. Thus, by having a successful professional career, but also putting his art at the service of the church he became something of the epitome of a Methodist artist.

Jackson's portrait of Wesley was engraved in the USA by a Methodist, James Barton Longacre (1794–1869). Longacre's chief, numismatic, fame rests on his designs for US coinage; he was Chief Engraver to the Mint from 1844. His career was as an engraver and he is noted for publishing *The National Portrait Gallery of Distinguished Americans*.[51] His son, Andrew, was a minister in Paris in the 1860s, and also a competent amateur artist.[52]

John Jackson was active during the culturally fluid era around the Regency. The careers of two later Methodist artists who were contemporaries serve to illustrate some tensions during the nineteenth century. James Clarke Hook (1819–1907) and James Smetham (1821–1889) were both Wesleyan Methodists and both career artists based in London. If they ever met each other it is not recorded and their lives followed contrasting trajectories.

Hook was the grandson of the Methodist minister and polymath Adam Clarke, probably the most talented Wesleyan of his time. Clarke was a gifted linguist, speaking some twenty languages, specializing in Middle-Eastern and Oriental tongues; he edited a substantial tranche of historic state papers and wrote an eight-volume Bible commentary – as well as being a career Methodist minister and three times President of Conference.

James Hook was proud of his grandfather, and in ways modeled his life on him. He was a lifelong Methodist, a (lay) preacher and committed socialist. As an artist, he studied at the Royal Academy and was introduced to Constable by John Jackson. A traveling scholarship enabled him, with his fellow-artist wife, to spent two years in Italy where he was influenced by Venetian painting. Although he started with historical painting, in the 1850s he turned to landscapes and seascapes, particularly specializing in celebrating manual labor. His career prospered and in the 1860s he built himself a country house in rural Surrey where he lived until his death.

Smetham was born in Yorkshire, but subject to a peripatetic lifestyle as the son of a Wesleyan minister. Perhaps he was happiest in the early 1830s while his father was minister in Madeley, Shropshire. He attended the Methodist Woodhouse Grove School, but suffered from the harsh regime. Initially apprenticed to an architect, he studied briefly at the Royal Academy, but the early and tragic death of his brother affected him deeply and triggered the onset of a mental condition which was to plague his life.

He returned to Shropshire and began to establish himself as a local portrait artist, but drifted back to London where he became drawing master at the newly established Wesleyan college for teachers in 1851. This work was to provide some stability for the remainder of his life, with a consistent, albeit limited, income. Here he also met his wife, who taught music.

Smetham's frenzied and increasingly sporadic attempts to activate his career, and sell his pictures, were unproductive although he sold to some wealthy Wesleyans. During periodic bouts of mental illness, his wife's teaching enabled the family to survive financially. His work was characterized by a vast output of minute 'squarings' (miniature visual jottings) and 'ventilations' (penning of passing thoughts). He also wrote poetry.

Associated with the Pre-Raphaelite movement, particularly with D. G. Rossetti, Smetham was sensitive to the tensions between their sometimes Bohemian lifestyle and the mores of his Wesleyan adherence. He used his art in teaching his Sunday school class where, like the college, he found a degree of fulfillment. In 1877 he had a final breakdown, after which he produced no art, and was confined to his room for much of the remaining years of his life.

Thus, two artists with comparable backgrounds, gifts, training, and connections had very different career patterns. Hook established a successful professional life which sat easily with his Wesleyanism and his (then radical) political views, while Smetham's perhaps slavish adherence to Methodist piety and lifestyle negatively affected his prospects. They also practiced in a different world from Russell or Jackson, a Victorian England caught in a sharp contrast between the filthy grind of the burgeoning industrial revolution and the cultural counterpoint of romanticism, Pre-Raphaelitism and, much later, Arts and Crafts.

A generation later Herbert Beecroft (1864–1951), from a Reading Wesleyan family, emigrated to Australia in 1904 and established himself for his caricatures, portraits of Aboriginal people and landscapes. His c.1927 painting 'And the Lord turned and looked upon Peter' in which the eyes seem to follow the viewer, became a hugely popular evangelical image.[53]

Arthur T. Nowell (1862–1940) was son of a Wesleyan minister. Like Hook, awards from the Royal Academy enabled him to travel in Europe and he built up a successful portraiture practice (including King George V and Queen Mary), maintaining a seasonal studio in New York in the 1920s, and (often biblical) scene painting. In 1926 he observed, 'I suppose I may claim to have painted more Wesleyans, ministerial and lay, than any living artist.'[54] Perhaps this was a comment on his near contemporary Frank O. Salisbury (1874–1962), with whom he seems to have had no links – a parallel similar to Hook and Smetham.

Salisbury's background was with stained glass, but he is known better for his portraits and history paintings. Oozing with self-confidence, he cultivated an elite (and transatlantic) clientele and made a fortune. He boasted of painting six US Presidents, 25 members of the British Royal Family, and a phalanx of other notables including Sir Winston Churchill (twice). Yet, Salisbury was in some ways a contradictory enigma. His initial success, and first introduction to Royalty, came through the Great War, although he was a convinced pacifist. His grand studio mansion in Hampstead, 'Sarum Chase,' was hardly the home of a typical Methodist, yet he was staunchly loyal to the denomination and its tenets. Before his time, his Methodism made him a keen ecumenist, leaving 'Sarum Chase' to the British Council of Churches.

Most controversially, at a time when art was moving rapidly into the modern period, Salisbury was an arch-conservative who deplored the work of near-contemporaries such as Picasso and Chagall and unequivocally practiced an outmoded photo-realistic style. He also painted some forty 'pageant' canvases of historic scenes. He was not entirely without influence; of a later generation, the railway and big game artist Terence Cuneo (1907–1996), although he did not share Salisbury's religion, artistically followed in his footsteps.[55] And it could be argued that an emerging realism in art in the late twentieth century owes a debt to such forbears. Reciprocally, Salisbury was ostracized by contemporary artistic circles. Ironically illustrative of these two worlds, in the same month that Frank Salisbury was painting his sumptuous and traditional 1937 Coronation scene, Picasso was working on *Guernica*.[56]

Methodism and the Struggle for Modernity

Even before the Great War of 1914–1918, art was taking new directions. Roger Fry's influential 'post-impressionist' exhibitions of 1910 and 1912 gave confidence to changing approaches, art which criticized its subject (rather than flattered), which was influenced by a 'plein air' approach (rather than being studio-bound) and by non-Western traditions such as Japan. But it was the horrors of the war which impelled artists to explore disjunctive styles. Art which looked only at beauty ceased to be valid; in its place came approaches such as surrealism, cubism, and abstraction.

The Great War marked a transition in many ways. In music, architecture, or dress new fashions were heard and seen – Schoenberg, the Bauhaus, and flappers. No longer could religion consist of unchallenged platitudes and conformist behavior. Church attendance ceased to be a matter of social expectation. How did Methodism and its artists adjust, if at all?

Frank Salisbury, as has already been seen, was an arch-traditionalist who believed that an artist's prime duty was to capture beauty, pointing humanity toward a God who is the source of all good. Although isolated in his views, he was not alone and among Methodists A. T. Nowell and the illustrator H. E. Tidmarsh (1855–1939) seemed to have been of a similar traditionalist stamp. However, by this time they were reaching the ends of their careers and were not inclined to pursue the strident advocacy of 'high art' trumpeted by Salisbury. Nowell's 'seasonal studio' in New York possibly reflected a continuing traditional taste (as well as rising wealth) in America that was declining in Europe.

On both sides of the Atlantic the denomination has been in slow decline, especially in Britain since the 1960s[57] and churches are no longer havens for a cultural and political avant-garde. Art colleges and studios were becoming places of social and political ferment. It might be argued that it became less easy for artists in an increasingly agnostic environment to retain their religious tenets.

Moreover, popular culture was moving away from painting to other media. Talking pictures became the dominant visual art where a giant of the cinema industry, J. Arthur Rank (1888–1972),[58] was to have a massive impact. Rank was a Methodist and philanthropist, a hugely wealthy businessman and staunch supporter of mission causes. As well as heading the largest sector of the entertainment industry, he clearly saw (and exploited) the role of film in evangelism.[59] The wheel had come full circle; as Gregory the Great might have appreciated, movies might embody religious parable as frescoes and stained glass once had done.

Contemporary Art

While philanthropy has a long Methodist tradition, patronage of art was hardly so. Individuals had paid painters – usually for portraits – while artists such as James Smetham benefited from new (Methodist) money in the decoration of Victorian homes. Instances of church adornment are rarer; Methodist interiors were generally plain.

So the emergence in mid-twentieth century of a prominent Methodist layman, Dr. John M. Gibbs (1912–1996),[60] knowledgeable about contemporary art and with the wherewithal to support it financially, came as a new development in Methodism's engagement with art. He supported art in his native South Wales as well as across Methodism, but perhaps his most enduring achievement was the gathering of an outstanding collection of modern paintings depicting scenes from the Christian narrative.

The collection may be the most significant denominational collection of modern religious art in Europe outside the Vatican. Given Methodism's long reputation for philistinism, it comes as something of a surprise to those in the art world to discover that while this collection contains no works by Methodists, it does include prominent artists such as Edward Burra, Elisabeth Frink, Eric Gill, Patrick Heron, William Roberts, Francis Souza, and Graham Sutherland. Originally conceived as an exercise to raise esthetic appreciation in congregations in the late 1950s, it has had a varied history, but is recently in considerable demand (and being expanded) by the British Methodist Church as a tool for mission.[61]

The late twentieth century has seen, across many churches, a flowering of interest in creativity and art. What was formerly a largely peripheral interest among the cognoscenti has become an important aspect of church life and mission. Music has long been central to many churches' life, but dance, drama, painting, sculpture – artistic expressions – are generally an innovation in Protestantism. Workshops, books, creative arts networks all are evidence of new approaches to being church – echoes of the beginnings of Methodism. The visual is no longer a closed world but an acknowledged means of Christian worship.

Esthetics and the Wesleyan Tradition

The foregoing narrative of the inter-relation of Methodism with art has so far not raised matters of principle which underlie how the tradition understands or practices any engagement with fine art. The point has now come where the question needed to be asked, what, if any, conceptual structure might be discerned which can provide an overarching dogmatic framework in this area?

There are two starting points by which to approach this: the contemporary and the historical. From a contemporary perspective, during the twentieth century two formative theologians in particular explored the area of esthetics: Paul Tillich (Protestant and pragmatic) and Hans Urs von Balthasar (Catholic and conceptual). Their thinking, which coheres in many ways, is contained in a number of works and to distil it to any extent is to risk distortion.[62] But risk that we must.

Their fundamental conclusions may be stated as, first, that much of life is, whether we are aware of it or not, deeply influenced by esthetic stimuli. We live through our senses: touch, taste, sight, smell, and sound guide our thoughts and actions; from these we cannot escape. Tillich states, for instance, 'If art expresses reality in images and religion expresses ultimate reality in symbols then religious art expresses religious symbols in artistic images. . . .' Yet Tillichian theological esthetics ventures wider than religious art as he writes, philosophically, of the essential sacramentalism of the whole of life experience.

Secondly, the Christian religion holds that humanity's ultimate purpose is to glorify the Divine Creator. Von Balthasar's preoccupation was with the glory of God as the central focus of life, the source and reason of all that is created and creative:

> God's attribute of beauty can certainly also be examined in the context of a doctrine of the divine attributes. Besides examining God's beauty as manifested by God's actions in his creation, his beauty would also be deduced from the harmony of his essential attributes, and particularly from the Trinity.[63]

In a landmark essay *In the Beauty of Holiness*[64] Kenton Stiles tackled the whole area of 'Wesleyan aesthetics' particularly with reference to theology and worship, or, perhaps, the theology of worship. In outlining the issues, Stiles considers aspects of contemporary theology in the Wesleyan tradition and considers 'the aesthetic dimension and holiness,' before suggesting new directions for Wesleyan worship and esthetics. Central to these approaches seems to be the identity and recovery of the 'Imago dei' in the life of the believer and of the church. The image of God is to be reflected, created, or re-created in and through worship – worship construed broadly.

If these are contemporary perspectives, what of the historical? The Methodist tradition, to a greater or lesser extent, regards John Wesley as its founding father, and his doctrinal tenets as normative. Fittingly, Stiles opens his essay with an analysis of Wesley's position, showing how Wesley was inconsistent in his attitude to art in general. Yet for an eighteenth-century gentleman such as Wesley, 'taste' was an inbuilt aspect of cultural perception, whether visual, musical, architectural, or other. Coming, as he did, from a clergy family with assumptions of gentility and education, he might be expected to have developed notions of 'taste' and would also have understood what was meant by the 'sublime' – words whose currency has changed.

Stiles suggests that Wesley's relevant comments indicate a juvenile understanding, 'the simple perspective of a boy who was raised in a rural setting.'[65] Stiles continues:

> Another disturbing feature of Wesley's aesthetic observations is the personal conflict that appears in his Journal entries . . . [which] clearly indicate that Wesley enjoyed his aesthetic encounters. Yet . . . felt compelled to qualify his positive remarks.[66]

Wesley's evangelical belief, fundamentally in the transience of the material world, constantly halted his appreciation as he reminds the reader, and himself, that all this beauty will be destroyed on the Day of Judgment.

Yet, one senses, even as he wrote, Wesley was himself in two minds – whether a landscape, building, picture, or piece of music is a vehicle for divine beauty or merely a worldly bauble. Should he admire or deplore? This schizophrenia continues to be reflected in Methodism's attitude to art, a grudging engagement coupled with a sense of moral dubiety. It has arguably led to a further, and more significant, inconsistency on which Stiles also touches, 'What is missing [from Wesleyan-Holiness theology] are the theoretical and practical frameworks necessary for effectively situating the aesthetic within the whole of Wesleyan theology and implementing it in Wesleyan worship.'[67]

Conclusion: Aldersgate, Audience, and Artist

The underlying ethos of the Methodist movement is surely experience. John Wesley's heartwarming on Aldersgate Street in May 1738 has become paradigmic. It was added to by the expectation of the need for holiness, not a striving toward sanctity, but a divinely gifted experience of perfection. Wesley's defining statement of purpose for the movement was that Methodism was raised up 'to reform the nation, particularly the Church; and to spread scriptural holiness over the land.'[68]

This essay has sought to demonstrate that, far from being an area where there is nothing to say because nothing has ever been, in fact the Wesleyan/Methodist tradition is imbued with artistic implications. Methodist worship, especially hymnody, and holiness of life are esthetic in character. The ongoing Methodist experience at its most basic has to do with sensual perceptions of creative community and a worshipping life centered on music. In fuller form, it embodies at least evangelical conversion and a salvific assurance which is a participation in the beauty and glory of God. These are fundamentally esthetic in nature.

Yet in coming, as it has, to describe and define these mechanistically (as Wesley tended to) means that Methodism is in danger of self-denial, it has been hinted above that Methodism is in essence characterized by tensions; like the Wesley family itself, there is a tendency toward the bipolar.[69]

There are challenges here for scholars and congregations alike. Methodist history has sometimes been overly parochial, an insider view of the tradition. It may be possible to point a finger similarly at Methodist or Wesleyan theology. While this essay might seem an example of that approach, it has endeavored to reach beyond the received narrative, to explore a holistic context, and start to provide some terms of reference whereby the interaction of Methodism and visual culture (in the many incarnations of both) may be interrogated.

But if Methodist scholars have operated in ignorance of art, cultural historians have not been at the forefront of engagement with the world of nonconformist religion. A recent biography of James Smetham woefully overlooks the religious connotations of much of his art.[70] The tide has turned; the very existence of this essay indicates that.[71] The task ahead is to progress beyond a narrative of common ground to explore methodological approaches which take cognizance of the protocols of historical sectors while also relating intelligibly to the discourse of theologians and philosophers.

Wesley wrote, 'It were well you should be thoroughly sensible of this – the heaven of heavens is love. There is nothing higher in religion – there is, in effect, nothing else. . . .'[72]

'If music be the food of love, play on, give me excess of it. . . .'[73] While music has indeed been meat and drink to Methodist devotion, even to excess, the challenge for congregations, particularly as Methodism increases in the 'global south,' is to make real and extend diversities of artistic creativity. In all that is created, in all that is creative, the church as Audience (passive and active) refers to One who is Artist and Author, whose *poesi* (handiwork, poetry)[74] is love. Such is the quest for the recovery of the *imago dei*, the pursuit of an image, the 'likeness' of God.

For Further Reading

Forsaith, Peter. *John Wesley: Religious Hero*? Oxford: Applied Theology Press, 2004.

Forsaith, Peter. 'Permission, Prohibition, Patronage and Methodism: A Denomination Engages with Art,' in Michelle P. Brown, ed., *The Lion Companion to Christian Art*. Oxford: Lion-Hudson, 2008: 312–314.

Lee, Roger. *Wesleyana and Methodist Pottery, A Short Guide*. Weymouth, 1988.

Stiles, Kenton M. 'In the Beauty of Holiness: Wesleyan Theology, Worship and the Aesthetic,' *Wesleyan Theological Journal*. Sloane and Partner: 194–217.

21 Methodist Printed and Archival Research Collections: A Survey of Material in UK/USA Repositories

Gareth Lloyd

Scholars interested in Methodism and related evangelical movements are fortunate that there is a wealth of accessible primary and secondary sources in libraries and archival institutions. This material includes thousands of manuscripts documenting the eighteenth-century birth and antecedents of the Methodist movement as well as archival collections charting post-1800 institutional development and global expansion. These rich collections of personal and official papers are complemented by a vast array of printed works ranging from the official minutes of the British and American conferences to publications setting out views on the major societal issues of the last 250 years from slavery and temperance to homosexuality and abortion. Publications and records of the Methodist denominations as central institutions are more than equalled by material produced by local congregations and thousands of individuals as well as groups that are affiliated with Methodism, but do not constitute a formal part of the church structure.

One of the greatest challenges facing researchers is not lack of material, but a proliferation that can often cause confusion and misunderstanding. Methodists in the eighteenth and nineteenth centuries took advantage of an explosion in inexpensive publishing opportunities to generate a huge catalogue of publications. The result is that any comprehensive Methodist bibliography in English-language works alone would run to many thousands of titles, often in multiple editions and revised for different markets. A similar situation exists with regard to archives. It is only in recent years that churches and related institutions have introduced records management systems in an effort to regulate the flow of information and ensure the preservation of documents of historic or legal significance. Prior to this development, survival was often accidental in nature and while much was lost, a great deal was kept, which today would not be considered worthy of preservation and which often serves to distract rather than inform. The problem of accessing Methodist material is exacerbated when related parts of collections are split between repositories, sometimes in different countries.

This chapter will attempt to make some sense of what can be a confusing picture by providing a brief survey of major Methodist printed and archival sources. The approach will necessarily be general in nature; the greatest restriction will be geographical as the survey will concentrate entirely on research collections located in the British Isles and the USA. This is not simply a result of limited space or Anglo–American bias, but is instead a reflection of where the centers of Methodist gravity have been located during much of the more than 270-year history of the movement. It was from Britain and the USA that Methodism spread to other parts of the world and while membership in the mother denominations is now in relative decline compared with many developing countries, Britain and the USA still possess the largest and best-known research collections in the fields of Methodist history, theology, and doctrine. These collections, in addition to documenting the church in the British Isles and the USA, also represent the greatest concentrations of information concerning global Methodism. Material relating to overseas missions is frequently found in repositories in countries from where such activities were directed rather than in the former mission field itself. Given this pattern of development, it is inevitable that this survey is focussed on collections located in Britain and the USA.

The remainder of this chapter will be arranged according to geographical area looking first at research resources located in the British Isles. Each section will describe three broad categories of records and printed items; namely, material produced at a central administrative level; collections created by local churches, circuits, and districts together with the papers of related institutions; and finally the records of overseas missions.

British Methodism

Connexional

Methodist use of the word 'Connexion' originated in the idea that the preachers and people were 'in connexion' with each other and with John Wesley. Over time it became a label attached to the workings and agencies of British Methodism at a central institutional level. The term 'Connexional' records and printed books denotes material either created by Methodism as a national policy-making and administrative body as distinct from a congregation, circuit or district, or items that are considered to have a greater than local significance.

Methodist Printed and Archival Research Collections

The Connexional archive and printed book collection of the Methodist Church of Great Britain is deposited at the Methodist Archives and Research Centre (MARC) located at the John Rylands University Library, The University of Manchester. The material consists of institutional archives, personal papers, and associated print items, and first took shape as a discrete collection at the beginning of the nineteenth century. This early body of material consisted of the personal papers and printed books created or owned by John Wesley (1703–1791) and other members of his family, together with the records of Conference (the policy-making body of the church), its constituent committees, and the Wesleyan publishing concern known as the Book Room. Over the course of time the collection was augmented by the personal papers of many Wesleyan itinerant preachers. The archives were kept at City Road in London either at John Wesley's House and Chapel, or a short distance away at the Book Room and Conference Office.

As the Methodist Church expanded in size during the nineteenth century, so did the number and sophistication of its administrative structures; this is reflected in the huge expansion in the Connexional archive during the Victorian period. Within the denominational family, it was Wesleyan Methodists who paid the greatest attention to record keeping and the archives of that church represent the bulk of material created during the nineteenth and early twentieth centuries. When the several national Methodist denominations united in 1932, the archives of the constituent churches were merged, although the integrity of each sub-collection was carefully preserved.

In 1977 it was decided by the Methodist Conference that the MARC could no longer be located at City Road in London. This decision was prompted by the need to make financial savings and the realization that the physical conditions in which the collection was housed were inappropriate for an archive of its size and international significance. After lengthy negotiations, the Conference transferred the collection on permanent loan to the John Rylands Library which remains the home of the MARC.

The size of the collection transferred from London was estimated at over 26,000 printed items and approximately 600 feet of manuscript shelving. Since 1977 the archive has expanded considerably, with approximately 60,000 deposits of new material. Many of these acquisitions were deposited by the Methodist Church as a result of the ongoing process whereby modern administrative records are selected for permanent preservation once they are no longer required by their creating department. This material is supplemented by deposits made by other individuals or institutions. New acquisitions are either donated to the MARC or are placed there on permanent loan.

The MARC collection is generally acknowledged to be one of the finest research resources in the world for the study of evangelical religion. It has particular significance as the home of the largest collection of papers and printed books relating to the founders of Methodism John and Charles Wesley (1707–1788). This body of material includes more than seven hundred manuscript letters written by John Wesley, together with his diaries, sermons, annotated printed material, and miscellaneous notebooks. John's brother Charles is represented by over five hundred autograph letters, the manuscript of his journal, all of his extant sermons, and other miscellaneous papers. Of particular note is the fact that the collection contains several thousand of Charles Wesley's manuscript poems including well-known hymns such as 'Love Divine, All Loves Excelling' and 'Hark the Herald Angels Sing' – this vast literary archive dwarves most single-author manuscript poetry collections from this period.

Additionally, the Wesley archive includes papers created by other leaders of the Evangelical Revival, including George Whitefield (1714–1770), John Fletcher (1729–1785) and his wife the former Mary Bosanquet (1739–1815), Benjamin Ingham (1712–1772), and Selina Hastings, the Countess of Huntingdon (1707–1791). There are also early examples of institutional records such as the Stewards Book of the London Society compiled between 1759 and 1802; this valuable but little-used manuscript volume is one of the earliest financial records of what became the Methodist Church.

The Wesley archive is complemented by several thousand discrete collections of personal papers created by Methodists or people associated with Methodism. These range in size from tens of thousands of items to individual manuscripts and date from the early eighteenth century to the present. There are a large number of medium-sized collections relating to significant ministers, missionaries, laypeople, and educators, including the missionary Thomas Coke (1747–1814), the lawyer and anti-slavery campaigner Thomas Allan (1774–1845), and the minister and scholar A. Raymond George (1912–1998). The papers include sermons, letters, diaries, illustrations, and drafts of printed publications. The focus is not exclusively Methodist or religious. The Allan collection, for example, includes material relating to emancipation and the fight for religious and political toleration in the early nineteenth century, while the papers of the well-known artist Frank Salisbury (1874–1962) contain versions of many of his portraits, together with signed correspondence with clients like US President Dwight Eisenhower and British Prime Minister Sir Winston Churchill.

In addition to large and medium sized collections are smaller deposits relating to nearly 4,000 individuals – laypeople, preachers, and ministers whose significance ranged from being founders of large break-away churches like the Primitive Methodist Hugh Bourne (1772–1852) to ordinary members of chapel congregations.

The wealth of personal papers deposited in the MARC is matched in importance by institutional archives. The papers of Methodist administration have not typically received the same attention from scholars as the letters and diaries of the early leaders of the movement, but they should nevertheless be regarded as possessing extraordinary research significance across a range of subject areas from education to social policy. The most important part of the institutional archive is the series of records relating to the Methodist Conference, the policy-making body of the church since the early days of the movement. The records of the Wesleyan Methodist Conference, which was the largest and oldest of the pre-1932 churches, include the official minutes kept from 1744 to the present; these document the decisions of Conference and also include details of ministers' circuit appointments, obituaries, and key financial business. Associated with the minutes are Conference journals, agendas, letter books, and the daily record of proceedings.

In the course of its business, Conference created a number of committees, which were charged with consideration of a large range of business between the annual meetings of the full Conference body, including education, chapels, home missions, armed forces chaplaincies, church-state relations, temperance, and urban mission. As Methodism increased in size and sophistication, the committees spawned sub-committees and governing bodies to provide detailed oversight in areas such as schools, colleges, individual city missions, and Lord's Day observance. It would be no exaggeration to say that the records of Conference and its constituent bodies provide a comprehensive picture of British Methodism as a national church with a local, international, and ecumenical outreach.

During the nineteenth century, sophisticated bureaucratic machinery evolved around Conference and its committees. The records of these departments are deposited at MARC as significant collections in their own right providing a detailed picture of Methodism as it developed from the early nineteenth century until the present. Much of this material is arranged in divisional sequences which correspond to the following broad areas of Church life: Education and Youth; Finance; Home Mission; Ministries; Overseas Mission; Property; and Social Responsibility.

This divisional structure was created in the 1970s, but the collections contain a considerable amount of material created by predecessor departments. The records of the property division, for example, contain the papers of the Wesleyan department of chapel affairs dating back to the early nineteenth century.

All pre-1932 Methodist denominations in Britain adopted the Wesleyan Conference model and their institutional record-keeping displays similar characteristics to the parent Wesleyan body, but while there are discrete Conference collections in the MARC for each of the major churches, there are also considerable differences in the range and quantity of the archival material that was produced. The largest and most comprehensive collection is that of Wesleyan Methodism, but there are significant collections also surviving for the Primitive Methodist and United Methodist Churches, as well as, the modern Methodist Church of Great Britain.

The non-archival holdings of the MARC comprise approximately 100,000 printed items arranged in discrete collections, and general or subject-based sequences. As with the archives, the MARC printed collections are subject to regular accruals with the result that modern works of scholarship appear alongside items dated as early as 1530. The material consists of a mix of monographs, tracts, pamphlets, and a small number of miscellaneous publications including theses, leaflets, and annual reports. The majority of items were published before 1850 and tend to fall into the category of pamphlet or tract.

The wealth of the published collections of the MARC defies easy description. Holdings include annotated copies of books owned by the Wesley brothers and their associates, including a personal library of over 430 volumes compiled by Charles Wesley and his family. The MARC is also home to the world's largest discrete collection of anti-Methodist tracts comprising 396 copies of 348 works, published mainly in the eighteenth century, but with some nineteenth-century editions. The institution also has an outstanding collection of hymnals that includes many eighteenth-century titles authored or compiled by John and Charles Wesley, John Newton (1725–1807), and Isaac Watts (1674–1748). The general subject-based printed sequences are exceptionally rich in the fields of Methodist and evangelical history, sermons, biography, theology, and church government. The main focus of the collection is Methodism in the British Isles, but there is also considerable coverage of overseas missions and the history of the movement in the USA, as well as a large number of works relating to the Church of England, the wider Christian church, and interaction with the secular world through books and tracts concerned with issues such as slavery, social justice, and education. Many of the volumes were annotated by their original owners and multiple editions of works are commonplace.

Many of the printed works deposited in the MARC are available in only a very small number of specialist libraries; exceptionally rare titles include John Jackson, *Index Biblicus or an Exact Concordance to the Holy Bible* . . . (Cambridge, 1668),[1] and James Morgan, *An Extract of the Life of Ignatius Loyola* (London, 1764).[2] Some of the titles appear to be unique to the MARC with no extant copies recorded elsewhere. Worthy of special note is the MARC copy of *A collection of psalms and hymns* compiled by John Wesley (Charlestown, 1737). This slim volume is of enormous significance on a number of levels; it was the first hymn book compiled by either John or Charles Wesley, the first hymnal produced for an Anglican congregation, and the first hymn book published in what became the USA. There are only two original copies of this book in the world and the one in the MARC is the only complete copy.

The MARC is also home to one of the world's finest collections of British Methodist and Methodist-related periodical publications. The bibliographer E. A. Rose listed 142 separate titles in his checklist of periodicals published in Britain, excluding titles relating to overseas missions and publications produced by individual circuits and chapels. The majority of these, together with the missionary titles not included in the Rose checklist, are represented in the MARC, although the collection does not include chapel and circuit material.

The MARC periodical collection can usefully be considered as falling into three broad categories. The first of these sub-divisions consists of official publications produced by denominations and includes Connexional magazines and newspapers published by all the major British Methodist churches before the union of 1932. These magazines and newspapers were the primary means of circulating news and views to the membership; contents included news of national or denominational interest, reports from foreign missions, obituaries, portrait engravings/photographs of ministers, local information such as chapel openings/anniversaries, and articles on theology, history, and religious affairs. Well-known titles that fall into this group include the *Methodist Magazine*, which was published in monthly issues between 1778 and 1969,[3] and *The Methodist Recorder*, which commenced publication in 1861 and remains the main serial publication of the British Methodist Church.

The second category contains materials that were not necessarily official publications of the church, but which were directed at a national readership and covered matters of general interest. Some of these publications like the Wesleyan *Methodist Times* were opposed to the leadership of their particular denomination and represent an aspect of the internal strife that was a feature of the nineteenth-century movement.

The final grouping of Methodist serial publications can best be termed special interest periodicals. From the nineteenth to the twentieth centuries the several Methodist denominations and related societies, institutions, and pressure groups published specialist magazines on an exceptionally wide range of subjects including overseas missions, academic research in history and theology, temperance, colleges, Sunday schools, youth and education, worship and liturgy, music, and theology. Many of these periodicals are represented in the MARC, although there are often gaps in the holdings. The majority of the titles were published in Britain, but there is also some North American representation.

In addition to the MARC, there are several other institutions in the UK that hold records and printed books that are of Connexional rather than local significance. Such collections relate mainly to the early years of the Wesleyan movement and the life and ministry of John Wesley. The most significant such collection outside of the MARC is that deposited in the library at Wesley College, Bristol. In addition to the institutional records of the college and its predecessor institutions, Wesley has an exceptionally fine archive relating to John Wesley and his contemporaries. Highlights of the collection include Wesley's ordination certificate, manuscript minutes of the first four Conferences, a book of autograph sermons preached by Samuel Wesley, Sr. (1662–1735) and a large collection of personal papers and printed books owned by eighteenth- and nineteenth-century Methodist ministers and laity.

Also of Connexional importance is the material held at the Methodist Studies Unit (MSU) of the Wesley Centre at Oxford Brookes University. This collection has a much broader coverage than the eighteenth and early nineteenth centuries and includes the Westminster College archive, the records of the AVEC consultancy relating to church and community development between 1976 and 1994, and personal papers of the prominent ministers Donald English (1930–1998) and Bill Gowland (1911–1991). Of particular interest is the library of the Wesley Historical Society; this has the second largest collection of Methodist books and related literature in Europe and has particular strengths in biography and local history.

Small collections of manuscripts and printed books can also be found at the following Methodist museums and heritage sites: The New Room, Bristol; John Wesley's Chapel and Museum of Methodism, City Road, London; and Epworth Old Rectory. This material is open to the public, but researchers should be aware that because the institutions concerned are museums rather than research libraries, advance notice of visits is necessary and conditions and rights of access may be subject to change. The same principle applies to the collection of memorabilia, documents, and books held in the Wesley Center at Kingswood School near Bath.

Mention should also be made of the large collection of Methodist records and printed material deposited in the National Library of Wales, Aberystwyth. The bulk of this material relates to the Welsh Calvinistic Methodist Church,[4] which originated within the Evangelical Revival at the same time as the Wesleyan movement, but differed fundamentally from it with regard to theology and developed into a separate evangelical denomination. The collection includes personal papers, which often shed light on the early years of the evangelical movement as a whole, together with records of a later date created by local congregations, institutional material, and associated print items.

British Methodist Local Records
Local records are defined for the purpose of this chapter as papers and associated print material created by churches, circuits, and districts,[5] or institutions affiliated with individual church congregations, such as Sunday schools and local branches of Methodist organizations such as the Wesley Guild. Such material, where it has survived, tends to be kept either in the relevant church or chapel, or in the custody of a local government administered archive

service depending on whether the record concerned is still in active use. For example, once a baptism register is full, then the current policy of the British Methodist Church requires that it be transferred on permanent loan to an archival holding institution designated as the appropriate place of deposit for Methodist material in that area. In most cases, this is to a county record office established to act as the custodian for records created within a county boundary. There are also some record offices attached to cities and a few large towns, sometimes operated as part of a reference or local history library.

Record offices will consider for deposit, archival and associated print material of all types from personal papers to the records of business, schools, hospitals, local government, law courts, churches, and social clubs. Public access to these collections is largely unrestricted, although material can only be consulted on site and there is often a requirement for researchers to provide identification. Depositors can also impose a closure period; in the case of the Methodist Church, this embargo extends to Connexional and local material created within the last thirty years, but this can be extended to one hundred years for certain categories of disciplinary records and other sensitive material.

To facilitate the process of deposit, each Methodist district and some circuits, have a volunteer archivist, who acts as the liaison between the record office and the church and who often makes arrangements for the transfer of material. These archivists tend to be people with a passion for local history and in many cases, their interest and involvement in local Methodist archival matters extends beyond their specific duties.

The above procedure represents in general terms the current policy for managing local Methodist records, but researchers should be aware that it has not guaranteed the survival of important material in every case. The district archivists' system was only introduced in the 1970s and there are often sizeable gaps in record office collections reflecting the period when there was no official archives policy within the church. Many records were disposed of either in periodic clear-outs of church safes or as a result of the merger of congregations following the two major Methodist unions in 1907[6] and 1932.[7] This problem was compounded by the fact that the modern county record office as a standard feature of local government was essentially a post-1945 development[8]; prior to that date, there was often no local repository in which records could be deposited once they were deemed surplus to requirements.

However, while many records have been destroyed or have otherwise vanished from sight, there is still a huge wealth of local Methodist material accessible to researchers. These collections are typically arranged chronologically by record type under the name of the creating body, whether that be a church, circuit, district, or affiliated organization. The records of a church will normally include registers of baptisms, marriages, and burials together with administrative material such as building fund accounts, the minutes of trustees' meetings, and schedules of trust property. Printed items often include church magazines, service sheets, and local histories. A church archive might also include records of groups affiliated with the congregation such as sporting clubs and youth associations, or these might be arranged into a separate collection.

Circuit material typically includes the minutes of quarterly meetings,[9] records of local preachers meetings, and schedules of circuit trust property. There can often appear to be overlap between circuit and chapel material; this is a product of a situation where some circuits either contained very few churches or where the records of the lead congregation in the circuit became mixed up with those of the circuit itself. For example, it is not unknown for the minutes of circuit committees and church committees to be recorded in the same volume, especially if one individual served as the secretary of both.

At the district level, records include the minutes of district meetings, schedules of property, and the minutes of committees such as finance, chapel building, sustentation fund, and local preachers. The names of committees are often the same at the church, circuit, and district level, and this can cause confusion; the best way of understanding this overlap is to view Methodist grassroots organization as having elements that were duplicated across all three levels – for example, the preachers at each church met together periodically as a committee or as a preachers' meeting to discuss matters of concern and engage in fellowship; representatives would have occasionally met their counterparts in the circuit and there also would have been a district preachers committee. Another reason for duplication of information and record types is that the district often received statistics from congregations and circuits, so that for example, information about property that appears in circuit property schedules is also duplicated in district schedules.

It is worth noting that the MARC also includes a very large district collection by virtue of the fact that districts submitted copies of their minutes to the Conference office. This Conference collection of district material was deposited in Manchester with the rest of the Connexional material.

Researchers should be aware that particular types of record will only appear in local Methodist collections at certain times and then not in every case. For example, registers of marriages, baptisms, and burials are rare in eighteenth-century British Methodism and even in the Victorian period, not all churches sought registration as a place where marriages could be legally performed.[10] The several pre-1932 Methodist denominations also had specific types of record, which were not always shared across British Methodism. For example, Primitive Methodist district collections often include lists of officials who had left the church, which was not something about which other denominations seemed to be overly concerned. When one takes into account such nuances and adds them to a situation where records have been lost or destroyed, then it becomes easy to understand why there is no such thing as a typical collection of local Methodist material. This situation of course also applies to other Methodist churches around the world.

The most common Methodist collection found in record offices other than those created by a chapel, circuit, or district is associated with Sunday schools. These were often linked to a particular congregation, but such was the volume of material that could be created, that they are frequently arranged into sequences separate from those associated with a church. Records that typically occur in a Sunday school deposit include log-books, registers of admissions, financial papers, photographs, and printed lists of rules for school governance.

Records of British Methodist Overseas Missions

British Methodist missionary records and associated print items are considered to be part of the Connexional archive in common with the material held at the MARC. However, because of the size and specialized nature of the overseas collection, it is held not in Manchester, but at the library of the School of Oriental and African Studies (SOAS) at the University of London.[11] The collection consists of 1,341 boxes of archive material and a library of approximately 6,500 books and pamphlets. It was deposited on permanent loan at SOAS in 1978; since that time, there have been regular accruals of material from the offices of the Overseas Division of the Methodist Church.[12]

The archival part of the collection contains material dating between 1736 and 1976, and documents the work of the Methodist Missionary Society and the following predecessor organizations: the Wesleyan Methodist Missionary Society; United Methodist Missionary Society; Methodist New Connexion Missionary Society; Bible Christian Home and Foreign Missionary Society; United Methodist Free Churches Foreign Missions; and the Primitive Methodist Missionary Society. The collection contains material relating to countries in most regions of the world.

The collection includes the personal papers of many prominent missionaries including Thomas Birch Freeman (1809–1890), David Hill (1840–1896), and Samuel Pollard (1864–1915), but the greatest strength of the archive rests in its extensive series of institutional records. The largest sequence relates to the work of the Wesleyan Methodist Missionary Society and its post-1932 successor institution, the Methodist Missionary Society. It includes material from the Mission House in London, which was the effective headquarters for overseas outreach; this discrete archive includes minutes and associated papers of the General Committee of Management and related bodies, such as its various sub-committees; documentation relating to candidates, 1829–1869; financial papers, 1817–1945; and correspondence sent to the Mission House from within the UK as well as from the Mission House to overseas stations. In addition to this 'home' material, there is a separate series of overseas records, comprising material sent back to Britain by the missionaries and associated workers employed overseas[13]; these papers, which are arranged by region, include the minutes of the annual Synods and official reports and correspondence. There are collections relating to the other pre-1932 denominations, but with the exception of the Primitive Methodist Missionary Society only minutes are extant. Material created before 1945 is arranged and listed separately from the later material for 1945 to 1950.

In addition to the 'home' and 'overseas' sequences, there is a third subdivision of material containing 'special' records; this includes biographical material relating to missionaries from nearly all the Methodist Missionary districts or churches; logs and associated papers of the Wesleyan mission ships dating from 1838 to 1865; anti-slavery papers and a large general collection of miscellaneous documents including research notes, unpublished articles, government publications, and histories. In addition, there is a very large image collection, including approximately 2,500 photographs illustrating aspects of the work in India, Burma, Sri Lanka, Australasia, Africa, China, and the Caribbean and Americas. Special mention should also be made of the 'Women's Work' collection, which documents the contribution made by Wesleyan women missionaries and the work of women in the Methodist Missionary Society after the Methodist union of 1932.

The SOAS Methodist printed collection consists of the Methodist Missionary Library, which comprises approximately 6,500 books and pamphlets, accessible by means of an online catalogue. A significant amount of the material was originally published by the MMS (and its predecessors) as well as by its partner churches overseas. Periodicals principally comprise printed annual reports and missionary magazines (with some similar material originating from overseas mission districts and mission stations). Not surprisingly, there are a number of books (many written by Methodist missionaries) on individual missionaries as well as the history of mission regions, districts, and individual stations. These are complemented by more general histories on geographic areas, countries, people, and cultures. There are also a small but important number of books written on the indigenous languages encountered by missionaries as well as the subsequent translations of Christian texts by missionaries.

The missionary collections of the British church document the birth and early development of a considerable part of what became one of the world's major Christian denominations. The nature of the relationship between the Methodist Church of Great Britain and overseas churches has evolved considerably over the years, from a paternal role to one of equal partnership. Many of the former overseas 'districts' have become autonomous Methodist churches in their own right, while others, such as the Canadian and Australian denominations have united with other Protestant churches and no longer have the name Methodist. Researchers will, therefore, encounter the problem of split collections, but there can be no doubting the importance of the SOAS missionary material as a major resource, not simply for charting the global evolution of Methodism, but also for illuminating a range of related nineteenth- and twentieth-century topics from imperialism in its wider aspects to anti-slavery, anthropology, and education.

Most of the material up to 1945 has been catalogued and the bulk of this material has been microfiched. Some archives created between 1945 and 1950 (mainly synod minutes and correspondence) have also been catalogued, but not microfiched. Until the process of cataloguing is complete, post-1950 records are currently unavailable. Copies of the microfiche are available at SOAS and, by prior appointment, at the MARC.

Researchers should be aware that there are many collections at the MARC that complement and overlap the SOAS material. It was commonplace for missionaries to spend at least part of their ministry in British circuits and the MARC collection of personal papers often includes material relating to overseas service. Mission related institutional records in the MARC include Conference reports and district material relating to home support for missions. Published sources include specialist periodicals such as *Work and Workers in the Mission Field*, and regular missionary reports and statistics are also included in the Connexional magazines. In addition, there are thousands of monographs and pamphlets in the MARC collection relating to the overseas work, including biographies, country-studies, and Bibles translated into local languages.

US Methodism

There has always been tremendous interest in the USA in the life and ministry of John Wesley. This fascination resulted over time in the acquisition by several Methodist affiliated colleges and universities of substantial collections of Wesley manuscripts and printed books. In most cases, this special material is not owned by the United Methodist Church (UMC),[14] but by the school or special collections library concerned and should, therefore, be considered as separate from the United Methodist Archives (UMA), which is the main institutional archive of the church.[15]

This is subtly different from the situation in Britain where most collections of Methodist material remain in the ownership of Methodism at both the local and Connexional level. The first subdivision of this section on research collections in the USA will therefore be concerned with substantial discrete collections of Wesleyana and related material owned by schools and specialist libraries outside of the UMA. The two following sections will look in turn at the resources of the UMA (including the records of overseas missions) and locally created US Methodist material held in conference archives.

Wesley-related and other early Methodist collections held by US special collections libraries:

Duke University
One of the largest collections of archives and printed material in the USA relating to the Wesley brothers and the early years of the Methodist movement is deposited in the Rare Books, Manuscript and Special Collections Library at Duke University in Durham, North Carolina. The backbone of the collection consists of material acquired over the course of more than fifty years by Frank Baker (1910–1999), a professor at Duke University and one of the world's greatest authorities on early Methodism. The collection contains manuscript letters and associated papers written by John and Charles Wesley, members of their family, and contemporaries in the early Methodist movement. The manuscript material is complemented by a large collection of publications authored by the Wesley brothers and other early evangelicals. The Baker collection also contains transcripts and photocopies or photographic copies of Wesley material held by other repositories or owned by private individuals. Frank Baker's frequent annotations and research papers add tremendously to the value of the archive.

Duke University Divinity School Library, which is separate from the Rare Books, Manuscript and Special Collections Library, but still within the Duke University system, also contains many general Methodist reference works as well as editions of works by the Wesleys and other early evangelicals.

Emory University
The Robert W. Woodruff Library at Emory University in Atlanta, Georgia, has a large collection of Wesleyana, other early Methodist manuscripts, and associated print items.[16] The discrete Wesley collection includes papers relating to John and Charles Wesley and Charles' wife (Sarah) and their children. Of particular note is an autograph diary written by John Wesley in 1736 and a discrete collection of twenty-three letters from Charles Wesley to John Langshaw, the organist of Lancaster Parish Church.[17] The library also contains a substantial microfilm collection of Wesley and related material, the originals of which are held elsewhere.

The Pitts Theology Library is the specialist theological library for Emory University and has its own collection of Wesleyana, including several autograph letters of John Wesley, and a notebook containing verse in the hand of Charles Wesley. Other early Methodist papers at Pitts include a manuscript by the pioneering British itinerant preacher John Bennet (1714–1759). The library also has strong printed holdings in the field of British religion and hymnody.

Garrett Evangelical Theological Seminary
The United Library of Garrett Evangelical Theological Seminary and Seabury Western Theological Seminary, Evanston, Illinois, has a rich collection of early Methodist material, including several autograph letters of John and Charles Wesley. Printed holdings include approximately five hundred titles of eighteenth-century imprints by the Wesley brothers, together with works authored by other early Methodist leaders including John Fletcher and George Whitefield.

Southern Methodist University
Bridwell Library, Southern Methodist University, Dallas, Texas, has one of the largest collections of Wesley publications and manuscripts in North America comprising more than 4,000 autograph letters and associated items. Papers of particular interest to students of British and North American Methodism include correspondence of the Wesley brothers and other members of their family together with papers of other evangelicals including Thomas Haweis (1734–1820), Thomas Coke (1747–1814), and Francis Asbury (1745–1816). Printed works include multiple editions of nearly four hundred Wesley publications, a significant number of which are first editions, together with substantial collections of hymn books, general Methodist reference works, and publications relating to nineteenth-century disputes and developments within the British and American churches. The library also has extensive holdings in historical and current periodical literature.

United Methodist Denominational Archives (UMA) amd Drew University
The UMA is the official archive of the UMC and is the American equivalent of the British Connexional archives located in Manchester and London. The UMA collections are owned and funded by the church under the specific administrative charge of the General Commission on Archives and History (GCAH) and are managed in partnership with Drew University, Madison, New Jersey.[18] Since 1982, the archives have been stored in the specially built United Methodist Archives and History Center on the Drew campus. The center contains a museum, library, archival storage providing approximately six miles of shelving with a capacity of 180,000 cubic feet, and the administrative offices of the GCAH.

The center houses the largest and most comprehensive collection of Methodist material in the world. It is rich in the manuscripts of John Wesley, his family, and his associates,[19] and in discrete collections of letters, sermons, diaries, and associated papers of thousands of ministers, missionaries, and laity representing 250 years of Methodist history. British and American individuals of note represented in the personal collections, include John Fletcher (1729–1785), William McKendree (1757–1835), Henry Boehm (1775–1875), Freeborn

Garretson (1752–1827) and his wife Catherine (1752–1849), Joseph Crane Hartzell (1842–1928), Leontine T. C. Kelly (1920–) and Judith Craig (1937–).

The UMA also houses the records of the general agencies of the denomination and its antecedents from the earliest days of the church.[20] It is possible to give only a very brief indication of the wealth of material, but the institutional collections include papers of the following bodies: the General Conference, annual conferences and local churches of the United Brethren in Christ, 1810–1946; Commission on Christian Higher Education, 1956–1960; Health and Welfare Ministries Division (part of the General Board of Global Ministries), 1881–1986; National Division of the General Board of Global Ministries, 1880–2000; The Council of Bishops, 1870–2002; General Board of Discipleship, 1890–1992; Women's Division of the General Board of Global Ministries, 1838–2001; Division of Human Relations and Economic Affairs of the General Board of Church and Society, 1950–1986; and the General Board of Higher Education and Ministry, 1883–1992.

The UMA is also responsible for the records of American overseas missions. This collection is the largest single record group in the UMA and is the world's most important resource for the study of Methodist global expansion. The archives include the personal papers of individual missionaries, such as the Luther and Jennie Burtner Collection relating to work in the Philippines from 1901 to 1904, and the Herman C. and Ethel Anderson papers relating to Evangelical Church missionary work in China during the 1920s. Institutional material includes records of the World Division of the General Board of Global Ministries, 1808–2004; this discrete sequence extends to 347 cubic feet of shelving and documents American Methodist outreach on every continent. Related collections include the administrative papers of the Board of Foreign Missions of the Methodist Episcopal Church, 1819–1955, and a large archive (252 cubic feet) relating to the Women's Division of the General Board of Global Ministries, 1838–2001. Common record types in both the overseas and home collections include minutes, government publications, reports, policy documents, official correspondence, photographs, and financial papers.

The center's published collections are equally impressive. They include more than 15,000 tracts and pamphlets, 35,000 monographs, 4,000 hymn books and the world's largest collection of Methodist periodicals encompassing 2,000 titles issued by the church in Britain and the USA, as well as their overseas off-shoots. Many of these serial publications are unique to the UMA.

The collections, both published and archival, receive regular accruals of material – more than 100 cubic feet of manuscript material is processed every year. Collection level descriptions of many, but not all, of the archive collections are available on the UMA section of the GCAH website and a catalogue of a large percentage of the published holdings is also accessible online.

Locally Created US Methodist Material Held in Archive Institutions
The GCAH issues guidelines for the management of records created by annual conferences and local congregations,[21] but the records themselves are not subject to transfer to the UMA; instead, locally created material that has been identified as worthy of long-term or permanent retention is transferred, when no longer needed for current use, to a local archives repository, designated as the annual conference archive. Responsibility for ensuring that local records are managed properly falls to individual conference Commissions on Archives and History which essentially carry out many of the functions at a local level of the United Methodist GCAH.

Annual conference archives tend to be located in a college, university, or special collections library, where they often form part of a wider Methodist or general religious collection.[22] The detailed administrative and funding arrangements are worked out on the basis of a partnership between the school or library and the conference, but in all cases, ownership of annual conference and church material remains vested in Methodism. One such collection is that of the Alabama-West Florida Conference of the United Methodist Church and its predecessor organizations dating back to 1808. This archive is located in a dedicated Methodist Archives Center at the Houghton Memorial Library, Huntingdon College, Montgomery, Alabama. In common with many schools holding conference archives, Huntingdon was founded as a Methodist institution and retains close connection with the church. The Methodist center also holds the institutional archive of the college and a large published collection containing general reference works and local histories.

Conference material can cover a wide spectrum of document types including papers of the bishop's office and other conference officials, the records of districts and their agencies, minutes of the conference committees and subcommittees, the records of auxiliary agencies such as the Epworth League and its successors, and the archives of United Methodist related institutions such as retirement homes and community centers. Conference archives also contain collections of personal papers relating to ministers, local officials and laity.

The records of individual churches are kept by the congregation concerned as long as the church remains open. In the event of closure or merger with another congregation, records that are selected for permanent preservation are transferred to the annual conference archive.[23] Such collections can include registers of baptisms, marriages and burials, financial papers, trustees' minutes, membership records, title deeds, and Sunday school records. A list of local conference archives and their contact details is accessible on the GCAH website.

Conclusion

It is not possible in the context of one chapter to provide a comprehensive and up-to-date survey of Methodist research collections around the world given the sheer number of repositories, amount of material, and the ever-changing denominational and research picture. In the years since 1945 membership of the church has expanded by leaps and bounds in countries and regions that once comprised part of the mission field, such as Korea, Malaysia, and parts of Africa. Independent Methodist denominations in these areas are now developing their own archives and records management systems and while some of these are sophisticated and well-advanced in terms of technology and access, others are at a very early stage of evolution. It is hoped that future versions of this survey will be able to take a greater account of this wider picture and in so doing, give due acknowledgement to Methodism as a truly global church. Nevertheless, it is also important to acknowledge the fact that the largest and most important Methodist research collections, both nationally and internationally, are still located in British and American repositories and it is this material that documents the principal areas of Methodist development from the founding of the movement to the dawn of the twenty-first century.

Acknowledgment

The section of this chapter relating to the collections of the MARC is based on the text of the following forthcoming publication: Gareth Lloyd, *Guide to Methodist Resources and Research Opportunities at the University of Manchester* (The John Rylands University Library, 2009). It is reproduced by courtesy of the University Librarian and Director, The John Rylands University Library, The University of Manchester. The author is also grateful to Lance Martin, archivist in charge of the Methodist missionary collections at SOAS, and to Mark Shenise, associate archivist of the GCAH for their invaluable help and advice relating to the collections at their institutions.

Part II

This page intentionally left blank

Methodism A to Z

John G. McEllhenney and Charles Yrigoyen, Jr.

This section includes a series of short articles on important Methodist concepts, denominations, geographical areas, and personalities. Some of these are the principal focus of larger chapters which appear in Part I. While most of the subjects of the shorter articles are obvious, some readers may doubt the significance of others, or will question why some subjects have been omitted. The choice of what or whom to include is always hazardous, not so much for the subjects chosen, but for those excluded. Nevertheless, we offer the following chapters with short bibliographic references. Boldface type indicates an article on that subject is in this section. The authors of the articles are identified as follows: J.M. = John G. McEllhenney, C.Y. = Charles Yrigoyen, Jr.

Africa

Christianity has existed in Africa since the earlier centuries of the church. Its modern presence and numerical strength is a result of the nineteenth-century missionary movement. British and American missionaries expanded the reach of Methodism into Africa during this period. Much of their work is documented in the British and American Methodist denominations who preserved correspondence, reports, and statistics in their missionary archives. This documentary evidence is the principal source of information regarding the origin and development of Methodism on the African continent. There is a desperate need for a history of African Methodism.

Methodist presence in South Africa can be traced to 1806 when a Methodist society was formed in Cape Town by soldiers stationed there. William Shaw (1798–1872) and Barnabas Shaw (1788–1857) were early leaders in organizing South African Methodism among both English settlers and Africans. British Methodist missionaries also established enduring work in Sierra Leone on Africa's west coast in 1811 under the direction of George Warren (d. 1812). Many of the first Methodists in Sierra Leone and elsewhere were freed slaves. Other early British Methodist mission efforts were successful in Gambia (1821), Ghana (1838), and other areas.

American Methodist missionary endeavors began in Liberia in 1833 led by Methodist Episcopal missionary Melville Cox (1799–1833) who died within months of his arrival, but not before conducting a camp meeting, organizing a Sunday school, and plotting mission strategy. From Liberia, American work stretched into Angola, Mozambique, and other areas. Among the most important leaders in the American work were Methodist Episcopal missionary bishops William Taylor (1821–1902), Joseph C. Hartzell (1842–1928), and John M. Springer (1873–1963).

British and American Methodist denominations historically active in Africa include the British Methodist Church (and its predecessors), and American churches including the African Methodist Episcopal, African Methodist Episcopal Zion, Christian Methodist Episcopal, Free Methodist, Primitive Methodist, United Methodist (including its Methodist and Evangelical United Brethren predecessors), Wesleyan, and the Church of the Nazarene. In addition there are a number of autonomous Methodist denominations in Africa, most with British or American roots, including the Methodist Church of Southern Africa, the Methodist Church of Nigeria, and the Methodist Church of Zimbabwe.

While the churches' missionary efforts involved vibrant evangelistic emphases, they also succeeded in planting effective educational work in primary and secondary mission schools. In more recent years a few denominations have initiated institutions of higher education, for example, United Methodism's Africa University, which opened in 1992.

There are approximately ten million members of Methodist or Methodist-related churches in Africa. United Methodism leads with approximately 3.5 million African members.

Barclay, Wade Crawford, *The Methodist Episcopal Church, 1845–1939, Widening Horizons 1845–95*, History of Methodist Missions (1957), 3:869–931; Copplestone, J. Tremayne, *Twentieth-Century Perspectives, The Methodist Episcopal Church, 1896–1939*, History of Methodist Missions (1973), 4:3–113, 519–580, 930–974; *HDM*, 1–7; Isichei, Elizabeth, *A History of Christianity in Africa* (1995); *World Methodist Council Handbook of Information* (current edition).
C.Y.

African Methodist Episcopal Church (USA)

Racial discrimination experienced by **Richard Allen** and others at St. George's Methodist Episcopal Church in Philadelphia led ultimately, in 1816, to the formation of the African Methodist Episcopal Church. Some disenchanted black Methodists chose to affiliate with the Protestant Episcopal Church; not Allen, however, who founded, in 1794, what is now Bethel AME Church in Philadelphia, became its first pastor, and finally, in 1815, secured his church's legal separation from the **Methodist Episcopal Church**. The next year, Allen and other black Methodist leaders from the mid-Atlantic region founded the African Methodist Episcopal Church, which retained Methodist doctrine and polity; Allen was elected bishop. The new church expanded, first, in the northeast and midwest, but had congregations in California by the 1850s. During the Civil War, AME clergy followed the Union army into the Confederacy, with the result that the denomination experienced great growth in the postwar South. Missions were opened in Haiti (1824), Liberia and Sierra Leone (1891), and South Africa (1896). At the beginning of the twenty-first century, the denomination counted over 3,300,000 members in the United States, and congregations in more than 30 other countries.

DCA, 29–30; HDM, 7–9.
J.M.

African Methodist Episcopal Zion Church (USA)

Racial discrimination in John Street Methodist Church in New York City precipitated the founding of the African Methodist Episcopal Zion Church (AMEZ). **James Varick** and other black Methodists withdrew from John Street in 1796; five years later, they incorporated as an autonomous congregation. During the next fifteen years, Varick's congregation and similar ones in New York, Connecticut, and Pennsylvania decided to cut all ties with the Methodist Episcopal Church, choosing, however, not to affiliate with the **African Methodist Episcopal Church**. Instead, in 1821, they founded the African Methodist Episcopal Zion Church. The next year, Varick was elected the first superintendent; the title was changed to bishop in 1868. Expansion of the new church was limited to the northeastern states before the Civil War. Then the AMEZ, even before the war ended, moved into the South, with North Carolina becoming its first stronghold. Soon there were annual conferences in Louisiana, Virginia, South Carolina, and Alabama. A mission was opened in Liberia in 1876. By the early twentieth century, there were AMEZ annual conferences in Ghana, Nigeria, and South Africa. An annual conference was established in England in 1971. The church's members numbered over 1,500,000 in 2000.

DCA, 30; HDM, 9–11.
J.M.

African Union Methodist Protestant Church (USA)

This denomination traces its origin to 1813, when Peter Spencer (1779/1782–1843) withdrew from the **Methodist Episcopal Church**. He founded Ezion

Church, a predominantly black congregation in Wilmington, Delaware in 1805. Spencer, who had been born into slavery but became free when his owner died, gave the name Union Church of Africans to the new Methodist-type organization, which began to organize congregations, primarily, in the Mid-Atlantic states. A dispute over a proposal to introduce episcopal polity led, in the 1850s, to a breakaway group that founded the Union American Methodist Episcopal Church. The original church changed its name to the African Union Church, which merged in 1865–1866 with the Colored Methodist Protestant Church to form the African Union Methodist Protestant Church. Like the **Methodist Protestant Church**, the new denomination adhered to Wesleyan doctrine but rejected episcopacy. Although the title 'bishop' was being used by the 1920s, the denomination delayed formal acceptance of episcopal polity until 1967. The AUMP joined the Commission on Pan-Methodist Cooperation and Union in 2004; other members are the **African Methodist Episcopal, African Methodist Episcopal Zion, Christian Methodist Episcopal**, and **United Methodist** churches.

Lewis V. Baldwin, *Invisible Strands in African Methodism: A History of the African Union Methodist Protestant and Union American Methodist Episcopal Churches* (1983); *EWM*, I: 68–69; *HAM*, I: 616–617.
J.M.

Albright, Jacob (1759–1808)

German-speaking Albright, recognizing that Pennsylvania's German-speakers were not being reached by Methodist preachers, initiated his own itinerant ministry and, a few years later, founded the **Evangelical Association**. Born near Pottstown, Pennsylvania, Albright married Catherine Cope in 1785, and became a farmer and respected tile maker. Following the deaths of several of his children in 1790, Albright, nominally Lutheran, felt guilty about his religious indifference. Guided by **United Brethren** and **Methodist Episcopal** preachers, he experienced God's forgiving love, and found fellowship in a Methodist class meeting, where he learned Christian disciplines and began studying the Bible. In 1796, Albright launched an itinerant ministry among German-speaking people in southeastern Pennsylvania. Soon he was winning converts and, because of his condemnation of personal evils, encountering persecution. In 1800, Albright organized three Methodist-style classes. Three years later, he called a meeting of the lay leaders and lay preachers associated with him; they voted for his ordination as elder. That action and the meeting itself mark what is regarded as the founding of the **Evangelical Association**. It held its first regular annual conference in 1807, at which Albright was elected bishop. But within six months, debilitated by tuberculosis, self-imposed austerities, and the rigors of itinerancy, he died.

Albright, Raymond W., *A History of the Evangelical Church* (1942); *ANB*, 1:226–227; Behney, J. Bruce and Paul H. Eller, *The History of the Evangelical United Brethren Church* (1979).
J.M.

Allen, Richard (1760–1831)

Allen, the founder of the **African Methodist Episcopal Church**, was born into slavery. His family's first owner, a Philadelphian, sold them to a man in Delaware, from whom, in 1783, Allen and his brother purchased their freedom. Earlier, in 1777, Allen was converted by a Methodist preacher, and soon began his own preaching ministry. He returned to Philadelphia in 1785, where he affiliated with Methodism's St. George's congregation. That church's leaders permitted him to speak to blacks on special occasions, but racist incidents during Sunday services convinced Allen and others that they needed their own worship place. Therefore, in 1794, Allen established a Methodist meeting house for blacks called Bethel, which white Methodists soon tried to control. Allen filed several civil suits, resulting, in 1815, in a decision that granted Bethel legal independence. The next year, he gathered black Methodists from the mid-Atlantic states to establish the African Methodist Episcopal Church, and was elected the church's first bishop. Under his leadership, the denomination spread out from its Philadelphia-Baltimore base. Allen received members from as far south as Charleston, South Carolina, and, in 1824, sent missionaries to Haiti. He produced his church's first Book of Discipline and three hymnals, and wrote an autobiography.

ANB, 1:341–342; *BDE*, 8–10; *HDM*, 14–15.
J.M.

Anglicanism

Anglicanism refers to churches worldwide that are in communion with the Archbishop of Canterbury, the senior prelate of the Church of England. Also the term highlights an outlook that seeks to incorporate what it believes is best in the Roman Catholic, Protestant, and Orthodox traditions. This inclusiveness was first outlined during the sixteenth century, with its principal documents being the Church of England's Book of Common Prayer, Thirty-Nine Articles of Religion, and Book of Homilies. During the seventeenth century, Anglicanism decisively rejected Calvinist-inspired, precisely worded confessional statements, opting instead for the doctrinal breadth made possible by authorizing a massive amount of doctrinal material expressed in liturgies, articles of religion, and sermons. Anglicanism appeals to Scripture as containing all things necessary to salvation, understands the Christian tradition of the first four centuries as key for interpreting the Bible, and legitimizes the role played by reason in defining doctrine. It was as a convinced Anglican that **John Wesley** developed Methodist doctrine, choosing to articulate it, not in a concise confession of faith, but rather in his published sermons and a commentary on the New Testament.

Buchanan, Colin, ed., *Historical Dictionary of Anglicanism* (2006); Quinn, Frederick, *To Be a Pilgrim: The Anglican Ethos in History* (2001); Rowell, Geoffrey, ed., *The English Religious Tradition and the Genius of Anglicanism* (1992).
J.M.

Anglican/Episcopal–Methodist Conversations

By the beginning of the twenty-first century, British Methodist discussions with the Church of England and American Methodist conversations with the Episcopal Church had achieved results. A proposal for union between the British Methodist Church and the Church of England was negotiated in the 1960s, but due to opposition on both sides was not carried forward. Conversations resumed in 1995, resulting in an Anglican-Methodist Covenant that was approved by the Methodist Conference and the General Synod of the Church of England during the summer 2003; it was signed in November. The Covenant affirms 'one another's churches as true churches,' in which 'the word of God is authentically preached' and the sacraments 'duly administered and celebrated.' The ministries of both churches are affirmed, but 'a united, interchangeable ministry' remains a goal to be achieved. In the United States, the **United Methodist Church's** bishops endorsed, in 2005, an agreement with the Episcopal Church that looks forward to full approval of intercommunion by the 2012 General Conference. In 2006, the Episcopal General Convention voted to enter into an interim Eucharist Sharing relationship with the United Methodist Church. Dialogue continues on reconciling the two churches' ordained ministries.

http://www.anglican-methodist.org.uk/history.htm.
J.M.

Antinomianism

Literally meaning *against law*, antinomianism is the theological proposition that justified believers are not bound by the moral law. Its advocates often quote Paul's statement that 'if you are led by the Spirit, you are not subject to the law' (Galatians 5:18); Paul's total theology, however, repudiates the antinomian use of that text. Responding to Martin Luther's emphasis on justification by faith, antinomian sects sprang up, making it necessary for mainstream Protestants to insist that ideas such as free love and indifference to good works perverted their doctrines. Two centuries later, **John Wesley** attacked not only the idea that Christians are by grace set free from the need of observing the moral law, but also the assertion that believers are not required to use the means of grace: attending worship, receiving Holy Communion, personal and corporate Bible study, fasting, and praying. But doing all those things, Wesley insisted, is not what saves us. They are, however, the way, first, that we show we are repentant; and then, after we have experienced justification, the way we reveal its presence in our lives. **John Fletcher** gave the Wesleyan anti-antinomianism position classic expression in his *Checks against Antinomianism*.

DMBI, 6–7; *HDM*, 17–18.
J.M.

Appenzeller, Henry G. (1858–1902)

One of the first Methodist missionaries in Korea, Appenzeller, a member of the Philadelphia Conference of the **Methodist Episcopal Church**, was born in Souderton, Pennsylvania, to Lutheran parents. After experiencing conversion at a Presbyterian revival, he joined First Methodist Episcopal Church in Lancaster, Pennsylvania, graduated from Franklin and Marshall College and Drew Seminary, where he became interested in missionary work in Japan and Korea. Ordained in 1885, he sailed via Japan to Korea, arriving in Seoul in June of that year. Given permission to teach but not preach, Appenzeller opened a school. The next year, he was allowed to hold the first public worship service. Soon he founded First Methodist Episcopal Church in Seoul and served as its pastor. Appenzeller traveled extensively, visiting six of Korea's eight provinces. He served the cause of translating the Bible and various tracts into Korean, managed a book store, helped establish a publishing house, and edited various periodicals. He and his wife, Ella J. Dodge, had four children, three of whom devoted a total of sixty-eight years to missionary service in Korea. He died when the boat on which he was sailing sank in a collision.

Davies, Daniel M., *The Life and Thought of Henry Gerhard Appenzeller (1858–1902)* (1988); *HDM*, 18–19.
J.M.

Arminius, Jacobus (1560–1609)

Wellspring of the **Arminian** theological tradition, Arminius was born in Oudewater near Utrecht, Holland. He studied, briefly or for extended periods, in Utrecht, Marburg, Rotterdam, Leiden, Geneva, Basle, Padua, and Rome. Then, in 1587, he returned to the Netherlands and, having accepted a call to be pastor of the 'Old Church' in Amsterdam, was ordained in the Dutch Reformed Church. His marriage in 1690 to Lijsbet Reael, an aristocrat, enabled him to move among Amsterdam's most prominent families. Arminius held the Amsterdam pastorate until, in 1603, having just received his doctorate from Leiden, he became professor of theology there; he also served as rector (president) of the university. At Leiden and Amsterdam, Arminius dealt in a conciliatory fashion with the theological fury of Calvinists who defended the doctrine of predestination, which his studies in the Epistle to the Romans had caused him to reject. He believed that fallen humans are not puppets manipulated by God, some to salvation, some to damnation; rather, even fallen humans have received grace sufficient to enable them to believe in God; therefore they are responsible for their belief or unbelief. Arminius published his views in *Examination of Perkins' Pamphlet* (1598) and *Declaration of Sentiments* (1608).

Bangs, Carl, *Arminius: A Study in the Dutch Reformation* (1971); HDM, 19.
J.M.

Arminianism

Taking its name from **Jacobus Arminius**, this theological tradition, one that significantly influenced **John Wesley**, rejects the Calvinist doctrine of predestination found in the writings of, among others, Theodore Beza (1519–1605), who argued that the Fall was part of God's eternal plan, that it followed the election of some to salvation and others to damnation, and that the death of Christ atones only for the sins of those predestined to be saved. The Arminian rebuttal of Calvinism, formally set forth in the *Remonstrance* of 1610, insists that the doctrine of predestination is unbiblical, that God's sovereignty is compatible with real human free will, and that Christ died for all, not just those elected to salvation. The Synod of Dort (1618–1619) condemned the Arminian position, resulting in the persecution of many Dutch Arminians and the expulsion of some. Soon a number of seventeenth century Church of England theologians were articulating Arminian views. In the eighteenth century, one of that church's priests, John Wesley, highlighted his opposition to the doctrine of predestination, which was preached by **George Whitefield** among others, by naming his monthly periodical the *Arminian Magazine*; its first issue (1777) featured a biography of Arminius.

ODCC, 107–108.
J.M.

Arts, The

Christianity opens its door to the arts, because it believes the Word of God became flesh in Jesus the Christ. It is not an unguarded door, however; ecclesiastics typically expect works of art to be doctrinally sound, with human flesh covered, and with nothing, in **John Wesley's** words, to 'give pain to the tenderest heart.' This guardedness makes artists restive: they see themselves as persons through whom truths, even raw truths, and emotions, sometimes painful, become visible.

Vincent van Gogh is perhaps the most renowned artist ever to be brushed by Methodism. Yet van Gogh's brilliantly colored distortions of 'reality' would likely elicit from Wesley the exclamation he used when objecting to the 'glaring' colors in Benjamin West's painting of the raising of Lazarus, 'When will painters have common sense!' No doubt van Gogh absorbed something of the Wesleyan heritage of compassion for the poor when he was a lay preacher on a British Methodist circuit (1876), but he would have found Wesley's taste for common-sense realism emotionally anemic. Van Gogh used exuberant colors and dramatic brushwork to express, for instance, his ecstatic response to a starry night.

Wesley objected to ecstasy in art as well as religion, even the ecstatic response of some people to mountains – 'horrid' was one of his epithets for jagged peaks, 'rough' another. He preferred nature converted, smoothed out by farmers and landscape gardeners.

Wesley toured stately houses and gardens, looked at paintings and sculptures, and decided he favored realism, 'an exact likeness.' But not too exact: Wesley expected works of art, unlike life itself, to be uncluttered, without 'glaring' colors, and with no one 'stark naked.'

Although Wesley's aesthetic stands opposed to Stanley Spencer's. Spencer (1891–1959) expressed in his paintings a key theme in Wesleyan theology – the belief that new life here is an 'antepast of heaven'; that, in **Charles Wesley's** words, 'Live we here to Heaven restor'd' (*Hymns for Our Lord's Resurrection* (1746), no. 7). Possibly Spencer absorbed that idea when he went with his mother to the Methodist chapel in Cookham, England. In his paintings, Cookham is a 'holy suburb of heaven'; and the dead are raised in Cookham churchyard, some in white robes, some in everyday clothes, some 'stark naked.' Just as early Christian mosaicists depicted Jesus with full frontal nudity in Jordan's baptismal waters, so Spencer used nudity as a visual metaphor for, in his words, the 'redeemed state.'

John Wesley's ministry centered on the conversion of men and women, but the idea of using nakedness as a visual metaphor for the converted state never entered his mind. And recognition that an artist can transform an unclothed model into a material expression of a spiritual reality is not common in Wesleyanism. Methodists tend to prefer the verbal metaphors of sermons and hymns to the visual metaphors of paintings and sculptures, especially those that shock tender hearts.

Methodism gave the world one master hymn-writer, Charles Wesley, but no poet to rank with the Anglican poet-priests John Donne (1571/2–1631), George Herbert (1593–1633), and R. S. Thomas (1913–2000). Charles' hymns feature memory-aiding rhymes, a variety of meters, and mind-opening images, such as the affirmation that eucharistic wine 'yields me larger Draughts of God'; and they, more than John's sermons, leave Wesleyan theology sticking like burrs to Methodist minds and hearts.

Methodism has continued to inspire hymn-writers – for example, Fanny Crosby (1820–1915), Charles Albert Tindley (1856–1933), and Fred Pratt Green (1903–2000); no one, however, has come close to equaling Charles Wesley's range of themes and depth of theology.

Methodism cannot claim any great novelist as a faithful worshiper; its puritanism, philistinism, and liturgical barrenness repel creative personalities. Generally speaking, Methodists appear in major fiction as hypocrites or figures of fun. 'Poor Mrs. Purefoy!' writes James Joyce in *Ulysses* (1922): 'Methodist husband. Method in his madness. . . . Eating with a stopwatch, thirtytwo chews the minute.'

In Britain, the mother of novelists Charlotte (*Jane Eyre*, 1847) and Emily (*Wuthering Heights*, 1847) Brontë was a staunch Methodist. When she died, her sister moved into the Brontë household, bringing with her a Methodist fervor, which her nieces later rejected. George Eliot's novel *Adam Bede* (1859) presents Methodists as instigators of dissension and, occasionally, as religiously sincere; for instance, a Methodist woman lay preacher.

In the United States, Edward Eggleston, son of Methodists, became a Methodist circuit rider. Later he abandoned Methodism and accepted the pastorate of a 'creedless' congregation. His *The Hoosier Schoolmaster* (1871) and *The Circuit Rider* (1874) are classics of regional Americana. Stephen Crane, the fourteenth child of a Methodist minister, published *Maggie: A Girl of the Streets* (1893) and *The Red Badge of Courage* (1895), books dealing with 'stark naked' prostitution and war. An Alabaman of Methodist background, Harper Lee wrote *To Kill a Mockingbird* (1960); voted 'Best Novel of the Century' (1999).

The art form Methodists find particularly appealing is Wesley's image. Numerous engravings of his portraits by artists such as Nathaniel Hone and

George Romney appeared. The English potter Enoch Wood made a Wesley bust that has been reproduced from the 1780s to the present day. Josiah Wedgwood created Wesley medallions, and other potters shaped Wesley busts and figurines of him in a pulpit. For nineteenth-century American Methodists, Nathaniel Currier issued a color lithograph of Wesley (1840s). In the twentieth century, just as Warner Sallman's 1941 'Head of Jesus' is *the* Jesus for Americans, so Frank Salisbury's 1932 Portrait of Wesley (Wesley's House, City Road, London) is the iconic Wesley for American and British Methodists alike.

It is a Wesley, whose definition of what constitutes good art – no nakedness, nothing to pain the tenderest heart – has produced a Methodism that appears to have closed its doors to many artists and writers.

DMBI, 11–12, 57–58, 206–207, 231, 362, 400–401; *EWM*, 2515–2519; Telford, John, ed., *The Letters of the Rev. John Wesley* (1931), 2:25–27; 4:232, 249, 256–258, 267; 6:283; 7:82; 8:107, 115; *WJW(B)*, 7:20, 81, 97, 104, 116, 472; 21:110, 443, 465; 22:305–306, 440–441; 23:33–34, 173–174, 181–182, 225, 283, 296–297, 359–360, 405; 24:118.
J.M.

Asbury, Francis (1745–1816)

English-born Asbury reshaped John Wesley's Methodism, enabling it to become an American church, one both democratic and authoritarian. His schooling lasted until age 13, when he was apprenticed to a craftsman. Influenced by his mother, he became a Methodist, soon a class leader, then a local preacher, finally one of Wesley's itinerant preachers. In 1771, Asbury volunteered for service in America, where his leadership qualities were quickly recognized. Because he took the American side during the Revolutionary War, he was Wesley's obvious choice to lead American Methodism when, in 1784, Wesley provided the basis for the **Methodist Episcopal Church**. Asbury insisted that Wesley's appointment be ratified by his fellow preachers. They voted for him unanimously, and he was ordained deacon, elder, and superintendent (bishop). Although Wesley appointed **Thomas Coke** to be co-superintendent, it was Asbury who, for the next thirty-two years, ruled American Methodism. He appointed and disciplined the itinerant preachers; traveled the settled areas and the frontier, evaluating progress and looking for mission opportunities; and guided the conferences in reaching the decisions he favored, although occasionally his proposals were voted down. By the time of his death, Asbury was one of the best known men in the United States.

ANB, 1:658–660; *BDE*, 24–27; Wigger, John H., *American Saint: Francis Asbury and the Methodists* (2009).
J.M.

Asia

Methodism's entry into Asia began with Thomas Coke's 1813 voyage to Ceylon (Sri Lanka), Java, and India. Although Coke died aboard ship before arriving at his destination, his fellow Methodist travelers founded a Sri Lankan mission which within six years was organized into two districts. Over the next century and a half, Methodist missionaries in Asia succeeded in founding schools, clinics, hospitals, and churches. One of Coke's companions James Lynch (1775–1858) extended British Methodist work from Sri Lanka to India in 1817. British missionary efforts were strongest in south India until 1947 when their missions united with Presbyterian and Anglican ministries to form the Church of South India, although some British Wesleyan churches in north India remained in the mother denomination.

The first official Methodist Episcopal Church missionaries, William Butler (1818–1899) and his wife, Clementina Rowe Butler (1862–1949), arrived in India in 1856. Later, Clementina was a founder of her denomination's Woman's Foreign Missionary Society which dispatched Clara Swain and Isabella Thoburn, two pioneer missionaries who initiated 'women's work for women,' emphasizing medical treatment and educational opportunities for Asian women. Northern episcopal Methodism extended its reach into Pakistan, Myanamar, Malaysia, Sarawak, and the Philippines. It posted missionaries to China in 1847, Japan in 1873, and Korea in 1885.

The Methodist Episcopal Church, South and the Methodist Protestant Church established missions and schools in China. Southern Methodists also organized ministries in Japan and Korea, and Methodist Protestants in India and Japan. In 1940 northern and southern episcopal Methodism and the Methodist Protestants joined their work to form the Methodist Church in China.

Among other Methodist denominations with missionary work in Asia, historically and at present, were Free Methodists, the Church of the Nazarene, the Wesleyan Church, the African Methodist Episcopal Church, and the Evangelical United Brethren Church and its predecessors.

Methodism in Asia remains numerically significant in India (where it is part of the churches of North and South India), Korea, Pakistan, and the Philippines. Several of the churches which trace their origins to missions of British and American Methodism have now become autonomous, for example the Korean Methodist Church, and the Methodist Church in Singapore. The World Methodist Council estimated about ten million Asians in Methodist or Methodist-related denominations in 2010.

Barclay, Wade Crawford, *The Methodist Episcopal Church, 1845–95: Widening Horizons*, History of Methodist Missions (1957), 3:367–757; Copplestone, J. Tremayne,

Twentieth-Century Perspectives, History of Methodist Missions, 4:646–861, 1130–1204; *DMBI*, various regional and biographical articles, e.g., India, China, and Sri Lanka; *EWM*, various regional and biographical articles, e.g., China, India, Japan, and Korea; *HDM*, 22–31; *World Methodist Council Handbook* (current edition).
C.Y.

Australasia

Methodism began in Australia in 1812 when to schoolmasters, Thomas Bowden and John Hosking, held meetings in their homes in New South Wales. They requested that the Methodist Mission Society in London send a qualified preacher. In 1815 Samuel Leigh was sent and two years later opened the first Methodist chapel in New South Wales. Over the ensuing years the initial work expanded to other settlements including Hobart (1820), Melbourne (1836), Adelaide (1837), and Perth (1840). British Wesleyan Methodism granted the Australians semi-autonomous status in 1854 and the first Australian conference was held the following year.

Other British Methodist denominations – Primitive Methodists, Bible Christians, Methodist New Connexion, and United Methodist Free Churches – were represented in Australia as some of their members migrated and established congregations. A union of the smaller denominations and the Wesleyan Methodists was accomplished in 1902 resulting in the formation of the Methodist Church of Australia and New Zealand. After several decades of negotiations with Congregationalists and Presbyterians, in 1977 Australian Methodism united with the other two denominations to become the Uniting Church of Australia.

New Zealand Methodism began in 1822 through the efforts of the British Methodist Missionary Society. Early work concentrated on the Maori, but the focus shifted to white migrants in the larger settlements and towns. Other British Methodist denominations were also established in New Zealand including the Bible Christians (1841), Primitive Methodists (1844), and the United Methodist Free Churches (1868). By 1913 these denominations had joined the Wesleyan Methodists to become the Methodist Church of New Zealand.

The South Pacific islands were the focus of mission efforts by the Wesleyan Methodist Missionary Society in the first half of the nineteenth century. Tonga was the first when Walter Lawry arrived, but permanent work was not established until 1826 with the ministry of John Thomas and John Hutchinson. The mission to Fiji began in 1835 with William Cross and David Cargill. Samoan Methodism was formally organized in 1835 when Wesleyan Methodist missionary Peter Turner arrived as the first resident missionary. Autonomy was achieved in each of three countries – Tonga

(1924), Fiji (1964), and Samoa (1964). Methodism remains numerically strong in Fiji.

DMBI, various articles, for example, Australia, New Zealand, Tonga, Fiji, and Samoa; Findlay, G. G. and W. W. Holdsworth, eds, *The History of the Wesleyan Methodist Missionary Society* (1924), III:13–61, 165–253; Forman, Charles W., *The Island Churches of the South Pacific: Emergence in the Twentieth Century* (1982); *HDM*, 36–8, 222–224, 297–299.
C.Y.

Báez-Camargo, Gonzalo (1899–1983)

Born in Oaxaca, Mexico, Báez-Camargo was a Methodist leader, educator, biblical scholar, editor, and writer. During the Mexican Revolution he served in the army, defending the nation and its new constitution. Following military service, he enrolled in Union Evangelical Seminary in Mexico City in 1918. Upon graduation in 1921 he served as pastor of several local congregations. Báez-Camargo's academic positions began with teaching in Puebla at the Instituto Metodista which he later directed. He taught at his seminary alma mater and managed Union Publishing House. In 1927 he was honored by appointment as General Secretary of National Council of Evangelical Churches of Mexico, the distinguished organization of Protestant churches, and was later chosen one of the translators for Mexico's Bible Society. In 1929 he chaired the notable Protestant assembly in Havana, Cuba, and was instrumental in writing its major report on the renewal of religion in **Latin America**. A journalist, editor, and poet, Báez-Camargo published a large number of books on Mexican and Latin American religion including works on Christian education (1933), Protestantism in Latin America (1945), Methodism (1952), **John Wesley** (1953), the biblical text (1975), and Israel (1981). He was one of Methodism's most important voices in Mexico.

EWM, I: 195.
C.Y.

Bangs, Nathan (1778–1862)

Theologian, historian, missions-advocate, and editor, Bangs was born in Connecticut, but grew up in New York State. After experiencing conversion in 1799, he prepared for ordination in the **Methodist Episcopal Church**, and was appointed in 1804 to missionary work in Canada; he returned four years later to preaching appointments in the United States. In 1819, Bangs helped organize the MEC's Missionary Society, which he later served as treasurer and corresponding secretary. He was selected in 1820 to head the church's publishing activities, becoming the editor at various times of *The Christian Advocate*, *The Methodist Magazine*, and *The Quarterly Review*. Beginning with *The Errors of Hopkinsianism* (1815), Bangs, 'the first significant Wesleyan theologian in the United States' (Thomas A. Langford), opposed the doctrine of predestination and articulated an **Arminian**-type theology. As a historian, he wrote a four-volume *History of the Methodist Episcopal Church* (1838–1842), which tells the church's story from 1776 to 1840. After a brief presidency of Wesleyan University, Bangs became controversial due to his espousal, for the sake of church unity, of compromise on the question of slavery. He returned to the pastorate in New York City and became the ministerial leader of **Phoebe Palmer's** holiness meetings.

ANB, 2:105–106; *HDM*, 40; Hermann, Richard E., *Nathan Bangs: Apologist for American Methodism* (thesis, Emory University, 1973).
J.M.

Bast, Anton (1867–1937)

The first Scandinavian elected bishop of the **Methodist Episcopal Church**, founder of the Central Mission in Copenhagen, and known across his home country as 'the minister of the poor,' Bast was born in Lokken, Denmark. After working as a fisherman, he received theological training in Copenhagen, was ordained, and served several Methodist parishes before being appointed to Jerusalem Church, Copenhagen, in 1906. While there, in 1910, he established the Central Mission, which ministered to the poor. Attached to it were several institutions for children. Bast was elected bishop at the 1920 Methodist Episcopal General Conference, but he was allowed to continue leading the Central Mission. In 1926, as the result of charges of financial dishonesty brought against him by a few members of Jerusalem Church, he was tried and convicted in a civil court. Previously, he had been released from his duties as bishop. The 1928 General Conference appointed a trial committee, with the outcome that Bast was permanently suspended from the episcopacy, but not deposed from the ordained ministry. He, however, withdrew from the annual conference and from the Methodist Episcopal Church.

EWM, I: 231–232.
J.M.

Bible Christians (Great Britain)

When, in 1815, mainstream British Methodism expelled **William O'Bryan**, a local preacher, for his freelance evangelistic activities, he founded the Bible Christians, popularly known as 'Bryanites.' O'Bryan, who said that **John Wesley** was 'ever near' him, argued that he and his church were truly Wesleyan in their teachings and practices. The Bible Christians expanded from their base in northeast Cornwall and Devon, England, spreading across the southern part of the country, into South Wales, and to the Channel Islands. Their first conference met in 1819; their 'Rules of Society' closely followed Wesley's General Rules; and, when they founded a magazine in 1822, they called it the *Arminian Magazine*, the same name Wesley used for his. O'Bryan left the Bible Christians in 1829, taking with him two preachers and several hundred members; they termed themselves Arminian Bible Christians. O'Bryan's departure meant that James Thorne (1795–1872), one of O'Bryan's earliest followers, assumed leadership of the Bible Christians. Growing during the nineteenth century, the church had 32,000 members when, in 1907, it joined the Methodist New Connection and the United Methodist Free Churches to create the United Methodist Church (see **Methodism, Britain**). Meanwhile, O'Bryan's itinerant evangelistic activities had taken the Bible Christians to Canada (1831) and the United States (1845).

DMBI, 29–30; HMGB, 3: 169–172; Wickes, Michael J. L., *The West Country Preachers. A new history of the Bible Christian Church (1815–1907)* (1987).
J.M.

Boehm, Martin (1725–1812)

Mennonite preacher and **United Brethren** bishop, Boehm was born in Lancaster County, Pennsylvania. About 1758, his Mennonite congregation chose him to be a minister, a role for which he felt spiritually unqualified until one day, while plowing, he experienced assurance of salvation, and soon became a fruitful evangelical preacher. The Mennonites advanced him to the status of bishop. But his preaching attracted many German-speaking non-Mennonites, one of whom was **Philip William Otterbein**, pastor of a German Reformed church in Lancaster. Around 1767, Otterbein, after hearing Boehm preach, greeted him, saying, 'We are brothers.' Soon those brothers in Christ became the informal leaders of an evangelical revival among German-speakers in Pennsylvania, Maryland, and Virginia. Boehm's openness to other denominations – a **Methodist Episcopal** class meeting was organized at his home – led the Mennonites, about 1775, to excommunicate him. Other preachers joined Boehm and Otterbein in their revival ministry. In 1800, thirteen of them met in conference, organized the United Brethren in Christ, and elected Boehm and Otterbein as bishops. By 1805, Boehm had become physically unable to provide day-to-day leadership. But in 1810, he traveled to Baltimore to meet with Otterbein and **Francis Asbury** to discuss, unsuccessfully, merging the German-speaking United Brethren ministry with English-speaking Methodism.

ANB, 3:99–100; Behney, J. Bruce and Paul H. Eller, *The History of the Evangelical United Brethren Church* (1979); *HDM*, 49–50.
J.M.

Bonino, José Míguez (1924–)

Born in Argentina, Bonino, a Methodist, is one of the leading **Latin American** liberation theologians. He received his basic theological training in 1948 at the Evangelical Faculty of Theology in Buenos Aires, Argentina, now known as the Instituto Universitario ISEDET (Instituto Superior Evangelico de Estudios Teologicos), a master's degree in theology from Emory University, Atlanta, Georgia in 1952, and a doctorate in theology from Union Theological Seminary, New York, in 1960. Bonino taught theology and ethics at the Evangelical Faculty of Theology from 1954 to 1969, and its successor ISEDET from 1970 to 1985. A Latin American Protestant observer at the Second Vatican Council, he was also a president of the World Council of Churches, and a founder of the organization, Church and Society in Latin America. He is the author of several important books including *Doing Theology in a Revolutionary Situation* (1975), *Christians and Marxists: The Mutual Challenge to Revolution* (1976), *Toward a Christian Political Ethics* (1983), and *Faces of Latin American Protestantism* (1997).

Gonzalez, Justo, ed., *The Westminster Dictionary of Theologians* (2006); Langford, Thomas A., *Practical Divinity: Theology in the Wesleyan Tradition* (1998), 1, 239–241; McGrath, Alister E., ed., *The Blackwell Encyclopedia of Modern Christian Thought* (1993), 376.
C.Y.

Booth, William (1829–1912) and Catherine (1829–1890)

Cofounders of the **Salvation Army**, Catherine Mumford, who was born in Derbyshire, England, and William Booth, who was born in Nottingham, married in 1855. William worked first as an apprentice pawnbroker, then, after his conversion, as a lay preacher in several Methodist denominations before being ordained, in 1858, in the **Methodist New Connection** (Great

Britain). Catherine, who played an active role in his work, shared his frustration with their denomination's polity. So in 1861 they severed their ties with it, and began a ministry in East London, where they formed the Christian Mission in 1865, out of which grew the Salvation Army in 1878. Catherine, who bore eight children, preached, advocated equal rights for women in church and society, and played a role in promoting in England the holiness movement led by American **Phoebe Palmer**. Catherine's reasoned yet passionate approach to ministry balanced William's rough-edged impatience. Together, they led the Salvation Army's street evangelism, with its signature brass bands playing saloon-like tunes. They attacked such social evils as drunkenness, gambling, and prostitution, and provided physical and social care for the poor. In 1890, William published a guide to the Salvation Army's social program, *In Darkest England and the Way Out*.

DMBI, 37; Green, Roger J., *The Life and Ministry of William Booth: Founder of the Salvation Army* (2005); *ODNB*, (William) 6:633–634, (Catherine) 6:602–605.
J.M.

Bourne, Hugh (1772–1852)

The shy, anxious son of a drunken, violent father, Bourne – who was converted at a Wesleyan Methodist love feast, but expelled by that church for failing to adhere to Wesleyan disciplines – co-founded **Primitive Methodism (Great Britain)**. He was born on a farm in England's pottery-making region, converted in 1799, and began, despite his shyness, to preach in 1801. His wide-ranging evangelistic ministry, which caused him to miss his Wesleyan Methodist class meetings, and his support of camp meetings led to his expulsion in 1808. Under the co-leadership of Bourne and **William Clowes**, Primitive Methodism took form during the next few years. Bourne became general superintendent of the movement, printed its first class tickets (1811), edited the Primitive Methodist *Magazine*, started a magazine for children, and wrote his church's history. Three times, he was secretary of the Primitive Methodist conference. He wrote hymns, compiled hymnbooks, and made his own study and library a base for other Primitive Methodist preachers. In 1844, he toured the United States and Canada. Although he and Clowes differed in temperament, with Clowes' easy ways making him more popular than the shy, awkward Bourne, they worked together to make certain the Primitive Methodist movement did not fracture.

DMBI, 38; *ODNB*, 6:851-852; Wilkinson, John T., *Hugh Bourne, 1772–1852* (1952).
J.M.

Bunting, Jabez (1779–1858)

Some of his contemporaries saw Bunting as a dictator. Others viewed him as the needed response to John Pawson's 1805 observation that Methodism was a headless body. Certainly, the perceived dictatorship of Bunting, who declared that 'Methodism was as much opposed to democracy as to sin,' led to two secessions from mainstream British Methodism: Protestant Methodists (1828) and the Wesleyan Association (1835). It is equally certain that Bunting, who was born in Manchester and studied medicine there before entering the ministry in 1799, provided the head that the Wesleyan Methodism needed to become a nineteenth-century church. In 1832, he settled in London and became the first secretary and master strategist of the Wesleyan Methodist Missionary Society; beginning in 1835, he was also the president of Hoxton Theological Institution. At various times, he served the conference as connectional editor, secretary, and president. Bunting promoted the election of younger ministers to the conference's legal corporation, worked for the right to petition conference, argued for the inclusion of laymen on key committees, promoted theological training for ministers and their ordination by the laying on of hands, and championed Methodist day schools. But Bunting's inflexible way of doing those things made a true partnership between clergy and laity impossible for a generation.

DMBI, 48; Hempton, David, *The Religion of the People: Methodism and popular religion, c. 1750–1900* (1996), 91–108; *ODNB*, 8:696–698.
J.M.

Butler, William (1818–1899)

A far-seeing, strong-willed, Dublin-born Irishman, Butler served as a Wesleyan Methodist minister during his country's potato-famine era. Then, in 1850, he and his second wife emigrated to the United States, where he became a minister of the **Methodist Episcopal Church** in Massachusetts. After the death of his second wife, he married Clementina Rowe; the two of them were selected by Bishop Matthew Simpson, in 1856, to begin a mission in India. Their work opened in Bareilly in 1858, with Butler promoting the use of printing presses, schools, orphanages, and agricultural projects as well as evangelism; and giving priority to women's education. The Butlers returned to pastoral appointments in the States in 1864. Five years later, Clementina Butler Rowe was a founder of the Woman's Foreign Missionary Society of the Methodist Episcopal Church. In 1872, Bishop Simpson asked the Butlers to establish a mission in Mexico, where Butler moved among Roman Catholics in a 'Christian and unsectarian manner.' His independent-minded handling of the mission's finances led to his recall in 1878, and he returned to the pastorate in New England. Later, he traveled to the Holy Land, returned to India and Mexico, and wrote books about the countries where he worked as a pioneer missionary.

Butler, Clementina, *William Butler, the Founder of Two Missions of the Methodist Episcopal Church* (1902); *EWM*, I: 365–366; *HDM*, 61–62.
J.M.

Calvinism

A theological tradition which originated with John Calvin (1509–1564), Calvinism has been foundational for the Reformed, Presbyterian, and Congregational traditions. It is rooted in belief in the sovereignty of God and God's exclusive role in human salvation. Some Calvinistic influence is detectable in the Thirty-Nine Articles of the Church of England. The Synod of Dort (1618–1619) is often cited as defining five main points of Calvinism: total sinful depravity of the human race and inability of humans to have a role in their salvation; God's unconditional election of some to salvation; the benefits of Christ's atoning death limited to those elected to salvation; the irresistibility of God's gracious election; and the perseverance of those elected who cannot lose their salvation. **John and Charles Wesley** were adamant that Calvinism of this sort is an erroneous and dangerous theology. In both brothers' journal entries, sermons by John (especially 'Free Grace'), and hymn-poems by Charles (e.g., 'Father, Whose Everlasting Love'), they held that by divine preventing (prevenient) grace, all are free to accept or reject God's offer of forgiveness and redemption. Historically, Methodism has always had serious reservations about Calvinism's denying human free will in the matter of salvation.

Coppedge, Allan, *John Wesley in Theological Debate* (1987); Gonzalez, Justo L., *Essential Theological Terms* (2005); Hart, Darryl G., et al., *Dictionary of the Presbyterian & Reformed Tradition in America* (1999); Rack, Henry D., *Reasonable Enthusiast: John Wesley and the Rise of Methodism* (1989).
C.Y.

Canada

Methodism entered Canada from both Britain and the United States. Beginning in the eighteenth century various Methodist groups planted work there.

The first preacher to introduce the Wesleyan message was Laurence Coughlan (d. c. 1784), an Anglican priest, who sympathetically implemented

Methodist beliefs and practices in Newfoundland in 1766. Coughlan organized classes following an evangelical awakening in the area. He left Newfoundland in 1773 to return to England. Another pioneer preacher was William Black (1760–1834) who founded Methodism in eastern Canada in 1781. Black's ministry was strengthened by loyalist Methodists migrating from the United States. He attended the Christmas Conference in Baltimore in 1784 and served as superintendent for Nova Scotia. British loyalist William Losee (1757–1832), another founder of Canadian Methodism, moved from New York to Nova Scotia in 1783 and four years later experienced conversion. He received deacon's ordination from Francis Asbury in 1789 and in 1791 established the first circuit in Ontario. Mental illness forced Losee to return to the United States, but his brief four-year ministry in Canada was significant in Methodism's expansion in Upper Canada.

Methodists in the maritime were supervised by the British Wesleyan Methodists. In 1855 the Canadian work continued to develop as the autonomous Wesleyan Methodist Conference of Eastern British America. In addition to the Wesleyan Methodists other British Methodist denominations who initiated work in Canada were the Primitive Methodists, Bible Christians, and the Methodist New Connexion. The Methodist Church of Canada was formed in 1874 by a union of the Wesleyan Methodists and New Connexion membership in Canada.

At the Methodist Episcopal Christmas Conference two preachers, Freeborn Garrettson and James O Cromwell, were set apart for mission work in Nova Scotia which began in 1785. Methodist Episcopal members from the United States were important in the spread of Wesleyanism, especially in Upper Canada. Among them were Paul (?–1795) and Barbara Ruckle Heck (1734–1804) who had been instrumental in organizing Methodism in New York City. More than forty Methodist Episcopal missionaries served in Canada between 1800 and 1813. The work stalled during the War of 1812, a conflict which created severe tensions between the United States and Canada. Several years after the war, in October 1828, the American mission to Canada was transformed into the Methodist Episcopal Church of Canada.

Canadian Methodists, Congregationalists, and Presbyterians joined in 1925 to form the United Church of Canada. It remains the largest Protestant Church in Canada and holds membership in the World Methodist Council. The African Methodist Episcopal and Wesleyan churches, as well as the Church of the Nazarene and Free Methodist Church of Canada also maintain congregations in Canada.

Barclay, Wade Crawford, *Early American Methodism, 1789–1844: Missionary Motivation* and *Expansion*, History of Methodist Missions, 1:166–200; *DMBI*, 54; *HDM*, 63–64; Semple, Neil, *The Lord's Dominion: The History of Canadian Methodism* (1996);

Van Die, Marguerite, *An Evangelical Mind: Nathaniel Burwash and the Methodist Tradition in Canada, 1839–1918* (1989); *EWM*, I: 385–394.
C.Y.

Camp Meeting

Popular with Baptists, Presbyterians, and Methodists in the United States, camp meetings were held in the outdoors for periods of several days, sometimes weeks. On the American frontier and in more populated areas people gathered for fellowship, to hear evangelistic preaching, to sing popular hymns, to engage in Bible study and prayer, to give personal testimonies, and to commit or recommit themselves to Christian faith and life. Originally, those attending lived in a tent community in an area conducive to camping. Later, the primitive tent camp meeting gave way to permanent sites with cottages and well-constructed wooden tabernacles for **worship** and preaching. Religious emotion often ran high at these meetings where spectacular conversions and experiences of sanctification were common. **Francis Asbury's** journal records the successes of early Methodist camp meetings in America. The camp meeting became an important institution for the **Holiness Movement**. In Great Britain the **Primitive Methodists**, much influenced by Lorenzo Dow (1777–1834), American Methodist evangelist, sponsored camp meetings, the first and most notable at Mow Cop on the border between Cheshire and Stafforshire, England, on 31 May 1807. A few Methodist camp meetings survive in the United States and elsewhere.

Brown, Kenneth O., *Holy Ground: A Study of the American Camp Meeting* (1992); Brown, Kenneth O., *Holy Ground Too: The Camp Meeting Family Tree* (1997); *DMBI*, 53–54; Clark, Elmer T., et al., *The Journal and Letters of Francis Asbury*, 3 vols. (1958); Semple, Neil, *The Lord's Dominion: The History of Canadian Methodism* (1997), 127–136, 213–225.
C.Y.

Castro, Emilio (1927–)

An ordained minister of the Evangelical Methodist Church of Uruguay, its president (1970–1972), and the fourth general secretary of the World Council of Churches, Castro was born in Montevideo, gained his basic theological education at Union Seminary, Buenos Aires, studied with Karl Barth at Basel, and received his PhD from the University of Lausanne. Early in his career, he pastored a Methodist church in La Paz, Bolivia, then one in Montevideo; while serving the latter church, he taught contemporary theological thought at the Mennonite Seminary, Montevideo. From 1965 to 1972, Castro was the executive secretary of the South American Association of

Theological Schools; moving on, in 1973, to the staff of the World Council of Churches as director of the Commission on World Mission and Evangelism. He became the Council's general secretary in 1985, a position he held until 1992. During his time at the World Council, he wrote, among others, the following books: *Amidst Revolution, Sent Free: Mission and Unity in the Perspective of the Kingdom*, and *When We Pray Together*. Church of India Bishop Lesslie Newbigin said Castro had 'a burning compassion for the victims of public wrong, a pastoral care for individual people, and a bubbling sense of humor.'

Lossky, Nicholas, et al., eds, *Dictionary of the Ecumenical Movement* (1991), 130.
J.M.

Chautauqua Institution

Founded in 1874 by **Methodist Episcopal** clergyman John Heyl Vincent (1832–1920) and layman Lewis H. Miller at Fairpoint (later Chautauqua), New York, as an assembly for training Sunday school teachers, Chautauqua grew into a full-scale summer school offering classes, lectures, and concerts. Vincent was especially active in Methodist Sunday school work and was elected to the episcopacy in 1888, and served in New York, Kansas, and Switzerland. The original Chautauqua assembly spawned hundreds of self-improvement 'chautauquas' across the United States which offered educational and cultural programs. In 1878 Vincent developed a four-year adult correspondence course, the Chautauqua Literary and Scientific Circle, which grew into approximately 10,000 organized circles during its first twenty years. The original assembly was chartered in 1902 as the Chautauqua Institution and continues to offer programs for thousands of visitors each summer.

EWM, I: 460; *HDM*, 68–9, 309–310; Irwin, Alfreda L., *Three Taps of the Gavel, Pledge to the Future: The Chautauqua Story* (1987); Morrison, Theodore, *Chautauqua: A Center for Education, Religion, and the Arts in America* (1974).
C.Y.

Chaves, Ottilia de Oliviera (1897–1983)

A leading Brazilian Christian, Chaves was born in Tombos, Brazil. She was raised a **Roman Catholic** who converted to Methodism in 1916 and joined the Methodist church. She received bachelors degrees in pharmacy and religious education from the Methodist Instituto Granbery in Brazil and a master's degree from Scarritt College in the United States. Chaves was highly regarded in both Methodist and ecumenical communities. She was president of the Methodist Women's Societies of the North and South Brazil annual conferences, served as editor of the **women's** periodical *Vox Missionaria*, and was elected a delegate to every annual and general conference in Brazil between 1930 and 1965. In the wider Methodist connection, she was president of the World Methodist Federation of Methodist Women (1952–1956) and was a delegate to the general conference of the **Methodist Church** in 1952. Among her many **ecumenical** activities were serving as a delegate to the World Sunday School Convention in Rio de Janeiro (1932) and the International Missionary Conference in Madras, India (1938). Chaves is the author of several books including works on religious education and the sexual education of children. She is one of the most important personalities in Brazilian Methodist history.

EWM, I: 461, 1226–1227.
C.Y.

Children

Methodists have shared with other faiths a concern for family life and children. **John Wesley**, despite whose marriage was not exemplary and had no children of his own, demonstrated a keen interest in children in his ministry. Two of his published sermons dealt specifically with children, 'On Family Religion' and 'On the Education of Children.' Although much of Wesley's interest was focused on their spiritual welfare, he also counseled Methodists to take responsibility for their physical care and nurture. As usual, Wesley not only offered advice, but also acted on behalf of children. Among his accomplishments he established Kingswood School near Bristol, England, in 1748 to educate the sons of Methodist families, founded an orphan house in Newcastle, and provided housing for widows and children. **Charles Wesley**, whose marriage was exceptionally sound and who was a father, shared his brother's attention to children, writing hymns for and about them (e.g., *Hymns for Children*, 1763). Every Methodist denomination supported **Sunday schools**. They founded secondary schools, colleges, and universities to educate children and young people. Furthermore, they have provided other services for children including shelters, foster parents programs, relief for children caught in poverty, and counseling to assist children and their families.

The Book of Resolutions of The United Methodist Church (current issue); Church, Leslie F., *Early Methodist People* (1948), 236–246; *DMBI*, 62–63; Paul Sangster, *Pity My Simplicity: The Evangelical Revival and the Religious Education of Children* (1963).
C.Y.

Christian Methodist Episcopal Church (USA)

Organized in 1870 by African American members of the **Methodist Episcopal Church, South**, and until 1954 known by its former name, the Colored Methodist Episcopal Church, its constituency was reluctant to join the **African Methodist Episcopal**, the **African Methodist Episcopal Zion**, or the **Methodist Episcopal** churches. Upon its organization it adopted a Wesleyan theology and a polity similar to the Methodist Episcopal Church, South. Its first elected bishops, **William Henry Miles** and Richard H. Vanderhorst, were consecrated by southern Methodist bishops Robert Paine and Holland N. McTyeire. Although originally a southern denomination, the Christian Methodist Episcopal Church expanded into the north and west. The denomination established an order of **deaconesses** in 1894, a women's missionary group in 1918, ordained women in the later twentieth century, and supported several colleges and a theological seminary. *The Christian Index*, the denomination's official periodical is the second oldest African American continuously published religious periodical in the United States. Among its ecumenical commitments are memberships in the National Council of Churches of Christ in the USA, the **World Methodist Council**, and the Pan-Methodist Movement.

EWM, I: 487–488; Lakey, Othal Hawthorne, *The History of the CME Church* (1985); Melton, J. Gordon, *A Will to Choose: The Origins of African American Methodism* (2007), 265–266.
C.Y.

CIEMAL (Concilio Iglesias Evangélicas Metodistas de America Latina)

Founded in February 1969 in Santiago, Chile, CIEMAL, the Council of Evangelical Methodist Churches in Latin America, assists autonomous and non-autonomous Methodist churches in **Latin America** and the **Caribbean**. It includes or represents Methodist bodies in Argentina, Belize, Bolivia, Brazil, Chile, Colombia, Costa Rica, Cuba, Dominican Republic, the Guyanas, Equador, Guatemala, Honduras, Mexico, Nicaragua, Panama, Puerto Rico, Uruguay, and Venezuela. Its stated purpose is, 'to make visible the connectionality and witness of the Methodist churches as they serve ... Latin American and Caribbean peoples....' CIEMAL maintains its historical Wesleyan and doctrinal heritage, the latter represented in its regard for scripture, **John Wesley's** sermons, and Methodism's traditional General Rules. It is governed by a board of directors composed of laity, pastors, men, women, and youth, and other indigenous persons. The Commission for Mission and Testimony, its program agency, emphasizes God's love for the poor and marginalized. CIEMAL is committed to strengthening the influence of Latin American and Caribbean people in the worldwide **mission** of the church.

HDM, 76.
C.Y.

Clarke, Adam (1760–1832)

Upholder of the orthodox view of biblical inspiration – 'We must ever consider these Scriptures as coming from *God*' – but unorthodox in his questioning of the eternal Sonship of Christ, Clarke was born in County Londonderry, Ireland. He became a Methodist in 1779, and, three years later, was accepted by **John Wesley** as an itinerant minister. Across his years of service, Clarke worked throughout the British Isles, including the Channel and Shetland islands and Dublin, where he, an advocate of caring for the poor, founded a branch of the Stranger's Friend Society; he also established six mission schools in counties Londonderry and Antrim. A voice of moderation, he was President of the British Methodist Conference three times; four, of the Irish. A gifted linguist, particularly in Middle Eastern and Oriental languages, Clarke was active in the British and Foreign Bible Societies, and published an eight-volume *Commentary on the Bible* (1810–1826), which was included in the course of study for British and American Methodist ministers for many years. He supported the creation of district missionary societies, and gave Christian instruction to two Buddhist priests from Ceylon. Baptized in 1820, they became controversial when they returned to Ceylon.

DMBI, 69; *ODNB*, 11:840–841; Taggart, Norman, *The Irish in World Methodism* (1986), 87–103.
J.M.

Clowes, William (1780–1851)

An unruly and dissipated young man, Clowes, the son of a Tunstall, England, potter, was converted in 1805, began to distribute Bibles and tracts, and became a Wesleyan Methodist class leader. An attendee at the 1807 Mow Cop camp meeting, he preached at the second one, and then became a Wesleyan preacher on trial. In 1810, he was expelled by the Wesleyans, perhaps because he was a camp-meeting enthusiast. But he continued to preach, and soon associated himself and his followers with **Hugh Bourne**, with whom he is linked as one of the founders, in 1811–1812, of the **Primitive Methodist Church (Great Britain)**. Based first in Tunstall, Clowes, a powerful and persuasive preacher, later made Hull his center of evangelistic activity, traveling from there as far as

London and Cornwall. For three years in the mid-1840s, he was president of the conference. Tension with Bourne was inevitable, given that Clowes was a more popular preacher than Bourne and that Bourne, as superintendent, felt that he was not in control of Clowes' Hull-based ministry. But Clowes' gentle and generous character and Bourne's determination not to let personal differences split Primitive Methodism, permitted them to continue working together.

DMBI, 72; Wilkinson, John T., *William Clowes, 1780–1851* (1951).
J.M.

Coke, Thomas (1747–1814)

Short of stature and sometimes of temper, trusted by **John Wesley** as a troubleshooter, Coke was born in Brecon, Wales. In 1764, he entered Jesus College, Oxford, was ordained a priest of the Church of England (1772), and obtained a doctorate in civil law (1775). His Methodist tendencies made him unpopular in his Anglican parish, with the result that after 1777 he was used by Wesley in various capacities: dealing with legal problems; alternating with Wesley in visiting Ireland and presiding over the Irish conference; aiding Wesley in preparing the Deed of Declaration (1784), which provided a legal basis for British Methodism after Wesley's death. The same year, Wesley prepared a plan for American Methodism, and ordained Coke to be one of its two superintendents (later bishops). Coke presented Wesley's plan, which included his nomination of **Francis Asbury** to be the other bishop, to a conference of Methodist preachers held at Christmastime 1784 in Baltimore. The conference organized the **Methodist Episcopal Church** and confirmed Wesley's nomination of Asbury. Although Coke visited American Methodists eight more times before 1805, Asbury was their dominant leader. Back in England, Coke administered Methodism's missions, with Henry Moore wrote a biography of Wesley, and he published a Bible commentary. Coke died aboard ship on his way to establish a mission in India and Ceylon.

Vickers, John A., ed., *The Journals of Dr. Thomas Coke* (2005); Vickers, John A., *Thomas Coke, Apostle of Methodism* (1969).
J.M.

Cook, Charles (?–1858)

Pioneer of French Methodism, Cook's early years, until he entered the Wesleyan ministry in 1816, are unrecorded. In 1818, he was appointed to

France, where Methodism had been introduced, in 1791, by William Mahy and Jean de Quetteville. At first, Cook found Paris to be 'hard ground,' but he was able to minister with some success in Normandy, the south of France, Sardinia, and French-speaking Switzerland. In 1824, he was sent to the Middle East to open a mission to Jews and Muslims; it closed after a trial period. Also he visited England and America in the cause of French-speaking Methodism. But it was in France that Cook found his appointed *métier*, developing a Methodism *du terroir*. For he did not allow French Methodism to be merely a French-language version of British Methodism; rather, he guided its development as a truly French Wesleyanism. Yielding to Cook's vision, the British Methodist Conference authorized him to organize an autonomous French Conference in 1852. Cook became its first president, and remained in that position until his death in Paris.

DMBI, 78; EWM, I: 62–63.
J.M.

Coughlan, Laurence (?–1784/1785)

Bringer of the first Methodist-type preaching to what is now Canada, Coughlan was born in Ireland and lived as a Roman Catholic until, at some point, he became a Methodist, and **John Wesley** began using him as a preacher. Wesley noted in 1758 that a society 'decreased' when Coughlan left; in 1763, Wesley described him as a 'hearty helper.' Two years later, after Coughlan obtained an irregular ordination, Wesley termed him 'a person who had no learning at all.' Not long after that, however, and apparently with Wesley's recommendation, Coughlan received regular Church of England ordination, and sponsored by the Society for the Propagation of the Gospel, went to Newfoundland in 1766. Two years into his ministry there, Wesley wrote to him, saying, 'By a various train of providences, you have been led to the very place where God intended you should be.' A revival broke out under Coughlan's leadership, he established Methodist societies, and a chapel was erected. In 1773, perhaps because his Anglican parishioners withheld his stipend, he returned to England, where he found a place in the **Countess of Huntingdon's** connection, and served a London chapel. Wesley reports that the last time he saw Coughlan, he was 'full of tears and contrition for his past unfaithfulness.'

DMBI, 80; Semple, Neil, *The Lord's Dominion: The History of Canadian Methodism* (1996), 28–29.
J.M.

Crosby, Fanny (1820–1915)

Although she lacked the theological range and depth of **Charles Wesley**, Crosby, who was born in Putnam County, New York, equaled Wesley in the number of hymns she wrote, and gave Christians some of their best remembered and easiest to sing gospel songs, such as 'Blessed Assurance,' 'I Am Thine, O Lord,' and 'Rescue the Perishing.' Poor treatment of an eye infection left Crosby blind six weeks after her birth; by age six, however, she was writing verse. In her teens and early twenties, while a student at the New York Institution for the Blind in New York City, she gained minor celebrity as a poet. Graduating in 1843, she taught at the school until 1858, when she married Alexander Van Alstyne, a blind musician, also a teacher at the school. Raised a Presbyterian, Crosby became a Methodist in 1850. First, in the early 1850s, she put her poems to music; then, by the mid-1860s, she was focusing on writing lyrics specifically for congregational singing. Among the composers who provided tunes for her lyrics were Ira Sankey, William Doane, and Robert Lowry. Crosby also ministered to railway workers and in city rescue missions, and promoted total abstinence.

ANB, 5:780–781; Blumhofer, Edith L, *Her Heart Can See: The Life and Hymns of Fanny Crosby* (2005).
J.M.

Dacorso, César (1892–1966)

One of Brazilian Methodism's outstanding leaders, Dacorso was born in Santa Maria, Rio Grande do Sul, Brazil. Elected to Methodist deacon's orders in 1916, his ordination did not occur until 1918 because in 1916–1917 it was too dangerous for an American bishop, needed to conduct ordination, to risk a voyage to Brazil with German submarines operating along the Brazilian coast. Dacorso's elder's ordination took place in 1918. His tenure in **ministry** lasted forty-three years and included almost every level of the connectional structure – local church pastor, district superintendent, editor of Sunday school literature, annual conference secretary and statistician, seminary teacher, and bishop. Dacorso was also a founder of the Bible Society of Brazil. After the Methodist Church of Brazil gained its autonomy in 1930 and elected its first bishop, it discovered the need for another episcopal leader. In 1934, it chose Dacorso who began a twenty-year episcopacy. Known for his vision, love for people, willingness to travel to almost inaccessible places, and his commitment to world peace and social action, Dacorso left a lasting mark on Brazilian and **Latin American** Methodism.

Costa, Nelson de Godoy, *César Dacorso Filho, Principe de Igreja Metodista do Brasil* (1967); *EWM*, I: 621.
C.Y.

Deaconess Movement

The New Testament office of deaconess (Romans 16:1; I Timothy 3:11) was revived in Protestantism by Theodor Fliedner in Kaiserswerth, Germany in 1836. A deaconess community was officially approved in the Church of England in 1862. In light of the temporal and spiritual needs of the urban poor, the American **Methodist Episcopal Church** was prompted by Lucy Rider Meyer (1849–1922) in 1887 to revive the biblical office of deaconess. The 1888 general conference officially approved the office. Over the next twenty years, deaconess organizations were approved by all of the predecessors of the **United Methodist Church**. British Wesleyan Methodists began to recognize the **ministry** of deaconess in 1890 when Thomas B. Stephenson (1839–1912) founded the Wesley Deaconess Institute, which marks the beginning of deaconess ministry in British Methodism. The **United Methodist Free Church** organized similar work in 1891 and **Primitive Methodism** in 1895. Until **women** were ordained and granted full clergy rights in the Methodist churches, the office of deaconess was a means for their exercising meaningful ministry in the church. Unlike United Methodists who commission deaconesses, British Methodism ordains them. Presently, in the United Methodist Church, the female office of deaconess is complemented by the male office of Home Missioner.

DMBI, 91–92; Dougherty, Mary Agnes, *My Calling to Fulfill: Deaconesses in the United Methodist Tradition* (1997); *EWM*, I:640–642; Semple, Neil, *The Lord's Dominion: The History of Canadian Methodism* (1996), 281–282.
C.Y.

Doctrinal Standards (American Methodism)

When, in 1773, the Methodist preachers in America met for their first conference, they accepted **John Wesley's** *Sermons* and *Explanatory Notes upon the New Testament* as their doctrinal guidelines for interpreting the scriptures and connecting with Wesley's teachings. They reiterated that acceptance in 1781. Three years later, Wesley sent instructions for constituting a Methodist church in the newly founded United States. Included in those instructions were twenty-four Articles of Religion, an abridgment by Wesley of the Thirty-Nine Articles (1563) of the Church of England.

The American preachers, meeting at Christmastime in 1784, adopted Wesley's Articles as the **Methodist Episcopal Church's** core doctrinal statement, but most scholars think they continued to regard Wesley's *Sermons* and *Explanatory Notes* as standard guides to biblical exposition and Wesleyan theology. A generation later, the 1808 General Conference decided that the 'General Conference shall not revoke, alter, or change our Articles of Religion, nor establish any new standards' of doctrine contrary to our present ones.

Meanwhile, the **United Brethren in Christ** and the **Evangelical Association**, the two churches that, along with the Methodists, created the **United Methodist Church**, were adopting their own doctrinal standards; as were the African American Methodist denominations that were founded during the early decades of the nineteenth century. The latter adopted Wesley's Articles of Religion with editorial revisions and a few substantive changes.

George Miller prepared a German translation of Wesley's Articles for the Evangelicals in 1809. Five polemical articles aimed primarily at Roman Catholic teachings were excised in 1816; a few textual changes were made in 1839, then it was mandated that 'the Articles of Faith ... should be constitutionally unchangeable among us.' Those Articles were brought by the Evangelicals into their union with the United Brethren in Christ in 1946. Christian Newcomer and Christopher Grosch formulated a summary of normative United Brethren teaching in 1813; slight revisions were made in 1815 and 1841, then it was stipulated that 'No rule or ordinance shall at any time be passed to change or do away with the Confession of Faith as it now stands.'

The history just reviewed indicates that doctrine was a living, changing reality for the early Methodists, Evangelicals, and United Brethren. Wesley felt no compunction about reducing the Thirty-Nine Articles of the Church of England to twenty-four, which he then edited for American Methodism; and he added his own *Sermons* and *Expository Notes* as standards of correct Methodist teaching. Evangelicals felt free to remove five articles that Wesley retained. The United Brethren composed their own Confession of Faith. Beginning in 1808, however, the churches authorized doctrinal cryogenics.

Only the United Brethren thawed their doctrine. They approved, by a large majority, a new Confession in 1889, an action that led to forming a new United Brethren denomination by those who adhered to the old Confession of Faith. The 1889 United Brethren Confession and the Evangelicals' 1839 Articles of Faith became the doctrinal standards of the **Evangelical United Brethren Church** when it was organized in 1946. The new church adopted a new Confession of Faith in 1962. That Confession, the Methodist Articles of Religion, and Wesley's *Sermons* and *Expository Notes*, now compose the United Methodist Church's constitutionally frozen doctrinal standards.

Those documents provide a massive amount of official doctrinal material – roughly three thousand pages in the editions listed in the United Methodist *Book of Discipline*. Because it is impossible to give equal weight to every page, Methodists have always attributed more heft to some doctrinal statements than to others. Usually, these weight-distribution decisions are made informally in the corridors of conferences, the classrooms of theological schools, and the studies of pastors. Occasionally, however, they take the form of general conference actions. The 2000 United Methodist general conference noted that seven of the Articles of Religion include 'strong statements against the Roman Catholic Church.' Responding to that fact, the conference declared that it is 'our official intent henceforth to interpret all our Articles, Confession, and other "standards of doctrine" in consonance with our best ecumenical insights and judgments.'

Weighty as that action was, more weighty is the section of the United Methodist *Book of Discipline* titled 'Doctrinal Standards and Our Theological Task,' which was first adopted in 1972; a new statement was approved in 1988. It places the Articles of Religion, Confession of Faith, and Wesley's *Sermons* and *Expository Notes* in an interpretative framework, at the center of which is the so-called Wesleyan Quadrilateral: 'Wesley believed that the living core of the Christian faith was revealed in Scripture, illumined by tradition, vivified in personal experience, and confirmed by reason.' When that sentence is unpacked, the Bible is identified as *primary*, which does not mean that its every passage is factual in the sense that history and science understand facts; it means, in the words of Article of Religion V, that Holy Scripture contains 'all things necessary to salvation.' Tradition, as presented in the Quadrilateral, illumines 'the living core of the Christian faith.' For United Methodists, the contents of tradition are, primarily, the doctrines of the first four or five centuries after Christ – doctrines found, among other places, in the Apostles' and Nicene creeds – and the Articles of Religion, the Confession of Faith, and Wesley's *Sermons* and *Expository Notes*.

In the Quadrilateral, experience and reason carry heavier doctrinal weight than is suggested by the words attached to them – 'vivified' and 'confirmed.' For tradition is simply past experience and reason applied to the Bible, written down, and handed on to future generations. Experience and reason applied to tradition and scripture in contemporary situations decide which portions of the Bible best reveal 'the living core of Christian faith.' The 'living core' never remains the same from generation to generation; different historical contexts shape and color how Christianity is lived and expressed.

Some United Methodists think that a mass of doctrinal material allows too much breathing room for doctrine, too much freedom for doctrine to live and grow. They prefer succinct formulations, such as the one attempted by Charles Keysor in 1966. Keysor, whose Good News movement continues to be a significant force in the United Methodist Church, listed five fundamental doctrines of Methodist 'orthodoxy': inspiration of scripture, virgin birth of Christ, substitutionary atonement of Christ, physical resurrection of Christ, and return of Christ. Wesley resisted the idea of *'fundamental* truths;' indeed, he called that term 'ambiguous' and charged it with provoking 'warm disputes.' When Wesley himself singled out the 'main doctrines' of Methodism, they were nothing like Keysor's five; instead, Wesley's are repentance, faith, and holiness.

In 1975, the Good News movement released a summary of core doctrine, the Junaluska Affirmation. The Confessing Movement, launched by United Methodist conservatives in 1994, continued the effort to get United Methodists to specify the 'things necessary to salvation' in a brief statement. Although the Good News and Confessing movements count many supporters, they have failed so far to convince United Methodism as a whole that a concise confession of faith is a good idea.

United Methodists, following Wesley, prefer to express their doctrinal standards in a mass of material. The roughly three thousand pages of the Articles of Religion, Confession of Faith, and Wesley's *Sermons* and *Expository Notes* provide room for doctrine to live and change as new occasions call forth fresh expressions of 'the living core of the Christian faith.'

Campbell, Ted A., *Methodist Doctrine: The Essentials* (1999); Oden, Thomas C., *Doctrinal Standards in the Wesleyan Tradition* (1988); Yrigoyen, Charles, Jr., John G. McEllhenney, and Kenneth E. Rowe, *United Methodism at Forty: Looking Back, Looking Forward* (2008), chap. 4, Doctrine and Theology; Yrigoyen, Charles, Jr., *Belief Matters: United Methodism's Doctrinal Standards* (2001).
J.M.

Doctrinal Standards (British Methodism)

As a priest of the Church of England, **John Wesley** adhered to that church's standards of doctrine as found in the Thirty-Nine Articles of Religion and the Book of Homilies, both of which received final authorization in 1571. They affirm the classic creeds of Christendom, such as the Apostles' and Nicene, and the doctrines of the trinity, the divine and human natures of Christ, the atonement, justification by faith, and other traditional Christian beliefs; also they define the Anglican position with regard to medieval corruptions of Catholic teaching, orthodox Roman Catholic doctrine, Calvinism, and Anabaptist teachings.

Against the backdrop of those Anglican doctrinal standards, Wesley staged the drama of Methodism, the three principal doctrinal actors being: grace-enabled freedom to accept God's gift of salvation in Jesus Christ, assurance of being accepted by God, and holiness of heart and life. He embodied his doctrinal emphases in his *Sermons on Several Occasions* (first edition, 1746) and his *Explanatory Notes upon the New Testament* (1755). In 1763, when he prepared a Model Deed for his preaching-houses, he included the stipulation that the trustees were responsible for making certain that the preachers affirmed 'no other doctrine than is contained in Mr. Wesley's *Notes Upon the New Testament* and four volumes of *Sermons*.'

Well into the twentieth century, British Methodism maintained the Model Deed's doctrinal standards. Occasionally someone's views were challenged in Conference; this was the case with Joseph A. Beet after he published *The Last Things* in 1897. A typical nineteenth-century statement of adherence to the provisions of Wesley's Model Deed is **Primitive Methodism's** declaration (1830) that its doctrinal clauses were to be interpreted agreeably to the 'first four volumes of John Wesley's *Sermons*' and his *Notes Upon the New Testament*. However, there were debates about the particular 'four volumes' of *Sermons* and therefore the number of 'official' sermons: Are there forty-four or fifty-three doctrinally significant sermons? Finally, in 1914, after seeking legal counsel, the Wesleyan Methodist Conference ruled that the phrase referred to the forty-four sermons published by Wesley before he set forth the Model Deed, in 1763.

The founding document of the British Methodist Church (1932) states that 'the doctrinal standards' cannot be altered or varied in any manner whatsoever by the Conference, and that the Conference is 'the final authority within the Methodist Church with regard to all questions concerning the interpretation of its doctrines.' Just over forty years later, however, the 1976 Methodist Church Act gave Conference power to amend the 1932 document in various ways, including the clause that denied Conference 'any power to alter or vary in any manner whatsoever the clauses ... which define the doctrinal standards of The Methodist Church.'

Whether officially or unofficially the range of permitted doctrinal diversity widened considerably in the twentieth century.

DMB I, 25, 97, 231; *EWM*, 698–703; Oden, Thomas C., *Doctrinal Standards in the Wesleyan Tradition* (1988), 163–166.
J.M.

Eastern Orthodoxy

A family of churches located mostly in eastern Europe, sharing the same faith, and relating to each other, Eastern Orthodoxy developed in the Byzantine empire and was much influenced by Hellenistic thought and culture. **Albert C. Outler** was among the first to emphasize its important impact on the theology of **John Wesley**. Outler claimed that Wesley's doctrine of Christian perfection was rooted in the theology of the eastern theologian Gregory of Nyssa through the writings of so-called Macarius the Egyptian. Wesley was also impressed with the thought of Ephrem Syrus, especially with the content of Ephrem's hymns and verse homilies. Echoes of the eastern doctrine of *theosis* (deification) are found in the theology of both Wesley brothers. Studies of John Wesley's thought by Randy L. Maddox and Kenneth J. Collins arrive at different conclusions regarding the eastern influence on Wesley, Maddox convinced of it, Collins expressing reservations. The **World Methodist Council** and the Orthodox began dialogues in 1992.

Campbell, Ted A., *Christian Antiquity: Religious Vision and Cultural Change* (1991); Collins, Kenneth J., *The Theology of John Wesley: Holy Love and the Shape of Grace* (2007); *DMBI*, 105; Maddox, Randy L., *Responsible Grace: John Wesley's Practical Theology* (1994).
C.Y.

Ecumenism

John Wesley's *Letter to a Roman Catholic* (1749) and his sermon, 'Catholic Spirit' (1750), may be seen as Methodism's ecumenical charter, stressing, as they do, the 'essentials' of the Christian gospel and tolerance concerning 'opinions.' Delegates from thirty Methodist churches gathered in London, in 1881, for the first Ecumenical Methodist Conference. In 1910, American Methodist layman John R. Mott chaired the first International [and inter-denominational] Missionary Conference in Edinburgh. Out of that meeting came two more interdenominational assemblies in which Methodists participated – Life and Work (1920) and Faith and Order (1927). Plans were made in 1939 for linking those two movements in a World Council of Churches. Meanwhile, in both Britain and the United States, Methodists were helping create councils of churches at local, regional, and national levels. At the founding assembly of the World Council of Churches (1948), American Methodist Bishop G. Bromley Oxnam became one of its presidents. Two general secretaries of the Council, **Philip A. Potter** and **Emilio Castro**, have been Methodists. In various countries, for example, Canada, India, and Japan, Methodist and other Protestant denominations have formed united churches. All these efforts may be seen as attempts to fulfill Jesus' prayer 'that they may all be one' (John 17:21).

DMBI, 106; *EWM*, 98–99.
J.M.

Education

Methodism strives, in the words of **Charles Wesley**, to 'Unite the pair so long disjoined, / Knowledge and vital piety.' Resistance to that union began, however, with some of **John Wesley's** preachers, who said, 'I have no taste for reading;' Wesley told them to develop a taste or leave his itinerancy. Some Methodists today imagine they honor the God of truth by denying evolution. To counter the supposition that piety compensates for ignorance, Methodists print books and establish schools. John Wesley published abridgments of Christian classics and an encyclopedia of science. Less than a decade after the **Methodist Episcopal Church** was organized, it set up a printing house. Sunday schools in Britain and America taught reading, writing, and arithmetic to children who worked the other six days. Wesley founded the Kingswood School in 1748 to educate the sons of Methodist families 'in every branch of useful learning.' In 1784, American Methodism authorized the building of Cokesbury College, named for Bishops **Coke** and **Asbury**. After it failed, thirty years passed, until the 1820 General Conference encouraged annual conferences to establish literary institutions. Soon American Methodists were funding academies, colleges, theological schools, and universities, first in the United States, then overseas. Similar steps were taken by British Methodism and Methodist denominations around the world.

DMBI, 107; *EWM*, I:748–754; *HMGB*, (1982), 3:279–308.
J.M.

Eklund, Anna (1867–1949)

'Sister Anna of Petrograd,' a Methodist deaconess who directed a relief program in St. Petersburg/Petrograd/Leningrad during the 1920s, was born in Turku, Finland. Trained as a deaconess nurse at the Methodist Deaconess Institute in Hamburg, Germany, she first did private nursing; then, in 1907, joined George A. Simons, the **Methodist Episcopal Church's** superintendent of the Finland and St. Petersburg Mission, in St. Petersburg, where she founded a deaconess institute and trained students who went on to serve in Estonia, other Baltic States, and Germany. Although Simons left St. Petersburg after the 1918 Russian Revolution, she remained and gained honor as Sister Anna of Petrograd. She cared for the congregation and church property, served as pastor and Sunday school teacher, nursed the sick and dying, dug graves, directed a steadily growing social work program, and, during the 1920s, was responsible for the Methodist Episcopal Church's relief work. At last, totally exhausted, she left Russia, fled to Estonia, and then returned, in 1931, to Finland. After months of rest, she regained sufficient strength to reestablish and maintain contacts with friends behind the Iron Curtain.

EWM, I: 759–760; Kimbrough, S T Jr., *Sister Anna Eklund, 1867–1949: A Methodist Saint in Russia. Her Words and Witness, St. Petersburg 1908–1931* (2001).
J.M.

Enthusiasm

Enthusiasm comes in three varieties: indifferent, bad, and good. Burbling excitement about a church's new praise band is indifferent enthusiasm, as are other things that spark animated chatter among religious people. Bad enthusiasts, according to **John Wesley**, are persons who imagine they can experience a transforming relationship with God without using the means of grace provided by God. Other bad enthusiasts suppose they have been told by God what to say and do, even though what they say and do is contradicted by scripture. In opposition to such 'madness,' Wesley insisted that 'religion is the spirit of a sound mind,' of a mind that applies reason to scripture, tradition, and experience as it develops its understanding of being in a true relationship with God. For Wesley, a good enthusiast is a person 'who says the love of God is shed abroad in his heart by the Holy Ghost given unto him;' who reveals the truth of that affirmation by living a life of ever-growing love of God, self, and neighbor; a life that is going on toward holiness of heart and life.

HDM, 103–105; WJW(B), 2: 44–60.
J.M.

Europe

Methodism in Europe must be understood in the broader context of European history and church life. Wesley's European offspring have struggled in the midst of state churches in some countries, with Roman Catholicism and Eastern Orthodoxy in others. Like other European denominations, Methodism has witnessed and experienced the consequences of two world wars, the Cold War, and the dissolution of the Soviet Union. It has been threatened by opposition and blessed with opportunity.

British and American Methodists were largely responsible for the origin and development of Methodism in Europe. The presence of the followers of **John Wesley** began as early as 1769 when British soldiers brought Methodism to Gibraltar and there constructed a chapel. Six years later Methodists inaugurated a ministry on the Channel Islands. Over the ensuing decades

British Methodists instituted ministries in France (in 1791, with a visit by **Thomas Coke**), Germany (1813), Sweden (1825), Spain (1832), Portugal (1853), Italy (1861), and Austria (1870).

European Methodism is also rooted in missions which originated in the United States by a variety of denominations. The **Evangelical Association/ Church** (EA) and the **Church of the United Brethren in Christ** (UB), two smaller Methodist-related churches, gave birth to work in German-speaking Europe. During their earlier years in the United States both were predominantly German language denominations. The EA began formal mission work in Germany in 1851 and later extended it to Switzerland and Alsace. It founded a publishing house at Stuttgart in 1875 and a theological seminary at Reutlingen in 1877. The 1869 UB general conference authorized work in Germany, but its ministry experienced only modest gains. When the EA and UB united in 1946 to become the **Evangelical United Brethren Church**, the denomination struggled to assist its European constituents with World War II's devastation and the challenge of a politically divided Germany.

The most extensive mission work by North American Methodists was supported by the **Methodist Episcopal Church**. Its mission to Germany began in 1848. Scandinavian Methodism was not originally an organized mission, but was the result of the MEC's Bethel Ship mission in New York City where Scandinavian seamen and immigrants were converted and carried their new Methodist faith back to their homelands – Norway (1849), Sweden (1850s), Denmark (1857), and Finland (1859). MEC missionaries were later dispatched to undergird Methodist ministries in those countries. Russia and the Baltic states were reached by MEC missions in 1889 (Russia), Lithuania (1905), Estonia (1907), and Latvia (1911). Other MEC mission work was opened in Switzerland, Bulgaria, Macedonia, Italy, and Serbia in the nineteenth century. **Methodist Episcopal Church, South** mission work in Europe did not commence until the conclusion of World War I when southern Methodists resolved to assist with European relief and reconstruction.

The missions of the EA, UB, MEC, and MECS are now incorporated into the **United Methodist Church**. Other Methodist denominations also organized in Europe including the Church of the Nazarene and the **Wesleyan Church**. European Methodism is well represented in the **World Methodist Council**.

Barclay, Wade Crawford, *The Methodist Episcopal Church 1845–1939, Widening Horizons 1845–95*. History of Methodist Missions (1957), 3: 933–1060; Copplestone, J. Tremayne, *Twentieth-Century Perspectives (The Methodist Episcopal Church, 1896–1939)*. History of Methodist Missions (1973), 4: 355–518, 975–1033; *DMBI*, 134, 179, 277–278, 330, 343; Streiff, Patrick Ph., *Methodism in Europe: 19th and 20th Century* (2003).
C.Y.

Evangelical Association/Church (USA)

During several early nineteenth-century gatherings held in central Pennsylvania, the Evangelical Association (later Church) took form. In 1803, a group of **Jacob Albright's** lay leaders and lay preachers voted for his ordination, which occurred when two of his lay preachers laid their hands on his head. Four years later, Albright's followers, informally known as 'Albright's People,' adopted the name 'The Newly-Formed Methodist Conference,' and elected Albright superintendent. After Albright died in 1808, George Miller edited Articles of Faith, based on the Methodist Articles of Religion, and a *Discipline* for the new ecclesiastical body; which, in 1816, at its first general conference, changed its name to Evangelical Association and approved a revised *Discipline*. Episcopacy formally entered the Association's polity in 1839, when John Seybert was elected bishop. The Association was Wesleyan in theology, but controversy swirled around the doctrine of sanctification after 1850. Personality conflicts, arguments about the use of episcopal powers, and alleged mistreatment of ministers resulted, in 1894, in a split. The new denomination chose the name United Evangelical Church. The two churches reunited in 1922 and selected the name Evangelical Church, which, in 1946, merged with the **United Brethren in Christ** to create the **Evangelical United Brethren Church**.

Albright, Raymond W., *A History of the Evangelical Church* (1942); Behney, J. Bruce and Paul H. Eller, *The History of the Evangelical United Brethren Church* (1979).
J.M.

Evangelical Congregational Church (USA)

When the **Evangelical Association** and the United Evangelical Church reunited in 1922 to form the Evangelical Church, there were members of the latter, especially in central and eastern Pennsylvania, but also a few in Ohio and Illinois, who refused to be part of the merger. They continued to call themselves United Evangelicals until 1928, when, after losing the legal right to retain that name, they formed the Evangelical Congregational Church, which has its headquarters and a seminary in Myerstown, Pennsylvania. The 'Evangelical' part of the name indicates the church's historical connection with **Jacob Albright**, while 'Congregational' part highlights congregational rights. The church, which rejected the Methodist-like polity of the Evangelical Church, limits the tenure and power of bishops, uses a Stationing Committee to determine the annual appointment of pastors, emphasizes the power of the laity, and adheres to Articles of Religion that are more conservative than those of its parent church.

Terry M. Heisey, ed., *Evangelical From the Beginning: A History of the Evangelical*

Congregational Church and its Predecessors – The Evangelical Association and the United Evangelical Church (2006).
J.M.

Evangelical United Brethren Church (USA)

Johnstown, Pennsylvania, witnessed the merger in 1946 of the **Evangelical Church** and the **United Brethren in Christ** to create the Evangelical United Brethren Church, which, in 1968, united with the Methodist Church to form the **United Methodist Church**. The new church accepted the doctrinal affirmations of its two predecessor churches until 1962, when its general conference approved a new Confession of Faith. In polity, the church had many similarities with Methodism, but also significant differences. There were local (congregational) and annual (regional) conferences, and a General Conference. Bishops were elected for four-year terms, with the possibility of reelection. Ordination was limited to one order, elder, not Methodism's two, deacon and elder. Women had been ordained since 1889 in the United Brethren tradition, but not the Evangelical one; isolated ordinations of women continued in the new denomination. The Evangelical United Brethren Church had a strong ecumenical commitment, participating in councils of churches at the local, state, national, and world levels. At the time of the 1968 merger, it had 750,000 members in thirty-two conferences in the United States and Canada, 42,000 in six conferences abroad, and missions in Africa, Asia, and Latin America.

Behney, J. Bruce and Paul H. Eller, *The History of the Evangelical United Brethren Church* (1979).
J.M.

Evangelism

Evangelism, in the sense of going out with the good news of God's love revealed in Jesus Christ to people wherever they are, began in Methodism on Monday, 2 April 1739, when **John Wesley** went out from the pulpit to people coming out from their workplaces. He declared, quoting Jesus (Luke 4:18–19), that he had come to evangelize the poor, proclaim release to the captives, recovery of sight to the blind, and liberation to the oppressed.

Modeling his evangelism on that declaration, Wesley went wherever people customarily gathered and urged them to admit they were blind to God's transforming love. Then Wesley described what they were missing and invited those captivated by his words to join one of his societies, where they learned methods for recovering their spiritual sight. Wesley's Methodist societies also provided relief for the poor, health care, job training, and centers of opposition to societal evils such as slavery.

Wesley deployed lay preachers, first in the British Isles, later in Britain's North American colonies. They went to people where they were, and presented **salvation** according to the Wesleyan way. When Britain's North American colonies became independent, so did the Methodist preachers. The bishops of the church they formed, the **Methodist Episcopal Church**, sent out preachers to follow the men and women who pushed the frontier westward. These preachers-on-the-move designed camp meetings as places for men and women to come together to overcome their social loneliness and spiritual emptiness. Soon, on both sides of the Atlantic, camp meetings were part of the Methodism's evangelism program.

Mass evangelistic rallies aimed at instantaneous conversions became features of British and American Methodism during the second half of the nineteenth century. Truer, perhaps, to the wholeness of Wesley's model was the Methodist **deaconess movement** founded by Lucy Rider Meyer in Chicago in the early 1880s. Deaconesses went to people living in urban and rural poverty and offered, in addition to the good news of Jesus Christ, a variety of educational and health care services. A similar combination characterized the programs of the Central Halls erected in Britain and the Institutional Churches founded in the United States during the last decades of the nineteenth century. Spellbinding preachers drew crowds into the auditoriums of those structures; once inside, people found, in addition to new life in Christ, a host of programs offered in classrooms and gyms: courses for job readiness and intellectual growth, physical fitness instruction, and special interest clubs.

In the twentieth century, Methodist evangelists continued to do what Wesley initiated on 2 April 1739: they went where people gathered, first by radio, then by television. These initiatives often failed, however, to plant persons in a modern equivalent of Wesley's societies. So by the close of the century, denominational ad campaigns were designed to attract women and men to local churches, many of which designed web sites that popped up near the top of the list when people typed certain words into their search engines.

EWM, 809–810; *HDM*, 120–122.
J.M.

Everett, James (1784–1872)

When Everett was six years old, he met **John Wesley**, with the result that Everett, for the remainder of his life, venerated Methodism's founder and became a vocal critic of some of his successors, in particular **Jabez Bunting**.

Born at Alnwick, England, Everett was converted in 1803 and, the next year, became a Wesleyan Methodist local preacher; he entered the itinerant ministry in 1811. His writing skills caught Bunting's attention, and Everett was appointed to assist at the Book Room in London. When chronic bronchitis forced him to leave the active ministry, he concentrated on writing, producing histories of Methodism in Sheffield and Manchester and a biography of **Adam Clarke**. By the early 1840s, anonymous pamphlets began to appear that criticized Bunting and the direction Wesleyan Methodism was taking. Although Everett was suspected of being their author, he refused to confirm or deny the charge, with the outcome that he was expelled from Wesleyan Methodism in 1849. By the early 1850s, he had become active in the cause of bringing together the Wesleyan Methodist Association and the Wesleyan Reform (Union). When those two groups united 1857 to found the **United Methodist Free Churches**, he became the first president.

Beckerlegge, Oliver A., *The Three Expelled* (1996); *DMBI*, 114; *ODNB*, 18:793–794.
J.M.

Fletcher, John William (1729–1785)

One of the most eminent and revered leaders in early Methodism, Fletcher was born Jean Guillaume de la Flechere in Nyon, Switzerland. He enrolled in Geneva University in 1746 and in 1748 engaged in military studies in Germany. Eager to find employment, he emigrated in England in 1750 and a year later began employment as a private tutor. In January 1754, Fletcher experienced a conversion under Methodist influence and was ordained into the priesthood of the Church of England in March 1757. He cultivated close friendships with the Wesleys and **Selina, Countess of Huntingdon**, becoming her household chaplain in 1760. That year he became vicar of Madeley, a Shropshire parish and a coal-mining area growing in importance as the Industrial Revolution progressed. While continuing his ministry at Madeley, Fletcher was appointed to the presidency of Lady Huntingdon's newly opened training college at Trevecca in 1769. Always doubtful about some of the main emphases of **Calvinism** and provoked by the Countess' attack on **John Wesley** in 1771, he resigned from the college presidency and issued a vindication of Wesley's anti-Calvinistic views. His most important published work is his *Checks to Antinomianism* (1771–1775) which argues for human free will and the necessity of faith with good works, and defends the Wesleyan doctrine of Christian perfection. In 1781 Fletcher married Mary Bosanquet (1739–1815), who was highly regarded among the Methodists. Both Fletcher and his wife were deeply spiritual and considered saintly by those acquainted with them. John Wesley thought of Fletcher as his successor to lead the

Methodist movement, a prospect Fletcher shunned and which was conclusively closed with his death more than five years before John Wesley's.

BDE, 228–230; DMBI, 124; Forsaith, Peter S., ed., *Unexampled Labours: Letters of the Revd John Fletcher to Leaders in the Evangelical Revival* (2008); Streiff, Patrick Ph., *Reluctant Saint? A Theological Biography of Fletcher of Madeley* (2001).
C.Y.

Free Methodist Church (USA, Great Britain)

Churches on both sides of the Atlantic call themselves Free Methodist. In the United States, during the pre-Civil War era, the bourgeoisification of the **Methodist Episcopal Church**, its practice of renting pews, its accommodation with slavery, its neglect of the poor, and its lack of enthusiasm for the doctrine of sanctification led **Benjamin T. Roberts** and others to found, in 1860, the Free Methodist Church, a denomination within the **Holiness Movement**. The 'Free' in the church's name stands for free seats in all meetinghouses, freedom from slavery, freedom from ecclesiastical authoritarianism, freedom from worldly behavior, freedom of the Spirit in worship, and freedom from sin in the experience of sanctification. Free Methodist discussions with the **Wesleyan Church** about union, initiated during the second half of the twentieth century, have so far proved unsuccessful, even though the two denominations share a similar ethos and history. In the British Isles, a number of Methodist churches have used, at one time or another, 'Free Methodist' to identify themselves. Resistance in North Lancashire to the **Anglican-Methodist Conversations** of the 1960s, led to the formation of the Free Methodist Church, which has Irish and British conferences.

DMBI, 128; *HDM*, 133–134.
J.M.

Hagen, Odd (1905–1970)

Norwegian pastor, seminary teacher, bishop, and president of the World Methodist Council, Hagen was born in Trondheim, Norway, and received his theological education at Union Scandinavian Theological School in Gothenburg, Oslo University, and Gothenburg University. Ordained a Methodist elder in 1932, he was a pastor in Norway before going on to teach at Union Scandinavian Theological School. He was the school's principal from 1947 to 1953, when he was elected bishop by the Northern Europe Central Conference of the Methodist Church. Assigned to the Stockholm Area, which meant that he became a Swedish citizen, he had episcopal responsibility for conferences in Denmark, Norway, Sweden, and Finland; also he supervised the Baltic and Slavic Conference, whose congregations he visited at some personal risk. Hagen was the host bishop for the World Methodist Conference in Oslo (1961); five years later, he became the World Methodist Council's president. Active during World War II in Methodist relief work for Norway, Hagen also aided relief efforts in Yugoslavia, traveled extensively, especially in Africa and the United States, and received honors from the kings of Norway and Sweden. He wrote articles for papers and magazines, books in the fields of philosophy, theology, and homiletics, and *Preludes to Methodism in Northern Europe* (1961).

EWM, I: 1053–1054.
J.M.

Harkness, Georgia (1891–1974)

The first woman to hold a prominent chair of theology in the United States, Harkness was born in Harkness, New York, received her PhD from Boston University, and taught at Elmira and Mt. Holyoke colleges before assuming major professorships at Garrett Biblical Institute (1939–1950) and Pacific School of Religion (1950–1961). She was, in the words of Thomas A. Langford, 'creative, poetic, devout, thoughtful, and able to express these qualities to others through her life and writing.' The author of more than thirty books, many of which attracted lay as well as clergy readers, Harkness believed, again in the words of Langford, 'there is a unity to knowledge found in faith, reason, and the Bible. Theology, which may begin at any of these points, moves toward the same center – that God is personal and gracious, that Jesus Christ renews human life for its highest achievement, and that the Holy Spirit is the continuing and sustaining expression of God's relation to humankind.' Harkness denounced the Versailles Treaty, racism, unbridled capitalism, war, and the internment of Japanese Americans in 1941; she defended women's rights, promoted the ordination of women, and supported ecumenism.

ANB, 10:88–90; Rosemary Skinner Keller, *Georgia Harkness: For Such a Time As This* (1992).
J.M.

Harris, William Wade 'Prophet' (1865?–1929)

Perhaps the most successful early native missionary in West **Africa**, Harris was raised in Liberia by a Methodist uncle. While in a Liberian prison in

1910 for political activism, Harris had a vision in which he was told that God intended to commission him to be a prophet. A mystical divine anointing followed. After unsuccessfully preaching in Liberia, Harris moved to Ivory Coast where he drew considerable attention. He wore a white prophet's robe and carried a Bible, cross, gourd rattle, and bowl for baptismal water. His appearance, charisma, and eloquent preaching persuaded many to surrender their traditional African religion for Christianity. It is believed that in one eighteen-month period he baptized approximately 120,000 into the Christian faith. Although most of the 'Prophet's' preaching was along coastal areas, his influence spread inland, even to places he never visited. Harris did not establish churches, but advised newly converted Christians to expect the coming of Christians with Bibles who would provide leadership and organization for them. When Bible-carrying denominational missionaries arrived in 1924, they discovered that Harris had laid the groundwork for their acceptance and ministry. In 1914 Harris returned to Liberia after he was banished from Ivory Coast by French officials. Ineffectual again in his native land, he died quietly in poverty in the home of a daughter. Methodism in Ivory Coast dates its beginning to 1914 when Harris began his ministry there rather than to 1924 when the first Methodist missionaries arrived.

EWM, I:1082–1083; Isichei, Elizabeth, *A History of Christianity in Africa* (1995), 284–286.
C.Y.

Hartzell, Joseph Crane (1842–1928)

Methodist Episcopal pastor, superintendent, and missionary bishop for Africa, Hartzell was born in Moline, Illinois. When he was sixteen he experienced conversion and a call to ministry. He received degrees from Illinois Wesleyan College and Garrett Biblical Institute, both in the same year (1868). Hartzell was ordained in the Methodist Episcopal Church, served churches in Illinois and New Orleans, Louisiana, and was appointed to superintend two districts. Throughout his **ministry** he was committed to improving race relations between blacks and whites. In 1896 Hartzell was consecrated missionary bishop for **Africa** to succeed William Taylor. Taking up the work with insight, commitment, and energy, he traveled an estimated 1.3 million miles by water, carriage and cart, on the backs of animals, and by foot to visit his constituency and promote missionary work in Africa. He successfully lobbied the heads of state and other officials in a number of nations including the United States, Great Britain, France, and Portugal to eliminate injustice and provide religious freedom. Hartzell worked effectively to cultivate indigenous leadership in the African church. He was at the forefront of Methodist Episcopal missions to Africa.

ANB, 10:268–269; Copplestone, J. Tremayne, *Twentieth-Century Perspectives (The Methodist Episcopal Church, 1896–1939)* (1973), History of Methodist Missions, IV: 3–17, 33–55, 59–85; *EWM*, I: 1088–1089.
C.Y.

Hedstrom, Olaf Gustav (1803–1877)

Pastoral skipper of *Bethel Ship*, a rehabilitated two-master in New York City's harbor that provided space for ministries with Scandinavian sailors and immigrants, Hedstrom was born in Kronberg Lans, Sweden. He traveled to the United States as a sailor, sold clothing in Pennsylvania, and married an American woman, Caroline Pinckney, who introduced him to Methodism. The New York Conference received him as a preacher on trial in 1835. Ten years later, after David Terry, an American, and Peter Berger, a Swede, purchased a condemned brig and refitted it as a house of God, rechristening it *Bethel Ship*, Hedstrom was appointed to take its helm. He evangelized Scandinavians arriving in New York City, and launched a Sunday school, tract mission, and Bible mission. In the wake of his ministries came the formation of Scandinavian Methodism in the United States and the introduction of Methodism to Norway, Sweden, and Finland by sailors who responded to God as a result of his pastoral care and preaching.

HDM, 154; Whyman, Henry C., *The Hedstroms and the Bethelship Saga* (1992).
J.M.

Hernández, Alejo (1842–1875)

Apostle of Methodism to Mexico and the first Mexican ordained by any Methodist church, Hernández enrolled as a young man in a Roman Catholic seminary in Mexico to prepare for the priesthood. Then, having lost his faith, he joined an army seeking to repel the 1862 French invasion of his home country. He was captured, and, escaping, made his way to Mexico's border with Texas, where he read an anti-Catholic pamphlet. Crossing to Texas, he met Methodists, received a Bible, and, although he did not understand the words of a Methodist revival service, 'became,' in the words of a later appraisal, 'a missionary forever.' Licensed to preach by the **Methodist Episcopal Church, South**, he ministered in the Corpus Christi area. In 1871, he was admitted on trial by the West Texas Conference, ordained deacon, and appointed to 'missionary work among the Mexicans.' Two years later, Bishop

John C. Keener chose Hernández to open a Methodist mission in Mexico City, where he experienced, in the words of the Board of Missions, 'the persecutions of superstitious ignorance and bigoted power.' Empowered by God, however, Hernández won a handful of converts; but within eighteen months, suffered a crippling stroke and returned to Corpus Christi, where he died.

HDM, 154.
J.M.

Holiness Movement/Churches

A revival movement focusing on **John Wesley's** doctrine of holiness of heart and life emerged in American Methodism in the 1830s during a time when that emphasis was waning in the **Methodist Episcopal Church**. It gained prominence through **Phoebe Palmer's** New York City-based 'Tuesday Meetings for the Promotion of Christian Holiness.' At the same time, 'New School' Calvinists, championed by Charles G. Finney, sparked the Oberlin holiness revival. In 1867, Methodist Episcopal Church clergyman John Inskip founded the National Campmeeting Association for the Promotion of Holiness. During the next decade, the lay ministry of English holiness evangelists Robert Pearsall Smith and Hannah Whitall Smith led to the organization of the Keswick Convention, which encouraged the higher-Christian life movement. Because holiness revivalists tended to be aggressive in their tactics and pointed in their criticism of the way mainstream Methodism was become more and more attuned to American culture, their movement spawned new churches: Wesleyan Methodist, **Free Methodist**, Church of God (Anderson, Indiana), Church of the Nazarene, Pilgrim Holiness Church, and the Oriental Missionary Society. Taylor University (Indiana) and Asbury College and Seminary (Kentucky) were founded by advocates of the holiness movement.

Burgess, Stanley M., Gary B. McGee, and Patrick H. Alexander, eds, *Dictionary of Pentecostal and Charismatic Movements* (1988), 406–409; DCA, 543–547; HDM, 327–329.
J.M.

Hoover, Willis C. (1856–1936)

The generator of Pentecostal Methodism in Chile, Hoover was born in Freeport, Illinois, and received his MD degree in 1884. While practicing medicine in Chicago, he kept hearing an inner voice, saying, 'South America, South America,' with the outcome that in 1889 he accepted appointment by **Methodist Episcopal** Bishop **William Taylor** to an English-language school in northern Chile. Belatedly studying theology, Hoover became a member of the Methodist Episcopal Church's South American Conference when it absorbed Bishop Taylor's independent mission in 1893. A pioneer of Spanish-language ministries as a pastor and district superintendent, Hoover's Methodist career climaxed when, in 1902, he became pastor of his conference's largest church in Valparaiso. Soon, hearing about pentecostal revivals, he prayed for one to occur in Chile. When it did, in April 1909, and quickly spread, Methodist Episcopal officials opened an investigation, concluded that Hoover was erring in doctrine and practice, and removed him as district superintendent, but not from his pastorate. He resigned, however, from the Methodist Episcopal Church in 1910, and became superintendent of a new pentecostal denomination, the *Iglesia Metodista Nacional*. When various tensions caused a split in that denomination, Hoover founded and led *Iglesia Evangelica Pentecostal de Chile*.

Burgess, Stanley M., Gary B. McGee, and Patrick H. Alexander, eds, *Dictionary of Pentecostal and Charismatic Movements* (1988), 445.

J.M.

Hughes, Hugh Price (1847–1902)

Methodist evangelist and preeminent social reformer, Hughes is considered the most influential leader in late nineteenth-century British Methodism. Born in Carmarthen, Wales, the young Hughes was educated at a Methodist school near Swansea and from 1865 to 1869 received his theological education at Richmond College, near London. In 1880 he completed a master's degree in modern philosophy at the University of London. Following ordination in 1869, Hughes served a series of three-year circuit appointments until 1887 when he became the superintendent of the West London **Mission**, a position held until his death. Hughes was perhaps Methodism's most vocal advocate for temperance. In 1884, declaring himself a Christian Socialist, he sought to awaken the church to its duty to care not only for people's spiritual needs, but also their social welfare. He was at the forefront of Britain's Forward Movement which called special attention to the desperate circumstances of the urban poor. Hughes was fervently committed to **ecumenism**, greater influence of the laity in church affairs, and the development of stronger leadership in Methodism. He was honored by his election to the one-year prestigious presidency of the Wesleyan Methodist Conference in 1898. Among his publications are *Social Christianity* (1889), *Ethical Christianity* (1892), and *Essential Christianity* (1894).

BDE, 315–316; DMBI, 167–168; Oldstone-Moore, C., *Hugh Price Hughes: Founder of a new Methodism, Conscience of a new Nonconformity* (1999).

C.Y.

Jacoby, Ludwig Sigismund (1813–1874)

German-born of Jewish descent, Jacoby worked as a shop assistant, largely educated himself, and received baptism from a Lutheran pastor before emigrating to the United States in 1838. There, while teaching school in Cincinnati, Ohio, he heard **Wilhelm Nast** preach, experienced conversion, and, in 1841, was appointed as a **Methodist Episcopal** missionary to German immigrants in St. Louis, Missouri. He became, in 1844, a district superintendent in a conference for German-speaking American Methodists. The 1848 Revolution in Germany, which brought religious liberty to some regions of that land, allowed the bishops of the Methodist Episcopal Church to appoint Jacoby to open, in response to repeated requests, a German mission. He landed at Bremerhaven in 1849, preached his first sermon in Bremen, and organized a local church. Soon he started a library, initiated periodicals for children and adults, published books, and founded a seminary. Functioning as a cross between district superintendent and bishop, Jacoby directed Methodist Episcopal work in many parts of Germany. Returning to the States in 1871, he served as a pastor and district superintendent in the Southwest German Conference. His *Geschichte des Methodismus* is a primary source of the history of Methodism in Germany.

Barclay, Wade Crawford, *The Methodist Episcopal Church, 1845–95, Widening Horizons 1845–95*, History of Methodist Missions (1957), 3:982–998; *EWM*, 1252–1253.
J.M.

Kilham, Alexander (1762–1798)

Founder of the **Methodist New Connexion**, Kilham was born in the village of Epworth, Lincolnshire, England, of Methodist parents and was converted in a revival in his home town. He enlisted in **John Wesley's** corps of intinerant preachers in 1785. As long as Wesley was alive, Kilham believed he was obliged to comply with the Methodist founder's wishes. After Wesley's death however, he became an advocate for political reform, and manifested hostility to the Established Church and its episcopacy. In his 1795 tract, *Progress of Liberty*, Kilham vigorously complained that Methodist laity should be granted more power in the life of the Connexion, that the Wesleyan Methodist hierarchy was unjust, and that the traveling preachers were embezzlers. After a trial in 1797 he was expelled from the Connexion. On 9 August 1797, Kilham and a few other itinerant preachers and lay people founded what became the Methodist New Connexion, which by 1850 had approximately 17,000 members. Published accounts of Kilham's life, politics, and ministry vary, often depending on the political and ecclesiastical positions of those who have assessed his accomplishments.

BDE, 315–316; DMBI, 191; HMGB, 2:280–294.
C.Y.

Laity

Lay participation and leadership has been important in Methodism from its earliest days. Realizing that he and his few clerical associates were unable to manage the temporal and spiritual supervision required by the growing Methodist movement, **John Wesley**, sometimes hesitantly, encouraged and endorsed lay leadership. In addition to his lay itinerant preachers, lay people were enlisted and, if possible, trained as class leaders, exhorters, society stewards, Sunday school teachers, trustees, and other positions. After Wesley's death, as the itinerant preachers gained more authority through the annual conference, the role and influence of the **laity** was somewhat diminished. This development, however, in no way meant that the support of lay people was unnecessary or dispensable. Throughout the nineteenth century there was a growing awareness that participation and leadership of laity had to be broadened. Clergy and laity by their baptism were partners engaged together in **ministry**. Lay representation at every level of the connection was advocated, depending on the **polity** or structure of the denomination. In the **United Methodist Church**, for example, there is lay and clergy parity in voting rights at the annual, jurisdictional (or central), and general conferences where much of the denomination's policies on the church's mission are decided.

Bucke, Emory Stevens, ed., *The History of American Methodism* (1964); *DMBI*, 195–196; *EWM*, II: 1401–1403.
C.Y.

Lambuth, Walter Russell (1854–1921)

Methodist Episcopal Church, South clergyman, medical missionary, and bishop, Lambuth was born of missionary parents in Shanghai, China. He received a bachelor's degree from Emory and Henry College, Emory, Virginia, in 1875 and a medical degree from Vanderbilt University, Nashville, Tennessee, in 1877. Ordained elder in the Tennessee annual conference, Lambuth was sent to China where he served Shanghai and its environs. In 1881 he returned to the United States, studied at Bellevue Hospital Medical College, New York, and was awarded a second medical degree. Lambuth traveled China in 1882 where he organized medical work and founded a hospital. In

1885 he and his father formed the denomination's Japan mission. Returning to the United States in 1891, Lambuth worked vigorously as an advocate for missions and was elected general secretary of southern Methodism's board of missions. The Methodist Episcopal Church, South elected him to the episcopacy in 1910 and assigned him to Brazil. In the years following he traveled to **Africa, Europe**, and Siberia. One of Methodism's outstanding mission leaders, Lambuth died and was buried in Yokohama, Japan.

EWM, II: 1375–1376; Lambuth, Walter Russell, *Medical Missions* (1924); Lambuth, Walter Russell, *Winning the World for Christ* (1915); Pinson, William W., *Walter Russell Lambuth: Prophet and Pioneer* (1925).
C.Y.

Latin America and the Caribbean

Although Methodism was carried to Latin America and the Caribbean by missionary efforts and committed lay people from England and the United States, the churches in the region have generally become autonomous and rely on indigenous leadership. Nathaniel Gilbert, a government official from Antigua and two of his slaves were converted on a visit to England under the preaching of **John Wesley** in 1758. Upon their return to Antigua they organized the first known Methodist work in the Caribbean. **Thomas Coke** is credited with inspiring the first officially organized Methodist mission in the West Indies. Between 1808 and 1811 he published a three-volume *History of the West Indies*. By the time of Coke's death in 1814 there were twelve Methodist circuits in the Caribbean. In 1967 much of the area's Methodism was consolidated when the Methodist Church in the Caribbean and the Americas (MCCA) was formed. The MCCA, which emphasizes evangelism, membership nurture, worship, and other ministries, is an active member of the **World Methodist Council**.

Methodism in Latin America is usually thought to have begun in 1832 when an anonymous layperson instituted a small Methodist class in Argentina and solicited the Methodist Episcopal Missionary Society for missionary support. The society dispatched Fountain E. Pitts (1808–1874) to Argentina, Brazil, and Uruguay to survey the prospects for MEC missionary work. As a result of Pitts' success, the 1836 MEC general conference formally approved sending missionaries to South America and Mexico. Over the ensuing decades, in spite of the disruption caused by the US Civil War and the resistance of entrenched Roman Catholicism in many areas, MEC missions advanced modestly. The Methodist Episcopal Church, South also established missionary work in Latin America and the Caribbean which was especially successful in Mexico, Brazil, and Cuba.

Other Methodist denominations also founded missions in Latin America and the Caribbean including the **Church of the United Brethren in Christ**, Church of the Nazarene, **Free Methodist Church**, and the **Wesleyan Church**.

Much of the mission work of the Anglo-American churches in Latin America and the Caribbean has resulted in the birth of autonomous churches in these regions. For example, the Methodist Church of Mexico and the Methodist Church of Brazil became autonomous in 1930, the Evangelical Methodist Church of Argentina in 1969, and the Methodist Church of Peru in 1970. Many of the autonomous churches are active members of **CIEMAL** and the **World Methodist Council**.

Barclay, Wade Crawford, *The Methodist Episcopal Church 1845–1939, Widening Horizons 1845–95*. History of Methodist Missions (1957), 3:758–868; Copplestone, J. Tremaye, *Twentieth-Century Perspectives (The Methodist Episcopal Church, 1896–1939)*. The History of Methodist Missions (1973), 4:240–314, 581–626, 1034–1129; *DMBI*, 387–388; *HDM*, 180–188.
C.Y.

Leigh, Samuel (1785–1852)

Born in Milton, Staffordshire, England, Leigh, originally raised a Congregationalist, was drawn to Methodism, served the Shaftesbury circuit, and was ordained by the Wesleyan Methodist Conference in 1814. After some confusion regarding an appointment to Lower Canada, Leigh was assigned to New South Wales and arrived there in 1815, becoming the first Wesleyan missionary to Australia. Finding the morality of the colony in danger, he sought to breathe new life into the small Methodist society in Sydney by organizing Bible classes and Sunday schools, and establishing a circuit of preaching places. In 1819, during a period of ill health, Leigh paid his first visit to New Zealand. Returning to England in 1820, he campaigned for the expansion of Wesleyan Methodist mission work in the South Pacific. Back in the South Pacific in 1821, Leigh served in New Zealand from 1822 until his health failed the following year. From 1823 to 1831 he ministered on an Australian circuit until his wife's death after which he rejoined the itinerant ministry in England. Leigh is credited with supervising the church's early ministries not only in New South Wales and New Zealand, but also in Tasmania. He is regarded as one of British Methodism's premier missionary pioneers.

DMBI, 203; *EWM*, II:1418; Strachan, Alexander, *Remarkable Incidents in the Life of the Rev. Samuel Leigh* (1855); Wright, Don and Eric Clancy, *The Methodists: A History of Methodism in New South Wales* (1993), 4–17.
C.Y.

Lutheranism

John Wesley both admired and detested Martin Luther (1483–1546), the great sixteenth-century reformer and patriarch of Protestantism, though obviously not at the same time. On 24 May 1738 Wesley attended the meeting on Aldersgate Street, London, where someone publicly read from Luther's preface to his commentary on St. Paul's letter to the Romans. Wesley was touched by the reformer's description of the change God makes in the life of those who have genuine faith in Christ. Luther's words began a transformation in Wesley's life. Three years later, however, 15–16 June 1741, Wesley read Luther's commentary on Galatians and was aghast at Luther's denigration of reason and good works. Whereas Luther found reason an enemy of the gospel, Wesley viewed reason as a way of understanding, judging, and speaking the good news. Furthermore, Wesley found Luther's comments on the role of good works and God's law leaning dangerously toward **antinomianism**. Wesley's opinion on Luther was somewhat tempered in a letter dated 22 August 1744 where he claimed, 'I love Calvin a little, Luther more; the Moravians, Mr. [William] Law, and Mr. [George] Whitefield far more than either.' Methodism and Lutheranism have not generally been antagonists, although relationships between the two have been strained in **European** nations where Lutheranism was the favored state church, making Methodist affiliation difficult for some. Among its ecumenical tasks, the **World Methodist Council** engaged in five dialogues with the Lutheran World Federation representatives beginning in 1979.

Hildebrandt, Franz, *From Luther to Wesley* (1957); Watson, Philip S., *The Concept of Grace* (1959).
C.Y.

Mashaba, Robert Ndevu (*c.* 1861–1939)

Born in Portuguese, East **Africa** near present-day Maputo Bay, Mashaba is credited with introducing Methodism to Mozambique. As a young man, he traveled to South Africa to find work. While in Port Elizabeth he attended worship with a friend at the Wesleyan Methodist Church and became interested in the Bible. He was converted, baptized, and became a Methodist. For three years he attended Lovedale Missionary Institute, Eastern Cape Province, South Africa, where he received religious training and became fluent in English. In 1885, Mashaba returned to Lorenco Marques, Mozambique, where he organized a school and initiated regular worship services among the inhabitants. Both Roman Catholics and Anglicans sought to assimilate his work, but Mashaba was intent on affiliation with Methodism. In 1892 or 1893 he became a candidate for the Methodist ministry. Mashaba was accused of complicity in a rebellion against the Portuguese colonizers, leading to his arrest and deportation in 1896. Methodist leaders were influential in his release which was secured after several years in prison on the condition that he would not return to Mozambique. He continued his ministry in South Africa and following his retirement in 1934 was able to live in Mozambique until his death.

EWM, II: 1530–1531, 1683.
C.Y.

Matthews, Marjorie (1916–1986)

The first woman to be elected bishop in any mainstream church, Matthews was born in Onawa, Michigan. Marrying early, she had a son, and lived on Army posts during World War II. After the war, she and her husband divorced and she took a job as an executive secretary with an auto parts manufacturer. In 1963, at age forty-nine, she was ordained in the **Methodist Church**, continuing, however, to pursue her education, earning college (Central Michigan) and seminary (Colgate Rochester) degrees, a master's in religion, and a PhD in humanities from Florida State (1976). During those years, Matthews served small churches in Michigan, New York, and Florida. She was the second woman to serve as a district superintendent in the **United Methodist Church**, filling that position in the West Michigan Conference. When, in 1980, she was elected bishop, headlines somewhat hysterically announced, 'The bishop is a woman.' She was assigned to the Wisconsin Area, where she served for four years before retiring. Two years later, she died of cancer.

HDM, 198.
J.M.

Methodism

Methodism is commonly viewed as the religion of persons who profess, in Samuel Johnson's words, 'to live by rules and in constant method.' **John Wesley** backs that view, reporting that an Oxford student – perhaps remembering doctors denominated 'Methodists' because they taught 'that almost all diseases might be cured by a specific *method* of diet and exercise' – applied the name to a group of Oxford men associated with John and **Charles Wesley**, who observed 'a more regular *method* of study and behaviour than was usual with those of their age and station.' Also, because theological **Arminianism** characterized the Wesley brothers' Oxford associates, the name may allude to the seventeenth-century **Calvinist** accusation that theological Arminians were 'new Methodists.'

Theologically, Methodism remains 'new Methodist.' It opposes the extreme Calvinist doctrine that God selects some persons to be saved, some to be damned. Rather, Methodism affirms that God gives every person sufficient grace to begin seeking, when awakened by something like Methodist **evangelism**, a personal relationship with God.

Methodism's theological breadth is grounded in Wesley's writings, which reflect his immersion in the theologians of the early church, especially the Greek Fathers; the Protestant reformers; **Pietism**, both Catholic and Protestant; his own Anglican tradition, both High Church and **Puritan**; and a spectrum of secular authors from the classical world to his own day.

Methodism's theological unity is founded in focusing more on the heart's reasons than the mind's reasonings. Often cited is Wesley's use of 2 Kings 10:15 – 'Is thine heart right, as my heart is with thy heart. . . . If it be, give me thine hand.' The sermon in which Wesley uses that text ('Catholic Spirit') outlines the theological basis of a 'right heart' – a clear, though implicit, Trinitarian belief, and faith that is 'filled with the energy of love.'

Wesley's approach to organizing Methodist institutions was methodical; its undergirding principle, connectional. His smallest groups were classes; several classes composed a society; a number of societies made up a circuit; a conference governed the whole. It was impossible to be an unconnected Methodist: either you actively participated in a class and society, or you were not a Methodist; and a society either received its preacher by conference appointment, or it was not Methodist.

Individual Methodists accepted a method for disciplining their life. They agreed to avoid all known evils, to do all the good they could, and to use the means of grace – worshiping God, listening to the Bible read and interpreted, receiving Holy Communion, sharing in family and private prayer, studying the Bible, and fasting.

Modern Methodist denominations maintain connectionalism as their organizational principle, although their particular forms of connectionalism often differ. The disciplining of individual Methodists depends in large measure upon the expectations of their local congregation: some 'live by rules and in constant method,' some do not.

DMBI, 230–231; *WJW(B)*, Vol. 9; Richard P. Heitzenrater, *Wesley and the People Called Methodists* (1995).
J.M.

Methodism (Great Britain)

British Methodism emerged in an officially Protestant country. The monarch headed the Church of England. Its bishops sat in the upper house of Parliament. Church steeples punctuated the landscape like giant exclamation marks. Most people were baptized, married, and buried by priests of the Established Church. Their lives, however, often showed scant evidence of being steeped in the church's teachings. In that context, Methodism provided spiritual disciplines to help men and women move forward from being cultural Protestants to becoming committed followers of Jesus Christ.

Initially, **John Wesley** saw Methodism as a renewal movement closely related to the Church of England. It offered meeting houses in which people could be taught Wesley's methods for preparing to experience God's forgiving love in a personal, transforming way. Methodists were still expected, however, to participate in Church of England worship services and to receive baptism and Holy Communion from the church's priests. Later, when British Methodism became a separate, legally recognized religious organization, it continued to stress disciplined Christian living. Class meetings remained the key structure for providing spiritual nurture and, when necessary, discipline.

For several decades after Wesley's death, the Wesleyan Connection in Britain worked to fashion its own distinctive silhouette, including the authorization of an ordained clergy, against the background of the Church of England. As it did so, it experienced some splintering: the **Methodist New Connection** (1797), **Primitive Methodists** (1811), **Bible Christians** (1815), and the **United Methodist Free Churches** (1857). The issues underlying these breakaway Methodist denominations varied: personality clashes, lay representation in the conference, lack of evangelical fervor, political conservatism, and growing autocracy in the Wesleyan ministry.

The nineteenth-century splintering of British Methodism was followed by unions in the twentieth century. In 1907, the Methodist New Connection, Bible Christians, and United Methodist Free Churches formed the **United Methodist Church (Great Britain)**. That denomination joined, in 1932, the Wesleyan Methodist Church and the Primitive Methodist Church to create the **Methodist Church** in Britain, which had almost 770,000 members at the time of union; a figure that dropped to 333,000 at the opening of the twenty-first century.

In Britain today, Protestantism as embodied in the Church of England continues to be the established religion, although it is a considerably weaker presence than it was in Wesley's day; and British Methodism's silhouette is no longer sharply outlined against the Anglican background as it was in the nineteenth century. One outcome of this changed situation is that, in 1955, representatives of British Methodism and the Church of England began discussions about the possibility of union. Many Methodists saw the first plan (1963) as a takeover of Methodism. A revised plan, put forward in 1968, was accepted by the Methodist Conference, but rejected by the Anglican General Synod. New talks were initiated in the 1990s.

HDM, 56–58; HMGB.
J.M.

Methodism (USA)

American Methodism evolved in a country whose Senate ratified a treaty with Tripoli in 1797 that declared that 'the Government of the United States . . . is not, in any sense, founded on the Christian religion.' References to God in the country's founding documents were to an aloof deist deity, not to the God and Father of Jesus Christ. A bishop did not administer the oath of office to the president of the United States. Many Americans were not baptized; many lacked even nominal church ties. There were no church steeples on the horizon beckoning adventurous men and women to trek westward. In that context, Methodism developed as one of a number of competing Protestant ways to be religious in the United States.

Early on, American Methodism maintained the Wesleyan disciplines, but when **John Wesley's** stands, such as his opposition to slavery, threatened church growth, they were shelved, if not jettisoned. Instead of being a small renewal movement with high expectations of its members, Methodism in the United States became a large evangelistic church with the goal of converting more persons and building more churches than the Baptists and Presbyterians. American Methodism continued to offer ways for its members to experience a heartfelt, personal relationship with Christ; but strict disciplines, while not abandoned, were enforced in ways that avoided membership decline.

The first Methodist denomination in the United States, the **Methodist Episcopal Church**, began to splinter early in its history. During the first two decades of the nineteenth century, racial discrimination led to the formation of the **Union Church of Africans**, and the **African Methodist Episcopal** and the **African Methodist Episcopal Zion** churches. A proposal to eliminate bishops and give laypersons representation in Methodism's conferences led to the founding of the **Methodist Protestant Church** (1828–1930). The denomination itself split in 1844 over the twin issues of slavery and the power of general conference, producing the **Methodist Episcopal Church, South**, leaving the Methodist Episcopal Church in the north. Other new Methodist denominations came into existence over such issues as slavery, the episcopacy, **holiness**, and **pentecostal** emphases; among these are the **Wesleyan** and **Free Methodist** churches.

The twentieth century witnessed two unions. In 1939, the Methodist Episcopal, Methodist Episcopal, South, and Methodist Protestant churches reunited to form the **Methodist Church**. That denomination and the **Evangelical United Brethren Church** (product of a union in 1946 of the **Evangelical Church** and the **Church of the United Brethren in Christ**) formed the **United Methodist Church** in 1968. Closer cooperation, if not union, discussions continue in the twenty-first century among the United Methodist, African Methodist Episcopal, African Methodist Episcopal Zion, **Christian Methodist Episcopal**, and the **Union American Methodist Episcopal** churches.

In the United States today, religion in general is 'established.' Many Americans consider it unpatriotic to be an atheist. In this context, Methodism offers a Protestant way to be a religious American. It is, however, a less influential way than it was in the nineteenth and early twentieth centuries. Methodism's percentage of the population has been decreasing since the 1930s.

HAM; McEllhenney, John G., ed., *United Methodism in America: A Compact History* (1992); *MEA*.

J.M.

Methodist Church (Great Britain)

While the years following **John Wesley's** death marked the creation of Methodist churches in Great Britain, the twentieth century was characterized by some of those churches uniting in 1932 to form the Methodist Church. This union was preceded by a smaller combination in 1907 when the **Methodist New Connection, Bible Christians**, and **United Methodist Free Churches** joined to form the **United Methodist Church**. The 1932 union included the United Methodists as well as the Wesleyan Methodists and the **Primitive Methodists**. The new church declared loyalty to the Holy Scriptures, John Wesley's *Explanatory Notes upon the New Testament*, and his *Forty-four Sermons*. To guide its **worship** *The Methodist Hymn Book* was published in 1933 containing representative texts of the three predecessor denominations. Since 1932 the Methodist Church has encountered numerous challenges including the fallout from World War II, theological disputes, questions about worship, liturgy, and structure, declining membership, and discussions regarding organic union with the Church of England.

HMGB, III: 309–390 (1983); Tabraham, Barrie W., *The Making of Methodism* (1995); Turner, John Munsey, *Modern Methodism in England, 1932–1998* (1998).

C.Y.

Methodist Church (USA)

On 26 April 1939 in Kansas City, Missouri, after several years of negotiation the **Methodist Episcopal Church**, the **Methodist Protestant Church**, and the **Methodist Episcopal Church, South** united to form the Methodist Church. The Methodist Episcopal Church, founded in 1784, was the oldest of the uniting denominations. Methodist Protestants seceded from the Methodist Episcopal Church in 1830 over dissatisfaction with the role and power of bishops, the southern Methodists over the issue of slavery. While the new denomination retained allegiance to Wesleyan theological standards, certain structural changes were incorporated in order to affect the union. The quadrennial general conference continued as the church's highest legislative authority. Six new jurisdictional conferences were instituted to elect bishops and conduct other business. Five of the six jurisdictions were geographical while the sixth, the central jurisdiction, was racial and included all of the African American annual conferences and local churches. A Judicial Council was created as the final court of appeal on matters of church law. Over the ensuing decades the denomination's membership grew. It produced a new hymnal in 1964 and granted **women** full clergy rights in 1956. In the early 1960s, the church began to struggle with the racial discrimination evidenced by the presence of the Central Jurisdiction. The Methodist Church united with the **Evangelical United Brethren Church** in 1968 to form the **United Methodist Church**.

HAM, III: 407–595; *EWM*, II: 1563–1567; Gesling, Linda, *Mirror and Beacon: The History of Mission of The Methodist Church, 1939–1968* (2005); Thomas, James S., *Methodism's Racial Dilemma: The Story of the Central Jurisdiction* (1992).
C.Y.

Methodist Denominations (Great Britain)

Although it was not **John Wesley's** expressed intent to form a Methodist church in England, within a few years of his death there were discussions and disagreements among Methodists about the movement's connection to the Church of England, the administration of sacraments by its preachers, the hours it held its preaching services, and the role of lay people in its governance. A dispute developed between 'church Methodists' who sought to hold the movement within the Anglican communion and those who argued for Methodist independence from the Established Church. In 1795 the Wesleyan Methodist Conference attempted to negotiate a compromise between the two positions by adopting a Plan of Pacification which stipulated provisions for sacramental administration, worship service times, and the role of the Conference in these and other organizational matters including the stationing of preachers. The Plan failed to gain complete acceptance and in the years following a number of Methodist denominations were formed.

Alexander Kilham (1762–1798), a lay preacher, led the first defection from Wesleyan Methodist Conference ranks when he and his followers formed the **Methodist New Connection** in 1797. In a series of pamphlets which led to his expulsion from the Conference in 1796, Kilham argued for a greater voice and vote for lay people in the business of Methodism. The Methodist New Connection joined two other denominations, the **Bible Christians** and the **United Methodist Free Churches**, to form the **United Methodist Church** in 1907.

Hugh Bourne (1772–1852) and **William Clowes** (1780–1851) were the prime figures in the formation of **Primitive Methodism** which favored revivalism and camp meetings in the life of Methodism. Both men were expelled from the Wesleyan Conference which judged camp meetings improper and disclaimed any connection with them. Primitive Methodism, which adopted its name in 1812, united with Wesleyan Methodism and the United Methodists in 1932 to become the Methodist Church.

The Bible Christians, a denomination founded in 1815 by **William O'Bryan** (1778–1868), a Wesleyan Methodist local preacher prone to freelance evangelism which led to his expulsion, had a strong evangelical and disciplinary emphasis. Bible Christians entered into the 1907 union with the Methodist New Connection and the United Methodist Free Churches.

In 1857 three other Methodist denominations, which had distinct histories, formed the United Methodist Free Churches. They included the Protestant Methodists founded in 1827, the Wesleyan Methodist Association organized in 1836, and the Wesleyan Reformers established in 1849.

Other small Methodist denominations were also formed during the nineteenth century. They included the Independent Methodists which traced its origin to 1806, the Methodist Unitarian Movement (1806), and the Magic Methodists (sometimes referred to as the Forest Methodists) founded in the first decade of the nineteenth century.

The major union in British Methodism occurred 1932 when the United Methodists, the Primitive Methodists, and the Wesleyan Methodists joined to form the Methodist Church.

DMBI; HMGB (1965–1988), especially vols. 2:276–329 and 4:242–494; Tabraham, Barrie, *The Making of Methodism* (1995); Turner, John Munsey, *Modern Methodism in England, 1932–1998* (1998); Turner, John Munsey, *Wesleyan Methodism* (2005).
C.Y.

Methodist Denominations (USA)

Methodism in the United States, which traced its origins to committed lay people as early as 1760, was formally organized, with the blessing of **John Wesley**, as the **Methodist Episcopal Church** in Baltimore, Maryland, in 1784 at what is known as the Christmas Conference. At the time of its formation it numbered about 15,000 members and 80 lay preachers. At the founding conference several lay preachers were ordained enabling them to administer the **sacraments**; an episcopal form of government was adopted; a mission statement was approved ('To reform the Continent and to spread scriptural Holiness over these lands'); slavery was denounced, and provisions were made to establish a school (Cokesbury College).

There were several schisms in the Methodist Episcopal Church in the decades following its establishment. One of the newly ordained preachers, James O'Kelly (1757–1826), and a group of dissidents broke away in 1792 over the issue of the authority of bishops to appoint preachers to congregations. O'Kelly and his followers formed the relatively short-lived Republican Methodist Church. Residual sentiment about the undue power of the episcopacy and advocacy for the rights of lay people and lay preachers led to the establishment of the **Methodist Protestant Church** in 1830.

Slavery and racial discrimination were factors in constituting three major black Methodist denominations in the nineteenth century. Former slave **Richard Allen** (1760–1831), because of ill-treatment at predominantly white St. George's Methodist Episcopal Church, Philadelphia, in 1816 founded the **African Methodist Episcopal Church**. Similar mistreatment of Blacks in New York City led **James Varick** (c. 1750–1827) and others to initiate the **African Methodist Episcopal Zion Church** in 1821. A third major black Methodist denomination, the Colored Methodist Episcopal Church (now the **Christian Methodist Episcopal Church**) was inaugurated in 1870 in the aftermath of the Civil War.

Dispute over slavery led to the largest rupture in the Methodist Episcopal Church in 1845 when southern Methodists, displeased with the antislavery drift of the denomination, left the fold to inaugurate the **Methodist Episcopal Church, South**. A decade earlier, a number of northern Methodists, unhappy that their church was too slow in renouncing slavery, in 1843 seceded from the denomination and organized the Wesleyan Methodist Church (now the **Wesleyan Church** after a union with the Pilgrim Holiness Church in 1968).

Disgruntled with Methodist Episcopal doctrine, government, and practices, including pew rent, a number of reformers led by **Benjamin T. Roberts** (1823–1893) in 1860 organized the **Free Methodist Church**.

The **Holiness Movement** of the nineteenth and twentieth centuries spawned a number of churches with theological ties to American Methodism.

They included the Church of the Nazarene (1907) and the **Salvation Army** (its mission to America in 1880). Holiness also gave rise to the modern diverse **Pentecostal** movement which began in the early twentieth century.

The largest worldwide Methodist denomination is the **United Methodist Church**, a 1968 union of the **Methodist Church** and the **Evangelical United Brethren Church**. Both uniting churches were themselves the products of unions in 1939 and 1946 respectively. United Methodism remains the largest of the present-day Methodist denominations.

EWM; HDM; Melton, J. Gordon, *A Will To Choose: The Origins of African American Methodism* (2007); DCA.
C.Y.

Methodist Episcopal Church (USA)

The Methodist Episcopal Church, founded in Baltimore, Maryland in December 1784, was formed with the authorization of **John Wesley** who ordered the organization of a Methodist church in the United States. He dispatched three emissaries, **Thomas Coke**, Richard Whatcoat, and Thomas Vasey, with orders to ordain some of his American lay preachers and to set aside **Francis Asbury** to be co-superintendent of the American Methodists with Coke. Wesley sent a worship book, *The Sunday Service of the Methodists in North America*, which included Twenty-four Articles of Religion, a distillation of **Anglicanism's** Thirty-Nine Articles. The organizing conference decided on the denominational name, adopted an episcopal form of government, founded a college (Cokesbury), and opposed slavery. In the decades following its formation, the Methodist Episcopal Church experienced several major schisms including the Republican Methodist, the **African Methodist Episcopal, African Methodist Episcopal Zion, Methodist Protestant, Wesleyan Methodist, Methodist Episcopal, South**, and **Free Methodist** churches. Despite these schisms, the Methodist Episcopal Church became one of the largest and most influential denominations in the United States. In 1939 it reunited with the Methodist Protestants and southern Methodists to form the **Methodist Church**.

HAM; EWM, II: 1555–1563; Norwood, Frederick C., *The Story of American Methodism* (1974).
C.Y.

Methodist Episcopal Church, South (USA)

The United States was embroiled in a sectional controversy over slavery in the middle decades of the nineteenth century. The dispute led to a painful civil war between north and south which cost thousands of lives and left the nation sectionally divided for decades. As the nation became split over slavery, so were the Protestant denominations which had large northern and southern constituencies. While the **Methodist Episcopal Church** originally held that slavery was incompatible with Christian faith, by the 1840s it had retreated from that position as most southerners found slavery an economic necessity and not contrary to their faith. The matter came to a head at the 1844 general conference when the two sides, pro-slavery and abolitionist, squared off on the case of Bishop James O. Andrew (1796–1871), a southern slave owner. Andrew was suspended from exercising his office by general conference vote. Southern delegates protested and when the issue could not be resolved, the southerners drew up a plan of separation which led to the formation of the Methodist Episcopal Church, South in May 1845 in Louisville, Kentucky. Following the civil war, southern Methodism resolved to continue as a separate denomination. They actively maintained effective **mission** work overseas, established schools and universities, and supported ministries throughout the south and other places in the nation. After extensive negotiations they reunited in 1939 with the Methodist Episcopal Church and the **Methodist Protestant Church** to form the **Methodist Church**.

HAM, II: 3–314; Sledge, Robert Watson, *'Five Dollars and Myself': The History of Mission of the Methodist Episcopal Church, South, 1845–1939* (2005), The United Methodist History of Mission, vol. 5; Sledge, Robert Watson, *Hands on the Ark: The Struggle for Change in the Methodist Episcopal Church, South, 1914–1939* (1975). C.Y.

Methodist New Connexion (Great Britain)

It is not surprising that following John Wesley's death there were some who sought changes in the Methodist movement. One Methodist itinerant preacher who was eager for change was **Alexander Kilham** who believed that lay people should have a larger role in the governance of Methodism. Kilham published his views in a document titled, *The Progress of Liberty, amongst the People called Methodist* (1795), which argued among other matters, for lay delegation in circuits, districts, and conference in a partnership with the preachers to deal with temporal and spiritual affairs. He was brought to trial in 1796 and was expelled from the Connexion and even forbidden to preach as a layman. Three preachers, William Thom, Stephen Eversfield, and Alexander Cummin, believing that Kilham was correct that there should be closer cooperation between the preachers and laymen, left the conference and joined Kilham in August 1797 to form the Methodist New Connexion. Within a short time of its founding the New Connexion drew approximately

5,000 members from the Wesleyan Connexion and by 1847, its Jubilee year, boasted almost 20,000 members in 579 societies with 327 chapels. In 1907 the Methodist New Connexion with a membership of 40,000 united with the **Bible Christians** and the **United Methodist Free Churches** to become the **United Methodist Church**.

DMBI, 233; HMGB, 2:280–294, 3:167–169.
C.Y.

Methodist New Connexion in Ireland

Similar tensions which led to the formation of the **Methodist New Connexion** in England also precipitated events in Ireland. In 1798 a group of Methodists in Lisburn petitioned the conference to grant lay representation at district and conference meetings. The 1798 Methodist New Connexion conference in England officially recognized the Irish dissenters, but the scattered Irish societies were generally isolated until 1824 when the Methodist New Connexion resolved to make Ireland a **mission** field. William Cooke (1806–1884), Methodist New Connection minister and theologian, is largely responsible for effectively reorganizing the Irish mission and encouraging its growth. British Methodist New Connexion financial difficulties led to diminished support for the Irish mission and the sale of its remaining Irish properties to the Methodist Church in Ireland in 1905 brought about its final demise.

Cooney, Dudley Levistone, *The Methodists in Ireland: A Short History* (2001); *DMBI*, 79, 233.
C.Y.

Methodist Protestant Church (USA)

The Methodist Protestant Church was organized in Baltimore, Maryland, in 1830 after more than a decade of attempts to reform the **Methodist Episcopal Church**. Reformers led by **Nicholas Snethen** and **Asa Shinn** pleaded for four significant changes in episcopal Methodism's structure: (1) elimination of the episcopacy which had become too authoritarian and powerful; (2) election of presiding elders (later called district superintendents) by the annual conference rather than their appointment by a bishop; (3) full conference membership for local pastors; and (4) official representation of the laity with the clergy in the policymaking bodies of the church. Advocates of reform held conventions in 1827 and 1828 to develop their views, consolidate their constituency, and map strategy. When the Methodist Episcopal Church refused to approve their reforms and actually suspended or expelled some of the reformers, the Methodist Protestant Church was founded with an appropriate constitution and Discipline. The office of bishop was replaced by an annual conference president whose pastoral appointments were subject to revision by an annual conference committee. At its origin the new denomination had 5,000 members. When it reunited in 1939 with the Methodist Episcopal Church and the **Methodist Episcopal Church, South**, its membership numbered nearly 200,000. During its tenure the Methodist Protestants founded educational institutions, carried on a vigorous publication program, and supported domestic and overseas **mission** work.

HAM, I: 636–684; Daugherty, Ruth A., *The Missionary Spirit: The History of Mission of the Methodist Protestant Church, 1830–1939* (2004), The United Methodist History of Mission, vol. 1; Drinkhouse, Edward J., *History of Methodist Reform and the Methodist Protestant Church, 1820–1898*, 2 vols. (1899).
C.Y.

Methodist Theology after John Wesley

John Wesley's theological writing was situational, not systematic. Sometimes the situation called for clarifying one of his distinctive themes, sometimes for critiquing the doctrines of others. Wesley repudiated the **Calvinistic** idea of double predestination, which, he said, represents God as an immoral deity, 'as worse than the devil.' Brushing aside biblical passages that seem to support predestination, Wesley argued that the Bible's core message is that a moral God, good and loving, graces everyone with sufficient freedom to seek God, or to turn aside. Once persons begin seeking God, their interactions with God's continuing gifts of grace allow them to find, if they do not call off the search, salvation in Christ and holiness of heart and life. Wesley presented this way of **salvation**, not in a systematic treatise, but in sermons, occasional tracts, and Bible commentaries.

John Fletcher (1729–1785) offered the first systematic treatment of Wesleyan theology in his *Checks to Antinomianism* (1771–1775). He rejected double predestination and irresistible grace, and defined God more in terms of moral qualities than of omnipotence. **Adam Clarke** (*c.* 1760–1832) carried forward Wesley's interest in biblical exposition, publishing a *Commentary on the Bible* (1810–1826). 'We must ever consider these Scriptures,' Clarke said, 'as coming from *God*, as divinely inspired, and as containing His infallible truth.' Richard Watson (1781–1833) provided a systematic Wesleyan theology in his *Theological Institutes* (1831); it served as the handbook of Methodist orthodoxy on both sides of the Atlantic until well into the second half of the nineteenth century.

Wesley, as a revival-movement leader, understood his theological writings as serving preaching and Christian formation. Watson, as a systematic theologian, saw himself as defending doctrines derived by deductive reasoning from God's 'infallible truth' contained in the Bible. It was assumed, by both Watson and Clarke, that divine revelation is not shaped and colored by the historical context in which it is received. That assumption was soon being challenged, however, by David Friedrich Strauss (1808–1874), who, in his *Life of Jesus* (1835), inaugurated modern biblical criticism.

Meanwhile, Methodist theologians in the United States, while joining their British colleagues in opposing Calvinistic double predestination, were laying philosophical foundations for their theologies. **Asa Shinn** (1781–1853) built his position upon Scottish common-sense philosophy. Both **Nathan Bangs** (1778–1862) and Wilbur Fisk (1792–1839) insisted, in an age devoted to scientific cause-and-effect thinking, on understanding salvation as a synergism between two causes: God's grace and human responses.

Slavery raised biblical and theological questions for American Methodists. Some used passages from the Bible to buttress their pro-slavery positions. Others argued that using the Bible to condone slavery makes God an immoral God. For them, thinking theologically about slavery meant thinking historically about the Bible. They considered the possibility that some passages tell us more about the culture of a particular time and place than they tell us about God.

While American Methodists were responding theologically to slavery, **Phoebe Palmer** (1807–1874) was providing a shortcut to holiness. For Wesley, the experience of having one's sins forgiven by God through Christ's atoning death (salvation) was not sufficient; the saved person needs to move on to holiness of heart and life (sanctification, Christian perfection). One may, in Wesley's view, experience sanctification instantaneously or gradually, but always paradoxically: no matter how perfect one's love is, it can always grow more perfect. Palmer offered a 'shorter way' to an unparadoxical 'second blessing': in the Bible, she asserted, God promises sanctification; so the 'first blessed' (the saved) need to accept God's promise, surrender entirely to God, and God will give them the 'second blessing,' the blessing of holiness.

The **Holiness Movement** gained followers on both sides of the Atlantic. British Methodist theologian William Arthur (1819–1901) published *The Tongue of Fire* in 1856, becoming an important influence on the developing holiness movement. About the same time, pentecostal-type experiences such as 'speaking in tongues' came to be seen as evidence of having received the 'second blessing.'

Most British and American Methodist theologians in the middle of the nineteenth century defended traditional doctrinal formulations. Among them are William Burt Pope (1822–1903) in Britain; and, in America, Thomas N.

Ralston (1806–1891), **Daniel A. Payne** (1811–1893), and John Miley (1813–1895). As those men continued to think traditionally, the nineteenth century's avant garde began to think historically.

Geologists studied the history of the earth and announced that it is millions of years old, not five or six thousand. Charles Darwin (1809–1882) examined the history of the species, tracking their evolution from the simplest life forms to human beings. Karl Marx (1818–1883) researched the history of human labor and found the rich using the promise of a better life hereafter to keep the poor from rebelling here and now. Hebrew and Greek scholars anatomized the Bible and displayed the various oral and written sources used by its authors.

American and British Methodist theologians dealt with those findings in various ways. Some, later dubbed fundamentalists, simply declared the historians and scientists wrong. Other Methodist theologians lived and worked in the new intellectual atmosphere. American biblical scholars Milton S. Terry (1846–1914) and Hinckley G. Mitchell (1846–1920) accepted the use of the historical-critical approach to the Bible.

Theologians, working with various late nineteenth-century intellectual developments, formulated a theology differing markedly from that of Wesley and early nineteenth-century Methodism. In the earlier period, it was assumed that divine revelation is not shaped and colored by the lives and times of the biblical authors; by the close of the nineteenth century, it was assumed that the authors expressed the truth they received from God in terms of the events, ideas, and biases of their own times.

The path toward liberal theology in the United States was blazed by Albert T. Bledsoe (1809–1877) and Daniel D. Whedon (1808–1885). Their work was carried forward by Borden Parker Bowne (1847–1910), who valued biblical criticism and based his Methodist theology on German philosophy.

The Social Gospel gained prominence in Methodism through the activities of Englishman **Hugh Price Hughes** (1847–1902) and American Frank Mason North (1850–1935). Hughes and North drew insights for reordering society from socialism's critique of capitalism, and espoused the liberal theology that was being articulated in their day. Hughes emphasized the fatherhood of God and the kingdom of God, and critiqued racism, militarism, irresponsible wealth, and the subjection of women. North wrote that the 'whole force of Christian thought and action' should be used 'to agitate against the overcrowding of the poor, the false methods of business, the public crime of monopoly, the injustice of the competitive system; the cruelty of child labor.'

British Methodist theologian John Scott Lidgett (1854–1953) exemplifies both the Social Gospel and liberal theology. His thinking was shaped by his decades-long ministry among the poor in southeastern London, inspired by the radical self-giving of Jesus, and informed by the new biblical criticism.

Lidgett highlighted the theme of grace and dealt with the tension between theory and practice.

Twentieth-century British Methodist theology retained Lidgett's concerns. Liberalism's optimism about human nature was sobered, however, by the experiences of two world wars, the Holocaust, and the possibility of nuclear annihilation. Among the century's British Methodist theologians are Charles Ryder Smith (1875–1956), Vincent Taylor (1887–1968), Frances M. Young (1939–), and Geoffrey Wainwright (1939–), whose *Doxology* (1980) is, perhaps, the most significant systematic theology written by a Methodist in the twentieth century.

Liberalism characterized American Methodist theology at the beginning of the twentieth century. It emphasized the immanence, rather than the transcendence, of God; the true humanity, rather than the divinity, of Jesus; the moral influence, rather than the satisfaction theory of the atonement; and it emphasized the realization in history of the kingdom of God. Among its proponents were Harris Franklin Rall (1870–1964), Albert C. Knudson (1873–1953), and **Georgia Harkness** (1891–1974). John A. Faulkner (1851–1931) and Edwin Lewis (1881–1959) raised their voices against this liberal tide, stressing the reality of sin, the centrality of Jesus Christ as the God-Man, the transcendence of God, and the authority of the Scriptures.

Wesley studies experienced a renaissance on both sides of the Atlantic. It was initiated in England by Philip S. Watson (1909–1983), Rupert E. Davies (1909–1994), and E. Gordon Rupp (1910–1986); and in the United States by Francis J. McConnell (1871–1953), George C. Cell, (1875–1937), **Albert C. Outler** (1908–1989), Frank Baker (1910–1999), William R. Cannon (1916–1997), and Richard P. Heitzenrater (1939–).

During the second half of the twentieth century in the United States, Carl Michalson (1915–1965) used existentialist concepts to interpret Christian doctrines; Thomas C. Oden (1931–) reaffirmed traditional doctrines; James H. Cone (1938–) developed a black theology; John B. Cobb (1925–) and Schubert M. Ogden (1928–) made theological use of process philosophy; Stanley M. Hauerwas (1940–) and Theodore W. Jennings, Jr. (1944–) worked at the interface of theology and social action. During the same period, Methodists around the world began to root Wesleyan emphases in the soil of their own cultures, with the dominant theme being liberation, the freeing of all life from economic, social, political, and spiritual bondage. Examples are Daniel T. Niles (1908–1970) in Sri Lanka, **José Miguez Bonino** (1924–) in Argentina, and Emerito P. Nacpil (1932–) in the Philippines.

Chiles, Robert E., *Theological Transition in American Methodism, 1790–1935* (1984); Langford, Thomas A., *Practical Divinity*, Volume One, *Theology in the Wesleyan Tradition* (1983).
J.M.

Miles, William Henry (1828–1892)

Methodist clergyman and first bishop of the **Colored (later Christian) Methodist Episcopal Church**, Miles was born a slave in Springfield, Kentucky, but was freed through his owner's last will and testament. In 1855 he became a member of the **Methodist Episcopal Church, South** and was licensed to preach two years later. Miles was the first bishop elected when the Colored Methodist Episcopal Church was formed in 1870. His consecration to the office was conducted by Methodist Episcopal Church, South bishops Holland N. McTyeire and Robert Paine. Miles served in the episcopacy until his death.

Lakey, Othal Hawthorne, *The History of the CME Church* (rev. ed., 1996); Phillips, C. H., *The History of the Colored Methodist Episcopal Church in America, Comprising Its Organization, Subsequent Development and Present Status* (1925). Posted at http://docsouth.unc.edu/church/phillips/phillips.html.
C.Y.

Ministry

Ministry is a term which is employed in at least two ways in Methodism's churches: (1) In a more general sense it refers to the service of the whole church to the world by its lay people and clergy as representatives of Christ. By their baptism all Christians are called by God into the ministry of the church. (2) Often the term is used in a narrower sense where it pertains to persons who occupy special roles in the church's life, especially those who serve as pastors of local congregations. In some Methodist denominations these men and women are called 'ministers.' Some persons have been set aside by the church through ordination as deacons and elders (presbyters in some Methodist denominations) and are described as having entered the 'ordained ministry.'

In general, the ministry of the **laity** and clergy is determined by the nature of the mission of the church. Many Methodist denominations have mission statements, for example, United Methodism which claims that its principal mission is to make disciples for Jesus Christ for the transformation of the world. At other levels of church life, conferences and local churches have also drafted mission statements as the basis for structuring their ministry. At least three considerations are often at the center of mission and ministry, namely, evangelism, Christian nurture, and engagement with social issues.

The mission and ministry of the church are promoted through literature, electronic media (e.g., email and web sites), workshops, conferences, and other means. Through these channels lay people and clergy are provided with information, instruction, and inspiration to equip them for ministry.

While the ministry of the clergy is critical to accomplishing the mission of the church, since the late nineteenth century lay people have been granted both voice and vote at policy-making level of Methodist denominations.

Considerable attention is paid to several requirements regarding those who serve in the pastoral ministry or in other settings in which they exercise the prerogatives of the clergy. Chief among these qualifications are: (1) an authentic call to ministry; (2) possession of talents and skills necessary to fulfill the calling; (3) soundness of the person's theology; (4) educational achievement which demonstrates ability to think and function theologically; (5) a period of trial ministry which allows for assessing effectiveness and potential for future ministry. Methodist denominations have various ways of judging these basic requirements.

Normally, persons in the ordained ministry are expected to preach and teach effectively, lead worship and administer the **sacraments** (baptism and the Lord's Supper) appropriately, offer pastoral care with sensitivity, and lead congregational life creatively. In most Methodist denominations there is also an assumption that ordained ministry usually involves commitment to itinerate. Other forms of pastoral ministry include persons not ordained, for example, local or lay pastors who may serve as the leaders of a local congregation which for a number of reasons, including financial, may not have ordained direction.

DMBI, 239; EWM, II: 1622–1626; Harnish, John E., *The Orders of Ministry in The United Methodist Church* (2000); Yrigoyen, Charles, Jr., John G. McEllhenney, and Kenneth E. Rowe, *United Methodism at Forty: Looking Back, Looking Forward* (2008), 89–121.

C.Y.

Minor, Rüdiger Rainer (1939–)

A leader of Methodism in East Germany during the end of the Cold War and the bishop who helped reestablish the **United Methodist Church** in Russia, Minor was born in Leipzig, Germany, the son of a Methodist family, received his doctorate of theology there at Karl Marx University (now the University of Leipzig), and prepared for ordination at the United Methodist Seminary in Bad Klosterlausnitz, Germany; both institutions played key roles in educating Christian leaders in East Germany before the collapse of communism. Ordained elder in 1966, Minor, while a pastor in Jena (1970–1976), became a part-time faculty member at Bad Klosterlausnitz, moved to full-time in 1976, and directed the seminary from 1984 to 1986, when he was elected bishop by the East German Central Conference and assigned to the Dresden Area. From 1993 until 2005, he was the bishop in residence in the Euro-Asia Area and bishop to the Northern Europe Central Conference; during that assignment he helped reestablish the United Methodist Church in Russia. Minor taught comparative Christianity at the United Methodist Seminary in Moscow, and currently is Professor of World Evangelism at Candler School of Theology in Atlanta, Georgia.

Harman, Robert J., *From Missions to Mission: The History of Mission of the United Methodist Church, 1968–2000*, The United Methodist History of Mission (2005), 5:307–309, 315, 327.
J.M.

Missions (American Methodism)

North American Methodism was a powerful force in the nineteenth-century missionary movement. Missionary endeavors by Methodists in the United States took two forms – domestic and foreign. The earliest cross-cultural domestic mission work of the MEC was begun in 1816 by an African American, John Stewart, who ministered to the Wyandotts in Ohio. Domestic missions included work in rural, town, and urban settings. Growing interest in missionary work in the MEC led to the formation of the Methodist Missionary Society in 1819. Its first overseas missionary, Melville Cox (1799–1833), was dispatched to Liberia in 1832 who died within months of his 1833 arrival.

American Methodism vigorously expanded its foreign missionary work in the nineteenth century. Much of the effort was centered on evangelism, education, and medical care. Missionaries of the MEC and MECS organized Methodist ministries in Asia, Europe, South and Central America, and the Caribbean. Methodist Protestants, Evangelical Association, and United Brethren also opened overseas work. Gradually, much of the mission work came under indigenous leadership and control. Indigenization and other factors contributed to, many of the churches begun by American missionaries, becoming autonomous, especially in the twentieth century. Among these are the Korean Methodist Church, the Methodist Church of Mexico, and the Methodist Church in Brazil. Some churches which trace their origins to Methodist missions were united in some nations with other denominations such as the United Church of Canada, the Uniting Church in Australia, and the United Church of Christ in Japan (known as the *Kyodan*).

Methodist churches in North America including the AME, AMEZ, CME, Free Methodist, Wesleyan, Church of the Nazarene, and other denominations supported effective missionary work in various countries.

It is impossible to consider denominational missionary work without reference to the role of women in enlisting as missionaries, recruiting others for the work, informing and educating the church about the missionary enterprise, and providing funds for the work. No other church constituency supplied more significant support for missions from local church to denominational societies than women.

By the end of the twentieth century denominations began to refer more generally to the church's mission rather than its missionary work since it was believed that speaking of the church's mission is a term which better describes the churches' work, both domestic and foreign.

Barclay, Wade Crawford and J. Tremayne Copplestone, History of Methodist Missions, 4 vols. (1949–1973); Campbell, James T., *Songs of Zion: The African Methodist Episcopal Church in The United States and South Africa* (1995); Semple, Neil, *The Lord's Dominion: The History of Canadian Methodism* (1996), especially 276–333; Robert, Dana L., *American Women in Mission: A Social History of Their Thought and Practice* (1996); The United Methodist History of Mission, six vols. (2003–2005).
C.Y.

Missions (British Methodism)

Although **John Wesley's** statement, 'I look upon all the world as my parish,' is often quoted to support Methodism's missionary efforts both at home and abroad, Wesley was not enthusiastic about missionary work overseas. Although he was a missionary to the American colonies in 1736–1738, his earliest overseas effort after organizing the Methodist movement included dispatching missionary preachers to America beginning in 1769.

Methodism's passion for overseas missions was conceived in the mind of **Thomas Coke** (1747–1814), generally considered the pioneer of Methodist mission work. Coke developed a plan for missions in 1786. It was endorsed by Wesley and included not only support for Scotland and the islands of Guernsey and Jersey, but also for the West Indies, Newfoundland, Nova Scotia, and Quebec. Gradually, the Methodist Conference began to take responsibility for overseas missionary work, especially its management and financing. Early mission work outside the British Isles extended to the West Indies, Sierra Leone, Ceylon (Sri Lanka), and India.

In 1818 the Conference formally organized the Wesleyan Methodist Missionary Society for the 'support and enlargement' of 'Foreign missions' for the preaching of the gospel and the conversion of the world. A major purpose in establishing the denominational society was to combine a variety of congregational and district missionary organizations which had originated over recent years. Its labors bore fruit in many places in **Africa, Asia**, and **Europe**. Other Methodist churches also organized overseas mission work. For example, the **Methodist New Connection, Bible Christians, Primitive Methodists**, and **United Methodist Free Churches** carried the gospel to a variety of nations and cultures. Missionary work often did not merely include preaching, but also the establishment of schools, medical clinics, and hospitals. The cooperative efforts of missionaries and indigenous leadership produced impressive results in conversions and other ministries. By the latter decades of the nineteenth century and throughout the twentieth century, indigenous initiative and control was critical to sustaining successful mission work. Effective indigenous leadership often prompted churches begun by missionary efforts to become autonomous.

Missionary magazines and other publications were effectively employed to tell the story of missionaries and their ministry. They carried extracts from the journals and letters of men and women in the field, as well as their reports to sponsoring agencies, and general news of the denominations' mission endeavors.

Women were an especially important force in Methodist mission work. They informed the church of missionary work, recruited people to serve, and generously financed mission labors.

With the union of 1932 all overseas mission ministries of the uniting bodies was integrated into the Methodist Missionary Society.

DMBI; *HMGB*, 3:1–116; 4:209–212, 343–346, 355–358, 381–388, 430–431, 439, 456, 469–471, 575–584.
C.Y.

Modern Media: Radio, Film, TV, Computer

John Wesley used the media of his day – preachers riding horses, the royal mails, printing presses – to disseminate his message; and ever since, his followers have been keen, if occasionally lagging, users of the evolving media. During the middle years of the twentieth century, there were 'name' radio preachers in Methodism, such as Ralph W. Sockman, who occupied America's National Radio Pulpit for thirty-six years. Film's possibilities, too, captured the Methodist imagination. In Britain, Methodist layman J. Arthur Rank, having recognized film (his personal business) as an important medium for evangelism, promoted the Religious Film Society (1933). Many Methodist congregations broadcast their Sunday services on local radio stations. Television, on the other hand, was dominated by independent fundamentalists who, because of their tear-jerking fund raising, could afford the costs. Methodist preachers did appear, however, on nationally televised programs, and toward the close of the twentieth century, the **United Methodist Church** mounted successful TV advertising campaigns. During the same period, pastors and local churches entered the kingdom of the computer: congregations, conferences, and denominations designed web sites, pastors became bloggers, bishops and district superintendents kept in frequent contact with their clergy via email.

DMBI, 243; Yrigoyen, Charles, Jr., John G. McEllhenney, and Kenneth E. Rowe, *United Methodism at Forty: Looking Back, Looking Forward* (2008), 36–39.
J.M.

Moravianism

Moravians played key roles at pivotal moments in **John Wesley's** spiritual development: by showing him during terrifying storms at sea that faith can throw fear overboard; by telling him to preach faith until he gained faith; and by assuring him that joy does not always accompany faith. Also they revealed to Wesley the value of congregational hymn singing, and provided models for Methodist love feasts and watchnight services. The name comes from a small group of Bohemian Brethren, followers of Jan Hus (*c.* 1372–1415), that existed as an underground movement in Moravia, now part of the Czech Republic, in the seventeenth century. In 1722, **Graf Nicholas von Zinzendorf** (1700–1760) invited those Moravians to settle on his Herrnhut estate in Saxony, Germany. Although Moravians accept the classic creeds of Christendom as well as the principal doctrinal statements of Protestantism, they do not make adherence to creeds and confessions a condition of membership, preferring to emphasize a personal experience of justification by faith, assurance of God's forgiveness, personal piety, and the missionary spirit. Both John and **Charles Wesley** owed much to the Moravian interpretations of conversion and assurance; John, however, adamantly rejected what he understood to be Moravianism's undervaluing of the sacraments and other means of grace.

DMBI, 245; HDM, 215; ODCC, 1112–1113.
J.M.

Müller, Christoph Gottlob (1785–1858)

Founder of British Wesleyan Methodism in Germany, Müller was born in Winnenden, Württemberg, Germany. He migrated to England in 1806 and was converted under Methodist preaching in London. Müller became active in British Methodism as an exhorter, class leader, circuit leader, and circuit steward. In 1813 he returned to Germany to visit his elderly ill father. In a Moravian meeting in his parent's home he offered a testimony of personal faith and salvation, a strikingly new message to many. A spiritual revival at Winnenden ensued with the newly converted requesting the Wesleyan Methodist Missionary Society to send a preacher. The society in 1831 responded by appointing Müller a lay missionary. His preaching and organization were largely successful so that by the time of his death his Methodist societies had more than a thousand members with fifty-seven preaching places and thirty-four class leaders and exhorters. Müller was also active in recruiting **women** for the Protestant **deaconess movement** in Germany.

Burkhardt, Friedemann W., *Christoph Gottlob Müller und die Anfange der Methodismus in Deutschland* (2003); Garber, Paul N., *The Methodists of Continental Europe* (1949); Sommer, Johann W. Ernst, *Christoph Gottlob Müller von Winnenden: der Gründer der ersten Methodistengemeinschaft in Deutschland* (1933); Streiff, Patrick Ph., *Methodism in Europe: 19th and 20th Century* (2003), 66–68.
C.Y.

Mysticism

John Wesley, while devoting himself at Oxford during the early 1730s to the pursuit of disciplined, holy living, received from William Law a copy of the medieval mystic classic *Theologia Germanica*. Soon Wesley was also reading the works of such Continental mystics as Madame Guyon, Antoinette Bourignon, Cardinal Fénelon, and the Marquis de Renty. Their emphasis on religion as a quest for perfect love and a personal encounter with the Divine appealed to Wesley. But by 1736–1737, when he was ministering in Georgia, Wesley had begun to question what he took to be mysticism's slighting of the means of grace. Several years later, in 1741, he noted in his journal: 'I read over once again *Theologia Germanica*. O how was it that I could ever so admire the affected obscurity of this unscriptural writer! Glory be to God that I now prefer the plain apostles and prophets before him and all his *mystic* followers.' Yet he continued to commend meditative reading of the works of Madame Guyon and de Renty, and Wesley's own message preserves what may be taken as the essence of mysticism: an experience of direct and loving union with God in Christ leading to holiness of heart and life.

DMBI, 248–249; *ODCC*, 1127–1128; Tuttle, Robert G., *John Wesley, his Life and Theology* (1978).
J.M.

Nast, Wilhelm [William] (1807–1899)

Considered the father of German Methodism, Nast was born in Stuttgart, Germany. He attended schools in Stuttgart and Baihingen-an-der-Enz before entering seminary in Blaubueren in 1821. Nast's seminary roommate was David Friedrich Strauss who later became a controversial rationalist biblical scholar. After a period of doubt regarding the ministry, Nast studied at the University of Tübingen (1825–1827) before migrating to the United States. In 1835 at a Methodist meeting in Ohio he had a religious experience and again seriously considered the ministry. He was appointed Methodist missionary to German immigrants in the Cincinnati, Ohio area. Effectively preaching, organizing, and supporting German-speaking people, his missionary work flourished in the American Midwest. Nast edited an influential German paper for the church, *Der Christliche Apologete*, from 1839 to 1892 and translated, edited, and wrote a number of biblical, historical, and theological works for German Methodists.

ANB, 16:245; Nast, William, *The Larger Catechism* (1892); Streiff, Patrick Ph., *Methodism in Europe: 19th and 20th Century* (2003), 66–68; Wittke, Carl F., *William Nast: Patriarch of German Methodism* (1959).
C.Y.

Nuelsen, John Louis (1867–1946)

German Methodist clergyman, scholar, teacher, **ecumenist**, and bishop, Nuelsen was born in Zurich Switzerland, the son of a Methodist clergyman. He began his education in Germany, but received his basic theological education (B.D.) in the United States at Drew University, Madison, New Jersey. Additional theological study in the United States was followed by academic work at German universities in Berlin and Halle. Nuelsen taught at Methodist colleges in St. Paul, Minnesota and Warrenton, Mississippi, as well as Nast Theological Seminary in Berea, Ohio, from 1899 to 1908 when he was elected to the episcopacy of the **Methodist Episcopal Church**. He was sent to **Europe** in 1912 where he supervised Methodist ministries in Europe and North **Africa**. Nuelsen was especially known for directing relief efforts in **Europe** following World War I. He also successfully endeavoured to build relationships between Germany and the United States. His scholarly publications included books on the history of Methodism, **John Wesley**, **John William Fletcher**, and the theology and practice of ordination. He retired from the **ministry** in May 1939.

EWM, II:1793; Hammer, Paul Ernest, *John L. Nuelsen: Aspekte und Materialien eines biographischen Versuchs* (1974); Streiff, Patrick Ph., *Methodism in Europe: 19th and 20th Century* (2003).
C.Y.

O'Bryan, William (1778–1868)

Founder of the **Bible Christians**, one of the Methodist denominations initiated after John Wesley's death, O'Bryan was raised in a Methodist household. In 1800 he became a local preacher, but by 1801 he was active as an unsanctioned itinerant evangelist. His application for the Wesleyan ministry in 1810 was rejected for several reasons including his unconventional evangelism, criticism of the Wesleyan itinerant preachers, and advocacy of voluntary offerings to support the itinerants. O'Bryan was expelled from membership in 1810 for failing to attend his class meeting, and again in 1815 for unauthorized preaching outside the Wesleyan circuit plan. On 1 October 1815 he organized an independent circuit in Cornwall and shortly thereafter formed additional classes in Devon. In 1819 the Bible Christians held their first conference and designated O'Bryan their president. Over the next two decades their membership increased to over 13,000. Opposition to O'Bryan's domineering style led to his emigration to North America and his effective withdrawal from the Bible Christians in 1829. In the decades following he crossed the Atlantic thirteen times, dying in the United States with burial in Brooklyn, New York.

BDE, 481–482; DMBI, 259; HMGB, 2:294–303; Shaw, Thomas, *The Bible Christians, 1815–1907* (1965).
C.Y.

Oldham, William F. (1854–1937)

Apostle of Methodism in Singapore, missionary bishop for Southern Asia, and the second resident **Methodist Episcopal** bishop in Latin America, Oldham was born in Bangalore, India, of parents whose ancestry was Indian and English. Hearing Methodist Episcopal missionary-evangelist Daniel Fox preach, Oldham experienced conversion, became a Methodist, traveled to the United States for college, joined the Michigan Conference, and was sent, in 1884, as a missionary to India. A few months later, Bishop **James Thoburn** ordained Oldham elder and appointed him to organize a mission in Singapore. Oldham developed ministries using Indian and Chinese languages as well as English, opened schools, and obtained financial support from persons of all races. After laying the foundations of Methodism in Malaysia, he returned to the United States and taught **missions** and comparative religion at Ohio Wesleyan University. In 1904, he was elected missionary bishop for Southern Asia, resident in Singapore. Eight years later, he became one of three co-ordinate secretaries of the Methodist Episcopal Board of Missions. The 1916 general conference elected him a regular, as differentiated from a missionary, bishop, and assigned him to South America, residing in Buenos Aires, from which area he retired in 1928.

EWM, II:1810–1811.
J.M.

Otterbein, Philip William (1726–1813)

German Reformed pastor and a founder of the **United Brethren in Christ**, Otterbein was born in Dillenburg, Nassau, Germany and educated at the University of Halle where Reformed confessionalism was combined with the personal devotion and evangelical methods of **Pietism**. Following his ordination in 1752, he responded to a call to emigrate to America. Over a period of twenty-two years of pastorates in Lancaster, Tulpehocken, and York, Pennsylvania; and Frederick, Maryland, Otterbein conducted an evangelical **ministry**. In 1767 he encountered **Martin Boehm** (1725–1812) at an evangelistic meeting near Lancaster, Pennsylvania. At the close of Boehm's preaching, Otterbein embraced him and declared, *'Wir sind brüder'* (We are brethren). The fruit of their subsequent friendship was a gathering of lay people and preachers who in 1800 organized the United Brethren in Christ. Otterbein never severed his ties with the German Reformed Church, but his final parish in Baltimore, Maryland, was known as the German Evangelical Reformed Church of Baltimore. His friendship with the Methodists was evident in his participation in the 1784 ordination of Methodist leader **Francis Asbury**. The United Brethren later united with the **Evangelical Church** and in 1968 the recently united **Evangelical United Brethren** became part of the **United Methodist Church**.

BDE, 492–494; Core, Arthur C., *Philip William Otterbein: Pastor, Ecumenist* (1968); O'Malley, J. Steven, *Pilgrimage of Faith: The Legacy of the Otterbeins* (1973).
C.Y.

Outler, Albert Cook (1908–1989)

Methodist clergyman, theologian, **ecumenist**, and teacher, Outler was born in Thomasville, Georgia. He was educated at Wofford College (B.A.), Spartanburg, South Carolina; Emory University (B.D.), Atlanta, Georgia; and Yale University (PhD), New Haven, Connecticut. Several institutions awarded him honorary doctorates. Following ordination in the South Georgia annual conference, Outler served several appointments. He later taught at Duke University, Durham, North Carolina (1938–1945), Yale University (1945–1951), and Southern Methodist University (1951–1977). Outler is considered one of the most important interpreters of **John Wesley's** life and theology. Editor of the four volumes of sermons in the most recent (Bicentennial) edition of Wesley's works, he is also credited with explicating Wesley's theological method, often referred to as the Wesleyan quadrilateral (Scripture, tradition, reason, and experience). As ecumenist, Outler served on the Faith and Order Commission of the World Council of Churches and was an official Protestant observer at the Second Vatican Council. In addition to the legacy of his leadership in the church and theological writings, Outler left an indelible impression on his students, some of whom have also become outstanding scholars of John Wesley and the Methodist tradition.

Outler, Albert C., *Evangelism and Theology in the Wesleyan Spirit* (1996); Outler, Albert C., ed., *John Wesley* (1964); Parrot, Bob W., *Albert C. Outler: The Gifted Dilettante* (1999).
C.Y.

Palmer, Phoebe Worrall (1807–1874)

Methodist Episcopal laywoman, holiness leader, and author, Palmer was born in New York City. Her parents were active members of the Methodist Episcopal Church and she was a leader in the church, including a weekly prayer and Bible study group. By 1837 this gathering devoted itself to promoting the Wesleyan doctrine of entire sanctification – being made perfect in love – and was known as the Tuesday Meeting for the Promotion of Holiness. This band included women and men, lay and clergy, Methodist and non-Methodist. Bible study, prayer, personal testimonies, and discussion were central features of the meetings. Her widely read book, *The Way of Holiness*, the editing of the periodical, *The Guide to Holiness*, and an active speaking schedule brought her to the attention of many and promoted her role as a principal leader of the **Holiness Movement** in both the United States and England. In her addresses and writings, Palmer described the path to holiness and insisted that entire sanctification is instantaneously available to every believer. She was also influential in popularizing the experience of being baptized with the Holy Spirit. Serving the poor, arguing for the ministry of women, and founding the Five Points Mission in New York City show that Palmer's advocacy of holiness had profound social implications for holiness theology.

Oden, Thomas C., ed., *Phoebe Palmer: Selected Writings* (1988); Raser, Harold E., *Phoebe Palmer, Her Life and Thought* (1987); White, Charles E., *The Beauty of Holiness: Phoebe Palmer as Theologian, Revivalist, Feminist, and Humanitarian* (1986).
C.Y.

Payne, Daniel Alexander (1811–1893)

African Methodist Episcopal clergyman, educator, historian, and bishop, Payne was born in Charleston, South Carolina. As a child of ten, he was orphaned and placed in the care of a great-aunt who oversaw his regular attendance at Methodist class meetings. In 1835 he moved north and studied for the **ministry** at the Lutheran Theological Seminary, Gettysburg, Pennsylvania. Although obtaining a Lutheran license to preach, he served a term as pastor of a Presbyterian congregation in Troy, New York. In 1841 Payne joined the **African Methodist Episcopal Zion Church** and the following year was admitted to the clergy ranks of its Philadelphia annual conference. He served churches in New York, Washington, DC, and Baltimore, Maryland. His influence in the denomination resulted in his election to the episcopacy in 1852. Through his preaching and writing Payne supported an educated ministry for his denomination. Wilberforce University, Xenia, Ohio, named for the British abolitionist William Wilberforce, in 1863 chose Payne its first president, and, it is believed, thereby made him the first black college president in the United States. He was one of the premier leaders in his church in the nineteenth century.

BDE, 510–512; Payne, Daniel Alexander, *Recollections of Seventy Years* (reprint, 1968); Tyler, Mark Kelly, *Daniel Alexander Payne of the African Methodist Episcopal Church: The Life of a 19th-Century Educational Leader, 1811–1865* (2007).
C.Y.

Pentecostalism

The gifts of the Spirit, according to Paul, are wisdom, knowledge, faith, healing, miracles, prophecy, discernment of spirits, tongues, and the interpretation of tongues (1 Corinthians 12:8–10). Among these gifts, the more sober ones, such as prophesying, seem to take precedence over the more ecstatic – tongues (14:1–5); with love being the greatest of all (13:13). **John Wesley** tended to view those who spoke in tongues (*glossolalia*) as **enthusiasts** in the negative sense. At the beginning of the twentieth century, however, pentecostal revivals broke out within the Methodist-related **Holiness Movement**; with the event that gained Pentecostalism worldwide attention being the 1906 Azusa Street Revival in Los Angeles led by William Seymour, who was raised a Baptist. Immediately, several Methodists joined the new movement: among others, Thomas B. Barratt and **Willis C. Hoover**. Barratt, a Norwegian Methodist minister of British descent, received the baptism of the Holy Spirit in New York City in 1906, returned to Norway, sparked a pentecostal revival there, and carried Pentecostalism to the British Isles in 1907. Two years later,

Hoover initiated a pentecostal revival in Chile. Pentecostalism is distinguished by the claim that speaking in tongues provides evidence that a person has been baptized by the Spirit.

Burgess, Stanley M., Gary B. McGee, and Patrick H. Alexander, eds, *Dictionary of Pentecostal and Charismatic Movements* (1988), 688–707; *HDM*, 241; *ODCC*, 1253–1254.
J.M.

Pietism

One of the colors woven into the tapestry of Methodism is Pietism, which, beginning in the late seventeenth century, was an attempt to reform German Protestantism, which was perceived to be so focused on doctrinal orthodoxy that it was failing to nourish personal faith and life. This movement was part of a larger interfaith emphasis on 'heart religion' that included Hasidism in eastern European Judaism, the Jansenists of French Roman Catholicism, and English Puritanism. Pietism's pivotal book is Phillip Jakob Spener's *Pia Desideria* (1675), which challenged the church to emphasize the devotional study of scripture; called upon the laity to become active in church renewal; elevated evangelical zeal over skill in theological debates; focused on Christian living rather than intellectual penetration; advocated preaching aimed at the salvation of the listeners, not simply their instruction or correction; and promoted theological training that developed the moral and spiritual qualities in the life of the pastor. Paul Gerhardt's German hymns, the first English translations of which were made by **John Wesley** in Savannah, Georgia, embodied Pietism's ideals. **Moravian** missionaries carried Pietist emphases to North America; the Danish-Halle mission planted them in Tranquebar, India.

Brown, Dale, *Understanding Pietism* (1978); *DMBI*, 272; *EWM*, II: 1912–1914; *HDM*, 242–243.
J.M.

Piety

Since its earliest days, Methodism has been keenly interested in the nature and practice of piety, that is, how one lives the Christian life. John and Charles Wesley taught that true piety is holiness of heart and life, loving God with all we are and have, and loving our neighbor as ourselves. The brothers urged their Methodist followers to make holy living their goal since God has ordained it as the only path to please God and enjoy genuine happiness.

Holy living cannot be accomplished privately or through human effort alone, but is nurtured by what John Wesley called 'works of piety.' These included, but were not limited to, the reading and study of scripture, private and corporate prayer, fasting, Christian fellowship, and the regular reception of the Lord's Supper. 'Works of piety' are rooted in gifts provided by God which, when faithfully exercised, nurture Christian life both individually and collectively.

According to the Wesleys, Christian discipleship is a disciplined way. An evidence of such discipline were the General Rules for the Methodist societies and classes, drawn up by John Wesley in 1743. These rules required Methodists to avoid evil of every kind, to do good to all people, and to engage in Bible study, prayer, worship, fasting, and to receive Holy Communion regularly.

Methodists were not only exhorted to employ 'works of piety,' they were also obliged to engage in 'works of mercy,' acts of justice and kindness to others. This, too, is indispensable to Christian living. Methodists were advised to be concerned about health (their own and that of others), warned against the misuse of money, and counseled to dress frugally and plainly (see John Wesley's sermon 'On Dress'). They were counseled on the importance of education and the wickedness of the slave trade. War was to be avoided and those in prison were to be cared for and ministered to.

Put in modern terms, the Wesleys held that the Methodist way of life was holistic. It included attention to peoples' physical health, their minds as a gift of God, and their spiritual welfare and growth.

While the churches that trace their origins to the eighteenth-century Wesleyan revival have identified themselves with the piety advanced by the Wesleys, they have not always been able to help their people adopt a holistic view of life which pays proper attention to the integrative importance of body, mind, and spirit. Sometimes they have emphasized evangelism, to the neglect of physical and educational needs. At other times their ministries have disregarded spiritual needs in favor of education and physical well-being.

Cracknell, Kenneth and Susan J. White, *An Introduction to World Methodism* (2005), 118–242; Gorrell, Donald K., *The Age of Social Responsibility: The Social Gospel in the Progressive Era, 1900–1920* (1988); Maddox, Randy L., *Responsible Grace: John Wesley's Practical Theology* (1994); Marquardt, Manfred, *John Wesley's Social Ethics: Praxis and Principles* (1992); Wakefield, Gordon S., *Methodist Spirituality* (1999); Yrigoyen, Charles, Jr., *John Wesley: Holiness of Heart and Life* (1996), 40–73.
C.Y.

Polity of John Wesley

In the polity of **John Wesley**, form follows the function of connecting persons to God and one another. He saw men and women who were not being reached by the Church of England. So, beginning in 1739, he preached outdoors or in secular structures, and formed societies in which those who responded to his message could connect with each other as they sought, through worship and fellowship, a personal connection with God. He divided the societies into small groups that met weekly for self-examination, mutual encouragement, and prayer.

Wesley viewed his connecting ministries as supplements to, not substitutes for, the traditional liturgical and sacramental roles of the ordained priests of the Church of England. So he sent his followers to their neighborhood parish churches for prayer-book worship and to receive the **sacraments**.

As time passed, Wesley, who was tireless in his travels, had more societies than he could visit and supervise. So he accepted men (later, a few women) who offered to serve as unordained preachers. He assigned two or more to each circuit (a group of societies in a geographical area) for a period of several months, then moved them to different circuits. These itinerant preachers visited each society regularly, preached, and reviewed the members' Christian growth. As the number of circuits increased, Wesley picked the best lay preachers to be his assistants, assigning to each the duty of supervising the work of a circuit's other itinerants.

Beginning in 1744, Wesley chose certain preachers to meet with him annually in conference, to advise him, but not to vote. Wesley's polity was not democratic: he made the final decisions on how to regulate Methodist doctrine, bring spiritual order to the lives of individuals, and organize the activities of the societies. Decisions with ongoing relevance were gathered in Large Minutes, the basic handbook of his connectional polity. The Large Minutes contained, among other items, a Model Deed for Methodist preaching-houses, which instructed the trustees to receive only the preachers appointed by Wesley and to guard against the preaching of any doctrine other than that contained in Wesley's *Sermons* and his *Explanatory Notes upon the New Testament*.

In addition to those volumes, Wesley, recognizing that his followers lacked reading materials they could afford, published hymnbooks, abridgments of classic Christian writings, volumes of his journal, and a book of home medical remedies. Some people needed food, clothing, and fuel; Wesley, or an assistant, selected two members in each Methodist society to distribute aid.

Polity's forms were important to Wesley, but only if they functioned effectively in meeting human needs and in connecting people to God and each other. Connectors were his polity's fundamental ingredient – group leaders, both women and men, at the local level; itinerant preachers traveling their circuits at the regional level, and these preachers meeting in conference with Wesley, the prime connector, at the national level.

Wesley could not, however, go on being the core connector forever. Therefore, in 1784, he devised ways to provide for a 'living Wesley' in the British Isles and the United States.

DMBI, 13, 18, 68, 69, 70, 75, 77, 92, 95, 110, 179, 195, 197, 200, 240, 243, 276, 279, 283–284, 286, 312, 325, 326, 359; Richard P. Heitzenrater, *Wesley and the People Called Methodists* (1995); WJW(B), vol. 9.
J.M.

Polity (American and British Methodism)

The principle that the connection, not the individual congregation, is the basic body of Methodism stands at the center of Methodist polity. Local Methodist congregations do not select their own preachers and do not make major decisions except at meetings presided over by someone representing the Methodist connection at large. This is true for British and American Methodism alike, yet the connectional polity of each has a distinctive tone that echoes polity decisions made by **John Wesley**.

Wesley ruled his people called Methodists as an absolute monarch: he alone appointed the lay preachers and made the final decisions about all things, temporal and spiritual, in the Methodist connection. Acknowledging that he could not live forever, he provided for a 'living Wesley' – a way to exercise the connectional oversight of Methodism after he died. His power to decide and act in the British Isles was to be carried forward by a Conference of one hundred members; in the United States, superintendents (bishops) and a Conference shared that authority.

In September 1784, Wesley sent a letter to the Methodist preachers in the United States. He acknowledged that the preachers, now ministering in a country that had achieved its independence from British rule, needed to form a church independent of his oversight. So he told them he had appointed **Thomas Coke** and **Francis Asbury** to be their 'joint *Superintendents*.' To deal with their need for an ordained ministry, he announced that he had ordained two elders who, with Coke and Asbury playing the principal role, would ordain additional elders to administer the **sacraments**. Also he sent Articles of Religion and a Sunday Service book that uses the Apostles' Creed as its summary of Christian doctrine.

Wesley did not mention the Conference, knowing it was already in place. Asbury made Conference's role explicit by saying he would accept Wesley's appointment only if elected by his fellow preachers. Meeting at Christmas in 1784, the preachers elected Asbury, and he was promptly ordained deacon, then elder, then superintendent. The new church took the name **Methodist Episcopal Church** in America, suggesting it saw itself as a denomination in which bishops play a key role; by 1787, the title 'superintendent' had become 'bishop.' To these bishops was given monarchical authority to appoint the itinerant preachers. Following the Christmas Conference, the first *Book of Discipline*, the denomination's polity handbook, was published.

By 1808, American Methodism's connectional polity was firmly in place. At the local level, several congregations (each with its own place to meet) were grouped in circuits governed by quarterly conferences. The circuits in a particular area composed a district, for which a presiding elder was responsible. Annual conferences included a number of districts in a geographical region. At the national level, there was a quadrennial general conference, which elected the bishops and made all connectional decisions. The bishops, exercising oversight and serving as the principal connectors of American Methodism, traveled throughout the whole church, presided at annual conference sessions, and appointed the presiding elders and itinerant preachers. The presiding elders (later called district superintendents) traveled around their districts and presided at quarterly conferences. Also in 1808, it was decided that the Articles of Religion and 'the present existing and established standards of doctrine' (usually assumed to mean Wesley's *Sermons* and *Explanatory Notes upon the New Testament*) could not be revoked, altered, or changed. A new *Book of Discipline* was published every four years, following the general conference.

The 'living Wesley' in the United States divides John Wesley's power of appointing preachers and making connectional decisions between bishops and the general conference. In the British Isles, both functions are lodged in the Conference.

In 1784, Wesley executed a Deed of Declaration for British Methodism, which created a hundred-member Conference to carry on his appointive and decision-making authority. Meeting after Wesley's death, the 1791 Conference elected a president and secretary and granted all preachers in full connection the same rights in Conference as the Legal Hundred, to the extent permitted by Wesley's Deed. That Conference grouped the circuits (composed of a number of societies) into districts, each, after 1792, with a chairman who also had pastoral responsibilities. The Conference appointed a Stationing Committee, with a representative from each district, to prepare an annual list of appointments for the Conference to approve.

In 1795, the Conference dealt with administering the **sacraments**. Wesley, trying to avoid an open break with the Church of England, refused to allow lay preachers to administer baptism and the Lord's Supper. But he himself courted such a rupture by ordaining preachers for American Methodism, a few for Scotland and overseas ministries, and one for England. The 1795 Conference adopted a plan that allowed itinerant lay preachers 'authorized by the Conference' to administer the Lord's Supper in Methodism's chapels, if a particular chapel's leaders gave their approval. Gradually, the idea developed that all preachers in full connection with the Conference were 'virtually' or 'in essence' ordained.

Wesley provided **doctrinal standards** for Methodism in his 1763 Model Deed, which declared his *Explanatory Notes upon the New Testament* and his four volumes of *Sermons* (later called his Forty-four Sermons) to be the templates of Methodist doctrine. Classic doctrines, such as the Trinity, the two natures of Christ, and atonement were generally assumed by British Methodism to be doctrinal standards, along with Wesley's own emphases, such as assurance and Christian perfection. But Wesley and his followers resisted calls for short lists of fundamental doctrines.

Wesley began, in 1753, the practice of gathering the Conference's key doctrine and polity decisions in *Large Minutes*. The 1789 edition continued in use in Britain until 1835, when it was replaced by the *Collection of Rules, or Code of Laws*, which had been adopted by the 1797 Conference.

By the mid-1790s, British Methodism had defined its connectional polity. Societies at the local level (usually each had its own chapel) were grouped in circuits governed by quarterly meetings and served by two or more ministers (one of whom was the superintendent) appointed by the Conference. The circuits in each geographical region were gathered into districts, presided over by a chairman. At the national level, the Conference made all decisions pertaining to British Methodism as a connection of societies, circuits, and districts.

The most important nineteenth-century polity development on both sides of the Atlantic was the gradual inclusion of the **laity** in governing conferences beyond the local level, where they shared decision-making responsibilities with the preachers from the earliest days. Laymen gained conference membership sooner than laywomen, but at various points in the twentieth century laypersons, female and male, were granted representation equal to that of the ordained.

DMBI, 68, 75–76, 77, 78, 92, 95, 95–96, 110, 179, 195–196, 197, 202, 243, 273, 279, 286, 312, 334, 342; *The Constitutional Practice and Discipline of the Methodist Church* (various dates); Frank, Thomas Edward, *Polity, Practice, and the Mission of The United Methodist Church* (2006); Waltz, Alan K., *A Dictionary for United Methodists* (1991).
J.M.

Potter, Philip A. (1921–)

Born in Roseau, Dominica, West Indies, Potter left a job as assistant to Dominica's attorney general to become a Methodist lay pastor. Then, in 1944, he began his theological training at Caenwood Theological Seminary in

Jamaica, followed, later, by postgraduate work at London University. After serving as a missionary to poor and mostly illiterate Creole-speaking Haitians, beginning in 1954, Potter worked in Youth Department of the World Council of Churches. In 1960, he was elected president of the World Student Federation, and became a secretary of the British Methodist Missionary Society. Potter directed the World Council's Division of World Mission and Evangelism from 1967 to 1972, when the Council selected him to be its third general secretary, a position he held until 1984. Then he returned to the Caribbean to work with students at the University of the West Indies. One of Potter's successors as general secretary, Samuel Kobia, identified some of Potter's accomplishments at the Council: 'the development of the theological consensus document *Baptism, Eucharist and Ministry*, the continuation of a courageous campaign against apartheid in southern Africa . . ., a vigorous debate on the nature of postcolonial Christian mission, . . .'

Lossky, Nicholas, et al., eds, *Dictionary of the Ecumenical Movement* (1991), 806.
J.M.

Primitive Methodist (Great Britain)

'Primitive' used to designate this Methodist denomination, and similar ones in **Ireland** and the **United States**, implies 'more pure,' as in water from a spring that has not yet been tainted by flowing through towns. Specifically, Primitive Methodism sought to return to the spring-like fervor of **John Wesley's** early Methodism, yet its founding initiative came from American evangelist Lorenzo Dow, who promoted camp meetings during a preaching trip to England. Among his listeners in 1807 were **Hugh Bourne** and **William Clowes**, who soon began to organize similar meetings, with the result that mainstream Methodism expelled them. Each man attracted followers, Bourne's 'Camp-Meeting Methodists' and the 'Clowesites,' that united as Primitive Methodists in 1811–1812. The first Primitive Methodist Conference was held in Hull in 1820. The denomination permitted women to preach, gained legal status in 1829, and authorized missions to the United States and various British colonies. Particularly successful among the rural working classes, Primitive Methodism's heartland was northern England, but it spread to other parts of England and Wales. Some of its preachers and members became leaders in organizing unions for agricultural workers and coal miners. Primitive Methodism published a newspaper, magazines, and books; and founded a theological institute, colleges, and orphanages.

DMBI, 281; Werner, Julia Stewart, *The Primitive Methodist Connexion: Its Background and Early History* (1984); Milburn, Geoffrey, *Primitive Methodism*, 2002.
J.M.

Primitive Methodist (USA)

Two Methodist groups in the United States chose the adjective 'primitive' to highlight their desire to revert to the early, more pure days of Wesleyan Methodism. The first, short-lived, was organized in 1792 by William Hammett in Charleston, South Carolina, as the outcome of his protest against Bishop **Francis Asbury** and his authoritarian leadership of the **Methodist Episcopal Church**. The second emerged from the transatlantic travels of Connecticut-born evangelist Lorenzo Dow. His camp-meeting mission to England in the first decade of the nineteenth century led, in 1811–1812, to the formation of the **Primitive Methodist** movement there. That new denomination sent four missionaries to the United States in 1829: William Summersides, Thomas Morris, Ruth Watkins, and Thomas Knowles. They evangelized in Connecticut, New York, New Jersey, and Pennsylvania; agreed to focus on the coalfields of western Pennsylvania, and, in 1840, decided to separate from British Primitive Methodism. In 1842, the American Primitive Methodist Church took form at Galena, Illinois. Several conferences were organized and a general conference was established in 1889. In 2009, this doctrinally fundamentalist denomination had 3,635 members in the United States, with overseas conferences in, among other countries, Guatemala, the Dominican Republic, and Columbia.

EWM, 1952–1953; *HDM*, 249.
J.M.

Primitive Wesleyan Methodists (Ireland)

John Wesley's insistence that his Methodist followers maintain their relationship with the **Anglicanism** through receiving the **sacraments** from priests of the Church of England was honored in Ireland longer than in England. It was not until 1816 that the Irish Conference authorized its ministers to administer Baptism and the Lord's Supper. Almost immediately, opponents of that action convened a conference and stationed nineteen itinerant lay preachers. A constitution was adopted in 1818, creating the Primitive Wesleyan Methodist Society, whose members continued to receive the sacraments in the Church of Ireland (Anglican). Beginning in the 1850s, the Primitive Wesleyans experienced declining membership, with the outcome that they and the Wesleyan Methodists united in 1878 as the Methodist Church in Ireland.

Cooney, Dudley Levistone, *The Methodists in Ireland: A Short History* (2001), 64–67, 75–76, 138–139; *DMBI*, 282.
J.M.

Publishing

No Protestant leaders in the eighteenth century made better use of the printed page than **John and Charles Wesley**. Between them the brothers published approximately five hundred titles, though most were from John's pen. Their published works included sermons, tracts, books, hymnals, biblical commentaries, prayer collections, and journals as well as other items. Among his most ambitious projects John published a fifty-volume *Christian Library* (1749–1755) containing selections of what he considered the best Christian literature from the early church to his own time. From the Wesleys' day to the present, Methodist denominations have engaged in publishing books, periodicals, Sunday school literature, and other printed pieces to inform and inspire their constituents. The larger churches established publishing houses. While print publications are a mainstay of most denominations, they have increasingly given attention to radio, television, and the internet as means of broadcasting their message and informing those interested in their ministries.

Cumbers, Frank H., *The Book Room: The Story of the Methodist Publishing House and Epworth Press* (1956); Ness, John H., *One Hundred Fifty Years: A History of Publishing in the Evangelical United Brethren Church* (1966); Pilkington, James P., *The Methodist Publishing House: A History*, vol. 1 (1968); Vernon, Walter N., *The History of the United Methodist Publishing House*, vol. 2 (1988).

C.Y.

Puritanism

Among the important movements influential in the life and the ministry of **John and Charles Wesley** was Puritanism. Their parents, Samuel and Susanna, while firmly committed to the Church of England, came from Puritan lineage. Evidence of the Puritan heritage is apparent in the family life of the Epworth parsonage, especially under the direction of Susanna. Her father, Samuel Annesley (1620–1696), an important Puritan divine in London, instilled in her the Puritan virtues of prayer, Bible reading, instruction in the Christian faith and life, and journaling. She emphasized these in the rearing of her children and they left their impression on the lives of sons John and Charles. Further proof of John's admiration of Puritanism is his generous inclusion of their writings in his *Christian Library*, his use of Richard Baxter's *Reformed Pastor* as a practical manual for his preachers, and his implementation of the Covenant Service derived from the Puritans Joseph and Richard Alleine. In some of his hymns Charles Wesley depended on the biblical exposition of Puritan biblical expositor Matthew Henry. He also highly respected the theological views of Richard Baxter on antinomianism.

EWM, II: 1966–1967; Monk, Robert C., *John Wesley: His Puritan Heritage*, 2nd ed. (1999); Newton, John A., *Methodism and the Puritans* (1964); Newton, John A., *Susanna Wesley and the Puritan Tradition in Methodism*, 2nd ed. (2002).
C.Y.

Quakerism

John Wesley was ambivalent regarding Quakerism. On the one hand, he was very critical of their approach to Christian faith. In his *Letter to a Person Lately Joined with the People Called Quakers* (1748), he argued that Quakers were wrong in their understanding of the nature and authority of scripture, soteriology, silent worship, and dispensing with the **sacraments** of baptism and the Lord's Supper. He closed the document with the following exhortation, 'Friend, you have an honest heart, but a weak head; you have a zeal, but not according to knowledge. . . . Come back, come back, to the weightier matters of the law, to spiritual, rational, scriptural religion.' On the other hand, Wesley found that many Quakers were both kind and generous. He expressed gratitude for a Quaker's liberal contribution to his Newcastle Orphan House and to Quakers who occasionally offered hospitality to Methodists for meetings. The first Methodist quarterly meeting was held in a Quaker home near Todmorden. Furthermore, his *Thoughts upon Slavery* (1774) was largely drawn from the Quaker Anthony Benezet's *Some Historical Account of Guinea with an Inquiry into the Rise and Progress of the Slave-Trade, Its Nature and Lamentable Effects* (1771). Methodist–Quaker relations today are mostly on a local community basis.

Baker, Frank, *The Relations between the Society of Friends and Early Methodism* (1949); *DMBI*, 285–286; *EWM*, II: 1969.
C.Y.

Reason

The relationship between reason and faith has been debated throughout the history of Christianity. **John Wesley** found himself caught between the extremes of those who argued that human reason was the enemy of genuine religion and, therefore, a threat to faith, and those influenced by the eighteenth-century Enlightenment who claimed that orthodox religious faith and reason are largely incompatible. The Oxford graduate and teacher sought a middle way in which reason is valued as a gift of God to be gratefully received and cultivated, but which has recognizable limits. By itself reason cannot produce faith, hope, and love, and, therefore, according to Wesley is helpless to give happiness. Much of his attention to the issue faith and reason is laid out in his, *An Earnest Appeal to Men of Reason and Religion* (1743), and *A Farther Appeal to Men of Reason and Religion* (1745). Reason, of course, occupies an important place in the so-called Wesleyan quadrilateral. Evidences of the importance of reason to Methodists are their schools, colleges, universities, and theological seminaries founded in various parts of the world.

Runyon, Theodore, *The New Creation: John Wesley's Theology Today* (1998).
C.Y.

Roberts, Benjamin Titus (1823–1893)

Founder and first general superintendent of the **Free Methodist Church**, Roberts graduated from Wesleyan University, Middletown, New York in 1848 with both bachelor's and master's degrees. Four years earlier he had a deep religious experience and decided for the **ministry**. Roberts affiliated with the Genesee annual conference of the **Methodist Episcopal Church** and served several congregations in upstate New York between 1848 and 1858. He became increasingly disturbed by the positions of the denomination on such issues as pew rent, secret society membership, and the church's worldliness. Those who sympathized with him were mockingly called Nazarites, beardless and ignorant followers. The Genesee conference expelled him in 1858 for unchristian conduct, though many laymen denounced his dismissal. The 1860 general conference upheld his expulsion, after which Roberts and a number of his supporters organized the Free Methodist Church in Pekin, New York. As general superintendent of the new church, Roberts carried on a tireless schedule of travel, preaching, editing, and writing. Some of his constituency accused him of an autocratic leadership style. At the time of his death Free Methodism had approximately 22,000 members and 1,000 preachers.

ANB, 18:594–595; Roberts, Benjamin Titus, *Why Another Sect* (1879); Roberts, Benjamin Titus, *Ordaining Women* (1891); Snyder, Howard A., *Populist Saints: B. T. and Ellen Roberts and the First Free Methodists* (2006).
C.Y.

Roman Catholicism

Although **John Wesley** at times demonstrated a very negative assessment of Roman Catholicism, in some of his writings at other times he also displayed a remarkably **ecumenical** spirit toward it. In his *Popery Calmly Considered* (1779) he complained about the theology and practices of the Roman church and in his earlier, *The Advantage of the Members of the Church of England over Those of the Church of Rome* (1756), he grumbled about its doctrine not being founded in scripture. Of the twenty-four Articles of Religion sent to the American Methodists, seven attacked Roman Catholicism. Yet, Wesley admired the holiness emphasis present in Catholic writers such as Gregory Lopez and Marquis de Renty. Furthermore, his irenic, *Letter to a Roman Catholic* (1749), pleaded, '... if we cannot as yet think alike in all things, at least we can love alike.' Relations between Methodists and Roman Catholics were generally strained, if not openly antagonistic, until post-World War II and the Second Vatical Council (1962–1965). Since 1967 dialogues between the **World Methodist Council** and the Roman Catholic Church have shown promise and have developed a more amicable relationship between the two traditions.

DMBI, 300; Butler, David, *Methodists and Papists* (1995); Wainwright, Geoffrey, *Methodists in Dialog* (1995).
C.Y.

Sacraments

Methodists follow **John Wesley** in recognizing Baptism and the Lord's Supper as their two sacraments, the means of grace through which God works invisibly, not only to quicken faith, but also to strengthen and confirm it. They do not, however, always adhere to Wesley's sacramental theology and practice.

Wesley attuned Methodism to the sacramental understanding of the early Christians, who, building theologically upon Jesus' metaphors, 'This is my body,' 'This is my blood,' believed in the real presence of Christ in the eucharist. Both John and **Charles Wesley** stressed the mystery of that presence: 'Who shall say how Bread and Wine / GOD into Man conveys?' Christ's presence is real; how it is realized is unknown. In the early church, the Lord's Supper climaxed every-Sunday worship; Wesley strove to restore that practice in Methodism.

Wesley, in harmony with the first Christians, understood the sacrament of baptism as a 'washing of the Holy Ghost.' Clement of Alexandria called it the sacrament 'by which we are cleansed from the filth of our sins.' Wesley never doubted that God washes us in baptism, but he emphasized that because we sin away that washing, we need to be regenerated.

Methodists after Wesley weakened his sacramental theology and frequently ignored his instructions concerning practice. British and American Methodists alike continued to baptize infants as well as adults, but theological erosion carried away major portions of the belief that God works in the sacrament to quicken, strengthen, or confirm faith. Often all that remained was the idea that baptism is a ceremony for naming children and dedicating them to God.

Methodists on both sides of the Atlantic never followed Wesley's injunction to celebrate the Lord's Supper every Sunday; quarterly or monthly communion was the norm. And the belief that the bread and wine mysteriously convey God into humans yielded to the view that the Lord's Supper is a time of remembering Jesus' last meal and death.

An ecumenical renaissance of liturgical studies, which began in the 1930s, focused, as Wesley did, on the sacramental theology and practice of the early Christians. Methodists rediscovered the pattern for Sunday worship that combines Word (Scripture readings, sermon) and Table (Lord's Supper). New books of worship of the British Methodists (1975, 1999) and the United Methodist Church in the United States (1989, 1992) feature a service of Word and Table as their basic worship plan. But most congregations do not celebrate the Lord's Supper every week at their principal Sunday services. Likewise, new rituals that present baptism as an act of God through the church do not seem to have significantly influenced most Methodists.

DMBI, 18–19, 211–212, 235, 305; *HDM*, 40–42, 108–109, 267; Felton, Gayle Carlton, *This Gift of Water: The Theology and Practice of Baptism Among Methodists in America* (1992); Stevick, Daniel B., *The Altar's Fire: Charles Wesley's Hymns on the Lord's Supper, 1745 – Introduction and Comment* (2004).
J.M.

Salvation, Wesleyan Way of

John Wesley, not a systematic theologian in the classical sense, described the pathway of Christian discipleship in his sermons and other writings. It consisted of at least six main themes, all centered around the God's grace, God's unmerited, undeserved, unearned love for all people.

(1) Original sin. While human beings, created in God's image, are made to enjoy life with God and each other, there is a great chasm between what God intends them to be and what they really are. They yield to idolatry, loving things more than the Creator and preferring to do what they please rather than doing the will of the One who made them. Furthermore, they exploit, neglect, are uncharitable, or in other ways unjustly offend their neighbors. Humans fail to love God and their neighbors as Jesus taught. The universal problem is sin which Wesley described as a 'fatal leprosy' which consumes human life. Who can cure them of this disease and renew God's image in them? See John Wesley's sermon, 'Original Sin' (1759).

(2) Preventing grace. The term literally means 'the grace that comes before,' and is usually today termed 'prevenient grace.' John Wesley spoke of it as

God's grace, 'free in all, and free for all.' It is present not only in the life of Christians, but in those of other faiths, even in the life of the atheist and agnostic. Preventing grace not only awakens humans to the gravity of sin and points them in the direction of new life, but most importantly, it frees them to accept God's offer of forgiveness and reconciliation, healing the disease of sin in each and all. Preventing grace moves people to repentant change. It was their commitment to the biblical notion of God's preventing grace, and the freedom it conveys, which led John and **Charles Wesley** to reject **Calvinistic** predestination which denied human free will. The writings and hymn-poems of the Wesley brothers rejected the teachings of the Calvinists and affirmed the reality of God's preventing grace available to all. See John Wesley's sermon, 'The Scripture Way of Salvation' (1765).

(3) Justification by faith. Setting their faith solidly in the message of scripture and the insights of the Protestant Reformation, the Wesleys declared that salvation from sin is a gift of God which is appropriated by faith. God's preventing grace prepares people for a new relationship with God. God's justifying grace accepts and sets them free from sin and its consequences. Justification is especially related to the life and ministry of Jesus, although salvation, just as creation, was understood by the Wesleys to be the work of all Three Persons of the trinitarian God. As the Second Person of the Trinity, Jesus occupied a special place in God's plan of salvation. John and Charles Wesley understood Jesus as Prophet, Priest, and King. As priest, Jesus offered his life as a sacrifice for sin and makes possible forgiveness, redemption, and justification. See John Wesley's sermon, 'Justification by Faith' (1746).

(4) New birth. There is an experiential dimension to salvation. Justification by faith is what God does for us. The new birth, which accompanies justification, is what God does in us. It is an inward, entire change which transforms the sinner from the image of Satan to the image of God. See John Wesley's sermon, 'The New Birth' (1760).

(5) Assurance. To those who are justified, the Spirit of God bears witness that they are God's children. This is apparently what John Wesley himself experienced on 24 May 1738 when he wrote that 'an assurance' had been given to him that Christ removed his sins and that he was indeed a child of God. See his sermon, 'Witness of the Spirit I' (1746).

(6) Holiness of heart and life, or sanctification. God intends all of his faithful people to live a life of holy thinking, speaking, and acting. Such holy living fulfills Jesus' summary of the commandments that we should love God with all we are and have, and love our neighbors (everyone else) as we love ourselves. This is the genuine substance of Christianity. Furthermore, John Wesley believed that it is God's intention that, by grace, we attain Christian perfection where love for God and neighbor becomes the controlling affection of one's life and we live as Jesus lived. John Wesley believed that by God's

grace the attainment of Christian perfection was possible in this life. His brother Charles disagreed, holding that it is only realized as believers pass from this life to the next. See John Wesley's sermon, 'Christian Perfection' (1741). Holiness of heart and life leading to Christian perfection is not achieved without the use of gifts, 'means of grace,' which God gives to nurture holy living. These include reading and studying scripture, prayer, fasting, Christian fellowship, and the Lord's Supper. Wesley referred to the use of such gifts as 'works of **piety**.' Authentic holy living is displayed in acts of love and justice, what Wesley called, 'works of mercy,' such as feeding the hungry, clothing the naked, caring for the sick, and resisting evil forces in the world. Important summaries of Wesley's views are found in his sermons, especially, 'The Scripture Way of Salvation' (1765), 'The Means of Grace' (1746), and 'Upon our Lord's Sermon on the Mount, VI' (1748).

Collins, Kenneth J., *The Theology of John Wesley: Holy Love and the Shape of Grace* (2007); Klaiber, Walter and Manfred Marquardt, *Living Grace: An Outline of United Methodist Theology* (2001); Maddox, Randy L., *Responsible Grace: John Wesley's Practical Theology* (1994).
C.Y.

Salvation Army

Originally known as the Christian Mission, the Salvation Army was founded in London's east end by British **Methodist New Connexion** clergyman **William Booth** and his wife **Catherine**. Its present name was adopted in 1878. By that time it had been organized along military lines with a general at its head and a requirement that its members render unquestioning obedience to its directives. Booth's son, William Bramwell Booth, assumed the generalship of the Army upon his father's death, but beginning in 1931 the High Council of the Army, which includes its commanders and leading officers, has chosen its leader. The Army's basic theology has traditionally been evangelical. It rejects both **sacraments** and emphasizes Christian morality. Although the Army operates headquarters and centers in a multitude of places, it has historically employed open-air meetings with its celebrated brass bands and banners. At its urban centers it oversees programs for the poor and homeless, alcoholics, hospitals, day care, and schools. While its ministry operates in more than a hundred nations, it is especially active in the United States.

Green, Roger J., *The Life and Ministry of William Booth, Founder of the Salvation Army* (2005); Sandall, Robert, Arch R. Wiggins, Frederick Coutts, *The History of the Salvation Army*, 7 vols. (1947–1986).
C.Y.

Schäfer, Franz Werner (1921–)

United Methodist bishop, Schäfer was born in Birsfelden, Basel, Switzerland. His early education was in local schools near his home. He received his basic theological education at the Theological Seminary of the Basel **Mission**. Admitted on trial by the Switzerland annual conference, Schäfer held conference positions in scouting work and men's ministries, was a board member of Methodism's Frankfurt seminary, and served as a superintendent of the West District of Switzerland from 1958 to 1966. He was elected to the episcopacy in 1966 at a special session of United Methodism's Central and Southern **Europe** central conference where he served until his retirement in 1989. In a time of political difficulty in Europe, Schäfer managed to maintain and strengthen the central conference over which he presided.

EWM, II: 2104; Streiff, Patrick Ph., *Methodism in Europe: 19th and 20th century* (2003), 254, 269.
C.Y.

Science

As one might expect, **John Wesley** was interested in science, primarily for its relationship to religion. His major work on the subject is, *A Survey of the Wisdom of God in the Creation* (1763). In another work, *Address to the Clergy* (1756), he argued that clerics should have some knowledge of science in order to understand the natural world and God's working in it. Perhaps his most famous foray into the practicality of science were his experiments with electricity, especially for its healing qualities. Wesley's interest in electricity was fanned by the studies and experiments of the American, Benjamin Franklin. Methodist scientists in Great Britain (e.g., Charles A. Coulson and W. Russell Hindmarsh), the United States, and other nations have made important contributions to various scientific disciplines and some have actively participated in the debate between science and religion from the nineteenth century to the present including the creationism controversy. Methodist scholar Herbert Butterfield, has provided historical perspective on the development of science in his, *Origins of Modern Science, 1300–1800* (1949).

DMBI, 309.
C.Y.

Selina, Countess of Huntingdon (1707–1791)

One of the most important figures in the origin and development of **Calvinistic** Methodism, Selina Hastings was born Lady Selina Shirley. In 1728 she married the ninth Earl of Huntingdon, hence her title. Using her wealth, rank, charisma, charm, and deep devotion to the Christian faith, she was a dominant force in the eighteenth-century British evangelical movement. She experienced conversion in 1739 and three years later became acquainted with **George Whitefield** and the Wesleys. She gradually rejected the Wesleyan brand of Methodism in favor of the Calvinistic variety which was represented in the preaching and ministry of George Whitefield and Howell Harris (1714–1773). In 1761 she built the first of many chapels which came to be associated with the Countess of Huntingdon Connexion which, though small, exists to this day. When a shortage of evangelical preachers threatened the future of her enterprise, she opened a theological college at Trevecca in Wales in 1768, the supervision of which she put in the hands of **John William Fletcher**. In 1905 the college was moved to Cambridge where it joined Westminster College. As the Countess was increasingly attracted to extreme Calvinism, she withdrew her friendship from the Wesleys, causing Fletcher to resign his Trevecca position. Unlike **John Wesley**, she published nothing, although her letters, a major source of knowledge about her views and accomplishments, have been published. She died within a few months of John Wesley, her evangelical rival. Her legacy to the revival was significant, but for several reasons not as sizable as Wesley's.

BDE, 318–321; DMBI, 171–172; Schlenther, Boyd S., *Queen of the Methodists: the Countess of Huntingdon and the Eighteenth-Century Crisis of Faith and Society* (1997); Tyson, John R. and Boyd S. Schlenther, *In the Midst of Early Methodism: Lady Huntingdon and Her Correspondence* (2006).
C.Y.

Shaw, William (1798–1872)

The father of South African Methodism, Shaw was born in Glasgow, Scotland. In 1819, he was appointed chaplain to British settlers in the Cape Colony and accepted as a missionary by the Wesleyan Methodist Missionary Society. Arriving in South Africa in 1820, he began immediately to establish Methodist societies and Sunday schools, recruit local preachers, and care for members of all denominations. In 1824, he started opening missions among the Xhosas, developing relationships, as he did so, with the tribal chiefs; there were six missions by 1830. Shaw visited England between 1833 and 1837, then went back to South East Africa as the general superintendent of Wesleyan Missions. He extended the chain of missions to Natal, with the result that Methodism had more black members than any other major denomination in the country. In 1855, with Shaw's encouragement, the colonial government opened four industrial schools on Methodist mission stations. Exhausted by his travels and responsibilities, Shaw returned to England in 1856, drafted a proposal for a South African Conference (which was not realized for twenty years), wrote *The Story of My Mission* (1860), and was president of the Wesleyan Conference in 1865.

Davies, Horton, *Great South African Christians* (1951), 30–39; *DMBI*, 315; Sadler, C., ed., *Never a Young Man* (1967).
J.M.

Shinn, Asa (1781–1853)

Clergyman, theologian, editor, author, and a principal figure in the founding of the **Methodist Protestant Church**, Shinn was born in New Jersey of Quaker parents. He was religiously awakened in 1798 by the ministry of a **Methodist Episcopal** circuit preacher and in 1800 became an itinerant Methodist preacher. The following year Shinn was admitted to the Baltimore annual conference and began several years of ministerial service in Pennsylvania, West Virginia, Ohio, Kentucky, and Maryland. He was an effective preacher and organizer whose talents led to his appointment to superintend two districts in western Pennsylvania. By 1824, Shinn began to support efforts to reform his denomination. He was especially troubled by the hierarchical nature of the church and its authoritarian leadership. The church, he held, must also be more open to a more active role of the laity. When the Methodist Episcopal 1828 general conference refused to adopt legislation proposed by the reform party, the reformers led by Shinn, Nicholas Snethen, and Alexander McCaine (1768–1856) in 1830 formed a new denomination, the Methodist Protestant Church, theologically Methodist, but without episcopal government. Shinn was an influential leader in the new church until mental illness forced his retirement from the **ministry**.

ANB, 19:846–847; Shinn, Asa, *An Essay on the Plan of Salvation* (1812); Shinn, Asa, *On the Benevolence and Rectitude of the Supreme Being* (1840).
C.Y.

Sigg, Ferdinand (1902–1965)

Methodist publisher, **ecumenical** leader, and bishop, Sigg was born in Thalwil, near Zurich, Switzerland. Initially prepared for a business career, he was called to ministry and trained at the Methodist seminary in Frankfurt, Germany from which he graduated in 1927. After a very brief period as a pastor, Sigg became secretary to Bishop **John L. Nuelson** and from 1936 to 1955 was general manager of the Methodist Publishing House in Zurich. As the church's publisher, he brought new life and sound business practices to his work. In October 1955, Sigg was elected and consecrated as the first bishop of the Central and Southern **Europe** central conference which he served until his untimely death. A dedicated ecumenist, his episcopal area included work with a diverse Protestant community, **Roman Catholics**, Muslims in North **Africa**, and eastern European Marxists. In this context Sigg learned the importance and skill of relating to people of other faiths. He was one of the founders of the European Council of Churches and served a term as its president.

EWM: II: 2154; *In Memoriam: Bischof Dr. Ferdinand Sigg* (1965?); Sigg, Ferdinand, *Das Versetzungssystem im Methodismus* (1959); Streiff, Patrick Ph., *Methodism in Europe: 19th and 20th Century* (2003).
C.Y.

Simons, George Albert (1874–1952)

American **Methodist Episcopal** clergyman and superintendent, Simons was born in Laporte, Indiana. He received degrees from Baldwin Wallace College, Berea, Ohio; New York University; and Drew Theological School, Madison, New Jersey. Entering **ministry** in 1899, Simons served several churches in the United States before appointment as superintendent of the Finland and St. Petersburg (Russia) Mission Conference from 1907 to 1911. From 1911 to 1921 he was superintendent of the Russia Mission, from 1921 to 1924 of the Russia Conference and Baltic Mission, and from 1924 to 1928 the Baltic and Slavic Mission Conference. While serving his last two superintendent appointments he was also the director of a Ministers' Training Institute in Riga, Latvia. Among other duties he served as editor and publisher of *Christiansky Pobornik* (Russian *Christian Advocate*) and the Baltic and Slavic *Bulletin*. He published many Methodist books and pamphlets in Russian. During the final years of his life, Simons returned to the United States where he died.

EWM, II: 2157–2158; Marshall, Leslie A., *Romance of a Tract and its Sequel: The Story of an American Pioneer in Russia and the Baltic States* (1928); Streiff, Patrick Ph., *Methodism in Europe: 19th and 20th Century* (2003), 142–145.
C.Y.

Snethen, Nicholas (1769–1845)

Clergyman and a founder of the **Methodist Protestant Church**, Snethen was born in Glen Cove, New York. In 1791 his family moved to Belleville, New Jersey where he affiliated with a **Methodist Episcopal** congregation. Convinced that he was called to preach, Snethen entered the denomination's itinerant **ministry**. He served circuits in Connecticut, Vermont, and Maine before appointment to Charleston, South Carolina. Ordained elder in 1800, he moved to Baltimore, then to New York City. Snethen left the itinerant ministry from 1806 to 1809 to take up farming, although he engaged in occasional preaching in the area. Reentering the itinerancy in 1809 he was appointed to churches in Baltimore and Fells Point, Maryland; Georgetown, District of Columbia; Alexandria, Virginia; and Frederick, Maryland. During his tenure in Georgetown he was chaplain of the United States House of Representatives. Leaving the intinerancy again in 1814 to return to farming, Snethen became increasingly interested and active in politics. He was convinced that lay people should have an official voice in the life of the denomination and that the power of the episcopacy should be limited. Snethen designed the reformers' petition which called for change at the 1828 general conference. When the petition was defeated, he joined those who founded the Methodist Protestant Church in 1830. He served churches in the new denomination, was elected president of its general conference in 1834, and was co-editor of the denominational periodical, *Mutual Rights and Methodist Protestant*.

ANB, 20:337–338; Freeman, Harlan L., *Francis Asbury's Silver Trumpet: Nicholas Snethen, Non-Partisan Church Statesman and Preacher of the Gospel, 1769–1845* (1950).
C.Y.

Social Thought and Action

From the beginning, Methodists have taken different sides on social issues. Concerning slavery, **John Wesley**, in 1774, declared: 'Liberty is the right of every human creature, as soon as he breathes the vital air; and no human law can deprive him of that right which he derives from the law of nature.' In 1784, American Methodists pronounced slavery 'contrary to the golden law of God' and 'the unalienable rights of mankind,' and ordered Methodists to free their slaves; six months later, they suspended the order, fearing it would hinder church growth. Methodist Abolitionists in New England insisted, in 1834, 'that no man has, or can have, a right to hold a fellow man for one moment in bondage as a piece of merchantable property.' Two years later, William Capers, reporting for the South Carolina Conference Missionary Society, wrote: 'We denounce the principles and opinions of the abolitionists *in toto*, . . . We believe that the Holy Scriptures . . . unequivocally authorize the relation of master and slave.'

From the first days of his ministry, Wesley recognized and responded to the desperation of the poor. On one occasion, he saw a woman 'gathering the bones which the dogs had left in the streets, and making broth of them, to prolong a wretched life!' To alleviate such misery, he raised money to provide food, clothing, and shelter. He established medical clinics, organized employment assistance, set up home workshops, and formed credit unions. He did not, however, limit his activities to ameliorating the plight of the poor. He analyzed the causes of poverty, maintained that the poor are not to blame for their plight, and criticized the rich for managing the economy to benefit themselves.

Since Wesley's day, Methodists have prescribed different remedies for poverty. Some favor untrammeled capitalism, insisting that the poor will benefit as money trickles down to them from a full-throttle pursuit of wealth by those at the top. Others promote socialism, believing that public control of the means of production is the best way to lift up the poor. Still others recognize the accomplishments of capitalism, the sinful greed of its managers, and the inability of private charity to meet all the needs of the poor; therefore they support a regulated capitalism, in which greed is restrained by law and the poor are protected by safety nets such as health, disability, and retirement insurance.

Methodist congregations, and regional, national, and world conferences deal in different ways with social questions. Some restrict their responses to private-sector activities, such as food kitchens, clothing cupboards, and shelters for the homeless. Others lobby governmental bodies to ban such things as slavery, alcoholic beverages, sweatshops, and child labor. Still others press their governments to support such things as labor unions, universal health care, and green energy.

Across the history of Methodism, agencies established by Methodist conferences have dealt with a broad spectrum of social concerns. British Methodism's Division of Social Responsibility has produced definitive statements on divorce, peace and war, industry, the treatment of animals, and race. The General Board of Church and Society of United Methodism in the United States is an advocacy agency for the denomination's Social Principles, among which are statements on 'the safe processing and disposal of toxic and nuclear waste,' 'the restriction of smoking in public areas and workplaces,' and abolishing the death penalty.

Methodists have been in the vanguard on a number of social issues, yet their overall record is mixed, occasionally reprehensible. Some American Methodists cited the Bible to fortify their antislavery stance during the first half of the nineteenth century; others quoted the Bible to justify their proslavery stand. It took the force of arms, however, not the Holy Scriptures, to settle the question.

Many pioneers of trade unionism in England were Methodists. Five of the six 'Tolpuddle Martyrs' – Dorset laborers who tried to form a union – were Wesleyan Methodists; convicted in 1834 and deported to Australia, they were pardoned after two years and brought home. Joseph Arch, a Primitive Methodist local preacher, founded the Agricultural Laborers' Union in 1837. A Wesleyan Methodist organized the Stonemasons' Union. Thomas Hepburn, a Primitive Methodist local preacher, in 1832 initiated the first Northumberland and Durham Miners' Union. In politics, some English Methodist labor leaders were Liberals; others became members of the Labour Party after it was organized in 1906. Seven years earlier, the president of the Wesleyan Methodist Conference, told its members: 'I believe that concerted action in the political sphere is about the last use we should make of our influence as a church.'

Homosexuality is Methodism's most contentious social question in the twentieth century, and it seems likely that it will not be answered by quoting the Bible; rather, the answer will track societal/cultural forces. In Europe, those forces are creating a climate of full acceptance for homosexual persons. Following that lead, the British Methodist Church 'reaffirms the traditional teaching of the Church on human sexuality; namely chastity for all outside marriage and fidelity within;' and it 'recognizes, affirms, and celebrates the participation and ministry of lesbians and gay men in the church.' There is, however, no authoritative interpretation of the interactions of those statements, and no procedures for questioning individuals about their adherence to them. In the United States, on the other hand, where society was largely antigay during the 1970s and 1980s, United Methodism formulated its position that the practice of homosexuality is 'incompatible with Christian teaching,' and banned 'self-avowed practicing homosexuals' from its ordained ministry. Then, when polls began showing a growing cultural acceptance of openly gay men and lesbians, the church started to surround its 'incompatible' position with softeners. In Africa, however, where the culture is generally adverse to homosexuality, United Methodists insist that their church must not deviate from a rigid antigay stance.

Taking its cue from John Wesley's mission statement, Methodism has always given reform a key place on its agenda. Wesley said the mission of Methodism was 'to reform the nation, particularly the Church; and to spread scriptural holiness over the land.' But there has never been a consensus about what is to be reformed and how this reform is to be accomplished.

The Book of Resolutions of The United Methodist Church (a new edition every four years); *Statements on Social Responsibility* [of the Methodist Church, Great Britain], *1946–1996* (1996); Hynson, Leon O., *To Reform the Nation: Theological Foundations of Wesley's Ethics* (1984); Jennings, Theodore W., *Good News to the Poor: John Wesley's Evangelical Economics* (1990); Marquardt, Manfred, *John Wesley's Social Ethics: Praxis and Principles* (1992).

J.M.

Sommer, Johann Wilhelm Ernst (1881–1952)

German Methodist clergyman, scholar, and bishop, Sommer was born in Stuttgart, Germany, the son of a British Methodist German pastor. He was educated at Kingswood School, Bristol, England; Cambridge University; and Lausanne, Switzerland. Sommer taught in London, served as dean at two schools – a teacher training college in Turkey (1906–1912) and a missionary training school near Berlin (1913–1920) – before becoming professor of Old Testament and ethics at the Methodist theological seminary in Frankfurt (1920–1946) where he also served as president for a decade beginning in 1936. In addition to being an outstanding academician, Sommer was an excellent church leader and administrator. These talents led to his election to the episcopacy in 1946. He founded Methodist relief work in Germany after World War II and was instrumental in Methodists joining other Protestant denominations in the relief efforts.

EWM, II: 2196–2197; Sommer, C. Ernst, *Bischof Dr. J. W. E. Sommer in Memoriam* (1952); Sommer, J. W. E., *John Wesley und die soziale Frage* (1930?).
C.Y.

Springer, John M. (1873–1963)

Pioneer, along with his wife, Helen, of Methodism in the Congo, Springer was born in Cataract, Wisconsin, educated at Northwestern University and Garrett Biblical Seminary, and appointed to **Methodist Episcopal** missionary service in Africa in 1901. Helen (1868–1949), who was born in New Sharon, Maine, graduated from Woman's Medical College in Philadelphia, went to Angola in 1891 as one of **William Taylor's** self-supporting missionaries, and married fellow missionary William Rasmussen, who died in 1895. In 1901, she went to Southern Rhodesia as the first missionary there of the Woman's Foreign Missionary Society of the Methodist Episcopal Church. She lived in Shona villages, translated hymns and several books of the Bible, and established girls' education. After she and Springer married in 1905 they traveled from northern Rhodesia to the Congo, from the Indian Ocean to the Atlantic, preparing themselves to speak effectively to Americans about Africa and the needs of its people. The Springers returned to the United States, dramatized the need for a Congo mission, and, receiving authorization, opened one in 1911. In 1936, Springer was elected missionary bishop for Africa. After he retired in 1944, he and Helen continued to live in the Congo, where she died.

HDM, 286; Springer, Helen, *Camp Fires in the Congo* (1936); Springer, John, *Pioneering in the Congo* (1916?)
J.M.

Stillness

A controversy erupted at the Fetter Lane Society in London in 1739–1740 over the matter of stillness. Philip Henry Molther, a **Moravian**, who visited the society was disturbed by the disorder and immoderate behavior (e.g., 'sighing and groaning') which he found there. He advised society members to be 'still' and to abstain from the Lord's Supper and other means of grace until God granted them the gift of faith. Associated with the society at the time, **John Wesley** renounced Molther's advice and separated from the Fetter Lane group. Wesley's position was that there are degrees of faith and that the means of grace including the Lord's Supper are provisions of God to nurture and strengthen faith at whatever stage it is. When Wesley withdrew from Fetter Lane, he and those who agreed with him moved to the Foundery which for several years became the center for his **ministry** in London. Passages in Wesley's journal provide further details about the stillness controversy.

DMBI, 337; Podmore, Colin, ed., *The Fetter Lane Moravian Congregation, London, 1742–1992* (1992); Rack, Henry, *Reasonable Enthusiast: John Wesley and the Rise of Methodism* (1989), 202–205.
C.Y.

Sunday School

Today, 'Sunday' signals a school offering religious education; originally, 'school' signaled a place where reading and writing were taught on Sundays. Hannah Ball is credited with opening the first Methodist Sunday school in England in 1769; **Francis Asbury** with starting one in the United States about 1786. On both sides of the Atlantic, the schools' initial goal was to provide rudimentary education, often using the Bible as the main resource, for children who worked the other six days. The **Methodist Episcopal Church** made the Sunday school an official part of the church in 1790, encouraging preachers to organize one wherever worship services were held. Wesleyan Methodism in Britain adopted rules for the schools in 1827. As the public-school movement grew, Sunday schools switched to providing Christian education for children, youth, and adults. Standardized curricula were developed, teacher training institutes organized, and conventions, often interdenominational, held at various levels. During the second half of the nineteenth century, Sunday schools replaced evangelistic campaigns as the principal source of new members for American Methodism. The twentieth century witnessed the schools' decline: their membership dropped by half in British Methodism between 1900 and 1932;

membership grew or held steady in American Methodism until 1960, then plunged.

DMBI, 340–341; *EWM*, II: 2276–2278; *HDM*, 288–290; *ODCC*, 1559.
J.M.

Sung, John (1901–1944)

An impassioned evangelist who influenced all the churches of eastern Asia, Sung was born in a Methodist parsonage in China, educated at Ohio Wesleyan University, began PhD work at Ohio State, and was attending Union Theological Seminary in New York City, when a religious experience so shattered his nerves that he was forced to spend six months in a mental hospital. Returning to China in 1927, he joined the Hinghwa Methodist Annual Conference, asked to be appointed as an evangelist-at-large, and began systematic campaigns, often stressing faith healing, in other regions of China. By the end of his career, he had visited nearly every province of that country, always leaving behind revitalized churches and individuals eager to buy Bibles. Sung made at least six visits to Singapore and Malaysia, and also preached in Indonesia, Siam, Indochina, Taiwan, and the Philippines.

EWM, II: 2283; Lyall, Leslie T., *John Sung* (1864).
J.M.

Swain, Clara (1834–1910)

Methodist Episcopal medical missionary and educator, Swain was born in Elmira, New York. From early childhood she had a deep interest in religion and was influenced by Methodist preaching. She was a graduate of Canandaigua Seminary in New York and Woman's Medical College in Philadelphia, Pennsylvania, from which she received her MD in 1869. In the same year Clementina (Mrs. William) Butler founded the Women's Foreign Missionary Society in Boston, Massachusetts. Butler secured the funds to support a modest mission to India and persuaded Swain to become the first female medical missionary in Asia. In November 1869 Swain, accompanied by **Isabella Thoburn**, another Methodist Episcopal missionary, embarked for India. Swain's aim was to provide medical care for women and to train young Indian women to offer medical treatment to those in need. Regarding the latter goal, Swain supervised the education of a number of women who expanded medical care in India. With regard to the former aim, the number of patients seeking help soon overwhelmed Swain's small clinic. Larger quarters were found and Swain opened the first woman's hospital in India on

1 January 1873 in Bareilly. Ill health caused Swain to return to the United States on three occasions, the final return a short time before her death. In 1912 the Bareilly hospital was renamed in Swain's honor.

ANB, 21:180–181; Swain, Clara A., *India* (1909); Wilson, Dorothy Clarke, *Palace of Healing, the Story of Dr. Clara Swain, First Woman Missionary Doctor, and the Hospital She Founded* (1968).
C.Y.

Taylor, William (1821–1902)

Ranging from a whiskey-keg pulpit in the goldfields of California to the missionary episcopacy of the **Methodist Episcopal Church**, Taylor, who was born in Rockbridge County, Virginia, was, perhaps, the most effective world-traveling evangelist of his era. He received his first appointment in the Baltimore Conference in 1842; seven years later, he was appointed to the California Mission. Beginning in 1857, Taylor traveled as an evangelist in New England, the Midwest, and Canada, followed by journeys to Australia, New Zealand, and Tasmania. From 1866 to 1868, he worked in South Africa, then spent two years in England, the West Indies, and Ceylon. Reaching Bombay in 1870, Taylor preached in India's principal cities, and developed a plan for self-supporting missionaries: the Board of Missions would fund their travel, but the salaries of the missionaries would be paid by the congregations they organized. Taylor left India in 1875, preached in London, visited his family in California, and then, in 1877, went to South America, where he planted self-supporting missions in Peru, Chile, and Brazil. The 1884 general conference elected him a missionary bishop and assigned him to supervise Methodist Episcopal missionary work in Liberia. Soon, however, he was opening missions in the Congo, Angola, and Mozambique. He retired in 1896.

ANB, 21: 406–407; HDM, 293–294; Taylor, William, *Story of My Life*, 2 vols. (1895).
J.M.

Theology of John Wesley

John Wesley never created a closely reasoned, systematic theology. Instead, he highlighted the 'main doctrines' of the Wesleyan way of **salvation** – repentance, faith, and holiness – and developed a system for handling theological questions. This began and ended with the Bible looked at through the lenses of tradition, reason, and experience (**Quadrilateral**).

Wesley found tradition in the Thirty-Nine Articles of Religion of the Church of England, which provided formulations of orthodox Christian doctrines;

insights drawn from Anglican writers (both High Churchmen and **Puritans**) and a variety of Protestant and **Roman Catholic** authors. He looked especially to the theology of the first three or four centuries after Christ, in particular the writings of the Greek Fathers. Then he subjected tradition and the Bible to logical analysis, formulating his own distinctive theological emphases.

With God's grace at the center of his theology, Wesley emphasized the biblical witness to God-with-us in Jesus Christ, provided ways for persons to experience the presence of Christ as Savior and Sanctifier, advocated a life of opposing all known evils and doing as much good as possible, and promoted a missional understanding of the Christian community.

The way Wesley's system for handling theological questions worked can be seen in his attempts to stake out a dynamic middle between rigid extremes. For example, when dealing with the doctrine of the Trinity (Sermon 55, 1775), he rejected the Unitarian left, arguing that the Bible makes clear that God is Father, Son, and Holy Spirit. He set his face equally against the dogmatic right, insisting that it is not even necessary to use the words 'Trinity' and 'Person.' In the middle stands the Bible: it reveals *that* God is Three-One, but leaves mysterious *how* God is Three-One – a mystery that theologians try to unlock at the risk of provoking unprofitable, unloving dissension.

The middle way also characterizes Wesley's delineation of the divine–human interaction in the process of being saved. Extremists of the left argue that humans save themselves by doing works acceptable to God (salvation by works). Extremists of the right believe that salvation is entirely God's work: God chooses some to be saved, others to be damned (double predestination). Wesley appeals to what he takes to be the Bible's central position: God works in you; therefore you *can* work. God works in you; therefore you *must* work. You must be workers together with God (Sermon 85, 1785; the text is Philippians 2:12–13).

Few Methodists question Wesley's view that God's grace empowers humans to choose to respond in faith to God-in-Christ, or to refuse; to co-operate with God in works of love, or to choose non-cooperation. But controversy swirls around his broadening of the category of persons God accepts as coworkers.

Wesley records a question-and-answer period with himself in his journal for 1 December 1767: To be saved, is it necessary to be able to articulate the meaning of *imputed righteousness*? No. To be saved, is it necessary to have a clear conception of *justification by faith*? No. To be saved, is it necessary to affirm *justification by faith*? No. What then? With regard to salvation, the plain message of Acts 10:35 is enough: God accepts those in every nation who fear God and do what is right.

Wesley laid the foundation for that conclusion in 1754, in his explanatory note on Acts 10:35, commenting, a person who 'reverences God, as great, wise, good; the Cause, End, and Governor of all things; and . . . not only avoids all known evil, but endeavours, according to the best light he has, to do all things well. *Is accepted of* [God] – Through Christ, though he knows him not. The assertion is express, and admits of no exception.' Thirty years later, in 1784, when Wesley adapted the Articles of Religion of the **Church of England** for the Methodists of America, he deleted the article that declared salvation is obtainable only by the name of Christ.

Wesley endeavored to outline and hold a dynamic middle in his theology. On the static left are persons who reverence nothing transcending themselves. On the static right are those who insist theirs is the only way of salvation. In the middle, Wesley holds two truths in tension. First, there is the truth that he found his salvation in Christ and was energized by God's love. That is the light he had, the basis for his evangelistic ministry, the message of his published sermons.

Wesley's second truth is that God 'is not the God of the Christians only, but the God of the heathens also; that he is "rich in mercy to all that call upon him", "according to the light they have", and that "in every nation he that feareth God and worketh righteousness is accepted of him" ' (Sermon 91, 1784).

In 1750, Wesley published 'Catholic Spirit' (Sermon 39), a summary of his middle-way theology. Its essence is Trinitarian, though the term is not used. Do you believe in God, he asks, God's 'eternity, immensity, wisdom, power; his justice, mercy, and truth?' Do you have 'a divine evidence, a supernatural conviction, of the things of God?' Do you 'believe in the Lord Jesus Christ, "God over all, blessed for ever"?' Is your 'faith filled with the energy of love?' Does your love of God cause you to ' "hate all evil ways"?' Do you love only those who love you, or do you also 'love your enemies'? 'Do you love even the enemies of God?' Do you do good to all – 'neighbours or strangers, friends or enemies, good or bad?' Do you try to meet their needs, 'assisting them both in body and soul to the uttermost of your power?' If the answers are yes, Wesley argues, the person is a Christian, even if his/her creed seems too liberal or too conservative.

Wesley's statement is noteworthy for what it does not say: no mention of inerrant scriptures, virgin birth, a particular theory of the atonement, the second coming. Those doctrines appear in Wesley's writings, but he does not single them out as must-believe fundamentals. Instead, he takes his theological stand in the middle, insisting against those on the left that Christian faith is much more than vague belief in a deist God; insisting against those on the right that true Christians may hang loose to certain doctrinal specifics so long as their faith is producing a life energized by love.

Collins, Kenneth J., *The Theology of John Wesley: Holy Love and the Shape of Grace* (2007); Maddox, Randy L., *Responsible Grace: John Wesley's Practical Theology* (1994);

Outler, Albert C., Thomas C. Oden and Leicester R. Longden, eds, *The Wesleyan Theological Heritage: Essays of Albert C. Outler* (1991); Outler, Albert C. and Richard P. Heitzenrater, eds, *John Wesley's Sermons: An Anthology* (1991); Runyon, Theodore H., *The New Creation: John Wesley's Theology Today* (1998).
J.M.

Thoburn, Isabella (1840–1901)

Methodist Episcopal laywoman, educator, and first missionary appointed by the denomination's Woman's Foreign Missionary Society, Thoburn was born in St. Clairsville, Ohio. After attending local schools, she studied at Wheeling Seminary in Virginia and the Cincinnati Academy of Design in Ohio after which she began a career in teaching. In 1866 her brother **James Mills Thoburn**, missionary to India wrote to his sister inviting her to travel to India to educate girls and young women. The recently formed Woman's Foreign Missionary Society dispatched Thoburn and **Clara Swain** to India in 1870 where Thoburn began educational and evangelistic work. She opened a school for girls in Lucknow on 18 April 1870, which grew steadily. She was instrumental in founding other schools for girls and the Lucknow Woman's College, which was named Isabella Thoburn College after her death. Thoburn was also active in cultivating **deaconess** ministries in Chicago and Cincinnati in the United States.

EWM, II: 2333–2334; Gesling, Linda Joyce, 'Gender, Ministry, and Mission: The Lives of James and Isabella Thoburn, Brother and Sister in Methodist Service,' (diss., Northwestern University, 1996); Thoburn, James M., *The Life of Isabella Thoburn* (reprint, 1987).
C.Y.

Thoburn, James Mills (1836–1922)

Methodist Episcopal missionary and bishop, Thoburn was born in St. Clairsville, Ohio, and was educated at Allegheny College, Meadville, Pennsylvania, graduating in 1857. He was converted, felt a call to the ministry, and affiliated with the Pittsburgh annual conference in 1858. Shortly after his ordination in 1859, Thoburn, under the sponsorship of the Methodist Episcopal Foreign Missionary Society, boarded a cargo ship bound for India. He returned to the United States in 1863 intending to form a missionary training school. At the 1864 general conference he effectively advocated denominational mission work. In 1865 he was again in India where he served several **mission** stations and superintended a district near Lucknow. Influenced by **William Taylor**, Thoburn moved to Calcutta where he served as pastor to a multiracial, multinational congregation. He moved on to Burma and

Singapore where he was instrumental in founding the first Methodist church in Malaysia. In 1888 the general conference elected him the first missionary bishop for India and Malaysia, a position he held until retirement in 1908. Thoburn was also an important figure in establishing churches in Java, Sumatra, British Borneo, and the Philippines. He is remembered as a major figure in the establishment of **Asian** Methodism.

ANB, 21:501–502; Garrett, Guy D., 'The Missionary Career of James Mills Thoburn,' (diss., Boston University, 1968); Thoburn, James M., *India and Southern Asia* (1907); Thoburn, James M., *Missionary Addresses* (1887).
C.Y.

Union American Methodist Episcopal Church (USA)

Divisive tendencies within the **Union Church of Africans** led to the formation of this denomination in the 1850s. The original church changed its name, first, to the African Union Church, then, in 1865–1866, after merging with the Colored Methodist Protestant Church, to **African Union Methodist Protestant Church**. As its name indicates, the Union American Methodist Episcopal Church adopted episcopal polity. It is generally Wesleyan in doctrine, but clergy are only asked to assent to the Apostles' Creed. A general conference is called whenever important decisions need to be made.

EWM, II: 2388.
J.M.

Union Church of Africans (USA)

Peter Spencer organized this denomination in 1813. It split in the 1850s, when **Union American Methodist Episcopal Church** was founded. The original church changed its name, first, to African Union Church, and then, in 1865–1866, after joining with the Colored Methodist Protestant Church, to **African Union Methodist Protestant Church**. Spencer was born, about 1779, into slavery in Kent County, Maryland. When his master died, he moved to Wilmington, Delaware, where he joined Asbury **Methodist Episcopal** Church. Spencer led a number of black members out of that congregation in 1805, began to hold outdoors meetings, then used a house. The Spencer group built their first church in 1812, naming it Ezion Methodist Episcopal Church. The next year, Spencer and about fifty other black persons withdrew from the Methodist Episcopal Church and organized the Union Church of Africans. In 1816, Spencer and others accepted **Richard Allen's** invitation to attend the organizational meeting of the **African Methodist Episcopal Church**; however, the Union Church of Africans chose not to join that denomination. Instead, it remained a group of churches, not a clearly defined denomination. But it expanded, developing new congregations and elementary school in several eastern states and Canada.

Lewis V. Baldwin, *Invisible Strands in African Methodism: A History of the African Union Methodist Protestant and Union American Methodist Episcopal Churches, 1805–1980* (1983).
J.M.

United Brethren in Christ (USA)

Founded in 1800, this church combined the ministries of **Philip William Otterbein** and **Martin Boehm**, who were elected bishops during its organizational conference held near Frederick, Maryland. Christian Newcomer and Christopher Grosch formulated a summary of United Brethren doctrine in 1813; it was based on the Apostles' Creed and other traditional doctrinal materials. In 1815, at the first general conference, a Discipline, modeled with modifications on the Methodist one, and a Confession of Faith, a slight revision of the Newcomer-Grosch document, were adopted. From the United Brethren heartland in Pennsylvania and Maryland, the denomination spread westward, especially into German-speaking communities. During the nineteenth century, the church opposed slavery, the use of beverage alcohol, and the growing popularity of secret societies. Constitutional changes in 1889, which permitted membership in secret societies and authorized a new confession of faith, caused a schism. Bishop Milton Wright, father of airplane-pioneers Wilbur and Orville Wright, was prominent in founding the breakaway United Brethren in Christ (Old Constitution). The original church developed missions in Sierra Leone, China, Japan, Puerto Rico, and the Philippines. It merged in 1946 with the **Evangelical Church** to create the **Evangelical United Brethren Church**.

Behney, J. Bruce and Paul H. Eller, *The History of the Evangelical United Brethren Church* (1979); Drury, Augustus W., *History of the Church of the United Brethren in Christ* (rev. ed., 1931).
J.M.

United Methodist Church (Great Britain)

Organized in 1907, this denomination brought together the **United Methodist Free Churches**, the largest of the uniting churches, the **Methodist New Connexion (Great Britain)**, and the **Bible Christians**. During its brief lifespan, before it became part of the union of 1932 that created the Methodist Church in Great Britain, little effort was made to undermine local customs or to merge congregations of the predecessor bodies in the same area. The year after the merger, a nationwide mission was held, with five thousand decisions recorded. Of its first nine presidents, there were three from each of the uniting churches.

DMBI, 361; Smith, Henry, John Edward Swallow, and William Treffry, *The Story of the United Methodist Church* (1932).
J.M.

United Methodist Church (USA)

The largest Methodist denomination in the United States, with a significant number of members worldwide, the United Methodist Church was created in 1968 by the union of the **Evangelical United Brethren** and Methodist churches; the latter was organized in 1939 when the **Methodist Episcopal, Methodist Episcopal, South**, and **Methodist Protestant** churches merged. The church's doctrinal position is found in the Methodist Articles of Religion, the Evangelical United Brethren Confession of Faith, and **John Wesley's** *Sermons* and *Explanatory Notes upon the New Testament*. United Methodism is governed by conferences at various levels, with a general conference, meeting every four years, empowered to legislate for the worldwide connection. Persons may be ordained to the permanent diaconate, whose key focus is service; or to the order of elders, whose members are authorized to administer the **sacraments**, and from whose membership are drawn local-church pastors, persons in other types of church-related service, and bishops. Bishops are elected for life, provide residential leadership for one or more annual conferences, and appoint the elders to their areas of service. During most of United Methodism's history, differences over the full acceptance of gay men and lesbians threatened its unity.

Yrigoyen, Charles, Jr., John G. McEllhenney, and Kenneth E. Rowe, *United Methodism at Forty – Looking Back, Looking Forward* (2008); *MEA*, vols. I and II.
J.M.

United Methodist Free Churches (Great Britain)

The culmination of a reform movement within British Methodism and an attempt to hold together congregationalism and Wesleyan connectionalism, the United Methodist Free Churches, organized in 1857, brought together the Wesleyan Methodist Association and the Wesleyan Reformers. After a period of considerable growth during the second half of the nineteenth century, it was the largest of the three denominations that formed the **United Methodist Church (Great Britain)** in 1907. The first president of the United Methodist Free Churches was **James Everett**, who also edited a hymnbook for the church that featured a portrait of **John Wesley**. An annual conference, called the Assembly, governed the denomination. Unlike mainstream Methodism, the circuits of the United Methodist Free Churches were autonomous, and free to choose clergy or laypersons to represent them at the Assembly. In other respects, such as circuit ministry, itinerancy, and class meetings, it followed traditional Wesleyanism. The denomination had a *Magazine*, and organized overseas missions.

Beckerlegge, Oliver A., *The United Methodist Free Churches* (1957); *DMBI*, 361; *EWM*, II: 2396.
J.M.

Varick, James (1750?–1827)

Methodist clergyman and a principal founder of the **African Methodist Episcopal Zion Church**, Varick was born near Newburgh, New York. His family later moved to New York City where he worked as a shoemaker, tobacco cutter, and taught school in his home. Drawn to Methodism, he affiliated with the John Street **Methodist Episcopal Church**, served as an exhorter, and was licensed to preach. In 1796 Varick and a number of African Americans left the John Street church to organize a separate black congregation which was incorporated in 1801 as Zion African Methodist Episcopal Church. The Zion congregation labored to attain a greater degree of self-determination within the denomination, but the Methodist Episcopal leadership in New York was reluctant to grant the measure of autonomy which Varick and others sought. Other black groups in New York City and Long Island; New Haven, Connecticut; and Philadelphia and Easton, Pennsylvania joined together in 1821 formally to constitute a new black Methodist denomination which by 1848 was known as the African Methodist Episcopal Zion Church. Varick was consecrated its first bishop. Varick was intensely committed to freedom and justice for black people, fought against the colonization movement, and was an important figure in establishing in 1827, *Freedom's Journal*, thought to be the first black newspaper.

ANB, 22:273–274; Melton, J. Gordon, *A Will to Choose: The Origins of African American Methodism* (2007); Walls, William J., *The African Methodist Episcopal Zion Church: Reality of the Black Church* (1974).
C.Y.

Welsh Methodism

A trinity of Methodisms characterizes Wales: Welsh-speaking, English-speaking, and Calvinistic. Methodist-type evangelistic activity began in Wales, when, in 1735, Howell Harris (1714–1773) experienced conversion and initiated a preaching ministry. **John Wesley** first preached in Wales in 1739, and soon agreed with Harris, a Calvinist influenced by **George Whitefield**, that they would not compete. Although Wesley preached often in Wales and appointed itinerant preachers to Welsh circuits, few Welsh English-speakers became Methodists in the eighteenth century, and the initial outreach to Welsh speakers was largely unsuccessful. Calvinistic Methodism, however, under the leadership of Harris and Daniel Rowland (1711–1790), grew. Two of its outstanding converts are the hymn-writers William Williams Pantycelyn (1717–1791) and Ann Griffiths (1776–1805). Thomas Charles (1755–1814), Calvinistic Methodist of Bala, responded to the demand for Welsh Bibles by helping establish the British and Foreign Bible Society in 1804. In the nineteenth-century, English-speaking Wesleyan Methodism grew as English workers moved into Wales; Welsh-speaking Wesleyan Methodism developed slowly; Calvinistic Methodism seceded from the Church of England and adopted a Confession of Faith. The twentieth century witnessed the development of official ways for English- and Welsh-speaking Wesleyan Methodists to work together, culminating in 1957 in the Standing Committee for Wales, which was superseded in 1997 by Y Gymanfa, or Welsh Assembly, which represents all districts in Wales. Calvinistic Methodism streamlined and modernized its structure, published a shorter Declaration of Faith, and gained clear legal identity.

A Dictionary of Methodism in Britain and Ireland, 366–367, 377–378.
J.M.

Wesley Family

Born in Epworth, a small village in Lincolnshire in northeastern England, **John and Charles Wesley** were two of nineteen children born to Samuel Wesley (1662–1735) and Susanna Annesley Wesley (1669–1742). Although both parents came from Puritan and Nonconformist ancestry, they were unwavering in their loyalty to **Anglicanism**. Samuel, an Oxford graduate and Anglican priest, became rector of the Epworth parish in 1695. In addition to his pastoral duties he was a scholar and writer. Unpopular with his parishioners, Samuel also served a short prison term for debt. Susanna, a person of deep piety and intellect, was very influential in the lives of her children. She was adept at managing the household despite her husband's inability to

Wesleyan Church (USA)

Formed in June 1968 by a union of the Wesleyan Methodist Church and the Pilgrim Holiness Church, the Wesleyan Church is rooted in the theology of the Wesleyan tradition, especially as it was influenced by the **Holiness Movement** of the late nineteenth and early twentieth centuries. Organized in 1843 by clergy and lay people who protested the leniency of the **Methodist Episcopal Church** on slavery, the Wesleyan Methodist Church not only supported the abolition of slavery, but also found the episcopacy distasteful, replacing it with an elected presidency, and implemented lay representation in the annual conference. As other holiness groups, it shunned the use of alcohol and tobacco, avoided indecent dress, and opposed membership in secret societies. Originally known as the International Holiness Union and Prayer League founded in 1897, the Pilgrim Holiness Church adopted their denominational name in 1922. At the top of the church's priorities were evangelism, holiness, and healing. The Wesleyan Church holds membership in the **World Methodist Council**, the National Association of Evangelicals, and the Christian Holiness Association. Its emphasis on overseas **missions** has resulted in congregations in more than fifty countries. The *Wesleyan Advocate* is the denominational periodical.

McLeister, Ira Ford and Roy Stephen Nichols, *Conscience and Commitment: The History of the Wesleyan Methodist Church of America* (1976).
C.Y.

Whitefield, George (1714–1770)

Known on both sides of the Atlantic, Whitefield was arguably the most prominent evangelical preacher of the eighteenth century. He was born in Gloucester, England, and educated at Pembroke College, Oxford. Influenced by a small group of students in Oxford calling themselves the Holy Club in which he was an active participant, Whitefield had a profound conversion experience in 1735. Ordained into the priesthood of the Church of England in 1736, Whitefield engaged in thirty-three years of preaching (1737–1770) in England, Scotland, and Wales in addition to seven visits to colonial America as one of the foremost leaders of its Great Awakening. On his first visit to America in 1739 he organized an orphanage and school near Savannah, Georgia, which he called Bethesda ('house of mercy'). When **Anglican** pulpits in his home country were closed to his preaching because of his evangelical message and his criticism of the spiritual lethargy of the church, he spoke wherever a crowd could be gathered. Whitefield was an outstanding dramatic orator who occasionally preached to crowds numbered in the thousands. Committed to the **Calvinist** understanding of the faith, in which humans are considered incapable of assisting in their own salvation, Whitefield was generously supported by the like-minded **Selina, Countess of Huntingdon**, but fell into disfavor with his friends **John and Charles Wesley** who held to human free will by God's prevenient grace. Whitefield is considered by many the forerunner of modern revivalism.

BDE, 716–719; Dallimore, Arnold A., *George Whitefield: The Life and Times of the Great Evangelist of the Eighteenth-Century Revival*, 2 vols. (1970, 1980); Gillies, John, ed., *George Whitefield's Journals*, 6 vols. (1771–1772); Lambert, Frank, *'Pedlar in Divinity': George Whitefield and the Transatlantic Revivals, 1737–1770* (1994); Stout, Harry S., *The Divine Dramatist: George Whitefield and the Rise of Modern Evangelicalism* (1991).
C.Y.

Women

Women have occupied a indispensable role in Methodism since its earliest period, though until recently their stories have not been widely researched, circulated, or celebrated. In the earliest period they were class leaders, teachers, housekeepers, exhorters, and ultimately preachers. Sarah Mallet (*c.* 1768–1845) is believed to be the first female preacher to receive **John Wesley's** official approval. After his death the conference imposed policies and regulations to make female preaching difficult, if not impossible. Women were held up as exemplars of the Methodist way including Wesley's own mother Susanna, Elizabeth Ritchie, Hester Ann Rogers, and Mary Bosanquet Fletcher – to name a few. In every place where Methodism has existed since its beginnings women have made impressive contributions as innovators, evangelists, theologians, **deaconesses**, missionaries, pastors, local preachers, superintendents, bishops, teachers, spiritual guides, writers and editors, local church officers, and just plain members and supporters of Methodist **ministry**. As individuals and in organizations they have accomplished this in spite of some who have denied them the roles to which they believed they were called. Late twentieth-century Methodist historiography began to recognize their importance and place in regional and world Methodism, though much more research on women is needed.

Chilcote, Paul Wesley, *She Offered Them Christ: The Legacy of Women Preachers in Early Methodism* (1993); Chilcote, Paul W., *Her Own Story: Autobiographical Portraits of Early Methodist Women* (2001); *DMBI*, 399; Schmidt, Jean Miller, *Grace Sufficient: A History of Women in American Methodism, 1760–1939* (1999); Sykes, Richard, ed., *Beyond the Boundaries* (1998), 58–86.
C.Y.

World Council of Churches

Founded in 1948, the World Council of Churches has its headquarters in Geneva, Switzerland. Its constitution defines it as, 'A fellowship of churches which confess the Lord Jesus as God and Saviour according to the scriptures and therefore seek to fulfill their common calling to the glory of the one God, Father, Son, and Holy Spirit.' Council membership includes approximately 350 denominations in more than 110 nations and territories. Nations in **Africa, Asia, Caribbean, Europe, Latin America**, Middle East, North America, and **Australasia** are represented. Visible unity in one faith and one eucharistic fellowship, common witness in mission and evangelism, serving human needs of all types, and fostering renewal, are its goals. Methodists have been active participants in council membership from the beginning.

Bell, G. K. A., *The Kingship of Christ: The Story of the World Council of Churches* (1954); Lossky, Nicholas, et al., eds, *Dictionary of the Ecumenical Movement* (1991), 1083–1100; ODCC, 1765–1766;
C.Y.

World Methodist Council

Known originally as the Ecumenical Methodist Council since its beginning in 1881, the name was changed in 1951 to the World Methodist Council. Its headquarters are in the United States at Lake Junaluska, North Carolina. It is an association of churches in the Methodist tradition throughout the world promoting unity and seeking to foster Methodist participation in the wider **ecumenical** movement, to encourage evangelism and Christian education, to support ministries of justice and peace, and to study union and reunion proposals which effect member churches. Among its important work is the quinquennial World Methodist Conference, a ministerial exchange program, a world peace award, and the Oxford Theological Institute which brings together world Methodist church leaders, theologians, and historians every five years. Groups with special interests in evangelism, men's and **women's ministry**, and history are affiliated with the council. It also publishes a newsletter, *World Parish*, and maintains a library and museum at its headquarters.

World Methodist Council Handbook of Information (published quinquennially).
C.Y.

Worship

Worship's components – words, music, and space – evolved in parallel during the course of Methodist history. **John Wesley** designated hymns, prayers, scripture readings, and a sermon as the *words* of worship, but insisted they were 'essentially defective' unless coupled with the words of the Church of England's prayer book. Therefore he admonished his followers to attend their Methodist preaching services *and* prayer-book worship at their parish church. In the former, unaccompanied *music* supported hymn singing. Wesley's 1780 *Collection of Hymns* became Methodism's model hymnbook. Choirs appeared during Methodism's third decade; Wesley approved of them so long as they sang understandable words to unadorned melodies. He advocated Methodist worship *space* that was plain outside and in, pulpit-centered, and inexpensive. Beginning in the 1760s, he promoted the octagonal design, but rectangles proved more successful, largely because they were easier to expand.

When American Methodists became independent in 1784 they accepted Wesley's plan for their worship. Soon, however, they laid aside his version of the Church of England's prayer book, the hymnbook he edited, and his recommendation for every-Sunday communion. Worship consisted of singing, praying, reading from the Old and New Testaments, preaching, and quarterly communion. Rectangular or square churches built of wood, brick, or stone, plain in style, provided pulpit-centered worship space.

British Methodism decided, shortly after Wesley died, to make the prayer-book liturgy he prepared for American Methodism the order for its own preaching service; however, some British Methodists remained nonliturgical; quarterly (monthly in some places) communion was usual. Four or five hymns, selected from Wesley's 1780 *Collection* or one of several new hymnbooks, were sung a cappella, or accompanied by a bass viol. Debates about permitting organs began in the 1790s; the 1820 Conference authorized them. Wesley's City Road Chapel in London (1778) served as the norm for building increasingly more impressive urban chapels for a half-century, signaling the growing prosperity of Methodists; many village chapels, however, remained modest.

Early nineteenth-century American Methodists shared their new nation's identification with ancient Greek democracy and the Roman republic by remodeling or building churches in Classic style. Inside, the rectangular preaching room remained the norm, with a high central pulpit and a small railed-in communion table. The basic worship service continued unchanged from the late eighteenth century, but hymnbooks moved upscale after 1821. Psalms and hymns from Europe were added; a tunebook appeared. Soon a two-hymnbook tradition developed: formal for church services, informal for **Sunday schools** and **camp meetings**. A debate about organs opened in the 1840s and went on for forty years. Until 1850, choirs existed to lead congregational singing; then they began to present anthems.

Starting in the 1830s, English churchmen promoted the Gothic style of church architecture, arguing that it was uniquely Christian; that its pointed arches provided a visual metaphor of the soul soaring upward to God. By the 1850s, Methodists, now rich enough to erect cathedral-like churches, were adopting Gothic architecture on both sides of the Atlantic. The interiors, however, unlike medieval cathedrals, were preaching rooms – the pulpit, not the altar, was the focal point.

Some Gothic-style Methodist churches in the United States were impressive stone or brick structures with stained glass windows; others were carpenter Gothic – clapboard buildings with pointed arch windows. The order of **worship** did not change, except for adding liturgical elements in a few congregations. Choirs in city churches grew larger and were given special places to sit; opponents of organs lost ground.

By the 1870s, nearly all British Methodists welcomed Gothic architecture for their pulpit-centered worship space. They retained Wesley's words for worship, either the nonliturgical ones of his preaching service, or his liturgical service of 1784, which provided the basis for their 1882 service book. His 1780 *Collection of Hymns* was reissued in 1876; other hymnbooks also appeared. During the same period, Methodist chapels added stained glass windows; at first, these had geometrical, multi-colored patterns; later they depicted biblical themes and Protestant heroes. Pulpit giants held large audiences enthralled; for those spellbinders, and to provide bases for urban mission, British Methodism built vast Central Halls in a modified Renaissance style.

Beginning around 1875, American Methodists selected Romanesque architecture for their city churches. Instead of the soaring Gothic, it was solid, down to earth, proclaiming the firm planting of Methodism. Inside, unlike rectangular gothic, Romanesque churches were square – new steel technology made it possible to roof broad spaces. This provided pulpit-centered, auditorium-style seating, allowing large genteel congregations to sit close to the now highly polished preacher. A mini liturgical revival in the 1890s produced two books of full liturgical texts to be placed in pew racks; quarterly communion continued. City and town churches had organs; country churches, pianos or melodeons; almost all had choirs that presented anthems. Wealthy congregations built organs that imitated orchestras; organists and quartets paraded their virtuosity; denominational musicologists stressed the need for 'quality music.' Meanwhile, the opening and closing Sunday school 'exercises' offered an alternative form of worship, less formal, with catchy songs and choruses.

Early in the twentieth century, British Methodists built modernized Gothic churches, then slowly switched to various modern designs. They published a new hymnbook in 1904, the first to be organized thematically; Wesley's model

1780 *Collection* was organized according to aspects of Christian experience. After the union of British Methodism's two major branches in 1932, a new hymnal (1933) and service book (1936) were published.

American Methodists continued to build Romanesque churches until the 1920s, then returned to Gothic with altar-focused interiors, even though worship continued to be sermon-centered. The front of the 1905 hymnal carried an order of worship that included a prayer of confession; soon a creed, psalter readings, and chants appeared. Another mini liturgical revival led to an unofficial book of services and prayers (1918). Quarterly communion was usual. During the 1920s, Methodist musicians planned several conferences to improve church music's quality. Another hymnal appeared in 1935. Churches organized children's and youth choirs. Electronic organs gained favor in the early 1940s, and altar-centered, colonial architecture joined the list of styles.

After the Second World War, British Methodists accented community as well as religious needs as they replaced destroyed churches or remodeled damaged ones; often the worship space was flexible, allowing the pulpit, table, and chairs to be arranged variously. The 1975 service book bypassed Wesley's 1784 prayer book in favor of an ecumenical order based on the worship of the early Christians, who maintained the unity of Word and **sacrament** in their services. A new hymnal appeared in 1983, and a revised edition of the book of services arrived in 1999. Instrumental groups sometimes supplemented, sometimes supplanted, organs.

When World War II ended, **American Methodism** resumed building colonial churches, then switched to contemporary, often A-frame, construction. By the end of the twentieth century, it avoided building churches that looked like churches; often the worship space was windowless or easily darkened. Changes in the words and music of worship paralleled changes in the space. During colonial's popularity, worship leaders looked backward to Wesley, taking up the words of his 1784 prayer book and the music of classical composers; these were enshrined in a new book of worship (1964) and hymnal (1966). With A-frame churches came chatty liturgies, guitar music, and Coke-and-crackers communions. The 1970s and 1980s, when few churches were built, witnessed a liturgical renaissance. Monthly or every-Sunday communion gained favor. A new order of worship, featured in the 1989 hymnal and 1992 book of worship, restored the early church's unity of Word and sacrament. But as those books were being published, advocates of contemporary worship discarded books in favor of Bible texts and praise choruses projected on a screen. Organs bowed out, instrumentalists strolled in, and the message took center stage.

DMBI, 8–9, 36, 60, 63, 74, 81, 172–173, 213, 235, 236, 260–261, 271, 278, 283, 333, 341, 372; *EWM*, 126–128, 1691–1694, 2605–2609; *HDM*, 217–220, 290–291, 342–346; *New*

Dictionary of Liturgy and Worship (2002), 47–48, 81–82, 186–188, 316–318; Tucker, Karen Westerfield, *The Sunday Service of the Methodists: Twentieth-Century Worship in Worldwide Methodism* (1996); Tucker, Karen Westerfield, *American Methodist Worship* (2001).
J.M.

Youth

Recognizing the importance of youth in the **ministries** of the church, and its future, the various Methodist denominations formed organizations for their young people. The earliest effort of the British Methodists occurred in 1896 when they organized the Wesley Guild. In 1945 they formed the Methodist Association of Youth Clubs (MAYC) which was one of the largest church youth organizations in Europe. For some years youth work in the United States centered in Christian Endeavor (CE), a nondenominational youth organization begun in 1881 and was supported by many Methodist congregations for at least another generation. CE was largely succeeded by the Epworth League which had origins as early as 1884 and eventually became the official youth organization of the **Methodist Episcopal Church** and its central conferences, the **Methodist Episcopal Church, South**, and the Methodist Church of Canada. The League was followed by the Methodist Youth Fellowship after the 1939 union and United Methodist Youth following the 1968 **United Methodist** union. As more opportunities have become available for youth, the churches' youth programs, especially in **Europe** and the United States, have experienced declining membership and participation.

DMBI, 407; *EWM*, I: 783–784.
C.Y.

Zinzendorf, Nikolaus Ludwig Graf von (1700–1760)

Founder of the **Moravian** Brethren, Zinzendorf was born in Dresden, Germany, educated at Wittenberg University, and in 1722 organized the Moravians on his estate called Herrnhut. He was opposed to the rationalism of the Enlightenment and traditional Lutheran orthodoxy, and favored **Pietism's** approach to the faith. **John Wesley** was impressed by Moravian spirituality during and after his American mission to Georgia. He visited Zinzendorf in 1738 following his Aldersgate experience and conversed extensively with Zinzendorf in London in 1741. Wesley became increasingly critical of Zinzendorf's autocratic leadership, and of the Moravians for their emphasis on **'stillness'** and what Wesley considered their **antinomianism**.

Three of Wesley's evangelical friends, John Cennick, John Gambold, and James Hutton, were much influenced by Zinzendorf's understanding of Christianity and became leaders of the Moravian church in England.

BDE, 759–761; DMBI, 408; Freeman, Arthur J., *An Ecumenical Theology of the Heart: The Theology of Count Nicholas Ludwig von Zinzendorf* (1998); Podmore, Colin, *The Moravian Church in England, 1728–1760* (1998); Towlson, Clifford W., *Moravian and Methodist: Relationships and Influences in the Eighteenth Century* (1957).
C.Y.

Part III

This page intentionally left blank

Bibliography

Susan E. Warrick

General Reference Works

Anderson, Christopher J., and Arturo L. Razon. *The Methodist Library Pamphlet Collection.* Madison, NJ: Methodist Library, Drew University, 2008–2009.

Anderson, Christopher J., and Kenneth E. Rowe. *United Methodist Studies: Basic Bibliographies.* 5th ed. Nashville, TN: General Board of Higher Education and Ministry, 2009. http://www.drew.edu/depts/library/methodist.aspx (accessed 1/14/10).

Baker, Frank. *A Union Catalogue of the Publications of John and Charles Wesley.* Stone Mountain, GA: George Zimmerman, 1991.

Batsel, John, and Lyda Batsel. *Union List of United Methodist Serials 1773–1973.* Evanston, IL: General Commission on Archives and History, UMC, with the United Methodist Librarians' Fellowship and Garrett Theological Seminary, 1974.

Calkin, Homer L. *Catalog of Methodist Archival and Manuscript Collections.* Alexandria, VA: World Methodist Historical Society, 1982–1991.

Collins, Kenneth J. *Wesley Bibliography.* Wilmore, KY: Asbury Theological Seminary. http://www.asburyseminary.edu/resources/wesleybibliography (accessed 1/14/10).

Gage, Laurie E. *English Methodism: A Bibliographical View.* Westcliff-on-Sea: Gage Postal Books, 1985.

Gray, C. Jarrett, Jr., comp. *The Racial and Ethnic Presence in America Methodism: A Bibliography.* Madison, NJ: General Commission on Archives and History, UMC, 1991.

Green, Charles A., comp. *Methodist History Cumulative Index, 1982–1997.* Madison, NJ: General Commission on Archives and History, UMC, 1998.

Hatcher, Stephen. *A Primitive Methodist Bibliography.* Westcliff-on-Sea: Gage Postal Books, 1980.

John Rylands University Library of Manchester. *Methodist Archives: Catalogues, Handlists, Bibliographies and Some Important Reference Works.* 2nd ed. Manchester: John Rylands University Library, 1991.

Jones, Charles Edwin. *Black Holiness: A Guide to the Study of Black Participation in Wesleyan Perfectionist and Glossolalic Pentecostal Movements.* Metuchen, NJ: Scarecrow Press, 1987.

———. *The Holiness-Pentecostal Movement: A Comprehensive Guide.* Lanham, MD: Scarecrow Press, 2008.

———. *The Wesleyan Holiness Movement: A Comprehensive Guide.* Lanham, MD: Scarecrow Press; Chicago: American Theological Library Association, 2005.

Bibliography

Lloyd, Gareth. *Sources for Women's Studies in the Methodist Archives*. Manchester: Methodist Archives and Research Centre, John Rylands University Library, 1996.
Miller, William C. *Holiness Works: A Bibliography*. Rev. ed. Kansas, MO: Nazarene, 1986.
Queen, Louise L., comp. *Methodist History Index, 1962–1982*. Madison, NJ: General Commission on Archives and History, UMC, 1984.
Rose, E. Alan. *A Checklist of British Methodist Periodicals*. London: World Methodist Historical Society, 1981.
Rowe, Kenneth E., ed. *Methodist Union Catalog, Pre-1976 Imprints*. Lanham, MD: Scarecrow Press, 1975–. 7 vols. (A-Le) published to date.
Turner, Kristen D. *A Guide to Materials on Women in the Untied Methodist Church Archives*. Madison, NJ: The General Commission on Archives and History, UMC, 1995.
Walls, Francine E. *The Free Methodist Church: A Bibliography*. Winona Lake, IN: Free Methodist Historical Center, 1977.
Warrick, Susan E. *Women in the Wesleyan and United Methodist Traditions: A Bibliography*. Madison, NJ: General Commission on Archives and History, UMC, 2003.

Encyclopedias/Dictionaries

Abraham, William J., and James E. Kirby, eds. *The Oxford Handbook to Methodist Studies*. Oxford: Oxford University Press, 2009.
Daniel, W. Harrison. *Historical Atlas of the Methodist Movement*. Nashville: Abingdon Press, 2009.
Harmon, Nolan B., ed. *Encyclopedia of World Methodism*. 2 vols. Nashville, TN: United Methodist Publishing House, 1974.
Kostlevy, William C., and Gari-Anne Patzwald. *Historical Dictionary of the Holiness Movement*. Lanham, MD: Scarecrow Press, 2001.
Lewis, Donald M. *The Blackwell Dictionary of Evangelical Biography*. 2 vols. Oxford: Blackwell, 1995.
Matthews, Rex D. *Timetables of History: For Students of Methodism*. Nashville, TN: Abingdon Press, 2007.
Vickers, John A., ed. *A Dictionary of Methodism in Britain and Ireland*. Peterborough: Epworth Press, 2000. Expanded edition available online at http://www.wesleyhistoricalsociety.org.uk (accessed 1/14/10).
Yrigoyen, Charles, Jr., and Susan E. Warrick, eds. *Historical Dictionary of Methodism*. Lanham, MD: Scarecrow Press, 2005.

General Histories

World Methodism

Born, Ethel. *From Memory to Hope: A Narrative History of the Areas of the World Federation of Methodist Women*. Ferrum, VA: Ferrum College, 2000.
Cracknell, Kenneth, and Susan J. White, eds. *An Introduction to World Methodism*. Cambridge: Cambridge University Press, 2005.
Hempton, David. *Methodism: Empire of the Spirit*. New Haven, CT: Yale University Press, 2005.
Yrigoyen, Charles, Jr., ed. *The Global Impact of the Wesleyan Traditions and Their Related Movements*. Lanham, MD: Scarecrow Press, 2002.

Great Britain and Ireland

Bebbington, David. *Holiness in Nineteenth Century England*. Carlisle, PA: Paternoster, 2002.
Beckerlegge, Oliver A. *The United Methodist Free Churches*. London: Epworth Press, 1957.
Brake, George Thompson. *Policy and Politics in British Methodism, 1932–1982*. London: Edsall, 1984.
Carwardine, Richard. *Trans-Atlantic Revivalism: Popular Evangelicalism in Britain and America, 1790–1865*. Westport, CT: Greenwood Press, 1978.
Chilcote, Paul Wesley. *Early Methodist Spirituality: Selected Women's Writings*. Nashville, TN: Kingswood Books, 2007.
——. *John Wesley and the Women Preachers of Early Methodism*. ATLA Monograph Series No. 25. Metuchen, NJ: Scarecrow Press, 1991.
Church, Leslie F. *The Early Methodist People*. London: Epworth Press, 1948.
——. *More About the Early Methodist People*. London: Epworth Press, 1949.
Cooney, D. Levistone. *The Methodists in Ireland: A Short History*. Dublin: Blackrock, 2001.
Davies, Rupert E. *Methodism*. 2nd ed. London: Epworth Press, 1985.
Davies, Rupert E., and Gordon Rupp, eds. *A History of the Methodist Church in Great Britain*. 4 vols. London: Epworth Press, 1975–1987.
Ditchfield, B. M. *The Evangelical Revival*. London: UCL Press, 1998.
Dreyer, Frederick. *The Genesis of Methodism*. Bethlehem, PA: Lehigh University Press, 1999.
Graham, E. Dorothy. *Saved to Serve: The Story of the Wesley Deaconess Order, 1890–1978*. Werrington: Methodist Publishing House, 2002.
Graham, E. Dorothy, and Verna E. Mossong. *Women Local Preachers in the British Isles*. New Zealand: Wesley Historical Society, 1999.
Harding, Alan. *The Countess of Huntingdon's Connexion: A Sect in Action in Eighteenth-Century England*. Oxford: Oxford University Press, 2003.
Heitzenrater, Richard P. *Mirror and Memory: Reflections on Early Methodism*. Nashville: Kingswood Books, 1989.
Hempton, David. *The Religion of the People: Methodism and Popular Religion c.1750–1900*. London: Routledge, 1996.
Jeffery, Frederick. *Irish Methodism: An Historical Account of its Tradition, Theology and Influences*. Belfast: Epworth House, 1964.
Kent, John. *The Age of Disunity*. London: Epworth Press, 1966.
——. *Wesley and the Wesleyans: Religion in Eighteenth-Century England*. Cambridge: Cambridge University Press, 2002.
Noll, Mark A. *The Rise of Evangelicalism: The Age of Edwards, Whitefield, and the Wesleys*. Leicester: Inter-Varsity, 2004.
Olsen, Gerald W., ed. *Religion and Revolution in Early Industrial England: The Halevy Thesis and its Critics*. Lanham, MD: University Press of America, 1990.
Shaw, Thomas. *The Bible Christians, 1815–1907*. London: Epworth Press, 1965.
Taggart, Norman E. *The Irish in World Methodism, 1760–1900*. London: Epworth Press, 1986.
Turner, John Munsey. *John Wesley: The Evangelical Revival and the Rise of Methodism in England*. Peterborough: Epworth Press, 2002.
——. *Modern Methodism in England, 1932–1998*. Peterborough: Epworth Press, 1998.

Bibliography

Valenze, Deborah Mary. *Prophetic Sons and Daughters: Female Preaching and Popular Religion in Industrial England*. Princeton, NJ: Princeton University Press, 1985.
Vickers, John, ed. *The Journals of Dr. Thomas Coke*. Nashville, TN: Kingswood Books, 2005.
Watson, David L. *The Early Methodist Class Meeting: Its Origins and Significance*. Nashville, TN: Discipleship Resources, 1985.
Werner, Julia S. *The Primitive Methodist Connexion: Its Background and Early History*. Madison, WI: University of Wisconsin Press, 1984.
Wickes, Michael J. L. *The West Country Preachers: A New History of the Bible Christian Church (1815–1907)*. London: Appledore, 1987.

North America

Canada
Airhart, Phyllis D. *Serving the Present Age: Revivalism, Progressivism and Methodist Tradition in Canada*. Montreal: McGill-Queens University Press, 1992.
Clifford, N. Keith. *The Resistance to Church Union in Canada, 1904–1939*. Vancouver: University of British Columbia Press, 1985.
Grant, John Webster, ed. *The Church in the Canadian Era*. Toronto, ON: Ryerson, 1972.
Grant, John Webster, and Charles H. H. Scobie. *The Contribution of Methodism to Atlantic Canada*. Montreal: McGill-Queen's University Press, 1992.
Jesske, Theodore. *Pioneers of Faith: A History of the Evangelical Church in Canada*. Three Hills, Alberta: EMF Press, 1985.
Muir, Elizabeth. *Petticoats in the Pulpit: The Story of Early Nineteenth Century Methodist Women Preachers in Upper Canada*. Toronto, ON: United Church Publishing House, 1991.
Rawlyk, George A. *The Canadian Protestant Experience, 1760–1990*. Montreal: McGill-Queen's University Press, 1984.
Semple, Neil. *The Lord's Dominion: The History of Canadian Methodism*. Montreal: McGill-Queen's University Press, 1996.
Van Die, Marguerite. *An Evangelical Mind: Nathanael Burwash and the Methodist Tradition in Canada, 1839–1918*. Montreal: McGill-Queen's University Press, 1989.

United States
Andrews, Dee. *The Methodists and Revolutionary America, 1760–1800: The Shaping of an Evangelical Culture*. Princeton, NJ: Princeton University Press, 2000.
Bailey, Julius. *Around the Family Altar: Domesticity in the African Methodist Episcopal Church, 1865–1900*. Gainesville, FL: University Press of Florida, 2005.
Baker, Frank. *From Wesley to Asbury: Studies in Early American Methodism*. Durham, NC: Duke University Press, 1976.
Baldwin, Lewis V. *'Invisible' Strands in African Methodism: A History of the African Union Methodist Protestant and Union American Methodist Episcopal Churches, 1805–1980*. Metuchen, NJ: Scarecrow Press, 1983.
Behney, J. Bruce, and Paul H. Eller. *The History of the Evangelical United Brethren*. Nashville, TN: Abingdon Press, 1979.

Bibliography

Born, Ethel W. *By My Spirit: The Story of Methodist Protestant Women in Mission, 1879–1939.* New York: Women's Division, General Board of Global Ministries, UMC, 1990.

Bradley, David H. *A History of the A.M.E. Zion Church, 1796–1968.* 2 vols. Nashville, TN: AME Zion Publishing House, 1956–1960.

Brooks Blair, Sarah D. *The Evangelical United Brethren Church: A Historical Sampler.* Nashville, TN: United Methodist Publishing House, 2000.

Bucke, Emory S., ed. *History of American Methodism.* 3 vols. Nashville, TN: Abingdon Press, 1964.

Case, Riley B. *Evangelical and Methodist: A Popular History.* Nashville, TN: Abingdon Press, 1964.

Clark, Elmer T., J. Manning Potts, and Jacob S. Payton, eds. *The Journal and Letters of Francis Asbury.* London: Epworth Press; Nashville, TN: Abingdon Press, 1958.

Daniels, George M. *Turning Corners: Reflections of African Americans in The United Methodist Church from 1961 to 1993.* Dayton, OH: General Council on Ministries, UMC, 1997.

Davis, Morris L., Jr. *The Methodist Unification: Christianity and the Politics of the Jim Crow Era.* New York: New York University Press, 2007.

Dayton, Donald W. *Discovering an Evangelical Heritage.* Peabody, MA: Hendrickson Publishers, 1988. Reprint of the 1976 edition.

Dickerson, Dennis C. *A Liberated Past: Explorations in A.M.E. Church History.* Nashville, TN: AME Sunday School Union, 2003.

Dodson, Jualynne E. *Engendering Church: Women, Power, and the AME Church.* Lanham, MD: Rowman & Littlefield, 2002.

Dougherty, Mary Agnes Theresa. *My Calling to Fulfill: Deaconesses in the United Methodist Tradition.* New York: Women's Division, General Board of Global Ministries, UMC, 1997.

Frey, Robert L. *The Making of an American Church: Essays Commemorating the Jubilee Year of the Evangelical United Brethren Church.* Lanham, MD.: Scarecrow Press, Center for the Study of World Christian Revitalization Movements, 2007.

Frey, Sylvia R., and Betty Wood. *Come Shouting to Zion: African American Protestantism in the American South and British Caribbean to 1830.* Chapel Hill, NC: University of North Carolina Press, 1998.

George, Carol V. R. *Segregated Sabbaths: Richard Allen and the Rise of the Independent Black Churches, 1760–1840.* New York: Oxford University Press, 1973.

Gonzalez, Justo L., ed. *Each in Our Own Tongue: A History of Hispanic United Methodism.* Nashville, TN: Abingdon Press, 1991.

Gregg, Howard D. *History of the African Methodist Episcopal Church: The Black Church in Action.* Nashville, TN: AME Church Sunday School Union, 1980.

Guillermo, Artemio R., ed. *Churches Aflame: Asian Americans and United Methodism.* Nashville, TN: Abingdon Press, 1991.

Hatch, Nathan O. *The Democratization of American Christianity.* New Haven, CT: Yale University Press, 1989.

Hatch, Nathan O., and John H. Wigger. *Methodism and the Shaping of American Culture.* Nashville, TN: Kingswood Books, 2001.

Heisey, Terry M., Robert George Hower, Leon O. Hynson, and John E. Moyer. *Evangelical from the Beginning: A History of the Evangelical Congregational Church and its Predecessors – the Evangelical Association and the United Evangelical Church.* Lexington, KY: Emeth, 2006.

Hildebrand, Reginald F. *The Times Were Strange and Stirring: Methodist Preachers and the Crisis of Emancipation.* Durham, NC: Duke University Press, 1995.
Kaufman, Paul Leslie. *'Logical' Luther Lee and the Methodist War against Slavery.* Lanham, MD: Scarecrow Press, 2000.
Keller, Rosemary Skinner, Hilah F. Thomas, and Louise L. Queen, eds. *Women in New Worlds: Historical Perspectives on the Wesleyan Tradition.* 2 vols. Nashville, TN: Abingdon Press, 1981–1982.
Kinghorn, Kenneth C. *The Heritage of American Methodism.* Nashville, TN: Abingdon Press, 1999.
Kirby, James E., Russell E. Richey, and Kenneth E. Rowe. *The Methodists.* Westport, CT: Greenwood Press, 1996.
Lakey, Othal L. *The History of the C.M.E. Church.* Memphis, TN: CME Publishing House, 1985.
Lawrence, William B., Dennis M. Campbell, and Russell E. Richey. *The People(s) Called Methodist: Forms and Reforms of Their Life.* Nashville, TN: Abingdon Press, 1997.
McEllhenney, John G., ed. *United Methodism in America: A Compact History.* Nashville, TN: Abingdon Press, 1992.
McLeister, Ira Ford. *Conscience and Commitment: The History of the Wesleyan Methodist Church of America.* 4th ed. Wesleyan History Series, vol.1. Marion, IN: Wesley Press, 1976.
Marston, Leslie Ray. *From Age to Age a Living Witness: A Historical Interpretation of Free Methodism's First Hundred Years.* Winona Lake, IN: Light and Life Press, 1960.
Melton, J. Gordon. *A Will to Choose: The Origins of African American Methodism.* Lanham, MD: Rowman & Littlefield, 2007.
Murray, Peter C. *Methodists and the Crucible of Race, 1930–1975.* Columbia, MO: University of Missouri Press, 2004.
Noley, Homer, ed. *First White Frost: Native Americans and United Methodism.* Nashville, TN: Abingdon Press, 1991.
Norwood, Frederick A. *The Story of American Methodism: A History of the United Methodists and Their Relations.* Nashville, TN: Abingdon Press, 1974.
———, ed. *Sourcebook of American Methodism.* Nashville, TN: Parthenon Press, 1996.
O'Malley, J. Steven. *Early German American Evangelicalism: Pietist Sources on Discipleship and Sanctification.* Lanham, MD: Scarecrow Press, 1995.
Ortiz, Leonard. *The Preservation of Native American Practices in The United Methodist Church: A Case Study in Recent Protestant Missions.* Lewiston, NY: Edwin Mellen Press, 2008.
Richardson, Harry V. *Dark Salvation: The Story of Methodism as It Developed Among Blacks in America.* New York: Doubleday, 1976.
Richey, Russell E. *Early American Methodism.* Bloomington, IN.: Indiana University Press, 1991.
———. *The Methodist Conference in America: A History.* Nashville, TN: Kingswood Books, 1996.
Richey, Russell E., Dennis M. Campbell, and William B. Lawrence, eds. *Methodism and American Culture.* 3 vols. Nashville, TN: Abingdon Press, 1997–1999.
Richey, Russell E., and Kenneth E. Rowe, eds. *Rethinking Methodist History.* Nashville, TN: Kingswood Books, 1985.

Bibliography

Richey, Russell E., Kenneth E. Rowe, and Jean Miller Schmidt, eds. *The Methodist Experience in America: A Sourcebook*. Nashville, TN: Abingdon Press, 2000.
Richey, Russell E., Kenneth E. Rowe, and Jean Miller Schmidt, eds. *Perspectives on American Methodism: Interpretive Essays*. Nashville, TN: Kingswood Books, 1993.
Salter, Darius. *America's Bishop: The Life of Francis Asbury*. Nappanee, IN: Evangel Publishing House, 2003.
Sano, Roy I. *From Every Nation without Number: Racial and Ethnic Diversity in United Methodism*. Nashville, TN: Abingdon Press, 1982.
Schneider, A. Gregory. *The Way of the Cross Leads Home: The Domestication of American Methodism*. Bloomington, IN: Indiana University Press, 1993.
Schmidt, Jean Miller. *Grace Sufficient: A History of Women in American Methodism, 1760–1939*. Nashville, TN: Abingdon Press, 1999.
Shockley, Grant S., ed. *Heritage and Hope: The African American Presence in United Methodism*. Nashville, TN: Abingdon Press, 1991.
Sledge, Robert Watson. *Hands on the Ark: The Struggle for Change in the Methodist Episcopal Church, South, 1914–1939*. Lake Junaluska, NC: General Commission on Archives and History, United Methodist Church, 1975.
Strong, Douglas M. *Perfectionist Politics: Ecclesiastical Abolitionism and the Tensions of American Democracy*. Syracuse, NY: Syracuse University Press, 1997.
Sweet, Leonard I., ed. *The Evangelical Tradition in America*. Macon, GA: Mercer University Press, 1984.
Sweet, William W. *Methodism in American History*. Rev. ed. Nashville, TN: Abingdon Press, 1953. First published in 1933.
——— . *Religion on the America Frontier, 1783–1940: The Methodists, a Collection of Source Materials*. New York: Cooper Square, 1964. Reprint of 1946 edition.
Thomas, James S. *Methodism's Racial Dilemma: The Story of the Central Jurisdiction*. Nashville, TN: Abingdon Press, 1992.
Tipton, Steven M. *Public Pulpits: Methodists and Mainline Churches in the Moral Arguments of Public Life*. Chicago, IL: University of Chicago Press; Bristol: University Presses Marketing, 2007.
Wacker, Grant. *Heaven Below: Early Pentecostals and American Culture*. Cambridge, MA: Harvard University Press, 2001.
Washburn, Paul. *An Unfinished Church: A Brief History of the Union of the Evangelical United Brethren Church and The Methodist Church*. Nashville, TN: Abingdon Press, 1984.
Wigger, John H. *Taking Heaven by Storm: Methodism and the Rise of Popular Christianity in America*. Urbana, IL: University of Illinois Press, 2001.
Williams, William H. *The Garden of Methodism: The Delmarva Peninsula, 1769–1820*. Wilmington, DE: Scholarly Resources, 1984.
Yrigoyen, Charles, Jr., John G. McEllhenney, and Kenneth E. Rowe. *United Methodism at Forty: Looking Back, Looking Forward*. Nashville, TN: Abingdon Press, 2008.

Africa

Atwell, Peggy. *Take Our Hands: The Methodist Church of Southern Africa Women's Auxiliary, 1916–1996*. Cape Town: Methodist Church of Southern Africa Women's Auxiliary, 1997.
Banana, Canaan S. *A Century of Methodism in Zimbabwe, 1891–1991*. Gweru: Mambo Press, 1996.

Bibliography

Bartels, Francis L. *The Roots of Ghana Methodism*. Cambridge: Cambridge University Press, 1965.
Campbell, James T. *Songs of Zion: The African Methodist Episcopal Church in the United States and South Africa*. New York: Oxford University Press, 1995.
Coan, Josephus R. *Flying Sparks: The Genesis of African Methodism in South Africa*. Nashville, TN: AMEC Publishing House, 1987.
Dong, Peter Marubitoba. *The History of the United Methodist Church in Nigeria*. Nashville, TN: Abingdon Press, 2000.
Hastings, Adrian. *The Church in Africa: 1450–1950*. New York: Oxford University Press, 1994.
Isichei, Elizabeth. *A History of Christianity in Africa*. Grand Rapids, MI: Wm. B. Eerdmans, 1995.
Kasongo, Michael O. *History of the Methodist Church in Central Congo, 1912–1997*. Lanham, MD: University Press of America, 1997.
Kurewa, John Wesley. *The Church in Mission: A Short History of The United Methodist Church in Zimbabwe, 1897–1997*. Nashville, TN: Abingdon Press, 1997.
Mears, W. Gordon. *Methodism in the Cape: An Outline*. Cape Town: Methodist Publishing House, 1973.
Nthamburi, Zablon. *A History of the Methodist Church in Kenya*. Nairobi: Uzima Press, 1982.
Okpo, S. K. *A Brief History of the Methodist Church in Eastern Nigeria*. Oron: Manson, 1985.
Potter, Jennifer. *The Origins and Development of Methodist Mission Work in the Area of Present Day Botswana*. Botswana: University of Botswana, 1995.
Taunyane, L. M., and Gabriel J. Leeuw. *The Methodist Church in Africa, 1933–2001*. Wellington: Lux Verbi, 2001.
Theilen, Uta. *Gender, Race, Power, and Religion: Women in the Methodist Church of Southern Africa in Post-apartheid Society*. New York: Peter Lang, 2005.
Xozwa, L. W. M. *Methodist Church in Africa: History of the Church*. Grahamstown: Cory Library for Historical Research, Rhodes University, 1989.

Asia/Australasia

Alejandro, Dionisio Diesta. *From Darkness to Light: A Brief Chronicle of the Beginnings and Spread of Methodism in the Philippines*. Quezon City: United Methodist Church, Philippines Central Conference, Board of Communications and Publications, 1974.
Allardice, R. W. *The Methodist Story in Samoa, 1828–1984*. Apia: Methodist Conference of Samoa, 1984.
Baker, Marcia. *For Others with Love: A Story of Early Sisters and Methodist Deaconesses*. Christchurch: Baker Family Publishing, 2007.
Breward, Ian. *A History of the Australian Churches*. St. Leonards: Allen & Unwin, 1993.
Champness, Beryl. *The Servant Ministry: The Methodist Deaconess Order in Victoria and Tasmania*. Melbourne: Uniting Church Press, 1996.
Cunningham, Floyd T. *Holiness Abroad: Nazarene Missions in Asia*. Lanham, MD: Scarecrow Press, 2003.
Davidson, Allan. *Christianity in Aotearoa*. Wellington: Education for Ministry, 1991.

Dawson, J. B. *Your Kingdom Come on Earth: Methodist Social Concerns in New Zealand.* Christchurch: Christchurch Methodist Mission, 1998.
Deats, Richard L. *The Story of Methodism in the Philippines.* Manila: Union Theological Seminary, 1964.
Forman, Charles W. *The Island Churches of the South Pacific: Emergence in the Twentieth Century.* Maryknoll, NY: Orbis Books, 1982.
Garrett, John. *Footsteps in the Sea: Christianity in Oceania to World War II.* Suva: Institute of Pacific Studies, 1992; Geneva: World Council of Churches, 1992.
Goh, Robbie B. H. *Sparks of Grace: The Story of Methodism in Asia.* Singapore: The Methodist Church in Singapore, 2003.
Grayson, James H. *Korea: A Religious History.* New York: Oxford University Press, 1989.
Hollister, John N. *The Centenary of the Methodist Church in Southern Asia.* Lucknow: Lucknow Publishing House, 1956.
Hunt, A. D. *This Side of Heaven: A History of Methodism in South Australia.* Adelaide: Lutheran Publishing House, 1985.
Krummel, John W., ed. *A Biographical Dictionary of Methodist Missionaries to Japan, 1873–1973.* Tokyo: Kyo Bun Kwan, 1996.
Krummel, John W. *The Methodist Protestant Church in Japan.* Two parts. Tokyo: Aoyama Gakuin University, 1982–1983.
Lacy, Walter N. *A Hundred Years of China Methodism.* Nashville, TN: Abingdon-Cokesbury, 1948.
Latukefu, Sione. *Church and State in Tonga: The Wesleyan Methodist Missionaries and Political Development, 1822–1875.* Honolulu: University Press of Hawaii, 1974.
Maiuka, Eare. *Methodist Church in Papua New Guinea.* Papua: University of Papua New Guinea Library, 1975.
Senior, Geoffrey R. *The China Experience: A Study of the Methodist Mission in China.* Peterborough: WMHS Publications, 1994.
Walker, Alan. *Heritage without End: A Story to Tell to the Nation.* Melbourne: Methodist Church of Australia, 1953.

Latin America and the Caribbean

Bastian, Jean-Pierre. *Protestantismo yo sociedad en México.* México: CUPSA, 1984.
Braithwaite, Joan A. *Methodism in the Caribbean: 200+ and Moving On: A Synopsis with Biographical Sketches and a Select Bibliography.* Bridgetown: Methodist Church in the Caribbean and the Americas, 1998.
Díaz Acosta, Juan. *Historia de la Iglesia Evangélica Unida de Puerto Rico: Obra Evangélica para el Cincuentenario en Puerto Rico, 1899–1949.* San Juan: Iglesia Evangélica Unida de Puerto Rico, 1949.
Duque Zúñiga, José, ed. *La Tradición Protestante en la Teologia Latinoamericana.* San José: DEI, 1983.
Forker, Wilbert. *Born in Slavery: The Story of Methodism in Anguilla and Its Influence in the Caribbean.* Edinburgh: Dunedin Academic Press, 2003.
González, Justo L. *The Development of Christianity in the Latin Caribbean.* Grand Rapids, MI: Wm. B. Eerdmans, 1969.
Griffiths, Leslie. *History of Methodism in Haiti.* Port-au-Prince: Imprimerie Méthodiste, 1991.
Literature Department of the Methodist Church. *For Ever Beginning: Two Hundred*

Bibliography

Years of Methodism in the Western Area. Kingston: Literature Department of the Methodist Church, Jamaica District, 1960.

Methodist Church. *Kindling of the Flame: How the Methodist Church Expanded in the Caribbean*. Grand Rapids, MI: Wm. B. Eerdmans, 1969.

Míguez Bonino, José. *Faces of Latin American Protestantism*. Grand Rapids, MI: Wm. B. Eerdmans, 1997.

Neblett, Sterling A. *Methodism's First Fifty Years in Cuba*. Macon, GA: Wesleyan College, 1966.

Sánchez, Beatriz Cano. *El Protestantismo en México, 1850–1940: La Iglesia Metodista Episcopal*. México: Instituto Nacional de Antropologia e Historia, 1995.

Yaremko, Jason M. *U.S. Protestant Missions in Cuba: From Independence to Castro*. Gainesville, FL: University of Florida Press, 2000.

Europe

Garber, Paul Neff. *The Methodists of Continental Europe*. New York: Board of Missions and Church Extension, the Methodist Church, 1949.

Hagen, Odd. *Preludes to Methodism in Northern Europe*. Oslo: Norsk Forlagsselskap, 1961.

Istomina, Lydia P. *Bringing Hidden Things to Light: The Revival of Methodism in Russia*. Nashville, TN: Abingdon Press, 1996.

Kimbrough, S T, Jr. *A Pictorial Panorama of Early Russian Methodism, 1889–1931*. Madison, NJ: General Commission on Archives and History, UMC, 2009.

——— . *Methodism in Russia and the Baltic States: History and Renewal*. Nashville, TN: Abingdon Press, 1995.

Kissack, Reginald. *Methodists in Italy*. London: Cargate Press, 1960.

Ludlow, Peter W. *The Churches in the European Union*. London: Methodist Church Division of Social Responsibility, 1994.

Nausner, Wilhelm. *Be Eager to Maintain the Unity of the Spirit Through the Bond of Peace: A Short History of the Geneva Area of The United Methodist Church*. Cincinnati, OH: General Board of Global Ministries, UMC, 1985.

Ramet, Sabrina P., ed. *Protestantism and Politics in Eastern Europe and Russia: Communist and Postcommunist Eras*. Durham, NC: Duke University Press, 1992.

Short, Roy H. *History of Methodism in Europe*. Nashville, TN: Office of the Secretary of the Council of Bishops, UMC, 1980.

Streiff, Patrick Ph. *Methodism in Europe, 19th and 20th Century*. Tallinn: Baltic Methodist Theological Seminary, 2004.

Van den Berg, Johannes, and W. Stephen Gunter. *John Wesley and the Netherlands*. Nashville, TN: Kingswood Books, 2002.

Topical Studies

Evangelism

Brown, Kenneth O. *Holy Ground: A Study of the American Camp Meeting*. New York: Garland, 1992.

Chilcote, Paul Wesley. *The Wesleyan Tradition: A Paradigm for Renewal*. Nashville, TN: Abingdon Press, 2002.

Collins, Kenneth J., and John R. Tyson, eds. *Conversion in the Wesleyan Tradition*. Nashville, TN: Abingdon Press, 2001.

Dunnam, Maxie D. *Going on to Salvation: A Study in the Wesleyan Tradition.* Nashville, TN: Discipleship Resources, 1990.
Jones, Scott J. *The Evangelistic Love of God and Neighbor.* Nashville, TN: Abingdon Press, 2003.
Logan, James C. *Theology and Evangelism in the Wesleyan Heritage.* Nashville, TN: Kingswood Books, 1994.
Outler, Albert C. *Evangelism and Theology in the Wesleyan Spirit.* Nashville, TN: Discipleship Resources, 1996.
Tuttle, Robert G., Jr. *On Giant Shoulders: The History, Role and Influence of the Evangelist in the Movement called Methodism.* Nashville, TN: Discipleship Resources, 1984.

Holiness
Black, Robert E., and Wayne E. Caldwell, ed. *Reformers and Revivalists: The History of the Wesleyan Church.* Indianapolis, IN: Wesley Press, 1992.
Dayton, Donald W. *Discovering an Evangelical Heritage.* Peabody, MA: Hendrickson Publishers, 1988. Reprint of the 1976 edition.
―――. *The Theological Roots of Pentecostalism.* Metuchen, NJ: Scarecrow Press, 1987.
Dieter, Melvin E. *The 19th Century Holiness Movement.* Kansas, MO: Beacon Hill Press of Kansas City, 1998.
Jones, Charles Edwin. *Perfectionist Persuasion: The Holiness Movement and American Methodism, 1867–1936.* Metuchen, NJ: Scarecrow Press, 2002.
McKenna, David L. *A Future with a History: The Wesleyan Witness of the Free Methodist Church.* Indianapolis, IN: Light and Life Press, 1995.
Robb, Edmund W. *The Spirit Who Will Not be Tamed: The Wesleyan Message and the Charismatic Experience.* Anderson, IN: Bristol House, 1997.
Smith, Timothy L. *Called unto Holiness: The Story of the Nazarenes, the Formative Years.* Kansas, MO: Nazarene, 1962.
Snyder, Howard A., with Daniel V. Runyon. *The Divided Flame: Wesleyans and the Charismatic Renewal.* Grand Rapids, MI: William B. Eerdmans, 1997.
Stanley, Susie Cunningham. *Holy Boldness: Women Preachers' Autobiographies and the Sanctified Self.* Knoxville, TN: University of Tennessee Press, 2002.
Synan, Vinson. *The Holiness-Pentecostal Tradition: Charismatic Movements in the Twentieth Century.* Grand Rapids, MI: William B. Eerdmans, 1997.
―――. *The Century of the Holy Spirit: 100 Years of Pentecostal and Charismatic Renewal, 1901–2001.* Nashville, TN: Thomas Nelson Publishers, 2001.
Thomas, Paul W. *The Days of Our Pilgrimage: The History of the Pilgrim Holiness Church.* Wesleyan History Series, vol. 2. Marion, IN: Wesley Press, 1976.

Missions
Barclay, Wade C., and J. Tremayne Copplestone. *History of Methodist Missions.* 4 vols. New York: Board of Missions, the Methodist Church, 1949–1957.
Daugherty, Ruth. *The Missionary Spirit: The History of Mission of the Methodist Protestant Church, 1830–1939.* New York: General Board of Global Ministries, The United Methodist Church, 2004.
Gesling, Linda. *Mirror and Beacon: The History of Mission of The Methodist Church, 1939–1968.* New York: General Board of Global Ministries, The United Methodist Church, 2004.

Harman, Robert J. *From Missions to Mission: The History of Mission of The United Methodist Church, 1968–2000*. New York: General Board of Global Ministries, The United Methodist Church, 2005.

Hill, Patricia R. *The World Their Household: The American Women's Foreign Mission Movement and Cultural Transformation, 1870–1920*. Ann Arbor, MI: University of Michigan Press, 1985.

Hutchison, William R. *Errand to the World: American Protestant Thought and Foreign Missions*. Chicago, IL: University of Chicago Press, 1987.

Koga, Sumio, comp. *A Centennial Legacy: History of the Japanese Christian Missions in North America, 1877–1977*. Chicago, Nobart, 1977.

O'Malley, J. Steven. *'On the Journey Home': The History of Mission of the Evangelical United Brethren Church, 1946–1968*. New York: General Board of Global Ministries, 2003.

Robert, Dana Lee. *American Women in Mission: A Social History of Their Thought and Practice*. Macon, GA.: Mercer University Press, 1996.

Sledge, Robert W. *Five Dollars and Myself: The History of Mission of The Methodist Episcopal Church, South, 1845–1939*. New York: General Board of Global Ministries, The United Methodist Church, 2005.

Yrigoyen, Charles, Jr. *The Global Impact of the Wesleyan Traditions and Their Related Movements*. Lanham, MD: Scarecrow Press, 2002.

Social Reform

Brendlinger, Irv A. *Social Justice through the Eyes of Wesley: John Wesley's Theological Challenge to Slavery*. Guelph, ON: Joshua Press, 2006.

Edwards, Wendy J. Deichmann, and Carolyn De Swarte Gifford. *Gender and the Social Gospel*. Urbana, IL: University of Illinois Press, 2003.

Eli, R. George. *Social Holiness: John Wesley's Thinking on Christian Community and its Relationship to the Social Order*. New York: Peter Lang, 1993.

Gorrell, Donald K. *The Age of Social Responsibility: The Social Gospel in the Progressive Era, 1900–1920*. Macon, GA: Mercer University Press, 1988.

Heitzenrater, Richard P., ed. *The Poor and the People Called Methodists*. Nashville, TN: Kingswood Books, 2002.

Jennings, Theodore W. *Good News to the Poor: John Wesley's Evangelical Economics*. Nashville, TN: Abingdon Press, 1990.

Keller, Rosemary Skinner, ed. *Spirituality and Social Responsibility: The Vocational Vision of Women in the Methodist Tradition*. Nashville, TN: Abingdon Press, 1993.

Knepper, Jeanne Gayle. *Thy Kingdom Come: The Methodist Federation for Social Service and Human Rights, 1907–1948*. Staten Island, NY: Methodist Federation for Social Action, 1996.

Knotts, Alice G. *Lifting Up Hope, Living Out Justice: Methodist Women and the Social Gospel*. S.I.: Frontrowliving Press, 2007.

Long, Stephen D. *Living the Discipline: United Methodist Theological Reflection on War, Civilization and Holiness*. Grand Rapids, MI: Eerdmans, 1992.

Meeks, M. Douglas, ed. *The Portion of the Poor: Good News to the Poor in the Wesleyan Tradition*. Nashville, TN: Kingswood Books, 1992.

Methodist Federation for Social Action. *Pioneers in the Faith: The Methodist*

Federation for Social Action at 100 Years, 1907–2007. Washington, DC: MFSA, 2007.
Muelder, Walter G. *Methodism and Society in the Twentieth Century*. Nashville, TN: Abingdon Press, 1961.

Sunday Schools
Bowen, Cawthon A. *Child and Church: A History of Methodist Church School Curriculum*. New York: Abingdon Press, 1960.
Boylan, Anne M. *Sunday School: The Formation of an American Institution, 1790–1880*. New Haven, CT: Yale University Press, 1988.
Lynn, Robert W. *The Big Little School: Two Hundred Years of the Sunday School*. Birmingham, AL: Religious Education Press, 1980.
Sangster, Paul. *Pity My Simplicity: The Evangelical Revival and the Religious Education of Children, 1738–1800*. London: Epworth Press, 1963.
Seymour, Jack. *From Sunday School to Church School: Continuities in Protestant Christian Education in the U.S., 1860–1929*. Washington, DC: University Press of America, 1982.
Wimberly, Anne Streaty. *Soul Stories: African American Christian Education*. Nashville, TN: Abingdon Press, 1994.

Theology and Doctrine

John and Charles Wesley
Abelove, Henry. *The Evangelist of Desire: John Wesley and the Methodists*. Stanford, CA: Stanford University Press, 1990.
Baker, Frank. *John Wesley and the Church of England*. 2nd ed. London: Epworth, 2000.
Beckerlegge, Oliver A., ed. *John Wesley's Writings on Roman Catholicism*. London: Protestant Truth Society, 1995.
——, ed. *The Shorthand of Charles Wesley*. Madison, NJ: Charles Wesley Society, 2002.
Brown, Earl Kent. *Women of Mr. Wesley's Methodism*. New York: Edwin Mellen Press, 1983.
Bullen, Donald A. *A Man of One Book? John Wesley's Interpretation and Use of the Bible*. Milton Keynes: Paternoster, 2007.
Campbell, Ted A. *John Wesley and Christian Antiquity: Religious Vision and Cultural Change*. Nashville, TN: Kingswood Books, 1991.
Chilcote, Paul Wesley. *Recapturing the Wesleys' Vision: An Introduction to the Faith of John and Charles Wesley*. Downers Grove, IL: InterVarsity Press, 2004.
Edwards, Maldwyn. *Family Circle: A Study of the Epworth Household in Relation to John and Charles Wesley*. London: Epworth Press, 1949.
——. *My Dear Sister: The Story of John Wesley and the Women in His Life*. Manchester: Penwork, 1980.
Green, V. H. H. *John Wesley*. Lanham, MD.: University Press of America, 1987.
Heitzenrater, Richard P. *The Elusive Mr. Wesley*. 2 vols. Nashville, TN: Abingdon Press, 1984.
——. *Wesley and the People Called Methodists*. Nashville, TN: Abingdon Press, 1995.

Bibliography

Hynson, Leon O. *To Reform the Nation: Theological Foundations of Wesley's Ethics.* Grand Rapids, MI: Zondervan, 1984.
Kinghorn, Kenneth C., ed. *The Standard Sermons in Modern English.* Nashville, TN: Abingdon Press, 2003.
Kimbrough, S T, Jr., ed. *Charles Wesley: Poet and Theologian.* Nashville, TN: Kingswood Books, 1992.
Kimbrough, S T, Jr., and Kenneth G. C. Newport, eds. *The Manuscript Journal of the Rev. Charles Wesley, M.A.* Nashville, TN: Kingswood Books, 2007.
Kimbrough, S T, Jr., and Oliver A. Beckerlegge, eds. *The Unpublished Poetical Writings of Charles Wesley.* 3 vols. Nashville, TN: Kingswood Books, 1988–1992.
Lloyd, Gareth. *Charles Wesley and the Struggle for Methodist Identity.* Oxford; New York: Oxford University Press, 2007.
McEllhenney, John G. *John Wesley: A Man Who Shook the Spiritual Earth.* Madison, NJ: General Commission on Archives and History, 1996.
Maddox, Graham, ed. *The Political Writings of John Wesley.* Bristol: Thoemmes, 1998.
Maddox, Randy L., ed. *Aldersgate Reconsidered.* Nashville, TN: Abingdon Press, 1990.
—— and Jason E. Vickers, eds. *The Cambridge Companion to John Wesley.* Cambridge: Cambridge University Press, 2010.
Marquardt, Manfred. *John Wesley's Social Ethics: Praxis and Principles.* Nashville, TN: Abingdon Press, 1992.
Newport, Kenneth G. C. *The Sermons of Charles Wesley: A Critical Edition with Introduction and Notes.* Oxford: Oxford University Press, 2001.
Newport, Kenneth G. C., and Ted Campbell, eds. *Charles Wesley: Life, Literature and Legacy.* Peterborough: Epworth, 2007.
Outler, Albert C. *Theology in the Wesleyan Spirit.* Nashville, TN: Discipleship Resources, 1975.
——. *The Wesleyan Theological Heritage: Essays of Albert C. Outler.* Edited by Thomas C. Oden and Leicester R. Longden. Grand Rapids, MI: Zondervan, 1991.
——, ed. *John Wesley (Library of Protestant Thought).* New York: Oxford University Press, 1964.
Outler, Albert C., and Richard P. Heitzenrater, eds. *John Wesley's Sermons: An Anthology.* Nashville, TN: Abingdon Press, 1991.
Rack, Henry D. *Reasonable Enthusiast: John Wesley and the Rise of Methodism.* London: Epworth Press, 1989.
Rogal, Samuel J. *Susanna Annesley Wesley (1669–1742): A Biography of Strength and Love.* Bristol, IN: Wyndham Hall Press, 2001.
Rowe, Kenneth E., ed. *The Place of Wesley in the Christian Tradition.* Rev. ed. Metuchen, NJ: Scarecrow Press, 1980.
Stone, Ronald H. *John Wesley's Life and Ethics.* Nashville, TN: Abingdon Press, 2001.
Tyson, John R. *Assist Me to Proclaim: The Life and Hymns of Charles Wesley.* Grand Rapids, MI: William B. Eerdmans, 2007.
——, ed. *Charles Wesley: A Reader.* New York: Oxford University Press, 1989.
——. *Charles Wesley on Sanctification: A Biographical and Theological Study.* Salem, OH: Schmul, 1992.
Vickers, John A. *Charles Wesley.* Peterborough: Foundery Press, 1990.

Bibliography

Wallace, Charles, Jr. *Susanna Wesley: The Complete Writings.* Oxford: Oxford University Press, 1997.
Wesley, John. *The Works of John Wesley.* Bicentennial ed. Projected 35 vols. Nashville, TN: Abingdon Press, 1978–.
Yrigoyen, Charles, Jr. *John Wesley: Holiness of Heart and Life.* Nashville, TN: Abingdon Press, 1999.

Doctrine

Campbell, Ted A. *Methodist Doctrine: The Essentials.* Nashville, TN: Abingdon Press, 1999.
Collins, Kenneth J. *John Wesley: A Theological Journey.* Nashville, TN: Abingdon Press, 2003.
——— . *The Scripture Way of Salvation: The Heart of Wesley's Theology.* Nashville, TN: Abingdon Press, 1997.
——— . *The Theology of John Wesley: Holy Love and the Shape of Grace.* Nashville, TN: Abingdon Press, 2007.
Cushman, Robert E. *John Wesley's Experimental Divinity: Studies in Methodist Doctrinal Standards.* Nashville, TN: Kingswood Books, 1989.
Gunter, W. Stephen, ed. *Wesley and the Quadrilateral: Renewing the Conversation.* Nashville, TN: Abingdon Press, 1997.
Jones, Scott J. *United Methodist Doctrine: The Extreme Center.* Nashville, TN: Abingdon Press, 2002.
Langford, Thomas A., ed. *Doctrine and Theology in The United Methodist Church.* Nashville, TN: Kingswood Books, 1990.
——— , comp. *Practical Divinity: Theology in the Wesleyan Tradition.* Nashville, TN: Abingdon Press, 1983.
——— , comp. *Wesleyan Theology: A Sourcebook.* Durham, NC: Labyrinth Press, 1984.
Long, D. Stephen. *John Wesley's Practical Theology.* Nashville, TN: Kingswood Books, 2005.
Maddox, Randy L. *Responsible Grace: John Wesley's Practical Theology.* Nashville, TN: Kingswood Books, 1994.
——— , ed. *Rethinking Wesley's Theology for Contemporary Methodism.* Nashville, TN: Abingdon Press, 1998.
Meeks, M. Douglas. *Trinity, Community, and Power: Mapping Trajectories in Wesleyan Theology.* Nashville, TN: Kingswood Books, 2000.
Oden, Thomas C. *Doctrinal Standards in the Wesleyan Tradition.* Rev. ed. Nashville, TN: Abingdon Press, 2008.
——— . *John Wesley's Scriptural Christianity: A Plain Exposition of His Teaching on Christian Doctrine.* Grand Rapids, MI: Zondervan, 1994.
Yrigoyen, Charles, Jr. *Belief Matters: United Methodism's Doctrinal Standards.* Nashville, TN: Abingdon Press, 2001.

Representative Methodist Theologians

Cobb, John B., Jr. *Grace and Responsibility: A Wesleyan Theology for Today.* Nashville, TN: Abingdon Press, 1995.
Cone, James H. *A Black Theology of Liberation.* Philadelphia, PA.: J. B. Lippincott, 1970.

González, Justo L. *Mañana: Christian Theology from a Hispanic Perspective*. Nashville, TN: Abingdon Press, 1990.
Harkness, Georgia. *Understanding the Christian Faith*. New York: Abingdon-Cokesbury, 1947.
Jones, E. Stanley. *The Christ of the Indian Road*. New York: Abingdon Press, 1925.
Kirkpatrick, Dow, ed. *The Doctrine of the Church*. Papers from the Second (1962) Oxford Institute of Methodist Theological Studies. Nashville, TN: Abingdon Press, 1964.
——. *The Finality of Christ*. Papers from the Third (1965) Oxford Institute of Methodist Theological Studies. Nashville, TN: Abingdon Press, 1966.
——. *The Holy Spirit*. Papers from the Fifth (1973) Oxford Institute of Methodist Theological Studies. Nashville, TN: Abingdon Press, 1974.
——. *The Living God*. Papers from the Fourth (1969) Oxford Institute of Methodist Theological Studies. Nashville, TN: Abingdon Press, 1971.
Klaiber, Walter, and Manfred Marquardt. *Living Grace: An Outline of United Methodist Theology*. Nashville, TN: Abingdon Press, 2001.
Langford, Thomas A. *God Made Known*. Nashville, TN: Abingdon Press, 1992.
——. *Methodist Theology*. Peterborough: Epworth Press, 1998.
Meeks, M. Douglas, ed. *The Future of the Methodist Theological Traditions*. Papers from the Seventh (1982) Oxford Institute of Methodist Theological Studies. Nashville, TN: Abingdon Press, 1985.
——. *What Should Methodists Teach? Wesleyan Tradition and Modern Diversity*. Papers from the Eighth (1987) Oxford Institute of Methodist Theological Studies. Nashville, TN: Abingdon Press, 1990.
Michalson, Carl. *The Hinge of History: An Existentialist Approach to the Christian Faith*. New York: Charles Scribner's Sons, 1959.
Oden, Thomas C. *Agenda for Theology: Recovering Christian Roots*. San Francisco, CA: Harper & Row, 1979.
——. *Systematic Theology*. 3 vols. San Francisco, CA: Harper & Row, 1987–1992.
——. *To Will and to Work: The Transforming Power of Grace*. Nashville, TN: Abingdon Press, 1993.
Runyon, Theodore H., ed. *Sanctification and Liberation: A Reexamination in the Light of the Wesleyan Tradition*. Papers from the Sixth (1977) Oxford Institute of Methodist Theological Studies. Nashville, TN: Abingdon Press, 1981.
——. *The New Creation: John Wesley's Theology Today*. Nashville, TN: Abingdon Press, 1998.
Wainwright, Geoffrey. *Doxology: The Praise of God in Worship, Doctrine and Life – A Systematic Theology*. New York: Oxford University Press, 1980.
Watson, David L. *God Does Not Foreclose: The Universal Promise of Salvation*. Nashville, TN: Abingdon Press, 1990.

Worship, the Sacraments, and Hymnody

Allen, Richard. *A Collection of Hymns and Spiritual Songs*. Reprint of 1801 edition. Nashville, TN: African Methodist Episcopal Church Sunday School Union, 1987.
Bowyer, O. Richard, Betty L. Hart, and Charlotte Meade. *Prayer in the Black Tradition*. Nashville, TN: Abingdon Press, 1986.

Chapman, David M. *Born in Song: Methodist Worship in Britain*. Warrington: Church in the Marketplace Publications, 2006.
Felton, Gayle Carlton. *This Gift of Water: The Theology and Practice of Baptism among Methodists in America*. Nashville, TN: Abingdon Press, 1992.
——. *United Methodists and the Sacraments*. Nashville, TN: Abingdon Press, 2007.
Graham, Fred Kimball. *'With One Heart and One Voice': A Core Repertory of Hymn Tunes Published for Use in the Methodist Episcopal Church in the United States, 1808–1878*. Lanham, MD: Scarecrow Press, 2004.
Job, Reuben. *A Wesleyan Spiritual Reader*. Nashville, TN: Abingdon Press, 1997.
Khoo, Lorna Lock-Nah. *Wesleyan Eucharistic Spirituality: Its Nature, Sources, and Future*. Adelaide: ATF Press, 2002.
Kimbrough, S T, Jr. *Orthodox and Wesleyan Spirituality*. Crestwood, NY: St. Vladimir's Seminary Press, 2002.
Knight, Henry H., III. *The Presence of God in the Christian Life: A Contemporary Understanding of John Wesley's Means of Grace*. Metuchen, NJ: Scarecrow Press, 1992.
Lawson, John. *The Wesley Hymns as a Guide to Scriptural Teaching*. Grand Rapids, MI: Zondervan, 1987.
Lorenz, Ellen Jane. *Glory Hallelujah: The Story of the Camp Meeting Spiritual*. Nashville, TN: Abingdon Press, 1980.
Rogal, Samuel J., comp. *Guide to the Hymns and Tunes of American Methodism*. New York: Greenwood Press, 1986.
Ruth, Lester. *Early Methodist Life and Spirituality: A Reader*. Nashville, TN: Kingswood Books, 2005.
——. *A Little Heaven Below: Worship at Early Methodist Quarterly Meetings*. Nashville, TN: Abingdon Press, 2000.
Staples, Rob L. *Outward Sign and Inward Grace: The Place of Sacraments in Wesleyan Spirituality*. Kansas, MO: Beacon Hill Press, 1991.
Steele, Richard B. *'Heart Religion' in the Methodist Tradition and Related Movements*. Lanham, MD: Scarecrow Press, 2001.
Stookey, Laurence H. *Eucharist: Christ's Feast with the Church*. Nashville, TN: Abingdon Press, 1993.
Tucker, Karen B. Westerfield. *American Methodist Worship*. New York: Oxford University Press, 2001.
Wainwright, Geoffrey. *Eucharist and Eschatology*. New York: Oxford University Press, 1982.
Wakefield, Gordon S. *Methodist Spirituality*. Peterborough: Epworth Press, 1999.
Warren, James I., Jr. *O for a Thousand Tongues: The History, Nature, and Influence of Music in the Methodist Tradition*. Grand Rapids, MI: Zondervan, 1988.
White, James F. *Sacraments as God's Self-Giving*. Nashville, TN: Abingdon Press, 1983.
White, James F, and Karen B. Westerfield Tucker. *The Sunday Service of the Methodists: Twentieth-Century Worship in Worldwide Methodism – Studies in Honor of James F. White*. Nashville, TN: Kingswood Books, 1996.
Young, Carlton R. *Music of the Heart: John & Charles Wesley on Music and Musicians: An Anthology*. Carol Stream, IL: Hope Publishing, 1995.
Yrigoyen, Charles, Jr. *Praising the God of Grace: The Theology of Charles Wesley's Hymns*. Nashville, TN: Abingdon Press, 2005.

Church Organization

Bowmer, John C. *Pastor and People: A Study of Church and Ministry in Wesleyan Methodism*. London: Epworth Press, 1975.

Burdon, Adrian. *The Preaching Service – The Glory of the Methodists: A Study of the Piety, Ethos and Development of the Methodist Preaching Service*. Bramcote: Grove Books, 1991.

Campbell, Dennis. *The Yoke of Obedience: The Meaning of Ordination in Methodism*. Nashville, TN: Abingdon Press, 1988.

Frank, Thomas Edward. *Polity, Practice, and the Mission of The United Methodist Church*. Nashville, TN: Abingdon Press, 2006.

Kirby, James E. *The Episcopacy in American Methodism*. Nashville, TN: Kingswood Books, 2000.

Oden, Thomas C. *Ministry through Word and Sacrament*. New York: Crossroad, 1988.

——— . *Pastoral Theology: Essentials of Ministry*. San Francisco, CA: Harper & Row, 1983.

Oh, Gwang Seok. *John Wesley's Ecclesiology: A Study in its Sources and Development*. Lanham, MD: Scarecrow Press, 2008.

Richey, Russell E. *The Methodist Conference in America: A History*. Nashville, TN: Kingswood Books, 1996.

Richey, Russell E., and Thomas Edward Frank. *Episcopacy in the Methodist Tradition: Perspectives and Proposals*. Nashville, TN: Abingdon Press, 2004.

Tuell, Jack M. *The Organization of The United Methodist Church*. Rev. ed. Nashville, TN: Abingdon Press, 2009.

Wilson, Robert L., and Steve Harper. *Faith and Form: A Unity of Theology and Polity in the United Methodist Tradition*. Grand Rapids, MI: Zondervan, 1988.

Representative Journals of History and Theology

Methodist History. Published by the General Commission on Archives and History, The United Methodist Church.

Proceedings of the Charles Wesley Society. Published by the Charles Wesley Society.

Proceedings of the Wesley Historical Society. Published by The Wesley Historical Society in Great Britain.

Wesleyan Theological Journal. Published by the Wesleyan Theological Society.

Contributors

Thomas R. Albin is Dean of the Chapel and Team Leader for the Upper Room Chapel, Nashville, TN.

Ted A. Campbell is Associate Professor of Church History, Perkins School of Theology, Southern Methodist University, Dallas, TX.

Paul Wesley Chilcote is Professor of Historical Theology and Wesley Studies, Ashland Theological Seminary, Ashland, OH.

Peter Forsaith is Research Fellow of the Oxford Centre for Methodism and Church History, Oxford Brookes University, UK.

Thomas Edward Frank is Professor of Religious Leadership and Administration at Candler School of Theology, Emory University, Atlanta, GA.

Richard P. Heitzenrater is William Kellon Quick Professor emeritus of Church History and Wesley Studies, Divinity School, Duke University, Durham, NC.

S T Kimbrough, Jr. is Editor of the *Proceedings of The Charles Wesley Society* and was the Society's first President.

John Wesley Z. Kurewa holds the E. Stanley Jones Chair of Evangelism at Africa University, Old Mutare, Zimbabwe.

Gareth Lloyd is Archivist of the Methodist Church of Great Britain, at the John Rylands University Library, Manchester, UK.

Randy L. Maddox is William Kellon Quick Professor of Theology and Wesley Studies, Divinity School, Duke University, Durham, NC.

Manfred Marquardt is retired Professor of Theology and Ethics, School of Theology, Reutlingen, Germany.

Paulo Ayres Mattos is Professor, Faculty of Theology, Methodist University of Sao Paulo, Brazil.

Contributors

John G. McEllhenney is a retired United Methodist pastor who has taught Methodist history, doctrine, and polity, and has written articles and books in those areas of study.

Rüdiger R. Minor holds the Daniel and Lillian Hankey Chair of World Evangelism, Candler School of Theology, Emory University, Atlanta, GA.

Luther J. Oconer is an ordained United Methodist elder in the Philippines currently serving a pastorate in Sitka, AK.

Russell E. Richey is William R. Cannon Distinguished Professor of Church History, Candler School of Theology, Emory University, Atlanta, GA.

Ulrike Schuler is Professor of Church History, Methodism, and Ecumenism, School of Theology, Reutlingen, Germany.

Laurence Hull Stookey is Hugh Latimer Elderdice Professor emeritus of Preaching and Worship, Wesley Theological Seminary, Washington, DC.

Norman E. Thomas is Professor emeritus of World Christianity at United Theological Seminary, Dayton, OH.

Karen B. Westerfield Tucker is Professor of Worship, Boston University School of Theology, Boston, MA.

Geoffrey Wainwright holds the Robert Earl Cushman Chair of Systematic Theology, Divinity School, Duke University, Durham, NC.

Susan E. Warrick is former Assistant General Secretary, General Commission on Archives and History, United Methodist Church, Madison, NJ.

Martin Wellings is President of the World Methodist Historical Society and Superintendent Minister of the Oxford Methodist Circuit, UK.

Charles Yrigoyen, Jr. is General Secretary emeritus, General Commission on Archives and History, United Methodist Church, Madison, NJ.

Notes

Chapter 1
1 E.g., see Chapter 2 for a discussion of the historical precedents and context for Wesley's theological development.
2 Maximin Piette, a Belgian priest, suggested several alternative views in his biographical study of Wesley, *John Wesley in the Evolution of Protestantism* (Bruxelles: Albert Dewit, 1927), followed by major works by Methodist theologians George Croft Cell, *The Rediscovery of John Wesley* (New York: H. Holt, 1935), and William Ragsdale Cannon, *The Theology of Wesley* (New York: Abingdon-Cokesbury Press, 1946).
3 See Frank Baker, 'Unfolding John Wesley: A Survey of Twenty Years' Studies in Wesley's Thought', in *Quarterly Review* 1 (Fall 1980): 44–58.
4 Such an approach had appeared in European historical studies over a century earlier with the work of such writers as Leopold van Ranke.
5 Albert Outler, 'A New Future for Wesley Studies', in *The Future of the Methodist Theological Traditions* (Nashville: Abingdon, 1985), 34–52.
6 Three recent examples would be Theodore Runyon, *The New Creation: John Wesley's Theology Today* (Nashville: Abingdon, 1998); Theodore Weber, *Politics and the Order of Salvation* (Nashville: Kingswood Books, 2001); and Stephen Long, *John Wesley's Moral Theology* (Nashville: Kingswood Books, 2005).
7 See comment by his son Samuel, quoted by Carleton Young in 'The Musical Charles Wesley,' in Kenneth C. G. Newport and Ted A. Campbell, eds, *Charles Wesley: Life, Literature, & Legacy* (Peterborough: Epworth Press, 2007), 415. This article also indicates that, although Charles was not much of a musician, he did play the flute (recorder) while in college at Oxford (as did his brother, John).
8 Reported by John Wesley in his obituary for his brother Charles, included in the 1788 *Minutes* of the Methodist conference.
9 See the work of Robert L. Moore, from the point of view of Eric Erickson's psychology, *John Wesley and Authority: A Psychological Perspective* (Missoula: Scholars Press, 1979); Thorvald Källstad's work from a Swedish point of view using theories such as cognitive dissonance, *John Wesley and the Bible: A Psychological Study* (Uppsala: Uppsala University, 1974); and a study by Henry Abelove, using Michel Foucault's views as a focus, *The Evangelist of Desire* (Stanford, CA: Stanford University Press, 1990).
10 See, for instance, the work of Earl Kent Brown, *Women of Mr. Wesley's Methodism* (New York: Edwin Mellen Press, 1983), and Paul Chilcote, *John Wesley and the Women Preachers of Methodism* (Metuchen, NJ: Scarecrow Press, 1991). Susan E. Warrick has produced a bibliography that is useful to anyone entering this field, *Women in the Wesleyan and United Methodist Traditions* (Madison, NJ: Commission on Archives and History, UMC, 2003).

Notes

11 See especially the work of Theodore W. Jennings, Jr., *Good News to the Poor* (Nashville: Abingdon, 1990), and the essays in M. Douglas Meeks, ed., *The Portion of the Poor* (Nashville: Kingswood Books, 1995), and Richard Heitzenrater, ed., *The Poor and the People Called Methodists* (Nashville: Kingswood Books, 2002).
12 See John Walsh, *Elie Halévy and the Birth of Methodism* (London: Royal Historical Society, 1975).
13 Some important beginning work was done by Thomas Walter Herbert, *John Wesley as Editor and Author* (Princeton: University Press, 1940).
14 See Richard P. Heitzenrater, 'Wesley and Children,' in Marcia Bunge, ed., *Children in the History of Christian Thought*, (Grand Rapids: Eerdmans, 2000).
15 *WJW(B)*, (Nashville: Abingdon Press, 1975–).
16 Originally published privately in 1966 at Duke University; more recently reissued in a second edition with new numbering and information related to the *Bicentennial Edition* (Stone Mountain, GA: G. Zimmerman, 1991).
17 S. T. Kimbrough, Jr. and Kenneth G. D. Newport, eds, *The Manuscript Journal of the Reverend Charles Wesley, M.A.* (Nashville: Kingswood Books, 2008), 2 vols.
18 Kenneth G. C. Newport, ed., *The Sermons of Charles Wesley: A Critical Edition* (New York: Oxford University Press, 2001).
19 S. T. Kimbrough and Oliver Beckerlegge, *The Unpublished Poetry of Charles Wesley* (Nashville: Kingswood Books, 1988–1992), 3 vols.
20 The category 'Wesley Texts' contains a variety of new manuscript materials, available at http://www.divinity.duke.edu/wesleyan/texts/index.html.
21 See two articles by Randy Maddox on 'John Wesley's Reading' in *Methodist History* 41 (Jan. and Apr. 2003), and Appendix IV in Richard Heitzenrater, 'John Wesley and the Oxford Methodists' (PhD diss., Duke University, 1972).
22 Donald Kirkham, *Pamphlet Opposition to the Rise of Methodism* (PhD diss., Duke University, 1973); and Clive D. Field, *Anti-Methodist Publications of the Eighteenth Century; A Revised Bibliography* (Manchester: John Rylands Library, 1991).
23 (London: Epworth Press, 2002).
24 *Wesley and the People Called Methodists* (Nashville: Abingdon, 1995), and *The Elusive Mr. Wesley* (Nashville: Abingdon, 2005).
25 Randy Maddox, *Responsible Grace* (Nashville: Kingswood Books, 1994), and Kenneth J. Collins, *The Theology of John Wesley; Holy Love and the Shape of Grace* (Nashville: Abingdon, 2007).
26 See Randy Maddox, 'A Decade of Dissertations in Wesley Studies, 1991–2001,' in *Wesleyan Theological Journal* 37 (Fall 2002): 103–113.
27 Zele's PhD diss., 'Wesley and America,' was completed at Duke University in 2008; Hammond's PhD diss., 'Restoring Primitive Christianity: John Wesley and Georgia, 1735–1737,' was completed at the University of Manchester in 2008 and is forthcoming from Epworth Press.
28 Rex D. Matthews' work on Wesley's epistemology is entitled ' "Religion and Reason Joined": A Study in the Theology of John Wesley' (ThD diss., Harvard University, 1983), and Thomas Albin's work at Cambridge University on early Methodist spirituality is reflected in his article, 'Inwardly Persuaded': Religion of the Heart in Early British Methodism,' in *'Heart Religion' in the Methodist Tradition and Related Movements* (Lanham, MD: Scarecrow Press, 2001), 33–66.
29 The category 'Resource Materials' contains a wide variety of resources available at http://www.divinity.duke.edu/wesleyan/texts/index.html.

Chapter 2
1 A good survey of scholarship on this period is Dewey D. Wallace, Jr., 'Via Media? A Paradigm Shift,' *Anglican and Episcopal History* 72 (2003): 2–21.

2 Leslie W. Barnard, 'The Use of the Patristic Tradition in the Late Seventeenth and Early Eighteenth Century,' in R. Bauckham and B. Drewery, eds, *Scripture, Tradition and Reason* (Edinburgh: T & T Clark, 1988), 174–203; and Robert D. Cornwall, 'The Search for the Primitive Church: The Use of Early Church Fathers in the High Church Anglican Tradition, 1680–1745,' *Anglican and Episcopal History* 59 (1990): 303–329.
3 William Laud, 'Answer to the Lord Say's Speech,' in *The History of the Troubles and Trial of ... William Laud*, 2 vols. (London: Richard Chiswell, 1695–1700), 1:503.
4 Compare the negative evaluation of Taylor in C. FitzSimons Allison, *The Rise of Moralism: The Proclamation of the Gospel from Hooker to Baxter* (Wilton, CT: Morehouse Barlow, 1966) with the positive evaluation in Rowan A. Greer, *Christian Hope and Christian Life* (New York: Herder, 2001).
5 *Jurare* in Latin means to take an oath.
6 See John Walsh and Stephen Taylor, 'Introduction: the Church and Anglicanism in the "long" Eighteenth Century,' in *The Church of England, c. 1689–1833* (New York: Cambridge University Press, 1993), 1–64.
7 Cf. Roy Porter, 'The Enlightenment in England,' in R. Porter and M. Teich, eds, *The Enlightenment in National Context* (New York: Cambridge University Press, 1981), 1–18; and David Bebbington, 'Revival and Enlightenment in Eighteenth-Century England,' in A. Walker and K. Aune, eds, *On Revival. A Critical Examination* (Carlisle: Paternoster, 2003), 71–86.
8 Good overviews are Ted Campbell, *The Religion of the Heart* (Columbia: University of South Carolina Press, 1991); and W. R. Ward, *The Protestant Evangelical Awakening* (New York: Cambridge University Press, 1992).
9 Cf. Robert Clarence Monk, *John Wesley: His Puritan Heritage*, 2nd edn. (Lanham, MD: Scarecrow Press, 1999); and Jean Orcibal, 'The Theological Originality of John Wesley and Continental Spirituality,' in R. E. Davies and E. G. Rupp, eds, *A History of the Methodist Church in Great Britain* (London: Epworth, 1965), 1:83–111.
10 See http://www.divinity.duke.edu/wesleyan/research/wesley.html for a set of articles detailing these collections.
11 See the analysis in Monk, 247–254.
12 For more details on what follows, see Randy L. Maddox, 'Opinion, Religion, and "Catholic Spirit": John Wesley on Theological Integrity,' *Asbury Theological Journal* 47/1 (1992): 63–87.
13 E.g., *A Plain Account of the People Called Methodists*, I.2, *WJW(B)*, 9: 254–255.
14 E.g., Sermon 55, 'On the Trinity,' §3, *WJW(B)*, 2:376–377.
15 Sermon 39, 'Catholic Spirit,' *WJW(B)*, 2:81–95.
16 His fluctuating sense of what is at stake in the debate over unconditional election is traced in Allan Coppedge, *John Wesley in Theological Debate* (Wilmore, KY: Wesley Heritage Press, 1987).
17 For a more detailed discussion of what follows, see Randy L. Maddox, 'John Wesley – Practical Theologian?' *Wesleyan Theological Journal* 23 (1988): 122–147.
18 George Bull, *A Companion for the Candidates of Holy Orders* (London: Richard Smith, 1714), 18. John Wesley records reading this in his Oxford diary on 18 September 1725.
19 Anglican worship to that point was typically restricted to singing psalms. Hymns were more common in dissenting traditions and the continental pietists. Wesley's early collections are available at http://www.divinity.duke.edu/wesleyan/texts/jw_poetry_hymns.html.
20 See the preface, §4, *WJW(B)*, 7:74.
21 Cf. Samuel Wesley, *Advice to a Young Clergyman* (London: Rivington, 1735), 56.
22 See Isabel Rivers, 'Dissenting and Methodist Books of Practical Divinity,' in Isabel

Rivers, ed., *Books and their Readers in Eighteenth Century England* (New York: St. Martins, 1982), 152.
23 E.g., *Journal* (19 November 1751), *WJW(B)*, 20:407; and Letter to Joseph Benson (31 July 1773), *Letters* (Telford), 6:35.
24 For John, see the survey volumes by Collins and Maddox in the select bibliography; for Charles, see the volumes by Rattenbury and Yrigoyen.
25 See *The Doctrine of Salvation, Faith, and Good Works, Extracted from the Homilies Of the Church of England* (Oxford, 1738), Sections I.9, I.13–15, II.2, and II.3. There is no such use of italics for these passages in any prior edition of the *Homilies*.
26 E.g., *The Character of a Methodist*, §1, *WJW(B)*, 9:33.
27 They could also use the term 'preventing grace.' In both cases, the emphasis is on God's grace coming before (*pre vene*) our response.
28 *Farther Appeal to Men of Reason and Religion, Pt. I*, I.3, *WJW(B)*, 11:106.
29 See Daniel B. Stevick, *The Altar's Fire: Charles Wesley's 'Hymns on the Lord's Supper'* (Peterborough: Epworth, 2004).
30 Cf. Bryan P. Stone and Thomas J. Oord, eds, *Thy Nature and Thy Name is Love: Wesleyan and Process Theologies in Dialogue* (Nashville: Kingswood Books, 2001).
31 See John R. Tyson, *Charles Wesley on Sanctification* (Grand Rapids: Zondervan, 1986) 115–155; and Peter Schmiechen, *Saving Power: Theories of Atonement and Forms of the Church* (Grand Rapids: Eerdmans, 2005), 298–299, 305.
32 James Clark, *Montanus Redivivus: or, Montanism revived, in the Principles and Discipline of the Methodists* (Dublin: Aunders, 1760).
33 E.g., Jason E. Vickers, 'Wesley's Hymns and Prayers,' in *Invocation and Assent: the Making and Remaking of Trinitarian Theology* (Grand Rapids: Eerdmans, 2008), 169–189.
34 See Gareth Lloyd, *Charles Wesley and the Struggle for Methodist Identity* (New York: Oxford University Press, 2007).
35 Note John's description of this difference in his *Journal* (15 December 1788), *WJW(B)*, 24:116–117.
36 See Charles Wesley, *Short Hymns on . . . Holy Scriptures* (Bristol: Farley, 1762), 2:184; and the comparison of the brothers in Tyson, *Charles Wesley*, 261–268.
37 For more details see Tyson, *Charles Wesley*; and S T Kimbrough Jr., 'Charles Wesley and the Journey of Sanctification,' *Evangelical Journal* 16 (1998): 49–75.
38 See Randy L. Maddox, 'Nurturing the New Creation: Reflections on a Wesleyan Trajectory,' in M. D. Meeks, ed., *Wesleyan Perspectives on the New Creation* (Nashville, TN: Kingswood Books, 2004), 21–52.
39 Compare his *Hymns for the Year 1756* to hymn 16, stanzas 5–6, in *Hymns for the Nation* (1781).
40 See Ted A. Campbell, *Methodist Doctrine: The Essentials* (Nashville: Abingdon, 1999).
41 For details on what follows, see Randy L. Maddox, 'Reclaiming an Inheritance: Wesley as Theologian in the History of Methodist Theology,' in R. Maddox, ed., *Rethinking Wesley's Theology for Contemporary Methodism* (Nashville: Kingswood Books, 1998), 213–226.
42 A convenient list of these centers can be found on the website of the Duke Center for Studies in the Wesleyan tradition: http://www.divinity.duke.edu/wesleyan/research/index.html.
43 See Randy L. Maddox, 'Reading Wesley as Theologian,' *Wesleyan Theological Journal* 30/1 (1995): 7–54.
44 Albert C. Outler, 'A New Future for "Wesley Studies": An Agenda for "Phase III",' in M. D. Meeks, ed., *The Future of the Methodist Theological Traditions* (Nashville: Abingdon, 1985), 34–52. See also Richard P. Heitzenrater, *The Elusive Mr. Wesley*, 2nd edn. (Nashville: Abingdon, 2003), 387–394; and Henry Derman Rack, 'Some

Recent Trends in Wesley Scholarship,' *Wesleyan Theological Journal* 41/2 (2006): 182–199.
45 Cf. http://www.divinity.duke.edu/wesleyan/docs/Recent_Dissertations.pdf.
46 On this topic, see especially the expansion of a portion of his dissertation by Mark T. Mealey, 'Tilting at Windmills: John Wesley's Reading of John Locke's Epistemology,' *Bulletin of the John Rylands Library* 85/2–3 (2003): 331–346.
47 The most detailed dissertation has just been published: Edgardo Colón-Emeric, *Wesley, Aquinas, and Christian Perfection: An Ecumenical Dialogue* (Waco, TX: Baylor University Press, 2009). See also D. Stephen Long, *John Wesley's Moral Theology . . . The Quest for God and Goodness* (Nashville: Kingswood Books, 2005).
48 Joanna Ruth Cruickshank, *Pain, Passion and Faith: Revisiting the Place of Charles Wesley in Early Methodism* (Lanham, MD: Scarecrow, 2009).
49 Cf. Deborah Madden, *'A Cheap, Safe and Natural Medicine': Religion, Medicine and Culture in John Wesley's 'Primitive Physic'* (Atlanta: Rodopi, 2007); Madden, ed., *'Inward and Outward Health': John Wesley's Holistic Concept of Medical Science, the Environment and Holy Living* (London: Epworth, 2008); and Thomas J. Oord, ed., *Divine Grace and Emerging Creation: Wesleyan Forays in Science and Creation* (Eugene, OR: Pickwick, 2009).
50 For a sense of this discussion, see the dedicated issue of *Journal of Psychology and Christianity* 23/2 (2004); and the website for SSPWT, http://home.snu.edu/~brint/sswpt/.
51 See Frank Baker, 'The Oxford Edition of Wesley's Works and Its Text,' in K. E. Rowe (ed.), *The Place of Wesley in the Christian Tradition* (1976), 117–33.
52 The current CD-ROM does not include every volume published, only completed sections, so it contains the four volumes of *Sermons*, the seven volumes of *Journals*, and the *Collection of Hymns* (vol. 7).
53 The best organized site for this and other public-domain Wesley texts is the Wesley Center at Northwest Nazarene University: http://wesley.nnu.edu/.
54 Kingswood Books is planning to issue his 'journal letters.' Editions of his broader correspondence are underway at both Kingswood and Oxford University Press.
55 See: http://www.divinity.duke.edu/wesleyan/texts/index.html.

Chapter 3
1 Henry Moore published five such examples in his *Life of the Rev. John Wesley*. See Frank Baker, *Representative Verse of Charles Wesley* (Nashville, TN: Epworth, 1962), 258–259. Baker's introduction to this volume, which was later published separately in a revised and expanded edition, *Charles Wesley's Verse* (London: Epworth, 1964, 1968), is the best study of the characteristics of Wesley's poetry, particularly vocabulary, structure, meter, rhyme, and rhetoric.
2 Charles is probably quoting from memory, for Horace's original text is *cunnus* instead of *mulier*.
3 Original text = *illi* instead of *omnes*.
4 S T Kimbrough, Jr. and Oliver A. Beckerlegge, eds, *The Unpublished Poetry of Charles Wesley*. 3 vols. (Nashville, TN: Abingdon/Kingswood, 1988, 1990, 1992), 3: 393. Henceforth cited as *Unpub. Poetry* followed by volume and page number.
5 Henceforth cited as *BCP*.
6 Donald Davie, *A Gathered Church: The Literature of the English Dissenting Interest, 1700–1930*, The Clark Lectures 1976 (New York: Oxford University Press, 1978), 48.
7 (London: Epworth Press, 1913).
8 (New York: New York Public Library, 1966).
9 England and Sparrow, 66.
10 England and Sparrow, 93.

Notes

11 England and Sparrow, 71.
12 Franz Hildebrandt and Oliver A. Beckerlegge, eds, with assistance by James Dale (Nashville, TN: Abingdon, 1983), 38–44.
13 Hildebrandt, Beckerlegge, and Dale, 43.
14 (Peterborough: Epworth Press, 2007), 361–367.
15 Newport and Campbell, 363.
16 James Dale, 'Charles Wesley and the Line of Piety: Antecedents of the Hymns in English Devotional Verse,' *Proceedings of the Charles Wesley Society*, 8 (2002): 55–64. See also James Dale, 'Holy Larceny? Elizabeth Rowe's Poetry in Charles Wesley's Hymns,' *Proceedings of the Charles Wesley Society*, 3(1996): 5–20.
17 *Miscellaneous Works in Prose and Verse of Mrs. Elizabeth Rowe* (London, 1739), No. 65, line 25. This work was published posthumously and was, according to Dale, most certainly read by Charles Wesley.
18 Kimbrough and Beckerlegge, *Unpub. Poetry*, see n. 4.
19 Kimbrough and Beckerlegge, *Unpub. Poetry*, 1:41–57.
20 Kenneth D. Shields, 'Charles Wesley as Poet,' in *Charles Wesley: Poet and Theologian*, ed. S T Kimbrough, Jr. (Nashville, TN: Abingdon/Kingswood, 1992), 67.
21 (2nd edition, Bristol: F. Farley, 1756), 11–12.
22 J. R. Watson, 'Charles Wesley and the Thirty-Nine Articles of Religion of the Church of England,' *Proceedings of the Charles Wesley Society*, 9 (2003–2004): 27–38.
23 Watson, 32.
24 Stanza three of 'Hymn for Christmas-Day,' *Hymns and Sacred Poems* (London: W. Strahan, 1739), 206–207.
25 (Bristol: F. Farley, 1745).
26 *Hymns on the Lord's Supper*, 134–135.
27 *Hymns on the Lord's Supper*, 136.
28 *Hymns for Our Lord's Resurrection* (London: W. Strahan, 1746), 10.
29 J. R. Watson, 'Charles Wesley's Hymns and the *Book of Common Prayer*,' in *Thomas Cranmer: Essays in Commemoration of the 500th Anniversary of His Birth*, ed. Margot Johnson (Durham, NC: Turnstone Ventures, 1990), 206. See also Kathryn Nichols, 'Charles Wesley's Eucharistic Hymns: Their Relationship to the *Book of Common Prayer*,' *The Hymn* 39, no. 2 (April, 1988): 13–21.
30 Robin A. Leaver, 'Charles Wesley and Anglicanism,' in *Charles Wesley: Poet and Theologian*, ed. S T Kimbrough, Jr. (Nashville, TN: Abingdon/Kingswood, 1992), 167. See also Henry Bett, *The Hymns of Methodism* (3rd edition, London: Epworth, 1945), 129–135; and J. R. Watson, 'Charles Wesley's Hymns and the *Book of Common Prayer*,' 205–208.
31 J. Ernest Rattenbury, *The Evangelical Doctrines of Charles Wesley's Hymns* (London: Epworth, 1941), 48.
32 Frank Baker, ed., *Representative Verse of Charles Wesley* (London: Epworth, 1962), xxv.
33 Rattenbury, 48.
34 (Grand Rapids, MI: Francis Asbury Press, 1987). See also the study by John W. Waterhouse, *The Bible in Charles Wesley's Hymns* (London, 1941).
35 See also: *Hymns and Sacred Poems* (1740), *Hymns on God's Everlasting Love* (1741), *Hymns and Sacred Poems* (1742), *Hymns for Times of Trouble and Persecution* (1744), *Hymns on the Lord's Supper* (1745), *Hymns for the Nativity of our Lord* (1745), *Hymns for our Lord's Resurrection* (1746), *Hymns for Ascension-Day* (1746), *Hymns of Petition and Thanksgiving for the Promise of the Father* (1746), *Hymns and Sacred Poems* (1749), *Hymns on the Trinity* (1767).
36 See S T Kimbrough, Jr., 'Charles Wesley as a Biblical Interpreter,' *Methodist History* 26, no. 3 (1988): 139–153.
37 (Bristol: F. Farley, 1749), 1:59, stanza 5.

38 2 vols. (Bristol: F. Farley, 1762); henceforth cited as *Short Hymns* followed by volume and page number.
39 See S T Kimbrough, Jr., 'Charles Wesley's Lyrical Commentary on the Holy Scriptures,' in *Orthodox and Wesleyan Scriptural Understanding and Practice*, ed. S. T. Kimbrough, Jr. (Crestwood, NY: St. Vladimir's Seminary Press, 2005), 171–206.
40 Of particular interest to this discussion is volume 2 which bears the subtitle, *Hymns and Poems on Holy Scripture.*
41 *Short Hymns*, No. 663, 2:337.
42 *Hymns and Sacred Poems* (Bristol: F. Farley, 1742), 96–98.
43 Nicholas Lossky, 'Lancelot Andrewes: A Bridge between Orthodoxy and the Wesley Brothers,' in *Orthodox and Wesleyan Scriptural Understanding and Practice*, 154.
44 *Hymns and Sacred Poems* (1739), 37–38.
45 Peter Bouteneff, 'All Creation in United Thanksgiving: Gregory of Nyssa and the Wesleys on Salvation,' in *Orthodox and Wesleyan Scriptural Understanding and Practice*, ed. S T Kimbrough (Crestwood, NY: SVS Press, 2002), 194.
46 *Hymns for Those that Seek and Have Redemption in the Blood of Jesus Christ* (London: W. Strahan, 1747), 12.
47 (London: Darlton, Longman and Todd, 1988).
48 Kallistos Ware, *The Orthodox Way* (Crestwood, NY: St. Vladimir's Seminary Press, 1998), 74.
49 *Hymns for the Nativity of our Lord* (London: W. Strahan, 1745), 18.
50 *Hymns for the Nativity of Our Lord*, 18.
51 S T Kimbrough, Jr., 'Theosis in the Writings of Charles Wesley,' *St. Vladimir's Theological Seminary Quarterly* 52, no. 2 (2008): 207.
52 (Bristol: F. Farley, 1745), 133.
53 *Hymns on the Lord's Supper*, 138, stanza 7 of Hymn 164.
54 *Hymns on the Lord's* Supper, 138, stanzas 2 and 3 of Hymn 165.
55 John Wesley was usually the editor of Charles' hymns and the publication of the volume, *A Collection of Hymns for the Use of the People Called Methodists* (1780), which included over 500 hymns by Charles, was primarily the editorial work of John. This volume, which was arranged according to the *ordo salutis*, is considered by many hymnographers to have changed the course of English-language hymnody.
56 For a brief analysis of John and Charles Wesley's treatment of Brevint see Geoffrey Wainwright's Introduction to *Hymns on the Lord's Supper*, published by the Charles Wesley Society in 1995. *Hymns on the Lord's Supper*, a facsimile reprint of the first edition (Madison, NJ: Charles Wesley Society, 1995, second printing 2001). In addition, to Charles Wesley's appropriation of language, imagery, and phraseology from the Bible and the *BCP* Psalter, Wainwright stresses the influence of the *Apostolic Constitutions* on *Hymns for the Lord's Supper*. For further study of the importance of this volume see John C. Bowmer, *The Sacrament of the Lord's Supper in Early Methodism* (London: Dacre Press, 1951) and Daniel B. Stevick, *The Altar's Fire: Charles Wesley's Hymns on the Lord's Supper, 1745, Introduction and Exposition* (Peterborough: Epworth, 2004).
57 *Hymns on the Lord's Supper* (Bristol: F. Farley, 1745), 45.
58 *Hymns on the Lord's Supper*, Hymn 40.
59 *Hymns on the Trinity* (Bristol: W. Pine, 1767), 28.
60 *Hymns on the Trinity*, 28.
61 Introduction to the facsimile reprint of *Hymns on the Trinity* (Madison, NJ: Charles Wesley Society, 1998), ix.
62 *Hymns on the Trinity*, stanza two, Hymn 35.
63 Stanzas two and three of the hymn, 'Ye servants of God, your Master proclaim,'

Notes

which are usually excluded in modern versions of the hymn. *Hymns for Times of Trouble and Persecution* (London: W. Strahan, 1744), No. 1, 43.
64 (London: W. Strahan, 1746).
65 *Hymns for the Public Thanksgiving-Day, October 9, 1746*, 4.
66 (London: W. Strahan, 1750).
67 (London: W. Strahan, 1759).
68 *Hymns on the Lord's Supper*, 139.
69 *Short Hymns* (1762), 2:380, No. 738, based on James 1:27.
70 *Charles Wesley: Poet and Theologian*, see n. 20.
71 Kenneth G. C. Newport and Ted A. Campbell, eds (Peterborough: Epworth, 2007), 533–564.
72 *Hymns for the Nativity of our Lord* (1745), *Hymns for Our Lord's Resurrection* (1746), *Hymns for Ascension-Day* and *Hymns for Whitsunday* (in one volume), *Hymns on the Lord's Supper* (1745), *Hymns on the Great Festivals* (1746), *Hymns on the Trinity* (1767), *Hymns and Sacred Poems* (1739).
73 *Unpub. Poetry*, see n. 4.
74 Kenneth G. C. Newport, ed., *The Sermons of Charles Wesley: A Critical Edition* (Oxford and New York: Oxford University Press, 2001.
75 S T Kimbrough, Jr., Kenneth G. C. Newport, eds, *The Manuscript Journal of the Reverend Charles Wesley, M.A.* 2 vols. (Nashville, TN: Abingdon/Kingswood, 2008).

Chapter 4

1 *The Book of Discipline of the United Methodist Church, 1972* (Nashville, TN: United Methodist Publishing House, 1972; hereafter cited as, UMC *Discipline 1972*), 75–79; *The Book of Discipline of the United Methodist Church, 1988* (Nashville, TN: United Methodist Publishing House, 1972; hereafter cited as, UMC *Discipline 1988*), 77–90.
2 (Munich: Verlag Ernst Reinhardt, 1938).
3 Colin W. Williams, *John Wesley's Theology Today* (Nashville, TN: Abingdon, 1960), 23–38.
4 The Theological Study Commission on Doctrine and Doctrinal Standards, 'An Interim Report to the General Conference' (n.p.: [1970]).
5 'An Interim Report to the General Conference,' 8.
6 UMC *Discipline 1972*, 75–79.
7 UMC *Discipline 1972*, 78–79.
8 Fourth World Conference on Faith and Order (Montreal 1963), report on 'Scripture, Tradition, and traditions,' par. 39; in Günther Gassmann, ed., *Documentary History of Faith and Order, 1963–1993* (Faith and Order paper no. 159; Geneva: World Council of Churches, 1993), 10–11.
9 UMC *Discipline 1972*, 76–77.
10 UMC *Discipline 1972*, 77–78.
11 Dennis M. Campbell, *Doctors, Lawyers, Ministers: Christian Ethics in Professional Practice* (Nashville, TN: Abingdon, 1982).
12 Jerry L. Walls, *The Problem of Pluralism: Recovering United Methodist Identity* (Wilmore, KY: Bristol Books, 1986; revised edition, 1988).
13 Ted A. Campbell, 'The "Wesleyan Quadrilateral": The Story of a Modern Methodist Myth' in (a) *Methodist History* 29:2 (January 1991): 87–95; and in (b) Thomas A. Langford, ed., *Doctrine and Theology in the United Methodist Church* (Nashville, TN: Abingdon/Kingswood Books, 1991), 154–161. Although the article was not published until 1991, it had been given as a series of lectures at St. Paul School of Theology, Kansas City, Missouri early in 1988, and was written in the context of the reconsideration of the notion of the Wesleyan Quadrilateral leading up to the 1988 revision of 'Our Theological Task.'

14 UMC *Discipline 1988*, 81.
15 UMC *Discipline* 1988, 86. On the issue of biblical primacy in this statement, cf. Charles M. Wood, *Love that Rejoices in the Truth: Theological Explorations* (Eugene, OR: Cascade Books, 2009), 42.
16 UMC *Discipline 1972*, 75.
17 UMC *Discipline 1988*, 77–78. Cf. Wood, 39–40.
18 Wood, 41–42.
19 William Abraham, *Waking from Doctrinal Amnesia: The Healing of Doctrine in the United Methodist Church* (Nashville, TN: Abingdon, 1995), 56–65; and an article responding to the question 'What Should United Methodists Do with the Quadrilateral?' in *Quarterly Review* 22:1 (Spring 2002): 85–88.
20 Donald Thorsen, *The Wesleyan Quadrilateral: Scripture, Tradition, Reason and Experience as a Model of Evangelical Theology* (Grand Rapids, MI: Zondervan, 1990).
21 W. Stephen Gunter, Scott J. Jones, Ted A. Campbell, Rebekah L. Miles, and Randy L. Maddox, *Wesley and the Quadrilateral: Renewing the Conversation* (Nashville, TN: Abingdon, 1997).
22 *Book of Discipline of the Methodist Church in India* (2nd edition, after 1982), 60.
23 World Methodist Council, statement of 'Wesleyan Essentials of Christian Faith,' a document available on the web site of the World Methodist Council (http://www.worldmethodistcouncil.org), section on 'Our Beliefs.'
24 John Wesley, 'The Doctrine of Original Sin, According to Scripture, Reason, and Experience' (in Thomas Jackson, ed., *The Works of the Reverend John Wesley, A.M.* [14 volumes; London: Wesleyan Conference Office, 1872], 9:191).
25 Preface to the 1771 edition of the *Works*, par. 4 (cited in Jackson, ed., *Works*, 1:iv).
26 Albert C. Outler, 'The Wesleyan Quadrilateral – in John Wesley,' *Wesleyan Theological Journal* 20:1 (Spring 1985): 16.
27 Albert C. Outler, 'History as an Ecumenical Resource: The Protestant Discovery of "Tradition," 1952–1963,' presidential address, American Catholic Historical Association, 28 December 1972; in *Catholic Historical Review* 59:1 (1973): 1–15.
28 Scott J. Jones, *John Wesley's Conception and Uses of Scripture* (Nashville, TN: Kingswood Books, 1995), 160–184.
29 John Wesley, *Explanatory Notes upon the New Testament*, comment on Romans 12:6 (London: Epworth Press, 1976), 569 (in footnote).
30 Guillaume du Buc (Bucanus), *Institutiones Theologicae seu Locorum Communium Christianae Religionis ex Dei Verbo et Praestantissimorum Theologorum Orthodoxo Consensu Expositorum Analysis* (Geneva, 1609), 4:21–24; English translation as given in Heinrich Heppe, *Reformed Dogmatics: Set Out and Illustrated from the Sources* (Ernst Bizer, ed., and G. T. Thompson, tr.; London: Allen and Unwin, 1950), 35.
31 Cf. Ted A. Campbell, 'The Image of Christ in the Poor: On the Medieval Roots of the Wesleys' Ministry with the Poor' in Richard P. Heitzenrater, ed., *The Poor and the People Called Methodists* (Nashville, TN: Kingswood Books imprint of the Abingdon, 2002), 39–57.
32 UMC *Discipline 1988*, 41.
33 D. W. Bebbington, *Evangelicalism in Modern Britain: A History from the 1730s to the 1980s* (London: Unwin Hyman, 1989), 50–55; Henry D. Rack, *Reasonable Enthusiast: John Wesley and the Rise of Methodism* (Philadelphia: Trinity Press International, 1989), 30–33, 383–388.
34 Frederick Dreyer, 'Faith and Experience in the Thought of John Wesley' in *American Historical Review* 88 [1983], 12–30); Richard E. Brantley, *Locke, Wesley, and the Method of English Romanticism* (Gainesville, FL: University Presses of Florida, 1984); Gregory Clapper, 'John Wesley on Religious Affections' (PhD diss., Emory University, 1985).

Notes

35 Rack, 386.
36 Rex Dale Matthews, ' "Religion and Reason Joined": A Study in the Theology of John Wesley' (PhD diss., Harvard University, 1986). D. Stephen Long has similarly observed that Wesley 'presents us with a "spiritual sensorium" that uncritically mixes an Augustinian theory of illumination (mediated through Cambridge Platonism) with the sensibility of knowledge plundered from Locke ...': *John Wesley's Moral Theology: The Quest for God and Goodness* (Nashville, TN: Kingswood Books, 2005), 13.
37 Rebekah L. Miles, 'The Instrumental Role of Reason,' in *Wesley and the Quadrilateral*, ed. Gunter (Nashville, TN: Abingdon, 1997), 77–106.
38 The wording proposed to the 1972 General Conference was, 'All religious experience affects all human experience; all human experience affects our understanding of religious experience.' (The Theological Study Commission on Doctrine and Doctrinal Standards, report to the General Conference, April 1972 [n.p., n.d. [1972]), 34. This makes perfectly good sense. Unfortunately, when published this was reduced to the nearly nonsensical, 'All religious experience affects our understanding of religious experience.' UMC *Discipline 1972*, 78.
39 Randy L. Maddox, 'The Enriching Role of Experience' in *Wesley and the Quadrilateral*, ed. Gunter (Nashville, TN: Abingdon, 1997), 107–127 and esp. 126–127.
40 See the works by Abraham cited above.
41 UMC *Discipline 1972*, 75.
42 If in fact the 1972 statement had been adopted by the General Conference with the status of a constitutionally protected doctrinal statement (which would have required a three-quarters majority of the General Conference and subsequent approval by delegates to annual conferences), this language would indeed have directly contradicted the legal or juridical status of the historic doctrinal standards. However, although members of the Commission understood that the 1972 statement was to be accorded this status, the denomination's Judicial Council declared (prior to the vote) that it was simple legislation (which required a simple majority of the General Conference) and thus it was not accorded the status of a constitutionally protected doctrinal standard. Only the Confession of Faith, the Articles of Religion, and the General Rules retained that status.
43 This is my own interpretation of the intent of the 1972 statement of 'Our Theological Task' and I admit (as stated in the text) that there are warrants for the view that the 1972 statement subverted traditional teachings and practices.
44 UMC *Discipline 1972*, 69. This section was moved to the conclusion of the statement in the 1988 revision: UMC *Discipline 1988*, 87–88.
45 UMC *Discipline 1972*, 71–75; cf. UMC *Discipline 1988*, 42–50.
46 UMC *Discipline 1988*, 41.
47 Ted A. Campbell, *The Gospel in Christian Traditions* (New York: Oxford University Press, 2009).

Chapter 5

1 *Proceedings of the Oecumenical Methodist Conference, held in City Road Chapel, London, September 1881* (London: Wesleyan Conference Office, 1881), v–vi.
2 British Methodism is honored by this, but does not feel that it deserves it!
3 A useful and accessible guide to recent publications in Methodist history may be found in the bibliographies compiled by Clive Field and published annually in the *Proceedings of the Wesley Historical Society*. These serve as a continuation of the bibliographical section of Rupert Davies, A. Raymond George, and Gordon Rupp, eds, *A History of the Methodist Church in Great Britain*, (London: Epworth, 1988), 4:656–800.

4 Richard P. Heitzenrater, *The Elusive Mr Wesley* (Nashville: Abingdon, 1984) and *Wesley and the People called Methodists* (Nashville: Abingdon, 1995); Henry D. Rack, *Reasonable Enthusiast. John Wesley and the Rise of Methodism* (London: Epworth, 1989).
5 The pioneering study in this field is David W. Bebbington, *Evangelicalism in Modern Britain. A History from the 1730s to the 1980s* (London: Unwin Hyman, 1989). See also Mark D. Noll, *The Rise of Evangelicalism. The Age of Edwards, Whitefield and the Wesleys* (Leicester: IVP, 2004).
6 See John Walsh, Colin Haydon, and Stephen Taylor. eds, *The Church of England c. 1698–c. 1833. From Toleration to Tractarianism* (Cambridge: Cambridge University Press, 1993).
7 John Walsh and Stephen Taylor, 'Introduction: The Church and Anglicanism in the "Long" Eighteenth Century,' in Walsh, Haydon, and Taylor, 1. For an example of local studies, see Jeremy Gregory and Jeffrey S. Chamberlain, eds, *The National Church in Local Perspective* (Woodbridge: Boydell, 2003). For a nuanced study of Dissent in the early eighteenth century, see Geoffrey F. Nuttall, 'Methodism and the Old Dissent: Some Perspectives,' in *Studies in English Dissent* (Oswestry: Quinta, 2002), 263–281.
8 See W. R. Ward, *The Protestant Evangelical Awakening* (Cambridge: Cambridge University Press, 1992) and *Early Evangelicalism. A Global Intellectual History 1670–1789* (Cambridge: Cambridge University Press, 2006).
9 A theme pursued by Bruce Hindmarsh in *The Evangelical Conversion Narrative* (Oxford: Oxford University Press, 2005), by John Kent, *Wesley and the Wesleyans* (Cambridge: Cambridge University Press, 2002), 104–139, and most recently by Phyllis Mack, *Heart Religion in the British Enlightenment* (Cambridge: Cambridge University Press, 2008).
10 Kenneth G. C. Newport, *The Sermons of Charles Wesley* (Oxford: Oxford University Press, 2001); S T Kimbrough, Jr. and Kenneth G. C. Newport, eds, *The Manuscript Journal of the Reverend Charles Wesley, M.A.* (Nashville: Kingswood, 2008); Gareth Lloyd, *Charles Wesley and the Struggle for Methodist Identity* (Oxford: Oxford University Press, 2007).
11 David Hempton identifies this task in his *Methodism: Empire of the Spirit* (New Haven: Yale University Press, 2005), 78–79, 137–138, 145–146, 149–150.
12 Rack, 533.
13 J[ohn] A. V[ickers], 'America,' in John A. Vickers, ed., *A Dictionary of Methodism in Britain and Ireland* (Peterborough: Epworth, 2000), 5.
14 Dissenters were so named because they dissented from the formularies of the Church of England. The term was usually applied to the Presbyterians, Congregationalists, Baptists, and members of the Society of Friends.
15 In the British context, the continuing Connexion adopted the name 'Wesleyan,' so for British historical writing 'Wesleyan Methodist' generally refers to a denomination rather than to a theological position.
16 John Munsey Turner, 'Methodism and the Oxford Movement – Aggressive Anglicanism and Militant Dissent,' in *Conflict and Reconciliation. Studies in Methodism and Ecumenism in England 1740–1982* (London: Epworth, 1985), 160–165; Mats Selén, *The Oxford Movement and Wesleyan Methodism in England 1833–1882* (Lund: Lund University Press, 1992); Frances Knight, *The Nineteenth Century Church and English Society* (Cambridge: Cambridge University Press, 1995), 202.
17 John C. Bowmer, *Pastor and People* (London: Epworth, 1975); David Hempton, *The Religion of the People. Methodism and Popular Religion c. 1750–1900* (London: Routledge, 1996), especially chapters 5 and 6.
18 Julia Stewart Werner, *The Primitive Methodist Connexion. Its Background and Early History* (Madison: University of Wisconsin Press, 1984).

19 John K. Lander, *Itinerant Temples. Tent Methodism 1814–1832* (Carlisle: Paternoster, 2003); John Dolan, *The Independent Methodists. A History* (Cambridge: James Clarke, 2005).
20 Hempton, 162–178. Thompson was the grandson of a Wesleyan missionary.
21 A convenient summary of these groups may be found in John T. Wilkinson, 'The Rise of Other Methodist Traditions,' in Davies, George, and Rupp, 2: 276–329. The allocation of a single chapter to seven Connexions indicates the historiographical balance in favor of the Wesleyans.
22 Martin Wellings, *Evangelicals in Methodism: Mainstream, Marginal or Misunderstood?* (Ilkeston: Moorley, 2005), 18–19.
23 See, for example, references in Hempton, *Empire of the Spirit*, 162–163, and the first chapter in his *Religion of the People*.
24 Summarized by Henry Rack, 'Wesleyan Methodism 1849–1902,' in Davies, George, and Rupp, 3:119–166.
25 Christopher Oldstone-Moore, *Hugh Price Hughes. Founder of a new Methodism, Conscience of a new Nonconformity* (Cardiff: University of Wales Press, 1999).
26 For instance, Brian Harrison, *Drink and the Victorians* (London: Faber, 1971) and George Thompson Brake, *Drink. Ups and Downs in Methodist Attitudes to Temperance* (London: Oliphants, 1974).
27 David W. Bebbington, *The Nonconformist Conscience. Chapel and Politics 1870–1914* (London: George Allen and Unwin, 1982); Timothy Larsen, *Friends of Religious Equality. Nonconformist Politics in Mid-Victorian England* (Woodbridge: Boydell, 1999); Timothy Larsen, 'A Nonconformist Conscience? Free Churchmen in Parliament in Nineteenth-Century England,' in Stephen Taylor and David L. Wykes, eds, *Parliament and Dissent* (Edinburgh: Edinburgh University Press, 2005).
28 N. Allen Birtwhistle, 'Methodist Missions,' in Davies, George, and Rupp, 3:1–116.
29 The work of Brian Stanley, beginning with *The Bible and the Flag. Protestant Missions and British Imperialism in the Nineteenth and Twentieth Centuries* (Leicester: Apollos, 1990), is significant in this field.
30 Phrase taken from James F. Hopewell, *Congregation. Stories and Structures* (London: SCM Press, 1987), 4.
31 This approach has been modelled by Charles D. Cashdollar, *A Spiritual Home. Life in British and American Reformed Congregations, 1830–1915* (University Park, PA: Pennsylvania State University Press, 2000).
32 The present writer is not aware of any single-volume treatment of the period.
33 For instance, Dorothy Graham's work on the deaconess movement, *Saved to Serve* (Peterborough, Methodist Publishing House, 2002), and Michael Hughes' study of Methodist attitudes to peace and war, *Conscience and Conflict* (Peterborough: Epworth, 2008).
34 Martin Wellings, 'A Time to be born and a time to die? A historian's perspective on the future of Methodism,' in Jane Craske and Clive Marsh, eds, *Methodism and the Future* (London: Cassell, 1999), 148–149.
35 See, for example, A. J. P. Taylor, *English History 1914–1945* (Oxford: Oxford University Press, 1992), 168–169; Arthur Marwick, *British Society since 1945* (London: Penguin, 2003), 392.
36 G. I. T. Machin, *Churches and Social Issues in Twentieth-Century Britain* (Oxford: Clarendon, 1998); Bebbington, Evangelicalism in Modern Britain.
37 Adrian Hastings, *A History of English Christianity* (London: Collins, 1987), 714; Callum G. Brown, *The Death of Christian Britain* (London: Routledge, 2001), 253.
38 Hughes.
39 John Kent, *The Age of Disunity* (London: Epworth, 1960), 1–43; Robert Currie, *Methodism Divided* (London: Faber and Faber, 1968).

40 David Butler, *Dying to be One* (London: SCM Press, 1996), Chapters 10 and 12; David M. Chapman, *In Search of the Catholic Spirit. Methodists and Roman Catholics in Dialogue* (Peterborough: Epworth, 2004).
41 Two may be mentioned: George Thompson Blake, *Policy and Politics in British Methodism 1932–1982* (London: Edsall, 1984) and J. Munsey Turner, *Modern Methodism in England 1932–1998* (Peterborough: Epworth, 1998).
42 Particularly the celebrated triumvirate of London preachers, W. E. Sangster, Leslie Weatherhead, and Donald Soper, each of whom is the subject of several biographical studies.
43 The classical theory is set out by Robin Gill, *The Myth of the Empty Church* (London: SPCK, 1993), 1–13. For the debate, see Steve Bruce, ed., *Religion and Modernization. Sociologists and Historians debate the Secularization Thesis* (Oxford: Clarendon, 1992).
44 Approaches associated respectively with Steve Bruce, Grace Davie, and Callum Brown.
45 A program of the British Methodist Conference from the 1980s.
46 Irish ministers have been listed in different ways in the *Minutes* of the British Conference, sometimes as part of a single list, sometimes in a separate category.
47 To appreciate some of the similarities and differences between Great Britain and Ireland, see for example, Toby Barnard, *A New Anatomy of Ireland. The Irish Protestants, 1649–1770* (New Haven: Yale University Press, 2003).
48 Hempton, *Religion of the People*, 48.
49 The challenge of secularization in the Republic is identified by Dudley Levistone Cooney in his, *The Methodists in Ireland. A Short History* (Blackrock: The Columba Press, 2001), 248.
50 Hempton, *Religion of the People*, 29–48, 130–139.
51 Norman W. Taggart, *The Irish in World Methodism 1760–1900* (London: Epworth, 1986) and William Arthur: *First among Methodists* (London: Epworth, 1993).
52 Chapman, 6–43, discusses Wesley's attitude toward Roman Catholicism.
53 For example, Richard Watson's *Theological Institutes* was used as the textbook for Methodist preachers in Britain and America in this period.
54 The fourth volume consists of illustrative documents and a bibliography.

Chapter 6
1 This chapter draws upon, distills, and summarizes parts of *The Methodist Experience in America: A Narrative* by Russell E. Richey, Kenneth E. Rowe, and Jean Miller Schmidt (Nashville: Abingdon, forthcoming). Readers may wish to consult the companion volume, *The Methodist Experience in America: A Sourcebook*, Russell E. Richey, Kenneth E. Rowe, and Jean Miller Schmidt, eds. (Nashville: Abingdon, 2000), II, which contains several primary source documents related to this chapter.
2 Dee E. Andrews, *The Methodists and Revolutionary America, 1760–1800: The Shaping of An Evangelical Culture* (Princeton: Princeton University Press, 2000), 31. See also John H. Wigger, *Taking Heaven by Storm: Methodism and the Rise of Popular Christianity in America* (New York and Oxford: Oxford University Press, 1998) and David Hempton, *Methodism: Empire of the Spirit* (New Haven and London: Yale University Press, 2005).
3 *A Form of Discipline, For the Ministers, Preachers, and Members of the Methodist Episcopal Church in America* (New York, 1787), 3–7. Hereinafter the varying names of the Disciplines, minutes and journals of the Methodist movements will be cited with the abbreviated designation: Discipline, Church, year, so Discipline, MEC, 1787, 3–7.
4 Discipline, MEC, 1785, 3–4.
5 Neil Semple, *The Lord's Dominion: The History of Canadian Methodism* (Montreal and Kingston: McGill-Queen's University Press, 1996), 24, 42, 58.

6 Andrews, 32.
7 On Asbury see, John H. Wigger, *Francis Asbury: American Saint* (New York: Oxford University Press, 2009).
8 Andrews, 47–62.
9 Semple, 30–52.
10 *Minutes*, MEC (1773–1828), 1780: 13.
11 On Coke see Richard P. Heitzenrater, *Wesley and the People Called Methodists* (Nashville: Abingdon Press, 1995), 281–292 and John Vickers, *Thomas Coke: Apostle of Methodism* (London: Epworth Press; New York: Abingdon Press, 1969).
12 On Garrettson see Robert D. Simpson, *American Methodist Pioneer: The Life and Journals of the Rev. Freeborn Garrettson, 1752–1827* (Rutland, Vermont: Academy Books, 1984), especially p. 411 for Garrettson's appointments.
13 Semple, 30–52.
14 Cf. *Minutes*, MEC (1780) 3–4.
15 On black Methodism see J. Gordon Melton, *A Will to Choose: The Origins of African American Methodism* (Lanham: Rowman & Littlefield Publishers, 2007).
16 On Methodist women's experience, including the modeling by Rogers, elaboration of informal offices, creation of women's organizations, quest for lay rights and pursuit of ordination, see Jean Miller Schmidt, *Grace Sufficient: A History of Women in American Methodism, 1760–1939* (Nashville: Abingdon, 1999).
17 J. Bruce Behney and Paul H. Eller, *The History of the Evangelical United Brethren Church*, ed. Kenneth W. Krueger (Nashville: Abingdon, 1979).
18 Jesse Lee, *A Short History of the Methodists* (Baltimore, 1810; Rutland, VT: Academy Books, 1974), 149–150.
19 Lee, 178–179.
20 *The Doctrines and Discipline of the Methodist Episcopal Church in America, with Explanatory Notes by Thomas Coke and Francis Asbury* (Philadelphia, PA: Henry Tuckniss, 1798; reprint: Rutland, VT: Academy Books, 1979).
21 *Causes* (Philadelphia: Printed by Parry Hall and sold by John Dickins, 1792). Nicholas Snethen, *A Reply to an Apology for Protesting Against the Methodist Episcopal Government. Compiled principally from original manuscripts* (Philadelphia: Printed by Henry Tuckniss, 1800). See also Harlan L. Feeman, *Francis Asbury's Silver Trumpet* (Nashville: Parthenon Press, 1950).
22 Robert Paine, *Life and Times of William M'Kendree*, 2 vols. (Nashville, 1872), I, 397–404.
23 Paine, I, 419–421.
24 Created as a vehicle for the Baltimore Union Society, it is considered a continuation of the *Wesleyan Repository and Religious Intelligencer*. On the Methodist Protestant movement see William R. Sutton, *Journeymen for Jesus: Evangelical Artisans Confront Capitalism in Jacksonian Baltimore* (University Park, PA: Pennsylvania State University Press, 1998).
25 Reproduced in *The General Conferences of the Methodist Episcopal Church From 1792–1896*, Lewis Curts, ed. (Cincinnati: Curts & Jennings, 1900), 95–97.
26 See Edward J. Drinkhouse, *History of Methodist Reform. Synoptical of General Methodism 1703 to 1898 with special . . . reference to the History of the Methodist Protestant Church*, 2 vols. (Baltimore: Board of Publication of the Methodist Protestant Church, 1899) II, 62–63.
27 (Baltimore, 1827), 74.
28 Both appeared in 1827. Emory's bore the full title, *A Defense of 'Our Fathers,' and of the Original Organization of the Methodist Episcopal Church, Against the Rev. Alexander McCaine, and Others* (New York: N. Bangs and J. Emory, for the Methodist Episcopal Church, 1827). Bond's was reprinted in Thomas E. Bond, *The Economy of Methodism Illustrated and Defended* (New York: Lane & Scott, 1852), 9–56.

29 James E. Kirby, *The Episcopacy in American Methodism* (Nashville: Abingdon/Kingswood Books, 2000), 105–126.
30 *Zion's Herald* (Dec. 7, 1842), 190.
31 Robert T. West, reporter, *Report of Debates in the General Conference of the Methodist Episcopal Church . . . 1844* (New York: G. Lane & C. B. Tippett, 1844).
32 *Journal*, MEC (1844), 65–66.
33 Morris L. Davis, *The Methodist Unification: Christianity and the Politics of Race in the Jim Crow Era* (New York and London: New York University Press, 2008).
34 See the four-volume History of Methodist Missions series (New York: Board of Missions and Church Extension of The Methodist Church, and the Board of Global Ministries of The United Methodist Church, 1949–1973), and the seven-volume The United Methodist History of Mission series (New York: General Board of Global Ministries of The United Methodist Church, 2003–2005).
35 Riley B. Case, *Evangelical and Methodist: A Popular History* (Nashville: Abingdon Press, 2004), James V. Heidinger II and Steve Beard, eds, *Streams of Renewal: Welcoming New Life into United Methodism* (Wilmore, KY: Living Streams Publications, 2004), Leon Howell, *United Methodism @ Risk: A Wake-Up Call*, a study guide by Bishop C. Dale White and the Rev. Scott Campbell (Kingston, NY: Information Project for United Methodists, 2003). See also Steven M. Tipton, *Public Pulpits: Methodists and Mainline Churches in the Moral Argument of Public Life* (Chicago and London: University of Chicago Press, 2007) and Charles Yrigoyen, Jr., John G. McEllhenney, and Kenneth E. Rowe, *United Methodism at Forty: Looking Back, Looking Forward* (Nashville: Abingdon, 2008).
36 *Discipline*, UMC, 1972, 39–82, 83–97. See especially 68–70, 79–81.
37 See the four-volume Methodism and Society series (Nashville: Abingdon Press, 1961).

Chapter 7
1 See A. Scott Moreau, ed., *Evangelical Dictionary of World Missions* [*EDWM*] (Grand Rapids, MI: Baker, 2000), 636–637, on varied meanings and usages of the terms 'missions' and 'mission'; Niles, *Upon the Earth* (New York: McGraw-Hill, 1962), 10–11.
2 *Encyclopedia of World Methodism* (Nashville, TN: United Methodist Publishing House, 1974), II: 1634–1640. *The Encyclopedia of Modern Christian Missions: The Agencies* (Camden, NJ: Nelson, 1967) contains essays on the MC, AME, AMEZ, and Nazarene mission boards in the USA as well as Methodism in the UK, Australia, and New Zealand.
3 Gerald H. Anderson, ed., *Biographical Dictionary of Christian Missions* (Grand Rapids, MI: Eerdmans, 1998) contains short biographies and sources for further information for most persons included in this essay. See also Anderson, et al., eds, *Mission Legacies* (Maryknoll, NY: Orbis, 1995), and biographical entries in Moreau, ed., *EDWM*.
4 Elmer T. Clark, J. Manning Potts and Jacob S. Payton, eds, *The Journal and Letters of Francis Asbury* (Nashville, TN: Abingdon, 1958), III, 491–492.
5 Winthrop Hudson, 'The Methodist Age in America,' in *Methodist History* 12 (1974): 3–15.
6 Robert W. Sledge, *'Five Dollars and Myself': The History of Mission of the Methodist Episcopal Church, South, 1845–1939* (New York: GBGM, 2005), 74–83, 258–261.
7 Wade Crawford Barclay, History of Methodist Missions, I/II: 41–42. See also Dana L. Robert, *American Women in Mission* (Macon, GA: Mercer University Press, 1996), 126–127 and 170–173.
8 Robert, 413.

Notes

9 Neill, *A History of Christian Missions* (Harmondsworth: Penguin Books, 1964), 322–396.
10 See Charles W. Forman, 'The Legacy of George Brown,' *IBMR* 22 (1998): 28–33, and Alan R. Tippett, *Deep Sea Canoe: The Story of Third World Missionaries in the South Pacific* (Pasadena, CA: William Carey Library, 1977).
11 Sannah, *Translating the Message: The Missionary Impact on Culture*, rev. ed. (Maryknoll, NY: Orbis, 2009), 12.
12 For a detailed history see R. Pierce Beaver, *American Women in World Mission*, rev. ed. (Grand Rapids, MI: Eerdmans, 1980), 95–101; Sledge, 257–265; and Robert, 125–188.
13 Montgomery, *Western Women in Eastern Lands: An Outline Study of Fifty Years of Woman's Work in Foreign Missions* (New York: Macmillan, 1910), 32; Robert, 137.
14 Latourette, *History of the Expansion of Christianity*, vol. 7 (New York: Harper, 1945).
15 Charles Howard Hopkins, 'John R Mott 1865–1955: Architect of World Mission and Unity,' in *Mission Legacies*, 79.
16 See J. Stephen O'Malley, *'On the Journey Home': The History of Mission of the Evangelical United Brethren Church, 1946–1968* (New York: General Board of Global Ministries, 2003), 79–149.
17 Robert, 303.
18 Nicholson, *The Place of Women in the Church on the Mission Field* (London: IMC, 1927).
19 Their autobiographies are Dodge, *The Revolutionary Bishop* (Pasadena, CA: William Carey, 1986), and Muzorewa, *Rise Up and Walk* (Nashville, TN: Abingdon, 1978).
20 John W. Egerton, 'The New Missionary,' in *The Christian Century* 82 (December 8, 1965): 1509.
21 For papers from the 1950s consultations see Gerald H. Anderson, ed., *Christian Mission in Theological Perspective* (Nashville, TN: Abingdon, 1967). For details of the efforts in the 1980s see Harmon, *From Missions to Mission* (New York: GBGM, 2005), 169–172, and Cole, ed., *Initiatives for* Mission (New York: GBGM, 2003), 25–38. For a more detailed treatment of theologies of mission by Methodists see Dana Robert, 'Traditions and Transitions in Mission' in Abraham and Kirby, eds, *The Oxford Handbook of Methodist Studies* (Oxford: Oxford University Press, 2009).
22 Missiology is the 'science of missions, missionary history, missionary thought and missionary methods.' See 22 David Barrett, George Thomas Kurian, Todd M. Johnson, eds, *World Christian Encyclopedia*, 2nd ed. (New York: Oxford University Press, 2001), 2:666.
23 Walls, *The Cross-Cultural Process in Christian History* (Maryknoll, NY: Orbis, 2002), 69.

Chapter 8
1 *WJW(B)*, 21:172.
2 *WJW(B)*, 21:172.
3 J. Kofi Agbeti, *West African Church History* (Leiden: E. J. Brill, 1986), 19.
4 Elizabeth Isichei, *A History of Christianity in Africa: From Antiquity to the Present* (Grand Rapids, MI: Eerdmans, 1995), 162–163.
5 Isichei, 163.
6 Agbeti, 20.
7 Isichei, 162.
8 Agbeti, 49.
9 Agbeti, 50.
10 Agbeti, 50.
11 *World Methodist Council Handbook of Information* (Lake Junaluska, NC: World Methodist Council, 2003), 227.

12 J. Bruce Behney and Paul H. Eller, *The History of the Evangelical United Brethren Church* (Nashville, TN: Abingdon Press, 1979), 170–172.
13 *World Methodist Council Handbook of Information* (2003), 225–226.
14 Agbeti, 54.
15 Agbeti, 54.
16 Agbeti, 54.
17 Agbeti, 54.
18 Agbeti, 56.
19 Isichei, 169.
20 Agbeti, 57.
21 Isichei, 170.
22 *World Methodist Council Handbook of Information* (2003), 159–161.
23 Agbeti, 144.
24 Agbeti, 147.
25 *World Methodist Council Handbook of Information* (1992), 32.
26 Harvey J. Sindima, *Drums of Redemption* (Westport, CT: Greenwood Press, 1994), 76.
27 *The Book of Discipline of The United Methodist Church, Africa Central Conference Edition, 1988* (n.p., 1990), 3.
28 Frederick Perry Noble, *The Redemption of Africa* (n.p., 1899), 304.
29 Wade Crawford Barclay, *Early American Methodism 1769–1844*, History of Methodist Missions (New York: Board of Missions and Church Extension of the Methodist Church, 1949), 330.
30 Noble, 305.
31 Barclay, 330.
32 J. Tremayne Copplestone, *Twentieth-Century Perspectives (The Methodist Episcopal Church, 1896–1939)*, History of Methodist Missions (New York: Board of Global Ministries of The United Methodist Church, 1973), 519.
33 Copplestone, 526.
34 Copplestone, 527.
35 Copplestone, 527.
36 Agbeti, 143.
37 Isichei, 171.
38 *World Methodist Council Handbook of Information* (1992), 87.
39 Agbeti, 60.
40 Agbeti, 60.
41 Agbeti, 61.
42 Agbeti, 61.
43 *World Methodist Council Handbook of Information* (1992), 87.
44 Peter Marubitoba and Peter Marubitoba Dong, *The History of the United Methodist Church in Nigeria* (Nashville, TN: Abingdon Press, 2000), 21.
45 Dong, 22.
46 Dong, 28.
47 Dong, 32.
48 Dong, 32.
49 Dong, 71.
50 Jane M. Sales, *The Planting of the Churches in South Africa* (Grand Rapids, MI: Eerdmans, 1971), 60.
51 Sales, 60.
52 Nontshakaza Bulelani, 'A Brief History of Methodism in South Africa,' unpublished paper presented in 2008 at Africa University, Old Mutare, Zimbabwe.

53 Kenneth Scott Latourette, *A History of the Expansion of Christianity* (New York: Harper and Brothers, 1943), IV: 330.
54 *World Methodist Council Handbook of Information* (1992), 114.
55 Bulelani, 2.
56 Copplestone, 569–570.
57 Adilson L. S. de Almeida, 'A Challenge to the Ministry of Evangelism for the Deaf in Africa in the 21st Century: A Case Study of the West Angola and Zimbabwe East Annual Conferences of the United Methodist Church,' PhD diss., Africa University, 2007, 63f.
58 Copplestone, 572
59 Copplestone, 572.
60 Copplestone, 572.
61 Peter Bolink, *Towards Church Union in Zambia* (n.p.: T. Wever Franeker, 1967), 68.
62 Bolink, 73.
63 Bolink, 75
64 Bolink, 75.
65 Noble, 313.
66 Michael C. Kasongo, *History of the Methodist Church in Central Congo, 1912–1997* (Lanham, MD: University Press of America, 1998), 7.
67 Kasongo, 10ff.
68 Kasongo, 37.
69 Copplestone, 92.
70 Copplestone, 93ff.
71 Copplestone, 104–105.
72 Copplestone, 913.
73 Copplestone, 928.
74 Copplestone, 929.
75 Bulelani, 2.
76 Alf Helgesson, *Church, State and People in Mozambique: An Historical Study with Special Emphasis on Methodist Developments in the Inhambane Region* (Uppsala: International Tryck AB, 1994), 60.
77 Bulelani, 2.
78 Helgesson, 89.
79 John Wesley Z. Kurewa, *The Church in Mission: A Short History of The United Methodist Church in Zimbabwe, 1897–1997* (Nashville, TN: Abingdon Press, 1997), 20.
80 Helgesson, 205.
81 Helgesson, 204.
82 Helgesson, 207.
83 Helgesson, 207.
84 Helgesson, 208.
85 Helgesson, 209.
86 Helgesson, 343
87 Canaan Sodindo Banana, ed., *A Century of Methodism in Zimbabwe, 1891–1991* (Harare: Causeway, 1991), 8.
88 Banana, 114.
89 *World Methodist Council Handbook of Information* (1992), 132–133.
90 Zablon John Nthamburi, *A History of the Methodist Church in Kenya* (Nairobi: Uzima Press, 1982), xvff.
91 Nthamburi, 71.
92 Nthamburi, 64.
93 Jean Ntahorturi, 'Evangelistic Challenge to a Church in a Conflict-Ridden Region:

An Assessment of the Evangelistic Mission of the United Methodist Church in Burundi, 1962–2002,' unpublished dissertation (n.p., 2004), 51.
94 Ntahorturi, 51.
95 Ntahorturi, 99.
96 Ntahorturi, 99.
97 Peter Stephens, *Methodism in Europe* (Cincinnati, OH: Service Center, General Board of Global Ministries of the United Methodist Church, 1981), 50.
98 Stephens, 50.
99 Stephens, 51.

Chapter 9
1 Philip Jenkins, *The Next Christendom: The Coming of Global Christianity* (New York: Oxford University Press, 2002), 2–6. See also Andrew F. Walls, *The Missionary Movement in Christian History: Studies in the Transmission of Faith* (New York: Orbis Books, 1996), chap. 6 passim; and Dana L. Robert, 'Shifting Southward: Global Christianity since 1945,' International Bulletin of Missionary Research 24 (2000): 53–56.
2 The use of the word 'translated' is based on a discussion by Andrew Walls on the 'translation principle,' in Walls, 26–42. Dana Robert also argues that 'that scholarship ignored the way in which ordinary people were receiving the gospel message and retranslating it into cultural modes that fitted their worldviews and met their needs.' See Robert, 53.
3 See Robbie B. H. Goh, *Sparks of Grace: The Story of Methodism in Asia* (Singapore: Methodist Church in Singapore, 2003), chap. 2 passim.
4 See Andrew F. Walls, 'Methodists, Missions and Pacific Christianity: A New Chapter in Christian History,' in Peter Lineham, ed., *Weaving the Unfinished Mats: Wesley's Legacy-Conflict, Confusion and Challenge in the South Pacific* (Auckland, New Zealand: Wesley Historical Society, 2007), 18–24.
5 For a comprehensive historical account on the WMMS, see George G. Findlay and William W. Holdsworth, *The History of the Wesleyan Methodist Missionary Society*, 5 vols. (London: Epworth Press, 1921–1925). Hereafter the Society is referred to as WMMS. David Hempton has acknowledged the difficulty of establishing a precise date for the origin of the WMMS and pointed to the year 1786, which occasioned Thomas Coke's address calling for monetary support for Methodist missions in the Scottish Highlands and its adjacent islands, the West Indies, and Quebec, as its possible beginning. See David Hempton, *Methodism: Empire of the Spirit* (New Haven: Yale University Press, 2005), 158–159. Hempton has also argued that the formation of the society can be attributed to Wesleyan Methodist 'expansive optimism.' See David Hempton, *Methodism and Politics in British Society* (Stanford, CA: Stanford University Press, 1984), 96–98. For details and issues surrounding the society's launching, see Findlay and Holdsworth, 1: 36–55. Further reflection is found in Walls, 'Methodists, Missions and Pacific Christianity,' 16–26, and David Hempton, *The Religion of the People: Methodism and Popular Religion c. 1750–1900* (London: Routledge, 1996), 103–105.
6 See Walls, 'Methodists, Missions and Pacific Christianity,' 21–24, and Hempton, Religion of the People, 103.
7 Kenneth Cracknell and Susan J. White, *An Introduction to World Methodism* (Cambridge: Cambridge University Press, 2005), 78–80. For a comprehensive history of Wesleyan Methodist work in Ceylon, see Findlay and Holdsworth, 5: pt. 1 passim.
8 Findlay and Holdsworth, 5: 176–180.
9 For a short history of Methodism in Myanmar, see Goh, 88–90.
10 A quick summary of Wesleyan Methodist mission to Australia and the Pacific

is found in Cracknell and White, 83–85. For a comprehensive early history, see Findlay and Holdsworth, vol. 3.
11 A short history of Methodism in Hong Kong is found in Goh, 152–154.
12 Hempton, *Empire of the Spirit*, 157. For a comprehensive history of the MSMEC see Wade Crawford Barclay, *Methodist Episcopal Church, 1845–1939: Widening Horizons, 1845–1895*, History of Methodist Missions, (New York: Board of Missions and Church Extension of the Methodist Church, 1957), 3:194–364. Hereafter, HMMMEC.
13 Russell E. Richey, 'Organizing for Missions: A Methodist Case Study,' in Daniel H. Bays and Grant Wacker, eds, *Foreign Missionary Enterprise at Home* (Tuscaloosa and London: University of Alabama Press, 2003), 77, 89. This view is reinforced and argued as similar with British Methodism in Walls, 'Methodists, Missions and Pacific Christianity,' 18–24.
14 Hempton, *Empire of the Spirit*, 156–157.
15 HMMMEC, 3: 367–369.
16 HMMMEC, 3: 449–451.
17 Cracknell and White, 80–81. For Pakistan, see Goh, 73–74.
18 HWMMS, 1:139; cf. Cracknell and White, 78–79.
19 HWMMS, 5: 176–180. For a brief summary on the British East India Company, see 'East India Company, British,' in *The Columbia Encyclopedia* (New York: Columbia University Press, 2008).
20 I digress, to some degree, from White and Cracknell's positive assessment of missionary participation in the Waitangi Treaty. See Cracknell and White, 84. For some the history and helpful insights on missionary role behind the treaty, see Douglas Pratt, 'From Missionary Paternalism to Bicultural Partnership: Aspects of Anglican and Methodist Experience in Aotearoa-New Zealand,' *International Review of Mission* 82/327 (1993): 305–308; W. Jim Stuart, 'Enduring Tensions in New Zealand Methodism,' in Peter Lineham, ed., *Weaving the Unfinished Mats: Wesley's Legacy-Conflict, Confusion and Challenge in the South Pacific* (Auckland, New Zealand: Wesley Historical Society, 2007), 140–141.
21 This does not mean, however, that missions is a 'moral equivalent of imperialism' as argued, for example, in William R. Hutchison, *Errand to the World: American Protestant Thought and Foreign Missions* (Chicago: University of Chicago Press, 1987), 91–124; Arthur Schlesinger, Jr., 'The Missionary Enterprise and Theories of Imperialism,' in John K. Fairbank, ed., *Missionary Enterprise in China and America*, (Cambridge, MA: Harvard University Press, 1974), 336–373. A counter argument can be found in Andrew Porter, ' "Cultural Imperialism" and Protestant Missionary Enterprise, 1780–1914,' *Journal of Imperial and Commonwealth History* 25/3 (September 1997): 367–391.
22 Barclay claims that government relations between the United States and China 'for the most part were good.' See HMMMEC, 3: 432–435.
23 HMMMEC, 3: 367–448.
24 HMMMEC, 3: 664–667.
25 HMMMEC, 3: 741–757; Goh, 163–170.
26 See J. Tremayne Copplestone, *Twentieth-Century Perspectives, the Methodist Episcopal Church, 1896–1939*, History of Methodist Missions (New York: United Methodist Church, 1973), chap. 4 passim. Hereafter HMMMEC, 4. It is also important to note that Homer C. Stuntz, for instance, in comparing membership statistics in other MEC fields showed that by 1903, a four-year-old Philippine Methodism had already outpaced MEC membership rolls in Japan, Korea, Mexico, South America, and Africa. See Homer C. Stuntz, *The Philippines and the Far East* (Cincinnati: Jennings and Pye, 1904), 453–454. For a survey of MEC attitudes toward the annexation of the Philippines, see Kenneth M. Mackenzie, *The Robe and the Sword: The*

Methodist Church and the Rise of American Imperialism (Washington, DC: Public Affairs Press, 1961), chap. 6 passim.
27 For this analysis on early Philippine Methodist history, see Luther J. Oconer, 'The Culto Pentecostal Story: Holiness Revivalism and the Making of Philippine Methodist Identity, 1899–1965' (PhD diss., Drew University, 2009), 66–74.
28 William B. Scranton, 'Korea,' Annual Report of the Missionary Society of the Methodist Episcopal Church (1893), 255; cf. HMMMEC, 3: 756.
29 See Findlay and Holdsworth, 5: 31–35, 97–101. An interesting summary is also found in Goh, 41–48.
30 See Findlay and Holdsworth, 5: 203–206.
31 See Findlay and Holdsworth, 5: 170–173. A comprehensive history of the WA can be found in Findlay and Holdswoth, 4: pt. 1 passim. Robert deals with the 'Woman's Work for Woman' missiological concept in her *American Women in Mission: A Social History of Their Thought and Practice, The Modern Mission Era, 1792–1992* (Macon, GA: Mercer University Press, 1996), 130–137.
32 See HMMMEC, 3: 367–370.
33 HMMMEC, 3: 414–415. The story is detailed in Frances J. Baker, *The Story of the Woman's Foreign Missionary Society of the Methodist Episcopal Church, 1869–1895* (Cincinnati: Curts & Jennings, 1898), 147–151.
34 Robert, American Women in Mission, 162–167; HMMMEC, 3: 506–508. For Clara Swain's biography, see [Mrs.] Robert Hoskins, *Clara A. Swain, M.D.: The First Medical Missionary to the Women of the Orient* (Boston: Woman's Foreign Missionary Society Methodist Episcopal Church, 1912).
35 HMMMEC, 3: 370–371.
36 The early history of Nanking University is given in HMMMEC, 3: 410.
37 HMMMEC, 3: 416, 443–444.
38 See Baker, 189–194; James M. Thoburn, *Life of Isabella Thoburn* (New York: Eatons & Mains, 1903), 181–194.
39 HMMMEC, 3: 744–746.
40 For Wesley's notion on real Christianity, see John Wesley, *The Almost Christian: A Sermon Preached at St. Mary's, Oxford, before the University, on July 25, 1741* (London: W. Strahan, 1741). For his intent on the Methodist societies, see John Wesley, *The Nature, Design, and General Rules of the United Societies in London, Bristol, Kingswood, and Newcastle Upon Tyne*, 2nd ed. (Bristol: Felix Farley, 1743).
41 Walls also raised a similar question. See Walls, 'Methodists, Missions and Pacific Christianity,' 26. This question is also addressed in the Oconer dissertation, 38–40.
42 See George S. Rowe, *The Life of John Hunt: Missionary to the Cannibals* (London: Hamilton, Adams, and Co., 1860), 41–54. Hunt's summary of his work in Fiji is quoted on 191–192. See also Walls, 'Methodists, Missions and Pacific Christianity,' 26.
43 For the shifts in the doctrine of holiness and its relationship to Pentecostalism, see Donald W. Dayton, *Theological Roots of Pentecostalism, Studies in Evangelicalism*, no. 5 (Metuchen, NJ: Scarecrow, 1987).
44 Robert, American Women in Mission, 144–148; idem, 'Holiness and the Missionary Vision of the Woman's Foreign Missionary Society of the Methodist Episcopal Church, 1869–1894,' *Methodist History* 39/1 (October 2000): 15–27.
45 For the influence of holiness piety on the SVM, see Michael Parker, *The Kingdom of Character: The Student Volunteer Movement for Foreign Missions (1886–1926)* (Lanham, MD: American Society of Missiology and University Press of America, Inc., 1998), 36–41. Cf. Oconer, 61–62.
46 Percentage extracted from 'Appendix A: List of Sailed Volunteers,' in *Students and the Present Missionary Crisis: Addresses Delivered before the Sixth International Convention of the Student Volunteer Movement for Foreign Missions, Rochester, New York,*

Notes

December 29, 1909, to January 2, 1910 (New York: Student Volunteer Movement for Foreign Missions, 1910), 513–532; 'Appendix A: List of Sailed Student Volunteers,' in Fennell P. Turner, ed., *Students and the World-Wide Expansion of Christianity: Addresses Delivered before the Seventh International Convention of the Student Volunteer Movement for Foreign Missions, Kansas City, Missouri, December 31, 1913 to January 4, 1914* (New York: Student Volunteer Movement for Foreign Missions, 1914), 641–670. A similar argument is made, in the case of the revivalistic character of Korean Protestantism, by Dae Young Ryu, 'The Origin and Characteristics of Evangelical Protestantism in Korea at the Turn of the Century,' *Church History* 77/2 (June 2008): 390.

47 For a comprehensive account of William Taylor's self-supporting ministry in India, see William Taylor, *Four Years' Campaign in India* (New York: Phillips & Hunt, 1875); idem, *Ten Years of Self-Supporting Missions in India* (New York: Phillips & Hunt, 1882). See also David T. Bundy, 'Bishop William Taylor and Methodist Mission: A Study in Nineteenth Century Social History, Part II,' *Methodist History* 28/1 (October 1989): 3–7; idem, 'The Legacy of William Taylor,' *International Bulletin of Missionary Research* 18 (1994): 172–176; Guy D. Garrett, 'The Missionary Career of James Mills Thoburn' (PhD diss., Boston University, 1968), 69–74; David Hempton, *Methodism: Empire of the Spirit* (New Haven: Yale University Press, 2005), 168–176.

48 See David O. Ernsberger, 'Story of the South Indian Conference,' in Frederick B. Price, ed., *India Mission Jubilee of the Methodist Episcopal Church in Southern Asia: Story of the Celebration Held at Bareilly, India, from December 28th, 1906, to January 1st, 1907, Inclusive* (Calcutta: Methodist Publishing House, 1907), 168; Bessie R. Beal, *Bishop John Edward Robinson* (Lucknow, India: Centenary Forward Movement Methodist Church in Southern Asia, 1958), 7.

49 Francis W. Warne, 'Jottings from Manila,' *Indian Witness* 27 (April 1900): 2.

50 For details of Moots' revival work among soldiers, see Cornelia C. Moots, *Pioneer 'Americanas' or First Methodist Missionaries in the Philippines* (Bay City, MI: Cornelia Chillson Moots, 1903), 52; cf. Oconer, 77–78.

51 Janet L. Luckcock, *Thomas of Tonga 1707–1881: The Unlikely Pioneer* (Peterborough, UK: Methodist Publishing House, 1992), 108–109; Alfred H. Wood, *Overseas Mission of the Australian Methodist Church*, (Melbourne: Aldersgate Press, 1975), 1: 54–57. A summary is found in Manase Koloamatangi Tafea, 'The Tongan Pentecost of 1834. A Revival in the Kingdom of Tonga: A Possible Key for Renewal and Unity for the Tongan Church Today' (D.Min. thesis, Asbury Theological Seminary, 1999), 16–20.

52 See Rowe, 178–192.

53 For more about the MEC Indian mass movements, see HMMMEC, 4: 787–833; Francis W. Warne, *India's Mass Movement* (New York: Board of Foreign Missions of the Methodist Episcopal Church, 1915). A recent related study can be found in James E. Taneti, 'Dalit Conversions to the Methodist Episcopal Church in Karnataka,' *Methodist History* 45/4 (2007): 204–213.

54 See, for example, a concern raised by Amy Wilson Carmichael of the Church of England Zenana Missionary Society in her *Things as They Are: Mission Work in Southern India* (London: Morgan and Scott, 1905), 286–288.

55 Oconer, 43–47.

56 See John E. Robinson, 'Days of Power and Blessing at Asansol,' *Indian Witness*, 21 December 1905, 3–4; Francis W. Warne, *The Revival in the Indian Church* (New York: Board of Foreign Missions Methodist Episcopal Church, 1907), 9–11. For secondary literature, see e.g., Gary B. McGee, 'Pentecostal Phenomena and Revivals in India: Implications for Indigenous Church Leadership,' *International Bulletin of Missionary Research* 20/3 (July 1996): 114, 16; idem, ' "Baptism of the Holy Ghost

& Fire!" the Mission Legacy of Minnie F. Abrams,' *Missiology* 27/4 (October 1999): 517–519.
57 Homer C. Stuntz, 'Missionary Outlook in the Philippines,' *The Gospel in All Lands*, (October 1901): 452. The development of this shift to holiness revivalism is detailed in Oconer, 93–102; idem, 'Holiness Revivalism in Early Philippine Methodism.' Methodist *History* 44/ 2 (January 2006): 80–93.
58 See, e.g., Young Hoon Lee, 'Korean Pentecost: The Great Revival of 1907,' *Asian Journal of Pentecostal Studies* 4/1 (2001): 73–83; Myung Soo Park, ' "The Korea Pentecost": A Study of the Revival of 1903–1910 in Relationship to Contemporary Worldwide Holiness Revival Movements,' in Charles Yrigoyen, Jr., ed., *The Global Impact of the Wesleyan Traditions and Their Related Movement* (Lanham, MD: Scarecrow Press, Inc., 2002), 185–200. Park has also effectively demonstrated the strong relationship of the Holiness movement with bishops and missionaries connected with the MEC mission in Korea.
59 A description of the Hinghwa Revival and its influenced on John Sung is explored in Leslie T. Lyall, *A Biography of John Sung* (Singapore: Armour Publishing, 2004), chap. 2 passim; Timothy Tow, *John Sung My Teacher* (Singapore: Christian Life Publishers, 1985), chap. 3 passim.

Chapter 10
1 This chapter focuses on Europe except the United Kingdom, Ireland, Russia, and the Baltic states; other essays focus on these countries. The term 'Northern Europe' is insofar conditionally accurate as the Baltic States and Russia also belong to it.
2 Strictly speaking Europe is only a subcontinent of Eurasia. Because of its special historical and cultural background it is common to speak about Europe as a continent.
3 Because of the legal rule of the Peace of Augsburg (1555), 'cuius region, eius religio' (whose region, whose religion), through the centuries the areas were largely homogeneous according to the confession of the inhabitants.
4 Soviet Union (1922–1991): a federal state made up of fifteen republics (sixteen between 1946 and 1956): Armenia, Azerbaijan, *Belarus, Estonia,* Georgia, Kazakhstan, Kyrgyzstan, *Latvia, Lithuania, Moldova, Russia,* Tajikistan, Turkmenistan, *Ukraine,* Uzbekistan (underlined states are European states); other communist governments in Europe existed after World War I or II up to the 1990s in the Czech Republic (1918–1992), Poland (1945–1989), Yugoslavia (1945–1963, later independent from the Soviet Union – socialistic), Hungary (1949–1989), Bulgaria (1944–1989), Rumania (1947–1989), Albania (1948–1992); under communistic influence, from 1952 with socialistic government: East Germany/German Democratic Republic (1949–1990).
5 The European Union was originally founded in 1951 by six western European countries basically because of collective economical interests. It emerged with enlarged political interests (e.g., foundation of a European parliament in 1979) and more member states – today twenty-seven states (without Switzerland with a declared neutrality since 1647, continued realized since 1815; Croatia, Macedonia, Albania, Serbia, Montenegro, Bosnia-Herzegovina).
6 The listed aspects are very striking only to make aware the specific situation that has to be in mind when reflecting the mission circumstances – the particular local situation is much more complicated and a conglomerate of different aspects as social, political, economical, cultural as well as personal aspects.
7 The explanation below relates largely to Streiff, *Der Methodismus in Europa im 19. und 20. Jahrhundert.* Based on quite different secondary literature, subscripts, conference minutes and mission board reports Patrick Streiff carried a remarkable inventory on the history of the Methodists of the different European countries. It is

Notes

a survey that needs more detailed researches in various regions and stimulates lots of research questions. The main used publications see listed below.
8 E.g. in France where the WM tied in with people of the minority Reformed Church around Nimes or Paris, or in the French-speaking Switzerland. It was also the case in Germany, Norway, Sweden, and Finland inside the Lutheran Church as well and in the German-speaking Switzerland, there again inside the main Reformed Church.
9 That was also the case with Macedonia, where a Congregational mission answered the call and later on handed the mission over to the MEC (in 1921; at that time Macedonia became part of Yugoslavia).
10 That is how P. Streiff interprets this advance (see Streiff, *Der Methodismus in Europa*, 58).
11 Portugal, Spain, Austria-Hungary, France, Italy. After the Italian Revolution in 1848, the national Italian Union as well as the annexation of the Vatican State (1861) the euphoric thought arose to enter Italy and for all Rome to convert liberal roman catholic priests (what really happened) and introduce Methodism. A growing identity and lay piety of Roman Catholicism developed not least because of the pressure in some states (e.g., the so-called 'Kulturkampf,' a struggle between the Catholic Church and the Prussian state 1872–1887, similar in Switzerland while in Austria the power struggle succeeded more moderate). Also results of the Vaticanum I and the founding of Roman Catholic political parties growing 'ultramontanism' were observed very sceptical from Protestant perspectives and forced the fear of Roman Catholic imperialism. At the beginning of the twentieth century a very aggressive 'Los-von-Rom-Bewegung' ('exempt-of-Rome-movement') started. It was rooted in Austria after a long suffered counter-reformation period and carried by Protestants and Old-Catholics broadening to other countries.
12 That is the reason why this article mainly focuses on these areas with short notes about the other European countries where detailed historical researches are needed.
13 Here and below some examples making no claim to be complete: Bulgaria 1864 Zornitza (MEC), Italy 1870 Il Corriere Evangelico (WM), Denmark 1873 Missionstidende (MEC), Sweden 1868 Lilla Sändebudet (MEC); Germany 1850 Der Evangelist (MEC), 1863 Der Evangelische Botschafter (EA), 1873–1889 Methodisten-Herold, 1890–1897 der Sonntagsgast (WM), Die Geschäftige Martha/Der Deutsche Telescope/Der Froehliche Botschafter; 1883 Der Heilsbote (UBC); France 1853 Les Archives du Méthodisme/later: L'Evangéliste (WM); Norway Kristelig Tidende (MEC).
14 Examples: Germany 1850 Bremen (MEC), 1871 Nürtingen (EA); Norway 1867 (MEC), Sweden ca. 1874 (MEC), Switzerland 1895 (EA), Norway 1867 Oslo (MEC).
15 Examples: Germany 1858 Bremen (MEC), 1864 Waiblingen (WM), 1877 Reutlingen (EA), 1952 Bad Klosterlausnitz/GDR (EA/MC); Switzerland (French-speaking area) 1850h Lausanne (MEC together with the Free Reformed Church), Sweden 1874 Orebro → Stockholm → Uppsala (MEC), Denmark/Norway 1874 Oslo (MEC); Finland 1897 Tampere → Helsinki (MEC); 1924 Goteborg for all Scandinavian Countries (MEC); Italy 1893 Rom (MEC); France 1889 Paris (WM); Baltic States 1994 Tallinn/Estonia; Russia 1991/95 Moscow; Austria 1986 Graz/Waiern; Belgium 1950 Protestant Theological Faculty Brussels (MC and two other Protestant Churches); Czechoslovakia 1950 'Comenius Faculty Prague' (MC and Protestant Churches); Poland 1983 (UMC).
16 The centers were founded in Germany and spread out to other countries: Germany 1874 'Bethanien-Verein Frankfurt a.M.' (MEC), 1886 'Bethesdaverein für allgemeine Krankenpflege zu Elberfeld' (EA); 1889 'Martha-Maria-Verein Nürnberg' (WM); Norway 1897 'Sosternhjemmet Bethanien' (MEC), 1900 'Diakonissenschwesternschaft in Sweden' (MEC); Denmark 1895 'Bethanienverein' (MEC).

17 Examples: Different types of schools for girls (later on also boys) in Italy, Spain, Portugal, Hungary, Yugoslavia, Macedonia, Bulgaria, residential school in Albania. Very popular became up to today the 'International School Monte Mario,' 'International Crandon Institute,' and as social institution the children's home 'Casa Materna' in Italy.
18 Nowadays there are in Europe: the Austria Provisional Annual Conference, Bulgaria Provisional Annual Conference, Hungary Provisional Annual Conference, and Serbia/Macedonia Provisional Annual Conference.
19 This was according to John Wesley's understanding of a 'world parish' that was rediscovered.
20 In times of national exaltation the demand for independence from alien influences easily arose.
21 In 1893 a central council for Europe was initialized ('Zentralrat der Konferenzen und Missionen der Bischöflichen Methodistenkirche in Europa'). It met 1895 in Berlin (Germany), 1903 in Zürich/Switzerland (than named 'Methodist Episcopal Church Congress'), and 1907 in Copenhagen (Denmark).
22 1911 the first MEC bishop (Bishop Burt) was stationed in Europe, namely in Zurich/Switzerland. 1912 Bishop John Nuelsen, a German-American was elected and worked in continuity up to 1940 in Europe – from 1924 on as bishop of the Middle European Central Conference. In 1928 the right to elect their own bishops was given to the CCs by the GC.
23 The most painful shift happened in 1936 when – because of the difficult political situation – Germany organized a single German Central Conference with bishop parish (see Schweizer, Urs. *Mit dem Feuer der ersten Liebe und dem tiefen, stillen Wasser des bewährten Glaubens. 50 Jahre Zentralkonferenz von Mittel- und Südeuropa der Evangelisch-methodistischen Kirche*. Zurich 2005) As a consequence of the Iron Curtain a second German Central Conference for the GDR was established in 1970.
24 The *Northern Europe Central Conference* (Denmark, Estonia, Finland, Latvia, Lithuania, Moldavia, Norway, Russia, Sweden, Ukraine), the *Central and Southern Europe Central Conference* (Albania, Algeria, Austria, Bulgaria, Croatia, Czech Republic, France, Hungary, Republic of Macedonia, Poland, Serbia-Montenegro, Slovak Republic, Switzerland, Tunisia) and the *Germany Central Conference*, the only CC of one nation and language.
25 Although the name was changed in the USA in 1922 into 'Evangelical Church' there came about no Union in Europe. The church maintained the title 'Evangelische Gemeinschaft.' The same happened at the EUBC union in 1946 – the name 'Evangelische Gemeinschaft' retained only with a subtitle 'Evangelical United Brethren Church'. Translating 'Evangelical Church' would have implicated problems in a German speaking context; it is how the main Protestant church (Church Union) is entitled.
26 Different from the MEC the EA retained its border-crossing CC also in times of German National Socialism.
27 Methodist mission approaches from Great Britain to Continental Europe: only begun by Wesleyan Methodists. There was also a minister sent from the 'Wesleyan Methodist Association' (separation from the Wesleyan Methodists in 1836) to an English-speaking congregation in Hamburg. That work remained marginal and was later on handed over the MEC mission.
28 See also Note 11.
29 The described coherence as well as the WM mission to Germany is very good deployed in a nonpublished dissertation of Helen Wright, a Nazarene. Her thesis was adopted by Brunel University in London, 2006. The title is: The Wesleyan

Notes

Methodist Missionary Society and its Mission to Germany and Austro-Hungary. 1859–1897.
30 Christoph Gottlob Müller (1785–1858): butcher, who left Germany to avoid the Napoleonic conscription in 1806, becoming a member of WMs in London, classleader, steward and lay preacher. After some home leaves in the 1820s he remigrated in 1831 to Winnenden/Kingdom Württemberg. His class meetings and Sunday schools initiated a local awakening that later spread to the Black Forrest. When he died, the society had 1040 members with 82 preaching places. Mueller is the founder of Wesleyan Methodism ('Wesleyanische Methodistengemeinschaft') in Germany. Karl Heinz Voigt wrote more than 150 articles about Methodists with included adjuvant sources. All in the following mentioned person will be found in an internet encyclopaedia (see www.kirchenexikon.de).
31 The whole story is very well researched and documented in the dissertation of Burkhardt, Friedemann. *Christoph Gottlob Müller und die Anfänge des Methodismus in Deutschland*. Göttingen 2003 [Arbeiten zur Geschichte des Pietismus 43].
32 John Lyth (1821–1886): apprenticed to a bookseller, lay preacher, 1843 minister in the Methodist Conference. After some appointments in Great Britain he was sent as General Superintendent to Germany in 1859. In 1865 he returned to Great Britain beginning a regular circuit work. He was elected as one of the Legal Hundred in 1878, became chairman in some districts before he retired in 1883. Lyth wrote the song 'There is a better world, they say, so bright.' Biographical information about person of the WMs in the United Kingdom is also available via internet in the *Dictionary of Methodism in Britain and Ireland*, edited by John Vickers (see homepage of the Wesley Historical Society, www.wesleyhistoricalsociety.org.uk; s. also www.kirchenlexikon.de).
33 John Cook Barratt (1832–1892): educated as landscape gardener, lay-preacher, 1855–1864 Methodist missionary on the West Indies, foremost Barbados, and 1865–1892 General Superintendent of the WMs German district. Barratt organized and led the Methodist mission to be state acknowledged. Under his guidance the mission spread to Bavaria and Austria.
34 The provisional training center moved from Waiblingen to a new building in Cannstatt in 1875. The history of the German Methodist preacher training institutions is described in: Schuler, Ulrike (ed.). *Glaubenswege – Bildungswege. 150 Jahre theologische Ausbildung im deutschsprachigen Methodismus Europas*. Reutlingen 2008 [EmKG 29/2008, 1–2].
35 1872 tolerance of the state.
36 1885 as 'Privatkirchengesellschaft' (private church society).
37 This transfer was at least enabled by the financial compensation of the Austrian Baroness Amelie von Langenau who also played an important role in the Austrian Methodist history (see Hammer, Paul Ernst. *Baronin Amelie von Langenau. Methodistenkirche in Österreich*. Wien 2001).
38 Statistics – published from 1820 on – prove the enormous immigration waves from Europe to the USA (see the according graphic in: Schuler, Die Evangelische Gemeinschaft, 361).
39 1789 French Revolution, between 1804 and 1815 some wars between France, Prussia, and Russia, 1812–13 Balkan War, 1818 Russian Revolution, 1820 Revolution in Spain and Portugal, 1821–1829 war and independency of Greece, 1830 Revolution in Belgium, 1830–31 Revolution in Poland, 1847 Risorgimento in Italy, 1848 German Revolution und February Revolution in France, 1853–1856 Crimean War, 1859 War of Sardinia and France against Austria, 1864 Austrian and Prussian War against Denmark, 1870–71 German-France War.
40 Johann Hinrich Wichern (1808–1881), famous German theologian, pedagogue,

founder of the Protestant home mission ('Innere Mission') in Germany in 1848 and prison reformer.
41 German-speaking mission in Cincinnati/Ohio (1935), founding of three German-speaking Annual Conferences in 1864; mission to people from Scandinavia in Illinois, Wisconsin, Iowa, Minnesota; first Swedish Conference 1876, Welsh Conference in the 1830, Portuguese Conference and under Bohemian in the middle of the 1880, Italian Conference end of 1880, Spanish Conference early 1890 (s. Streiff, *Der Methodismus in Europa*, 41–43).
42 Nuelsen states that in that time about 200,000 Scandinavians arrived in the USA (see Nuelsen, *Geschichte des Methodismus*, 737).
43 Olof Gustaf Hedstrøm (1803–1877): born nearby Karlskrona/Sweden, sailor, conversion in the USA, from 1845 on harbor missionary at the Bethel ship mission. Hedstrøm went back to Sweden on several occasions visiting his family and meeting with the people who had met him at Bethel ship. At last he returned to Sweden.
44 Ole Peter Peterson (1822–1901), a Norwegian sailor, met Methodism in Boston in 1843–1844, conversed on the *Bethel ship*, went back to Norway and started preaching in 1849. Peterson returned to the USA and became missionary among Norwegian immigrants in Iowa. Meanwhile those people who were awakened in Norway by his preaching came under the influence of Mormons. In 1853 Peterson was ordained and sent to Norway by the MEC. When other missionaries were sent, Peterson went back to the USA in 1858 and worked at the Bethel ship mission. During 1869–1871 he was appointed as superintendent again in Norway.
45 Christian Edvard Baltør Willerup (1815–1886), a salesman, emigrated to the USA, worked in Savannah at a Methodist employer. He is the founder of a Norwegian Methodist congregation in the USA, founder of Methodism in Denmark, and was appointed superintendent for Scandinavia by the MEC.
46 For centuries Finland was part of Sweden. From the eighteenth century on Sweden lost more and more parts of Finland to the Russian empire. Finland became independent in 1917. Methodism in Finland will be mentioned in the chapter about Russia and the Baltic states.
47 More about Scandinavia see paragraph 'holiness movement' below.
48 The beginning of this mission is well explained according to minutes of the General Conference and citations from periodicals, in: Voigt, Karl Heinz: Warum kamen die Methodisten nach Deutschland. Eine Untersuchung über die Motive für ihre Mission in Deutschland. Stuttgart 1975 [BGEmK, Beiheft 4].
49 Wilhelm Nast (1807–1899), studied theology in Blaubeuren and Tübingen, emigrated to the USA in 1828 working henceforth as language teacher and librarian; converted to Methodism, became lay preacher and in 1835 an appointment as MEC missionary among Germans in the USA, founder of the German MEC branch beginning in Cincinnati/Ohio, published from 1839 on the periodical 'Der christliche Apologete', an important periodical for German immigrants. In 1844 Nast visited Germany to examine the possibility of a MEC mission to Germany. Nast visited Christoph Gottlob Müller (see Note 30) with the conclusion that because of a lack of religious freedom a mission is not advisable. Cofounder of the German Wallace College in Berea where he became president in 1865.
50 That impression later on proved to be wrong. The first attempt to install a democratic composed national state collapsed in 1849 – most of the liberal laws were withdrawn.
51 Ludwig Sigismund Jacoby (1813–1874), educated in Jewish tradition, converted at the age of 23 (baptism in a Lutheran church), commercial apprenticeship, 1838

Notes

emigration to the USA, connections to Methodism, conversion, becoming lay preacher. In 1841 Jacoby was appointed as minister of the MEC for working with German immigrants, in 1849 sent to Germany where he became the founder of the MEC in Continental Europe. After extremely spreading and organizing the Methodist mission work, Jacoby went back to the USA in 1871. He died in St. Louis/Missouri.

52 Ernst Gottfried Mann (1830–1915): in the turmoil of the German revolution Mann decided to emigrate to the USA. At the port Bremen his spiritual life was revolutionized by a Methodist bible peddler. He went back to his family in Pirmasens/Palatinate, deployed an awakening, in 1855 Mann was appointed as Methodist circuit minister, sent to Alsace, in 1856 to Lausanne/Switzerland where he worked in cooperation with WMs; mission spread to other Swiss cities. In 1867 Mann finished his work as minister and founded a commercial enterprise. He was accountable for a kind of state acknowledge ('Privatkirchengesellschaft') of the MEC in Bavaria in 1883.

53 In 1856 the GC formed the 'German-Switzerland-Mission Conference'.

54 At that time Germany was composed by 39 autonomic states (empires, kingdoms, dukedoms, princedoms, and free imperial cities) with different laws and nowhere religious liberty that complicated the mission a lot. Encroachments by the particular state authorities forced by state church ministers were a daily occurrence (e.g., banishment, penalty, punishment).

55 Erhard Wunderlich (1830–1895): emigration to the USA in 1849, conversion to Methodism in Dayton/Ohio, returning to his native place Rüßdorf/Thuringia in 1850, worshipping and preaching at his patent's estate with his family and workers, expanding to evangelize when a regional awakening began; after persecution, imprisonment, fines, punishment he returned to the USA in 1853. There Wunderlich was ordained and worked among German immigrants. His brother Friedrich continued the mission work that was soon integrated into the MEC mission under the supervision of Ludwig Sigismund Jacoby (see Note 51).

56 Again: first date marks the approach by lay persons, the date being put in parentheses gives the date of official acceptance by the mission board.

57 Work among Italian speaking foreign workers in Switzerland.

58 The American Board of Commissioners for Foreign Missions (short-form: American Board) was the first American Christian foreign mission agency (nondenominational). It was officially chartered in 1812.

59 Macedonia was from 1371 to 1913 part of the Ottoman Empire. After the second Balkan War it was cantoned in a Greece, Albanian, Bulgarian, and Serbian part. After World War II the Macedonian's identity was again nationally divided accompanied by violent relocations and displacements. After World War I and during World War II Macedonia became occasionally under Bulgarian statute of occupation; in 1944 it was part of Yugoslavia. In 1991 Macedonia became independent with the problem to unite an ethnically complicated 'patchwork'-society.

60 Serbia from 1459 to 1804 was a part of the Ottoman Empire. In 1882 after some revolts and wars Serbia became an autonomous kingdom. At the end of World War I the Kingdom Serbia, Croatia, and Slovenia constituted Yugoslavia. After further wars and World War II Serbia became one of six-part republics of Yugoslavia later on called Socialistic Republic Serbia. After 1991 Serbia became – as the other republics – independent. After further wars (e.g., Kosovo War) and federation era with Montenegro, Serbia is an independent republic since 2006.

61 In several states of the USA, it was forbidden to speak German anymore; also names were anglicized.

62 The 'Christlicher Botschafter' is the EA's periodical – a good informative source

where news from Germany, letters, mission reports, all important information about the church was published. It is the longest abroad in German published church newsletter (published 1836 to 1946). *'Die Geschäftige Martha'* – the periodical of the UBC – had an erratic history: first published in 1841, it discontinued in June 1846, 1846 to 1848 published as *'Der Deutsche Telescope'*, 1849 again named *'Die Geschäftige Martha'*, 1851 changed in *'Der Fröhliche Botschafter.'*

63 The creative so-called 'Zehn-Thaler-Plan' is described in Schuler, *Die Evangelische Gemeinschaft*, 124–127. Nicolai's plan is printed in: *Christlicher Botschafter* No. 22 from 15.11.1849, 170–171 (also in: Schuler, *Die Evangelische Gemeinschaft*, 362–364).

64 Johann Conrad Link (1822–1883): 1836/37 emigration to the USA became member of the EA and minister of the West-Pennsylvanian Conference, 1850 appointed as missionary to Germany. Link became – together with Johannes Nikolai (1818–1912), the second sent missionary – the founder of the EA in Germany, after some disagreements Link left the EA in 1865 and became a Baptist minister.

65 Sebastian Kurz (1789–1868): emigrated in the early 1830s to the USA, became member of the EA in Pennsylvania, remigrated in 1845 to Bonlanden/Württemberg and started class meetings, wrote letters that were printed in the EA periodical, *'Der Christliche Botschafter,'* became later a colporteur of the MEC.

66 See article of C. G. Koch, Cleveland/Ohio, 27.11.1849. In: *Christlicher Botschafter* No. 24, 15.12.1849, 188.

67 E.g. 'Preußen Mission' (Prussian mission) in Ruhr (mission among coal miners).

68 See O'Malley, *On the Journey Home*, 36.

69 The Alsatian people suffered living in boundary area between Germany and France that was occupied several times from both sides – always followed by the change of the main language and persecutions. From 1871 to 1918 Alsace and Lorraine were composed as administrative district 'Alsace-Lorraine' of the German Empire ('Deutsches Reich'). Today the territory is part of France.

70 East- and West-Prussia were in the late Medieval and Reformation times the territories of the Teutonic Knights, became in the sixteenth century part of the Ducal Prussia (later Kingdom Prussia). 1871 to 1945 it was part of the German Empire, than after World War II under Polish and Soviet control, respectively; from 1992 the area is part of Poland, the northerly part of East Prussia belongs to Russia. The EA recorded in the beginning of the twentieth century up to the thirtieth in East- and West-Prussia revivals and emerging congregations. The statistic speaks in 1945 of forty-two emerging congregations. 1945 the twenty-three church buildings were occupied and the German inhabitants were banished.

71 More details about these meetings, see Ulrike Knöller/Doris Sackmann, *Erste Zusammenkünfte von Vertretern der drei Gemeinschaften methodistischen Ursprungs in Deutschland: Sitzungsprotokolle 1881–1885*. EmKG 28/2, 2007, 83–86.

72 There is a very illuminating discussion about this coherence as reason to open a mission in Germany at the GC of the UBC in 1869 (see *Proceedings of the Fifteenth General Conference of the United Brethren in Christ, held in Lebanon, Pennsylvania, 20 May to 1 June 1869* (Dayton, Ohio, 1869) especially 175f, 183f).

73 Georg Christian Heinrich Bischoff (1829–1885): Bischoff was a member of a pietistic Lutheran society in Naila/Franconia. His brother emigrated to the USA and wrote letters about his conversion. Bischoff followed his brother in 1867, became a member and contributor of the UBC, was ordained in 1869 and sent as missionary to Germany. He evangelized unremittingly. He died in an accident. Bischoff was the founder of the UBC in Germany.

74 See Streiff, *Der Methodismus in Europa*, 168.

75 Bohemia and Moravia are the two historical areas of today's Czech Republic. After

the collapse of the Austro-Hungarian Empire after World War I, the independent republic of Czechoslovakia was created in 1918. This country incorporated regions of Bohemia, Moravia, Silesia, Slovakia, and the Carpathian Ruthenia with significant German, Hungarian, Polish, and Byelorussian-speaking minorities. In 1993 they emerged as succeeding states the Czech Republic and Slovenia.
76 See details in Vilém Schneeberger, 'Der Methodismus in der Tschechoslowakei,' in: Hecker, Schneeberger, Zehrer, *Methodismus in Osteuropa*, 40.
77 Poland's history is shaped very tragically from the seventeenth century on. It is branded by divisions (by Austria, Prussia and Russia), occupations, oppression, and fighting for freedom and independence – in details much too close and complicated to explain in a footnote.
In parts of Poland also other Methodist mission had started before but did not survive: the UBC in 1880 in Pomerania – there are no sources and information what has happened to this mission; the WM 1876 in Silesia, soon abandoned because of preacher deficits; a Moravian Congregation was affiliated to the MEC in 1914. The MEC evangelized in Polish areas based from north Germany (for details see Zehrer, Karl *Der deutsche Methodismus im heutigen Polen*, in: Hecker, Schneeberger, Zehrer, *Methodismus in Osteuropa*, 9–29).
78 Roots of Methodist missions to Czechoslovakia are also earlier. The story about those cautious beginnings link to a conversion of a director of a theater, Václav Pázdral (1845–1919), in 1879. Looking for a congregation to join, he received a theological education at the WM, emigration to the USA, cared over there for immigrants from Moravia and Bohemia (see Vilém Schneeberger, 'Der Methodismus in der Tschechoslowakei,' in: Hecker, Schneeberger, Zehrer, *Methodismus in Osteuropa*, 30–166).
79 Instead of Belgium they first had decided to go to South Russia but the political development had anticipated this plan. The MECS already had a mission in Congo/Africa that was at that time a Belgian colony.
80 More specified s. Streiff, *Der Methodismus in Europa*, 210ff.
81 Streiff, 218ff.
82 Streiff, 214ff.
83 In view on the EA Karl Steckel proves this very clearly in his article *Die Veränderung des Traktats zur Christlichen Vollkommenheit in den verschiedenen Kirchenordnungsausgaben der früheren Evangelischen Gemeinschaft (1809–1968)*. In: Mitteilungen der Studiengemeinschaft für Geschichte der EmK 11/2 (1990).
84 That led at least to the more precise definition in the discipline of the United Methodist Church in 1968.
85 Voigt describes this relationship in his monograph *Die Heiligungsbewegung zwischen Methodistischer Kirche und Landeskirchlicher Gemeinschaft. Die Triumphreise von Robert Pearsall Smith im Jahre 1875 und ihre Auswirkungen auf die zwischenkirchlichen Beziehungen* (Wuppertal, 1996).
86 Not being allowed to celebrate the sacraments, not being allowed to conduct funerals in churchyards, etc.
87 To learn more about the Holiness movement in the German-speaking area, see Michel Weyer, *Heiligungsbewegung und Methodismus im deutschen Sprachraum. Einführung in ein Kapitel methodistischer Frömmigkeitsgeschichte und kleine Chronik einer Bewegung des 19. Jahrhunderts*. Stuttgart 1991 [BGEmK 40].
88 These and the following consolidated findings are specified in Streiff, *Der europäische Methodismus um die Wende vom 19. zum 20. Jahrhundert*, 81–89.
89 Thomas Ball Barratt (1862–1940): minister, evangelist, founder of the Norwegian Pentecostal movement and European Pentecostalism at all. Barratt was born in Great Britain, studied theology, arts, and music (at Edward Grieg). He went to

Notes

Oslo, Norway to become a minister of the MEC. He wrote songs and poems. In 1902 he became superintendent of the supra-denominational 'Christiana City Mission' and experienced the 'second anointing' in 1906. Up to 1916 Barratt was a Methodist speaker and writer in the Pentecostal movement. He published a Pentecostal periodical, 'Korsets Seier' in Swedish, Finnish, Russian, German and Spanish.

90 Research about Methodist attitudes toward Pentecostalism in Europe is in its infancy. Three newer articles are concerned with that question: Christoph Raedel, 'Der Methodismus und das Aufkommen der Pfingstbewegung in Deutschland'; Peter Borgen, 'Der Methodismus und die Anfänge der Pfingstbewegung in Norwegen'; Jorgen Thaarup, 'Der Methodismus und die Pfingstbewegung in Dänemark', in: Streiff, *Der europäische Methodismus um die Wende vom 19. und 20. Jahrhundert.*

91 Detailed statistics according to Germany that had the greatest disorganization, see Schuler, *Methodisten in Deutschland nach 1945.* In: KZG 2/2000, S. 429–455.

92 The 'Kingdom Advance Program' of the 1946 united churches, EUBC, also merged the 'Kingdom Service Fund' of the EA and the 'Advance Program' of the UBC.

93 'Evangelische Kirche in Deutschland' (EKD), at that time 27 autonomous Protestant (former state) churches (Lutheran, Reformed, Uniate).

94 The relief program is described in: Schuler, *Die Evangelische Gemeinschaft.*

95 Participating institutions: Centre Méthodiste de Formation Théologique, Lausanne, Switzerland (today Strasbourg, France), Eesti Metodisti Kiriku Teologilinke, Tallinn, Estonia, Hoyskolen for Kistendom, Metodistkirkens Studiesenter, Bergen, Norway, Theological Seminary of the Russia United Methodist Church, Moskau, Russia, Theological Training Center for the Balkans, Graz-Waiern, Austria (is not existing anymore), Theologisches Seminar der Evangelisch-methodistischen Kirche, Reutlingen, Germany (since 2008 Reutlingen School of Theology), Wyzsze Seminarium Teologiczne in Jana Laskiego, Warsaw, Poland.

96 All 'Free Churches' (independent from the state) total about one percent of all Christians in Europe (according to the whole population that characterizes itself as Christians).

97 Ulrike Schuler, 'Chancen und Grenzen freikirchlicher Organisationsstrukturen im ökumenischen Prozess', in: Holger Eschmann, Jürgen Moltmann, Ulrike Schuler, eds, *Freikirchen – Landeskirchen. Historische Alternative – Gemeinsame Zukunft?* Neukirchen-Vlyn 2008, 36–56 [Theologie interdisziplinär, Bd. 2].

98 The German Theological Seminary was the first theological institute of the free churches that became state acknowledged in Germany in 2005.

99 According to the need of historical work, agencies, and archives, see *Discipline of the UMC (2004)*: § 104 Our Theological Task, §§ 530 (Archives and History), 606 (Records and Archives), 640 (Conference Commissions on archives and history).

100 The goal of the historical society ('Studiengemeinschaft') was and is to do and support historical research; and to publish articles, research reports and reviews of new historical publications, information, and reports about historical conferences. Therefore the 'Studiengemeinschaft' published from 1962 on the 'EmK Geschichte. Quellen-Studien-Mitteilungen' (up to 2001 named *MITTEILUNGEN der Studiengemeinschaft*), a journal that appears twice a year and a monograph in the series EmK Geschichte. Monografien (formerly 'Beiträge zur Geschichte der EmK') generally once a year. All published articles and monographs up to now are listed (see www.emk-studiengemeinschaft.de).

101 At the fourth Ecumenical Methodist Conference in Toronto in 1911, historical researches were encouraged by founding the 'Ecumenical Methodist Historical Union.' Initially it had two sections: Western (i.e., American) and Eastern (i.e.,

Notes

British). Its first task was that of 'discovering, cataloguing, and making available the historical documents – Wesleyana and other materials connected with the origin and development of Methodism.' The two Sections worked largely independently of each other. Reports were printed from time to time in the 'Proceedings' of the 'Wesley Historical Society.' In 1947 the name was changed to the 'International Methodist Historical Society' (IMHS) and the 'Eastern Section' became known as the 'British Section.' In 1971 the 'World Methodist Historical Society' was formed and representatives from other parts of the world began to be involved (for further details, see the WHS Proceedings, 13: 73ff, 26: 120ff.).

102 Some are just at the beginning of archives collections, so that e.g. Christina Cekov from Macedonia can speak about her 'shoe-box-archives' or 'drawer-archives.'

Chapter 11

1 The story has been told most recently and succinctly in Patrick Streiff, *Methodism in Europe: 19th and 20th century* (Frankfurt: EmK-Geschichte 2003), 140–146, 183–189, 241–245. The best overview of dates and events is given in a collection of excerpts from books and articles by S T Kimbrough, Jr. *Methodism in Russia and the Baltic States. History and Renewal.* (Nashville: Abingdon, 1995; Russian [enlarged] edition: Yekaterinburg 2003) Especially helpful are the chronological tables, 212–222.

2 The exact location of those villages needs to be verified. There are at least two places by the name of Sigalovo that could fit the description about trips to this place, as given in the Methodist periodical *Khristianski Pobornik* (*Christian Advocate*) hereafter *KP*.

3 *KP* (1910).

4 *American Orthodox Messenger* (Amerikanski Pravoslavni Vestnik) 13 (1–15 July 1912): 249.

5 For sister Anna Eklund's ministry see S. T. Kimbrough, Jr., *Sister Anna Eklund. 1867–1949. A Methodist Saint in Russia. Her Words and Witness. St. Petersburg 1908–1931.* (New York: General Board of Global Ministries, 2001).

6 The beginning of Russian Baptism, strongly favored by several representatives of St. Petersburg aristocracy, were met with full scale persecution by the government and the Russian Orthodox Church in the last third of the nineteenth century.

7 For Baptists and Evangelicals in St. Petersburg see, S. Shults Jr., *Khramy Sankt Peterburga. Istoria I sovremennost.* (*Churches of St. Petersburg. History and Present.*) (St. Petersburg: Glagol, 1994), 262.

8 *KP* seldom mentions events beyond Methodism in St. Petersburg, though it was the stronghold of Russian evangelicalism and Baptism [*KP* (1909): 7; (1910): 144]. There are, however, long reports about the 'Molokans,' a Russian evangelical group from the Odessa region [*KP* (1909): 45, 53, 98; (1911): 38].

9 John Dunstan, 'George A. Simons and the "Khristianski Pobornik," Unknown Source of Witness About Methodism in St. Petersburg, *Methodist History* 19:1 (October 1980): 21–40, presents an interesting analysis of the Russian Methodist publication. What he does not mention is also interesting, for example, the overwhelming presence of material from European Methodism.

10 Facsimile of the document in S T Kimbrough, Jr., *A Pictorial Panorama of Early Russian Methodism 1889–1931* (Madison, NJ: General Commission on Archives and History, 2008), 10. Permission is given 'on condition that he (Salmi) must not discuss political questions . . . and in general must fulfill all demands of the law.'

11 Facsimile of letters pertaining to the registration in Kimbrough, 22. The letters state that 'its members comprised not only people of foreign confessions but also those who had left Orthodoxy.'
12 'Orthodoxy was for Simons a write-off' in Dunstan, 67.
13 'Iskateli Boga' (God-seekers), *KP* (1914): 357.
14 Photographs of the building in Kimbrough, *A Pictorial Panorama*, front page, 26, 27.
15 Shults, 262. 'Methodist-episcopal church of the "Bethany" society (Bolshoy prospect, house no. 58) Closed according to the decree of the Presidium of the Executive Committee of the Leningrad region of December 2, 1931.'
16 Photographs of both buildings in Kimbrough, *A Pictorial Panorama*, 8.
17 'Evangelische Gemeinschaft,' the German name of the Evangelical Church, a predecessor denomination of the United Methodist Church.
18 Priit Tamm, 'Die methodistische Mission in Estland an der Wende vom 19. zum 20. Jahrhundert' (Methodist Mission in Estonia at the turn of the nineteenth to the twentieth century), Patrick Streiff, ed., *Der europäische Methodismus um die Wende vom 19. und 20. Jahrhundert*. (Frankfurt: Medienwerk der Evangelisch-methodistischen Kirche, 2005), 61–66, tries to discover 'reasons or motives' for the beginnings of Estonian Methodism, and states that Methodism was helpful 'to translate a formal and inconsequential Christianity into daily life,' 62.
19 *KP* (1910): 169.
20 The reason might be found in the personal character of both Simons and Eklund and their conviction that Methodism in Russia would vanish with them. Subsequently, it did.
21 While serving in Russia in the 1990s, this author was told stories from the civil war that men carried hats of the Red Army as well as the White, to wear the right one as they encountered armed groups.
22 A good source that tries to do justice to the reform groups is Edward E. Roslof, *Red Priests. Renovationism, Russian Orthodoxy, and Revolution, 1905–1946* (Bloomington: Indiana University Press, 2002). Reformers were widely seen as under the influence and employed by the Communist government. The Orthodox Church, one of the strongest pillars of the Tsarist regime, was the main target of antireligious measures of the Communist party and its Soviet power by disestablishment, the separation of church and state as well as church and school, wholesale nationalization of property, and other means.
23 Roslof, 110–146, speaks of a 'Religious NEP' in the Soviet Union with regard to the Russian Orthodox Church.
24 Shults, 263, gives the year 1926 as the end of this period.
25 The exact location of this place is not established. It was, however, close to the town of Luga, south of Leningrad. The person appointed to Jablonitzy was also working there. There is a village named Jaskovitzy about 20 km from Luga.
26 The involvement of the Methodist Church with the 'Living Church' faction of Russian Orthodoxy needs more study and a new assessment. So far it has been treated from an almost exclusive anti-Soviet, anti-Bolshevist point of view. Carl Malone, 'A Methodist Venture in Bolshevik Russia,' *Methodist History* 18:4 (1980): 239–261 is a striking example of such an assessment, written in 1980, the heyday of the Cold War.
27 'I confess that I have more confidence in the judgment of Dr. Hecker than in that of some good men of decidedly reactionary tendencies.' John Nuelsen, letter of 6 February 1923, quoted in S. T. Kimbrough, Jr., 'The Living Church Conflict in the Russian Orthodox Church and the Involvement of the Methodist Episcopal Church,' *Methodist History* 40:2 (January 2002): 10–118.
28 A biography of Hecker is highly desirable. An academically trained sociologist

(Ph. D. from Columbia University), he had a thorough knowledge of Russian history and society. His writings on religion and Communism under the Soviets in the 1920s are well informed. Aware of the hostility and shortcomings of atheist propaganda, he maintained a positive attitude toward the goals of a socialist society and the role of the Christian faith in it. There is only scarce information about his later life, though he is said to have died a political prisoner in 1943. The most comprehensive information about him is found in Streiff, 184–187.

29 Gita Metis, 'Die methodistische Bewegung in Lettland vor dem Ersten Weltkrieg' (The Methodist Movement in Latvia prior to World War I), in Patrick Streiff, ed., *Der europäische Methodismus*, 67–86. Metis argues that Freiberg had been a 'Methodist in his heart' since 1911, however was waiting for a time when it would be less difficult openly to do Methodist work (81), using the Moravian church as organizational protection.

30 See below, part II.3.

31 See Heigo Ritsbek, 'The Development of Estonian Methodism' in S T Kimbrough, Jr., *Methodism in Russia & the Baltic States*, 130–144.

32 The papers of the missionary Rev. J. O. J. Taylor, now in the Archives of Pitts Library at Candler School of Theology, Emory University, Atlanta, Georgia, report of meetings with and mutual support of the United States forces in Vladivostok.

33 Church use of the Vladivostok building was restricted to the basement only – see copies of documents in the Vladivostok State archives in the episcopal office of the Russia United Methodist Church, Moscow.

34 See S T Kimbrough, Jr., 'Methodism in Siberia,' *Methodist History* 36:3 (1998): 153–161.

35 A biographical notice in 'Religioznye deyateli russkogo zarubezhja' (Religious leaders of Russia abroad) Pejsti Nikolai Ivanovich (N. J. Poysti) (1892–1947): http://zarubezhje.narod.ru/mp/p_090.htm, accessed 4 April 2009.

36 The story of the Far East mission and its discontinuation is Dana Robert, 'The Methodist Episcopal Church, South, Mission to Russian in Manchuria, 1920–1927,' *Methodist History*, 26:2 (1988): 67–83. Robert puts her finger on some problems, typical not only for events in Russia. Main decisions about mission are made by mission boards (and bishops) often without knowing the real situation in the 'field.'

37 The Rev. Jan Piotrowski in his memoirs states that Vilna 'was and is a Belarusian city on Belarusian soil.' Jan Piotrowski Memoir, *A Century in Retrospect. Book One* (Gainesville, 1988, in Belarusian language), 65. The book is an interesting primary source for this almost unknown part of Methodist mission history.

38 Kindly provided by his sons, this author is in the possession of some of the memories of this pioneer preacher who later became the Methodist superintendent in Austria. Despite considerable resistance from traditional forces, he formed a cooperative, building a mill, and starting the first village school among the poor farmers.

39 The Soviet time 'Byelorussian Encyclopedia' mentions Methodist churches in several Belarusian cities and emphasizing the use of the Belarusian language. 'Metadisty' in *Byelorussian Soviet Encyclopedia* (Minsk, 1969) in Belarusian language.

40 Heigo Ritsbek, 'Estonian Methodism During the First Year Under the Plague of the Red Commissars,' *Methodist History*, 31:4 (July 1993): 248–255.

41 The main emphasis of the KGB's church politics can be described as 'Unite and rule' (not, Divide and rule).

42 See Mark Elliott, 'Methodism in the Soviet Union since World War II,' *The Asbury Theological Journal* 46:1 (1991): 5–47.

43 Elliott, footnotes 4, 11, 22.

44 The Soviet Union has been treated by many Methodists as an appendix to Estonia, a complete misunderstanding of dimensions and potentials.
45 This raises the question about how identity is found and experienced. How much are Estonian heritage and history a part of a Russian, Latvian, and Lithuanian self-understanding after the empire and the Soviet Union are gone?
46 See *Mission in the Commonwealth of Independent States. A Report to the World Division. Spring Meeting March 1992* (New York: General Board of Global Ministries, 1992).
47 Although the 'Russia Initiative' of the General Board of Global Ministries has been mentioned widely in pronouncements and publications of the board as a new model of grassroots support of, and involvement in, mission, its story and, most of all, the role and leadership of Dr. Bruce R. Weaver (of Dallas, Texas) still needs to be written.
48 See also Rüdiger Minor, 'Erfahrung im Dienst' *EmK Geschichte* 24:2 (2003): 21–30. (Russian publication in Kimbrough, *Methodism in Russia & the Baltic States* [Russian edition], 9–18.

Chapter 12
1 The expression 'mainline Methodism' in this chapter applies to the British Methodist 'Wesleyan Connection,' established in Great Britain in 1795 after John Wesley's death, and to the two main bodies of North American episcopal Methodism (the Methodist Episcopal Church, organized in 1784, and the Methodist Episcopal Church, South, organized in 1845). This chapter gives particular attention to the churches established in Latin America and the Caribbean resulting from missionary work of those three Methodist denominations in the nineteenth century and the first half of the twentieth century. With few exceptions, other Methodist bodies in Great Britain and the United States have not played a major role in the establishment and development of Latin American Methodism. The exceptions are the African Episcopal Methodist Church, established in the USA in 1816 (under the leadership of Bishop Richard Allen), Salvation Army, established in Great Britain in 1878 (under the leadership of William and Catherine Booth), and the Church of the Nazarene, established in the USA in 1895 (under the leadership of Phineas F. Breese).
2 Wade Crawford Barclay, *History of Methodist Mission*, (New York: Board of Missions, The Methodist Church, 1949), I: 345.
3 D. A. Reily, 'Justin Spaulding,' in *Encyclopedia of World Methodism* [hereafter *EWM*], (Nashville: United Methodist Publishing House, 1974), II: 2223.
4 Ernest R. Case, 'John Dempster,' in *EWM*, I: 655.
5 Barclay, 1: 346–347, 353.
6 Barclay, 1: 351, 355–357.
7 Edwin H. Maynard, 'William H. Norris,' in *EWM*, II: 1763.
8 Barclay, 1: 352.
9 Isnard Rocha, 'Daniel Parish Kidder,' in *EWM*, I: 1331.
10 D. A. Reily, 'Junius Newman,' in *EWM*, II: 1749.
11 Edwin H. Maynard, 'Thomas Bond Wood,' in *EWM*, II: 2594–2595.
12 Jesse A. Earl, 'Mexico,' in *EWM*, II: 1596.
13 J. Waskom Pickett and Albea Godbold, 'William Butler,' in *EWM*, I: 365–366.
14 Nolan B. Harmon, 'John Christian Keener,' in *EWM*, I: 1318.
15 Eula K. Long, 'John James Ransom,' in *EWM*, II: 1987.
16 Marvin H. Harper, 'William Taylor,' in *EWM*, II: 2317–2318.
17 Edwin H. Maynard, 'Adelaide Whitefield LaFetra,' and 'Ira Haynes LaFetra,' in *EWM*, II: 1368.

18 Daniel P. Monti and Edwin H. Maynard, 'Francisco G. Penzotti,' in *EWM*, II: 1881–1882.
19 D. A. Reily, 'Justus Nelson,' in *EWM*, II: 1715.
20 Eula K. Long, 'Martha Hite Watts,' in *EWM*, II: 2473.
21 Justo L. González, 'Enrique Benito Someillán,' in *EWM*, II: 2196.
22 Barclay, 3: 773–774, 776, 778.
23 João Prado Flores, 'Carmen Chacon,', in *EWM*, I: 442–443.
24 Antonio Campos de Gonçalves, 'Hugh ClarenceTucker,' in *EWM*, 2: 2372–2373.
25 The organizers of that missionary meeting decided to call it *'Congress on Christian Work in Latin America'* instead of *'Congress on Missionary Work in Latin America'* because the word 'missionary' could be displeasing to the sensibility of educated Latin Americans. This decision brought strong reactions among the missionaries in the field and national workers as well. See Panama Congress Report, Vol. 1, 17.
26 *World Methodist Council, Handbook of Information, 2007–2011* (Waynesville, NC: Cornerstone Printing & Design, 2007), 279.
27 When she was appointed Minister of Justice by the Bolivian President Evo Morales in 2006, a Bolivian household worker-turned-activist and recipient of the 2003 World Methodist Peace Award, Methodist Casimira Rodriguez Romero was secretary general of Bolivia's National Federation of Domestic Workers, an organization of indigenous women that supported development and peace for many years. The National Federation was instrumental in convincing Bolivia's congress to pass legislation that improved working conditions and defined fair labor practices for more than 130,000 domestic workers.
28 'For over thirty years of internal politics and violence, Maria Sumire has worked with the Quechua communities of Cuzco [Peru], advocating human rights. She has fought for and affirmed the Quechua identity [in the Methodist Church of Peru].' http://gbgm-umc.org/global_news/full_article.cfm?articleid = 4651.
29 Robert J. Harman, 'A History of Relationships – The United Methodist Church and Methodist Churches in Latin America [and] Caribbean.' Paper presented at the consultation of the General Board of Global Ministries of the United Methodist Church and CIEMAL (Consejo de Iglesias Evangélicas Metodistas de América Latina e Caribe), Panama City, Panama, 1–4 March 2007.

Chapter 13
1 *The Book of Discipline of the United Methodist Church* (Nashville: The United Methodist Publishing House, 2004), 386 (¶629.1).
2 See Paul W. Chilcote, ed., *The Wesleyan Tradition: A Paradigm for Renewal* (Nashville: Abingdon, 2002), esp. 23–37.
3 See the excellent discussion by Dana L. Robert, *Evangelism as the Heart of Mission*, (New York: General Board of Global Ministries, 1997). See also S. T. Kimbrough, Jr., ed., *Evangelization, the Heart of Mission: A Wesleyan Imperative* (New York: General Board of Global Ministries, 1995).
4 In his Denman Lectures of 1971, *Evangelism in the Wesleyan Spirit* (Nashville: Tidings, 1971), Albert Outler identified three great components of evangelism in the Wesleyan spirit, namely, heralding, martyrdom, and servanthood.
5 See Tore Meistad, 'The Missiology of Charles Wesley and Its Links to the Eastern Church,' in S T Kimbrough, Jr., ed., *Orthodox and Wesleyan Spirituality* (Crestwood, New York: St. Vladimir's Seminary Press, 2002), 205–231.
6 J. Ernest Rattenbury, 'Methodist Evangelism,' in J. Scott Lidgett and Bryan H. Reed, eds, *Methodism in the Modern World* (London: Epworth, 1929), 190–191.
7 Paul W. Chilcote and Laceye C. Warner, eds, *The Study of Evangelism: Exploring a Missional Practice of the Church* (Grand Rapids: Eerdmans, 2008), xxvi–xxvii.

Chapter 14
1 London: [William Strahan], 1784. Available in facsimile as *John Wesley's Prayer Book: The Sunday Service of the Methodists in North America* (Cleveland, Ohio: OSL Publications, 1991).
2 For some of these revisions, see A. Elliott Peaston, *The Prayer Book Reform Movement in the XVIIIth Century* (Oxford: Basil Blackwell, 1940), though it does not mention Wesley's revision.
3 See, for example, James F. White's 'Introduction' and 'Notes' in *John Wesley's Prayer Book*.
4 T. O. Summers, ed., *The Sunday Service of the Methodist Episcopal Church, South* (Nashville: A. H. Redford, 1867). For a study of Summers' liturgical contributions, see L. Edward Phillips, 'Thomas Osmond Summers: Methodist Liturgist of the Nineteenth Century,' *Methodist History* 27.4 (1989), 241–253.
5 *Minutes of the Methodist Conferences, from the First, Held in London, by the Late Rev. John Wesley, A.M. in the Year 1744*, vol. 1 (London: Printed in the Conference Office by Thomas Cordeux, 1812), 191 (*Minutes* for 1786).
6 Wesley F. Swift, ' "The Sunday Service of the Methodists": A Study of Nineteenth-century Liturgy,' *Proceedings of the Wesley Historical Society* 31 (1957–1958), 142. See the rest of the essay (112–118, 133–43) for a brief study of these editions.
7 F. E. Brightman, *The English Rite; Being a Synopsis of the Sources and Revisions of the Book of Common Prayer, with an Introduction and an Appendix* (London: Rivingtons, 1921).
8 Nolan B. Harmon, Jr., *The Rites and Ritual of Episcopal Methodism, with Particular Reference to the Rituals of the Methodist Episcopal Church and the Methodist Episcopal Church, South, Respectively* (Nashville: Publishing House of the M. E. Church, South, 1926).
9 See the various essays by international authors in Karen B. Westerfield Tucker, ed. *The Sunday Service of the Methodists: Twentieth-century Worship in Worldwide Methodism* (Nashville: Kingswood Books, 1996).
10 *The Doctrines and Discipline of the Methodist Episcopal Church in America. With Explanatory Notes by Thomas Coke and Francis Asbury*, 10th ed. (Philadelphia: Printed by Henry Tuckniss, 1798); facsimile ed., Frederick A. Norwood (Rutland, VT: Academy Books, 1979), 121.
11 Thomas O. Summers, *Commentary on the Ritual of the Methodist Episcopal Church, South* (Nashville: A. H. Redford for the M. E. Church, South, 1873).
12 R. J. Cooke, *History of the Ritual of the Methodist Episcopal Church, With a Commentary on Its Offices* (Cincinnati: Jennings & Pye; New York: Eaton & Mains, 1900).
13 John Paris, *History of the Methodist Protestant Church* (Baltimore: Printed by Sherwood & Co., 1849) 313–314.
14 Preface, *The Book of Offices; being the Orders of Service authorized for use in the Methodist Church* (London: Methodist Publishing House, 1936), 9.
15 Silas Told, *An Account of the Life and Dealings of God with Silas Told, Late Preacher of the Gospel* (n.p.: Printed by W. Cowdroy, 1805), 73–74.
16 Joseph Nightingale, *A Portraiture of Methodism: Being an Impartial View of the Rise, Progress, Doctrines, Discipline, and Manners of the Wesleyan Methodists. In a Series of Letters, Addressed to a Lady* (London: Printed by C. Stower, 1807), 251–253.
17 An older, but still useful, book is Frank Baker's *Methodism and the Love-Feast* (London: Epworth, 1957).
18 A full history of the covenant service in British Methodism is contained in David Tripp's *The Renewal of the Covenant in the Methodist Tradition* (London: Epworth, 1969).

Notes

19 George Coles, 31 December 1829, Journal, Ms., Drew University Library, Madison, NJ.
20 Maria Dyer Davies, 21 April 1853, Diary, Ms., Special Collections Library, Duke University Library, Durham, NC.
21 J. Ernest Rattenbury, *Vital Elements of Public Worship* (London: Epworth, 1936).
22 John Bishop, *Methodist Worship in Relation to Free Church Worship* (London: Epworth, 1950).
23 Lester Ruth, 'Urban Itinerancy: "Stational" Liturgy in Early American Methodism,' *Studia Liturgica* 32 (2002) 222–239.
24 A list of these tunes, with introduction and annotation, may found in Appendix J of *WJW(B)*, Franz Hildebrandt and Oliver A. Beckerlegge, eds, *A Collection of Hymns for the Use of The People Called Methodists* (Nashville: Abingdon Press, 1983), 7:770–787.
25 Linda J. Clark, Joanne Swenson, and Mark Stamm, *How We Seek God Together: Exploring Worship Style* (Bethesda, MD.: The Alban Institute, 2001); and C. Michael Hawn, *One Bread, One Body: Exploring Cultural Diversity in Worship* (Bethesda, MD.: The Alban Institute, 2003).
26 See, for example, Karen B. Westerfield Tucker, *American Methodist Worship* (New York: Oxford University Press, 2001); and David M. Chapman, *Born in Song: Methodist Worship in Britain* (Warrington: Church in the Market Place Publications, 2006).

Chapter 15
1 Anglican Articles of Religion, cited here and later, can be found in any edition of *The Book of Common Prayer*. EUB and Methodist Articles are in *The Book of Discipline of The United Methodist Church* in any quadrennial version from 1968 onward.
2 (Geneva: World Council of Churches in Geneva, 1982).
3 Henry Rack, *Reasonable Enthusiast: John Wesley and the Rise of Methodism* (London: Epworth, 1963), 152.
4 Sermon 101 in *WJW(Jackson)* and *WJW(B)*. Also found with helpful commentary in Albert C. Outler, ed., *John Wesley*, A Library of Protestant Thought (London: Oxford University Press, 1964), 332–344.
5 J. Ernest Rattenbury, *The Eucharistic Hymns of John and Charles Wesley* (London: Epworth, 1948), 195–249.
6 John Calvin, *Institutes of the Christian Religion* (any edition), IV.XVII.32.
7 Rattenbury 233. Also in *The Faith We Sing* (Nashville: Abingdon, 2000), no. 2259.
8 The Episcopal Church, *The Book of Common Prayer* (New York: Oxford University Press, 1990), 372.
9 World Council of Churches as in Note 2.

Chapter 16
1 *WJW(B)* 4:90.
2 Jordan Aumann, O.P., *Christian Spirituality* (San Francisco: Ignatius Press, 1985), 10.
3 Gordon S. Wakefield, *Methodist Devotion* (London: Epworth Press, 1966), 9.
4 Richard J. Payne, ed., *Classics of Western Spirituality*, 30 vols. (New York: Paulist Press); Ewert Cousins, ed., *World Spirituality: An Encyclopedic History of the Religious Quest*, 25 vols. (New York: Crossroad, 1985–); Adrian Van Kaam, *Formative Spirituality*, 4 vols. (New York: Crossroad, 1983–1987); L. Bouyer, *History of Christian Spirituality*, 3 vols. (London: Burns & Oats, 1969); P. Pourrat, *Christian Spirituality*, 4 vols. (Newman Press, 1953).
5 Philip Sheldrake, ed., *The New Westminster Dictionary of Christian Spirituality* (Louisville, KY: Westminster John Knox Press, 2005); Arthur Holder, ed., *The Blackwell Companion to Christian Spirituality* (Oxford: Blackwell Publishing, 2005).

6 David Hempton, *Methodism: Empire of the Spirit* (New Haven: Yale University Press, 2005); Cheslyn Jones, Geoffrey Wainwright, Edward Yarnold, eds, *The Study of Spirituality* (Oxford: Oxford University Press, 1986); R. F. Lovelace, *Dynamics of the Spiritual Life* (Downers Grove, IL: IVP, 1979); J. Aumann, T. Hopko, and Donald Bloesch, *Christian Spirituality, East & West* (Boston: Priory Press, 1968); Louis Bouyer, *Introduction to Spirituality* (New York: Desclee Company, 1961).
7 For example, *Weavings: A Journal of the Christian Spiritual Life* (1986–), *Studies in Formative Spirituality: The Journal of Ongoing Formation* (1979–).
8 Academic forums include the Working Group on Spirituality, and the Study Group on Personality, Religion, and Culture; both meet regularly at the American Academy of Religion annual meeting.
9 Romans 8:9–11, 14–16.
10 Sheldrake, 2.
11 Sheldrake, 2. For a full discussion of the term 'spirituality' and 'Christian spirituality' see Kenneth J. Collins, ed., *Exploring Christian Spirituality: An Ecumenical Reader* (Grand Rapids, MI: Baker Books, 2000), 21–91; and Alister E. McGrath, *Christian Spirituality: An Introduction* (Malden, MA: Blackwell, 1999).
12 Holder, 10–16.
13 Holder, 19–29.
14 Richard P. Heitzenrater, *Wesley and the People Called Methodists* (Nashville: Abingdon, 1995), 1–95.
15 John D. Walsh, 'Origins of the Evangelical Revival,' in G. V. Bennett and J. D. Walsh, eds, *Essays in Modern English Church History* (New York: Oxford University Press, 1966), 132–162; W. R. Ward, *The Protestant Evangelical Awakening* (Cambridge: Cambridge University Press, 1992).
16 *HMGB*, 1; 1–79, 115–144.
17 Irenaeus, 'Against Heresies,' in Alexander Roberts and James Donaldson, eds, *The Ante-Nicene Fathers*, 10 vols. (Grand Rapids, MI: Eerdmans, reprint, 1950) 1: 526. For the second Adam see Romans 5:12–21 and I Corinthians 15:20–29. For a rich theological and biblical discussion see John R. Tyson, ed., *Invitation to Christian Spirituality* (New York: Oxford University Press, 1999), 1–52.
18 *WJW(B)*, 4: 305–317.
19 John Norris, *Practical Discourses on Several Divine Subjects in Four Volumes* (London, 1707) 1:10.
20 The best study to date is J. Steven Harper 'The Devotional Life of John Wesley (diss., Duke University, 1981).
21 Preface from the first edition printed in Fredrick C. Gill, ed., *John Wesley's Prayers* (London: Epworth, 1951), 19.
22 *WJW(Jackson)* 11: 203–237. This prayer book went through ten editions by 1755 and was included in the 1772 edition of the collected *Works*.
23 *WJW(B)* 2: 193.
24 *WJW(B)* 1: 575, 'Sermon on the Mount, VI (1760) II.1.
25 *WJW(Jackson)*, 11: 433–435.
26 John Telford, ed., *The Letters of the Rev. John Wesley*, 8 vols. (London: Epworth Press, 1931), 5: 283.
27 *WJW(B)*, 7: 347.
28 *WJW(B)* 1: 408.
29 *WJW(B)* 2: 155–169.
30 Henry Knight, *The Presence of God in the Christian Life* (Metuchen, NJ: Scarecrow Press, 1992), 11, 35ff.
31 *WJW(B)* 1: 396.
32 See Robert G. Tuttle, Jr., *Mysticism in the Wesleyan Tradition*, esp. 151–185; and, W. R.

Ward, *Early Evangelicalism: A Global History, 1670–1789* (Cambridge University Press, 2006), chap. 7, esp. 129–132. According to Tuttle, the concept of infinite progress comes most directly from Francois Fenelon.
33 For example, the society in Hutton Rudby had two bands for children, one for boys and the other for girls. See *WJW(B)* 21:330f.
34 *WJW(B)* 19:461, diary.
35 *WJW(B)* 9:270.
36 *WJW(B)* 9:270.
37 Thomas R. Albin. 'Inwardly Persuaded: Religion of the Heart in Early British Methodism' in Richard B. Steele, ed., *'Heart Religion' in the Methodist Tradition and Related Movements* (Lanham: Scarecrow Press, 2001), 33–66.
38 *WJW(B)*, 9:70–73, emphasis added.
39 *WJW(B)*, 7:73–74.
40 Wakefield, 50.
41 *The Book of Resolutions of The United Methodist Church*, para. 324. These Guidelines were updated at the request of the General Conference of 2004 and the revised text approved in 2008.
42 Wakefield, 65.
43 Association of Theological Schools, *Accreditation Handbook*, 2008, 180.
44 Holder, 10.
45 See Gordon S. Wakefield, *Fire of Love: The Spirituality of John Wesley* (London, 1976); and 'La littérature de Désert chez John Wesley,' *Irénekon*, 51 (2e trimestre, 1978) 155–170; *HMGB*, vol. 1; Robert C. Monk, *John Wesley: His Puritan Heritage* (London, 1966); J. Brazier Green, *John Wesley and William Law* (London, 1945).
46 Frank Baker, *Charles Wesley as Revealed by His Letters* (London: Epworth, 1948) and *Representative Verse of Charles Wesley* (London: Epworth, 1964).
47 For the shorthand sermons, see my article on 'Charles Wesley's Earliest Evangelical Sermons,' *Methodist History* (October 1982), 60–62; for the sermon texts see T. R. Albin and O. A. Beckerlegge, *Charles Wesley's Earliest Evangelical Sermons* (Wesley Historical Society Occasional Publication, 1987). For new shorthand passages of Charles' journal, see John R.Tyson, 'Charles Wesley, Evangelist,' *Methodist History* (Oct. 1986), 41–60. For the shorthand verse, see S T Kimbrough, Jr. and O. A. Beckerlegge, *The Unpublished Poetry of Charles Wesley*, 3 vols. (Nashville: Kingswood Books, 1988–1992).
48 Kenneth G. C. Newport, ed., *The Sermons of Charles Wesley* (Oxford: Oxford University Press, 2001) and S T Kimbrough, Jr. and Kenneth G.C. Newport, eds *The Manuscript Journal of the Reverend Charles Wesley, M.A.* 2 volumes (Nashville: Kingswood Books, 2008).
49 At this time, with the help of the Literary and Linguistic Computing Centre of Cambridge University in England, I developed a database of more than 500,000 words of text transcribed for over 150 manuscript letters, journals, and diaries.
50 The summary of this work is presented in M. Douglas Meeks, ed., *The Future of Methodist Theological Traditions* (Nashville: Abingdon, 1985), chap. 5: 172–202.
51 Paul W. Chilcote's other publications on this subject include *She Offered Them Christ* (Nashville: Abingdon, 1993), and *Her Own Story: Autobiographical Portraits of Early Methodist Women* (Nashville: Kingswood Books, 2001).
52 Lester Ruth, *Early Methodist Life and Spirituality: A Reader* (Nashville: Kingswood Books, 2005).
53 D. Bruce Hindmarsh, *The Evangelical Conversion Narrative* (Oxford: Oxford University Press, 2005).

Chapter 17
1 *WJW(B)*, Sermon 1, 'Salvation by Faith,' 1: 125.
2 *WJW(B)*, Sermon 112, 'On Laying the Foundation of the New Chapel,' 3: 580f.
3 *WJW(Jackson)*, 11: 53–59.
4 See *WJW(B)*, Sermon 50, 'The Use of Money,' 2: 263–282; Manfred Marquardt, *John Wesley's Social Ethics: Praxis and Principles* (Nashville, TN: Abingdon, 1992), 36f. John Locke also argued that private property is a positive good.
5 *WJW(B)*, Sermon 122, 'Causes of the Inefficacy of Christianity,' 4: 95.
6 'Bristol was . . . the second slaving port in England during the 1750s and the third from the seventies onward.' Kenneth Morgan, *Bristol and the Atlantic Trade in the Eighteenth Century* (Cambridge: Cambridge University Press, 1993), 145.
7 Marquardt, 67–75.
8 *WJW(Jackson)*, 13: 153.
9 *WJW(B)*, 11: 233.
10 *WJW(Jackson)*, 13: 153.
11 *WJW(Jackson)*, 11: 59–79.
12 See Kenneth Cracknell and Susan J. White, *An Introduction to World Methodism* (Cambridge: Cambridge University Press, 2005), 225f.
13 Cracknell and White, 221. They could have added other biblical references like John the Baptist's advice to soldiers, 'Do not extort money from anyone by threats or false accusation, and be satisfied with your wages' (Luke 3:14), or the Roman officers approaching Jesus for help (Matt. 8).
14 See the letter to James West (MP), 1 March 1756. John Telford, ed., *The Letters of the Rev. John Wesley* (London: Epworth Press, 1931), 3: 165.
15 *WJW(Jackson)*, 9: 191–464.
16 *WJW(Jackson)*, 9: 221.
17 *WJW(Jackson)*, 9: 222.
18 *WJW(B)*, Sermon 23, 'Sermon on the Mount III,' 1: 518.
19 *WJW(B)*, Sermon 112, 'On Laying the Foundation of the New Chapel,' 3: 592.
20 Quoted in Theodore Runyon, *The New Creation: John Wesley's Theology Today* (Nashville, TN: Abingdon, 1998), 173.
21 *WJW(Jackson)*, 11: 81.
22 *The Wesley Study Bible* (Nashville, TN: Abingdon, 2009), 1405, correctly comments, 'These verses . . . do not fit well into Paul's argument. If original, they likely address the issue of some women disputing worship with questions, not their praying or prophesying during worship.' Wesley, of course, shared the traditional interpretation of his century.
23 Letter to Mary Bosanquet, 13 June 1771. Telford, 5: 257.
24 Runyon, 197.
25 *WJW(B)*, Sermon 98, 'On Visiting the Sick,' 3: 396.
26 Cracknel and White, 218. The authors give examples from the Methodist Episcopal Church in the nineteenth century; similar procedures could be added from other countries, although other branches of Methodism, like the Methodist Protestant Church, were more faithful to Wesley's teaching and practice.
27 Runyon, 200.
28 Other churches in the Wesleyan tradition (Methodist Protestant Church, some African American churches, the Salvation Army, etc.) were much earlier in ordaining women. In mostly Roman Catholicism and Eastern Orthodoxy countries as well as some Protestant churches the ordination of women is still disputed.
29 Runyon, 146–167.
30 Randy L. Maddox, *Responsible Grace: John Wesley's Practical Theology* (Nashville, TN: Abingdon, 1994), 213. See also *WJW(B)*, Sermon 4 'Scriptural Christianity,' 1:

Notes

      159–180), in which Wesley considered 'Christianity as beginning, as going on, and as covering the earth' in order to 'close the whole with a plain practical application' (172).
31. See Manfred Marquardt, 'Methodism in the Nineteenth and Twentieth Centuries,' in W. Abraham and J. Kirby, eds, *Oxford Handbook of Methodist Studies* (Oxford: Oxford University Press, 2009), chapter 5.
32. See Barrie W. Tabraham, *The Making of Methodism* (Peterborough: Epworth Press, 2009), 81f.
33. Mary Lou Barnwell, 'Deaconess Movement,' in *EWM*, I: 640.
34. Christopher H. Evans, *The Kingdom Is Always but Coming: A Life of Walter Rauschenbusch* (Grand Rapids, MI/Cambridge, UK: William B. Eerdmans, 2004), 68.
35. *The United Methodist Hymnal* (Nashville, TN: United Methodist Publishing House, 1989), # 427, and *Hymns and Psalms* (Peterborough: Methodist Publishing House, 1983), # 431.
36. *The Doctrines and Discipline of the Methodist Episcopal Church, 1908*, 481. The authors of the report 'The Church and Social Problems' were Harry Ward (1873–1966) and Herbert G. Welch (1862–1969). During a year of postgraduate studies in Oxford, Welch learned to know the *Wesleyan Methodist Union for Social Service* which became a model for the *Methodist Federation for Social Service*.
37. Number 59, 'The Church and Social Problems,' in the 1908 *MEC Discipline*, 479–481.
38. Other burning social problems like racial discrimination or equal rights for women, in spite of the pertinent Wesleyan teaching, did not appear in this text.
39. Robin Lovin, *Christian Ethics: An Essential Guide* (Nashville, TN: Abingdon, 2000), 109.
40. The National Council of Churches of Christ in America chose a different way for updating the Social Creed of 1908; together with Church World Service it updated the 1908 declaration as 'A Social Creed for the 21st Century.' http://www.ncccusa.org/news/ga2007.socialcreed.html (accessed 6 August 2009).
41. *Book of Discipline of the United Methodist Church* (Nashville, TN: United Methodist Publishing House, 2008), 130f.
42. *Book of Discipline of the United Methodist Church*, any edition since 1972.

Chapter 18
1. James M. Buckley, *Constitutional and Parliamentary History of the Methodist Episcopal Church* (New York: Methodist Book Concern, 1912); Thomas B. Neely, *The Evolution of Episcopacy and Organic Methodism* (New York: Phillips and Hunt, 1888).
2. On Methodist unions in the USA, see John M. Moore, *The Long Road to Methodist Union* (New York: Abingdon-Cokesbury Press, 1943); James H. Straughn, *Inside Methodist Union* (Nashville, TN: Methodist Publishing House, 1958); Nolan B. Harmon, *The Organization of The Methodist Church*, 2nd ed. (Nashville, TN: Abingdon Press, 1962); Paul Washburn, *An Unfinished Church: A Brief History of the Union of the Evangelical United Brethren Church and The Methodist Church* (Nashville, TN: Abingdon Press, 1984).
3. On the struggle of African Americans for equal participation in predominantly white American Methodist bodies, see James S. Thomas, *Methodism's Racial Dilemma: The Story of the Central Jurisdiction* (Nashville, TN: Abingdon Press, 1992); Grant S. Shockley, ed., *Heritage and Hope: The African American Presence in United Methodism* (Nashville, TN: Abingdon Press, 1991); William B. McClain, *Black People in the Methodist Church: Whither Thou Goest?* (Cambridge, MA: Schenkman, 1984). On the changing role of women in United Methodism, see Jean Miller Schmidt, 'Denominational History When Gender is the Focus: Women in American

Methodism,' in *Reimagining Denominationalism: Interpretive Essays*, ed. Robert Bruce Mullin and Russell E. Richey (New York: Oxford University Press, 1994) 203–221; Judith Craig, *The Leading Women: Stories of the First Women Bishops of The United Methodist Church* (Nashville, TN: Abingdon Press, 2004).

4 One exception, on the political prospects for a global Methodist church, is Bruce Robbins, *A World Parish? Hopes and Challenges of The United Methodist Church* (Nashville, TN: Abingdon Press, 2004).

5 All paragraph references are from *The Book of Discipline of The United Methodist Church 2008* (Nashville, TN: United Methodist Publishing House, 2008).

6 E.g., Wilbert R. Shenk, 'Recasting Theology of Mission: Impulses from the Non-Western World,' *International Bulletin of Missionary Research* 25, no. 3 (July 2001): 98–107.

7 See Sarah Heaner Lancaster, 'Our Mission Reconsidered: Do We Really "Make" Disciples?' *Quarterly Review* 23, no. 2 (Summer 2003): 117–130.

8 For further discussion of the synthesis, see Thomas Edward Frank, *Polity, Practice, and the Mission of The United Methodist Church* (Nashville, TN: Abingdon Press, 2006), 55–65.

9 On the corporatization trends in Methodism, see Thomas Edward Frank, 'From Connection to Corporatization: Leadership Trends in United Methodism,' *Journal of Religious Leadership* 5, nos. 1–2 (Spring/Fall 2006): 109–130.

10 Russell E. Richey, 'History in the Discipline,' in *Doctrine and Theology in The United Methodist Church*, ed. Thomas A. Langford (Nashville, TN: Kingswood Books, 1991), 193–194; Frank, *Polity*, 141–143.

11 E.g., the open letter from Francis Asbury and William McKendree on the first pages of *Doctrines and Discipline of the Methodist Episcopal Church 1808*.

12 E.g., S T Kimbrough, Jr., ed., *Methodism in Russia and the Baltic States: History and Renewal* (Nashville, TN: Abingdon Press, 1995).

13 E.g., Larry M. Goodpaster, *There's Power in the Connection: Building a Network of Dynamic Congregations* (Nashville, TN: Abingdon Press, 2008).

14 Frank, *Polity*; Jack M. Tuell, *The Organization of The United Methodist Church*, rev. ed. 2005–2008 (Nashville, TN: Abingdon Press, 2005); Robert L. Wilson and Steve Harper, *Faith and Form: A Uniting of Theology and Polity in the United Methodist Tradition* (Grand Rapids, MI: Francis Asbury Press, 1988). For a historical and typological account of polity development in Methodism, see Thomas Edward Frank, 'Discipline,' in *Oxford Handbook of Methodist Studies*, ed. William J. Abraham and James E. Kirby (Oxford: Oxford University Press, 2009) 245–261.

15 John J. Tigert, *A Constitutional History of American Episcopal Methodism*, 6th ed., revised and enlarged (Nashville, TN: Methodist Episcopal Church Publishing House, South, 1916), esp. 15.

16 Russell E. Richey, *The Methodist Conference in America: A History* (Nashville, TN: Kingswood Books, Abingdon Press, 1996).

17 John Wesley, 'Minutes of Several Conversations,' in *The Works of John Wesley*, ed. Thomas Jackson, vol. VIII (Grand Rapids, MI: Zondervan, reprint of 1872 edition), 322–323.

18 E.g., 'Guidelines for Holy Conferencing' distributed to delegates of the 2008 UM General Conference, *Daily Christian Advocate*, vol. 1, 'Handbook for Delegates' (distributed by the General Conference Commission of the UMC, 2008), 18.

19 E.g., Decisions 893 and 909, available at the website of UMC, in which Judicial Council decision are recorded: http://archives.umc.org/interior_judicial.asp?mid = 263 (accessed April 2009).

20 Russell E. Richey, *Marks of Methodism: Theology in Ecclesial Practice*, United Methodism and American Culture Series, Chap. 1 (Nashville, TN: Abingdon Press, 2005), 5.

Notes

21 (Werrington: Methodist Publishing House, 2003), 11.
22 In Clive Marsh et al., eds, *Unmasking Methodist Theology* (New York: Continuum, 2004), 29–40.
23 (Zurich: Methodist Church Publishing House, 1964).
24 James K. Mathews, *Set Apart to Serve: The Meaning and Role of Episcopacy in the Wesleyan Tradition* (Nashville, TN: Abingdon Press, 1985).
25 E.g., L. Bevel Jones, *One Step Beyond Caution: Reflections on Life and Faith* (Decatur, GA: Looking Glass Books, 2001).
26 Russell E. Richey and Thomas Edward Frank, *Episcopacy in the Methodist Tradition: Perspectives and Proposals* (Nashville, TN: Abingdon Press, 2004); James E. Kirby, *The Episcopacy in American Methodism*, (Nashville, TN: Kingswood Books, Abingdon Press, 2000).
27 Richard Heitzenrater reviewed the history of studies of the ministry in the UMC and predecessor bodies in 'A Critical Analysis of the Ministry Studies Since 1948,' in *Perspectives on American Methodism: Interpretive Essays*, ed. Russell E. Richey, Kenneth E. Rowe, and Jean Miller Schmidt (Nashville, TN: Abingdon Press, 1993), 431–447. The 2008 study document of the General Conference Ministry Study Commission, and related resources, is posted online: General Board of Higher Education and Ministry, available at http://www.gbhem.org/site/c.lsKSL3POLvF/b.3744969/k.DCE9/Study_of_Ministry_Commission.htm (accessed May 2009). See articles discussing the study document and current issues in ministry in *Circuit Rider* (November/December/January, 2007–2008) also available at http://www.umph.org/resources/publications/circuitrider.asp?act=displayissue&cr_issue_id=75 (accessed May 2009).
28 Dennis M. Campbell, *The Yoke of Obedience: The Meaning of Ordination in Methodism* (Nashville, TN: Abingdon Press, 1988).
29 John E. Harnish, *The Orders of Ministry in The United Methodist Church* (Nashville, TN: Abingdon Press, 2000).
30 Margaret Ann Crain and Jack Seymour, *The Deacon's Heart: The Ministry of the Deacon in The United Methodist Church* (Nashville, TN: Abingdon Press, 2000); Ben L. Hartley and Paul E. Van Buren, *The Deacon: Ministry Through Words of Faith and Acts of Love* (Nashville, TN: General Board of Higher Education and Ministry, The United Methodist Church, 1999).
31 Donald E. Messer, ed., *Send Me? The Itineracy in Crisis* (Nashville, TN: Abingdon Press, 1991).
32 (Nashville, TN: General Board of Higher Education and Ministry, The United Methodist Church, 2008).
33 An attempt at an ethnographic approach was conducted through the research for the United Methodist Council of Bishops episcopal teaching document on *Vital Congregations: Faithful Disciples; Vision for the Church* (Nashville, TN: Graded Press, 1990), in which anecdotes and reflections from local churches were printed as commentary on the bishops' statement on congregational vitality.
34 The formative and continuing influence of the General Rules was interpreted by Nolan B. Harmon, *Understanding The United Methodist Church* (Nashville, TN: Abingdon Press, 1955, 1983), 75–94, and by Reuben P. Job, *Three Simple Rules: A Wesleyan Way of Living* (Nashville, TN: Abingdon Press, 2007).
35 Roger Finke and Rodney Stark, *The Churching of America 1776–1990: Winners and Losers in Our Religious Economy* (New Brunswick, NJ: Rutgers University Press, 1992), 56.
36 *Religious Congregations and Membership in the United States 2000* (Nashville, TN: Glenmary Research Center, 2002), 86, 191.
37 Frank, *Polity*, 255–268.

38 General Conference adopted a statement on Holy Communion as an official document, but it is not published in the *Book of Discipline* nor is its implementation mandated; see 'This Holy Mystery: A United Methodist Understanding of Holy Communion,' General Board of Discipleship, available at http://www.gbod.org/worship/thisholymystery/default.html (accessed May 2009).
39 For survey of how the Social Principles are adapted in various cultures, see Darryl W. Stephens, 'Face of Unity or Mask over Difference? The Social Principles in the Central Conferences of The United Methodist Church,' *Thinking About Religion* 5 (2005), available at http://organizations.uncfsu.edu/ncrsa/journal/v05/stephens_face.htm (accessed May 2009).
40 See Richey and Frank, *Episcopacy*, 89–103.
41 See Frank, *Polity*, 229–240.
42 James A. Coriden, *An Introduction to Canon Law* (New York: Paulist Press, 1991), 12–14.
43 On the intersection of Methodist polity with civic constitutional law, see William.
44 Johnson Everett and Thomas Edward Frank, 'Constitutional Order in United Methodism and American Culture,' in *Connectionalism: Ecclesiology, Mission and Identity*, ed. Russell E. Richey et al. (Nashville, TN: Abingdon Press, 1997), 41–73.
45 Coriden, *Canon Law*, 194.
46 Coriden, *Canon Law*, 191–192.
47 Robbins, *A World Parish?*; Elaine A. Robinson, 'Restructuring The United Methodist Church In an Age of Empire,' General Board of Higher Education and Ministry, The UMC, available at http://www.gbhem.org/atf/cf/%7B0BCEF929-BDBA-4AA0-968F-D1986A8EEF80%7D/pub_restructuringrobinsonmono.pdf (accessed May 2009). Other global church perspectives may be found in *Circuit Rider* February/March/April 2008, 'Shaping Our Global Future,' available at http://www.umph.org/resources/publications/circuitrider.asp?act=displayissue&cr_issue_id=77 (accessed May 2009).
48 This principle was articulated by Tigert in his *Constitutional History* and is sustained in the UM constitutional provision for amendments (para. 59).
49 The 'four areas of focus' for UM ministries adopted by the 2008 General Conference are described available in the website of the UMC at http://www.umc.org/site/c.lwL4KnN1LtH/b.4443111/k.D720/Four_Areas_of_Ministry_Focus.htm (accessed May 2009).

Chapter 19
1 'The Character of a Methodist' (1742), 17; see *WJW(B)*, 9: 41.
2 *WJW(Jackson)*, 10: 80–86. See also the significant edition by the Irish Jesuit, Michael Hurley, *John Wesley's Letter to a Roman Catholic* (London and Dublin: Geoffrey Chapman, 1968).
3 *WJW(B)*, 3: 48–51.
4 *WJW(B)*, 3: 52.
5 *WJW(Jackson)*, 10: 86.
6 *WJW(B)*, 2: 79–95.
7 Letter to James Harvey, in *WJW(B)*, 19: 66–67.
8 Letter to 'John Smith,' in *WJW(B)*, 26: 197–207.
9 *WJW(Jackson)*, 8: 280–281.
10 See the sermon 'On Schism' (1786), in *WJW(B)*, 3: 58–69.
11 *WJW(B)*, 9: 331–341; cf. 567–580.
12 *WJW(B)*, 3: 464–478.
13 The observation on Wesley's oarsmanship is attributed to Dr. Joseph Beaumont;

Notes

see Benjamin Gregory, *Sidelights on the Conflicts of Methodism* (London: Cassell, 1898), 161.
14 Frank Baker, *John Wesley and the Church of England* (London: Epworth, 1970), 162.
15 *WJW(Jackson)*, 8: 320–321.
16 The quoted phrases are from John Wesley's letter of 10 September 1784 to 'our brethren in America'; see for context *John Wesley*, ed. Albert C. Outler (New York: Oxford University Press, 1964), 82–84.
17 *WJW(B)*, 2: 485–499.
18 For an enthusiastic contemporary account, see *Methodist Quarterly Review*, 65 (July 1883): 447–473. Theologically, some remarkable anticipations of the twentieth-century ecumenical movement are found in the Fernley Lecture by the British Wesleyan, Benjamin Gregory (1820–1900), *The Holy Catholic Church, the Communion of Saints* (London: Wesleyan Conference Office, 1873).
19 Biographically, see Robert C. Mackie and others, *Layman Extraordinary: John R. Mott 1865–1955* (London: Hodder & Stoughton, 1965); C. H. Hopkins, *John R. Mott 1865–1955* (Grand Rapids, MI: Eerdmans, 1979). Mott was a Nobel peace-prize winner in 1946.
20 Robert Newton Flew, ed., *The Nature of the Church* (London: SCM Press, 1953). At a time when Roman Catholics were forbidden to associate with ecumenical gatherings, Flew himself wrote the descriptive chapter on Roman Catholic ecclesiology.
21 See Max Thurian, ed., *Churches Respond to BEM* (Geneva: World Council of Churches 1986), 2:177–199.
22 For a long-term view of the 'home front,' see John Munsey Turner, *Conflict and Reconciliation: Studies in Methodism and Ecumenism in England, 1740–1982* (London: Epworth, 1985).
23 See the chapter by Eric J. Lott, in Karen Westerfield Tucker, ed., *The Sunday Service of the Methodists: Twentieth-Century Worship in Worldwide Methodism* (Nashville, TN: Abingdon, 1996), 53–66.
24 For the former figure, see Alan Turberfield, *John Scott Lidgett – Archbishop of British Methodism?* (Peterborough: Epworth, 2003). For his part, Robert Newton Flew contributed a chapter on Methodism to N. P. Williams, ed., *Northern Catholicism: Centenary Studies in the Oxford and Parallel Movements* (London: SPCK, 1933) and wrote, *Jesus and His Church: A Study of the Idea of the Ecclesia in the New Testament* (London: Epworth, 1938). As a learned and ecumenically committed ecclesiologist, Flew was the leading light behind the British Methodist Conference's 1937 statement, *The Nature of the Christian Church*. There we read: 'The Church today is gathered for the most part in certain denominations or "churches". These form but a partial and imperfect embodiment of the New Testament ideal. It is their duty to make common cause in the search for the perfect expression of that unity and holiness which in Christ are already theirs.'
25 In the early 1990s, the WMC explored with the Patriarchate of Constantinople the possibility of moving toward a dialogue with the Orthodox, but nothing further resulted than a booklet of mutual self-introductions, *Orthodox and Methodists* (1995). In 2003 the WMC began a modest dialogue with the Salvation Army, whose origins reside in the work of the Methodist William Booth (1829–1912).
26 See Geoffrey Wainwright, 'Is Episcopal Succession a Matter of Dogma for Anglicans? The Evidence of Some Recent Dialogues' in *Community, Unity, Communion: Essays in Honour of Mary Tanner*, ed. C. Podmore. (London: Church House Publishing, 1998), 164–179. The Anglican-Methodist International Commission had envisaged that, without 'calling into question the ordination or apostolicity of any of those who have been ordained as Methodist or Anglican ministers according

to the due order of their churches,' those churches would 'work towards the establishment of that ministry in its traditional three-fold form, including, in ways which still need to be worked out, the historic episcopate.' In 2007 some attempt was begun to re-open the international conversation between the WMC and the Anglican Communion.

27 In 1996, seven Methodist churches in Europe, including this time the British, signed a 'joint declaration of church fellowship' associating themselves with those Lutheran and Reformed churches that have over the years endorsed the bilateral Leuenberg Concordat of 1973. The 'Community of Protestant Churches in Europe' includes mutual recognition of ordination and the practice of reciprocal presidency at the Lord's table.

28 It is noteworthy that ecclesiological themes figure prominently in the topics listed by the Joint Declaration as needing further clarification in light of the 'consensus in basic truths of the doctrine of justification': 'the relationship between the Word of God and Church doctrine,' 'ecclesial authority, Church unity, ministry, the sacraments and the relation between justification and social ethics' (43).

29 See Albert C. Outler, *Methodist Observer at Vatican II* (Westminster, MD: Newman Press, 1967).

30 The Reports, written in English, are published officially in the *Information Service* of the Secretariat (now Pontifical Council) for Promoting Christian Unity, and as brochures by the World Methodist Council (Lake Junaluska, North Carolina). They can be found, also in translated form, in various journals and collections of dialogue documents. The Centro pro Unione in Rome has produced a compact disk containing all the original texts. As of 2007, the joint commission has been engaged also in drawing up a 'synthesis' that will document thematically the convergences that have been registered over the entire course of the dialogue and identify the remaining issues for settlement.

31 From this point on, I write as an insider: I joined the Commission in 1983 and have been chairman on the Methodist side since 1986.

32 Albert Outler had described Methodism as 'an evangelical order' needing 'a church catholic' within which to function; see, for instance, his essay, 'Do Methodists have a Doctrine of the Church?' in *The Doctrine of the Church*, ed. Dow Kirkpatrick (Nashville, TN: Abingdon, 1964), 11–28. Within his own United Methodist Church, at the General Conference in 1970, Outler sponsored the 'resolution of intent' whereby the anti-Roman elements in the historic Articles of Religion that John Wesley had borrowed for American Methodism from the Church of England were to be interpreted 'in consonance with our best ecumenical insights and judgment.' See Albert C. Outler, 'An Olive Branch to the Romans, 1970s style: United Methodist initiative, Roman Catholic response,' in *Methodist History* 13.2 (January 1975): 52–56.

33 One such event may have been the service of word and song shared between Catholics, Anglicans, and Methodists at the Roman basilica of St. Paul Outside the Walls in late 2007 to celebrate the three-hundredth anniversary of Charles Wesley whose hymns all three bodies share.

34 For the full text, see *Proceedings of the Seventeenth World Methodist Conference, Rio de Janeiro, Brazil, August 1966*, Joe Hale, ed. (Lake Junaluska, NC: World Methodist Council, 1997), 266–269; or (with another related text) *Proceedings of the Nineteenth World Methodist Conference, Seoul, Korea, 2006: God in Christ Reconciling* (Lake Junaluska, NC: World Methodist Council, 2007), 151–158.

35 See *WJW(Jackson)*, 8: 275. For possible application to ecumenical ecclesial structures in the twenty-first century, see Geoffrey Wainwright, 'A primatial ministry of unity in a conciliar and synodical context' in *One in Christ* 38, no. 4 (October 2003): 3–25;

also forthcoming in James F. Puglisi, ed., *How Can the Petrine Ministry Be a Service to the Unity of the Universal Church* (Grand Rapids, MI: Eerdmans, 2010).

Chapter 20
1. Amal Asfour and Paul Williamson, *Gainsborough's Vision* (Liverpool: Liverpool University Press, 1999), 23 ff.
2. Quoted in Helen de Borchgrave, *A Journey into Christian Art* (Oxford: Lion, 1999), 7.
3. For a good introduction, see William Vaughan, *British Painting: The Golden Age from Hogarth to Turner* (London: Thames & Hudson, 1999).
4. John Wesley's active ministry was between 1739 and 1791; Sir Joshua Reynolds floreat c.1744–1792; Thomas Gainsborough floreat c.1748–1788.
5. *The Methodist Hymn-Book* (London: Methodist Conference Office, 1933), iii.
6. See Dan Cruickshank, *A Guide to the Georgian Buildings of Britain and Ireland* (New York: Rizzoli, 1985), 170, 176.
7. Wesley's Large Minutes, 1770, in *Minutes of the Methodist Conferences* (London: John Mason, 1862), 612–614.
8. British governments levied taxes on windows in Acts of 1696, 1766, and 1784.
9. *WJW(B)*, 21:131 (Journal, 23 November 1757).
10. Fifteen octagonal chapels were built between 1761 and 1776. See Alan Smith, 'John Wesley's Octagonal Preaching House,' *London Society Journal* 454 (Winter 2007): 8–11; also articles in *EWM, DMBI*.
11. Known as the 'City Road arrangement.' See 'Architecture' in *DMBI*.
12. R. Furneaux Jordan, *Western Architecture* (London: Thames & Hudson, 1983), 125ff.
13. Kenneth Cracknell and Susan J. White, *An Introduction to World Methodism* (Cambridge: Cambridge University Press, 2005), 134, 194–195.
14. Stourport Methodist Church, Worcestershire, built in 1788.
15. D. Bruce Hindmarsh, *The Evangelical Conversion Narrative* (Oxford: Oxford University Press, 2005).
16. J. M. Williams also painted the most reliably authenticated portrait of Susanna Wesley. See Peter Forsaith, 'The Curious Incident of Susanna Wesley's Rosebud Lips,' in N. Virgoe, ed., *Angels and Impudent Women* (Loughborough: Wesley Historical Society, 2008), 31ff.
17. *WJW(B)*, 22: 436 (Journal, 4 November 1774).
18. See Tim Clayton, *The English Print 1688–1802* (New Haven, CT/London: Yale University Press, 1997); Vic Gattrell, *City of Laughter* (London: Atlantic, 2006).
19. Hone, from an Irish artistic family, was an important London painter known for his sympathetic portraits of children (including one of Charles Wesley's son, Samuel) and for a furor created by his 1775 painting 'The Conjuror Unmasked' which lampooned Sir Joshua Reynolds, the leading artist of his day and the founding President of the Royal Academy. See Martin Butlin, 'An Eighteenth-Century Art Scandal: Nathaniel Hone's "The Conjuror",' *The Connoisseur* (May 1970), 1–9; John Newman, 'Reynolds and Hone, "The Conjuror" Unmasked,' in Nicholas Penny, ed., *Reynolds* (London: Royal Academy of Arts, 1986), 344.
20. 'Hone Pinxt./Blood Sculp.' John Wesley, *Explanatory Notes upon the Old Testament* (Bristol: Pine, 1765).
21. Joseph G. Wright 'Wesley Portraits,' *PWHS*, 2: 49–51; John Kerslake, *Early Georgian Portraits*, 2 vols (London: H.M.S.O., 1977), 302.
22. J. Wesley to Henry Brooke (Dublin artist and drawing master), letter of 15 October 1771, *PWHS*, xx: 51; *WJW(B)*, 24:118 (Journal, 5 January 1789).
23. Peter Forsaith, 'The Romney portrait of John Wesley,' *Methodist History* XLII, no. 4 (July 2004): 249–255, esp.251.

24 E. Wood to A. Clarke, 6 October 1830, ms. in United Library, Garrett Theological Seminary, Evanston, IL.
25 Richard P. Heitzenrater, *The Elusive Mr. Wesley*, vol. 2 (Nashville, TN: Abingdon Press, 1984), 180ff.
26 For the best guide to the subject, see Roger Lee, *Wesleyana and Methodist Pottery, A Short Guide* (Weymouth: Sloane & Partner, 1988).
27 See Donald Ryan, 'The Edinburgh Wesley Portraits,' *PWHS*, 55, no. 1 (February 2005): 1.
28 Oliver Cromwell to Sir Peter Lely, c.1653–1654 (attrib.) 'I desire you would use all your skill to paint your picture truly like me, and not flatter me at all; but remark all these roughness, pimples, warts, and everything as you see me.'
29 *WJW(B)*, 24:68 (Journal, 22 December 1787).
30 Tim Clayton, *The English print, 1688–1802* (New Haven, CT/London: Yale University Press, c.1997).
31 See Peter Forsaith, *John Wesley, Religious Hero*? (Oxford: Applied Theology Press, 2004).
32 E.g., by Claxton (1849); Hunt (undated); Brownlow (1860) and a number of prints.
33 William Hatherell, 'John Wesley Preaching at a Market Cross' (1904) and 'John Wesley preaching at Bath in 1739' (1917) sold through Berry-Hill Galleries, New York, c.1976. Location presently unknown.
34 In The Mansion House, Bristol. The other was a sketch of Wesley preaching on a Bristol street and survives only as a squared sketch. See David Tovey, *W. H. Y. Titcomb: Bristol, Venice and the Continental Tours* (Tewkesbury: Wilson Books, 2003), plate 10.
35 *WJW(B)*, 24: 71 (Journal, 16 March 1788).
36 Such as those by A. G. Walker (1932), New Room, Bristol, and a similar c.1961 at Wesley Theological Seminary, Washington, DC.
37 John Pudney, *John Wesley and His World* (London: Thames & Hudson, 1978), 70.
38 Later known as, *A Midsummer's Afternoon with a Methodist Preacher*, in the National Gallery of Canada, Ottawa (NGC 4057).
39 See Bernd Krysmanski, 'We See a Ghost: Hogarth's Satire on Methodists and Connoisseurs,' *Art Bulletin* 80, no. 2 (June 1998): 292–310.
40 At the American Tract Society, New York, NY.
41 Titcomb was in fact based in St. Ives rather than Newlyn, but this has become a generic term.
42 David Tovey, *W. H. Y. Titcomb: A Newlyner from St. Ives* (Tewkesbury: Wilson, 2003).
43 Tom Norgate, *From Pedagogy to Photography: The Life and Work of John William Righton* (Hampshire: 613 Books, 2008).
44 Antje Matthews, *John Russell (1745–1806) and the Impact of Evangelicalism and Natural Theology on Artistic Practice* (PhD diss., University of Leicester, 2005), also 'John Russell's Mysterious Moon,' *PWHS*, 55 (2006): 252ff.
45 Leonard Robinson, *William Etty: The Life and Art* (Jefferson, NC: McFarland, 2007), 29ff.
46 Hockney's brother remained a local preacher and was prominent in the civic life of Bradford ('Art' in DMBI).
47 The Spencer Gallery, Cookham, Berks., is in the former Methodist chapel which Spencer and family attended. His father was a Methodist local [lay] preacher.
48 *Dictionary of American Biography*, quoted in *EWM*, but for a discussion of Jarvis' relationship to John Wesley, see Ann Onstott and F. F. B[retherton], 'Two Wesley Letters in America,' *PWHS*, xix (1934–1935): 89–92.
49 He named his son John Wesley Paradise (Paradise, John) in *EWM*.
50 'He did a great deal of good, much more, I believe, than is generally known, and

he never did harm to any living creature.' See Hugh Honour, 'John Jackson, R.A.,' *The Connoisseurs' Year Book* (1957): 91–95.
51 James Herring and James B. Longacre, eds, *The National Portrait Gallery of Distinguished Americans*, 4 vols (New York: Bancroft, 1834).
52 'Longacre, James' in *EWM*; Wanda Willard Smith, ed., *A Methodist Minister in Paris* (Dallas, TX: Bridwell Library, 2002).
53 'Beecroft family' in *DMBI*. Original canvas is at the Museum of Methodism, London.
54 'A. T. Nowell' in *DMBI*.
55 *The Times*, 5 January 1996, 1.
56 George VI was crowned 12 May 1937; Picasso commenced work on *Guernica* 1 May 1937.
57 See Calum McCleod, *The Death of Christian Britain* (London: Routledge, 2001), 170ff.
58 'Rank family' in *DMBI*. J. Arthur Rank was created Baron Rank of Sutton Scotney in 1957.
59 Michael Wakelin, *J. Arthur Rank: The Man Behind the Gong* (Oxford: Lion, 1996).
60 Peter Wakelin, *An Art-Accustomed Eye: John Gibbs and Art Appreciation in Wales 1945–1996/Celf drwy lygad craff* and *John Gibbs a gwerthfawrogi celf yng Nghymru, 1945–1996* (Caerdydd: Amgueddfeydd ac Orielau Cenedlaethol Cymru, 2004); 'Gibbs, Dr. J.' in *DMBI*.
61 See R. Wollen, *An Introduction to the Methodist Church Collection of Modern Christian Art* (Oxford: Trustees of the Methodist Church Collection of Modern Christian Art, 2001).
62 See Gesa E. Thiessen, *Theological Aesthetics: A Reader* (London: SCM, 2004).
63 Thiessen, 324.
64 Kenton M. Stiles, 'In the Beauty of Holiness, Wesleyan Theology, Worship and the Aesthetic,' *Wesleyan Theological Journal* xxx: 194–217.
65 Stiles, 199.
66 Stiles, 199.
67 Stiles, 201.
68 *WJW(Jackson)*, 8: 299.
69 See Philip Olleson, *Samuel Wesley, The Man and His Music* (Woodbridge: Boydell, 2003), 3, 31.
70 Susan Casteras, *James Smetham* (Aldershot, UK: Scolar Press, 1995).
71 See also Jeremy Black, *A Subject for Taste* (London/New York: Hambledon & London, 2005), esp. chap. 4; Clare Haynes, *Pictures and Popery* (Aldershot: Ashgate, 2006).
72 John Wesley, *A Plain account of Christian Perfection* (London: Epworth, 1952), 90.
73 William Shakespeare, *Twelfth Night*, Act 1, scene 1, 1–3.
74 Ephesians 2: 10.

Chapter 21
1 The English Short Title Catalogue (ESTC) lists one other copy-holding institution in the UK and one in the USA.
2 ESTC lists one other copy-holding institution in the UK and none in the USA.
3 During its long history, the magazine was renamed several times as follows: *Arminian Magazine* (1778–1798); *Methodist Magazine* (1798–1822); *Wesleyan Methodist Magazine* (1822–1913); *The Magazine* (1913–1932) and the *Methodist Magazine* (1932–1969).
4 Also referred to as The Presbyterian Church of Wales.
5 The Methodist circuit and district is broadly analogous to the Anglican or Catholic parish and diocese.
6 In 1907, the British UMC (not to be confused with its American counterpart)

was created as a result of the merger of the Bible Christians, the Methodist New Connexion, and the United Methodist Free Churches.
7 In 1932, the Methodist Church of Great Britain was born from the union of the UMC with the Wesleyan Methodist and the Primitive Methodist denominations.
8 The first county record office was established in 1913 in Bedfordshire, but it was not until after World War II that the system was adopted more generally.
9 Quarterly meetings originated in 1748 and evolved as gatherings of preachers and lay officials to discuss financial, spiritual, and administrative matters of general relevance to the churches in a particular circuit.
10 Until 1837, all marriages, other than those of Quakers and Jews, by law had to take place according to Anglican rites. With regard to baptism, celebration was officially restricted to Anglican ministers working in association with the societies. Some preachers baptized anyway and Methodist registers begin to appear from 1772, but for most people having a child christened in a Methodist chapel was not an option. Chapel burials in the eighteenth century were also rare, with the exception of London's City Road which opened its own burial ground in 1779.
11 SOAS contains several other non-Methodist missionary collections, including the records of the London Missionary Society, China Inland Mission and the foreign mission of the Presbyterian Church of England.
12 In the major administrative restructuring of the early 1970s, departments of the Methodist Church became to known as divisions, with the Methodist Church Overseas Division (MCOD) assuming responsibility for overseas work. In 1996, further large-scale administrative restructuring removed these divisions and the Methodist Church became a single Connexional team. It is anticipated that the only transfers to SOAS of material created after 1996 will consist of archives relating to those overseas districts for which the Methodist Church of Great Britain retains a measure of responsibility.
13 These non-ordained workers included deaconesses and medical staff.
14 The UMC is the largest Methodist denomination in the world with a membership in 2010 of approximately eight million in the USA and 3.5 million in Africa, Asia, and Europe. It is the result of a merger of the Evangelical United Brethren Church and the Methodist Church in 1968. The Methodist Church was in turn, a product of a 1939 merger between the Methodist Episcopal Church, the Methodist Episcopal Church, South, and the Methodist Protestant Church.
15 The UMA is under the supervision of a general church agency termed the GCAH.
16 *Special Collections: Manuscript Sources for Methodist History – A descriptive List of Holdings in the Special Collections Department* (Atlanta, GA: Robert W. Woodruff Library, Emory University, January 1990).
17 *Wesley/Langshaw Correspondence: Charles Wesley, His Sons and the Lancaster Organists*, ed. Arthur W. Wainwright in collaboration with Don E. Saliers (Atlanta, GA: Emory University, Emory Texts and Studies in Ecclesial Life, 1993).
18 As part of this arrangement, the GCAH processes and handles Drew's collection of Methodist archives as well as its own.
19 Including approximately 150 autograph letters.
20 Predecessor denominations include the Methodist Episcopal Church, 1784–1939; Methodist Protestant Church, 1830–1939; Methodist Episcopal Church, South, 1844–1939; Methodist Church, 1939–1968; Church of the United Brethren in Christ, 1800–1946; Evangelical Association/Church, 1806–1946; and Evangelical United Brethren Church, 1946–1968.
21 The UMC is organized into a large number of geographical annual conferences, for example New England and Kansas East. A General Conference is usually held every four years and acts as the supreme legislative body of the UMC.

Notes

22 Sometimes annual conference archives are also located in museums; for example, Barratt's Chapel and Museum near Dover, Delaware, houses a research library that contains the archives of the Peninsula-Delaware Annual Conference.
23 See the online *Guidelines for Managing Records of the Annual Conference and Local Church* (Madison, NJ: GCAH, 2005).

Index

Abingdon Press 32
abolition of slavery 104–107
Abraham, William J. 65, 70, 235
Academy for Evangelism in Theological Education 234
accountable discipleship 226–227
Act of Toleration of 1689 22
Act of Uniformity of 1662 21
Act of Union of 1804 85
active presence of Christ (in the eucharist) 265–266
adaptation 324–325
administrators of baptism 269–270
Advance for Christ and His Church 129
advocacy 109–110
aesthetics 13–14
  and the Wesleyan tradition 365–366
Africa 133–151, 389–390
  East Africa 147–149
  North Africa 149
  Southern Africa 140–147
  West Africa 115–116, 121, 133–140
Africa University 147, 150
African American Methodism 95–96, 108, 109, 121, 212
African Methodist Episcopal Church (AME) 137, 141, 323, 337, 390–391, 449
African Methodist Episcopal Zion Church (AMEZ) 121, 136, 138, 337, 391, 449

African Union Methodist Protestant Church 391–392, 498
age
  baptism 268–269
  and receiving the eucharist 273
Aggrey, James Emman Kwegyri 136
Albin, Tom 227
Albright, Jacob 97–98, 266–267, 392–393, 427
Allan, Thomas 372
Allchin, A. M. 51
Allen, Horace Newton 123
Allen, Richard 95, 390–391, 393, 449
Alley, Mary 205
American Academy of Religion, Wesleyan Studies Group 32
American Civil War 106, 284
American Methodism *see* United States of America (USA)
American Society of Missiology 131
amillennialism 30
'analogy of faith' 67–68
Anderson, Gerald H. 131
Andrew, James O. 104, 106, 451
Andrewes, Lancelot 50
Anglican/Episcopal-Methodist conversations 341–342, 394
Anglican-Methodist International Commission 343
Anglicanism 393–394
  see also Church of England

Angola 141–142
Anne, Queen 23
Annesley, Samuel 24, 477
annual conferences 100–101, 169, 315, 319, 325
  foreign language annual conferences 168
  records 384–385
Anta, James 145
Antigua 205–206
anti-Methodist literature 16, 17, 374
antinomianism 394–395
Apiri, James 146
apostolic witness 69
Appenzeller, Henry G. 122, 157, 395
Aquinas, Thomas 295
architecture 351–353, 509–510
archives 369–386
  American Methodism 381–385
  British Methodism 370–381
  Europe 183–184
archivists 377
Argentina 206–207, 217
Arias, Mortimer 126–127, 235, 237
Aristotle 317
Arminian Magazine 14, 354, 356, 396–397
Arminianism 396–397
Arminius, Jacob 22, 396
Arndt, Johann 90
Arthur, William 85
Articles of Religion 65, 67, 71, 418–419, 419–420
arts, the 13–14, 350–368, 397–399
  contemporary art 364

587

Index

cultural context of Methodism 351–353
images of John Wesley 353–357, 398–399
images of Methodism 358–359
Methodist artists 359–362
struggle for modernity 363–364
Asbury, Francis 76–77, 91, 92, 94, 101, 322, 334, 399, 472
 conflict in American Methodism 98–100
 'explanatory notes' on the *Discipline* 245
 missionary 113–114
 ordination 94
Asia 152–165, 400–401
 agents of 'civilization' and social change 158–160
 colonialism 155–158, 164
 holiness revivalism 160–163, 164–165
 Methodist denominational identity 153–155, 163–164
Association of Theological Schools 288
assurance 482
Australasia 116, 155–156, 401–402
Australia 340–341, 401
'Author of life divine' (Charles Wesley) 54
authority 61–72
autonomy 208–209

Báez-Camargo, Gonzalo 402
Baker, Frank 6, 11, 14, 45, 288, 334, 382
Baker, John 135
Baltic countries 188–203
 blooming of Methodism 194–196
 Methodist beginnings 191–192
 renewal 202–203
Baltic Mission Centre 202
Baltimore Union Society 103
bands 281, 282
Bangs, Nathan 94, 105, 206, 402–403, 454
baptism 242, 259–263, 480–481
 agreed statement 339
 practical questions and implications 267–271

baptismal formula 268
Baptists 31, 258
Barchet, Reinhold 191
Barclay, Wade 118
Barratt, John Cook 171, 560
Barratt, Thomas Ball 180, 468, 564–565
Barth, Karl 262
Bast, Anton 403
Baxter, John 205–206
Bebbington, D. W. 69, 83
Beckerlegge, Oliver A. 45
Beecroft, Herbert 362
Belarus 197–198
Belgium 177
Benedict XVI 348
Benedict, Dan 236
Benezet, Anthony 295
Bengelius 47
Benin 135
Bethel Ship mission 173, 426, 434
Bett, Henry 38
Beza, Theodore 396
Bible *see* scripture
Bible Christians 78, 284, 404, 448
Bible Women 124
Bicentennial Edition of the Works of John Wesley 8–9, 11, 33
bilateral dialogues and relations 342–348
Bischoff, Christian 176, 563
Bishop, John 252
Black, William 94, 409
Black Methodists for Church Renewal 109
Blake, Edgar 193, 194
Blake, William 39
'Blow Ye the Trumpet, Blow' (Charles Wesley) 226
Blyden, Edward 121
Boardman, Richard 91
Boehm, Martin 89, 91, 266, 404–405, 466
Boggs, John 117
Bolivia 218
Bonino, José Míguez 212, 213, 405
Book of Common Prayer (BCP) 38, 42–44, 240–241, 242, 243
Book of Offices, The 246
Book of Resolutions 110
Book of Worship 247
Book of Worship for Church and Home 246–247

Booth, Catherine 405–406, 483
Booth, William 118, 405–406, 483
Bosanquet, Mary 224, 372, 430
Bossuet, Jacques-Bénigne 329
Bourne, Hugh 284, 372, 406, 414–415, 448, 475
Bouteneff, Peter 51
Bowmer, John 78
Brantley, Richard 69
Brazil 206–207, 208, 217
Brethren in Christ 286
Brett, Pliny 100
Brevint, Daniel 42, 53
Brightman, F. E. 244
British East India Company 155, 156
British Methodism 73–84, 86–88, 337, 444–445
 growth and division 76–79
 heyday of Nonconformity 79–82
 missions 80, 84, 460–461
  Asia and the Pacific 153–154, 155–156, 158–159
  Europe 169, 170–172
 polity 473–474
 printed and archival research collections 370–381
 twentieth century 82–84
 Wesleys' Methodism and the Evangelical Revival 74–76
Broadman, Richard 113
Brontë family 398
Brown, Callum 83
Brown, George 120
Brown, Marcus 139
Brown, Maria 124
Bruce, Philip 101
Buc, Guillaume du (Bucanus) 68
Buckenham, Henry 142
Bullen, Donald A. 59
Bulu, Joeli 117
Bunting, Jabez 78, 85, 153, 407
Burundi 148–149
Butler, Clementina Rowe 400, 493
Butler, William 120, 155, 400, 407–408

Index

Calixt I 295
Calvin, John 264, 265
Calvinism 408
Cambodia 127
camp meetings 284, 410
Campbell, Dennis M. 64, 316
Campbell, Sophia 205
Campbell, Ted A. 39, 64, 66
Camphor, Alexander P. 138
Campolo, Tony 286
Canaanite woman 48–50
Canada 93, 94–95, 340–341, 408–410
Cape Coast Bible Band 115
Capers, William 104
Carew, Benjamin A. 135
Cargill, David 117
Caribbean *see* Latin America and the Caribbean
Carlson, Bengt A. 189
Caroline divines 21–22, 24
Cartwright, Andrew 121, 138
Carvalho, Emilio J. M. de 142
Case, William 95
case study methodology 255–256
Castro, Emilio 126, 231, 338, 410–411
caucuses 109–110
causes 109–110
Centenary Movement 177–178
Central Conferences 170, 326
Central Jurisdiction 108, 109, 310
Centre for the Study of Christianity 131
Ceylon 158
Chadwick, Samuel 285–286
Charismatic movement 286
Charles I 21
Charles II 21–22
Charles, Thomas 502
Charles Wesley: Poet and Theologian 59
Charles Wesley Society (CWS) 32, 59, 289
Chautauqua Institution 411
Chaves, Ottilia de Oliveira 411–412
Chilcote, Paul W. 236, 237, 238, 289
children 412
Chile 212, 217
China 122, 124, 156, 159–160, 163

Cho Young Cheul 200
chrismation 269
Christian Advocates 96
Christian antiquity 66–67
Christian Library 14, 24
Christian Methodist Episcopal Church (formerly Colored Methodist Episcopal Church) 337, 413, 449
Christian Realism 305
Christian spirituality 275–277
Christian Year, hymns for 58
Christmas Conference 94, 95, 241–242
Church, The: Community of Grace 344–345
Church of England 20–23, 28, 75, 340, 343–344
  Anglican/Episcopal-Methodist conversations 341–342, 394
  bilateral dialogue with Methodists 343–344
  Charles Wesley's hymns for 57–59
  colonies 93
  divergences between John and Charles Wesley 29
  sacraments 257, 258–259
  separation of Methodism from 77, 333–334
  Thirty-Nine Articles of Religion 41–42
church extension 114–115
Church Missionary Society (CMS) 153
Church of the Nazarene 107, 119, 211, 286
Church of North India 341
church records 377–378, 385
Church of Scotland 340
Church of South India (CSI) 341
church unions 340–342
Churches Uniting in Christ 342
CIEMAL 209–210, 211, 413–414
Cikala 142–143
cinema 363–364
circuit records 378
civil war
  American 106, 284
  English 21

'civilization', agents of 158–160
Clapper, Gregory 69
Clarke, Adam 361, 414, 453
class meetings 282
Claxton, Marshall 356
Clemens Alexandrinus 51
Clement, Shirley 235
Clowes, William 284, 414–415, 448, 475
Coke, Thomas 94, 98, 99–100, 241, 334, 372, 415, 472
  'explanatory notes' on the *Discipline* 245
  overseas missionary work 117, 134, 153, 171, 400, 460
  Latin America and the Caribbean 113, 205, 206, 439
Coker, Daniel 115, 137
Cole, Richard Lee 85
Coleman, Robert E. 232
Coles, George 251
Collection of Forms of Prayer for Every Day in the Week 278
Collection of Hymns for the Use of the People Called Methodists 58, 253, 283
Collection of Psalms and Hymns 253, 374
Collection of Psalms and Hymns for the Lord's Day 253
Collins, Judson D. 154, 159
Colombia 211, 219
colonialism 114, 118–124
  Asia and the Pacific 155–158, 164
Colored Methodist Church (later Christian Methodist Episcopal Church) 107
Commission on the Structure of Methodism Overseas (COSMOS) 209
Committee of Nine on the Division of the Church 106
common discipline 320–321, 324
common witness 126–127
Commonwealth government 21

589

Index

Commonwealth of
 Independent States
 (CIS) 200–202
communicants 273
communism 192–194,
 198–200
Community of Protestant
 Churches in Europe
 182
compendiums of theology
 31
comprehensive studies 7–8
conciliar structures 338–340
conference 323
 governance by 314–315,
 321–322
 records 373–374
 representation 325–326
 *see also under difference types
 of conference*
Conference of European
 Churches 182
Confessing Movement 421
Confession of Faith 65, 67,
 71, 419–420
confirmation 262–263
Congo, Democratic Republic
 of 143–144
Congo Institute–
 Mulungwishi 144
Congregationalists 31
congregations 81
 congregation and baptism
 270–271
Congress on Christian Work
 in Latin America
 207–208, 570
connection principle 319,
 327
Connectional records and
 archives 370–376
Connectional Table 312
consecration at a distance
 271
consecratory prayer 263–264
Constable, John 360
constitutional principles
 323–327
constitutional rights 326
Consultation on Church
 Union (COCU) 109,
 342
contemporary art 364
contemporary events 55–56
context
 cultural context of
 Methodism 351–353
 evangelism and 237–238

literary context of Charles
 Wesley's verse 38–40
contextual approach 11
controversial divinity 26–27
conversion 230
convictions, theological
 27–29
Cook, Charles 415–416
Cooke, R. J. 245
Cooke, William 452
Coombs, Lucinda L. 123
Cooper, Ezekiel 101
cooperative missionary
 work 208
core doctrinal convictions 25
corporate capitalism 312
'Corpus Christianum' 166
Costa Rica 218
Coughlan, Laurence
 408–409, 416
Council of Bishops 110
Council of Evangelical
 Methodist Churches
 in Latin America and
 the Caribbean
 (CIEMAL) 209–210,
 211, 413–414
covenant renewals 250–251,
 283
Cowman, Lettie Burd 119
Cox, Melville 137, 389–390
Cracknell, Kenneth 353
Crain, Margaret Ann 316
Crandall, Ron 235–236
Crane, Stephen 398
Cranmer, Thomas 257
creation 222
critical decade of
 missiological
 reflection 232–234
Cromwell, James O. 94
Crookshank, C. H. 85
Crosby, Fanny 417
Cross, William 117
Crusade for Christ program
 181
Crusade for a New World
 Order 109
Cuba 209, 218
Culloden, Battle of 56
cultural context 351–353
cultural shifts 237
Cuneo, Terence 362–363
Cyrus, Ephrem 52
Czechoslovakia 177

Dacorso, César 417–418
Dale, James 39, 40

Darwin, Charles 261, 455
Davie, Donald 38
Davies, Maria Dyer 251
De Graft, William 116, 138
De Loutherbourg, Philip
 358
deaconess movement 124,
 301–302, 418
deacons 270
decoration of churches 353
Democratic Republic of
 Congo 143–144
Dempster, John 206
Denman, Harry 231
Denmark 179
denominational identity
 153–155, 163–164
denominational Methodism
 329, 334–337
denominations 5, 15
 see also Methodist
 denominations
descriptive primary sources
 248–252
'Desiring to Love' (Charles
 Wesley) 45–46
development 129
devotion 276
diaspora, Irish 85
disciple-making slogan
 311–312
Discipline 91–92, 95, 99–100
 Coke and Asbury's
 'explanatory notes'
 245
 Miller's version 98
 1972 innovations 109
 'Our Theological Task'
 statement *see* 'Our
 Theological Task'
 statement
Dissent 75
Dissenters 77, 545
district records 378
divines (pastoral
 theologians) 25–27
Dix, Dom Gregory 265
doctrinal/speculative
 divinity 26–27
doctrinal standards
 American Methodism 65,
 67, 70–71, 418–421
 British Methodism
 421–422, 474
doctrine 23, 25, 28, 65, 86
Doctrine of Original Sin, The
 (John Wesley) 27, 28
Dodge, Ralph Edward 130

Dominican Republic 208, 218
Dow, Lorenzo 100, 284, 476
Downes, John 354
Dress Reform Society 121
Drew University 383–384
Dreyer, Frederick 69
Duke University 382
  Divinity School Center for Studies in the Wesleyan Tradition 59–60
  Divinity School Library 382
  Divinity School Summer Wesley Seminar 11–12
Dunnam, Maxie 235
Dunwell, Joseph R. 135
Durdis, Georg 191

Early Fathers of the Church 50–52
East Africa 147–149
Eastern Orthodox Church 166, 168–169, 422–423
ecclesiology 271–272, 313
economics 12–13
Ecuador 208, 219
ecumenical Methodism 329, 337–349
  bilateral dialogues and relations 342–348
  church unions 340–342
  conciliar structures 338–340
  ecumenism 82, 83, 287, 329–349, 423
  denominational Methodism 329, 334–337
  Europe 182
  Latin America and the Caribbean 213–214
  Wesleyan Methodism 329, 330–334
editing 14–15
education 84, 122–123, 158–160, 164, 216, 423
Edward VI 20
Eggleston, Edward 398
Ehnes, Morris 146
Ehwa Haktang 122, 160
Eighteenth Century Collections Online (ECCO) 17
ekklesia 317–318

Eklund, Anna 189, 192, 193, 194, 424–425
El Salvador 210–211
elements, eucharistic 272–273
Eliot, George 398
Elizabeth I 20–21
Elliker, S. 148
Ellis, Joseph 144
Elmer, Charles 119
Ely, Richard 302
Embury, Philip 89, 91
emerging churches 210–211
Emory, John 102
Emory University 382
emotion 39
empiricism 32
England, Martha Winburn 38–39
English, Donald 376
English Civil War 21
Enlightenment 23, 112
Ensley, Gerald 233
enthusiasm 425
episcopacy 314, 315–317, 322–323
Episcopal Church 342
Erwin, George 196
Escher, John J. 175, 178
essays 27
Estonia 191, 195, 196, 198–200, 202
'Ethiopians' 141
Etty, William 360
eucharist 263–267, 480–481
  evangelism 227–228
  hymns for 52, 53–54, 57, 264–265
  practical questions and implications 271–274
Europe 166–187, 425–426
  American Methodist missions 169–170, 172–178
  British Methodist missions 169, 170–172
  historical organizations and archives 182–184
  turning points in European Methodism 178–182
European Central Conference of the Methodist Episcopal Church 170
European Commission on Mission 181
European Historical Commission 182–183

European Historical Conference of 2010 183
European Methodist Council 181
European Methodist E-Academy 181
European Union 167, 557
Evangelical Association/ Church 98, 107, 108, 427
  doctrinal standards 419
Europe 170, 175–176
Evangelical Congregational Church 427–428
Evangelical Episcopal Church 149
Evangelical Reformed Church of Baltimore 91
evangelical renewal 310–313
Evangelical Revival 23, 24, 73, 74–76
Evangelical Theological Seminaries 213
Evangelical United Brethren Church (EUB) 107, 109, 127, 419, 428
  sacraments 258–259
evangelism 215–216, 221–239, 335–337, 428–429
  developments within Methodism 229–237
  principles 238–239
  rethinking at the close of the Millennium 234–237
  Wesleyan practice 225–229
  Wesleyan theory of 221–225
evangelization 125
Everett, James 429–430
Every Creature Crusade 119
expansion 119–120
experience
  hymns for Christian experience 58–59
  spirituality and religious experience 276
  Wesleyan Quadrilateral and authority 62–66, 70, 71–72
exploration 114
extra-sensory perception 14
eyewitness accounts 248–252

591

Index

faith
'analogy of faith' 67–68
justification by 482
'Wesleyan essentials of Christian faith' 66, 348
Faith and Order movement 63–64, 65, 68, 338
family 284–285
Fante Christians 115–116, 135–136
Federal Council of Churches of Christ in America 305
Few, Ignatius A. 105
Fiji 116–117, 120
Findlay, G. G. 80
Findlay, J. Alexander 287
First World War 210, 363
Fisher, Geoffrey 341
Fisk, Wilbur 105, 454
Fletcher, John 75, 372, 430–431, 453, 485
Flew, Robert Newton 287, 338, 341
Flickinger, D. K. 134
Fliedner, Friederike 301–302
Fliedner, Theodor 301–302
Fluvanna conference 93–94
foot binding 124
foreign language annual conferences 168
Forsaith, Peter 16
Forward Movement 80, 81
Foundation for Evangelism 231, 234
Fowler, James W. 289
Fox, H. Eddie 233
France 56
Francke, August Hermann 90
Frank, Thomas Edward 316
Frederick, John Richard 121
Free Church 80, 82, 258
Free Church Association 182
Free Methodist Church 78, 119, 337, 431
freedom 214
religious 190
Freeman, Thomas Birch 116, 135, 136, 138, 140, 379
Freiberg, Alfred 195
Freud, Sigmund 261
Frost, Stanley 61, 71
Fry, Roger 363
fundamentalism 83

Gainsborough, Thomas 351
Gambia 135
Gamewell, Frank Dunlap 122
Gamewell, Mary Porter 122
Garrett Evangelical Theological Seminary 382–383
Garrettson, Freeborn 93, 94
Garrison, William Lloyd 104
Gebhardt, Ernst 178
Geeting, George Adam 91
Gell, Dr 47
Geller, William 357
gender 12, 310
see also women
General Board of Global Ministries of the UMC 210, 211
General Commission on Archives and History (GCAH) 383, 384, 385
general conference 98–99, 100–104, 314–315, 320, 325–326
General Council on Ministries 110
General Rules 65, 71, 318, 320–321, 470
George II 23, 56, 296
George, A. Raymond 372
George, Enoch 102, 105
Germany 171, 173–174, 175–176, 178–179, 181
Ghana 115–116, 121, 135–136
ghosts 14
Gibbs, John M., collection 364
gifts of the Spirit 29
Gilbert, John Wesley 120, 143
Gilbert, Nathaniel 112–113, 133, 205, 439
Gladden, Washington 302
'Glory be to God on High' (Charles Wesley) 43
God 29
authority of 61, 71–72
beauty of 365–366
union with 279
Goh, Robbie H. 152
Gold Coast/Ghana 115–116, 121, 135–136
Golden Rule 301
Gomer, Joseph 134–135
Gomer, Mary 134–135
Good News 109, 110, 241
Gorham, Sarah 121
Gothic architecture 352

Gowland, Bill 376
grace
means of 278, 280–281, 483
prevenient 28, 481–482
Graf, J. F. 148
Graham, Billy 232, 286
Great Awakenings 89, 90, 114, 118, 119, 230
Great Litany, The 43–44
Great War 180, 363
Gregory the Great 350
Gregory of Nyssa 51
Griffiths, J. B. 148
Guatemala 219
Guinter, C. W. 139
Gunter, W. Stephen 66
Gurney, Samuel 146, 147
Guyana 212
Gwennap Pit, Cornwall 357
Gwynne, Sarah 11

Hagen, Odd 199, 431–432
Halévy, Elie 13, 78
Haley, John Wesley 148–149
Hammett, William 100, 476
Hanoverian kings 23
Harbin 197
Harkness, Georgia 432
Harman, Robert J. 215
Harmon, Nolan B. 244
Harnish, John E. 316
Harris, Howell 75, 502
Harris, William Wade 'Prophet' 121, 140, 432–433
Hartzell, Joseph Crane 137, 138, 141, 146, 433–434
Hastings, Adrian 83
Hastings, Selina, Countess of Huntingdon 75, 77, 372, 484–485
Hatherell, William 357
Hearn, J. Woodrow 200
heart religion 160–163, 164–165
Heath, Elaine 236
Heck, Barbara 89, 92
Hecker, Julius F. 189, 194
Hedding, Elijah 103, 105
Hedstrom, Olaf Gustav 173, 434, 561
Heinkel, Herman 143
Heitzenrater, Richard 74
Hempton, David 78, 79, 85, 86, 87
Hena, Chris 200
Henry VIII 20, 25, 257
Henry, Matthew 47

592

Herbert, George 253
Hernández, Alejo 434–435
Hill, David 379
Hindmarsh, D. Bruce 16, 289
historical organizations 182–184
History of the Methodist Church in Great Britain, A 87
Hockney, David 360
Hogarth, William 358
Holdsworth, W. W. 80
Holiness Movement 119, 211, 284, 285–286, 435, 449–450
  Europe 178–180
  holiness revivalism in Asia and the Pacific 160–163, 164–165
holistic soteriology 222–223
Holy Club 281, 292, 503, 504
holy communion *see* eucharist
holy living 4, 32
holy living divines 22, 24
Holy Spirit 29
home missions 81, 84
Home Rule 85, 86
homosexuality 306, 490
Honduras 211
Hone, Nathaniel 355, 582
Honolulu Report 346–347
Hook, James Clarke 361–362
Hoover, Willis Collins 212, 435–436, 468–469
Horace 37–38
Hosier, Harry 95
Howard, Leona 159, 160
Hughes, Hugh Price 80, 82, 230, 436, 455
Hughes, Michael 83
human rights 214, 216, 297–299
Hunt, Earl G. 231, 235
Hunt, John 117, 161, 162
Hunter, George G. 234–235, 237
Huntingdon College 385
Hwa Yung 237–238
'Hymn upon the pouring out of the Seventh Vial . . .' (Charles Wesley) 41
hymns 26, 351, 398, 508
  Charles Wesley 3, 10, 26, 27, 32, 36–60, 86
  evangelism and 225–226

literary context of sacred verse 38–40
sources of the hymns 41–56
John Wesley 26
  spirituality 283
  worship 253–255
Hymns on the Expected Invasion 56
Hymns on the Lord's Supper 42, 53–54, 57
Hymns occasioned by the Earthquake 56
Hymns for the Public Thanksgiving-Day 56
Hymns and Sacred Poems 36, 40
Hymns for Times of Trouble and Persecution 55–56
Hymns on the Trinity 54–55

images *see* arts, the
immersion, baptism by 268–269
immigrants/immigration 84, 172–173
incarnation, doctrine of 222
inclusive ministry 224–225
Independent Methodists 78
India 120–121, 122, 155, 158–159, 162, 163, 341
Indian Manual Labor Training School 115
individualism 214
industrialization 78, 79
influence of the Wesleys 15
Ingham, Benjamin 372
institutional archives 372–374, 379–380
instrumental role of reason 70, 72
intentional community 281–283
'interim eucharistic sharing' agreement 342, 394
International Association for Mission Studies 131
International Consultation on English Texts (ICET) 287
International Missionary Council (IMC) 126, 231, 338
internet 10
interpretation 47
Ireland 73–74, 84–88, 452
Irenaeus 277
Istomina, Lydia 200

itinerant general superintendency 316, 322–323
Ivory Coast 140

Jackson, John 355, 356, 360, 374
Jackson, Thomas 33, 288
Jacobite Revolution 55–56
Jacoby, Ludwig Sigismund 173–174, 437, 561–562
James I 21
James II 22
Japan 156–157
Jarratt, Devereaux 93
Jarvis, John Wesley 360
Jenkins, Philip 152
'Jesu, show us thy salvation' (Charles Wesley) 43–44
Jesus Christ 29
  encounter with the Canaanite women 48–50
  presence in the eucharist 265–266
Jobson, F. J. 352
John Paul II 349
John Rylands University Library 76, 79
  MARC 371–375, 378, 381
Johnson, James 'Holy' 121
Joint Commission on Unification 108
'Joint Declaration on the Doctrine of Justification' 345
Joint Task Force on Extended Mission to the CIS 201
Jones, E. Stanley 125
Jones, Robert 108
Jones, Scott J. 66, 67, 236
Jones, William 54–55
Journal of Charles Wesley 33
Joyce, James 398
judiciary 326
justice 130, 214
justification by faith 482

Kafue Training Institute 142
Kansas Bible College 286
Kay, John 356
Kelley, Margaret Lavinia 124
Kelsey, Morton 287
Kenya 147–149
Keswick Convention 285–286

593

Index

Keysor, Charles 109, 420–421
Kilham, Alexander 284, 437–438, 448, 451
Kim, Helen 128
Kingdom Advance program 181
Kingswood Book series 32
Klaiber, Walter 236
Kobia, Samuel 231, 338
Korean Bible 122
Korean Methodism 122–123, 128, 157, 196–197
Krapf, Johann Ludwig 148
Kumler, D. C. 134
Kumm, Karl 139
Kurewa, John W. Z. 238
Kurz, Sebastian 175, 563
Kuum, Alexander 199
Kuum, Karl 191

Ladies' China Missionary Society 118
Ladies Committee for the Amelioration of the Conditions of Women in Heathen Countries 123
Ladies Repository 96
laity 438
Lambuth, James William 117
Lambuth, Mary McClellan 117
Lambuth, Walter Russell 120, 143, 196, 438–439
Lampe, John F. 55, 58
Lankford, Sarah Worrall 97
Latin America and the Caribbean 204–220, 439–440
  autonomy 208–209
  CIEMAL 209–210, 211, 413–414
  emergence of new Methodist churches 210–211
  establishment and development of Methodism 205–208
  meaning of Methodist presence and witness 212–217
Latin American Evangelical Conferences (CELA) 213
latitudinarianism 23, 25
Latourette, Kenneth Scott 125

Latvia 191, 195, 196, 202–203
Laud, William 21
Lausanne Committee for World Evangelization 232
Lausanne Covenant 232
Lawson, John 45
Leaver, Robin 44
Lee, Jarena 97
Lee, Jason 115
Lee, Jesse 98–99, 101
Leech, Kenneth 287
legacy of the Wesleys 15
legislative conferences 313–314
Leigh, Samuel 116, 154, 440
letter days 283
liberalism 31, 286–287, 455–456
liberation 130
Liberia 137–138
Lidgett, John Scott 341, 455
Link, Johann Conrad 175, 563
Lithuania 191, 195, 196, 204
Liturgical Movement 247
living faith 335
Livingstone, David 114, 118, 141, 142
'local' church 332
local records 376–379, 384–385
Locke, John 32, 69
Logan, James 235
London Missionary Society (LMS) 153
Longacre, Andrew 360
Longacre, James Barton 360
'Lord, and God of heavenly powers' (Charles Wesley) 42–43
'Lord, regard my earnest cry' (Charles Wesley) 48–50
Losee, William 409
Lossky, Nicholas 50
love 58
love feasts 250–251, 283
Loveness, Henry 142
Lucknow Women's College 122, 160
Lutheran World Federation 344–345
Lutheranism 97, 344–345, 441
Lynch, James 154, 155, 400
Lyth, John 171, 560

Machin, Ian 83
Maclay, Robert S. 157
Maddox, Randy L. 66, 70
Mahlatsi, Joseph M. 141
majority world missions 128–129
Maltby, W. R. 287
Mann, Ernst Gottfried 174, 562
Maolosi, Robert 142
marriage 284
Marsden, Samuel 116
Martin, John 357
Marx, Karl 455
Mary I (Mary Tudor) 20
Mashaba, Robert Ndevu 144, 441–442
Mason, Mary W. 118
mass movements 120–121, 162–163
Mathews, James K. 316
Matthews, Marjorie 108, 442
Matthews, Rex Dale 69, 72
Maweni, Jacob 143
Mazonya, John 146
McCaine, Alexander 103
McCarthy, Charles 135
McKendree, William 101, 102
means of grace 278, 280–281, 483
media, modern 461–462
medical work 123, 158–159, 164
'Meet and right it is to sing' (Charles Wesley) 43
Meistad, Tore 226
Melanesia 120
Mennonites 91
Merritt, Timothy 102
Messer, Donald E. 316
Methodism 442–446
Methodist Archives and Research Centre (MARC) 371–375, 378, 381
Methodist artists 359–363
Methodist Church (Great Britain) 82, 83, 337, 444, 446
Methodist Church (USA) 107, 108, 178, 337, 447
Methodist Church in the Caribbean and the Americas (MCCA) 209, 439

Methodist denominations
  denominational identity
    and missions in Asia
    and the Pacific
    153–155, 163–164
  Great Britain 447–448
  USA 449–450
  see also denominational
    Methodism
Methodist Episcopal Church
  (MEC) 92, 94–95,
  106–107, 107–108, 329,
  334, 337, 449, 450
  China 159
  divisions over slavery and
    race 104–107
  doctrinal standards 419
  Europe 169–170, 172–174,
    177
  general conferences 98–99,
    100–104
  John Wesley and 30–31,
    94, 334, 450
  Latin America 206–207
  Missionary Society 154
  restructuring 107
  slavery 295–296
  Social Creed 304–305
  union with MECS and
    Methodist Protestant
    Church 178, 337, 450
  WFMS 123, 124, 127, 172
Methodist Episcopal Church,
  South (MECS)
  106–107, 117, 449,
  450–451
  Europe 176–178
  Russian Far East and
    Belarus 196–198
  union with MEC and
    Methodist Protestant
    Church 178, 337, 450
  WMS 124
Methodist Federation for
  Social Service 304, 305
Methodist History 32
Methodist Homes for the
  Aged 84
Methodist Magazine, The 375
'Methodist militia' 13
Methodist Missionary
  Library 380
Methodist Missionary
  Society (MMS)
  American 97, 102, 115
  Women's Auxiliary 97,
    102, 118
  British 80, 84, 117, 129

Methodist New Connection
  78, 451–452
  Britain 284, 448, 451–452
  Ireland 452
Methodist Oecumenical
  Conference of 1881
  73, 87, 337
Methodist people 76
Methodist Protestant
  Church 103–104, 246,
  449, 452–453
  union with MEC and
    MECS 178, 337, 450
Methodist Quarterly Review
  96
Methodist Recorder, The 375
Methodist Relief and
  Development Fund
  (MRDF) 129
Methodist Service Book 247
Methodist Times 375
Methodist United Society
  282
Methodist Worship Book 247
Mexico 208, 217
Michelangelo 350
Micronesia 120
Miles, Rebekah L. 66, 70,
  72
Miles, William Henry 457
Miller, Craig 236
Miller, George 98
Millsburg Female Academy
  118
Milton, John 39
ministry 457–458
Minor, Rüdiger Rainer
  458–459
Mission alongside the Poor
  84
mission associations 131
'Mission Conference' 169
missions 112–132
  Africa 115–116, 121,
    133–151
  American Methodism see
    United States of
    America (USA)
  Asia and the Pacific
    116–117, 120, 152–165
  British Methodism see
    British Methodism
  church, evangelism and
    mission 223–224
  ecumenical movement
    335–337
  and eucharists 272
  Europe 168–178

expansion and
  colonialism 118–124
founders 112–114
home missions 81, 84
Irish 85
Latin America and the
  Caribbean 204–209
Methodist theology of
  mission 130–131
from mission to church
  125–131
mission as core value 285
pioneers 114–118
records 379–381, 384
rise of Methodist
  denominational
  identity 153–155
Russia and the Baltics
  188–203
to slaves 104
M'noti, Philip 148
'Model Deed' (1763) 30, 422,
  471, 474
'model deeds' for local
  church property 327
modern media 461–462
modernist theologies 31
modernity 363–364
Moede, Gerald F. 316
Mokone, Mangena 141
Moleli, Mudumeni 145
money 293
monographic studies 6, 7–8,
  17–18
Montgomery, Helen Barrett
  124
Montreal Faith and Order
  statement 63–64, 65
Moody, Dwight L. 118, 126
Moots, Cornelio C. 162
Moravianism 462
Morgan, James 374
Morgan, John 135
Morgan, William 281
Morris, Colin 130
Morrison, Henry Clay 286
Mott, John R. 126, 231, 338
Mozambique 144–145
Müller, Christoph Gottlob
  171, 462–463, 560
museums 376
music 283, 351
  see also hymns
Mutembo, Kayeka 143
Mutual Rights of Ministers and
  Members of the
  Methodist Episcopal
  Church 102, 103

595

Index

Muzorewa, Abel Tendekai 130
mysticism 463

Nairobi Report 347
Nanking, Treaties of 156
narrative 314
narrative poems 48–50
Nast, Wilhelm 173, 463–464, 561
National Camp Meeting Association for the Promotion of Holiness 284
National Children's Home 80, 84
'national' church 331
National Council of Churches (USA) 287
National Library of Wales 376
Native Americans 115
Nauka I Religia 199
Nausner, Ernst 198
Navess, Tizore 145
Nazarene, Church of the 107, 119, 211, 286
Ndoricimpa, Alfred 149
Neill, Stephen 118
Nemapare, E. 146
Neo-orthodoxy 31
Neuformirten Methodisten Conferenz 97–98
New Age movement 285, 287
new birth 482
New Chapel, London 352
New Economic Policy (NEP) (Russia) 193
New England Wesleyan Anti-Slavery Society 105
New Room, Bristol 352
New York Female Missionary and Bible Society 118
New Zealand 156, 401
Newbury Biblical Institute 114
Newcomer, Christian 91
Newell, Fanny 97
Newport, Kenneth G. C. 39
Nicaragua 211, 219
Nicholson, Evelyn Riley 128
Niebuhr, Reinhold 262, 305
Nigeria 138–140
Nightingale, Joseph 250
Niles, Daniel T. 126, 227, 338

nominal Christianity, struggle against 160–163
Nonconformity, heyday of 79–82
nonjurors 22–23
Norris, John 277–278
Norris, William H. 207
North, Frank Mason 302–303, 305, 455
North Africa 149
Northern Ireland 83
Norway 179–180
Nowell, Arthur T. 362, 363
Ntahorturi, Jean 149
Nuelson, John Louis 193, 194, 464, 559
Nugent, Randolph 200

'O the Depth of Love Divine' (Charles Wesley) 264–265
'O for a thousand tongues to sing' (Charles Wesley) 226
Oath of Allegiance 22–23
O'Bryan, William 404, 448, 465
O'Connor, Anthony 140
octagons 352
Oduyoye, Mercy Amba 127
Oecumenical Methodist Conference of 1881 73, 87, 337
O'Kelly, James 99–100, 449
Oldham, J. H. 126
Oldham, William F. 465–466
Oliver, Anna 97
Opon, Sampson 136
Oppong, Kwame Sampson 121
ordinances 257–258, 258–259
see also sacraments
ordination 242–243, 271–272, 311
organic union 340–342
Oriental Missionary Society (later OMS International) 119
original sin 260–261, 481
originative principles 318–323
orthopathy 300
Orwig, William W. 178
Osborn, George 34, 288
Otterbein, Philip William 89, 90–91, 94, 266, 404–405, 466

'Our Theological Task' statement 61–66, 68–69, 70–71
1972 statement 61, 63–64, 69, 70, 71, 72, 109
revised statement 64–65, 69
Outler, Albert C. 6, 11, 31, 32, 62, 66, 67, 68, 233, 338, 466–467
Ovid 39
Oxford Brookes University Wesley Centre 376
Oxford Institute of Methodist Theological Studies 31–32, 213–214
Oxford Movement 75, 77

Pacific, the 116–117, 120, 152–165, 401–402
agents of 'civilization' and social change 158–160
colonialism 155–158, 164
holiness revivalism 160–163, 164–165
Methodist denominational identity 153–155, 163–164
Pacification, Plan of 283–284, 334, 447–448
Palmer, Phoebe 97, 284, 454, 467
Panama 218
paradigm shifts 230–231
Paradise, John 360
Paraguay 219
Parham, Charles 286
Parker, H. Perlee 356
'Partner of our flesh and blood, The' (Charles Wesley) 55
partnership 127
'pastoral office' 78
pastoral theologians (divines) 25–27
Payne, Daniel Alexander 468
peace 296–297
Pentecostalism 107, 119, 212, 286, 468–469
Percival, Peter 158
periodicals 374–375
Perks, Sir Robert 82
personal papers 371–372
Peru 218
Petersen, Ole Peter 173, 561
philanthropy 84
Philippines, The 157–158, 162, 163

596

photography 359
Piercy, George 154
Pietism 23, 24, 75, 89–90, 112, 469
piety 276, 469–470
Pilmoor, Joseph 91, 113
Piotrowski, Jan 198
Pitts, Fountain E. 206, 439
Pitts Theology Library, Emory University 382
plagiarism 9
Plan of Pacification 283–284, 334, 447–448
Platt, William J. 140
Poetical Works of John and Charles Wesley 34
poetry, sacred 10–11, 40–56, 264
  see also hymns
Poland 177
politics 13
polity 309–328
  American Methodism 310–313, 315, 319–320, 472–473
  British Methodism 473–474
  of John Wesley 470–472
  present state of research and writing 313–317
  for the twenty-first century 317–328
  constitutional principles 323–327
  discernment of principles 327–328
  nature of polity 317–318
  originative principles 318–323
Pollard, Samuel 379
Pope-Levison, Priscilla 237
popular works 7–8
Porter, Mary 124
portraiture 351, 353–357
postmillennialism 30
Potter, Philip A. 126, 231, 338, 474–475
pouring, baptism by 269
Pourrat, Abbé 275
poverty 12–13, 84, 292–293, 488–489
Poysti, N. J. 197
practical divinity 26–27
practical theology 4
prayer 278–279
Prayer Book 38, 42–44, 240–241, 242, 243
prayer meetings 283

preachers 318–319
preaching 26, 225, 285
preaching assignment plans 252
premillennialism 30
Presbyterian Church 31, 246
presiding elders, election of 101–102
prevenient (preventing) grace 28, 481–482
Prikask, Martin 198
primary sources 7–9, 17, 76
  archives *see* archives
  worship 248–252
Primitive Methodism 301
  Britain 78, 82, 284, 448, 475
  USA 100, 476
Primitive Wesleyan Methodists 476
principles 317–328
  constitutional 323–327
  discernment of 327–328
  originative 318–323
printed and archival collections *see* archives
printed engravings 354
'printer's flowers' 14
'Process Theology' 287
property, social obligations of 293–294
proportionality 325
Protestant Evangelical Alliance 201
'Provisional Conference' 169
psychological studies 12
publishing 14–15, 477
Puerto Rico 208, 209, 218
Pugin, Augustus 352
Puritanism 21, 22, 257, 477–478

Quakerism 258, 478
Quaque, Philip 115

racism 95–96, 104–107, 108, 310
Rack, Henry D. 69, 74
Ramsey, Dwight 200
Rank, J. Arthur 363–364
Rankin, Thomas 92
Rattenbury, J. Ernest 45, 230–231, 252
Rauschenbusch, Walter 302
reason 39, 478–479
  Wesleyan Quadrilateral and authority 62–66, 69–70, 72

reception 324
record offices 377
Reformation 257–258
Reformed Churches 344
'Reformed Methodists' 100
regional variations 267
Reids, the 146
relief 129, 180–181
religious freedom 190
religious poetry 10–11, 40–56, 264
  see also hymns
remaining elements 272–273
representation 101–102, 325–326
Republican Methodists 99
Restrictive Rules 101, 103, 316
reverse mission 129
revivalism 284, 285–286
revolution 13, 78
Russia 192–194
Revolutionary crisis 93–95
Reynolds, Hiram Farnham 119
Reynolds, Sir Joshua 351, 355
Richards, Erwin 144
Richardson, Jonathan 356
Richey, Russell E. 315, 316
Righton, John 359
rights
  constitutional 326
  human 214, 216, 297–299
ritual commentaries 245
ritual texts 240–247
Robert, Dana L. 127, 161
Roberts, Benjamin Titus 479
Roberts, Robert Richford 102, 105
Rodriguez Romero, Casimira 214, 570
Rogers, Hester Ann 96
Roman Catholicism 20, 22, 166, 169, 342–343, 479–480
  bilateral dialogue with Methodists 345–348
  evangelism 233
  Ireland 85, 86
  Latin America 215
  Second Vatican Council 233, 247, 342–343, 345, 346
Romney, George 355
Roosevelt, Theodore 304
Rose, E. A. 375
Rowe, Elizabeth Singer 40

597

Index

Rowlandson, Thomas 358
Runyon, Theodore 300
Rural Educational Activities for Development (READ) 129
Russell, John 355, 359
Russell, William 359–360
Russia 188–203
   after the collapse of the Soviet Union 200–202
   Methodist beginnings 189–190
   Revolution and interwar period 192–194
   Russian Far East 196–198
   see also Soviet Union
Russia United Methodist Theological Seminary 201
Russian Orthodox Church 190, 192, 193, 201
Ruth, Lester 289
Rwanda 148–149
Ryan, Henry 95

sacraments 257–274, 480–481
   baptism *see* baptism
   early Methodism's reliance on Anglican understandings 258–259
   eucharist *see* eucharist
   practical questions and implications 267–274
   Reformation roots of Methodist perspective 257–258
sacred poetry 10–11, 40–56, 264
   see also hymns
Sahu, Manjulata 129
Salisbury, Frank O. 362–363, 363, 372
Salmi, Hjalmar 189, 190
salvation 28, 51, 222–223, 277, 495–496
   and social action 230–231
   Wesleyan Way of 279–280, 481–483
Salvation Army 118, 211, 483
Samoa 120
sanctification 28, 30, 161, 280, 300–301, 482–483
Sangster, William 231
Sanneh, Lamin 121
Sarah Gorham Mission School 121
Sayer, Robert 356

Scandinavia 173, 179–180
Scaramelli, Giovanni 275
scene paintings 356–357
Schäfer, Franz Werner 484
schism 332–333
Schneiders, Sandra M. 276–277
School of Oriental and African Studies (SOAS), University of London 379–381
science 484
Scott, Isaiah B. 138
Scott, Orange 105
Scranton, Mary F. 122–123, 157, 160
Scranton, William Benton 123, 157, 158
scripture
   Enlightenment tendencies and 23
   primacy of 27
   sources of Charles Wesley's hymns 45–50
   translation of the Bible 121–122
   Wesleyan Quadrilateral and authority of 62–66, 67–68, 71–72
Sears, Anna B. 160
Second Great Awakening 90, 114, 230
Second Vatican Council 233, 247, 342–343, 345, 346
Second World War 180–181, 196, 198
secondary sources 17–18
secularization 83
select bands (select societies) 281–282
Selections from the Sunday Service of the Methodists 243
self-sacrifice 228–229
self-supporting missions 119–120
self-transcendence 276
Seoul Report 347–348
servanthood 228–229
Seward, William 16
Seymour, Jack 316
Shaw, Anna Howard 97
Shaw, Barnabas 140, 389
Shaw, William 389, 485–486
Shier-Jones, Angela 315
Shimmin, Isaac 145
Shinn, Asa 452, 454, 486

Shodeke, Chief 138
Short Hymns on Select Passages of the Holy Scriptures (Charles Wesley) 46–47
Shubotham, Daniel 284
Shuey, W. J. 134
shut-ins 274
Sierra Leone 115, 134–135
Sigg, Ferdinand 486–487
Sikobele 144–145
Simons, George Albert 189, 191, 192, 193, 194, 487
sin 260–261, 481
singing 225–226
   see also hymns
slavery 92, 95–96, 104–107, 294–296, 488
Small, John Bryan 121, 136
small groups 226–227, 281–283
Smetham, James 361–362, 364, 367
Smith, Edwin 142
Smith, John 142
Smith, Joseph 135
Smith, Robert Pearsall 178
Snethen, Nicholas 100, 452, 487–488
social action 13, 230–231, 488–490
   American Methodism 110
   British Methodism 79–80, 84, 281, 489–490
   Latin America 216
   missions in Asia and the Pacific 158–160
social ethics 292–308
   John Wesley's seminal contribution 292–301
   in the nineteenth and twentieth centuries 301–307
   in the twenty-first century 307
Social Gospel Movement 302–303, 455
Society of Friends (Quakers) 258, 478
Society for the Study of Psychology and Wesleyan Theology 33
Sommer, Johann Wilhelm Ernst 491
Soper, Donald Lord 231
Soule, Joshua 101, 102, 103, 105

South Africa 140–141
Southern Africa 140–147
Southern Methodist University 383
Southport Convention 285–286
Soviet Union 192–194, 198–200
  collapse 166, 167, 200
  see also Russia
Sparrow, John 38
Spaulding, Justin 206
speaking in tongues 286
Spektorov, Vladislav 200
Spencer, Peter 391–392
Spencer, Stanley 360, 397–398
Spener, Philipp Jakob 90, 469
Spilsbury-Taylor, Maria 356
spirit world 14
spirituality 28, 30, 275–291
  Christian 275–277
  distinctive Methodist 277–281
  enduring qualities of Wesleyan spirituality 289–290
  intentional community 281–283
  nineteenth century Methodist 283–285
  research agenda 288–289
  twentieth century Methodist 285–288
Springer, Helen 143, 491
Springer, John M. 143–144, 491
sprinkling, baptism by 269
St. Petersburg 188, 189–190, 192–193
Stephenson, Thomas Bowman 80
Stevens, Abel 105, 106
Stewards Book of the London Society 372
Stewart, John 115, 137
Stiles, Kenton 365–366
stillness 492
Stockton, William S. 102, 103
Stone, Bryan 236, 237
Strawbridge, Elizabeth 92
Strawbridge, Robert 89, 91, 93
Student Volunteer Movement (SVM) 161–162, 338

subsidiarity 324–325
Sudan 148–149
suffering 30, 32
Sumire de Conde, María Cleofé 214, 570
Summers, Thomas O. 242, 245
Sunday Morning Service of the Methodists, The 243
Sunday schools 379, 492–493
Sunday Service of the Methodists, The 240–245
Sunday Service of the Methodists in North America 94
Sunderland, La Roy 105
Sung, John 163, 493
superintendency, itinerant general 316, 322–323
Swain, Clara 123, 159, 493–494
Swanson, Roger 235
Sweet, Leonard 237
Switzerland 178

Taggart, Norman 85
Täht, Vassili 191
'take away communion' 273–274
Tamutsa (or Tsiga), Job 146
Tanzania 148–149
Tattersall, Edward 359
Taylor, J. O. J. 196
Taylor, Jeremy 22
Taylor, William 119, 119–120, 494
  Africa 120, 137, 141, 143, 144
  India 162
Tent Methodists 78
Thakombau, Chief 117
'Thanks be to God, the God of Power' (Charles Wesley) 56
Theological Institution 78
theological pluralism 64
Theological Study Commissions on Doctrine and Doctrinal Standards 62, 63, 64–65
theology 86
  after John Wesley 453–456
  and doctrine 65
  of mission 130–131
  Wesleyan see Wesleyan theology

'Theology and Evangelism in the Wesleyan Heritage' conference 235
theosis 51–52
Thirty-Nine Articles of Religion 41–42
Thoburn, Isabella 122, 123, 124, 160, 497
Thoburn, James Mills 120–121, 157, 497–498
Thomas, John 116
Thompson, E. P. 78
Thorsen, Donald 66
'Thou God of boundless power and grace' (Charles Wesley) 53–54
Thunyiswa, Ben 141
Tidmarsh, H. E. 363
Tigert, John J. 314–315
Tiki, Stephen 146
Tillich, Paul 365
Tindal, Matthew 23
Ting Ang 156
Titcomb, William 357, 358–359
Together in God's Grace 344
Togo 140
Toland, John 23
Told, Silas 248–249
Tonga 116, 120
Tongan Pentecost 162
tongues, speaking in 286
Toogood, Jacob 92
Tozzo, James 142
tracts 27
trade unionism 489–490
tradition 62–66, 66–67, 68–69, 71–72
translation 47
  of the Bible 121–122
  liturgical texts 244–245
trial bands 282
Trinity 54–55, 222, 495
Tull, L. E. 147
tune books 254
Tupou, Taufa'ahau 116
Turner, Nat 104
Twentieth Century Fund 82

Uganda 148–149
Ukraine 199
unconditional predestination 25
Union American Methodist Episcopal Church 498

599

Index

Union Church of Africans 498–499
United Brethren in Christ (UB) 91, 107, 108, 175, 499
  doctrinal standards 419
  mission in Germany 176
United Church of Canada 95, 340
united churches 340–342
United Irishmen 85
United Methodist Archives (UMA) 381, 383–384
United Methodist Church (Great Britain) 82, 499–500
United Methodist Church (Nigeria) 139–140
United Methodist Church (USA) 128, 342, 500
  constitution 320–321
  formation in 1968 107, 109, 337, 450
  Judicial Council 315, 326
  mission statement 311–312, 321
  'Our Theological Task' statement *see* 'Our Theological Task' statement
  polity 310–313, 315, 319–320
  Social Creed 305–307
  Social Principles 305–307, 321
  theology of mission 130–131
United Methodist Committee in Relief 129
United Methodist Free Churches 500–501
United Methodist Hymnal 262
United Methodist Renewal Services Fellowship 286
United Methodist Theological Schools in Europe 181
United States of America (USA) 30–31, 76–77, 79, 334–335, 337, 445–446
  differentiation, division and constitution-making 97–100

divisions over slavery and race 104–107
growth and reform 100–104
history of Methodism 89–111
John Wesley and 89, 92–93, 94, 334, 472
  appointment of superintendents 94, 334
  doctrinal standards 418–419
missions 119, 129, 459–460
  Asia and the Pacific 154–155, 156–158, 159–160, 161–163
  Europe 169–170, 172–178
  origins 90–93
  race and gender 95–97
reorganization and unifications 107–108
Revolutionary crisis 93–95
women in mission 127–128
polity 310–313, 315, 319–320, 472–473
printed and archival research collections 381–385
Wesley's appointment of superintendents 94, 334
unity
  in diversity 318
  visible 340
Upper Room 287
  Academy for Spiritual Formation 287
urbanization 79
Uruguay 206–207, 217

Van Gogh, Vincent 397
Varani 117
Varick, James 391, 449, 501
Vasey, Thomas 94, 334
Venezuela 211
Vesey, Denmark 104
Viksna, Arijs 202–203
virtue ethic 32
Vladivostok 196–197
Von Balthasar, Hans Urs 365
Vovole, 'Aisea 162
Vuksta, Ivan 199

Wainwright, Geoffrey 338
Waitangi, Treaty of 156
Wakefield, Thomas 148
Wales 502
Walker, Sir Alan 233
Walls, Andrew F. 131, 153
Walls, Jerry L. 64
Walpole, Sir Robert 296
Walsh, John 15–16
Wanghia, Treaty of 156
war 13
  social ethics 296–297
  see also civil war; World Wars
Ward, Harry F. 303
Ward, Reginald 11, 16
Ward, W. R. 78
Warner, Laceye C. 236, 237
Warren, George 115, 140, 389
Warrener, William 206
watch nights 250–251, 283
water, baptismal 268
Waters, Francis 103
Watkins, Owen 145
Watson, J. R. 39–40, 41–42, 44
Watson, Richard 31, 453–454
Watts, Isaac 11, 36, 253
Waugh, Beverly 102
wealth 12–13
  social obligations of 293–294
Weatherhead, Leslie 287
Webb, Thomas 89, 92
Wembo-Nyama Mission 143
Wesley, Charles 89, 277, 288–289, 503, 503–504
  death 283
  divergences from John Wesley 29–30
  editions of theological writings 33–34
  hymns *see* hymns
  life, ministry and legacy 3–19
  materials in MARC 372
  means of grace 280
  origins of Methodism 75–76
  prayer 278–279
  sacred poetry 10–11, 40–56, 264
  studies 10–11, 59–60
  theology *see* Wesleyan theology
  see also Wesleyan studies
Wesley, John 36, 37, 226, 289, 366–367, 503, 504
  advice on preaching 225

Index

Antigua 205
attitude to art 366, 397
authentic worship 227
author or originator of the Wesleyan Quadrilateral 62–63, 66–67
baptism 260–261, 262, 480
of Gilbert's slaves 133
Brevint's *On the Christian Sacrament and Sacrifice* 53
conference 315
death 76–77, 283
Directions for Renewing Our Covenant with God 250–251
divergences from Charles Wesley 29–30
doctrinal standards for British Methodism 421–422
ecumenism 330–334
editions of theological writings 33
eucharist 264, 480
evangelism 224–225, 428–429
experience 70
funeral 76
General Rules 65, 71, 318, 320–321, 470
'The General Spread of the Gospel' 335–337
holistic soteriology 222–223
images of 353–357, 398–399
Ireland 85, 86
laity and administering the sacraments 274
learning from 299–301
life, ministry and legacy 3–19
materials in MARC 372
means of grace 280
ministry to the poor 13, 292–293, 488–489
and missions 112–113, 460
Model Deed of 1763 30, 422, 471, 474
mysticism 463
origins of Methodism 73, 74–76
polity of 470–472
British Methodism 473–474
prayer 278–279

preachers 318–319
reason 69, 478–479
salvation 277, 279–280, 481–483
seminal contribution to social ethics 292–301
Sermons and *Expository Notes* 418–419, 420, 422, 474
social thought and action 488–489
The Sunday Service of the Methodists 240–243
theology *see* Wesleyan theology
USA *see* United States of America (USA)
view of authority 62–63
worship 507–508
see also Wesleyan studies
Wesley, Mehetabel 37
Wesley, Samuel (father) 16, 24, 36–37, 89, 260, 277, 502
Wesley, Samuel (son) 37, 503
Wesley, Susanna 24, 89, 277, 477, 502–503
Wesley College, Bristol 375–376
Wesley family 15, 502–503
Wesley Historical Society 376
Wesley Works Editorial Project 6, 33, 87
Wesleyan aesthetics 365–366
Wesleyan Church 119, 505
Wesleyan Connection 77, 78, 82, 105–106, 337
Wesleyan Missionary Society (WMS) 78, 153
Women's Auxiliary 158–159
Wesleyan Quadrilateral 61–72, 420
evolution of the concept 61–66
issues associated with 66–72
Wesleyan Repository and Religious Intelligencer 102
Wesleyan spirituality 277–281
enduring qualities 289–290
Wesleyan Spirituality and Faith Development Working Group 289

Wesleyan studies 3–19, 31–32
areas requiring further attention 11–18
Charles Wesley studies 10–11, 59–60
methodology and techniques 7–10
Wesleyan Theological Journal 32
Wesleyan Theological Society 32
Wesleyan theology 20–35, 453
divergences between Charles and John 29–30
evangelism 221–225
forms of theological activity 25–27
historical background 20–23
John Wesley's theology 494–497
reception and transmission in Methodism 30–32
shared convictions 27–29
Wesley brothers' stance within their theological context 24–25
West Africa 115–116, 121, 133–140
West African Methodist Church 140
Westley, John 24
Westminster Central Hall 82
Whatcoat, Richard 94, 334
Whedon, Daniel D. 105
'Where cross the crowded ways of life' (North) 303
White, John 142
White, Moses C. 154, 159, 160
White, Susan J. 353
Whitefield, George 16, 75, 89, 92, 372, 504, 505–506
Whitehead, Alfred North 287
Wichern, Johann Hinrich 172, 301, 560–561
Wilberforce, William 295
Wilkins, Ann 118
Willard, Frances 107
Willerup, Christian 173, 561
William of Orange 22–23, 24

601

Index

Williams, Colin 61–62, 64, 68
Williams, J. M. 354
Williams, John 116
Williams, Robert 93
Winston, W. R. 154
Winter, Ralph 131
Withey, Amos 142
Witt, Jan 198
women 12, 237, 506
  American Methodism 92, 96–97, 107–108
  John Wesley and the role of 298–299
  in mission 118, 123–124, 127–128
Women's Foreign Missionary Society (WFMS) of the MEC 123, 124, 127, 172
Women's Missionary Movement 124
Women's Missionary Society (WMS) of the MECS 124
Wood, Enoch 355
Woolner, James 148
Works of John Wesley, The 33
World Alliance of Reformed Churches 344
World Congress on Evangelism 1966 232
World Council of Churches (WCC) 126, 182, 231, 287, 338–340, 423, 507
Bangkok world mission conference 232
Baptism, Eucharist and Ministry 262, 267, 338–339
Mission and Evangelism 233–234
theology of mission 130
World Federation of Methodist Women 128
World Gospel Mission (WGM) 148–149
World Methodist Council (WMC) 15, 112, 125, 287, 337, 343, 507
  and Lutheran World Federation 344–345
  and the Roman Catholic Church 345–348
  'Wesleyan essentials of Christian faith' 66, 348
  and World Alliance of Reformed Churches 344
World Methodist Evangelism division 233
World Missionary Conference of 1910 231
World Student Christian Federation (WSCF) 126, 338
World Wars
  First World War 180, 363
  Second World War 180–181, 196, 198
worship 240–256, 507–511
  authentic 227–228
  descriptive primary sources 248–252
  hymns, song and tunes 253–255
  ritual texts 240–247
  see also hymns; sacraments
Worthington, Reginald T. 148
Wright, Frank Lloyd 352
Wright, Richard 91
Wunderlich, Erhard Friedrich 174, 562

'Ye servants of God, your Master proclaim' (Charles Wesley) 56
Yi Su-Jong 122
youth work 84, 511

Zambia 142–143
Zeller, Andrew 91
Zimbabwe 130, 145–147
Zinzendorf, Nikolaus Ludwig Graf von 462, 511–512
Zunuze, Escrivao 145
Zwinglianism 258, 264